BRIEF CONTENTS

{ FIFTH EDITION }

Choices
A Writing Guide with Readings

Kate Mangelsdorf | **Evelyn Posey**
The University of Texas at El Paso

Bedford/St. Martin's
Boston • New York

For Bedford/St. Martin's

Developmental Editor: Erica T. Appel
Production Editor: Peter Jacoby
Senior Production Supervisors: Nancy Myers, Jennifer Peterson
Marketing Manager: Christina Shea
Editorial Assistant: Amy Saxon
Copy Editor: Jamie Thaman
Indexer: Melanie Belkin
Photo Researcher: Julie Tesser
Permissions Manager: Kalina K. Ingham
Art Director: Lucy Krikorian
Text Design: Castle Design
Cover Design: Donna Lee Dennison
Cover Photo: © Donna Lee Dennison. *Photograph of a Window Display at Paragon Sports*, New York, NY.
   Photograph taken on March 28, 2012.
Composition: Jouve
Printing and Binding: RR Donnelley and Sons

President, Bedford/St. Martin's: Denise B. Wydra
Presidents, Macmillan Higher Education: Joan E. Feinberg and Tom Scotty
Editor in Chief: Karen S. Henry
Director of Development: Erica T. Appel
Director of Marketing: Karen R. Soeltz
Production Director: Susan W. Brown
Associate Production Director: Elise S. Kaiser
Managing Editor: Shuli Traub

Library of Congress Control Number: 2012938886

Manufactured in the United States of America.

7 6 5 4 3 2
f e d c b a

For information, write: Bedford/St. Martin's, 75 Arlington Street, Boston, MA 02116   (617-399-4000)

ISBN 978-0-312-61140-8 (student edition)

Acknowledgments

In our early years of teaching, we searched for a textbook that would actively lead students through each step of writing an essay. Our ideal text would be complete, offering a rhetoric, readings, and a handbook. It would also let students choose their own topics and enable them at the outset of the course to write whole essays. It would offer engaging readings to model the writing process; teach critical thinking; provide collaborative learning activities; and help students apply what they learn in class to their other courses, the workplace, and the community. Above all, it would respect the wealth of knowledge and experience that students bring to the writing classroom. Because we were never able to find such a book, we decided to write *Choices: A Writing Guide with Readings*.

Choices offers student writers comprehensive step-by-step instruction for writing expressive, informative, and persuasive essays. It showcases the writing process; offers a variety of engaging assignments; and strengthens students' reading, thinking, and writing skills. Most important, it builds students' confidence by encouraging them to think of themselves as writers with important ideas to communicate. Rather than simply talking about how to write, *Choices* gets students actively involved in writing.

Working on the fifth edition of *Choices*, we decided to make the book even more engaging and helpful to students. We began by introducing a student writer at the opening of each assignment chapter, along with a quote, a photo, and an activity based on that student's writing topic. Throughout the book, we updated both the professional and the student essays, and we added a brand-new student essay in Chapter 3 to show how to write using multiple patterns of development. We added annotations to the first reading in each chapter, and we included a writing activity following each reading, to help students better understand the connection between reading and writing. To help students discover why they write, we increased the emphasis on the purposes for writing. To help students become better academic writers, we added more coverage of source-based writing.

Finally, we thought about the diverse ways our students already communicate and considered how we could help them build on existing strengths. They text their friends and family, sometimes using multiple languages; they celebrate special events by creating videos; and they post frequent updates on Facebook and Twitter. To build on these interests and skills, we added tips for writing using digital technologies, especially social media, to encourage students to use the knowledge and skills they already have in their everyday writing as they learn to become competent, confident academic writers.

❰ How *Choices* Works

Choices is divided into four parts. Part One, "Composing Ourselves, Writing for Others," has three introductory chapters that present writing as purposeful and creative:

- Chapter 1 introduces the stages of the writing process and follows one student through each stage.
- Chapter 2 focuses on the elements of good paragraphs, showing the development of a sample student paragraph.
- Chapter 3 describes nine common patterns of development and follows one student through the process of using some of these patterns to develop an essay.

Part Two, "Writing to Share Ideas," consists of six chapters organized by purpose and theme—for example, "Explaining: Cultural Symbols, Traditions, and Heroes" (Chapter 5). Each chapter includes three professional readings and a step-by-step guide for writing essays, complete with student models. Each chapter also highlights two patterns of development, includes group and peer review activities, and gives helpful sentence editing and grammar tips. A Chapter Checklist and the opportunity for students to reflect on their own writing appear at the end of each chapter.

Part Three, "Writing for Different Situations," provides support for the writing assigned in Part Two, as well as for other academic and work situations.

Part Four, "Handbook with Exercises," is a practical, concise resource that shows students how to identify and correct errors, rather than explaining grammatical concepts and terms at length. A separate section provides guidelines and grammar for multilingual students.

Finally, an appendix, "Additional Readings," provides students and instructors with more models and ideas for writing.

❰ The Features

Complete, Accessible Instruction for Writing, at an Affordable Price

Choices contains everything students need to become effective writers, including a clear explanation of the writing process; six assignment chapters covering expressive, informative, and argument-based writing; excellent model essays that generate ideas for writing; in-depth information on conducting research; chapters on writing for different situations; and a comprehensive handbook—all at a price students can afford.

Step-by-Step Guidance through the Process of Writing an Essay, Illustrated with Student Models

At the heart of *Choices* are the six writing assignment chapters in Part Two, which guide students through the steps of the writing process:

- exploring choices
- drafting
- revising
- editing
- sharing their work with others

The focus on sharing work as the last step in the writing process is part of the book's overall emphasis on helping students communicate effectively *to a specific audience* rather than simply practicing a particular mode of writing. Each chapter's abundant writing activities, examples of student writing, and helpful "how-to" boxes give students the support they need.

Unique Guidance on Choosing Topics That Matter

Each assignment chapter offers three engaging topic suggestions, illustrated with professional readings. Students are invited to try out each topic using different invention strategies and then choose the topic that is most meaningful to them. This unique approach (which inspired the title of the text, *Choices*) makes writing relevant for students and provides flexibility for instructors.

Help with Writing Paragraphs and Understanding the Patterns of Development

Chapter 2, "Crafting Paragraphs," helps students develop and organize paragraphs, teaching them about topic sentences, introductions, and conclusions. Chapter 3, "The Patterns of Development," illustrates each of the rhetorical patterns using example paragraphs. Additional coverage of the patterns can also be found in each assignment chapter.

Advice for Special Writing Situations

Part Three gives students advice on dealing with writing situations they will encounter in other college courses and on the job. Separate chapters focus on keeping journals, writing summaries, conducting research, taking essay exams, and writing résumés and cover letters.

Comprehensive Handbook with Extensive ESL Coverage

The handbook in Part Four covers sentence grammar, word choice, spelling, punctuation, and mechanics, with more than 150 exercises for practice correcting sentences, editing paragraphs, and combining sentences. The handbook concludes with a newly revised "Guide for Multilingual Writers" chapter, which covers ESL issues.

New to This Edition

A New Focus on the Reading-Writing Connection

In the readings section that opens each assignment chapter, the first reading has been annotated to show students the features of an effective essay. To get students thinking about the chapter theme in relation to their own writing, a new writing activity, Share Your Ideas, follows each reading. Later, as they work through the steps of the writing process, students are invited to refer to the writing they did earlier.

A Stronger Focus on Academic Writing

Coverage on using sources, first introduced in Chapter 6 ("Analyzing"), has been expanded in Chapter 9 ("Proposing a Solution"), which gives step-by-step guidance on writing a source-based paper. In addition, Chapter 12 ("Conducting Research") has been updated and expanded to help beginning writers better understand how to evaluate and integrate sources into their writing.

Engaging New Chapter Openers That Emphasize the Purposes for Writing

Revised assignment chapter openers bring into focus that chapter's writing purpose—such as remembering, explaining, or arguing a position—and tie it into the chapter's theme. To further engage students, a student writer is introduced in each opener, accompanied by a full-page photo, a quote from that student's essay, and a writing activity based on the photo.

New Readings to Spark Ideas for Writing

For the fifth edition, we have replaced approximately 40 percent of the readings with timely and engaging pieces, such as

- **Anna Quindlen** on censorship of books in the high-school classroom,
- **Jhumpa Lahiri** on the unique way Indian families celebrate a baby's coming of age,
- **Nicholas Carr** on the iPad's popularity and what it means.

We have also added four new student essays, which include a personal reflection on the writing process, an argument essay on children's exposure to violence on television, a review of a museum exhibit, and a proposal for adopting veganism as a solution to our environmental problems.

New "Writing Digitally" Tips

Boxed tips throughout the book help students use digital and social media to improve their writing. Topics include blogging to test out ideas, using social networking sites to share ideas and write drafts, and using word-processing programs to help organize thoughts.

An Attractive New Design

A new design helps students and instructors better navigate the chapters. Design features include striking opening photos; clearly marked introductions to the writing guides; and a dedicated type font for activities, making them easy to see on the page.

Support for Instructors and Students

Choices does not stop with a book. Online and in print, you will find both free and affordable premium resources to help students get even more out of the book and your course. You will also find convenient resources for instructors, such as a downloadable instructor's manual and supplemental exercises. For information on ordering and to get ISBNs for packaging these resources with your students' books, see pages ix–x or contact your Bedford/St. Martin's sales representative, e-mail sales support (**sales_support@ bfwpub.com**), or visit **bedfordstmartins.com/choices/catalog**).

📖 = print resource

🖥 = online resource

💿 = CD

Free Instructor Resources

📖 *The Instructor's Annotated Edition of Choices* provides practical page-by-page advice on teaching with *Choices*, Fifth Edition, as well as answers to all the exercises. It includes discussion prompts, strategies for teaching ESL students, ideas for additional classroom activities, suggestions for using other print and media resources, and cross-references useful to teachers at all levels of experience. ISBN 978-1-4576-2378-3

🖥 📖 *Additional Resources for Instructors Using Choices*, prepared by Craig Wynne, Sandra Blystone, and Bruce Thaler, provides new and seasoned instructors alike with the support they need for teaching writing. Part One includes information and advice on working with student writers, facilitating collaborative learning, teaching ESL students and speakers of nonstandard dialects, and assessing student progress. Part Two includes grammar diagnostics, mastery, and exit tests. Available in print ISBN 978-1-4576-2372-1. Or, to download, see **bedfordstmartins.com/choices/catalog**.

Bedford Coursepacks allow you to plug *Choices* content into your own course management system. For details, visit **bedfordstmartins.com /coursepacks**.

Testing Tool Kit: Writing and Grammar Test Bank CD-ROM allows instructors to create secure, customized tests and quizzes from a pool of nearly two thousand questions covering forty-seven topics. It also includes ten prebuilt diagnostic tests. ISBN 978-0-312-43032-0

Teaching Developmental Writing: Background Readings, Fourth Edition, is edited by Susan Naomi Bernstein, former cochair of the Conference on Basic Writing. This professional resource offers essays on topics of interest to basic writing instructors, along with editorial apparatus pointing out practical applications for the classroom. ISBN 978-0-312-60251-2

Teaching Composition: Background Readings, Third Edition, is edited by T. R. Johnson of Tulane University. This collection includes thirty professional readings on composition and rhetoric written by leaders in the field, accompanied by helpful introductions and activities for the classroom. It includes up-to-date advice on helping students avoid plagiarism, improving online instruction, blogging, and more. ISBN 978-0-312-46933-7

E-Book Options

The Choices e-Book, available for the first time and value priced, can be purchased in formats for use with computers, tablets, and e-readers. Visit **bedfordstmartins.com/ebooks** for more information.

Student Resources

The Student Site for Choices at **bedfordstmartins.com/choices** provides students with additional exercises from *Exercise Central*, helpful guidelines on avoiding plagiarism and doing research, annotated model essays, reading-comprehension quizzes, additional writing assignments, supplemental exercises, and links to other useful resources from Bedford/St. Martin's.

Exercise Central 3.0 at **bedfordstmartins.com/exercisecentral**, a free and open database of over nine thousand exercises, offers immediate **feedback**, recommends personalized study plans, and provides tutorials for common problems. Best of all, students' work is automatically reported to a gradebook, allowing instructors to track students' progress quickly and easily.

WritingClass provides students with a dynamic, interactive online course space preloaded with book-specific exercises, diagnostics, video tutorials, writing and commenting tools, and more, including **new Learning-Curve activities**, which adapt the pace to each student—and lead every student to success. To learn more, visit **yourwritingclass.com**. ISBN 978-0-312-57384-3

💻 *Re:Writing Plus,* **now with VideoCentral,** gathers all our premium digital content for the writing class into one online collection. This resource includes innovative and interactive help with writing a paragraph; tutorials and practices that show how writing works in students' real-world experience; VideoCentral, with over 140 brief videos for the writing classroom; the first-ever peer-review game, *Peer Factor; i-cite: visualizing sources;* plus hundreds of models of writing and hundreds of readings. *Re:Writing Plus* can be purchased separately or packaged with *Choices* at a significant discount. ISBN 978-0-312-48849-9

💻 *Exercise Central to Go: Writing and Grammar Practices for Basic Writers* **CD-ROM** provides hundreds of practice items to help students build their writing and editing skills. No Internet connection is necessary. **Free** when packaged with the print text. ISBN 978-0-312-44652-9

📖 *The Bedford/St. Martin's ESL Workbook* includes a broad range of exercises covering grammar issues for multilingual students of varying language skills and backgrounds. Answers are at the back. **Free** when packaged with the print text. ISBN 978-0-312-54034-0

💿 *Make-a-Paragraph Kit* is a fun, interactive CD-ROM that teaches students about paragraph development. It also contains exercises to help students build their own paragraphs, audiovisual tutorials on four of the most common errors for basic writers, and the content from the *Exercise Central to Go* CD-ROM. **Free** when packaged with the print text. ISBN 978-0-312-45332-9

📖 *The Bedford/St. Martin's Planner* includes everything that students need to plan and use their time effectively, with advice on preparing schedules and to-do lists plus blank schedules and calendars (monthly and weekly). The planner fits easily into a backpack or purse, so students can take it anywhere. **Free** when packaged with the print text. ISBN 978-0-312-57447-5

Ordering Information

To order any ancillary or ancillary package for *Choices,* Fifth Edition, contact your local Bedford/St. Martin's sales representative, e-mail **sales_support@bfwpub.com**, or visit our Web site at **bedfordstmartins.com**. Use these ISBNs when ordering the following supplements packaged with your students' copy of *Choices.*

The Bedford/St. Martin's ESL Workbook ISBN 978-1-4576-4119-0
The Bedford/St. Martin's Planner ISBN 978-1-4576-4123-7
Exercise Central to Go CD-ROM ISBN 978-1-4576-4127-5
Make-a-Paragraph Kit CD-ROM ISBN 978-1-4576-4116-9

Bedford/St. Martin's Writing Journal ISBN 978-1-4576-4117-6
WritingClass access card ISBN 978-1-4576-3739-1
Re:Writing Plus access card ISBN 978-1-4576-4121-3
The Bedford/St. Martin's Textbook Reader ISBN 978-1-4576-4122-0
A Commonsense Guide to Grammar and Usage ISBN 978-1-4576-4126-8

Acknowledgments

Choices reflects years of collaboration with students, teachers, and editors, and we are grateful to the many people whose inspiration and hard work helped us improve this fifth edition. We are especially indebted to students Andrea Benitez, Kathy Chu, Sandra Cordero, Reginald Jones, Paul LaPrade, Leslie Lozano, Charles Lujan, Carlos Montijo, Jesus Ramirez, Melissa Ruiz, and Rachel Serrano, who allowed us to use their essays in this book. We also thank student Todd Ruecker, who contributed a model survey, and Craig Wynne, who helped with the revision of the instructor's manual.

We especially want to thank Traci Gardner, Virginia Tech, who suggested many of the digital tips, and Mary Duffy, University of South Alabama, who suggested revisions for conducting electronic library research. We also thank the following reviewers for their many helpful suggestions: Richard L. Babik, Barry University; Alena Balmforth, Salt Lake Community College; Andrea Berta, University of Texas at El Paso; Patti Casey, Tyler Junior College; Elijah M. Coleman, Idaho State University; Barbara Cox, Redlands Community College; Janet Cutshall, Sussex County Community College; Steve Daubs, University of Wisconsin–Parkside; William Durden, Clark College; Steffeny Fazzio, Salt Lake Community College; Jean Louise Ferguson, Garden City Community College; Joanne Gabel, Reading Area Community College; Monique Harris, University of Wisconsin–Parkside; Leslie J. Henson, Butte-Glenn Community College District; Desha Hill, Tyler Junior College; Nicole Jackson, Abraham Baldwin Agricultural College; Billy Jones, Miami Dade College; Linda Koffman, College of Marin; Dawn Lattin, Idaho State University; Christopher Morelock, Walters State Community College; Patricia Moseley, Central Carolina Technical College; Linda Mulready, Bristol Community College; Jeffrey L. Newberry, Abraham Baldwin Agricultural College; Michele Peterson, Santa Barbara City College; Deborah Pollack, Ventura College; Robert Saba, Florida International University; Rebecca Samberg, Housatonic Community College; Esther Sampol, Barry University; Caroline Seefchak, Barry University; Gwynda Shields, Abraham Baldwin Agricultural College; Billie Unger, Blue Ridge Community and Technical College; Maria C. Villar-Smith, Miami Dade College; Dr. Raymond Watkins, Central Carolina Technical College; Vita Watkins, Ventura College, Glendale Community College, and East Los Angeles College; Gwenna Weshinskey, College of DuPage; Sylvia

Wilhelm, Colorado Mesa University; and Kelly Lynn-Ford Zepp, Colorado Mesa University.

For over fifteen years, we have had the pleasure of working with truly dedicated and talented professionals at Bedford/St. Martin's. For the extraordinarily fine improvements to this edition, we thank our editor, Erica Appel, who provided exceptional guidance, attention to detail, and an insistence on excellence that has resulted in our best edition yet. She is not only an exceptionally capable editor but also a delight to work with. We also thank Karrin Varucene, Amy Saxon, and Peter Jacoby for ably guiding the text through the revision and editing process, and Christina Shea and Alexis Walker for their unflagging enthusiasm. Finally, we thank Karen Henry, Joan Feinberg, Nancy Perry, and Denise Wydra, who have always encouraged our work; no words can adequately describe our appreciation for their continued support.

Kate Mangelsdorf
Evelyn Posey

CONTENTS

9 Proposing a Solution: Health, Education, and the Environment   275

PART THREE Writing for Different Situations   313

10 Keeping Journals   315

14 Writing Résumés and Cover Letters 389

PART FOUR
Handbook with Exercises 397

15 Writing Sentences 399

16 Expanding Sentences 421

17 Combining Sentences 436

Composing Ourselves, Writing for Others

Writing is an important way to communicate—in class, in the workplace, and for personal enjoyment. Many of us are writing more than ever, whether it be sending texts to friends, e-mailing coworkers, or updating our Facebook pages. No matter what the writing task, good writing skills are a must.

In Part One, you'll explore why writers write and how they go about getting their ideas down on paper. You'll discover your own writing process and begin to use it to communicate the important ideas you have to share. You will learn how to write effective paragraphs, an important step when putting your ideas in writing. And you'll learn about patterns you can use to develop your writing.

The Writing Process

What comes to mind when you think of a writer? You might picture a writer whose works you like to read, such as J. K. Rowling, Malcolm Gladwell, or Stephenie Meyer. Or you might think of the stereotypes we have of writers, such as the newspaper reporter who submits a late-breaking story minutes before a deadline, or the tortured poet who wears a beret, lives in a cold attic, composes brilliant sonnets on scraps of paper, and dies before receiving any recognition.

Writers are more common than you might imagine. A consumer who writes a letter to the electric company is a writer, as is a student who completes a report for a course, a child who writes her name for the first time, a father who records the birth of his baby in a journal, and an engineer who writes a proposal to build a bridge. A lover who sends a valentine is a writer, and so is an angry voter who composes a letter to the city council. A writer is anyone who uses written language to communicate a feeling, a fact, or an opinion.

If the idea of writing frightens you, you are not alone. Even the most experienced writers get anxious when faced with a new project. But understanding how writers find ideas, organize them, and complete a piece of writing can help relieve any fears you might have about writing. How do writers transform their ideas into a polished piece of writing to be

> **In this chapter, you will write a brief essay about your attitude toward writing. As you work on your essay, you will**
>
> - Learn how to read to improve your writing.
> - Learn how to analyze your audience.
> - Examine different purposes for writing.
> - Explore the steps of the writing process.
> - Discover several strategies for gathering ideas.
> - Learn the importance of standard written English.
> - Follow one student through the writing process.

shared with readers or turned in for a grade? What do they do first, next, and last? As you'll learn in this chapter, writing is best completed over a period of time in distinct steps. In this chapter, you'll follow a student writer, Charles Lujan, as he completes the steps of the writing process for a college essay. As you progress through this book, you'll see that although good writing takes effort, it's not nearly as frightening or mysterious as it may seem. ■

Writing Assignment

Your first assignment is to "compose yourself" as a writer. Think back over your life to consider when and to whom you have written. Consider all types of writing, such as sending texts, posting to Web sites, writing complaint letters, responding to essay exams, and filling out forms. How frequently do you write? Who reads your writing? What are your purposes for writing? In addition, make a note of your feelings about writing. Do certain types of writing interest you more than others? Does writing excite you or make you anxious? Does writing come easily to you, or do you struggle to find the right words? You might want to get your ideas flowing by writing for a few minutes nonstop in response to the following questions:

- What have been some of the most important writing events in your life? Consider not only formal writing assignments for school or work but also e-mails, texts, and posts on social media sites such as Facebook and Twitter.

- What are the most common types of writing that you do? What are your purposes for writing, and who reads your writing? What happens as a result of your writing?

- What languages have you used for writing? Do you enjoy writing in one language more than another, or do you prefer to go back and forth between two languages? Why?

- Who was most influential in your development as a writer? How did this person influence you?

- Can you recall any time when you felt inadequate as a writer? What was the event? Why did you feel this way? What changes did you make as a result?

- What are three words that best describe you as a writer? Discuss these three words.

Use your best ideas to write a brief essay for your classmates and instructor explaining how you feel about yourself as a writer. Follow the steps of the writing process described in this chapter.

❨ Reading to Improve Writing

Throughout this book, you'll have the opportunity to read sample essays written by both professional and student writers. Before every writing assignment in Part Two, for example, you will find three essays on the topics you will be asked to write about. You will also follow the progress of a college student as he or she completes the same assignment that you are working on.

As a college student, you're already familiar with at least some of the benefits of reading. You know that textbooks and other assigned readings can teach you new skills or give you information about a subject. You might read a newspaper, either in print or online, to keep up with what's going on around you, or you might enjoy reading a novel and comparing it with the movie version of the same story. Some people read as they commute to and from work to make the ride pass more quickly.

The advantages of reading multiply when you read as writers read—to observe the techniques of others and therefore improve your own writing. When you examine a piece of writing to learn how the author communicates a certain idea, you're like an athlete who watches a game to observe the moves of the players. Examining the writing strategies of a particular author helps you use these strategies in your own writing. If you read like a writer, you can learn ways to organize, develop, and express your ideas in your own writing.

Suppose you can't decide how to begin a paper on whales for your biology course. Around the same time, you read an article on hallucinogenic drugs in *Outside* magazine called "One Toad over the Line," written by Kevin Krajick. Here is its beginning:

> It's big, it looks like a cowpie with eyes, and many people believe it can bring them face to face with God. It's the Colorado River toad, a once obscure amphibian whose fame has spread in recent years thanks to the venom secreted by its skin. When dried and smoked, the venom releases bufotenine, a substance that one California drug agent calls "the most potent, instantaneously acting hallucinogen we know."

From this paragraph, you learn two strategies for beginning an essay. First, a startling comparison ("a cowpie with eyes") can get your audience's attention. Second, stating the topic of an essay (in this case, the hallucinogen bufotenine) at the beginning helps your audience understand right away what your piece is about.

Reading can also improve your vocabulary. Suppose that one of your favorite authors is the suspense novelist Mary Higgins Clark. On the next page is an excerpt from Clark's *While My Pretty One Sleeps*, a book about a fashion designer named Neeve:

To Neeve's dismay, as she crossed Thirty-Seventh Street she came face to face with Gordon Steuber. Meticulously dressed in a tan cashmere jacket over a brown-and-beige Scottish pullover, dark-brown slacks and Gucci loafers, with his blaze of curly brown hair, slender, even-featured face, powerful shoulders and narrow waist, Gordon Steuber could easily have had a successful career as a model. Instead, in his early forties, he was a shrewd businessman with an uncanny knack of hiring unknown young designers and exploiting them until they could afford to leave him.

The word *meticulously* might not be familiar to you, but from the context of this passage you can guess that it means "carefully" or "precisely." From this passage, you can also guess that *uncanny* means "unusual" or "remarkable" and that *exploit* means "to use." Verify your guesses by looking up unfamiliar words in a dictionary, and keep a list of new words and their meanings so that you can refer to them when you read and write.

▌**HOW TO** Be an Active Reader

- Preview the text.
  - Think about the title and what it means to you.
  - Think about whether you recognize the author's name.
  - Read any headings, captions, charts, and lists.
- Read the text.
  - Read carefully, underlining the most important points.
  - Circle and look up the meanings of words you don't know.
  - Briefly list the main points in the margin.
- Write to comprehend and remember.
  - List or outline the most important points.
  - Write your personal reactions to what you have read.
- Review these notes before class.

◖ A Writer's Composing Process

Although it's easy to think of writing as simply putting words on paper, most writers use a particular *writing process*, or method, to turn ideas into finished essays. Generally, here is a typical writing process that many writers follow:

Step 1   **Explore your choices.**
Step 2   **Write a draft to discover your ideas.**
Step 3   **Revise the draft to make your ideas clearer for readers.**

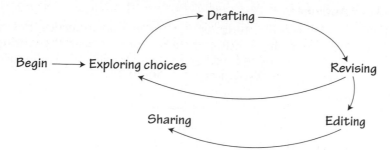

Figure 1.1 The Recursive Nature of the Writing Process

Step 4   Edit the draft for grammar, spelling, and punctuation.
Step 5   Share the final draft of your essay with an audience.

You'll probably find that your writing process does not exactly follow the steps in the order outlined here but that you prefer to move back and forth among the various steps. For example, while revising an essay, you may discover you need more information. To get that information, you have to return to exploring your choices. You may discover, too, that you prefer to revise for quite a while, producing perhaps three or four revised drafts. Figure 1.1 illustrates the recursive nature of the writing process.

To discover your own writing process, experiment with the various ways of exploring choices, drafting, revising, editing, and sharing explained in this chapter and throughout Part Two of this book. The methods that work best for you will lead you to discover your preferred writing process. Let's get started.

Step 1   Explore Your Choices

The first step of the writing process, often called *prewriting*, includes all that you do before you actually begin to write a draft. This step involves activities such as writing, talking, reading, and thinking. But first, you must think about who will read your essay and why you're writing it.

Analyzing Your Audience and Purpose

As you begin to work on an assignment, you want to keep your reader in mind. After all, you're writing to communicate something of interest, so you want to be sure the reader gets your message. It's also important to understand why you are writing and the kind of message you want to communicate. The more you know about your audience and your purpose, the easier it will be for you to write.

A Writer's Audience

No matter what you're writing about, your *audience* influences how you write. A writer's audience consists of those who will read the writing—yourself, family members, friends, classmates, instructors, colleagues at work, political leaders. The possibilities are limitless.

Writing to an audience is not the same as speaking to an audience. In fact, writing has some advantages. Have you ever said something you wished you could take back? This is less likely to happen when you write because you can revise your words before your audience sees them.

Writing is also different from speaking because your audience isn't actually in front of you. When you speak, your audience can smile, frown, or ask questions. When you write, however, you must envision, or picture in your mind, how your readers will respond to your words. To envision your audience, ask yourself these questions:

- *Who are my readers?* Sometimes your audience is someone specific, such as the sociology professor who will read your term paper or the fellow students who will see your flyer about an upcoming event at the student union. At other times, your readers will be the general public, such as subscribers to the local print or online newspaper who read your letter to the editor.

- *What do my readers know about my topic?* Your readers' knowledge of the topic is important because you don't want to bore people by telling them what they already know. Instead, you want to tell them something new—where they might go for career counseling, how to speed up their wireless connection, whom they should vote for in the next election.

- *What do my readers need to know about my topic?* Answering this question can help you decide how much information you need to give your readers. For instance, if you're explaining how to change a tire, will your readers know what a tire jack is? Or must you describe it and explain how to use it?

- *How do my readers feel about my topic?* If your readers know nothing about your topic or might even find it dull, you'll want to find a way to capture their interest. Alternatively, your readers might be opposed to your message. If you're writing an e-mail asking your supervisor for a raise, don't assume that he or she will automatically agree to it. Instead, try to anticipate your supervisor's reasons for not giving you a raise and take them into account when you make your case.

A Writer's Purpose

Whenever you write, whether for yourself or others, you have a *purpose*. Most writing is primarily expressive, informative, or persuasive.

Expressive Writing   In *expressive writing*, writers communicate their thoughts, feelings, and personal history. When you write about the day's events in a journal, describe your vacation on Facebook, or blog about your children, you're writing expressively.

In the following example of expressive writing, student Scott Weckerly describes the morning he left home for college:

> The impact of saying good-bye and actually leaving did not hit me until the day of my departure. Its strength woke me an hour before my alarm clock would, as for the last time Missy, my golden retriever, greeted me with a big, sloppy lick. I hated it when she did that, but that day I welcomed her with open arms. I petted her with long, slow strokes, and her sad eyes gazed into mine. Her coat felt more silky than usual. Of course, I did not notice any of these qualities until that day, which made me all the sadder about leaving her.

This sample paragraph is expressive because it describes Weckerly's thoughts and feelings at an important time in his life. When he tells us that the reality of his departure didn't sink in until that morning, we understand what he was thinking. By describing his reactions to his dog, we know he was sad about leaving home. In re-creating an important incident in his life, Weckerly's writing is expressive.

Informative Writing   Sometimes we write not to express ourselves but to convey information. *Informative writing* explains: it tells how something works, how you can do something, what something looks like, how two things are alike or different, or what the cause or outcome of an event is. Informative writing typically uses facts, examples, or statistics. Most writing we encounter is informative. Nutritional labels on food containers are informative, as are directions for going through airport scanners or for administering CPR. Textbooks, including the one you're reading now, are also in this category. Most sections of the newspaper are informative.

The following is an example of informative writing:

> Studies based on 2010 census data show that a college student's future income may be directly related to his or her choice of major. Over a lifetime, individuals with a college degree will make 84 percent more than those with only a high school diploma. Among college graduates, however, average incomes differ greatly. Math, engineering, and computer science majors make between $98,000 and $120,000 annually, whereas counseling psychology majors and early childhood education majors make roughly $30,000 to $35,000 annually.

This piece of writing is informative because the author uses facts and statistics to compare the amount of money that college graduates who major in different fields make in the workforce.

Persuasive Writing *Persuasive writing* differs from expressive and informative writing because it attempts to change a reader's opinion or convince a reader to take a particular action. Newspaper editorials and advertisements are two types of persuasive writing. The *Times Picayune* wants you to support the school bond issue, and Ben and Jerry's wants you to buy its brand of ice cream. Some of the world's most memorable writing is persuasive, such as these words from President John F. Kennedy's 1961 inaugural address: "Ask not what your country can do for you; ask what you can do for your country."

Martin Luther King Jr.'s famous "I Have a Dream" speech is another example of persuasive writing. His purpose was to motivate civil rights workers to continue striving for racial equality. Here's an excerpt:

> Go back to Mississippi, go back to Alabama, go back to South Carolina, go back to Georgia, go back to Louisiana, go back to the slums and ghettos of our northern cities, knowing that somehow this situation can and will be changed. Let us not wallow in the valley of despair.

As with many persuasive pieces, King's audience is urged to believe something—in this case, that the battle for civil rights will be won. At the same time, the audience is told to do something: King wants the marchers to return home to continue the fight.

◼ HOW TO Know Your Purpose for Writing

- *Expressive:* You write to communicate your thoughts, feelings, and personal history.
- *Informative:* You write to explain something you know about—how it works, what it looks like, what caused it, or what outcome it had.
- *Persuasive:* You write to convince others to accept your opinion.

While most writing is primarily expressive, informative, or persuasive, rarely is a piece of writing entirely one type. Much of the time, all three types occur in a single piece. The *primary purpose* is the one that you consider the most important reason for writing your piece.

◼ GROUP ACTIVITY 1 Identify Purposes

Working in groups of two or three, identify the following paragraphs as primarily expressive, informative, or persuasive.

1. From the Leukemia & Lymphoma Society Web site:

> Whether you chose The Leukemia & Lymphoma Society's traditional Team In Training program, or TNT Flex, a flexible, customized, online training option de-

veloped by TNT's renowned coaches, you get all the support you need to cross the finish line at the marathon, half marathon, triathlon, century ride, and hike adventure of your choice. Both offer a choice of world class events, travel arrangements to your exciting destination, and a fabulous, activity-filled weekend once you're there.

Purpose: _____

2. From *In a Sunburned Country* by Bill Bryson:

And so, because we know so little about it, perhaps a few facts would be in order: Australia is the world's sixth largest country, and its largest island. It is the only island that is also a continent, and the only continent that is also a country. It was the first continent conquered from the sea, and the last. It is the only nation that began as a prison.

Purpose: _____

3. From Frommer's *Australia* by Elizabeth Hansen:

Is Paul Hogan in *Crocodile Dundee* a typical Aussie? Some Australians might like you to think so, but facts show that less than 15% of the population lives in rural areas. Instead, the average Australian lives in one of eight capital cities and has never seen native fauna anywhere but in a zoo or wildlife park.

Purpose: _____

4. From the *AARP Bulletin*:

We must create a more positive and accurate image of aging and help people recognize that people are living longer, more productive lives. As a nation, we must let go of our obsession with the number of years in life and focus instead on the life in those years.

Purpose: _____

5. From *One Writer's Beginnings* by Eudora Welty:

Of course it's easy to see why they both overprotected me, why my father, before I could wear a new pair of shoes for the first time, made me wait while he took out his thin silver pocket knife and with the point of the blade scored the polished soles all over, carefully, in a diamond pattern, to prevent me from sliding on the polished floor when I ran.

Purpose: _____

Gathering Ideas

Once you know your audience and purpose, you can begin to gather ideas for any topic you might want to write about.

Imagine, for example, that you are taking a course in criminal justice and your instructor gives you the following essay assignment: "Write a two- to three-page essay in which you explain a problem in the criminal justice system. Suggest a solution for the problem." Any of the following methods could help you explore possibilities for your essay.

Brainstorming

When you brainstorm, you list all the thoughts that come into your head on a topic. You don't consider whether your ideas are good or bad; you just write them down. For the criminal justice assignment, you could brainstorm a list of problems in the criminal justice system, such as prisons that are overcrowded or innocent people who are jailed.

Here is student writer Jerry's list of problems in the criminal justice system:

> Some problems
> should kids be tried as adults?
> does it make them more responsible?
>
> Another problem
> racial profiling
> can it be prevented?
> prisoners being released and doing more crimes
> no schools in prison
> you just get out of prison and do more crimes
> how to stop this?

In addition to brainstorming by yourself, you can brainstorm in a group. In this case, you would name a topic and then ask each group member to call out ideas on it. Asking others to brainstorm with you greatly increases the number of ideas you have to choose from for your essay.

Freewriting

Freewriting means writing for a specific period of time without pausing or until reaching a certain page limit. You don't stop, go back, or correct freewriting. You can focus on one topic or go on to new ones as they pop into your mind. Freewriting helps you develop fluency as a writer.

Here is student writer Crystal's freewriting about the use of DNA evidence in the court system:

> Heard on the news that they released another prisoner because DNA
> evidence showed he was innocent. He'd been in jail for eleven years! How sad.
> DNA evidence is so much better than any other way of seeing if someone is

guilty. They gather DNA evidence from a tiny piece of skin. It's like fingerprints. Everyone has their own DNA. I hope more innocent prisoners can be released. They should be given money for the time they had to spend in jail.

 Use your computer to freewrite

If you find it hard to resist correcting your writing, try using invisible writing. Simply turn down the brightness on your monitor so that you can't see what you're writing. This forces you to stay in touch with your thoughts instead of worrying about what you have already written. As with all the writing you do on a computer, remember to save your work.

Clustering

Clustering is similar to brainstorming, but instead of listing your ideas, you draw a cluster of those ideas. To begin clustering, you write your subject in the center of a blank page, and draw a small circle around those words. Then, as ideas about the topic come to mind, you write them down, put circles around them, and draw lines from them to the center circle. As you think of additional details, you circle and join them to their main ideas. Clustering can thus help you organize your ideas as well as generate ideas.

Figure 1.2 on page 14 shows how student writer Lee used clustering to gather ideas about problems in the criminal justice system.

 Do your clustering online

Online graphic organizers and mind-mapping tools can help make clustering an easy and productive activity. Go to http://ncteinbox.blogspot.com/2008/08/mind -mapping-graphic-organizers.html for links to some of these tools.

Asking Questions

The six questions that journalists use to gather details about the news can also help you discover ideas about your topic:

- Who?
- What?
- When?
- Where?
- How?
- Why?

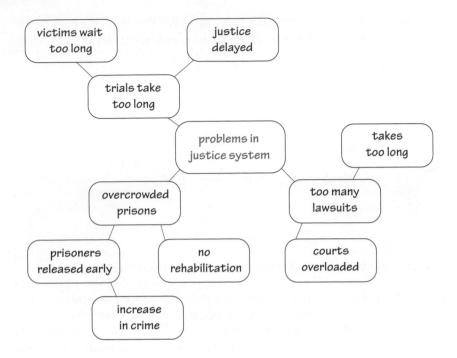

Figure 1.2 Lee's Clustering

Researching

As you gather ideas for an essay, you may discover that you need to learn more about your topic. The more you learn about your topic, the more supporting details you'll find. Research can also spark your own ideas for writing.

You can do firsthand, or primary, research by surveying or observing people. Alternatively, you can conduct secondary research by reading articles, books, or Web sites on your topic. When you conduct secondary research, keep in mind that some sources are better than others. To find reliable information, examine the writer's credentials, point of view, and purpose. Knowing these things will help you decide whether the information is something you should use. When conducting research, be sure to avoid just cutting and pasting information into your paper. Instead, integrate your researching by paraphrasing and quoting your sources. Cite your research both in the essay itself and at the end. For more help in conducting and using research, see Chapter 12.

Consulting with Others

Consulting with people who know about your topic is an excellent way to gather information and interesting details for your paper. Also, you can enliven your writing by using quotations from the discussion.

The first step is finding someone to consult with. For the criminal justice assignment, for instance, you could talk to a family member or friend involved in the criminal justice system, such as a police officer or an attorney. You could also consult with someone who has been a victim of a crime or has been accused of committing a crime.

■HOW TO Consult with Others

- Prepare questions to ask. You might begin with the journalists' questions: Who? What? When? Where? How? Why? Avoid yes-no questions.
- Listen carefully, and take notes.
- Ask questions when you don't understand something.
- Go over your notes with the person to fill in any gaps in your understanding.

Relating Aloud

Relating aloud simply means talking about your topic with others. Tell friends or classmates about what you plan to write, and get their feedback. Do they ask questions that indicate you need to supply more details or background information? Talking through what you plan to write is also a good way to realize that you have more to say than you think.

 Record your thoughts on your topic

If you are feeling reluctant to share your thoughts, you might consider using a digital recorder, computer, or smartphone to talk about your topic, and then share this with others later.

■HOW TO Gather Ideas

Use one or more of these strategies:

- *Brainstorming:* List all thoughts that come to mind about a topic.
- *Freewriting:* Write without stopping for a certain period of time (five to ten minutes) or until you reach a certain page length.
- *Clustering:* Write down your topic in the middle of a page, and circle it. Write down more specific ideas, circle them, and draw lines to connect them to the larger idea.

(continued)

- *Asking questions:* Ask a series of questions about the topic, such as, Who? What? When? Where? Why? How?
- *Researching:* Read and take notes on your topic.
- *Consulting with others:* Ask a knowledgeable person about your topic.
- *Relating aloud:* Talk about your topic with others.

After you have tried some of these ways to gather ideas, be sure to reflect on your topic possibilities for a few hours or days, letting your ideas develop before you begin to write.

(Step 2 Write Your Discovery Draft

A *discovery draft* is a first attempt at getting your ideas down on paper. When you write a discovery draft, concentrate on writing down your ideas without being too concerned about things like sentence structure, word choice, grammar, spelling, or punctuation.

Drafting styles vary widely. Some writers draft quickly and spend considerable time revising; others draft more slowly and write fewer drafts. The more you practice and experiment with writing, the better you'll know what works for you.

⏻ Turn off your word-processing tools

Before beginning your discovery draft, consider turning off the grammar- and spell-check features on your word-processing program so that you won't be distracted by the squiggly lines that appear under words as you type. You can turn them back on when you revise and edit your draft. (Keep in mind that these tools will not spot all of your errors.)

Choosing a Topic

Sometimes a topic will be given to you. For instance, your psychology instructor might ask you to write a definition of *psychosis*, or your supervisor at work might ask for a brief report on your visit to a local manufacturing plant. In such cases, you'll know what to write about, although you may not always be interested in the topic.

Often you'll have more of a choice. All of the writing assignments in Part Two of this book, for instance, ask you to gather ideas on three broad topics before you select one to write about. In such cases, your job is to select a topic that will interest you and your readers. In the criminal justice assignment, for example, you would need to first select a problem in the criminal justice system to write about and then think of a solution to that problem.

■HOW TO Select a Topic

Make a list of possible topics. Then answer the following questions:

- How much does this topic interest me?
- How much do I know about this topic?
- If I select this topic, how much, if any, research will I have to do? Is this research available to me? Can I complete the research in time to write the paper?
- Is the topic narrow enough to be explained in detail, given the word or page limit?
- How well does this topic satisfy the audience? For instance, if the reader wants an informative essay, will this topic lead to an informative essay?

Use your responses to these questions to decide on a good topic.

Once you have identified a general topic, you need to make sure that it is narrow enough to be sufficiently developed in the space you have. For instance, suppose you want to write about how advertising on television has changed. As you start to write, you realize you could probably write a book on that topic. To narrow the topic, ask yourself questions such as What kind of advertising? What time period should I cover? What particular change do I want to focus on? Questions like these help you narrow a broad topic so that you can go into more depth.

■HOW TO Narrow a Topic

Break the topic into parts by asking these questions:

- What particular thing happened?
- Who is involved?
- What is the time period?
- What type is it?
- Where does it happen?
- Why does it happen?
- How does it happen?
- What is the result of it?

GROUP ACTIVITY 2 Narrow Topics

Working with two or three other students in your writing class, assume that a sociology instructor has asked you to write a three-page essay about how technology has changed American life. Using the questions in How to Narrow a Topic, rewrite the following topics to make them narrow enough for a three-page essay.

EXAMPLE: BROAD TOPIC   How transportation has changed American life

NARROWED TOPIC   The influence of cars on the creation of the suburbs in the 1950s

1. How computers have changed our lives
2. Recent changes in telephone technology
3. How technology has changed the home
4. Negative effects of technology
5. How travel has changed in recent years

Sharing Your Ideas

Once you have selected and narrowed your topic, the next step is to write a discovery draft that puts your ideas together. Most of the time, this first draft will be very rough. Paragraphs might be skimpy; the organization might not make any sense; sentences will probably have mistakes in them. That's fine. The purpose of a discovery draft is to see what you have to say. Nobody writes a perfect, finished essay in one try.

Write a Preliminary Thesis Statement

As you begin a draft, first think about your *thesis statement*, the sentence (or sentences) that explains the main point of the essay. This thesis statement will probably change as you refine your ideas when revising, but it's a good place to start.

From your readers' point of view, a good thesis statement makes an essay easier to understand. From your point of view, an effective thesis statement gives you a solid place to work from. It also helps you keep track of your ideas as you write.

A good thesis statement does three things:

- It announces the topic of your essay.
- It shows, explains, or argues a particular point about the topic.
- It gives the reader a sense of what the essay will be about.

Compare the following ineffective and effective thesis statements.

INEFFECTIVE My daughter was arrested last week for shoplifting.

EFFECTIVE After my daughter was arrested for shoplifting, I made several important changes in how I raise my children.

INEFFECTIVE Some people think that having more female police officers is good.

EFFECTIVE Increasing the number of female police officers has helped the police department handle domestic violence and child abuse cases more effectively.

In the first example, we learn the topic, but a particular point isn't being made. In the second example, the point being made is too vague for the reader to predict what the essay will be about.

Where should your thesis statement appear in your essay? Usually, the thesis is given in the first or second paragraph. Knowing the main idea from the start gives your reader a road map for reading the whole essay.

▪ HOW TO Write a Thesis Statement

Ask yourself these questions about your topic:

- What point do I want to make about my topic?
- How can I show, explain, or argue this point?
- How can I break this point down so that I can develop one idea about it in each section of my essay?

◖ GROUP ACTIVITY 3 Evaluate Thesis Statements ▶

Working in small groups, identify the following thesis statements as either effective or ineffective. Then rewrite the thesis statements that need improvement.

1. Reality shows are some of the best shows on television.
2. A successful marriage requires patience, good communication, and a sense of humor.
3. There have been too many budget cuts at this university.
4. If you have time on your hands, do community volunteer work.
5. Even though I didn't make the Olympic ski team, my years of training taught me important skills, such as discipline, time management, focus, and persistence.

Get Organized

Once you have a topic and a preliminary thesis statement in hand, look back at the ideas you gathered. Decide which ones appear most promising, and use the techniques you have learned to gather as many additional ideas as you think you might need. Some writers prefer to organize their ideas before they begin to write. Others prefer to discover what they have to say while writing the discovery draft. Try to write your discovery draft in one sitting.

As you draft, use your thesis statement as a guide. Keep in mind that you are free to change your thesis statement later. After all, your discovery draft is for exploring your ideas. The most important thing is to write. If you reach a place where you need more information, write "add information here" in bold or colored type to remind yourself to add more to this part of your essay.

■ HOW TO Organize an Essay

- *Introduction:* Hook the reader, give background information, and state the thesis.
- *Body Paragraphs:* Give the main point of each paragraph in a topic sentence. Use details, facts, and examples to support each topic sentence.
- *Conclusion:* Refer back to the thesis. Explain the importance of the subject.

(Step 3   Revise Your Draft

Revising is an important part of the writing process. When you revise your discovery draft, you focus on developing and organizing your ideas while keeping your readers' expectations in mind. Usually, the more you revise, the better your essay will be.

Developing Your Ideas

The more you read, the more you'll notice that writers make their essays more interesting and convincing by developing them in detail. Supporting details increase interest, help readers understand the writer's thoughts, and support the writer's main ideas.

Writers use specific methods, or patterns, to develop the details in their paragraphs and essays. The most common of these patterns are description, narration, examples, process explanation, classification, definition, comparison and contrast, cause and effect, and argument. Chapter 3 explains in detail how each of these patterns works, and the Developing Your Ideas section in each chapter in Part Two shows you how to use them in your own writing.

Building Your Essay

When you build your essay, you look for ways to clarify your ideas for your readers, such as adding topic sentences to your paragraphs, giving more supporting details, or rearranging your points. The questions in How to Revise an Essay will help you find ways to improve the content and organization of your draft.

HOW TO Revise an Essay

Ask yourself these questions as you revise:

- Have I followed all the instructions for this assignment?
- Do I begin the essay in a way that encourages my reader to continue reading?
- Do I need to revise my thesis statement?
- Do I include enough main ideas to support my thesis statement?
- Do I support each main idea with details?
- Do I vary my sentences and use the appropriate words?
- Do I end the essay clearly?

One way to revise is to set your essay aside for a day or two, reread it, and then rewrite it as you see fit. A better way to revise is to enlist the help of others, a strategy that is often called *peer review*. Ask a friend or classmate to read your essay and suggest ways it could be improved.

⏻ **Share a draft of your essay online**

Your draft (or part of your draft) can be shared with others as a blog post, a note on Facebook, or a posting on a discussion forum. Be sure to let readers know the kind of feedback you want. For example, you might ask, "Here's a draft of an essay I'm writing about an important event in my life. Do you find the beginning interesting? Is there anything you want to know more about?"

> ## ▪ HOW TO Give and Receive Feedback on Your Writing
>
> When you're giving someone suggestions for revision, follow these guidelines:
>
> - Always say something positive about the piece.
> - Be specific. Don't say, "You need to improve the organization." Say, "Why don't you combine your second and third paragraphs?"
> - Don't make the feedback personal. Focus on the writing, not the writer. Don't say, "I can't believe you really believe that!" Say, "I was confused by your claim. Do you mean to say that the death penalty should be used for all convicted drug felons?"
>
> When you're receiving feedback, follow these guidelines:
>
> - Write down the suggestions you receive.
> - Ask questions to clarify what the readers are suggesting.
> - Don't take the suggestions personally. Remind yourself that your classmates are discussing your writing, not you. Consider all feedback you get. The more suggestions you receive, the better your essay will be.

❨Step 4 Edit Your Sentences

When you edit, you revise your sentences and words so that they communicate clearly. Since you have already devoted a great deal of time and effort to communicating your ideas, you don't want to spoil the essay with awkward sentences or distracting errors. Therefore, edit your essay carefully before sharing it with your readers.

Using Standard Written English

You may identify yourself as an English-speaking person, but actually you speak a dialect of English. A *dialect* is a variety of a language, and every language has many dialects. Dialects are characterized by pronunciation, word choice, and sentence structure. People speak different dialects based on where they live and their ethnic backgrounds. Here are some examples of dialects:

1. From *The Quilters: Women and Domestic Art.* Rosie Fischer is talking in 1974 about her life on a farm in Rowlett, Texas:

   > Well, anyway, I was dreaming on havin' all kinds of pretty things in my home after I married. Well, I found out right quick that livin' out on a farm, what with all the chores that had to be done, a person didn't have a whole lot of time for makin' pretty things.

2. From Robert Kimmel Smith's *Sadie Shapiro's Knitting Book*, a novel about a Jewish widow from Queens, New York:

   > "Listen, darling," Sadie said patiently, "we all have our ways and that's it. . . . I lived with my son Stuart and his wife for three years after my Reuben died, he should find eternal peace. And what happened? My daughter-in-law and I drove each other crazy. I'm a neat person, I think you can tell that, but she . . . Well, I wouldn't exactly call her a slob, but the best housekeeper in the world she isn't. Not that I want to talk badly about her, mind you. But by me you don't wash a floor with a mop. That's not what I call clean."

3. From "Black Children, Black Speech," an essay by Dorothy Z. Seymour:

   > "C'mon, man, les git goin'!" called the boy to his companion. "Dat bell ringin'. It say, 'Git in rat now!'" He dashed into the school yard.
   > "Aw, f'get you," replied the other. "Whe' Richuh? Whe' da muvvuh? He be goin' to schoo'."
   > "He in de' now, man!" was the answer as they went through the door.

Northern, southern, and midwestern dialects have developed from the languages spoken by European immigrants. The structure of African American spoken English is similar to several West African languages. In areas where people have emigrated from Latin America or Spanish-speaking parts of the Caribbean, dialects such as Spanglish have developed.

All these dialects are different from standard English, which is taught in American schools and used in business, government, and the media. The written version of standard English is known as standard written English (or SWE).

The following examples show the differences between standard written English and three dialects:

AFRICAN AMERICAN SPOKEN ENGLISH	He always be walkin' dere.
SWE	He always walks there.
SPANGLISH	They put his broken arm a cast.
SWE	They put his broken arm in a cast.
CREOLE ENGLISH	In Main Street have plenty shop.
SWE	Main Street has plenty of shops.

Because standard written English is generally considered the appropriate language to use in school and business, every chapter in Part Two of this book shows you how to use it in your writing. However, no language is better than another; languages are just different. Standard written English is a tool that will help you advance in college and in your workplace. It doesn't replace the other regional or ethnic dialects you might speak; it adds to them.

Correcting Errors

Before you can consider an essay finished, you must check your revised draft for any errors in grammar, spelling, and punctuation. It's perfectly acceptable to make mistakes when you're drafting and revising; most writers do. But if your readers are distracted by errors in your writing, they'll pay less attention to what you have to say. You'll have several opportunities throughout this book to learn what the most common errors are and how you can fix them. You should also refer to the Handbook in Part Four whenever you have a question about the correct way to structure a sentence. Remember: Editing is not a punishment; it is your final chance to make a good impression on your readers.

⏻ Use spell-check and grammar-check to edit

Be careful when you use the spell-check and grammar-check features of your word-processing program. While spell-check helps you spot typos and words that you have misspelled, it won't spot all errors. For instance, it won't notice if you use *their* when you're supposed to use *there* or *to* when you meant *too*. It also won't see when you use "textese" in your essay, such as *going 2 school* or *B4*. Grammar-check also has limitations. For example, it tends to label all long sentences as incorrect, when in fact the length of a sentence has nothing to do with its grammatical correctness.

◖Step 5 Share Your Essay

In the final step of the writing process, you share your revised and edited essay with your audience. You may just submit your essay to your instructor for a grade, but if you're proud of what you have written, you may wish to share it with your classmates as well.

At times, you may share your writing in a more public way. You may submit it to your local or campus newspaper for possible publication. Some magazines will share essays and articles submitted by their readers. If your essay proposes a change of some kind, you might want to use it as the basis of a letter that you send to a public official who can take action.

▪HOW TO Use the Writing Process

Exploring Your Choices
- Analyze your audience.
- Discover a purpose for writing.
- Brainstorm, freewrite, cluster, ask questions, research, consult with others, or relate aloud.

Drafting
- Select and narrow a topic.
- Write a tentative thesis statement.
- Get your ideas down on paper.
- Don't be concerned about sentence structure, word choice, grammar, spelling, or punctuation.

Revising
- Focus on helping your audience understand your essay.
- Improve your organization and supporting details.
- Strengthen the introduction, thesis statement, and conclusion.
- Polish sentence structure and word choice.
- Use peer review.

Editing
- Correct errors in grammar, spelling, and punctuation.
- Use a dictionary and the Handbook in Part Four.
- Don't rely on spell-check and grammar-check to catch all errors.

Sharing
- Share the final draft of your essay with your audience.

❰ One Student's Writing Process

On the following pages, you'll follow Charles Lujan, a student writer, as he writes a short essay in response to the writing assignment at the beginning of this chapter. As you recall, this assignment asks that you "compose yourself" as a writer by describing your writing experiences, influences on your writing, and your own attitude toward writing. (See p. 4 for the full assignment.) As you follow Charles through the writing process, think about your own writing process and the ways that it resembles or differs from his.

Charles's Ideas

After receiving the assignment, Charles thought first about his audience and his purpose. Although he planned to show his final draft to several classmates and a good friend from high school, he knew his primary audience was his English instructor. In his journal, Charles explained how he chose a topic and started to gather ideas for his paper:

> Jan. 18
>
> The first thing I thought about when my instructor gave this assignment on the first day of the semester was fear. This is because the last time I had to write for school I was taking an essay exam that I needed to pass in order to graduate. I did well on that exam, but the thought of writing a school assignment still bugs me even though I've been out of school for a few years. But I'm determined to get rid of that fear and do well on any writing assignment that I have to complete in college.

If you would like to start a journal, turn to Chapter 10 for more information.

Charles's Brainstorming

In order to gather ideas on his topic, Charles brainstormed about his previous experiences writing. He decided to use a chart to help him recall these experiences and organize his thoughts. (See Figure 1.3 on p. 27.)

Charles's Drafting

Using his journal writing and the brainstorming that he did on the topic (Figure 1.3), Charles wrote the following discovery draft. (Note that the draft includes the types of errors that typically appear in a first draft.)

> Thinking about Writing
>
> I write a lot more than I thought I did before I had to do this assignment. At first all I thought of was school writing. All I remember from high school was preparing for the tests that you had to take in order to graduate. You were given a topic and then you had about 30 minutes to write. This made me incredibly nervous. I'm determined that in college I'll get the help I need from the Writing Center so I'll do well. Also, I write texts and notes to my family, such as when I have to tell them where I am or when I'll get home. I'm not worried about how well I write these because my family just cares about the message. At the fire department I have to write e-mails, mostly to my supervisor. I have to be sure to get my facts straight. I wish I could have the

Writing for . . .	Kinds of writing	Thoughts
High school	Essay exam to graduate	Nervous about passing, even though I did well. I want to do better when I write in college.
Work	Forms and e-mails to my supervisor and other irefighters on my team	Just the facts. I use spell-check so I don't make stupid mistakes.
Family	Texts, notes	Let people know where I am, when I'll pick them up. No one cares how well I write.
Friends	Texts	Quick messages. Just the facts. Jim — loved to write short stories!

Figure 1.3 Charles's Brainstorming Chart

incredibly positive attitude about writing that my friend from high school Jim did. He wrote short stories and even won a contest. So I'm an anxious writer, but I'm also hopeful that I can be like Jim and start to really enjoy writing.

Charles's Revising

After finishing his discovery draft, Charles reflected again on his audience and purpose. He decided that his instructor would want an essay that would be easier to follow; after all, she had over a hundred students who would be turning in essays. This meant that his essay had to be better organized and more fully developed, with a good thesis statement. Charles asked several classmates in his class to read his discovery draft and give him suggestions for revision.

In his journal, Charles explained how he revised his essay:

Jan. 20

Before I revised my essay, I wrote an introduction with a thesis statement: "I write for many different reasons and occasions, and I have a different attitude toward each type of writing." I based the rest of the essay on this thesis statement. When I wrote the revised draft, I used a standard essay format — introduction, body paragraphs, and a conclusion. I decided to use a lot of examples to support my points, such as the phrase "catch a hydrant." I also wrote a conclusion that expressed my hope that I would write well in college. Then I went to the Writing Center for help with putting the sources into the essay and correctly using documentation.

Here is Charles's revised draft. (You may spot errors that Charles will correct when he edits his draft.)

Thinking about Writing

When I first began to think about writing, the first thing I remembered was the standardized essay exam I had to take in high school in order to graduate. But then I realized that I actually do a lot of writing, such as texts, e-mails, and forms. I write for many different reasons and occasions, and I have a different attitude toward each type of writing.   1

Some of the most important writing that I've done is related to my family. The overall conventions of our family are good honest values with the purpose of supporting and loving each other unconditionally. I and members of my family will use different types of writing. From short letters to family members of simple hellos and updates on our family, to notes being left to let someone know where we are. We often use texting for quick messages about personal family news or simple conversations. Different kinds of words are used depending on the situation, for example, when I text with my parents I try to use correct spelling, but when I text my brother I use shortcuts and slang. When I write something for my family, I'm usually in a good mood and don't worry about what the reader will think about how I write.   2

As a firefighter for the El Paso Fire Department, I know that the purpose of all my writing is to make sure everyone stays safe. I have written professional e-mails to my supervisor and fellow firefighters on subjects from training activity to actual live fire and medical calls that we have dealt with. Sometimes we use special jargon in e-mails or reports about fire events; this jargon lets us simplifie and deliver a clear message. For example, writing "catch a hydrant" means a firefighter pulled a five foot fire hose from the back of the fire truck, wrapped it around a fire hydrant, and then connected the hose to the fire hydrant. When I write for my job, I focus on getting the facts correct. As long as I dont have to rush, I don't feel stressed about how good the writing is because my readers are just interested in the message.   3

When I write for school, I can get anxious, mostly because of the standardizied writing tests I had to take in high school. Even though I'm no longer in high school, the anxiety remains. Because I've just started college, I haven't had to write much, but I know that I might get worried and not know what to say. I also don't have a lot of practice with using computers to write   4

The thesis statement tells the reader what the essay will be about.

The topic sentence states the main point of the paragraph. All of the paragraphs in the body of this essay begin with clear topic sentences.

Examples support the topic of the paragraph.

This example gives the reader a better understanding of the writing that Charles does on the job.

By talking about his attitude, Charles is directly responding to the writing assignment.

This topic sentence addresses another part of the writing assignment—the effects that previous writing experiences had on him.

essays. During orientation I was told about the Writing Center, where tutors can help you make your writing better. Going to the Writing Center will help me improve my mood and make me feel more confident.

The person who most helped me develop as a writer was my friend Jim from high school. He loved creative writing and even won a state writing contest for a short story. Jim used to talk to me about how much he loved to write. I had never met anyone who loved to write before, so he showed me that writing can be much more than just taking essay exams to graduate from high school. Because of Jim, one of the ways that I would describe myself as a writer is hopeful. I'm hopeful that my writing will continue to improve and that I will come to enjoy writing as much as he does.

By explaining how he plans to relieve his writing anxiety, Charles is giving the reader more information about the type of writer that he is.

5

In his conclusion, Charles looks to the future in an optimistic way.

> **GROUP ACTIVITY 4** Analyze Charles's Essay

Discuss the following questions with your classmates:

1. Charles was not satisfied with the title of his essay. What title would you suggest?
2. Does Charles's introduction make you want to read the essay? Why or why not?
3. How effective is Charles's thesis statement?
4. What details did Charles add to the revised draft to improve his essay?
5. How effective is Charles's conclusion? What more would you suggest he add?
6. What else could Charles do to improve his essay?

Charles's Editing

Charles described editing his essay in his journal:

> Jan. 22
>
> I used my spell-checker to catch some misspelled words. I also took my draft to the Writing Center, where a tutor showed me how to correct some errors. Finally, I proofread my essay by reading it from the end to the beginning.

Here is Charles's edited essay. (The brackets and underlining indicate where he corrected errors during the editing stage.)

Charles Lujan
Professor Evelyn Posey
English 1311
25 Jan. 2011

Thinking about Writing

When I first began to think about writing, the first thing I remembered was   1
the standardized essay exam I had to take in high school in order to graduate.
But then I realized that I actually do a lot of writing, such as texts, e-mails,
and forms. I write for many different reasons and occasions, and I have a
different attitude toward each type of writing.

Some of the most important writing that I've done is related to my family.   2
The overall conventions of our family are good honest values with the purpose
of supporting and loving each other unconditionally. I and members of my
family will use different types of writing, from short letters to family members

Sentence fragment corrected. —— of simple hellos and updates on our family, to notes being left to let someone
know where we are. We often use texting for quick messages about personal
family news or simple conversations. Different kinds of words are used

Comma splice corrected. —— depending on the situation; for example, when I text with my parents I try to
use correct spelling, but when I text my brother I use shortcuts and slang.
When I write something for my family, I'm usually in a good mood and don't
worry about what the reader will think about how I write.

As a firefighter for the El Paso Fire Department, I know that the purpose of   3
all my writing is to make sure everyone stays safe. I have written professional
e-mails to my supervisor and fellow firefighters on subjects from training
activity to actual live fire and medical calls that we have dealt with.
Sometimes we use special jargon in e-mails or reports about fire events; this

Spelling error corrected. —— jargon lets us <u>simplify</u> and deliver a clear message. For example, writing "catch
a hydrant" means a firefighter pulled a five foot fire hose from the back of the
fire truck, wrapped it around a fire hydrant, and then connected the hose to
the fire hydrant. When I write for my job, I focus on getting the facts correct.

Apostrophe added. —— As long as I <u>don't</u> have to rush, I don't feel stressed about how good the
writing is because my readers are just interested in the message.

When I write for school, I can get anxious, mostly because of the   4

Spelling error corrected. —— <u>standardized</u> writing tests I had to take in high school. Even though I'm no
longer in high school, the anxiety remains. Because I've just started college, I
haven't had to write much, but I know that I might get worried and not know
what to say. I also don't have a lot of practice with using computers to write
essays. During orientation I was told about the Writing Center, where tutors
can help you make your writing better. Going to the Writing Center will help
me improve my mood and make me feel more confident.

The person who most helped me develop as a writer was my friend Jim   5
from high school. He loved creative writing and even won a state writing
contest for a short story. Jim used to talk to me about how much he loved to
write. I had never met anyone who loved to write before, so he showed me
that writing can be much more than just taking essay exams to graduate from
high school. Because of Jim, one of the ways that I would describe myself as
a writer is hopeful. I'm hopeful that my writing will continue to improve and
that I will come to enjoy writing as much as Jim does.

_____ Unclear pronoun reference
corrected.

Charles's Sharing

Writing in his journal, Charles summed up his feelings about the final
draft of his assignment:

> Jan. 25
>
> I was really worried about the grade I would get for this essay because it
> was one of the first I've written in college. I was hoping for a B but was
> surprised when I received an A! All that revising paid off, and because I
> understand the writing process, I feel more confident about writing for
> my professors. The next time I have to write an essay, I'll have a plan for
> what to do.

CHAPTER CHECKLIST

- ❑ There are five steps in the writing process: exploring choices, drafting,
  revising, editing, and sharing.
- ❑ The writing process is recursive; that is, you often need to go back and
  forth among the steps.
- ❑ Your audience affects what you write. Identify your audience—your
  readers—and take into account what they know about your topic, what
  they don't know about your topic, and how they feel toward your topic.
- ❑ You may have three purposes for writing:
  - ❑ Expressive writing communicates thoughts, feelings, or personal
    history.
  - ❑ Informative writing conveys information.
  - ❑ Persuasive writing seeks to change the reader's opinion or to
    convince the reader to take a particular action.
- ❑ The techniques for gathering ideas include brainstorming, freewriting,
  clustering, asking questions, researching, consulting with others, and
  relating aloud.

❏ When you draft, focus on getting your ideas down on paper. Use a tentative thesis statement as a guide.

❏ When you revise, aim to improve your writing and to communicate your ideas effectively and clearly.

❏ Skilled writers usually revise a draft several times.

❏ Standard written English (SWE) is taught in American schools and used in business, government, and the media. It is important to learn SWE for writing in college and in the workplace.

❏ When you edit your writing, eliminate errors in grammar, spelling, and punctuation, which, if left uncorrected, may prevent your reader from focusing on your message.

❏ Share your finished writing with others.

REFLECTING ON YOUR WRITING

To help you reflect on the writing you did in this chapter, answer the following questions:

1. What did you learn from writing this essay?

2. How will your audience benefit from reading your essay?

3. If you had more time, what more would you do to improve your essay before sharing it with your readers?

4. How will learning about the writing process help you?

Using your answers to these questions, complete a Writing Process Report for this chapter (you can download a report form at **bedfordstmartins.com /choices**). Once you complete this report, freewrite about what you learned about the writing process and about yourself as a writer.

Crafting Paragraphs

Just as a football game is divided into quarters, an essay is divided into paragraphs. The quarters of a football game divide the game into shorter time periods so that athletes won't get overtired and spectators won't get bored or confused. Similarly, paragraphs divide information into chunks so that readers can more easily follow your ideas. Paragraphs separate the main ideas of an essay into easily understood sections. They tell your readers where one main idea ends and another begins. They also help your readers make connections between these ideas. This chapter focuses on important elements of good paragraphs: topic sentences, unity, and organization. You'll learn to write special types of paragraphs, such as introductions and conclusions. You'll also follow a student, Melissa Ruiz, as she uses the writing process to write a descriptive paragraph. ∎

In this chapter, you will write a paragraph about a meaningful photograph. As you work on your paragraph, you will

- Compose topic sentences.
- Learn about paragraph unity and organization.
- Practice writing special kinds of paragraphs.

Writing Assignment

Imagine you are applying for a job as an after-school tutor for children. You are required to submit an application form and letters of recommendation. Because your potential employer is interested in knowing something about your character, you also have to submit a writing sample in which you describe a photograph that is meaningful to you in some way. The photograph can show an important family occasion, such as a

(continued)

wedding or birthday, or it can depict a special place or a gathering of friends. Alternatively, you can select a photograph of either a historical event that captures your attention or a person who interests you. Write a paragraph in which you describe the photograph and explain what it reveals. Assume that your readers do not have a copy of the photograph.

Use the writing process when you compose your paragraph. As you learned in Chapter 1, the steps in the writing process are:

- exploring your choices
- drafting
- revising
- editing
- sharing

Topic Sentences

When it comes to paragraphs, the phrase "one thing at a time" is useful to remember. The "one thing" you explain in a paragraph is stated in a topic sentence. To write an effective topic sentence for each paragraph in your essay, follow these guidelines:

- Break up your thesis statement into several specific supporting ideas.
- Write a complete thought for each of these specific ideas.

A topic sentence functions as a mini-thesis for each paragraph. Here are some examples of thesis statements and the topic sentences that might follow from them:

To review the characteristics of a strong thesis statement, turn to pp. 18–19.

THESIS STATEMENT Hiking is excellent exercise because it strengthens muscles, offers a chance to enjoy nature, and relieves stress.

Topic Sentences

- Hiking provides a strenuous workout for many parts of the body, especially leg and back muscles.
- Whether in the desert or in the woods, hikers enjoy beautiful scenery and clear air.
- A hike in a beautiful area takes people completely away from the daily grind of school, family, and work.

These are effective topic sentences because they support the thesis statement that hiking is excellent exercise.

⏻ **Think of a topic sentence as a status update**

Writing a topic sentence is similar to posting a status update on Facebook or Twitter. Your update has to express your main idea in a sentence or phrase that is short, direct, and informative.

Here is another set of topic sentences that supports the thesis statement:

THESIS STATEMENT   If this university continues to increase tuition year after year, it will no longer be an asset to our community.

Topic Sentences

- As a result of tuition increases, families on limited incomes will not be able to send their children to college.
- Students who have already spent several years in college—and who have invested thousands of dollars in their education—will be forced to drop out.
- High school students will lack the motivation to study because they'll feel that college costs too much.
- Companies will decide not to locate here because they won't be able to find well-educated workers.

These topic sentences are effective because they explain the negative effect that tuition increases will have on the community. Consider one more set of examples:

THESIS STATEMENT   Before I moved to the United States, I lived in Japan, a very different country and culture.

Topic Sentences

- Housing is much more spacious in the United States than it is in Japan. Even small apartments in this country are large by Japanese standards.
- Americans are informal, and even strangers use first names, whereas people in Japan are reserved and formal.
- People in the United States emphasize individuality, whereas people in Japan emphasize conformity to a group.

▪ HOW TO Write a Topic Sentence

- Write several complete thoughts that make a point about your thesis statement. These are your topic sentences.
- Check that these topic sentences tell something informative and interesting about your thesis statement.
- Check that you can add details to show or explain these topic sentences.
- Check that you are writing on the topic assigned.

> **GROUP ACTIVITY 1 Write Topic Sentences**

With your classmates, write several topic sentences for each of the following thesis statements.

1. No two people could be more different than Matt and Jerry, but they are my two closest friends.

2. Living with your parents when you're an adult has its disadvantages, but so does living on your own.

3. Time management skills are important for students holding a full-time job while working toward a college degree.

4. Today's communications technology — from cell phones to Facebook — makes life more stressful, not more efficient.

5. Because anyone can use it, the Internet can be a dangerous place for children and adults alike.

Should your topic sentence appear at the beginning, middle, or end of the paragraph? A topic sentence can fall anywhere in the paragraph. Most often, however, it comes first. Just as placing the thesis statement at the beginning of an essay helps guide the reader through the paper, putting the topic sentence at the beginning of the paragraph helps guide the reader through the paragraph. To put it another way, giving the main idea at the beginning is like giving the reader a hook on which to hang the details that follow.

In the following paragraph, the topic sentence (highlighted) comes first. The author, Garrison Keillor, states in the topic sentence that when he was a child, denim pants represented freedom to him. In the rest of the paragraph, he gives facts and examples to support this idea.

> Thus denim came to symbolize freedom to me. My first suit was a dark brown wool pinstripe bought on the occasion of my Aunt Ruby's funeral, and I wore it to church every Sunday. It felt solemn and mournful to me. You couldn't run in a suit, you could only lumber like an old man. When church was over, and you put on denim trousers, you walked out the door into the wide green world and your cousin threw you the ball and suddenly your body was restored, you could make moves.
>
> —**GARRISON KEILLOR**, *"Blue Magic"*

Sometimes, however, you may need to provide background information or explain the connection between two paragraphs before the topic sentence can be presented. In either case, the topic sentence may fall in the middle of the paragraph. In the following paragraph, the topic sentence (highlighted) is given after the first sentence, which explains the connection between this paragraph and the previous one:

> I don't mean that some people are born clearheaded and are therefore natural writers, whereas others are naturally fuzzy and will never write well. Thinking clearly is a conscious act that writers must force upon themselves,

as if they were working on any other project that requires logic: adding up a laundry list or doing an algebra problem. Good writing doesn't come naturally, though most people obviously think it does. Professional writers are constantly being bearded by strangers who say that they'd like to "try a little writing sometime"—meaning when they retire from their real profession, which is difficult, like insurance or real estate. Or they say, "I could write a book about that." I doubt it.

—**WILLIAM ZINSSER**, *"Simplicity"*

Occasionally, placing a topic sentence at the end of a paragraph can dramatize the main idea. In the following example, the topic sentence (highlighted) appears at the end. By giving several specific examples before stating the generalization, the writer emphasizes the main point of the paragraph:

Most black Americans are not poor. Most black teenagers are not crack addicts. Most black mothers are not on welfare. Indeed, in sheer numbers, more white Americans are poor and on welfare than are black. Yet one never would deduce that by watching television or reading American newspapers and magazines.

—**PATRICIA RAYBORN**, *"A Case of 'Severe Bias'"*

GROUP ACTIVITY 2 Write Topic Sentences

With your classmates, brainstorm for several minutes about a photograph. In addition to describing the photograph, jot down ideas about what the photograph means to you. Then, as a group, write topic sentences that summarize each group member's thoughts about the photograph.

☾ Unity

Once you have an effective topic sentence, you need to make sure that all other sentences within the paragraph relate to that topic sentence. This is called *paragraph unity.* Paragraphs that lack unity contain sentences that distract and confuse readers because they aren't on the topic. These are called *irrelevant sentences.* In the following paragraph, several irrelevant sentences have been added (in italics); notice how these irrelevancies distract you from the topic of the paragraph.

I went to high school in the Fifties, when blue denim had gained unsavory cultural associations—it was biker and beatnik clothing, outlaw garb, a cousin to the ducktail, a symbol of Elvis, and as such, it was banned at our school. *Elvis Presley was my favorite singer at the time.* Every September, we were read the dress code by our homeroom teacher: you could wear brown denim, or grey, or green, but not blue. *Blue is my favorite color.* Why? "Because," she explained. *She lived a block away from me.* There have to be rules, and blue denim was a statement of rebellion, and we were in school to learn and not to flaunt our individuality. So there.

—**GARRISON KEILLOR,** *"Blue Magic"*

During the drafting stage, you may include irrelevant sentences as you focus on getting your thoughts on paper. When you revise, however, you need to eliminate them to achieve paragraph unity. Reread your paragraphs and topic sentences, and delete any statements that are off the topic.

GROUP ACTIVITY 3 Improve Paragraph Unity

With your classmates, read the following sentences. Place a checkmark next to the sentences that do not relate to this topic sentence: *I had defied a direct order, but I didn't expect my dad to do anything about it.*

_____ My dad looked as if he were trying to recover from a gunshot wound.

_____ Gun control is a topic I would like to write about some day.

_____ His eyes fluttered and his mouth gaped. "You're saying no to me?" was all he could say.

_____ "Yeah, I'm saying no to you."

_____ I felt like a newborn colt, prancing around, kicking, testing my limits.

_____ Riding horses is one of my favorite hobbies.

_____ "Well, pack your bags and leave," he shouted.

_____ Uh-oh, I hadn't expected that.

_____ My Samsonite bag is stored on the top shelf of my closet.

_____ "Okay, I will."

Organization

You must organize the ideas in your paragraphs. If you don't, your readers won't be able to follow what you're saying, they'll become frustrated, and they'll stop reading. You can use general-to-specific order, topic-illustration-explanation order, progressive order, directional order, question-and-answer order, or specific-to-general order to organize your ideas.

General-to-Specific Order

General-to-specific order is one way to organize ideas in a paragraph. Whereas general statements are broad, specific statements are more focused. For example, the statement "I love dogs" is general because it refers to all dogs. But the statement "I love my dog Rupert because he's smart, funny, and affectionate" is specific because it cites a particular dog and several details.

In general-to-specific order, the most general idea is given at the beginning of the paragraph in the topic sentence. The more specific ideas that follow help support and explain the general statement. The following paragraph illustrates this order:

> The *quinceañera*, or coming-out party, is a tradition for many young Latinas. In this ritual, parents proudly present their fifteen-year-old daughter to their community. The ceremony consists of a Mass followed by a dinner and dance. Fourteen young couples serve as the girl's court. Long formal dresses, tuxedos, live music, and video cameras are all part of the spectacle.

Topic-Illustration-Explanation Order

The *topic-illustration-explanation (TIE) order* is used to organize paragraphs that contain examples such as facts and expert testimony. As in general-to-specific order, the paragraph starts with a topic sentence. You can organize the paragraph in this way:

- State the topic.
- Give an illustration (such as a fact or expert testimony).
- Explain the significance of the illustration.

The topic-illustration-explanation method of organization is used in the following paragraph about an American cultural symbol—the T-shirt. Notice that the writer states the topic, gives an illustration, and then explains why the illustration is important.

> T-shirts with political or controversial statements can require the viewer to think about the message. A few years ago the slogan "A woman's place is in the House" was seen on many T-shirts. To understand this slogan, the viewer had to know the original saying, "A woman's place is in the home," and then realize that the word *House* on the shirt referred to the House of Representatives. The House of Representatives, a part of Congress, has always had fewer female than male members. A person wearing this T-shirt, then, advocated electing more women to political office.

In this paragraph, the topic is stated in the first sentence: T-shirts with political statements may require some thought. To illustrate, the writer uses a slogan—"A woman's place is in the House"—and then explains the significance of the slogan.

Progressive Order

Another way of organizing the ideas in your paragraphs is to use *progressive order*, in which ideas are arranged from least to most important. Since the final idea in a paragraph (or in an essay, for that matter) is the one that readers tend to remember most readily, ending with the most important idea is usually very effective. Thus, rather than presenting your examples randomly, you can arrange them progressively to emphasize the most important one.

Here's another paragraph from the essay about the American T-shirt. Notice that the writer uses progressive order to illustrate the various functions that the T-shirt serves in our culture.

> The common, ordinary T-shirt tells us much about the American culture. The T-shirt is a product of our casual lifestyle. People have been known to wear T-shirts under blazers at work and under evening dresses at the Academy Awards. The T-shirt is also associated with people of all ages, from the elderly to newborn babies. Most important, the T-shirt gives us a way to express ourselves. It tells others about our favorite schools, sports teams, or cartoon figures. It can also let others know our political views—whether or not they care to know.

In this paragraph, the most important function of T-shirts is stated at the end. The writer emphasizes this function with the introductory words *most important.*

(ᗑ) **The Top Ten list and progressive order**

Are you familiar with the Top Ten list from David Letterman's late-night television show? This list is an example of progressive order. Letterman always reads the most important item (#1) last.

Directional Order

When you use *directional order,* you describe something from one location to another, such as left to right, down to up, or near to far.

For example, suppose you want to describe a photograph of your brother taken while he was in the Air Force. To organize your description, you might use top-to-bottom directional order, as in the following example:

> This is my brother Antonio in his Air Force uniform. His face is clean shaven, and his haircut is regulation style. He's smiling his big lopsided smile. He has an athletic build, like a body builder's. He wears his uniform proudly. It is perfectly pressed, and every brass button is perfectly shined. The crease in his pants is as sharp as a blade. His shoes are like black mirrors.

Question-and-Answer Order

Question-and-answer order is another method for organizing ideas in a paragraph. It involves asking a question at the beginning of the paragraph and then answering that question in the rest of the paragraph. In the following paragraph, the writer uses the question-and-answer method when discussing the causes of homelessness:

What's the root of the homeless problem? Everyone seems to have a scape-goat: Advocates of the homeless blame government policy; politicians blame the legal system; the courts blame the bureaucratic infrastructure; the Democrats blame the Republicans; the Republicans, the Democrats. The public blames the economy, drugs, the "poverty cycle," and the "breakdown of society." With all this finger-pointing, the group most responsible for the homeless being the way they are receives the least blame. That group is the homeless themselves.

—L. CHRISTOPHER AWALT, *"Brother, Don't Spare a Dime"*

 Question-and-answer order and FAQs

Using question-and-answer order is similar to writing FAQs, or frequently asked questions. As with FAQs, you begin with a question and then follow with the answer.

Specific-to-General Order

In *specific-to-general order*, the most specific ideas are stated first, and the general idea appears at the end of the paragraph. Use this type of organization when you want to position a topic sentence at the end of a paragraph.

In the example that follows, the writer organizes ideas from the most specific to the most general:

The audience gasps as colors explode in the night sky—red, blue, yellow, green. The explosions grow bigger and bigger until they cover the night sky, and then they slowly disintegrate like silvery rain. Although everyone enjoys a fireworks spectacle on the Fourth of July, few understand the origin of this ritual celebration. The Fourth of July commemorates America's fight for independence, and the fireworks are to remind us of the historic battles that ended the Revolutionary War.

■ **HOW TO** Organize a Paragraph

The **topic sentence** states the main point of the paragraph. **Support sentences** include details that support your topic sentence, arranged using one of these orders: general-to-specific, topic-illustration-explanation, progressive, directional, question-and-answer, or specific-to-general. The **concluding sentence** restates the main point of the paragraph.

- Indent the first line of each paragraph five spaces.
- Use margins of one inch on each side of the page.
- Check that each sentence is a complete thought and ends with a period (.), question mark (?), or exclamation mark (!).

GROUP ACTIVITY 4 Identify Types of Paragraph Organization

With your classmates, identify the type of organization in each of the following paragraphs as general-to-specific, topic-illustration-explanation (TIE), progressive, directional, question-and-answer, or specific-to-general. Some types of organization may overlap.

1. With about a half-billion passengers a year boarding scheduled U.S. flights, air travel has become so routine that it's easy for people to forget what's outside their cabin cocoon. The atmosphere at 35,000 feet won't sustain human life. It's about 60 degrees below zero, and so thin that an inactive person breathing it would become confused and lethargic in less than a minute.
   —CONSUMER REPORTS, *"Breathing on a Jet Plane"*

   Organization: _____

2. When you need a new car, do you go to the nearest auto dealer and buy the first car you see? Most of us don't. We shop and compare features, quality, and price. We look for the best value for our money.
   —O. M. NICELY, *"Using Technology to Serve You Better"*

   Organization: _____

3. When you go on a hike in the desert, the least of your worries is snakes and scorpions. If you stay away from them, they'll stay away from you. Instead of worrying about reptiles and bugs, worry about the sun. To avoid a serious burn, apply sunscreen to exposed skin and wear a hat. Most important, bring plenty of water — at least a gallon per person.

   Organization: _____

4. When many dogs hear the words "Let's go on a hike!" they can't contain their excitement. They wag their tails, jump up and down, and even bring their leashes to their owners. Most dogs love to hike, and their owners love to take them. Just as with humans, though, dogs need to be prepared for a rigorous day on the trail.

   Organization: _____

5. Almost everyone knows that smoking is bad for one's health, yet young people continue to start smoking every day. According to the National Cancer Institute, 20 percent of U.S. high school students are tobacco smokers. Experts believe that many young people take up smoking because they think it will make them look cool.

   Organization: _____

◖ Special Kinds of Paragraphs

In addition to focusing on topic sentences and paragraph unity and organization, you need to keep in mind the special requirements of two different but important types of paragraphs: introductions and conclusions.

Introductions

First impressions are important. In a job interview, employers prefer someone who is well spoken and neatly dressed over someone who mutters and is dressed to go to the gym. Similarly, the introduction to an essay provides readers with a good first impression of your ideas.

In a short essay (two to three pages), the introduction usually consists of only the first paragraph; longer essays often have introductions that are several paragraphs in length. A good introduction has three characteristics: it gets readers' attention, narrows the topic, and states the thesis.

The technique of getting your readers' attention is often called the *hook*. You want your introduction to grab your readers and pull them into your essay, just as a hook lures a fish to bite on the line. In addition to getting readers' attention, the hook contains information relevant to the topic of your essay. A hook can consist of a question, an interesting fact, a brief story, or a vivid image, or it can be a definition or classification of key terms to help the reader begin to understand the topic.

Pose a Question

Posing one or more *questions* at the start of an essay can arouse readers' curiosity about your topic, making them want to read on to find the answers. In the following introduction, the author uses a question to begin her essay about her father's heroism during World War II.

> "Who is your hero and why do you admire him?" is the question my son, Andy, had to answer on his application to a private school. The school's headmaster made an eloquent speech linking the growing incidence of drug abuse, suicide, and violence among teenagers to the absence of heroes in contemporary life.
>
> —IRINA HREMIA BRAGIN, *"What Heroes Teach Us"*

Provide an Interesting or Surprising Fact

Introducing a topic with *facts*—statements that can be verified as true—has two important effects on readers. It signals them that you know your topic well, and it encourages them to read further to see what you have to say. An interesting or surprising fact can also get readers' attention, as in this essay on how to drive safely:

The first automobile crash in the United States occurred in New York City in 1896, when a car collided with a bicyclist. We've had 100 years since then to learn how to share the road, but with increasingly crowded and complex traffic conditions, we're still making mistakes, mostly because we assume that other drivers—and their vehicles—will behave the way we do.

—CAROLYN GRIFFITH, *"Sharing the Road"*

Most readers would be intrigued by the date of the first car accident and would want to read more about this topic.

Tell a Story

Beginning with a *brief story* or an *anecdote* related to a topic can help draw readers into your essay because most readers like to read about other people's lives:

The Hollywood blockbuster had been playing for about 20 minutes when one of the characters took a gunshot in the face, the camera lingering on the gory close-up. Fifteen rows from the big screen, a little girl—no more than six years old—began shrieking. Her mother hissed, "Shut up," and gave her a stinging slap.

—ALVIN POUSSAINT, *"Let's Enforce Our Movie Ratings"*

In addition to getting readers' attention, this story illustrates the writer's point that movie ratings need to be enforced.

Describe a Vivid Image

An introduction that contains vivid *description* sets the scene and draws readers into your essay. Because readers like to imagine scenes, a vivid image is another effective way to hook readers:

Joe Flom is the last living "named" partner of the law firm Skadden, Arps, Slate, Meagher and Flom. He has a corner office high atop the Condé Nast tower in Manhattan. He is short and slightly hunched. His head is large, framed by long prominent ears, and his narrow blue eyes are hidden by over-size aviator-style glasses. He is slender now, but during his heyday, Flom was extremely overweight. He waddles when he walks. He doodles when he thinks. He mumbles when he talks, and when he makes his way down the halls of Skadden, Arps, conversations drop to a hush.

—MALCOLM GLADWELL, *Outliers: The Story of Success*

This colorful description introduces an important character in the book.

Define a Term

Defining the meaning of a word works well in an introduction when you need to explain an unfamiliar topic for your readers. In the following introductory paragraph, the writer uses definition to ensure her readers' understanding of her topic and thesis statement. Notice also that she uses humor in the definition to further engage her readers. Her thesis sentence is the last one in the paragraph.

> As a lifelong crabber (that is, one who catches crabs, not a chronic complainer), I can tell you that anyone who has the patience and a great love for the river is qualified to join the ranks of crabbers. However, if you want your first crabbing experience to be a successful one, you must come prepared.
>
> —**MARY ZEIGLER**, *"How to Catch Crabs"*

Break the Topic into Categories

You may wish to use *classification* in an introduction when categorizing by types can help narrow your topic and focus your readers' attention on the one type discussed in your essay. For example, in the following introduction, the writer classifies various types of musicians before focusing attention on the essay's topic: the two types of musicians who play percussion instruments, drummers and percussionists. The writer's thesis statement comes last in the introduction.

> Quick—what do you call a person who plays a trumpet? A trumpeter, of course. A person who plays the flute is referred to as a flutist, or flautist, if you prefer. Someone who plays a piano is usually known as a pianist, unless of course he plays the player piano, in which case he is known as a player piano player rather than a player piano pianist. Got the hang of this yet? Okay, then, what do you call someone who plays that set of instruments belonging to the percussion family? Why, you call him a percussionist, don't you? Wrong! It's not quite as easy as all that. There are two types of musicians who play percussion instruments, "drummers" and "percussionists," and they are as different as the Sex Pistols and the New York Philharmonic.
>
> —**KAREN KRAMER**, *"The Little Drummer Boys"*

Narrow the Topic

An introduction announces the general topic of the essay and then narrows the subject to the more specific point stated in the thesis. Just as a photographer focuses the lens on a specific object for greater clarity, a writer narrows the scope of the essay.

In the following example, the writer introduces the general topic of the earth and its environment in the first paragraph before focusing on her main point—that human beings have been endangering the earth's environment—at the end of the first paragraph and into the beginning of the second paragraph:

> The history of life on earth has been a history of interaction between living things and their surroundings. To a large extent, the physical form and the habits of the earth's vegetation and its animal life have been molded by the environment. Considering the whole span of earthly time, the opposite effect, in which life actually modifies its surroundings, has been relatively

slight. Only within the moment of time represented by the present century has one species—man—acquired significant power to alter the nature of his world.

During the past quarter century this power has not only increased to one of disturbing magnitude but it has changed in character. The most alarming of all man's assaults upon the environment is the contamination of air, earth, rivers, and sea with dangerous and even lethal materials.

—RACHEL CARSON, *"The Obligation to Endure"*

By gradually narrowing her topic, Carson prepares her readers for her thesis statement (highlighted) that human contamination is damaging the environment.

State the Thesis

For more information about thesis statements, turn to pp. 18–19.

After getting your readers' attention and narrowing the topic, you're ready to state your thesis. Generally, the thesis appears at the end of the introduction; depending on the length and complexity of the essay, it can range from one sentence to several sentences long. As you read in Chapter 1, the thesis of an essay states the topic; shows, explains, or argues a particular point about the topic; and gives the reader a sense of what the essay will be about.

In the following introduction, notice how the writer attracts readers' attention, narrows her topic, and then states her thesis (highlighted):

"Welcome to Rio Bravo Grill! Can I get y'all a margarita?" With those words I began my stint as a full-time waitress, apartment renter, and bill payer in downtown Atlanta. It was the first time I had ever truly been on my own, with no help from my parents except for the occasional sardonic words of advice or chastisement. At that time I had no idea what I wanted to do with my life. I had recently been forced to leave the United States Air Force Academy, and I didn't know what to do next. My life had always been planned around a career in the Air Force, and I had never pictured myself as anything else. My leaving and subsequent return to the academy, as well as my experiences during the time I was out, taught me a lot about myself, the world around me, and where I want to go from here.

—ANDREA L. HOUK, *"The Honor Principle"*

▪ HOW TO Write an Introduction

- Use a hook—such as a question, an interesting fact, a brief story, a vivid image or description, a definition, or a classification—to get readers' attention.
- Narrow the topic to one main point.
- Write a thesis statement.

> ### GROUP ACTIVITY 5 Unscramble an Introduction

The following sentences are from the introduction of an essay about a young college student's reaction to the birth of his child. The sentences are out of order. With several other classmates, put the paragraph into the correct order.

_____ I thought I would have to give up my dream of graduating from college in four years.

_____ When I discovered I was going to be a father at age nineteen, I thought my life was over.

_____ Now, however, I can't imagine my life without my daughter.

_____ Instead, I would need to find a full-time job to support my new family.

_____ She has taught me that despite the responsibilities of parenthood, the joy and love make it worthwhile.

_____ In fact, I thought I would have to give up going to college altogether.

Conclusions

Often the last thing people read is what they remember the most. Therefore, your conclusion needs to be well written and memorable. The standard way to end an essay is to restate your thesis, summarize your major points, or broaden your focus.

Restate the Thesis

By restating your thesis, you ensure that your readers remember your main point. However, don't use the same words you used in your introduction. Instead, vary your word choice so that your main point isn't unnecessarily repetitive. The restated thesis can appear at either the beginning or the end of the conclusion.

STATEMENT OF THESIS IN INTRODUCTION	If we make it a point to be considerate of all the occupants of our roadways, from cars and trucks to motorcycles and pedestrians, we can make our streets much safer places to be.
RESTATEMENT OF THESIS (ITALICIZED) IN CONCLUSION	But no matter how much time elapses, the basic principles of sharing the road safely won't change much. Just watch out for *the big guys, cut the little guys some slack, pay attention to "vehicular diversity,"* and above all, enjoy the ride.

— **CAROLYN GRIFFITH**, *"Sharing the Road"*

By varying her word choice, Griffith restates her thesis in an interesting way.

Often, an *effective quotation* can restate your thesis in an interesting, attention-getting way that emphasizes your main point. In the conclusion to an essay on Olympic athletes' ability to focus intensely, Adam Rogers ends with a quotation that describes this mental process:

> Though the psychologists might not be sure what's going on in flow, they know a few things about how to get there. In a beautiful irony, the harder athletes try to win, the less likely they are to find their zone. "Any time you get into that state where you're thinking about the result instead of what you're doing, you're pretty much screwed, to use a scientific term," says Shane Murphy, a sports psychologist and consultant. That's an ancient notion—since the 13th century, students of kyudo, Japanese Zen archery, have been forbidden to even aim at a target until they perfect their drawing and firing. Even today, says Janet Dykman, a U.S. archer, "I try to have no emotion about what happens to the arrow. I just concentrate on my form." And the arrow lands smack in the bull's-eye of harmony.
>
> —**ADAM ROGERS**, *"Zen and the Art of Olympic Success"*

Summarize Your Points

For a lengthy and complex essay, a *summary* can pull ideas together and reinforce main points in the conclusion. The author of an essay on the New England clambake summarizes her important points about the clambake in her conclusion:

> A clambake may remind you of Boston and Paul Revere's ride, but to ensure a successful meal, remember these important points: start early, dig a pit that is at least two feet deep, feed the charcoal fire with hardwood, and use seaweed-soaked canvas. While your clams are cooking, get out the iced tea and beer and enjoy playing volleyball or strolling along the beach while taking part in this cherished New England tradition.

Broaden the Focus

In your introduction, you state the general topic and then narrow your focus until you give the thesis statement. In the conclusion, however, you want to broaden your focus—widen the lens of the camera—to tell your readers how your main point connects to other important ideas.

In the conclusion to her essay on illegal immigrants, Linda Chavez broadens the focus of her argument by pointing out that the immigration question is about more than whether or not to grant amnesty—it's about supporting values that are important to all of us:

> The fact that so many illegal immigrants are intertwined with American citizens or legal residents, either as spouses or parents, should give pause to those who'd like to see all illegal immigrants rounded up and deported or their lives made so miserable they leave on their own. A better approach would allow those who have made their lives here, established families, bought homes, worked continuously and paid taxes to remain after paying

fines, demonstrating English fluency and proving they have no criminal record. Such an approach is as much about supporting family values as it is granting amnesty.

—LINDA CHAVEZ, *"Supporting Family Values"*

Chavez's final sentence invites readers to think about the immigration question in a deeper way.

In the following example from an article about the popularity of collecting baseball cards, the writer concludes with a call for action by asking readers to consider joining a baseball card club:

> After collecting baseball cards for several years, our greatest desire is to start a baseball card club in Los Angeles. If you would be interested in joining such a club, write to the above address with a note, "Count me in!"

■ HOW TO Write a Conclusion

- Restate the thesis to remind readers of your main point.
- Sum up what has been said in the essay.
- Broaden the focus or make an additional observation about your main point.

GROUP ACTIVITY 6 Unscramble a Conclusion

The following sentences are from the essay about a young college student's reaction to the birth of his child. The sentences are out of order. With a group of your classmates, put the sentences in the correct order.

_____ Because of her, I get angry when I hear people talk about how bad it is when young people have children.

_____ In fact, for some people, it's the best thing that can ever happen to them.

_____ It's not always bad.

_____ My daughter has improved my life in many ways, from making me more responsible to teaching me what love really means.

◖ One Student's Paragraph

As you recall, the writing assignment for this chapter is to write a paragraph for part of a job application in which you describe a photograph and explain what it reveals about your life. On the following pages, you'll follow Melissa Ruiz, a student writer, as she writes her paragraph for this assignment. Use Melissa's writing process as a guide to writing your own paragraph.

Melissa's Choices

In her journal, Melissa freewrote about the assignment after she had looked through several photographs:

> I thought it would be easy to pick a photo. I guess I didn't realize a big part of this application is finding a good photo I'd really want to write about. I looked through my photo albums but couldn't decide. Should I write about my trip to Mexico? How my family celebrates Christmas? My younger sister? Then I saw it. On the floor was a stack of newspapers, and on the front page of one of them, there was a picture of a Red Cross worker helping victims of Hurricane Katrina. They look so sad, and I knew this was a better picture to write about, since it's so emotional, and Hurricane Katrina is something that everyone has feelings about.

After selecting the following photograph, Melissa brainstormed about it in her journal:

The young woman is wearing a white t-shirt with the big Red Cross logo
   on back.
Her back is to the camera, can't see her face.
Her hair is up in a bun.
The older woman's dark, sad eyes look through rose-tinted glasses.
She looks away, probably has been crying.
She looks old and sad, short hair.
The older man has white hair that is balding.

He looks down, his tiny eyes peek out, big bags under his eyes.
They both look lost.
What does this photo mean to me?
I appreciate what I have — a home, food, my family and friends.
Anything can happen; you just never know.

Melissa's Drafting

After studying the photograph again and referring to her brainstorming, Melissa wrote the following discovery draft. (Note that the example includes the types of errors that typically appear in a first draft.)

After Katrina

As soon as I look at this photograph, I get sad. I mean, I don't know this couple, I've never met them, but I know they're suffering because of what Hurricane Katrina did to their home. They look so sad, as if their about to cry, and they probably have been already. The wife's dark eyes look through her rose-tinted glasses and out into nothing. She folds her hands tightly and rests them under her chin. The husband's sad eyes barely peek through big bags. It's as if neither one of them are really there—they're lost in sadness. This photo makes me realize how fortunate I am to have a home and that my family and friends are safe, because you never know what can happen to you unexpectedly. My heart goes out to this couple, who are probably hundreds of miles away from their home, just wishing for the nightmare to be over.

Melissa's Revising

Melissa read her paragraph aloud to several classmates so that they could give her suggestions for revision. Because her classmates were confused about her main point, Melissa decided to begin her paragraph with a topic sentence that would be supported by the rest of the paragraph. Her classmates also suggested that Melissa organize the sentences in the paragraph and include more description.

Here is Melissa's revised draft. (Because she focused on getting down her ideas, you may spot editing errors she will still need to correct.)

After Katrina

This photograph I found in the newspaper reminds me to appreciate what I   —— Topic sentence added.
had in life. In the photo, a young woman with a big red cross on the back of her white T-shirt facing a couple who were victims of Hurricane Katrina. The couple is older, the husband's white hair is balding, and the woman's face is wrinkled. The wife folds her hands tightly and rests them under her chin. Her dark eyes   —— Details added.

look through rose-tinted glasses and out into nothing. She looks as if she wants to cry, and she probably has already. The husband's sad eyes barely peek through large puffy bags. His fist holds up his downturned face. He's probably thinking about how their lives and home has been torn apart, and he just wishes for the nightmare to be over. They both look as though they're not really there: they're lost in sadness. The misfortune they are suffering is a reminder that there's no telling what can come along to effect your life and change it forever. Seeing this photo makes me cherish the very simple and basic things in life, like a roof over my head, food to eat, and the safety of my family and friends. Its sad but true: we usually don't appreciate what we have until we have already lost it.

Conclusion added. —

Repetition of topic sentence. —[

Melissa's Editing

To help her edit her paragraph, Melissa sought help from a tutor at her college's writing center. She also used the spell-check on her word-processing program.

Here is Melissa's edited paragraph. (The underlining indicates where she corrected errors during the editing stage.)

After Katrina

Verb tense fixed. —

Comma splice fixed. —

Subject-verb agreement fixed. —

Spelling error corrected. —

Apostrophe added. —

This photograph I found in the newspaper reminds me to appreciate what I have in life. In the photo, a young woman with a big red cross on the back of her white T-shirt faces a couple who were victims of Hurricane Katrina. The couple is older; the husband's white hair is balding, and the woman's face is wrinkled. The wife folds her hands tightly and rests them under her chin. Her dark eyes look through rose-tinted glasses and out into nothing. She looks as if she wants to cry, and she probably has already. The husband's sad eyes barely peek through large puffy bags. His fist holds up his downturned face. He's probably thinking about how their lives and home have been torn apart, and he just wishes for the nightmare to be over. They both look as though they're not really there: they're lost in sadness. The misfortune they are suffering is a reminder that there's no telling what can come along to <u>affect</u> your life and change it forever. Seeing this photo makes me cherish the very simple and basic things in life, like a roof over my head, food to eat, and the safety of my family and friends. <u>It's</u> sad but true: we usually don't appreciate what we have until we have already lost it.

Melissa's Sharing

In a journal entry, Melissa explained how she shared her paragraph:

When I revised my paragraph, I made it more interesting to read. I read my revised paragraph aloud to my group and then showed them the photograph.

They told me that I really captured the details and emotion in the photo. They too could see how sad the couple looked. Then I turned the paragraph in to my teacher for a grade.

CHAPTER CHECKLIST

❑ Remember the phrase "one thing at a time" when you write paragraphs. The "one thing" you explain in each paragraph is stated in the topic sentence.

❑ Write effective topic sentences by breaking down your thesis statement into several specific supporting ideas. Then write a complete thought for each specific idea.

❑ Maintain paragraph unity by sticking to the topic introduced in your topic sentence.

❑ Organize the ideas in your paragraphs by using
   ❑ general-to-specific order.
   ❑ topic-illustration-explanation (TIE) order.
   ❑ progressive order.
   ❑ directional order.
   ❑ question-and-answer order.
   ❑ specific-to-general order.

❑ In your introduction, get the readers' attention, narrow the topic, and state the thesis.

❑ In your conclusion, restate the thesis, summarize your points, and broaden the focus.

REFLECTING ON YOUR WRITING

To help you reflect on the writing you did in this chapter, answer the following questions.

1. In your description of a photograph, which step of the writing process (exploring choices, drafting, revising, editing, and sharing) did you find the easiest to do? Which was most difficult? Why?

2. What pleases you most about your paragraph?

3. If you had more time, what parts of your paragraph would you continue to revise? Why?

Using your answers to these questions, complete a Writing Process Report for this chapter (you can download a report form at **bedfordstmartins.com /choices**). Once you complete this report, freewrite about what you learned in this chapter about crafting paragraphs and what you still hope to learn.

The Patterns of Development

Suppose you visit one of your favorite Web sites and find words scattered randomly over the screen. Photos and artwork are upside down or obscured by blotches of color. Incomprehensible music blares out from your speakers. The Web site has no order. You don't know what to look at first, and you can't understand what message is being conveyed. Similarly, an essay that lacks order will confuse and frustrate readers, who won't be able to understand the connection between your ideas or the main point you're trying to make.

As you learned in Chapter 1, when you write an essay, you write a thesis statement that focuses on your main point, and you organize, in a logical order, the paragraphs that support that thesis statement. And, as you learned in Chapter 2, each of these paragraphs contains a topic sentence that focuses on the main point of the paragraph. In this chapter, you will learn how to use the patterns of development to expand and structure your thoughts within those paragraphs and across the essay as a whole. Essays usually contain several patterns, but one pattern may be dominant. Using the patterns of development enables you to

- Increase interest in your topic.
- Communicate your thoughts clearly to your readers.
- Support your main ideas.

In this chapter, you will write a brief essay on a topic of your choice. As you work on your essay, you will

- Learn about the patterns of development: description, narration, examples, process explanation, classification, definition, comparison and contrast, cause and effect, and argument.
- Practice using each of these patterns of development.
- Follow one student through the process of using the patterns to develop an essay.

In this chapter, you'll practice using each of the patterns of development and then follow a student writer, Carlos Montijo, as he uses some of them to develop an essay. ■

Writing Assignment

Write a practice essay for your classmates in which you take a position on a topic of importance to you. You may choose the topic and the audience, but it should be a topic that everyone is talking about, on which people have differing opinions, and on which you would like to present your views. To find such a topic, read through some online newspapers, magazines, or blogs to find current issues, such as the effects of a toxic oil spill or the need for college students to vote in a local election. Use the steps of the writing process that you learned in Chapter 1—exploring your choices, drafting, revising, editing, and sharing—when composing your essay. Support your points by using some of the patterns of development described in the pages that follow.

Description

When you use description in your writing, you allow your readers to become more involved. The key is to go beyond describing experiences in general ways ("We had a great time; that day really changed me.") to describing them in enough detail that your readers relive those moments with you.

Notice how one writer, Benjamin Alire Sáenz, improves the following sentences from his short story "Cebolleros" by adding description in the revised version:

Original

He was getting good grades in everything except chemistry. And the teacher hated him. His brother wrote to him and told him to calm down, told him everything would be all right.

Revised

He was getting good grades in everything except chemistry. If he didn't pass, he'd have to go to summer school because it was a required course. All those good grades, and it had come down to this. He was a borderline student in that class and he knew it, but there wasn't any time. There wasn't any time.

And the teacher hated him. He could feel the teacher's hatred, the blue-eyed wrestling coach who favored athletes and nice-looking girls.

His brother wrote to him and told him to calm down, told him everything would be all right. "Just graduate and go to college. Do whatever it takes, just don't join the Army."

To use description, start with a general statement and then add details to make it more specific. Use these questions:

- Who is involved?
- What happens?
- When and where does it happen?
- Why does it happen?
- How does it happen?

Here's an example of a general statement to which detailed observations have been added:

Original

My cousin's wedding was really beautiful.

Revised

My cousin Veronica's wedding took place in the flower garden of Haven Park on a sunny June day. Veronica and Samuel took their vows surrounded by red, pink, and yellow roses. In addition to the three bridesmaids and the best man, there was a ring bearer—my four-year-old son, Jason. I've never seen Jason smile so much. Other family members were both smiling and crying. My aunt Liz had tears streaming down her face as she watched Veronica and Sam walk through the garden arm in arm. Even my uncle Albert, usually so stern, had tears in his eyes.

 Description on eBay or Craigslist

Read descriptions of items for sale on eBay or Craigslist. Which items appeal to you the most—the ones that have little description or the ones that give details on appearance, condition, and price? Why are these details important to you as a reader? Practice writing a few descriptions of your own.

 GROUP ACTIVITY 1 Use Description

With several classmates, add description to make the following paragraphs more interesting and vivid. Use the journalist's questions: Who? What? When? Where? Why? How?

1. The first time I baby-sat for my brother's children was a disaster. One of them kept throwing things around. The other one wouldn't stop crying. I was relieved when my brother and his wife returned home.

2. I was so happy when the Little League team I coach won the city tournament. The

final play was very suspenseful. The score was tied. The parents were probably more nervous than the players. But no one could have been happier than the kids when they won.

3. One of my favorite pastimes is backpacking in the mountains. I love the fresh air and the scenery. At night, my friends and I lie awake and look up at the stars. One night, we even saw a shooting star.

☾ Narration

Narration is writing that tells a story that is based on either fact or fiction. You use narration when you want to develop ideas by relating a series of events. In most cases, you will organize events in chronological order. Occasionally, however, you might use a flashback. You might also use dialogue to make a narrative more immediate and real.

Chronological Order

Generally, stories are told in the order in which they actually happened, called *chronological order.* Imagine that you want to narrate a story about your family's tradition of taking a family photograph at the start of every new year. Here's how you might organize a narrative paragraph in chronological order:

> On picture-taking day, we all rush around trying to get ourselves to look as good as possible for the camera. In the bathroom, my mother puts makeup on my stepfather's nose to hide the redness caused by a cold. I hear my stepsister tell my parents she refuses to be in the picture because her hair is too puffy. My brother rushes into the kitchen to clean up the grape juice he spilled on his shirt, while I look through the cupboards in the utility room for shoelaces. Finally, we're ready to make our trip to the photographer's studio.

Notice how the sentences in the paragraph are arranged in the order in which the events of the story occurred. This gives the reader a sense of the flow of the events in the story.

Flashback

An alternative way to organize a narrative is to use a *flashback*: you begin the story in the middle, flash back to the beginning, and then resume telling the story in the middle again. You often see this technique used in movies: the picture becomes fuzzy, and a scene from an earlier time appears. The flashback technique is useful when you want to contrast then and now or highlight a key scene. Here's how the paragraph about the picture-taking ritual might be organized using the flashback technique:

In the photograph, my family appears calm and relaxed. Our hair is perfectly combed, and our clothes are neatly pressed. The expressions on our faces seem calm and happy. But as I stare at the photograph, I recall the chaos that preceded the snap of the camera. My stepfather had such a terrible cold that my mother had to put makeup on his nose to cover the redness. My stepsister didn't want to be in the picture because her hair was too puffy. My brother had spilled grape juice on his shirt, and I had broken my shoelace. To make matters worse, we had a flat tire going to the studio. But when I look at this photograph, I know it was all worthwhile.

Dialogue

In a narration, *dialogue* consists of the actual words that people say, indicated by quotation marks. Use dialogue when you want to highlight an important scene or portray a certain person through his or her own words.

Dialogue can make a narration more interesting and fast paced. Consider this narrative paragraph:

> I couldn't have survived my first semester in college without my roommate, Lisa. She encouraged me to study harder, helped me find a job, and introduced me to new friends. One night, while I was studying for my calculus exam, I became so frustrated I yelled and threw the calculus book across the room. Lisa comforted me. That's the kind of roommate she was.

Here's the same paragraph, expanded to five paragraphs to include dialogue. Notice that the dialogue makes the scene more vivid.

> I couldn't have survived my first semester in college without my roommate, Lisa. She encouraged me to study harder, helped me find a job, and introduced me to new friends. One night, while I was studying for my calculus exam, I became so frustrated that I yelled as loud as I could, "I can't take it anymore!" Then I threw the calculus book across the room.
>
> Lisa, who was studying for her psychology exam, looked up at me from across the room. "What's wrong with you?"
>
> "I can't do this! I know I'm going to flunk!"
>
> "Calm down," she said, putting her book down. "Let me see if I can help." She spent the next hour explaining the problems to me.
>
> That's the kind of roommate she was.

⏻ **Text message your dialogue**

If you use text messaging, you already write dialogue every day. Look at a recent text message exchange, and imagine how you would include it in a written essay. How would you explain the context, introduce the names of the speakers, and add the correct punctuation?

> **WRITING ACTIVITY 1 Practice Narration**
>
> Write a paragraph in which you use narration to describe a scene that took place in one of your favorite movies or television shows. Relate the events in chronological order. If there was a flashback within the scene, describe that as well. Wherever possible, include some of the actual dialogue spoken by the actors. Read your paragraph aloud to your classmates, and listen to their paragraphs to develop your ear for narration.

Examples

In writing, examples are used to clarify, explain, and support ideas. Two of the most common types of examples are facts and expert testimony.

Facts

Facts provide support for your ideas. Unlike opinions or guesses, facts are statements that can be objectively verified as true. For example, the statement "Golden retrievers are beautiful" represents the opinion of the writer. In contrast, the statement "A golden retriever is a breed of dog" is a fact that can be verified in an encyclopedia or some other reliable source. Facts may include names, dates, numbers, statistics, and other data relevant to your topic or idea. Notice in the following paragraph that facts are used to support the idea that Asian Americans are an especially diverse group:

> Asian Americans are an especially diverse group, comprised of Chinese, Filipino, Japanese, Vietnamese, Cambodians, Hmong, and other groups. The largest Asian American groups are Chinese Americans (24 percent), Filipino Americans (20 percent), and Japanese Americans (12 percent). Other groups, such as Vietnamese, Cambodians, Laotians, and Hmong, are more recent arrivals, first coming to this country in the 1970s as refugees from the upheavals resulting from the Vietnam War. In the 1980s, Koreans and Filipinos began immigrating in larger numbers. The majority of Asian Americans live in the West.
>
> —**BRYAN STRONG** and **CHRISTINE DeVAULT**, *The Marriage and Family Experience*

Expert Testimony

Statements made by knowledgeable people are considered *expert testimony*. Examples supported by expert testimony make your writing more convincing. For example, citing the surgeon general's warning that cigarette smoking greatly increases your risk of lung cancer is more convincing than offering the statement without support or citing someone with no medical background or authority to advise American citizens on health matters.

Research facts on Wikipedia

Google the search term "researching with Wikipedia." What does the Wikipedia site say about using its entries for academic research? Is it a good idea? Why or why not? How will you use Wikipedia?

In the following paragraph, an author writing an article about how cooking has become an expensive hobby uses expert testimony to develop her point that the amount of time people spend cooking and preparing meals has dropped dramatically during the past century:

> When my grandmother was growing up in the 1920s, the average woman spent about 30 hours a week preparing food and cleaning up. By the 1950s, when she was raising her family, that number had fallen to about 20 hours a week. Now, according to the U.S. Department of Agriculture, women average just 5.5 hours—and those who are employed, like me, spend less than 4.4 hours a week. And that's not because men are picking up the slack; they log a paltry 15 minutes a day doing kitchen work. One market-research firm, the NPD Group, says that even in the 1980s, 72 percent of meals eaten at home involved an entrée cooked from scratch; now just 59 percent of them do, and the average number of food items used per meal has decreased from 4.4 to 3.5. That's when we're home at all: by 1995, we consumed more than a quarter of all meals and snacks outside the home, up from 16 percent two decades earlier.
>
> —MEGAN McARDLE, *"The Joy of Not Cooking"*

 WRITING ACTIVITY 2 Find Examples

Using the practice essay topic you chose for this chapter's writing assignment, find several facts and at least one piece of expert testimony to support your opinion. To do this, you may need to do some research: interviewing people with experience on your topic or reading what others have written about it. Read your facts and expert testimony to your classmates, asking them what more they would like to know about your topic.

Process Explanation

Writers use a technique called *process* to explain how something works or how to do something. Cookbooks and repair manuals come to mind when we think of process writing, but bookstore shelves are filled with all sorts of other "how to" books explaining processes—from how to use a computer to how to arrange your closet.

In a paragraph about your favorite hiking trail, for instance, you might explain the process of preparing to hike the trail and locating the trailhead, as Laurence Parent does in the following paragraphs about hiking to Wheeler Peak in New Mexico:

> Be sure to get a very early start on this hike. To minimize problems with storms, you ideally want to be on the summit before noon. Snow flurries are possible even in mid-summer. Be sure to take rain gear and extra-warm clothing. Lightning and hypothermia are real threats on Wheeler Peak and the exposed summit ridge.
>
> At just short of one mile you will pass marked Trail 63, the Long Canyon Trail to Gold Hill, coming in from the left. Ignore it and continue climbing up the northeast valley. Just past the trail junction, the trail hits an old road. Turn left onto the road and follow it the rest of the way up the valley.
>
> —**LAURENCE PARENT**, *The Hiker's Guide to New Mexico*

In process writing, it is important to use transitions and to present each step in the process clearly so that your readers can follow along with you.

❰ Classification

Writers use *classification* to organize their ideas and thus to aid their readers' understanding of those ideas. When you classify, you categorize something into types on some particular basis. For example, you might classify cars on the basis of their type or size (sports car, SUV, compact, midsize, and full size) or on the basis of their country of origin (Volvos and Saabs from Sweden, Hyundais and Kias from Korea). You might also classify cars on the basis of their resale value, safety record, popularity as indicated by sales, or some other basis you deem important.

In the following paragraph about her job as a store clerk in the women's clothing department at Walmart, Barbara Ehrenreich classifies women's clothing first by style and then by type of item:

> Moving clockwise, we encounter the determinedly sexless Russ and Bobbie Brooks lines, seemingly aimed at pudgy fourth-grade teachers with important barbecues to attend. Then, after the sturdy White Stag, come the breezy, revealing Faded Glory, No Boundaries and Jordache collections, designed for the younger and thinner crowd. Tucked throughout are nests of the lesser brands, such as Athletic Works, Basic Equipment, and the whimsical Looney Tunes, Pooh, and Mickey lines, generally decorated with images of their eponymous characters. Within each brand-name area, there are of course dozens of items, even dozens of each kind of item. This summer, for example, pants may be capri, classic, carpenter, clam-digger, boot, or flood, depending on their length and cut, and I'm probably leaving a few categories out.
>
> —**BARBARA EHRENREICH**, *Nickel and Dimed: On (Not) Getting By in America*

⏻ **Electronic file classification**

Think about the classification systems you have created when arranging your music files on iTunes or sorting your photos on Flickr. What are some of the different classifications you have used? Why did you choose to classify this way?

GROUP ACTIVITY 2 **Use Narration, Examples, Process Explanation, and Classification**

Following are several topic sentences. For each one, decide with your group whether you will use narration, examples, process explanation, or classification as the primary method of development. Then use that method to develop the topic sentence into a brief paragraph.

1. With the right tools, it's easy to change a flat tire.

   Primary method of development: _____

2. Rock music can be divided into various categories.

   Primary method of development: _____

3. I'll never forget the first time I tried to drive a car.

   Primary method of development: _____

4. The music on my iPod illustrates the different parts of my personality.

   Primary method of development: _____

◖ Definition

Writers use *definition* to explain and clarify. Thus, when you define something, you tell your reader what it means. A good definition has two parts: first the term being defined is placed in a general category, and then an explanation of how it fits within that category (a discussion of its distinguishing features) follows. For example, to define the term *skydiving*, you might first define it generally as a risky sport and then explain what distinguishes skydiving from other risky sports, such as rock climbing and hang gliding.

In the following paragraph, the writer defines the Khan Academy, a new online learning tool that has changed the way students learn math and science in schools. He begins by defining the topic generally as an education Web site, before pointing out its distinguishing feature: it focuses on math, science, and economics education.

Khan Academy is an education website that, as its tagline puts it, aims to let anyone "learn almost anything—for free." Students, or anyone interested enough to surf by, can watch some 2,400 videos in which the site's founder, Salman Khan, chattily discusses principles of math, science, and economics (with a smattering of social science topics thrown in).

—CLIVE THOMPSON, *"The New Way to Be a Fifth Grader: How Khan Academy Is Changing the Rules of Education"*

WRITING ACTIVITY 3 Practice Definition

Using the essay topic you chose for this chapter's writing assignment, define one key word that will help your readers understand your topic. For example, if you chose to write on a toxic oil spill, you might define the word *dispersant*, explaining how the word is used to describe the action taken to remedy the effects of the oil spill. Read your definition aloud to your classmates, and listen to their definitions. Create a vocabulary list of the words that are new to you.

Comparison and Contrast

When you *compare*, you identify the similarities between two or more things; when you *contrast*, you identify the differences between things. Sometimes the focus is on one or the other, but at other times both similarities and differences are included.

Writers use comparison and contrast to clarify relationships. How are people, places, or ideas alike? How are they different? For example, in the following paragraph, the author writes about the voluntary separation between black and white students at his high school. He contrasts the distance he now feels from his black friend with the closeness he felt when they were younger:

> Ten years ago, we played catch in our backyards, went bike riding, and slept over at one another's houses. By the fifth grade, we went to movies and amusement parks, and bunked together at the same summer camps. We met while playing on the same Little League team, though we attended different grade schools. We're both juniors now at the same high school. We usually don't say anything when we see each other, except maybe a polite "Hi" or "Hey." I can't remember the last time we talked on the phone, much less got together outside of school.
>
> —BRIAN JARVIS, *"Against the Great Divide"*

When you write a comparison, you can order your ideas point by point or subject by subject. Point-by-point organization means that you explain two topics according to points of comparison. For instance, you can compare two coworkers by examining their work habits, personalities, and professionalism. Each section in the body of the essay focuses on one of the points.

First section: work habits
    Explain work habits of coworker 1
    Explain work habits of coworker 2 (how they are similar to or different
        from those of coworker 1)
Second section: personalities
    Explain personality of coworker 1
    Explain personality of coworker 2 (how it is similar to or different from
        that of coworker 1)
Third section: professionalism
    Explain professionalism of coworker 1
    Explain professionalism of coworker 2 (how it is similar to or different
        from that of coworker 1)

Alternatively, you can organize your ideas subject by subject; each coworker is discussed only once in the body of the essay.

First section: coworker 1
    Work habits, personality, professionalism
Second section: coworker 2
    Work habits, personality, professionalism

GROUP ACTIVITY 3 Find Similar Subjects for Comparison

Work with your classmates on the following list of subjects. For each main subject,
identify three similar subjects that could be used to make a comparison.

EXAMPLE: SUBJECT Ford Explorer

SIMILAR SUBJECTS _____ Cadillac Escalade, Lincoln MKX, Nissan Murano

1. Subject: The movie *X-Men: First Class*

    Similar subjects: _____

2. Subject: McDonald's

    Similar subjects: _____

3. Subject: Buffalo wings

    Similar subjects: _____

4. Subject: Walmart

    Similar subjects: _____

Cause and Effect

When you use *cause and effect,* you explain why something happened
(the cause) and what the result of it was (the effect). Writers use cause and

effect to show a necessary or logical connection between two things. It is not enough to say that two things happened at the same time. For example, if a freeze ruins the orange crop and orange prices go up, that's cause and effect. If there also happens to be a full moon on the night of the freeze, that's a coincidence. It is the freeze, not the full moon, that ruins the crop.

In the following paragraph, the author explains the problems that arise when people unfairly stereotype each other. She shows a clear and logical connection between the cause (stereotyping) and the effect (a loss of individuality).

> In a primitive part of my parental mind, I figured that I would pick her up from school . . . well, if not forever, then at least until graduation. And then suddenly, she got her license. I was obsolete. Just like that! It took my breath away. Our old Volvo, long stationed like a stalwart in front of the house, was now her car.
>
> A hundred other things changed then, too, the most terrifying of which has been familiar to parents since the advent of the automobile. . . . My daughter was out driving at night. I had two strategies for coping with that development: text messaging (some evenings) and Ambien (others).
>
> —**ANN PACKER**, *"Life Lessons"*

◖ WRITING ACTIVITY 4 Use Cause and Effect

Using the practice essay topic you chose for this chapter's writing assignment, write a paragraph in which you explain why something happened (the cause) and what the result of it was (the effect). Read your cause-and-effect paragraph to your classmates, asking them if you've demonstrated a logical connection between the cause and the effect.

◖ Argument

When you make an *argument*, you try to persuade readers to change their perspectives or alter their behavior in some way. In an essay that uses argument, the thesis statement contains the *claim*, or your argumentative point. The rest of the paragraphs contain *reasons* and *evidence* that justify the claim.

In the following paragraph, the writer uses reasons and evidence to support the claim that student athletes should not be paid:

> The benefits of the student-athlete experience are many. Student-athletes graduate at a higher rate than the general student body. Most do so while playing the sport they love and preparing for a future as a professional in something other than sports. Many receive athletics grants-in-aid that can be worth more than $100,000. NCAA studies show that student-athletes enjoy

high levels of engagement in academics, athletics and community; have positive feelings about their overall athletics and academic experiences; attribute learning invaluable life skills to being a student-athlete; and are more likely to earn similar or higher wages after college than non-student-athletes.

Critics argue that student-athletes generate large amounts of money for the institution and therefore should be compensated. That argument ignores the fact that intercollegiate athletics programs are necessarily composed of many sports, many of which generate significant expenses over revenues. Only about two dozen programs nationally, all of them large Division I programs, actually yield revenues over expenses after the bills are paid. The remainder rely to varying degrees on institutional financial support. . . . Overall NCAA revenue, primarily derived from the Association's media agreements and the popularity of the Division I Men's Basketball Championship, helps 400,000 student-athletes at more than 1,000 member institutions learn and compete in 23 sports and 88 national championships.

—NCAA WEB SITE, *"Why student-athletes are not paid to play"*

WRITING ACTIVITY 5 Practice Argument

Using the essay topic you chose for this chapter's writing assignment, write a preliminary thesis statement that contains the argumentative claim that supports your position. List three pieces of evidence that support your argument.

▪ HOW TO Use the Patterns of Development

- In an introduction, write a thesis statement that states the main point of your essay.
- For each paragraph, write a topic sentence that supports your thesis statement.
- Support each topic sentence with details that increase interest and help readers understand your main point.
- Use one or more patterns of development, such as description, narration, examples, process explanation, classification, definition, comparison and contrast, cause and effect, or argument.
- Add or delete sentences to improve your paragraphs.
- Write a conclusion.

GROUP ACTIVITY 4 Develop Ideas Using Definition, Comparison and Contrast, Cause and Effect, and Argument

Following are several topic sentences. For each one, decide with your group whether you will use definition, comparison and contrast, cause and effect, or argument as the primary method of development. Then use that method to develop the topic sentence into a brief paragraph.

1. The meaning of *love* differs from person to person.

   Primary method of development: _____

2. Since the implementation of the TV rating system, violence in children's programming has decreased.

   Primary method of development: _____

3. Cheerleading is a sport in its own right, not just a peppy sideshow for a football game.

   Primary method of development: _____

4. Both my boss and my best friend are total introverts.

   Primary method of development: _____

❨ One Student's Writing Process

Look back at the writing assignment given at the beginning of the chapter (p. 60), which was to write an essay on a topic of importance to you, using some of the patterns of development to help support your points. On the following pages, you'll follow Carlos Montijo, a student writer, as he writes his essay. Carlos decided to write on the role that television plays in children's lives because this topic was being discussed in one of his education classes. As you follow Carlos through the writing process, you'll notice that he uses some of the patterns of development to strengthen his essay, make it more interesting, and support his ideas. You'll also notice that he conducted research on his topic, cited his sources within his paper, and added a Works Cited page at the end.

Note that some essays are written using one particular pattern of development. A piece about hiking to the top of a mountain, for example, might be written using narration. An essay about how to cook a five-course dinner for eight people in your tiny apartment kitchen might be written using process explanation. An article in a magazine on the different types of cell phones available today might use classification to show the choices on the market. But in most writing you will encounter, writers use a combination of patterns to produce an effective, clear, and compelling essay. This is what Carlos did when writing his essay.

Carlos's Ideas

After receiving the assignment, Carlos thought first about his audience and his purpose. Although he planned to show his final draft to a friend who had just had a child, he knew his primary audience was his writing instructor. He knew that the research he would do on the topic would help make his essay persuasive because it would show that he was knowledgeable about this subject. In his journal, Carlos explained how he chose a topic and started to gather ideas for his essay:

> Oct. 15
>
> A couple of weeks ago, I baby-sat my neighbors' two kids, who are four and seven years old. I was shocked when they told me they got to watch as much TV as they wanted. I know that their parents are really busy trying to make a living, but they are using TV as a babysitter. I think the seven-year-old is too aggressive when he plays with his friends, which is probably from watching violent TV shows. He's also kind of chubby because he's spending too much time watching TV. I decided that I wanted to research this topic and maybe show my paper to my neighbors to let them see that too much television watching might be harmful to their kids.

Carlos's Drafting

Using his journal writing and the clustering that he did on the topic (Figure 3.1), Carlos wrote the discovery draft shown on p. 72. (Note that the draft includes the types of errors that typically appear in a first draft.)

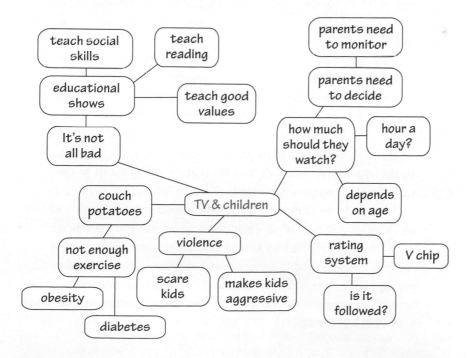

Figure 3.1 Carlos's Clustering

Too Much Television

Most children watch too much television. Parents use it like a babysitter, but this isn't good for their kids. Many shows on TV are violent, and young children can be disturbed by this. Everyone is susceptible to the influence of television, but children are especially gullible because they have not fully developed their critical sensibilities. Unfortunately, many television programs contain obscenity, violence, and sex. Which can be harmful to children, especially if they watch a great deal of it. They can become too aggressive and try to imitate what they see on TV. For instance, if they see a fight break out on a TV show, they might think this is a good way to solve a problem instead of trying to talk it out. The actors seem cool, which makes the kids want to be just like them. Plus if children are watching TV all the time, they aren't reading, which can make them bad students. They aren't playing with other children, which might hurt their social skills. They also might not get enough exercise, which can make them overweight and unhealthy. Excessive television viewing can decrease childrens activity levels, resulting in health problem such as obesity and diabetes. It is simply naive to think that viewing a great deal of television will not affect children's behavior or moods.

I know that not all TV is bad. Some children's shows are educational and some are pretty harmless. But the point is that children are watching too much TV, and they're watching shows that have too much violence or sex. The violence can make them scared or upset them. Almost all shows in the evening hours are unsuitable for children. TV violence is so grained in American culture that it is hard to find a dramatic program completely void of it. Critics like Jacob Weisberg argue that the problem is not the amount of violence shown on TV but the kind of violence, children may not be bothered by silly, cartoonish violence (Weisberg). Also, it's true that some children may stay out of trouble because "if you're at home watching TV, you're not out on the streets punching someone's head in" (Mackay 1). But is this how we want to protect children, by having them watch TV?

Children younger than two years however should not even be exposed to television because their minds are still very tender; the younger children are, the more susceptible they are to visual media (American Academy of Pediatrics). Parents need to be very careful about regulating their children's viewing habits. It might be hard for parents to do this because they can't be home all the time, but it's very important that children not be exposed to too much TV at an early age.

Carlos's Revising and Editing

After finishing his discovery draft, Carlos reflected again on his audience and purpose. He decided that his instructor would want an essay that would be easier to follow; after all, she had more than a hundred students who would be turning in essays. This meant that his essay had to be better organized and more fully developed, with a good thesis statement. Carlos asked several students in his education class to read his discovery draft and give him suggestions for revision.

In his journal, Carlos explained how he revised and edited his essay:

Oct. 20

Before I revised and edited my essay, I wrote a new thesis statement: "Parents need to regulate both the amount of time their kids spend watching television and the types of programs they watch." I based the rest of the essay on this thesis statement. I also went to the library and asked a librarian to help me find some good sources. He helped me find sources that were objective and well researched. When I wrote the revised draft, I used a standard essay format—an introduction, body paragraphs, and a conclusion. I decided to use cause and effect to help support my point about TV violence, and I also used comparison and contrast to add information about the positive things about television, such as how it can be educational, so that my audience would know I had considered both sides of the issue. I also worked hard on my introduction because sometimes people form their opinion of the essay based on the introduction. Then I went to the Writing Center for help with putting the sources into the paper and correctly using documentation. Finally, I used my spell-checker to catch spelling errors in my essay and proofread my draft by reading it from beginning to end.

Here is Carlos's revised and edited draft.

Carlos Montijo
Professor Al-Tabaa
English 0311
12 Nov. 2011

Television and Children

During the twentieth century, the invention of the television changed   1
American culture and paved the way for the modern era. Even though people today use many different kinds of media (such as Facebook and video games), television is still very popular. As a result, everyone is susceptible to the influence of television, but children are especially gullible because they

Sentence fragment is corrected.

Cause (too much television) and effect (results) is introduced.

Argument is the dominant pattern used in this essay.

Comparison and contrast is used to show both sides of the issue.

Comma splice is corrected.

Research is used throughout this essay to exemplify Carlos's points.

Cause and effect is used throughout this essay.

Spelling error is corrected.

This exemplifies the point that children watch too much TV.

When using research, Carlos relies mostly on paraphrasing (putting others' words into your own words) rather than quoting. This gives the essay a better flow.

Examples about the negative effects of TV help support Carlos's point.

have not fully developed their critical sensibilities. Unfortunately, many television programs contain obscenity, violence, and sex, which can be harmful to children, especially if they watch a great deal of it. Research has shown that this kind of exposure can result in overstimulation and sometimes even destructive behavior. Parents need to regulate both the amount of time their kids spend watching television and the types of programs they watch.

Naturally, not all television is bad for children. Some channels, such as PBS, have educational shows that can teach children important skills or show them interesting aspects of the world. One study found that watching certain TV shows may help 3- to 5-year-old children learn how to read (Stanton 1). Other channels, such as Nickelodeon and Disney, have shows that might have a positive message or that are at least harmlessly entertaining. Also, not all violence is always harmful to children. Critics like Jacob Weisberg argue that the problem is not the amount of violence shown on TV but the kind of violence; children may not be bothered by silly, cartoonish violence. Also, it's true that some children may stay out of trouble because "if you're at home watching TV, you're not out on the streets punching someone's head in" (Mackay 1). But is this how we want to protect children, by having them watch TV?

Children who watch a great deal of television are exposed to shows with inappropriate and possibly damaging content. Many experts have been concerned about this. According to Carter and Weaver, "For almost a century now, the apparent ability of the media to negatively affect individual behavior has been one of the foremost concerns around media violence for government officials, pressure groups, media scholars, and citizens" (2). TV violence is so ingrained in American culture that it is hard to find a dramatic program completely void of it. Moreover, the average American child is in a home with a television that is on for about seven hours a day (Gerbner 45). According to the American Academy of Pediatrics, violence in the media can make children aggressive and afraid of being harmed. It can also make children think that violence is a good way of settling arguments or solving problems (American Academy of Pediatrics). Children might start to believe that it is cool because the actors who are being violent on TV seem cool. Also, studies have found that watching television at a young age can lead to attention-deficit problems and disorders (Condon 1). Excessive television viewing can also decrease children's activity levels, resulting in health problems such as obesity and diabetes. It is simply naive to think that viewing a great deal of television will not affect children's behavior or moods.

Television warning labels are not very useful in helping to curb children's   4
television watching. Most prime-time TV shows are labeled TV14, meaning
they're not appropriate for children under fourteen, or TVPG, meaning that
children should watch these shows only with their parents. However, these
warning labels are not easy to spot; in TV Guide, for instance, the label for
each show appears in a tiny black box next to the description of the show.
Based on these ratings, virtually all shows that are on in the evenings are not
appropriate for children. Parents can use the V chip that comes with their
televisions to block certain shows from their sets. However, many adults might
want to watch these shows themselves, and so they don't bother with the
V chip or have problems understanding how to use it.

Parents need to become more aware and active in the lives of their kids and   5
regulate what they view at all times. According to the American Academy of
Pediatrics, a good plan is to allow a child to view no more than one hour of
safe, preferably educational television daily. Children younger than two years,
however, should not even be exposed to television because their minds are still
very tender; the younger children are, the more susceptible they are to visual
media (American Academy of Pediatrics). Excessive exposure to television will
hinder a child's potential because it easily distracts them, consumes their time,
encourages them to develop bad habits that are difficult to correct, and gives
them a false, distorted sense of reality. Parents must seriously consider the
consequences of exposing their kids to too much television.

Definitions are used to
define terms.

This example helps support
the main point of the
paragraph.

This description of using the
V chip comes from Carlos's
own personal experience.

Missing commas
are inserted.

This specific recommendation
strengthens Carlos's
conclusion.

These final sentences remind
the reader of the main points
of the essay.

Works Cited

American Academy of Pediatrics, "Media Violence." 124.5 (2009):
    1495–1503. Web. 5 Nov. 2010.

Carter, Cynthia, and C. Kay Weaver. *Violence and the Media*.
    Buckingham, Philadelphia: Open UP, 2003. Print.

Condon, Deborah. "TV Is Bad for Young Kids." *Irish Health*. Health on the
    Net Foundation, 4 July 2004. Web. 4 Oct. 2010.

Gerbner, George. "Television Violence at a Time of Turmoil and Terror."
    Critical Readings: Violence and the Media. Ed. Cynthia Carter and
    C. Kay Weaver. New York: Open UP, 2006. 45–53. Print.

Mackay, Hugh. "Answer to TV Violence: Turn It Off." *Sydney Morning
    Herald* 5 Mar. 2005. Web. 5 Nov. 2010.

Stanton, Carina. "TV Viewing Good and Bad for Kids, Seattle Study
    Says." *Seattle Times* 5 July 2005. Web. 14 Oct. 2010.

Weisberg, Jacob. "What Do You Mean by 'Violence'?" *Slate* 15 May
    1999. Web. 5 Nov. 2010.

The Works Cited page follows
correct MLA format.
Information about the sources
will help readers find the
sources themselves if they
want to read more about the
topic.

◀ **GROUP ACTIVITY 5** Analyze Carlos's Revised and Edited Essay ▶

Discuss the following questions with your classmates.

1. What do you think of the title of Carlos's essay? What title would you suggest?
2. Does Carlos's introduction make you want to read the essay? Why or why not?
3. How effective is Carlos's thesis statement?
4. What details did Carlos add to the revised and edited draft to improve his essay?
5. In what ways did Carlos's research help make his essay more persuasive?
6. How effective is Carlos's conclusion? What more would you suggest he add?
7. What else could Carlos do to improve his essay?

Carlos's Sharing

Writing in his journal, Carlos summed up his feelings about the final draft of his essay:

> Dec. 16
>
> Rereading my paper, I see how much I learned about my topic while I was writing it. I'm also glad I took the time to proofread and correct my errors, so my readers will take me seriously. The next time I babysit for my neighbors, I'll tell them about the research I did for this essay and ask if they want to read it. For the sake of their kids, I hope they learn from what I wrote.

CHAPTER CHECKLIST

❑ The patterns of development help readers make sense of your thoughts and can be used to write a more effective paragraph or essay.
❑ Description helps readers picture your ideas.
❑ Narration allows you to tell a story.
❑ Examples let you clarify, explain, and support ideas.
❑ Process explanation helps you explain how something works or how to do something.
❑ Classification leads you to categorize something into types.
❑ Definition allows you to tell the reader what something means.
❑ Comparison and contrast lets you explain similarities and differences.
❑ Cause and effect helps you to explain why something happened and its result.
❑ Argument lets you persuade readers to change their perspective or perform an action.

REFLECTING ON YOUR WRITING

To help you reflect on the writing you did in this chapter, answer the following questions:

1. Which patterns of development did you use in your practice essay on a topic of importance to you? Why did you choose these patterns to support your position?

2. Which pattern do you think is the easiest to use? The hardest to use? Why?

3. How did learning about the patterns of development help you as a writer?

Using your answers to these questions, complete a Writing Process Report for this chapter (you can download a report form at **bedfordstmartins.com /choices**). Once you complete this report, freewrite about what you learned in this chapter about the patterns of development and what you still hope to learn.

PART TWO

Writing to Share Ideas

Writing provides a permanent record of our ideas. Writing also allows us to communicate with others and to share what we know in ways that express our thoughts, inform, and persuade.

In Part Two, you'll learn how to improve your writing as you write to share your ideas. You'll read some sample essays to get you thinking about that chapter's writing purpose and topic. You'll experiment with different methods of gathering ideas and practice writing discovery drafts. You'll learn how to revise and how to use the patterns of development to expand and organize your thoughts. You'll improve your sentences and learn how to choose just the right word to communicate what you want to say. You'll edit your writing to ensure that you communicate your ideas clearly. Finally, you'll share your writing with an audience.

At the end of each chapter, you'll check to see that you've completed all the steps of the writing process, and you'll have an opportunity to reflect on your own writing process.

"What matters is that you get another chance to hit the ball."

— JESUS RAMIREZ, "BASEBALL MEMORIES"

Remembering
Significant People, Events, and Periods in Our Lives

We all have memories of important people, events, and periods in our lives. Some of these memories are happy: a supportive mentor, the birth of a child, a special vacation. Others are less pleasant: a cruel coworker, a serious traffic accident, a long-term illness.

Memories change who we are and how we see ourselves. To a great extent, we are all defined by important people, events, and times in our lives. In this chapter, you will learn how to write an essay that shows how someone or something in your past has changed you. You will begin by reading essays by professional writers about an important change in their lives. You will also follow a student, Jesus Ramirez, as he writes his essay, "Baseball Memories," in which he remembers how his father used their time together watching baseball games to teach him life lessons about having self-confidence and not giving up.

Exploring your own memories in writing will help you better understand who you are and what is meaningful to you. Working through the readings and activities in this chapter will guide you in the process of writing an essay about a personal experience that had an impact on your life. Once you have completed your essay, you can share your written memories with the people who are close to you. This is what good writing is about—communicating something important to readers so that they learn something new. ■

In this chapter, you will write about a significant person, event, or period in your life. As you follow the steps of the writing process, you will

- Explore the chapter topic by reading essays about a significant person, event, or period.
- Gather ideas by brainstorming, relating aloud, and clustering.
- Develop your ideas using **description** and **narration**.
- Practice writing effective thesis statements, topic sentences, and focused paragraphs.
- Combine sentences with coordinating conjunctions.
- Learn how to correct run-on sentences.
- Share your essay with your classmates.

The photograph on the previous page is of major league baseball player Rickey Henderson. What memories might he be having as he sits holding the bat? What can you tell about him from the expression on his face? How does the quote on the photograph fit his expression? Share some photographs of significant people, events, and periods of your life with your classmates.

Getting Started   Reading Essays That Remember a Significant Person, Event, or Period

Reading is an excellent way to start thinking about a topic. Learning other people's stories may spark some memories from your own past.

At the same time, examining what others have written will help you discover new strategies for sharing your ideas. Before you start work on your own essay, read the following short essays about how a significant person, a memorable event, or an important period changed someone. As you read, pay close attention to how the writers use description and narration to explain their thoughts to their readers and to make their stories interesting and compelling. Notice, too, how the writers introduce their topic and how they use paragraphs to develop each main idea. You can use what you learn from reading these essays to get you started writing your own essay. (For additional essays about a significant person, event, or period, see p. 545.)

A Significant Person

JOSHUA BELL
My Maestro

Joshua Bell became interested in music at an early age. His parents, eager to encourage their son's interests, gave him his first violin when he was four years old. Even though he liked to play computer games, basketball, and tennis, by the age of twelve he was committed to playing the violin. When he was fourteen, he made his professional debut with the Philadelphia Orchestra and later toured with major orchestras in the United States, Europe, Australia, and Asia. He has recorded numerous classical works and played with musical legends, such as the cellist Yo-Yo Ma. In this essay, Bell credits Josef Gingold—his maestro, or master teacher—for showing him that music could be "more than a hobby."

As a boy, I played the violin surrounded by ghosts. My teacher, Josef Gingold, plastered his Bloomington, Ind., studio walls with autographed photos of musical greats he admired or had met on his travels. Their faces watched our music-making, and inspired my small fingers to coax songs from the strings.

1 Bell uses the image of ghosts to get his reader's attention and to introduce his thesis statement.

When I became Gingold's pupil at age 12, he was already a legend at Indiana University, a gregarious Old World exile who had played under Arturo Toscanini and George Szell.

2 Bell begins to narrate his story.

We almost didn't meet. The day before my first solo recital—which someone had convinced him to attend—I was tossing a boomerang at my parents' farm. My mother fretted whether this was wise. Sure enough, the boomerang whirled back and sliced my chin open. The ER doctor stitched me up. Two inches to the left and I couldn't have held my violin. But I played, wounded.

3 Bell uses a short, catchy topic sentence and a description to paint a picture of himself as a child.

Gingold liked what he heard. I enrolled in a chamber music program he taught that summer in upstate New York. There, I realized I had never met anyone who found music so fun. He would play two parts of a string quartet at once. He laughed and laughed, and I left those lessons buzzing. My parents saw my excitement, and asked Gingold to continue to teach me back at home. He was wary. Too many children had been pushed on the violin, Gingold thought, and were living others' dreams. But he let me try.

4 In this unified paragraph, every sentence explains why Gingold was significant to Bell.

So I went to his studio with the ghosts on the walls, to enter the long tradition of one musician's hands guiding another's. My teacher taught me that music could be more than a hobby. It could be a life.

5 Bell explains another way Gingold was significant to him.

Born in Russia in 1909, he came to America in 1920 and studied violin with Vladimir Graffman. In 1937 he won a spot in the NBC Symphony Orchestra, and later was the Cleveland Orchestra's concertmaster.

6 Bell helps his reader get to know his teacher through narrating a bit of Gingold's life.

But Gingold found his true calling as a teacher. He was a musical inspiration for kids, who brought him joy. Unlike many maestros, he refused to scold his students, a decision that stemmed from a childhood horror. As a boy, he had once played his violin at a school assembly. His fellow students loved it, and applauded for so long the principal had to order them to stop. Later, Gingold's art teacher pulled him aside. "Let me see your hands," she said. "Are those the hands that made that beautiful music?" He beamed, so proud to be recognized for what he could do. Then she took a wooden pointer, smacking his palm so hard it damaged a nerve. Years later, he still felt pain. The teacher had decided he shouldn't feel so good about himself. That stuck with him. He went the opposite way with his students.

7

Bell uses the actual words of Gingold's art teacher to help his reader envision what happened.

Sometimes I wish he had been more strict. I was a kid, I goofed off. He wanted me to have a normal childhood and was secretly pleased when my mother told him I'd spent all day playing video games instead of music. During my afternoon lessons, we'd take breaks and listen to records. He let me play his Stradivarius. I was amazed by the depth of sound, the colors floating from that instrument. He helped me create a very personal relationship with music, but he did not teach me how to play every note. Many teachers have students copy all their fingerings. Gingold gave me the tools to teach myself—chamber music, solos, anything.

8 Yet another example of Gingold's significance.

Bell uses description to show how Gingold was like a grandfather to him.

I studied with him for nine years, and he became the grandfather I didn't   9 have. In my family, everyone played an instrument. During holidays, we gathered for informal concerts we called musicales. One year, Gingold joined us. He invited some of his international students to come play too. He led our little orchestra most of the night in this multicultural circle of warmth and music, tucked away from the Indiana cold. He couldn't stop smiling. With Toscanini or in a crowded living room, he was happy if he had a violin in hand.

Bell continues to tell the story.

Gingold didn't pull strings to further my career, but I pushed myself. Soon the   10 spotlight found me. I made my professional debut at 14, playing Mozart's Third Violin Concerto with the Philadelphia Orchestra. He flew to see me. At 17, I played at Carnegie Hall, and he saw me there, too, smiling like a proud grandpa.

Bell uses description to paint a picture of his last visit with Gingold.

When I moved to New York at 21, I couldn't see Gingold as much as I'd have   11 liked. His health was failing, and I dreaded the day he would leave me. On New Year's, 1995, I paid him a visit, bringing a photo of him I wanted autographed, to hang on my wall like the ghosts on his. I walked into his house, and in his hand he had one last gift for me — a rare picture of Niccolò Paganini, the crown jewel of his studio collection. He signed his own photo. I played. We talked through that last wonderful afternoon. The next day he had a stroke. He died two weeks later.

Early success can be dangerous for a musician. You hear of prodigies who rise   12 fast and flame out. Sometimes that's because teachers spoon-feed these young people every musical idea. At some point they feel they don't need teaching anymore, so they stop learning. Gingold was always learning. So am I.

Bell concludes by again referring to the ghosts, a good way to bring his essay full circle.

Someday I want to teach too. Gingold's ghost — the autographed photo on   13 my wall hung next to Paganini — will be watching.

READING ACTIVITY 1   Build Your Vocabulary

Determine the meanings of the following words from the context of Joshua Bell's essay. Then check their meanings by looking up the words in a dictionary: gregarious (2), fretted (3), wary (4), maestros (7), Stradivarius (8), fingerings (8), prodigies (12).

GROUP ACTIVITY 2   Discuss the Reading

Discuss the following questions about "My Maestro" with your classmates.

1. Why is Josef Gingold a significant person in Bell's life? Where does Bell express this main point?

2. Reread the paragraph about Gingold's childhood experience at a school assembly (7). How does this story help explain why Gingold is special to Bell?

3. What do you want to know about Josef Gingold that the writer doesn't tell you?

4. What details does Bell use to show how his violin teacher influenced his life?

WRITING ACTIVITY 1 Share Your Ideas

Write a paragraph or two about a significant teacher or coach, describing what the teacher or coach looked like and telling a story about this person. As you write, think about why this teacher or coach is important to you. Share what you have written with your classmates.

A Memorable Event

JAMES DILLARD
A Doctor's Dilemma

James Dillard is recognized as one of America's leading authorities on pain and pain management. A frequent lecturer and former clinical director of Columbia's Rosenthal Center for Complementary and Alternative Medicine, Dillard is known for integrating modern medicine and pharmaceutical practices with alternative treatments. He has appeared on national television multiple times and has written two books, *Alternative Medicine for Dummies* (1998) and *The Chronic Pain Solution* (2002). In this essay, Dillard describes how and why—as a doctor in training—he helped an accident victim despite the risks that a potential malpractice lawsuit could have posed to his career in medicine.

It was a bright, clear February afternoon in Gettysburg. A strong sun and layers   1
of down did little to ease the biting cold. Our climb to the crest of Little Roundtop wound past somber monuments, barren trees and polished cannon. From the top, we peered down on the wheat field where men had fallen so close together that one could not see the ground. Rifle balls had whined as thick as bee swarms through the trees, and cannon shots had torn limbs from the young men fighting there. A frozen wind whipped tears from our eyes. My friend Amy huddled close, using me as a wind breaker. Despite the cold, it was hard to leave this place.

Driving east out of Gettysburg on a country blacktop, the gray Bronco ahead of   2
us passed through a rural crossroad just as a small pickup truck tried to take a left turn. The Bronco swerved, but slammed into the pickup on the passenger side. We immediately slowed to a crawl as we passed the scene. The Bronco's driver looked fine, but we couldn't see the driver of the pickup. I pulled over on the shoulder and got out to investigate.

The right side of the truck was smashed in, and the side window was shattered.   3
The driver was partly out of the truck. His head hung forward over the edge of the passenger-side window, the front of his neck crushed on the shattered windowsill. He was unconscious and starting to turn a dusky blue. His chest slowly heaved against a blocked windpipe.

A young man ran out of a house at the crossroad. "Get an ambulance out here,"   4
I shouted against the wind. "Tell them a man is dying."

I looked down again at the driver hanging from the windowsill. There were six   5
empty beer bottles on the floor of the truck. I could smell the beer through the window. I knew I had to move him, to open his airway. I had no idea what neck injuries
he had sustained. He could easily end up a quadriplegic. But I thought: he'll be dead
by the time the ambulance gets here if I don't move him and try to do something to
help him.

An image flashed before my mind. I could see the courtroom and the driver of   6
the truck sitting in a wheelchair. I could see his attorney pointing at me and thundering at the jury: "This young doctor, with still a year left in his residency training, took
it upon himself to play God. He took it upon himself to move this gravely injured
man, condemning him forever to this wheelchair. . . ." I imagined the millions of dollars in award money. And all the years of hard work lost. I'd be paying him off for the
rest of my life. Amy touched my shoulder. "What are you going to do?"

The automatic response from long hours in the emergency room kicked in. I   7
pulled off my overcoat and rolled up my sleeves. The trick would be to keep enough
traction straight up on his head while I moved his torso, so that his probable broken
neck and spinal-cord injury wouldn't be made worse. Amy came around the driver's
side, climbed half in and grabbed his belt and shirt collar. Together we lifted him off
the windowsill.

He was still out cold, limp as a rag doll. His throat was crushed and blood from   8
the jugular vein was running down my arms. He still couldn't breathe. He was deep
blue-magenta now, his pulse was rapid and thready. The stench of alcohol turned
my stomach, but I positioned his jaw and tried to blow air down into his lungs. It
wouldn't go.

Amy had brought some supplies from my car. I opened an oversize intravenous   9
needle and groped on the man's neck. My hands were numb, covered with freezing
blood and bits of broken glass. Hyoid bone — God, I can't even feel the thyroid carti-
lage, it's gone. . . . OK, the thyroid gland is about there, cricoid rings are here . . . we'll
go in right here. . . .

It was a lucky first shot. Pink air sprayed through the IV needle. I placed a sec-   10
ond needle next to the first. The air began whistling through it. Almost immediately,
the driver's face turned bright red. After a minute, his pulse slowed down and his
eyes moved slightly. I stood up, took a step back and looked down. He was going to
make it. He was going to live. A siren wailed in the distance. I turned and saw Amy
holding my overcoat. I was shivering and my arms were turning white with cold.

The ambulance captain looked around and bellowed, "What the hell . . . who   11
did this?" as his team scurried over to the man lying in the truck.

"I did," I replied. He took down my name and address for his reports. I had just   12
destroyed my career. I would never be able to finish my residency with a massive
lawsuit pending. My life was over.

The truck driver was strapped onto a backboard, his neck in a stiff collar. The   13
ambulance crew had controlled the bleeding and started intravenous fluid. He was
slowly waking up. As they loaded him into the ambulance, I saw him move his feet.
Maybe my future wasn't lost.

A police sergeant called me from Pennsylvania three weeks later. Six days after   14
successful throat-reconstruction surgery, the driver had signed out, against medical

advice, from the hospital because he couldn't get a drink on the ward. He was being arraigned on drunk-driving charges.

A few days later, I went into the office of one of my senior professors, to tell the   15
story. He peered over his half glasses and his eyes narrowed. "Well, you did the right thing medically of course. But, James, do you know what you put at risk by doing that?" he said sternly. "What was I supposed to do?" I asked.

"Drive on," he replied. "There is an army of lawyers out there who would stand   16
in line to get a case like that. If that driver had turned out to be a quadriplegic, you might never have practiced medicine again. You were a very lucky young man."

The day I graduated from medical school, I took an oath to serve the sick and   17
the injured. I remember truly believing I would be able to do just that. But I have found out it isn't so simple. I understand now what a foolish thing I did that day. Despite my oath, I know what I would do on that cold roadside near Gettysburg to-day. I would drive on.

READING ACTIVITY 2 Build Your Vocabulary

Determine the meanings of the following words from the context of James Dillard's essay. Then check their meanings by looking up the words in a dictionary: somber (1), dusky (3), heaved (3), sustained (5), quadriplegic (5), thundering (6), gravely (6), condemning (6), traction (7), magenta (8), thready (8), intravenous (9), arraigned (14).

GROUP ACTIVITY 3 Discuss the Reading

Discuss the following questions about "A Doctor's Dilemma" with your classmates.

1. What is Dillard's thesis? Does he regret helping the victim of a car accident? Why or why not?

2. Examine how the author orders the events in his story. Why does he include details about things that happened before and after he helped the truck driver?

3. Compare how Dillard feels about this event now — as a licensed medical doctor — with how he felt about it as a medical student.

4. Reread paragraph 8, in which Dillard describes the truck driver's body. How does the author's use of description help explain why he was willing to risk his medical career?

WRITING ACTIVITY 2 Share Your Ideas

Write a paragraph or two about a time that you took a risk such as the one taken by Dr. Dillard. Describe what happened, and let your classmates know if you still think you did the right thing.

An Important Period

MALCOLM X
Prison Studies

Malcolm X (1925–1965) rose from a world of street crime in the Harlem section of New York City to become one of the most powerful African American leaders of the civil rights movement in the 1960s. On February 21, 1965, at the age of thirty-nine, he was shot and killed. Malcolm X told his life story in *The Autobiography of Malcolm X* (1964), written with the assistance of Alex Haley (1921–1992), author of the slave saga *Roots* (1976). The following selection from *The Autobiography* refers to a period that Malcolm X spent in federal prison. In the selection, Malcolm X explains how his inability to express himself led him to learn how to read and write.

1   Many who today hear me somewhere in person, or on television, or those who read something I've said, will think I went to school far beyond the eighth grade. This impression is due entirely to my prison studies.

2   It had really begun back in the Charlestown Prison, when Bimbi first made me feel envy of his stock of knowledge. Bimbi had always taken charge of any conversation he was in, and I had tried to emulate him. But every book I picked up had few sentences which didn't contain anywhere from one to nearly all of the words that might as well have been in Chinese. When I just skipped those words, of course, I really ended up with little idea of what the book said. So I had come to the Norfolk Prison Colony still going through only book-reading motions. Pretty soon, I would have quit even these motions, unless I had received the motivation that I did.

3   I saw that the best thing I could do was get hold of a dictionary — to study, to learn some words. I was lucky enough to reason also that I should try to improve my penmanship. It was sad. I couldn't even write in a straight line. It was both ideas together that moved me to request a dictionary along with some tablets and pencils from the Norfolk Prison Colony school. I spent two days just riffling uncertainly through the dictionary's pages. I'd never realized so many words existed! I didn't know which words I needed to learn. Finally, to start some kind of action, I began copying.

4   In my slow, painstaking, ragged handwriting, I copied into my tablet everything printed on that first page, down to the punctuation marks.

5   I believe it took me a day. Then, aloud, I read back, to myself, everything I'd written on the tablet. Over and over, aloud, to myself, I read my own handwriting.

6   I woke up the next morning, thinking about those words — immensely proud to realize that not only had I written so much at one time, but I'd written words that I never knew were in the world. Moreover, with a little effort, I also could remember what many of these words meant. I reviewed the words whose meanings I didn't remember. Funny thing, from the dictionary first page right now, that *aardvark* springs to my mind. The dictionary had a picture of it, a long-tailed, long-eared,

burrowing African mammal, which lives off termites caught by sticking out its tongue as an anteater does for ants.

– I was so fascinated that I went on — I copied the dictionary's next page. And the   7
same experience came when I studied that. With every succeeding page, I also learned of people and places and events from history. Actually the dictionary is like a miniature encyclopedia. Finally the dictionary's A section had filled a whole tablet — and I went on into the B's. That was the way I started copying what eventually became the entire dictionary. It went a lot faster after so much practice helped me to pick up handwriting speed. Between what I wrote in my tablet, and writing letters, during the rest of my time in prison I would guess I wrote a million words.

I suppose it was inevitable that as my word-base broadened, I could for the first   8
time pick up a book and read and now begin to understand what the book was saying. Anyone who has read a great deal can imagine the new world that opened. Let me tell you something: from then until I left that prison, in every free moment I had, if I was not reading in the library, I was reading on my bunk. You couldn't have gotten me out of books with a wedge. Between Mr. Muhammad's teachings, my correspondence, my visitors — usually Ella and Reginald — and my reading of books, months passed without my even thinking about being imprisoned. In fact, up to then, I never had been so truly free in my life. . . .

As you can imagine, especially in a prison where there was heavy emphasis on   9
rehabilitation, an inmate was smiled upon if he demonstrated an unusually intense interest in books. There was a sizable number of well-read inmates, especially the popular debaters. Some were said by many to be practically walking encyclopedias. They were almost celebrities. No university would ask any student to devour literature as I did when this new world opened to me, of being able to read and understand.

I read more in my room than in the library itself. An inmate who was known to   10
read a lot could check out more than the permitted maximum number of books. I preferred reading in the total isolation of my own room.

When I had progressed to really serious reading, every night at about ten P.M. I   11
would be outraged with the "lights out." It always seemed to catch me right in the middle of something engrossing.

Fortunately, right outside my door was a corridor light that cast a glow into my   12
room. The glow was enough to read by, once my eyes adjusted to it. So when "lights out" came, I would sit on the floor where I could continue reading in that glow.

At one-hour intervals the night guards paced past every room. Each time I   13
heard the approaching footsteps, I jumped into bed and feigned sleep. And as soon as the guard passed, I got back out of bed onto the floor area of that light-glow, where I would read for another fifty-eight minutes — until the guard approached again. That went on until three or four every morning. Three or four hours of sleep a night was enough for me. Often in the years in the streets I had slept less than that.

I have often reflected upon the new vistas that reading opened to me. I knew   14
right there in prison that reading had changed forever the course of my life. As I see it today, the ability to read awoke inside me some long dormant craving to be mentally alive. I certainly wasn't seeking any degree, the way a college confers a status symbol upon its students. My homemade education gave me, with every additional

book that I read, a little bit more sensitivity to the deafness, dumbness, and blindness that was afflicting the black race in America. Not long ago, an English writer telephoned me from London, asking questions. One was, "What's your alma mater?" I told him, "Books." You will never catch me with a free fifteen minutes in which I'm not studying something I feel might be able to help the black man. . . .

Every time I catch a plane, I have with me a book that I want to read — and that's   15 a lot of books these days. If I weren't out here every day battling the white man, I could spend the rest of my life reading, just satisfying my curiosity — because you can hardly mention anything I'm not curious about. I don't think anybody ever got more out of going to prison than I did. In fact, prison enabled me to study far more intensively than I would have if my life had gone differently and I had attended some college. I imagine that one of the biggest troubles with colleges is there are too many distractions, too much panty-raiding, fraternities, and boola-boola and all of that. Where else but in prison could I have attacked my ignorance by being able to study intensely sometimes as much as fifteen hours a day?

READING ACTIVITY 3 Build Your Vocabulary

Determine the meanings of the following words from the context of Malcolm X's essay. Then check their meanings by looking up the words in a dictionary: emulate (2), painstaking (4), inevitable (8), engrossing (11), intervals (13), feigned (13), vistas (14), dormant (14).

GROUP ACTIVITY 4 Discuss the Reading

Discuss the following questions about "Prison Studies" with your classmates.

1. In what ways is the period of time spent reading significant in Malcolm X's life?
2. How do you think this period in the author's life affected him after his release from prison?
3. Which details about Malcolm X's prison life do you find especially interesting? Why?
4. Go through Malcolm X's essay, and underline his topic sentences. Does the author include any details that don't directly support these points? If so, how do these details affect your response to his essay? Would "Prison Studies" be better or worse without them?

WRITING ACTIVITY 3 Share Your Ideas

Write a paragraph or two about an important period in your life when you went through a significant change or confronted a new challenge. What experiences made this period more or less difficult for you? What people helped you go through this change? How did going through this period make a difference in your life? Compare your experiences with those of your classmates.

Writing Your Essay   A Step-by-Step Guide

Now that you've read some essays remembering a significant person, event, or period in the writer's life, it's time to write your own essay. First, read the writing assignment that follows. Then, use the step-by-step advice that follows to discover ideas, develop them as you draft, and polish your writing into a finished essay that writers will find both interesting and expressive:

Step 1   Explore Your Choices 91
Step 2   Write Your Discovery Draft 97
Step 3   Revise Your Draft 99
Step 4   Edit Your Sentences 108
Step 5   Share Your Essay 112

Writing Assignment

What made you the person you are today? Introduce yourself to your classmates and your instructor by writing a brief essay that explains how something in your past changed your sense of who you are and what's important to you. You (or your instructor) may decide to approach this assignment in one of several ways:

- Write about a person who has had an impact on you.

  OR

- Write about an event that was memorable for you.

  OR

- Write about an important period in your life.

Step 1 Explore Your Choices

If you're like most people, choosing something to write about is a challenge. Of all the people you have known and things you have experienced, how can you possibly pick one to help explain who you are? Before you choose a topic to write about, you will first think about who your readers are and what you want them to know about you. Then you will learn some techniques for gathering ideas, and use those techniques to explore the three major topic possibilities (people, events, or time periods) presented in this chapter. Experimenting with your options will help you identify the most promising topic to write about and find good details to support your ideas.

Analyzing Your Audience and Purpose

For more on audience and purpose, see pp. 7–11.

You are writing an essay about a significant person, a memorable event, or an important period in your life because you want the other students in your class to know you better. Your classmates are your readers. Before you write for this audience, consider what you know about them as well as what they already know about you. What do you want your classmates to learn about you?

Consider also how this essay will help you explain something in your life that changed you. You may want to express your thoughts and feelings about someone important, as Joshua Bell does in "My Maestro," or like James Dillard, you might inform your readers of something you learned. You might even want to persuade your classmates to think differently about something that matters to you, as Malcolm X does in "Prison Studies." Always remember, though, that your primary purpose for this essay is expressive—to share your thoughts and feelings about an important person, event, or period in your life.

WRITING ACTIVITY 4 Analyze Your Audience and Purpose

Your responses to the following questions will help you decide how to approach this chapter's writing assignment. Be sure to come back to these questions after you have chosen a topic.

1. Does the assignment call for primarily expressive, informative, or persuasive writing?

2. What is the average age of your audience?

3. How many readers are female? How many are male?

4. What parts of the country or world are they from?

5. How many have had experiences like yours?

6. In what ways are your readers similar to or different from you?

7. How will these similarities and differences with your readers affect the way you write your essay?

Gathering Ideas

For more on ways of gathering ideas, see pp. 11–16.

When you gather ideas, or *prewrite*, you explore your thoughts about a topic without worrying about where those thoughts will lead you. Many different methods can help you discover ideas before you write. In this chapter, you will review three of these methods (brainstorming, relating aloud, and clustering), and use each method to explore one of the three possible topics: a significant person, a memorable event, or an important period in your life. As you practice these techniques, you may decide to apply the ones that work best for you to your other topic choices as well.

Brainstorming about a Significant Person

One of the most productive techniques for gathering ideas is *brainstorming*. When you brainstorm, you write down everything that comes to mind without judging which ideas are better than others or how they might connect. Instead, you express as many thoughts as possible so that you can go back and select the ones that are most helpful.

Think about the significant people in your life. Who would you name? You might name your parents, a partner, a friend, or a teacher or coach—such as the one you may have written about after reading Joshua Bell's "My Maestro" (p. 82).

You might even remember an acquaintance or a stranger you met only once but who nevertheless gave you a new perspective at a critical time in your life. Whomever you choose, the person should be someone who has influenced your sense of who you are and who you strive to be.

If you have trouble thinking of things to write about someone important to you, answering the following questions can help you get started:

- How would you describe this person to someone who has never met him or her?
- How would you describe some places you have visited with this person?
- What special objects do you associate with this person? Why?
- What song, book, or movie do you associate with this person? Why?
- What holidays or other special occasions are memorable because of this person? Why?
- How do you feel when you think of this person? Describe these feelings.
- Why is this person important to you?

 Use Google Docs

To gather ideas through brainstorming, create a document in Google Docs, and post the questions about a significant person listed above. After entering the questions, ask family and friends who know this person to join Google Docs and answer the questions. Use their answers to help you add additional details to your essay.

Here's how one student writer, Jesus Ramirez, brainstormed about his father. He started by answering a few of the preceding questions, and wrote down other ideas as they occurred to him.

My father
short (5' 6"), green eyes, brown hair, lots of hair
in good shape
kind

understanding

always tries to be helpful

soft-spoken but firm!

doesn't talk much, but when he does, everyone listens!

we've been so many places together that it's hard to name only a few:

    grandparents' house

    Uncle Jim's

    church

    the mall

    auto-parts store

    Disneyland

    fishing

    baseball games

rents movies for us to watch together

Field of Dreams — Dad loves baseball so much that if he had a cornfield, he'd
    turn it into a baseball field, too

anything about baseball

Cardinals' cap

remote control

favorite chair

newspaper

coffee mug

WRITING ACTIVITY 5   Brainstorm about a Significant Person

Think of someone who has meant a lot to you, and write that person's name at the top of a page. Then brainstorm whatever comes to mind. You may use the questions on page 93 to get started, but follow whatever direction your mind takes you.

Relating a Memorable Event

In addition to the people in your life, events have changed you in some way. Whether you did something to make these events happen (such as earning a scholarship or running a marathon) or saw them change your life unexpectedly (such as discovering a talent or learning you need surgery), such moments have influenced who you are.

One good way to explore ideas about an important event is to *relate* it—to talk about it with other people. By simply sharing a story or a thought orally without the pressure of having to write it down, you will usually discover that you have quite a bit to say about it. At the same time, you have the advantage of an audience that can provide immediate feedback—giving you a sense of what will interest your readers and how you can best explain your ideas. For example, you may want to tell more of the details of the risk you may have written about after reading James Dillard's "A Doctor's Dilemma" (p. 85).

After thinking about some of the important events in her life, student writer Karla Jaramillo decided that her classmates might be interested in the time her mother almost died. Karla told them about that event as another student took notes. This is her story:

> It all began on my first day in fifth grade. I wanted to go shopping for school supplies. My mom didn't really want to take me, but I just had to get some things. My older sister Ana offered to drive, since my mom has heart trouble, and my mom decided she wanted to go with us after all. We spotted another one of my sisters, Mary, driving my dad's truck. We knew she could only be going to her boyfriend's house. My mom had forbidden Mary to see him because he was separated but not divorced. "Do you want me to follow her?" Ana asked. My mother said yes.
>
> At last the truck stopped, and Mary went to the front door of the house. Her boyfriend came out and hugged her. My mother was hysterical! She leaped out of the car and ran toward the house, yelling at Mary to get in the car. Mary kept screaming, "I hate you! I hate you!" Then mom sank to the ground. She began to gasp for breath.
>
> Mary's boyfriend called 911, and Mom was taken to the hospital. I was really scared. I thought my mother was going to die. I prayed hard, and we all cried a lot. After a while, things turned out all right. She had had a heart attack, but she was going to live.

Karla's story prompted many questions from her peer response group. For example, one student asked, "Did your mom and sister make up?" Others asked, "Can you remember anything else that was said?" and "How did you feel during all of this?" Finally, someone asked Karla why this event was significant to her.

Relating the event aloud and reading over her classmate's notes from the discussion helped Karla focus on the details and understand what the story meant to her. Answering the group's questions also helped Karla identify her main idea: although it was a terrible crisis, her mother's heart attack brought the family closer together.

 Create a video

Ask someone to record a video of you relating a memorable event out loud. Upload the video to YouTube, then ask your group members to view it and ask any questions they may have about the memorable event. Use their questions to help you think of additional details to add to your essay.

> **GROUP ACTIVITY 5** Relate a Memorable Event

Working with a small group, relate a memorable event out loud. The moment may be happy or sad, but it should have markedly affected who you are. Ask someone to take notes on your story, or use a recording device. When you finish relating aloud, respond to the group's questions about your topic. Then read over your classmate's notes from the discussion (or listen to the recording) to gather additional ideas.

Clustering about an Important Period

Unlike an *event*, which occurs at a specific time or on a particular day, a *period* includes events that take place over days or months. For example, you could write about the summer you spent away from home, your first six months of marriage, or the year you shed a significant amount of weight. You may already have written about one important period in your life after reading Malcom X's "Prison Studies" (p. 88).

Clustering is another useful technique that can help you gather and organize your thoughts. Especially if you're a visual thinker, drawing connections can open your eyes to fresh ways of looking at something.

To begin clustering about an important time in your life, write a word or phrase that describes that time in the center of a blank page, and draw a circle around it. As ideas about the topic come to mind, write them down, put circles around them, and draw lines from them to the center circle. As you think of ways to describe your ideas, write down the descriptions, circle them, and join these circles to the ideas they describe.

Student writer Maria Talberg clustered her ideas about an important period in her life—the three years she worked at a job that made her so unhappy she decided to return to college. (See Figure 4.1 below.)

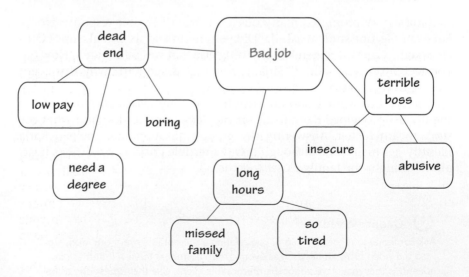

Figure 4.1 Maria's Clustering

WRITING ACTIVITY 6 Cluster about an Important Period in Your Life

Spend a few minutes thinking about a time in your life that was very happy or very un-happy and that had a profound effect on who you are today. In the center of a blank page, write a word (or phrase) that describes that time, and draw a circle around it. Then write down any words or phrases about the period that occur to you, and draw lines to connect related ideas. For each word or phrase you write, try to think of additional words and phrases related to them.

> ⏻ **Use a template to gather ideas**
>
> To make clustering easier, refer to the charts and diagrams templates on your word-processing program, or go to Office.com to find a template. Use this tem-plate to help you create a cluster of an important period in your life.

Step 2 Write Your Discovery Draft

It's time to move to the stage of the writing process where you put your ideas together so that you can see what you have to work with.

When you write a discovery draft, you aim to explore possibilities rather than follow a map that's already been drawn. You might find that your thoughts take you in an unexpected direction; follow the path that seems most interesting to you. You'll have time later on to revise and edit your discovery draft.

For more on drafting, see pp. 16–20.

Choosing a Topic

You have gathered ideas on three possible topics—a significant person, a memorable event, and an important period in your life—that changed you in a meaningful way. Before you can begin drafting, you must choose one topic to write about.

Review all of the material you compiled as you gathered ideas, and look for a promising topic that you can develop into an essay that explains how something changed you. You might discover that one option—a person, an event, or a period—gave you the best ideas. On the other hand, if you find that one theme emerged as you explored different topics, consider creating a topic that combines two or three ideas. For example, you might connect your significant person with a significant event or period in your life. Whatever you decide to do, be sure to choose a topic that you have many ideas about and that will interest both you and your readers.

Student writer Jesus decided to write about a significant person—his father—but he was also drawn to write about what attending baseball games with his father meant to their relationship. This combined topic allowed Jesus to provide supporting details and thereby develop his ideas more fully in his discovery draft.

> ◖ **WRITING ACTIVITY 7** Choose Your Topic ◗

Review your brainstorming, notes made by your classmates when you related aloud to other students, and your clustering. Based on the ideas you have gathered, decide which topic will be most interesting for you and your readers (and make sure you have something to say about it). To ensure that you have generated enough details to support a draft, you may want to do more brainstorming, relating aloud, and clustering on the topic of your choice.

Sharing Your Ideas

When you begin drafting, try to write a preliminary thesis statement that indicates the main point of your essay. You can then use this statement as a guide while you write. As you draft, feel free to use ideas that you have already gathered and to add new ones as they come to you. Remember that your main goal at the drafting stage is to get your ideas down on paper. You'll revise and edit your essay later.

A Student's Discovery Draft

Student writer Jesus, whose brainstorming you saw earlier in the chapter, wrote the following preliminary thesis statement and discovery draft about going to baseball games with his father. (Note that Jesus's draft includes the types of errors that typically appear in a first draft.)

Preliminary thesis statement: My father taught me valuable lessons.

I love this sport because of my father. My father is the reason I love baseball. He cares for his family. He's always putting them above everything else. He works hard at his job so that we have all of the necessities of life. He loves to rent DVDs for us to watch, too. Ever since I was two years old, my father has taken me to baseball games. My father taught me valuable lessons.

On one occasion, a player struck out two times. He threw his bat out onto the baseball field. My father told me that the next time, he would strike out again. I didn't believe him when the player was at bat again, I was ready to disprove my dad. But he was right. I asked him how he knew that the batter was going to strike out. He told me that it is very hard to get things accomplished through anger or frustration. Anger gets in the way of performance.

My father also used baseball to show me the importance of not giving up. During one ball game, a pinch hitter struck out three times. The American League has allowed designated hitters since 1973. As he stepped up to the plate for the fourth time, the crowd was booing and cursing him. I played little league baseball and nobody ever shouted bad things at us no matter how many times we struck out. The people in the stands always encouraged us. I asked my dad, "Why are all these people being rude to this player?" He said that it was because he was not doing well. He was having a bad night, but that did not make him a bad player. He said the important thing was that the player kept trying no matter how many times he struck out.

But of all the times I went with my father to the ball games, this one stands out. It was a warm afternoon when my father asked me to go with him. I love warm days in September. When we got there, it was very cold. The wind was blowing. I remember that I was just wearing shorts my legs were freezing. My father had to put his arms around my bare legs to protect me. My memories of my father at the ballpark will always be special to me. He used baseball games to teach me about life.

WRITING ACTIVITY 8 Write Your Discovery Draft

First, write a preliminary thesis statement that identifies your topic and explains why the person, event, or period you are writing about is important to you. Then write a discovery draft that explores your ideas. Don't worry about the details. For now, focus on getting all of your ideas in writing. If you wish, you may write drafts on two or three topics to see which one you prefer to continue working on.

Step 3 Revise Your Draft

When you revise a discovery draft, you focus not only on what you want to communicate to your audience but also on how you communicate it. In this stage, you concentrate on supporting your ideas and making your points easy to follow. Writers often move back and forth among the stages of the writing process. Thus, it's possible that as you revise, you might need to return to gathering ideas. After you've gathered enough ideas, you can go back to revising.

For more on revising, see pp. 20–22.

As you revise, always think about what your reader needs to know to understand the significance of that special person, event, or period in your life.

⏻ Create a Facebook group

Invite your classmates to join you in a Facebook group, and then post your discovery draft for your fellow students to read. Ask your readers (1) what interested them the most about your draft and (2) what they want to know more about. Use their responses to help you decide where to add supporting details.

Developing Your Ideas

For more on description and narration, see pp. 58–62

When you wrote your discovery draft, you probably wrote the story quickly, as Jesus did. When you revise, you want to add details that make your piece interesting and memorable. You need to go beyond describing experiences in vague, general ways to describing them with details that help your readers feel as if they were there with you.

For this chapter's writing assignment, you will develop your ideas and support your thesis statement by using description and narration. These strategies serve several important functions in an essay:

- They increase readers' interest in your topic.
- They help readers understand your main ideas.
- They help convince readers to accept your viewpoint.

Description

Although you have firsthand experience of the person, event, or period you're writing about, your readers don't. Consider adding description to make your essay more colorful and interesting. As you learned in Chapter 3, using description creates vivid images that explain how something looks, sounds, smells, tastes, or feels. For example, James Dillard, in "A Doctor's Dilemma," draws on sight, touch, and smell to describe the injured truck driver. This description of the accident victim helps readers feel as if they were at the scene themselves:

> He was still out cold, limp as a rag doll. His throat was crushed and blood from the jugular vein was running down my arms. He still couldn't breathe. He was deep blue-magenta now, his pulse was rapid and thready. The stench of alcohol turned my stomach, but I positioned his jaw and tried to blow air down into his lungs. It wouldn't go.

■ HOW TO Use Description

- Draw on as many senses—sight, sound, smell, taste, and touch—as you can.
- Be specific. Instead of "The apartment smelled bad," write "The apartment smelled of stale cigarettes and boiled cabbage."
- Make comparisons, such as "The baby's eyes are like gray marbles."
- Avoid common phrases, such as "as pretty as a picture" or "as cute as can be."

WRITING ACTIVITY 9 Use Description to Develop Your Ideas

Use the following questions to brainstorm for descriptive details about a person, thing, or place: How does it smell? Taste? Sound? What does it feel like? Look like? Review your answers, and select details to add interest to your essay.

Narration

Whether you're writing about a person, an event, or a period in your life, you probably have at least one story to tell. As you learned in Chapter 3, you can use *narration* to describe an event or a series of events as they happened in time. Good narration includes specific details, and it often contains dialogue in which people's actual words are quoted.

In the following example from "My Maestro," Joshua Bell explains in narrative form why his violin teacher never punished his students:

> As a boy, he had once played his violin at a school assembly. His fellow students loved it, and applauded for so long the principal had to order them to stop. Later, Gingold's art teacher pulled him aside. "Let me see your hands," she said. "Are those the hands that made that beautiful music?" He beamed, so proud to be recognized for what he could do. Then she took a wooden pointer, smacking his palm so hard it damaged a nerve. Years later, he still felt pain. The teacher had decided he shouldn't feel so good about himself. That stuck with him. He went the opposite way with his students.

■ HOW TO Use Narration

- To support your thesis, tell a series of events in the order in which they occurred.
- Narrate only the most important events.
- Use descriptive details and dialogue to illustrate important points.

Student writer Jesus reviewed his discovery draft and decided that he could use narration to explain the time his father kept him warm at a game. He drafted this narrative for his revision:

> I told my father that I was cold, but I didn't want to leave. He then suggested that we move to another place where the wind didn't blow as hard. But when we moved to the new place, it was still cold, so my father sat in back of me and said "bend your knees toward your chest and lean back." Then he put his warm hands on my legs, like a duck protecting his duckling from bad weather or a predator that might hurt him.

◖ WRITING ACTIVITY 10 Use Narration to Develop Your Ideas ◗

Review your discovery draft, looking for ideas that you could expand with a story. Draft at least one narrative paragraph that supports the main idea of your essay (you may or may not decide to use it in your revised draft). Include descriptive details, and if possible, quote some dialogue.

Building Your Essay

Once you have developed your ideas, you want to make sure that your essay communicates those ideas as clearly as possible. In this chapter, you will focus on organizing your thoughts so that your readers can understand your message.

To organize, first review your thesis statement to ensure that it is effective. Next, make sure that each of your preliminary paragraphs has a topic sentence, so that readers can follow your train of thought. Then check that the details in each paragraph support their topic sentences.

Revise Your Thesis Statement

When you started your discovery draft, you prepared a preliminary thesis statement to help guide your writing. When you revise, you need to make sure that your thesis statement reflects what you actually wrote and helps prepare readers to understand your ideas.

As you learned in Chapter 1, an effective thesis statement

■ Announces the topic of the essay.

■ Shows, explains, or argues a point about your topic.

■ Gives a sense of what the essay will be about.

For more on writing a thesis statement, see pp. 18–20.

A thesis statement may be one or two sentences, and normally it appears at the beginning of an essay. In the introduction to "Prison Studies," for example, Malcolm X provides the following thesis statement about a significant period in his life:

> Many who today hear me somewhere in person, or on television, or those who read something I've said, will think I went to school far beyond the eighth grade. This impression is due entirely to my prison studies.

In addition to indicating the topic of the essay (education), this thesis statement shows a point (the author is well educated even though he finished only the eighth grade) and gives a sense of what the essay will be about (how Malcolm X used his time in prison to educate himself).

For his discovery draft, student writer Jesus wrote the following preliminary thesis statement: "My father taught me valuable lessons." This early thesis statement was a good start because it announces a topic (Jesus's father) and shows a point about the topic (his father taught him valuable lessons). As he reviewed his draft, however, Jesus realized that what he wrote about was how his father used the sport of baseball to teach him about life. He revised his thesis statement to reflect the focus of his essay: "My father used baseball to teach me valuable lessons about life."

> **WRITING ACTIVITY 11** Revise Your Thesis Statement

Reread the preliminary thesis statement you wrote for your discovery draft. Does it announce the topic, show a point about the topic, and give a sense of what the essay will be about? Because your discovery draft may have gone in a different direction than you expected, revise your thesis statement as necessary to make it more effective.

Add Topic Sentences

Once you have a revised thesis statement, you need to show how the different parts of your essay develop your main idea. The best way to guide your readers is to provide topic sentences that explain how the details in each paragraph support the thesis statement. As you revise, make sure that every paragraph includes a topic sentence.

For more on topic sentences, see pp. 36–39.

As you learned in Chapter 2, effective topic sentences break up a thesis statement into several supporting ideas and express a complete thought for each of those specific ideas. For example, here is the thesis statement followed by some of the topic sentences Malcolm X provides in "Prison Studies." Notice how each of these topic sentences identifies a specific supporting idea that develops the thesis statement.

Thesis Statement

Many who today hear me somewhere in person, or on television, or those who read something I've said, will think I went to school far beyond the eighth grade. This impression is due entirely to my prison studies.

Topic Sentences

It had really begun back in the Charlestown Prison, when Bimbi first made me feel envy of his stock of knowledge.

I saw that the best thing I could do was get hold of a dictionary—to study, to learn some words.

I suppose it was inevitable that as my word-base broadened, I could for the first time pick up a book and read and now begin to understand what the book was saying.

I have often reflected upon the new vistas that reading opened to me.

A topic sentence may fall anywhere in the paragraph. Most often, however, it comes first. For example, in the following paragraph from "A Doctor's Dilemma," the topic sentence (italicized) comes first, and the rest of the paragraph tells us what Dillard imagined:

An image flashed before my mind. I could see the courtroom and the driver of the truck sitting in a wheelchair. I could see his attorney pointing at me and thundering at the jury: "This young doctor, with still a year left in his residency training, took it upon himself to play God. He took it upon himself to move this gravely injured man, condemning him forever to this wheel-chair. . . ." I imagined the millions of dollars in award money. And all the years of hard work lost. I'd be paying him off for the rest of my life. Amy touched my shoulder. "What are you going to do?"

◖ WRITING ACTIVITY 12 Revise and Add Topic Sentences ◗

Reread your discovery draft, and underline your thesis statement and the topic sentence in each paragraph. Where necessary, revise the topic sentences to show how each paragraph supports your thesis statement. If any paragraphs are missing their topic sentences, add them.

Strengthen Your Focus

As you learned in Chapter 2, once you have effective topic sentences for each paragraph, you need to make sure that all other sentences within a paragraph relate to its topic sentence. If a paragraph includes any sentences that do not support the topic sentence, you can revise them to make them clearly relate to your point, move them to another paragraph, or remove them from your essay.

The following paragraph from Jesus's discovery draft includes several sentences that do not support the topic sentence. Notice how these irrelevant sentences (in italics) detract from the topic sentence (highlighted):

> My father also used baseball to show me the importance of not giving up. During one ball game, a pinch hitter struck out three times. *The American League has allowed designated hitters since 1973.* As he stepped up to the plate for the fourth time, the crowd was booing and cursing him. *I played little league baseball and nobody ever shouted bad things at us no matter how many times we struck out. The people in the stands always encouraged us.* I asked my dad, "Why are all these people being rude to this player?" He said that it was because he was not doing well. He was having a bad night, but that did not make him a bad player. He said the important thing was that the player kept trying no matter how many times he struck out.

Here is the same paragraph from Jesus's draft with the irrelevant sentences removed:

> My father also used baseball to show me the importance of not giving up. During one ball game, a pinch hitter struck out three times. As he stepped up to the plate for the fourth time, the crowd was booing and cursing him. I asked my dad, "Why are all these people being rude to this player?" He said

For more on paragraph unity, see pp. 39–40.

that it was because he was not doing well. He was having a bad night, but that did not make him a bad player. He said the important thing was that the player kept trying no matter how many times he struck out.

GROUP ACTIVITY 6 Strengthen Focus

With the other members of your peer group, read the following paragraph, and underline the topic sentence. Cross out any irrelevant sentences that don't support the topic sentence.

> The results of the election for student body president would be revealed at the meeting that day. My stomach was in knots anticipating the outcome. I knew that being president would be trying, but it was a risk worth taking. Once I took a risk when I rode the Shock Wave roller coaster at Six Flags. "You can breathe," a classmate said, but I didn't want to miss a word of the announcement. I took a CPR course when I was thirteen and learned a lot about how to get someone breathing again. Slowly but surely, the dean of students announced the name of the next president. The dean of students is a really nice woman who just moved here from California. Holding my breath hadn't helped because I still didn't hear what she said. My friends gave a little cheer, and the rest of the group applauded and chanted, "Speech, speech, speech." I was an awful public speaker, but as the newly elected student body president, I gave it my best.

WRITING ACTIVITY 13 Strengthen Your Focus

Examine your current draft, checking each paragraph for sentences that don't support the topic sentence. Make your paragraphs more unified by deleting, relocating, or revising any irrelevant sentences that you find.

A Student's Revised Draft

Before you read Jesus's revised draft, reread his discovery draft on pages 98–99. Notice how in the revision he has used description and narration to develop his ideas, improved his thesis statement and topic sentences, and strengthened his focus. (You will notice a few errors in the revised draft; these will be corrected when Jesus edits his essay later on.)

Baseball Memories

To some, baseball is just a sport where someone tries to reach base before getting thrown out. To others, it is "America's pastime"—a baseball stadium filled with people cheering, eating hot roasted peanuts, and, when the seventh inning approaches, singing "Take Me Out to the Ball Game." To me, though, baseball will always be more than just a game because my father used baseball to teach me valuable lessons about life.

1

The introduction is more interesting.

From the time I was two years old, my father took me to baseball games.   2
On one occasion when we were at a game, a player struck out two times and
threw his bat out onto the baseball field. My father told me that the next
time, the player would strike out again. I didn't believe him when the player
was at bat again, I was ready to disprove my dad. But he was right. I asked
him how he knew the batter would strike out again. He told me that it is very
hard to get things accomplished through anger or frustration. Anger gets in
the way of performance. He added that I should not throw things when I get

The main point of the
paragraph is clearer.

mad because this could hurt someone else or myself. Instead, he suggested
that I take the time to think things over before I do something that I will
regret later on.

He also used baseball to show me the importance of not giving up. During   3
one ball game, a player struck out three times. As he stepped up to the plate
for the fourth time, the crowd booed and cursed him. I asked my dad, "Why
are all these people being rude to this player?" He replied, "He is one of the

Dialogue makes the father's
advice easier to understand.

best players the team has, but he is not doing too well. There are days when
we are not ourselves we are humans and make mistakes. Just because he
struck out three times does not make him a bad person. You should learn from
his experience: life is made of strikeouts, but it doesn't matter how many
strikeouts you have. What matters is that you get another chance to hit the
ball. If you are confident, you will succeed, but if you are not confident and
do not believe in yourself, you will fail."

But of all the times I went with my father to the ball games, one stands   4
out. It was a warm afternoon when my father asked me to go with him. When
we got there, it was very cold. The wind was blowing. I remember that I was
just wearing shorts my legs were freezing. I told my father that I was cold,
but I didn't want to leave. He suggested that we move to a place where the
wind didn't blow as hard. When we moved to the new place, it was still cold

This description makes the
essay more interesting and
the point clearer.

my father sat in back of me and said, "Bend your knees toward your chest and
lean back." Then he put his warm hands on my legs, like a duck protecting his
duckling from bad weather or a predator that might hurt him. Not only did I
feel warmed by my father, but I felt protected as well.

My memories of my father at the ballpark will always be special to me. He   5
used baseball to teach me the importance of controlling my temper. He taught

The conclusion is more
extended and doesn't leave
the reader hanging.

me not to throw or hit things when I become upset. He also used baseball to
teach me to work toward goals without giving up. Like a batter facing that
next pitch, he taught me to face life head-on.

GROUP ACTIVITY 7   Analyze Jesus's Revised Draft

Use the following questions to analyze how Jesus has improved his draft through revision.

1. What is Jesus's thesis statement? How did he improve it from his preliminary thesis statement?

2. How well does Jesus use topic sentences? After examining all of his topic sentences, focus on one paragraph. Identify the topic sentence, and explain how the idea in the topic sentence is developed in the paragraph.

3. What details has Jesus included to improve his essay?

4. Look back at paragraph 1 of Jesus's discovery draft (pp. 98–99). He omitted most of these sentences in his revision. Why do you think he decided to omit these? Was it a good decision?

5. Does Jesus convince you — his reader — that his father used baseball to teach him valuable lessons about life? Explain.

6. What other revisions could Jesus make to improve his draft?

GROUP ACTIVITY 8   Peer Review

Now that you have made some revisions to your discovery draft, form a group with two or three other students, and exchange copies of your drafts. Read your draft aloud while your classmates follow along. Then ask your group members the following questions about your essay. Write down your classmates' responses. If you don't understand what a classmate is suggesting, ask for clarification before you write it down. You will want to read these notes later for suggestions on how to improve your draft.

1. What do you like best about my essay?

2. What is my thesis statement? Do I need to make the thesis clearer?

3. Examine my topic sentences. How well do they connect to my thesis and indicate the main idea of each paragraph?

4. Where in the draft could I better develop my ideas by using description or narration?

5. Is each paragraph in my draft unified? Or do some paragraphs contain irrelevant sentences that need to be omitted or revised?

6. Where in my draft did my writing confuse you? How can I clarify my ideas?

7. Have I followed all the instructions for this assignment?

WRITING ACTIVITY 14   Revise Your Essay

You have already developed your ideas, revised your thesis statement, added topic sentences, and strengthened your focus. But your classmates have probably given you additional suggestions for improving your essay. Taking your classmates' peer review responses into consideration, revise your draft as a whole so that readers will understand how a significant person, event, or period in your life changed you.

◖Step 4 Edit Your Sentences

When you wrote and revised your discovery draft, you were busy getting your thoughts on paper. Your sentences may not have come out as clearly as you would have liked, and you probably made some mistakes. You're now ready to edit your draft for readability and correctness.

Read your revised essay carefully, looking at each word for errors in grammar, spelling, and punctuation and for awkward sentences. Consult the Handbook in Part Four of this book and a dictionary. As you edit your essay for this chapter's assignment, you will focus on combining sentences with coordinating conjunctions and on eliminating run-on sentences.

Combining Sentences Using Coordinating Conjunctions

One way to ensure that your ideas are well received is to consider sentence variety. Readers get bored easily when they read many sentences that are short and sound alike. You may have noticed, for example, that Jesus's drafts contained many short sentences. To improve his writing, Jesus decided to use a technique known as *sentence coordination*.

Like Jesus, you can combine short, closely related sentences with *coordinating conjunctions*. Here are seven coordinating conjunctions and their meanings:

for	because
and	in addition
nor	neither
but	opposite
or	alternatively
yet	opposite
so	as a result

One way to remember these words is to think of the word *FANBOYS*, which is spelled with the first letter of each of the seven coordinating conjunctions.

For more on sentence combining and coordination, see pp. 436–39.

Use an appropriate coordinating conjunction to combine short, closely related sentences. Put a comma before the conjunction.

Short Sentences

Last Saturday, I went to an outlet store to buy a business suit. I saw a movie with my best friend.

Combined Sentence with *And*

Last Saturday, I went to an outlet store to buy a business suit, and I saw a movie with my best friend.

Short Sentences

The plane was an hour late getting to Denver. I missed my connecting flight.

Combined Sentence with *So*

The plane was an hour late getting to Denver, so I missed my connecting flight.

Short Sentences

I gave my girlfriend another chance to show her commitment to me. She started dating my best friend.

Combined Sentence with *But*

I gave my girlfriend another chance to show her commitment to me, but she started dating my best friend.

> ### ▪ HOW TO Combine Sentences Using Coordinating Conjunctions
>
> • To be sure that two closely related sentences are complete, check that each one has a subject and a verb and that each conveys a complete thought.
> • Select an appropriate coordinating conjunction (*for, and, nor, but, or, yet, so*).
> • Use a comma before the coordinating conjunction.

EDITING ACTIVITY 1 Use Coordinating Conjunctions

Combine the following sentences with an appropriate coordinating conjunction.

EXAMPLE   I played baseball when I was young. I lost interest in the sport.
, but I

1. Baseball is a multimillion dollar business. It is also one of America's oldest organized sports.

2. Baseball is still popular. Newer sports, such as basketball and football, have become more popular.

3. Hundreds of Major League Baseball players earn more than a million dollars a year. Many athletes are attracted to the sport.

4. Women's softball has increased in popularity. This game is played at many colleges and at the Olympics.

5. At this time, a softball player can't earn a living playing softball. Not many athletes are interested in the sport professionally.

For additional practice with using coordinating conjunctions to combine sentences, go to **bedfordstmartins.com /choices** and click on **Exercise Central.**

For more on run-on sentences, see pp. 457–61.

WRITING ACTIVITY 15 Combine Your Sentences

Examine your revised draft for short, closely related sentences. Where it makes sense to do so, combine them with coordinating conjunctions.

Correcting Run-on Sentences

Remember, the more attention your readers pay to errors in your writing, the less attention they pay to what you have to say. Run-on sentences are an especially common mistake.

A *run-on sentence* occurs when two complete sentences, or *independent clauses*, are written together without any punctuation between them, as if they were one sentence. Here are some examples of run-on sentences:

RUN-ON   Arizona has some of the hottest spots in the country don't visit it in August.

RUN-ON   Going to college while working full time has been hard I never get enough sleep.

RUN-ON   Student athletes often experience great pressure to do well they might need extra support from their schools.

RUN-ON   I bought a minivan after I had my third child we needed the room.

Correct run-on sentences in one of three ways:

- Use a period.

  CORRECT   Arizona has some of the hottest spots in the country. Don't visit it in August.

- Use a semicolon. You may follow the semicolon with a conjunctive adverb (such as *however, in addition, also, therefore,* or *furthermore*) and a comma if you like.

  CORRECT   Going to college while working full time has been hard; I never get enough sleep.

  CORRECT   Student athletes often experience great pressure to do well; therefore, they might need extra support from their schools.

- Use a comma and a coordinating conjunction.

  CORRECT   I bought a minivan after I had my third child, for we needed the room.

EDITING ACTIVITY 2 Correct Run-on Sentences

Correct each of the following run-on sentences by adding a period, a semicolon, or a comma and a coordinating conjunction.

                                                      . Mine
EXAMPLE Everybody has at least one wacky relative ~~mine~~ is my uncle.
                                                   ^

1. My uncle has a plastic spider he likes to take it out of his pocket to frighten young children.

2. When there's a full moon, our cat gets crazy he climbs the curtains and howls when we try to get him down.

3. My youngest daughter is only three she can already write her name.

4. My father was treated for cancer he's doing well now.

5. I'm returning to school to enter one of the health-care professions I plan to be a physical therapist.

For additional practice with correcting run-on sentences, go to **bedfordstmartins.com /choices** and click on **Exercise Central**.

■ **WRITING ACTIVITY 16 Edit Your Sentences**

Read your essay carefully, looking at each word for errors in grammar, spelling, and punctuation. Focus on run-on sentences. Use a dictionary and the Handbook in Part Four of this book to help you find and correct any mistakes.

A Student's Edited Essay

Using the Handbook in Part Four, Jesus corrected the errors in his essay. His corrections are noted in the margin.

Jesus Ramirez
Professor Posey
English 0311
16 Apr. 2012

Baseball Memories

To some, baseball is just a sport where someone tries to reach base   1
before getting thrown out. To others, it is "America's pastime"—a baseball
stadium filled with people cheering, eating hot roasted peanuts, and, when
the seventh inning approaches, singing "Take Me Out to the Ball Game." To
me, though, baseball will always be more than just a game because my
father used baseball to teach me valuable lessons about life.

From the time I was two years old, my father took me to baseball   2
games. On one occasion when we were at a game, a player struck out two
times and threw his bat out onto the baseball field. My father told me that
the next time, the player would strike out again. I didn't believe him.
When the player was at bat again, I was ready to disprove my dad. But he   — A run-on sentence is corrected.
was right. I asked him how he knew the batter would strike out again.

Sentences are combined.

He told me that it is very hard to get things accomplished through anger or frustration, for anger gets in the way of performance. He added that I should not throw things when I get mad because this could hurt someone else or myself. Instead, he suggested that I take the time to think things over before I do something that I will regret later on.

He also used baseball to show me the importance of not giving up. During one ball game, a player struck out three times. As he stepped up to the plate for the fourth time, the crowd booed and cursed him. I asked my dad, "Why are all these people being rude to this player?" He replied, "He is one of the

A run-on sentence is corrected.

best players the team has, but he is not doing too well. There are days when we are not ourselves; we are humans and make mistakes. Just because he struck out three times does not make him a bad person. You should learn from his experience: life is made of strikeouts, but it doesn't matter how many strikeouts you have. What matters is that you get another chance to hit the ball. If you are confident, you will succeed, but if you are not confident and do not believe in yourself, you will fail."

But of all the times I went with my father to the ball games, one stands

Sentences are combined.

out. It was a warm afternoon when my father asked me to go with him. When we got there, it was very cold, and the wind was blowing. I remember that I

A run-on sentence is corrected.

was just wearing shorts, so my legs were freezing. I told my father that I was cold, but I didn't want to leave. He suggested that we move to a place where the wind didn't blow as hard. When we moved to the new place, it was still

A run-on sentence is corrected.

cold, so my father sat in back of me and said, "Bend your knees toward your chest and lean back." Then he put his warm hands on my legs, like a duck protecting his duckling from bad weather or a predator that might hurt him. Not only did I feel warmed by my father, but I felt protected as well.

My memories of my father at the ballpark will always be special to me.

Sentences are combined.

He used baseball to teach me the importance of controlling my temper, and he taught me not to throw or hit things when I become upset. He also used baseball to teach me to work toward goals without giving up. Like a batter facing that next pitch, he taught me to face life head-on.

3

4

5

◖Step 5   Share Your Essay

Share your finished essay with your instructor and classmates, either by e-mail or by posting it to a class Web site. Ask your peer review group to comment on the improvements you made. Don't be surprised if someone says, "I can't believe this is the same essay. It's so much better!"

CHAPTER CHECKLIST

❑ I read essays about a significant person, event, or period to explore and learn about the chapter's theme.

❑ I analyzed my audience and purpose.

❑ I gathered ideas on my topic by brainstorming, relating aloud, and clustering.

❑ I wrote a discovery draft.

❑ I revised my draft by

    ❑ using description and narration to develop ideas.

    ❑ revising my thesis statement.

    ❑ adding topic sentences.

    ❑ improving paragraph focus.

❑ I combined short, closely related sentences with coordinating conjunctions.

❑ I edited my draft to correct errors, including run-on sentences.

❑ I shared my draft with my instructor and classmates.

REFLECTING ON YOUR WRITING

To help you continue to improve as a writer, answer the following questions about this assignment:

1. Did you enjoy writing an expressive piece in which you shared your thoughts and feelings?

2. Which method of gathering ideas worked best for you?

3. Which details most improved your essay?

4. If you had more time, what parts of your essay would you want to improve before sharing it with readers? Why?

Using your answers to these questions, complete a Writing Process Report for this chapter (download a form at **bedfordstmartins.com/choices**). After completing this report, freewrite about what you learned in this chapter.

"Fireworks light up the night sky as everyone celebrates Mexico's independence."
— SANDRA CORDERO, "EL GRITO DE DOLORES"

Explaining
Cultural Symbols, Traditions, and Heroes

When you explain something, you are communicating what you know to others. You might explain a particular concept or idea, demonstrate how something works, or share information with others on a topic you know about. When you write an explanatory essay, your purpose is to teach or tell your readers something—to inform them about a subject. Your goal is to present your subject in a way that is interesting, that includes your own thoughts about the subject, and that teaches your readers something new. In this chapter, you will use this type of informative writing to examine a culture.

Have you ever traveled to another country? Were you surprised by what you saw and heard? Did people drive on the left or right side of the road? How did they entertain themselves? Were shopping practices different than what you are accustomed to? Were you introduced to new foods or styles of dress? Although they can be unsettling at times, such encounters enable us not only to learn about other cultures but also to better understand our own.

The term *culture* refers to the customs, beliefs, values, objects, and languages shared by members of a particular group. Although many people grow up as part of a single culture—Vietnamese, Brazilian, or German, for instance—more and more people are

In this chapter, you will write about a cultural symbol, tradition, or hero that is meaningful to you. As you follow the steps of the writing process, you will

- Explore the chapter topic by reading essays about a cultural symbol, tradition, or hero.
- Gather ideas by clustering, asking questions, and freewriting.
- Develop your ideas using **examples** and **process explanation**.
- Practice writing introductions and conclusions, and making connections with transitions and keywords.
- Combine sentences with conjunctive adverbs.
- Learn how to identify and correct sentence fragments.
- Share your essay with others.

recognizing themselves as *multicultural*, or as having roots in more than one culture. In addition to identifying ethnic heritage or national origin, *culture* can also refer to the beliefs and customs of any particular group. The hippie culture of the 1960s, for example, favored social and personal rebellion, encouraged a distinctive lifestyle, and came to use the peace sign as its symbol. Although members of a given culture might take its unique characteristics for granted, outsiders are sometimes fascinated, puzzled, or even frightened by things about that culture that they don't understand.

In this chapter, you will learn how to write an essay that explains a cultural symbol, tradition, or hero. You will begin by reading essays by professional writers about an aspect of culture. You will also follow a student, Sandra Cordero, as she writes about celebrating Mexico's independence day in her essay "El Grito de Dolores."

By examining a specific aspect of a culture, you will gain a stronger understanding of your own beliefs and values and will probably want to share your knowledge with others. The readings and activities in this chapter will help you explain your ideas about a particular culture to your readers. As you work through the readings and activities in this chapter, you will practice transforming your knowledge of and experience with a culture into an essay that teaches your readers about something important to you. ∎

GROUP ACTIVITY 1 Think about Cultures

The photo on page 114 shows a celebration of Mexico's independence day, which occurs on September 16, the day that marks the beginning of the Mexican war of independence from Spain in 1810. Looking at this photo, can you see similarities in the way that Mexicans and people of other countries celebrate their independence? Why do you think that many of these celebrations include a fireworks display? With several classmates, describe independence day celebrations in the cultures that you're familiar with.

Getting Started   Reading Essays That Explain a Cultural Symbol, Tradition, or Hero

Most of us are fascinated by how other people live, think, and behave. In fact, learning about unfamiliar cultures is one of the major reasons that people travel. But familiar cultures can also be fascinating. By examining what we value and whom we admire in our own culture, we can better understand the way we lead our lives. Cultural experiences, whether familiar or unfamiliar, make for interesting reading and can lead to important insights. Before you start considering possibilities for your own writing, read the following professional essays about a cultural symbol (the Korean delicacy kim chee), a cultural tradition (ice fishing in Minnesota), and a cultural hero (Captain Chesley Sullenberger). As you read, notice how the writers provide examples and explain processes to help readers understand what their subjects mean to them. Notice, too, how the writers use effective introductions to get their readers' attention and powerful conclusions to leave a lasting impression about their subject. (For additional essays about a cultural symbol, tradition, or hero, see p. 554.)

A Cultural Symbol

NORA OKJA KELLER
My Mother's Food

Nora Okja Keller is a freelance writer and journalist who often writes about the intersection of Korean and American cultures. Her articles have appeared in *Newsweek*, *Time*, and the *New York Times*. She has also written several books, including the novels *Comfort Woman* (1998), which won the American Book Award, and *Fox Girl* (2003).

Keller was born in Seoul, Korea, but her family immigrated to the United States, settling in Hawaii, when she was a young child. As a teenager, she rebelled against her mother's Korean culture in an effort to be seen as "American." In "My Mother's Food," Keller writes about the role food played in her rebellion.

I was weaned on kim chee. A good baby, I was "able to eat anything," my mother told me. But what I especially loved was the fermenting, garlicky Chinese cabbage my mother pickled in our kitchen. Not waiting for her to lick the red peppers off the won bok, I would grab and gobble the bits of leaves as soon as she tore them into baby-size pieces. She said that even if my eyes watered, I would still ask for more.

Propping me in a baby carrier next to the sink, my mother would rinse the cabbage she had soaked in salted water the night before. After patting the leaves dry, she would slather on the thick red-pepper sauce, rubbing the cloves of garlic and green onion into the underarms of the cabbage, bathing it as she would one of her own children. Then, grabbing them by their dangling leafy legs, she would push the wilting heads into five-gallon jars. She had to rise up on tiptoe, submerging her arm up to the elbow, to punch the kim chee to the bottom of the jar, squishing them into their own juices.

Throughout elementary school, our next-door neighbor Frankie, whose mother was the only other Korean in our neighborhood, would come over to eat kim chee with my sisters and me every day after school. We would gather in our garage, sitting cross-legged around a kim-chee jar as though at a campfire. Daring each other on, we would pull out long strips that we would eat straight, without rice or water to dilute the taste. Our eyes would tear and our noses start to run because it was so hot, but we could not stop. "It burns, it burns, but it tastes so good!" we would cry.

Afterward when we went to play the jukebox in Frankie's garage, we had to be careful not to touch our eyes with our wrinkled, pepperstained hands. It seemed

1   Keller captures her reader's attention by beginning her essay with a memorable image of a baby being "weaned" on kim chee.

2   Keller explains the process of making kim chee using descriptive examples.

3

This dialogue helps the reader imagine this scene.

4

as if the hot, red juice soaked through our skin and into our bones; even after we bathed, we could still feel our fingers tingling, still taste the kim chee on them when we licked them. And as my sisters and I curled into our bed at night, nestling together like sleeping doves, I remember the smell lingered on our hands, the faint whiff of kim chee scenting our dreams.

This description of the children in bed creates a vivid image.

We went crazy for the smell of kim chee—a perfume that lured us to the 5 kitchen table. When my mother hefted the jar of kim chee out of the refrigerator and opened the lid to extract the almost fluorescent strips of cabbage, she didn't have to call out to us, although she always did. "Girls, come join me," she would sing; even if we weren't hungry we couldn't resist. We all lingered over snacks that lasted two or three hours.

But I didn't realize that I smelled like kim chee, that the smell followed me to 6 school. One day, walking across Middle Field toward the girls' locker room, a girl I recognized from the gym class before mine stepped in front of me.

"You Korean?" she asked. She had narrowed eyes as brown as mine, shaped 7 like mine, like mock-orange leaves pinched up at the corners.

This dialogue slows down the action and helps the reader picture the event.

Thinking she could be my sister, another part-Korean, part-Caucasian *hapa* 8 girl, I nodded and welcomed her kinship with a smile.

"I thought so," she said, sneering. Her lips scrunched upward, almost folding 9 over her nostrils. "You smell like one."

I held my smile, frozen, as she flitted away from me. She had punched me in 10 the stomach with her words. Days later, having replayed this confrontation endlessly in my mind (in one fantasy version, this girl mutated into a hairy Neanderthal that I karate-chopped into submission), I thought of the perfect comeback: "Oh yeah? Well, you smell like a chimpanzee." At the very least, I should have said *something* that day. Anything—a curse, a joke, a grunt—anything at all would have been better than a smile.

Keller gives examples of how the encounter with her classmate affected her.

I smiled. And I sniffed. I smiled and sniffed as I walked to the locker room and 11 dressed for P.E. I smiled and sniffed as I jogged around the field, trying to avoid the hall and other girls wielding field hockey sticks. I smiled and sniffed as I showered and followed my schedule of classes.

I became obsessed with sniffing. When no one was looking, I lifted my arms 12 and, quick, sniffed. I held my palm up to my face and exhaled. Perhaps, every now and then, I would catch the odor of garlic in sweat and breath. I couldn't tell: the smell of kim chee was too much a part of me.

I didn't want to smell like a Korean. I wanted to be an American, which meant 13 having no smell. Americans, I learned from TV and magazines, erased the scent of their bodies with cologne and deodorant, breath mints and mouthwash.

So I erased my stink by eliminating kim chee. Though I liked the sharp taste 14 of garlic and pepper biting my tongue, I stopped eating my mother's food.

Keller feels shame over and rejects her culture because of peer pressure.

I became shamed by the kim chee that peeked out from between the loaf of 15 white bread and the carton of milk, by the odor that, I grew to realize, permeated the entire house. When friends pointed at the kim-chee jars lined up on the refrigerator shelves and squealed, "Gross! What's that?" I would mumble, "I don't know, something my mom eats."

I also stopped eating the only three dishes my mother could cook: *kalbi ribs*, 16
bi bim kooksoo, and Spam fried with eggs. (The first "American" food my mother
ever ate was a Spam and egg sandwich; even now she considers it one of her favorite foods and never tires eating it.)

I told my mother I was a vegetarian. One of my sisters ate only McDonald's 17
Happy Meal cheeseburgers (no pickle); the other survived for two years on a diet
of processed-cheese sandwiches on white bread (no crust), Hostess DingDongs,
and rice dunked in ketchup.

Keller gives examples of
American food that her
sisters ate.

"How can you do this to me?" my mother wailed at her American-born chil- 18
dren. "You are wasting away! Eat, eat!" She plopped heaps of kim chee and *kalbi*
onto mounds of steaming rice. My sisters and I would grimace, poke at the food,
and announce: "Too fattening."

My mother had always encouraged us to behave like proper Korean girls: 19
quiet, respectful, hardworking. She said we gave her "heartaches" the way we
fought as children. "Worse than boys," she'd say. "Why do you want to do things
like soccer, scuba, swimming? How about piano?"

This dialogue helps the reader
understand Keller's mother.

But worse than our tomboy activities were our various adolescent diets. My 20
mother grieved over the food rejected. "I don't understand you," she'd say. "When
I was growing up, my family was so poor, we could only dream of eating this kind
of food. Now I can give my children meat every night and you don't want it."
"Yeah, yeah," we said, as we pushed away the kim chee, the Koreanness.

As I grew up, I eventually returned to eating kim chee, but only sporadically. I 21
could go for months without it, then be hit with a craving so strong I would run to
Sack-n-Save for a generic, watery brand that only hinted at the taste of home. Kim
chee, I realized, was my comfort food.

When I became pregnant, the craving for my own mother accentuated my 22
craving for kim chee. During the nights of my final trimester, my body foreign and
heavy, restless with longing, I hungered for the food I had eaten in the womb, my
first mother-memory.

The baby I carried in my own womb, in turn, does not look like me. Except for 23
the slight tilt of her eyes, she does not look Korean. As a mother totally in love
with her daughter, I do not care what she looks like; she is perfect as herself. Yet I
worry that — partially because of what she looks like — she will not be able to identify with the Korean in me, and in herself. I recognize that identifying herself as
Korean will be a choice for her — in a way it wasn't for someone like me, who looks
pure Asian. It hit me then, what my own mother must have felt looking at each of
her own mixed-race daughters; how strongly I do identify as a Korean American
woman, how strongly I want my child to identify with me.

When my daughter was fifteen months old, she took her first bite of kim chee. 24
I had taken a small bite into my own mouth, sucking the hot juice from its leaves,
giving it "mothertaste" as my own mother had done for me. Still, my daughter's
eyes watered. "Hot, hot," she said to her grandmother and me. But the taste must
have been in some way familiar; instead of spitting up and crying for water, she
pushed my hand to the open jar for another bite.

This description of her daughter
eating kim chee echoes the
description at the beginning of
the essay.

"She likes it!" my mother said proudly. "She is Korean!" 25

I realized that for my mother, too, the food we ate growing up had always 26
been an indication of how Korean her children were — or weren't. I remember how
intently she watched us eat, as if to catch a glimpse of herself as we chewed.

Now my mother watches the next generation. When she visits, my daughter 27
clings to her, follows her from room to room. They run off together to play the
games that only the two of them know how to play. I can hear them in my daughter's room, chattering and laughing. Sneaking to the doorway, I see them "cooking" in the Playskool kitchen.

By using Korean words in this dialogue, Keller is showing the close connection between food and culture.

"Look," my mother says, offering her grandchild a plate of plastic spaghetti, 28
"noodles is *kooksoo*." She picks up a steak. "This *kalbi*." My mother is teaching her
Korean, presenting words my daughter knows the taste of.

My girl picks up a head of cabbage. "Let's make kim chee, *Halmoni*," she says, 29
using the Korean word for *grandmother* like a name.

"Okay," my mother answers. "First, salt." My daughter shakes invisible salt 30
over the cabbage.

This process analysis is similar to the process analysis earlier in the essay, which gives the end of the essay a sense of closure.

"Then mix garlic and red-pepper sauce." My mother stirs a pot over the stove 31
and passes the mixture to my daughter, who pours it on the cabbage.

My daughter brings her fingers to her mouth. "Hot!" she says. Then she holds 32
the cabbage to my mother's lips, and gives her *halmoni* a taste.

"Mmmmm!" My mother grins as she chews the air. "Delicious! This is the best 33
kim chee I ever ate." My mother sees me peeking around the door.

"Come join us!" she calls out to me and tells my daughter, who's gnawing at 34
the fake food. "Let your mommy have a bite."

READING ACTIVITY 1 Build Your Vocabulary

Determine the meanings of the following words from the context of Nora Okja Keller's
essay. Then check their meanings by looking up the words in a dictionary: won bok (1),
slather (2), nestling (4), extract (5), flitted (10), Neanderthal (10), wielding (11), permeated (15), sporadically (21), accentuated (22).

GROUP ACTIVITY 2 Discuss the Reading

Discuss the following questions about "My Mother's Food" with your classmates.

1. What did kim chee symbolize for Keller when she was a child? Why did she stop
   eating it?

2. How did Keller's mother react when her children refused to eat Korean food?
   What does her reaction suggest about what the dishes symbolized in her mind?

3. How did the meaning of kim chee change for the author after she had a child?

4. Why do you think the author wants her daughter to think of herself as Korean?

5. How does Keller use examples and process explanation to explain what kim chee
   is and what it means to her?

> **WRITING ACTIVITY 1 Share Your Ideas**

Write a paragraph or two about an important food in your culture, describing what this food represents. For instance, in U.S. culture, apple pie is thought to represent goodness, as in "as American as Mom and apple pie." Share your writing with your classmates.

A Cultural Tradition

KEVIN KLING
Hook, Line, and Television

Playwright and commentator Kevin Kling writes about the beauty and peculiarities of Minnesota, his home state, which is known for its frigid temperatures and adaptable citizens. Rather than stay indoors during the cold weather, Minnesotans have developed a tradition of winter sports, one of which is ice fishing. In "Hook, Line, and Television," Kling explains the tradition of ice fishing, which involves unique social interactions as much as it does fishing.

1   Every year the call goes out: the ice is safe. Open water has turned into prime real estate, and villages of tiny shacks pop up overnight. Thus ice-fishing season opens in Minnesota, home of the nation's icebox, where carpaccio is still made with carp and especially frigid winters are referred to by their year, like fine wine. Although months of subzero temperatures test the heartiest souls, some people actually live in this state on purpose. As I overheard one Northern gentleman say, "When you freeze paradise, it's bound to last a little longer."

2   Mille Lacs Lake is one of the most popular spots for ice fishing in the Land of 10,000 Lakes. It covers more than 200 square miles in the middle of Minnesota and is known for its walleye, arguably the best-tasting fish you can pull from fresh water. Once the ice sets — late November or early December, depending — local resort owners start renting out ice-fishing houses and hauling them out onto the lake, where bars, churches and the random bowling alley follow. By January, there will be around 5,000 angling abodes on the ice, which qualifies as a small city in Minnesota. (And at Gull Lake, more than 9,000 folks competed in last year's annual Brainerd Jaycees Ice Fishing Extravaganza, but that's a one-day affair involving less housing.)

3   To most people below the 48th parallel, ice fishing must seem like pounding your head against the wall, in that it's not doing it in the first place that makes the most sense. While it's true that it's not for everyone, it sure beats staying cooped up inside your house for six months. Here are some basics to get you started:

4   First, find a spot on the lake where the ice is thick enough to support your car without its dropping through. If you're unsure, watch someone else drive out first. Next, auger a fishing hole in the ice. An ice auger is like a posthole digger with a large screwlike cutting blade rotated by hand or motor. In the fun department, the powered ice auger sits just behind the chain saw and way ahead of the power leaf blower.

5   Most people opt for an ice-fishing house, a 10- by 16-foot shack with a propane

stove and holes in the floor. The holes are usually covered by hinged plywood that can be flipped up for fishing. Some fishing houses are rudimentary, but others come with stereos, TVs, kitchens, bunk beds, couches, or even hot tubs and saunas parked next door. Ice anglers tend to have a lot invested in their fish houses. The shacks are usually painted to reflect the owner's personality, hobby, favorite sports franchise or cause. On the lake, brilliant colors are an advantage. An all-white house probably wouldn't be found until spring.

6   You'll need an ice-fishing pole with a reel, monofilament line and bobber. An ice-fishing pole looks pretty much like any other fishing pole but shorter, since casting isn't an option. You'll need a skimmer, or slotted ladle, for clearing out the ice that will form on the hole, and a five-gallon plastic bucket to haul your gear and your catch, or "tonnage." For bait, use a minnow or wax worm on a hook with a brightly colored weight. The best fishing is usually just off the bottom of the lake, which is only about 40 feet deep at most. A slight tug, or "jigging," on the line every few seconds draws attention to the bait.

7   There are other ways to increase your luck, such as using feeding-time charts and depth finders and topographic maps of the lake bottom that show ridges and shoals. Every fisher man or woman has a secret weapon, a lure that will make a fish react against its better judgment, whether by seduction, rage or appetite. Some folks spray their lures with fish oil to take away the human scent. (A word of caution: keep the fish oil away from the beer.)

8   The fun of ice fishing is that you never know what you might catch: perch, trout, northern pike, muskie, crappie—even the coveted walleye. Or you can drop a line down deep and try to snag something prehistoric with a lantern on its head. You just don't know what's going to come out of that hole. Maybe a trophy fish—something to take to the taxidermist, maybe a reason to fix up the basement, put a piece of shag carpet over the oil stain, make wise investments with confidence gained and spend more time with the family. A whole world of new possibilities opens. I heard about one guy who felt a tug on his line and pulled up sharply to set the hook. There was a tremendous fight until finally up through the hole came a license plate. He threw the plate in the corner and was rebaiting his line when he had a fearsome epiphany. He ran outside to see the hole in the ice where his truck had been. (That one may be apocryphal.)

9   We used to call ice fishing "sitting around practicing for when we got old," but now we just call it "sitting around." Many fisherpeople use a "tip-up," a device that sends up a flag when a fish bites. This frees one to multitask—that is, fish and play cards, fish and watch TV, fish and learn Spanish, and so on. Other warning systems include buzzers, bells, whistles, car alarms and voice-activated computers ("I believe you have a fish, Dave"). I knew a high-school band teacher who rigged cymbals to crash when a fish took the bait.

10   Northern Minnesota is known for its stoic Nordic types, but to ice fish I think you also have to have a sense of humor. The people, like the weather, seem cold at first, but then you get used to them. Just remember: when a guy sitting next to you doesn't talk to you for hours, it doesn't mean he doesn't like you. If he then asks, "Cold enough for you?" take it as a sign of affection. Answer with, "I'd wear a coat," and you'll be fine.

> **READING ACTIVITY 2 Build Your Vocabulary**

Determine the meanings of the following words from the context of Kevin Kling's essay. Then check their meanings by looking up the words in a dictionary: carpaccio (1), angling (2), abodes (2), rudimentary (5), casting (6), taxidermist (8), epiphany (8), apocryphal (8), stoic (10), Nordic (10).

> **GROUP ACTIVITY 3 Discuss the Reading**

Discuss the following questions about "Hook, Line, and Television" with your classmates.

1. What did you learn about ice fishing from reading Kling's essay?
2. A culture consists of the behaviors and beliefs that are characteristic of a certain group of people. In what ways are people who fish in the Minnesota winters part of a culture?
3. In your own words, describe one of the processes that ice fishers use — for example, to set up their huts or to increase their luck.
4. Explain the significance of the title of the piece, "Hook, Line, and Television."
5. What other sporting events are similar to ice fishing in the way that people behave?

> **WRITING ACTIVITY 2 Share Your Ideas**

Write a paragraph or two about a cultural tradition that you know. For instance, tailgating before football games is a uniquely American pastime. Exchange your writing with your classmates so that you can learn about other cultural traditions.

A Cultural Hero

JEFFREY ZASLOW
What We Can Learn from Sully's Journey

Jeffrey Zaslow was a writer who specialized in writing about the lives of extraordinary people. He graduated from Carnegie Mellon University in 1980 and was a columnist for the *Wall Street Journal*. In addition to writing his regular column, he authored or coauthored three best-selling books, including *Highest Duty: My Search for What Really Matters*, the memoir of Captain Chesley "Sully" Sullenberger. The following piece about Captain Sullenberger first appeared in the *Wall Street Journal* in 2009.

US Airways Capt. Chesley "Sully" Sullenberger has flown thousands of flights   1
in the last 42 years. "But now," he says, "my entire career is being judged by how I performed on one of them." That flight, of course, came last Jan. 15, when his Airbus A320 suffered a bird strike en route from New York to Charlotte, N.C., and lost

both engines. Sully and First Officer Jeff Skiles executed an emergency landing later dubbed "The Miracle on the Hudson," but that description never felt right to Sully.

He is a precise, methodical, cerebral man who carefully chooses his words. In recent months, while working on his new book, *Highest Duty: My Search for What Really Matters*, Sully spent a great deal of time reviewing his life and career. He has tried to understand what experiences from his past prepared him for Flight 1549.   2

As Sully's co-author, I clearly saw that it wasn't only his skills as a veteran pilot that carried him in those tense moments over Manhattan. It was also his upbring-ing, his family bonds, his sense of integrity — and his own losses. Flight 1549 wasn't just a five-minute journey from LaGuardia Airport to the Hudson. Sully's entire life led him safely to that river.   3

He was born in Denison, Texas, the son of a dentist and a teacher who had high expectations. "I grew up in a home where each of us had our own hammer," says Sully. That was because his dad kept enlarging the family home with the help of three not-always-willing assistants: Sully, his sister and his mom. "The goal was to do everything ourselves, to learn what we didn't know and then have at it," Sully says. The house wasn't perfect, but Sully knew where every nail was. "Sometimes I'd brood, wishing we lived in a professionally built house like everyone else," he says. "But each time the house grew, I felt a sense of accomplishment."   4

As a boy, Sully was a classic introvert who felt things deeply. In 1964, for in-stance, he saw news reports about a New York woman named Kitty Genovese. Her neighbors heard her screams as she was being stabbed to death by a stranger outside her apartment. Allegedly, they did nothing to help. "I made a pledge to myself, right then at age 13," Sully recalls, "that if I was ever in a situation where someone such as Kitty Genovese needed my help, I would choose to act. No one in danger would be abandoned. As they'd say in the Navy: 'Not on my watch.'"   5

People tell Sully that his success on Jan. 15 showed a high regard for life. Their words led him to reflection. "Quite frankly," he says, "one of the reasons I think I've placed such a high value on life is that my father took his." Suffering from de-pression, Sully's father killed himself in 1995. "His death had an effect on how I view the world," he says. "I am willing to work hard to protect people's lives, to not be a bystander, in part because I couldn't save my father."   6

There are other moments in Sully's personal life that he feels helped prepare him for Flight 1549. Sully and his wife struggled with infertility, then endured the arduous journey of trying to become adoptive parents. "The challenges Lorrie and I faced made me better able to accept the cards I've been dealt," Sully says, "and to play them with all the resources at my disposal." The couple eventually adopted two daughters, now ages 16 and 14.   7

He first yearned to fly at age five. At 16, in 1967, he began taking lessons from a no-nonsense crop-dusting pilot named L. T. Cook Jr. Sully was an earnest, hard-working student who paid close attention. One day he noticed a crumpled Piper Tri-Pacer at the end of Mr. Cook's grass airstrip. A friend of Mr. Cook's had tried to land the plane and didn't realize that power lines stretched across a nearby high-way. The plane slammed into the ground nose first. The pilot died instantly.   8

Sully peered into the blood-splattered cockpit. "I figured his head must have   9
hit the control panel with great violence," he says. "I tried to visualize how it happened—his effort to avoid the power lines, his loss of speed, the awful impact. I
forced myself to look into the cockpit, to study it. It would have been easier to
look away, but I didn't." That sobering moment taught Sully to be vigilant and
alert. For a pilot, one simple mistake could mean death.

He went on to the U.S. Air Force Academy, then a military career, and contin-   10
ued to study accidents. Twelve fellow military pilots died on training runs. "I
grieved for my lost comrades," he says, "but I tried to learn all I could about each
of their accidents." As an airline pilot, he helped develop an air-safety course and
served as an investigator at crash sites. He'd page through transcripts from cockpit voice recorders, with the last exchanges of pilots who didn't survive.

Since childhood, Sully has been fascinated by Charles Lindbergh. In *We*,   11
Lindbergh's 1927 book, he explained that his success was due almost entirely to
preparation, not luck. "Prepared Lindy" wouldn't have had the same magic as his
nickname "Lucky Lindy," but his views resonated with Sully. One aspect of preparing
well is having the right mind-set, he says. "In so many areas of life, you need to be a
long-term optimist but a short-term realist. That's especially true given the inherent
dangers in aviation. You can't be a wishful thinker. You have to know what you know
and don't know, and what your airplane can and can't do in every situation."

Sully has always kept in mind the air-crew ejection study he learned about in   12
his military days. Many pilots waited too long before ejecting from planes that
were about to crash. They either ejected at too low an altitude, hitting the ground
before their parachutes could open, or they went down with their planes. Why did
these pilots spend extra seconds trying to fix the unfixable? The answer is that
many feared retribution if they lost million-dollar jets. And so they remained determined to try to save their airplanes.

Sully says he has never shaken his memories of fellow Air Force pilots who   13
didn't survive such attempts. Having those details in the recesses of his brain was
helpful as he made quick decisions on Flight 1549. "As soon as the birds struck," he
says, "I could have tried to return to LaGuardia so as not to ruin a US Airways air-
craft. I could have worried that my decision to ditch the plane would be questioned by superiors or investigators. But I chose not to."

Sully values the concept of "goal sacrificing." When it's no longer possible to   14
complete all your goals, you sacrifice lower-priority goals. He instinctively knew
that goal sacrificing was paramount on Flight 1549. "By attempting a water landing," he says, "I would sacrifice the 'airplane goal'—trying not to destroy an air-
craft valued at $60 million—for the goal of saving lives."

Able to compartmentalize his thinking, even in those dire moments over the   15
Hudson, Sully says his family did not come into his head. "That was for the best. It
was vital that I be focused; that I allow myself no distractions. My consciousness
existed solely to control the flight path."

Since saving 155 lives that day, Sully has received thousands of emails and   16
now has 635,000 Facebook fans. His actions touched people so deeply that they
felt compelled to reach out and share their own seminal experiences with him. "I
am now the public face of an unexpectedly uplifting moment," Sully says, and he

accepts that. Still, he's not comfortable with the "hero" mantle. A hero runs into a burning building, he says. "Flight 1549 was different because it was thrust upon me and my crew. We turned to our training, we made good decisions, we didn't give up, we valued every life on that plane — and we had a good outcome. I don't know that 'heroic' describes that. It's more that we had a philosophy of life, and we applied it to the things we did that day."

Sully has heard from people who say preparation and diligence are not the   17
same as heroism. He agrees. One letter that was particularly touching to Sully came from Paul Kellen of Medford, Mass. "I see a hero as electing to enter a dangerous situation for a higher purpose," he wrote, "and you were not given a choice. That is not to say you are not a man of virtue, but I see your virtue arising from your choices at other times. It's clear that many choices in your life prepared you for that moment when your engines failed. There are people among us who are ethical, responsible and diligent. I hope your story encourages those who toil in obscurity to know that their reward is simple — they will be ready if the test comes. I hope your story encourages others to imitation."

Sully now sees lessons for the rest of us. "We need to try to do the right thing   18
every time, to perform at our best," he says, "because we never know what moment in our lives we'll be judged on." He always had a sense of this. Now he knows it for sure.

READING ACTIVITY 3 Build Your Vocabulary

Determine the meanings of the following words from the context of "What We Can Learn from Sully's Journey." Then check their meanings by looking up the words in a dictionary: cerebral (2), introvert (5), arduous (7), inherent (11), ejection (12), retribution (12).

GROUP ACTIVITY 4 Read to Improve Your Writing

Discuss the following questions about "What We Can Learn from Sully's Journey" with your classmates.

1. What sentence or sentences in this piece best summarize the main point?
2. List three experiences from Captain Sullenberger's life that you think best prepared him for Flight 1549.
3. What is the concept of "goal sacrificing"? What goal did Captain Sullenberger sacrifice when he decided to land the plane on water?
4. Captain Sullenberger says that he is not a hero. Do you agree? Why or why not?

WRITING ACTIVITY 3 Share Your Ideas

Write a paragraph or two about your definition of a hero. In your writing, explain the characteristics and experiences that lead to heroic behavior. Who are some cultural heroes that fit your definition?

Writing Your Essay   A Step-by-Step Guide

Now that you've read some essays explaining a cultural symbol, tradition, or hero, it's time to write your own essay. First, read the writing assignment that follows. Then, use the step-by-step advice that follows to discover ideas, develop them as you draft, and polish your writing into a finished essay that readers will find both interesting and informative:

Writing Assignment

What cultures do you belong to? Consider your ethnic heritage, religion, age group, schools, workplaces, interests, social activities, and pastimes. Have you ever noticed that people who are unfamiliar with one of these cultures don't always understand it? No matter what your background is, your experience has given you specialized knowledge and a unique perspective. For this chapter's assignment, your goal is to teach readers something about a culture you know well. You (or your instructor) may decide to approach this assignment in one of several ways.

- Write about a cultural symbol you are familiar with.

  OR

- Write about a tradition that has special meaning for you.

  OR

- Write about a person who is a hero to members of a particular group.

Step 1   Explore Your Choices

After a little thought, you should be able to identify several different cultures that have influenced who you are and how you look at the world. Your family heritage and the region where you grew up, for example, probably hold special meaning for you. You might belong to a club or a sports team, identify with fans of a particular kind of music, or participate in an online community. In addition to having multiple cultures to consider, you will explore three topic possibilities—a cultural symbol, a cultural tradition, and a cultural hero—before you choose one topic to develop.

As you begin to search for essay ideas, think about who might read your essay and what they may already know (or not know) about a culture you belong to. For now, you will keep your options open by working with all three of the topics suggested in the assignment. Once you have tried out these possibilities, you will have a better idea of what topic—or topics—will be most productive.

Analyzing Your Audience and Purpose

For more on audience and purpose, see pp. 7–11.

In addition to your instructor and classmates, your audience may consist of family members, friends, and even complete strangers. Because your readers will come from different cultures, you need to figure out how much they might already know about your topic and what their attitude toward it might be. You will also need to provide plenty of context and detail so that a person who is unfamiliar with your culture will be able to understand what you have to say about it.

(ᐤ) Examine your online audience

If you're considering submitting your essay to a blog or Web site, find out as much as you can about the audience. Examine the comments readers have posted on the site in response to articles, photos, and so on. What do these comments reveal about the audience's interests and viewpoints? Use this information to make your essay appealing to your readers.

Consider, also, what you want to accomplish with your essay. Remember that the assignment is to teach readers something about a culture they might not fully understand. Although you may also be interested in expressing your feelings or persuading your readers to do something or think a certain way, always keep in mind that your goal is informative—to give them new information.

WRITING ACTIVITY 4 Analyze Your Audience and Purpose

Consider the audience that will be reading your essay. It can consist of your instructor, classmates, friends, and family. It can also consist of people you have never met if you decide to post your finished essay on a blog or another site on the Internet. Your responses to the following questions will help you decide how to approach your topic.

1. Does this assignment call for primarily expressive, informative, or persuasive writing?

2. What is the average age of your readers?

3. What percentage of your readers are likely to be female? Male?

4. What parts of the country or world could they be from?

5. What might your readers already know about your topic? If you asked them to list five words about your topic, which five might they list?

6. What do your readers need to know about your topic? What terms and concepts will you need to define? What objects or events would you need to describe in detail?

7. How might your readers feel about your topic? Will they find it interesting, or will you have to work to get their attention?

Gathering Ideas

Before you begin writing, it's always a good idea to explore a few topics by using different techniques. Trying out several possibilities often leads to unexpected ideas, and you might be surprised to discover which topic you have the most to say about. In the previous chapter, you gathered ideas by brainstorming, relating aloud, and clustering. In this chapter, you will again use clustering, but you will also add two more tools for gathering ideas about a cultural symbol, tradition, and hero—questioning and freewriting. Although the activities prompt you to use one technique for each topic possibility, don't hesitate to use additional approaches that work for you.

For more on gathering ideas, see pp. 11–16.

Clustering about a Cultural Symbol

A *symbol* is something that stands for or represents something else. For example, the American flag symbolizes the United States and also stands for freedom and democracy. The Star of David stands for Judaism, and a pink triangle symbolizes gay pride.

For more on clustering, see p. 13.

Some symbols are formal and permanent representations, such as the flag of the United States or the Statue of Liberty. As you discovered reading "My Mother's Food," however, symbols can be quite ordinary and represent any number of things for different people. Cultural symbols can take almost any form and often tell us what the people of the culture consider important.

To gather ideas about a cultural symbol that you might want to write about, try *clustering*, a technique that works especially well for visual topics. As you learned in the previous chapter, you start a cluster by putting a word or phrase in the center of a blank page and drawing a small circle around it. Write down other words or phrases that your topic brings to mind, draw small circles around them, and use lines to connect related ideas. If you need a starting point or if you get stuck, the following questions can help jump-start your thinking:

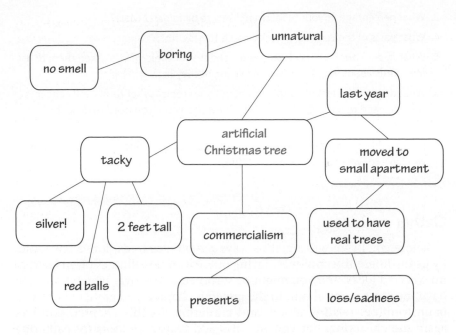

Figure 5.1 Clara's Clustering

- Describe the object to someone who has not seen it before.
- When was the last time you encountered or used the object?
- What ideas, events, or other objects do you associate with the object?
- How does the object symbolize the culture's lifestyle or beliefs?

Here's how one student, Clara, used some of these questions to create a cluster about a cultural symbol that interested her—an artificial Christmas tree.

WRITING ACTIVITY 5 Cluster about a Cultural Symbol

Select an object or image that symbolizes contemporary American culture or another culture that has influenced you. You could choose the food you wrote about after reading "My Mother's Food" (p. 117). Then create a cluster that connects the words and phrases you associate with this symbol. You may use the questions above to get started, but don't limit yourself to them.

Asking Questions about a Cultural Tradition

Put your clustering about a cultural symbol aside for the moment. Now you want to gather ideas about another possible topic for your essay—a cultural tradition.

A *tradition* is an event or activity repeatedly performed in the same way, usually to celebrate a culture's heritage and to bring people closer together. Many families develop traditions, such as annual reunions, that bring them together. A *cultural tradition*, however, extends beyond a family's rituals because it reflects the values of a whole culture. In "Hook, Line, and Television," for instance, Kevin Kling shows the cultural values of the coldest part of the United States when he describes the winter tradition of ice fishing.

Thanksgiving and the Fourth of July are cultural traditions unique to the United States. Some American cultural traditions have been adapted from other parts of the world and changed to suit American lifestyles and values. In Ireland, for example, St. Patrick's Day is a solemn Roman Catholic religious holiday, whereas in America, the day has lost most of its religious overtones and has become a public festival that celebrates Irish heritage. New cultural traditions develop all the time. Kwanzaa, for instance, was started in 1966 by African Americans who adapted the customs and beliefs of several African tribes to celebrate their heritage and to foster a sense of community among Americans of African descent.

A good way to gather ideas for an essay about a cultural tradition is to use the six questions reporters often ask to ensure that they get every detail of a news story:

- *Who* participates in this tradition?
- *What* happens during the tradition?
- *Where* is this tradition practiced?
- *When* does this tradition take place?
- *How* is this tradition celebrated? (For example, do special clothes, food, music, or dance accompany it?)
- *Why* is this tradition important to the participants?

Here is how one student, Sandra Cordero, answered the reporter's questions about a Mexican tradition, the holiday El Grito de Dolores:

Who? This tradition is celebrated by people in Mexico. The governor of each city pretends to be Miguel Hidalgo. The people of the city attend a parade.

What? This tradition has people reenact the time when Miguel Hidalgo persuaded the people of Dolores to fight for freedom from Spain.

Where? This tradition is celebrated in every town and city in Mexico.

When? El Grito de Dolores takes place on the evening of September 15 and the morning of September 16.

How? Fireworks are set off, a parade is held, and some people dress in traditional costumes.

Why? The Mexican people use this tradition to celebrate their freedom from Spain.

> **WRITING ACTIVITY 6**   Ask Questions about a Cultural Tradition

Select a tradition that you know well. You could choose the tradition you wrote about after reading "Hook, Line, and Television" (p. 121). Then use the journalist's questions — who, what, where, when, how, why — to generate ideas for an essay that could explain the tradition to readers who aren't familiar with it.

⏻ Use social media to ask questions

Post your cultural tradition and the six journalist's questions on your favorite social media site, such as your Facebook account or Twitter. You could also use an online survey site, such as SurveyMonkey. Use your friends' responses to gather more ideas about your topic.

Freewriting about a Cultural Hero

Put your writing about a cultural tradition aside for now. It's time to explore a third possible topic before you select one topic for your essay.

We all have personal heroes—family members, friends, teachers, or coaches—whom we admire because of their courage, dedication, or hard work and who serve as role models. *Cultural heroes* are known by many people within a culture and inspire an entire culture. Some cultural heroes are part of a group's heritage, others come from contemporary life, and still others are fictional characters. Sacagawea, the Dalai Lama, Mother Teresa, Martin Luther King Jr., Nelson Mandela, César Chávez, and Luke Skywalker are just a few examples of cultural heroes. In "What We Can Learn from Sully's Journey," you read about a cultural hero widely admired in the United States and around the world for saving hundreds of people's lives when he safely landed a disabled airplane

Who are some of your heroes? Although you may be able to list several people who have inspired you, you may not be certain that they are cultural heroes or that you know enough about them to fill a whole essay. You can find out if a person is a good subject for an essay by freewriting.

To freewrite, write without stopping for a certain period of time or until you reach a given page limit. Don't pause, go back, or make corrections, and don't try to put your thoughts in order; above all, don't worry about whether your ideas are good or not. Just keep writing, and see what you have to say. You can start by answering these questions:

- What facts do you know about this person (age, accomplishments, and so on)?
- Which five words best describe this person?
- What do you most admire about this person?
- What makes this person a cultural hero?

Here's how one student, Mark, gathered ideas about the reggae musician Bob Marley by freewriting:

> Bob Marley was a great musician. I love his music. Most people only know one or two of his songs, like Buffalo Soldier and No Woman, No Cry. But he wrote a lot of songs that celebrated Jamaican culture. Political too. Marley was a Rastafarian. People think it's all about marijuana, but it's a serious religion. Bob Marley is a famous and respected musician. His reggae popularized Jamaican music for the rest of the world. He also celebrated his Jamaican heritage by reminding people of the beauty and strength of Jamaican culture. My dream is to visit Jamaica someday. Bob Marley died tragically at age thirty-six, but his spirit lives on in his music. His son Ziggy is a reggae artist too.

GROUP ACTIVITY 5 Freewrite about a Cultural Hero

On your own or with a group of classmates, brainstorm a list of cultural heroes. Consider musicians, athletes, public officials, religious leaders, actors, entrepreneurs, celebrities, and ordinary people who are widely known because of their extraordinary talent, dedication, or achievements. Then select a hero who interests you, and freewrite about that person for at least ten minutes. If you like, you can write more about the hero you may have written about after reading "What We Can Learn from Sully's Journey" (p. 123).

Step 2 Write Your Discovery Draft

Now that you have experimented with at least three different topics that you might want to explore in an essay, you should be ready to begin a discovery draft. Remember that nobody creates a perfect essay in one try. Writing a discovery draft is a lot like the freewriting you did earlier in this chapter: experiment, let yourself wander, and feel free to make mistakes. You can focus on the details later when you revise and edit.

Choosing a Topic

You have gathered ideas on three aspects of culture—a symbol, a tradition, and a hero—and now have a rich source of material for writing. But you need to decide how to proceed.

Start by looking over the materials you wrote during your clustering, questioning, and freewriting. Which topic generated the most useful ideas? Which topic (or topics) are you most interested in pursuing? Which one will your readers want to learn about?

As you consider options for your discovery draft, you may stick with one of the three topics listed in the assignment (a cultural symbol, tradition, or hero), or you could decide to combine related topics. For instance, you could describe a cultural symbol that is part of a cultural tradition, or you could discuss a tradition that honors a cultural hero, as student writer Sandra Cordero does in the draft below.

Whatever you decide, the topic you choose should be one that interests you and that you are already fairly well informed about.

❮ WRITING ACTIVITY 7 Choose Your Topic ❯

Review your clustering, questioning, and freewriting, and identify or create a topic that you will enjoy writing about and that your audience will enjoy reading. If you wish, you may do more clustering, questioning, and freewriting (or whatever prewriting techniques work best for you) to gather additional ideas on one or more topics before you move forward.

Sharing Your Ideas

For more on thesis statements, see pp. 18–19.

Once you have settled on a topic, write a preliminary thesis statement to help focus your thoughts. As you draft and new ideas emerge, you can revise your thesis as many times as you need to.

If necessary, you might want to collect some basic information—such as dates and names—to get started. Most of the material for your discovery draft, however, should come from your own knowledge and experience. Keep your audience and purpose in mind as you decide what to include. Above all, remember that your main goal right now is to get your ideas down on paper. You'll have time later on to expand, fine-tune, and edit your draft.

⏻ **Share your preliminary thesis statement**

Share your thesis statement online so that your friends can give you feedback. You could post it as a status update on Facebook or Twitter. (If you use Twitter, you may need to condense the statement so you don't go over 140 characters.) After posting the statement, ask your friends if the topic interests them and if they know what your essay will be about. Use their responses to revise your thesis.

A Student's Discovery Draft

Student writer Sandra Cordero used the reporter's questions to gather ideas about a Mexican holiday called El Grito de Dolores. She then wrote the following discovery draft about this cultural tradition that is meaningful to her but unfamiliar to most people outside of Mexico and the American Southwest. Her preliminary thesis statement is highlighted. After reading the draft, discuss with your classmates what Sandra might do to revise it. (Note that the example includes the types of errors that typically appear in a discovery draft.)

El Grito de Dolores

I am proud to be part of the Mexican culture. The Mexican culture honors events important to its history. To celebrate Mexico's independence, Mexicans have El Grito de Dolores. El Grito de Dolores tells about what happened the day when the fight for our independence was over. Every Mexican participates in this event because it's the way we thank our heroes and ancestors for giving us freedom.

The preliminary thesis statement

Our celebration begins the night of the 15th of September. The main event is celebrated in Mexico's capital, which is El Distrito Federal. The holiday is celebrated everywhere in Mexico. Even the most little towns have their own celebration. People get together in the Main Plaza to celebrate the fiesta. Exactly at midnight, the governor of each city goes on top of the municipal building. "¡Viva Don Miguel Hidalgo!" he yells to honor the person who made our independence possible. The words "¡Viva México, Viva México, Viva México!" give honor to our country.

On the morning of the 16th of September, people get together on the main street to see the parade. The parade includes children, business leaders, government leaders, clubs, police officers, and firefighters. Everyone under the sun. On this day, everyone feels the freedom that this day brought. Every town in Mexico has a street called "16 de Septiembre" where it begins and ends.

We give honor to the men who made us free. Mexicans believe in traditions. By giving honor to the men who made us free, we thank them our ancestors for the freedom that they have given us.

WRITING ACTIVITY 8 Write Your Discovery Draft

Prepare a preliminary thesis statement, and build on the ideas you gathered during Step 1 to write a discovery draft. Remember that your purpose is to teach your audience something about a cultural symbol, tradition, or hero important to you. For now, focus simply on getting your ideas in writing. If you have any trouble, consider writing drafts on one or more topics before you decide which one to continue working on.

Step 3 Revise Your Draft

When you revise a discovery draft, you concentrate on clarifying and supporting your ideas. Resist the urge to correct errors when revising; you will do that during the editing stage.

The revision skills you learned in the previous chapter will also help you improve your essay about a cultural symbol, tradition, or hero. Check that (1) your thesis statement identifies your topic and expresses your main idea, (2) each paragraph has a topic sentence, and (3) your essay is well focused. In the rest of this chapter, you will learn how to use examples and process explanation to develop your ideas. You will also learn strategies for writing an effective introduction and conclusion, and you will practice connecting ideas with keywords and transitions.

Developing Your Ideas

An essay must be well developed to be convincing. In other words, you need to support your points with information. Detailed information helps readers understand your subject and makes your essay more interesting. Two methods of development—examples and process explanation—are especially appropriate for an essay on a cultural symbol, tradition, or hero.

Examples

For more on using examples, see pp. 62–63.

Examples provide specific details that make a main point vivid and concrete. The most common type of examples are facts, or statements that can be verified to be true. Examples may also be specific instances or events that illustrate your main point, relevant personal experiences, or other people's opinions.

In his essay "Hook, Line, and Television," writer Kevin Kling uses examples to support his point that ice fishing is enjoyable because of the surprises it offers. Notice that he starts that paragraph with a topic sentence (highlighted) and then provides several examples of surprises—verifiable facts, imagined possibilities, and specific instances—to support his idea:

> The fun of ice fishing is that you never know what you might catch: perch, trout, northern pike, muskie, crappie—even the coveted walleye. Or you can drop a line down deep and try to snag something prehistoric with a lantern on its head. You just don't know what's going to come out of that hole. Maybe a trophy fish—something to take to the taxidermist, maybe a reason to fix up the basement, put a piece of shag carpet over the oil stain, make wise investments with confidence gained and spend more time with the family. A whole world of new possibilities opens. I heard about one guy who felt a tug on his line and pulled up sharply to set the hook. There was a tremendous fight until finally up through the hole came a license plate. He threw the

Flight 1549 wasn't just a five-minute journey from LaGuardia Airport to the Hudson. Sully's entire life led him safely to that river.

Ask a Question   Posing one or more questions early in an essay can rouse readers' curiosity about your topic and encourage them to keep reading to find the answers to those questions. To improve her discovery draft (p. 135) about El Grito de Dolores, for example, student writer Sandra Cordero started her revised draft (p. 146) with a vivid description of the celebration and added a simple question to engage her readers:

> What is El Grito de Dolores?

Cordero uses the remainder of her essay to answer this question for her readers.

■ **HOW TO** Write an Effective Introduction

- Grab your readers' attention—perhaps with description, a surprising fact, a brief story or anecdote, or a question.
- Narrow your topic.
- Conclude with a thesis statement.

WRITING ACTIVITY 11 Revise Your Introduction

Reread the introductory paragraph of your essay. Then rate your introduction on a scale of 1 to 4 according to the following list:

1. Effective (forceful, attention-getting hook; clearly stated thesis statement)
2. Adequate (satisfactory hook; clearly stated thesis statement)
3. So-so (uninteresting hook; vague thesis statement)
4. Ineffective (no hook; no thesis statement)

Discuss your rating with your classmates. Then revise the introduction to your essay using one of the techniques discussed in this chapter. Also look at your thesis statement to see how you can make it more effective. It should announce your topic clearly and reveal its significance.

Write a Powerful Conclusion

The *conclusion* serves two major functions in an essay: it makes clear that you have made the point you introduced at the start of the essay, and it draws the essay to a satisfactory close. Thus, in the conclusion, you do not include new material or end abruptly; instead, you wrap up what you have already said. Try to leave your readers with a lasting impression about your topic and its significance. For most short essays, the most effective way to conclude is to reinforce your thesis and broaden your focus.

Reinforce the Thesis   By *reinforcing the thesis* using different wording in your conclusion, you remind readers of the significance of your topic and emphasize your main point or idea. For example, Jeffrey Zaslow provides versions of his thesis statement in both the introduction and the conclusion to "What We Can Learn from Sully's Journey":

STATEMENT OF THESIS IN INTRODUCTION	Flight 1549 wasn't just a five-minute journey from LaGuardia Airport to the Hudson. Sully's entire life led him safely to that river.
REINFORCEMENT OF THESIS IN CONCLUSION	Sully now sees lessons for the rest of us. "We need to try to do the right thing every time, to perform at our best," he says, "because we never know what moment in our lives we'll be judged on." He always had a sense of this. Now he knows it for sure.

Broaden the Focus   By *broadening the focus* of an essay in the conclusion, you connect your topic to something larger to show readers why it is important to them.

Because you have special knowledge of the topic, you can inform others about how to put the information you have provided to good use. A good way to broaden the focus of a personal essay about a cultural symbol, tradition, or hero is to conclude with a suggestion that your readers do something or that they continue thinking about how the topic affects them. In his conclusion to "Hook, Line, and Television," for example, Kevin Kling offers some tips for readers who might want to give ice fishing a try:

> Northern Minnesota is known for its stoic Nordic types, but to ice fish I think you also have to have a sense of humor. The people, like the weather, seem cold at first, but then you get used to them. Just remember: when a guy sitting next to you doesn't talk to you for hours, it doesn't mean he doesn't like you. If he then asks, "Cold enough for you?" take it as a sign of affection. Answer with, "I'd wear a coat," and you'll be fine.

GROUP ACTIVITY 6 Revise Your Conclusion

Ask several members of your peer group to rate the concluding paragraph of your draft on a scale of 1 to 4 according to the following list:

1. Powerful (memorable closure; main point reinforced)

2. Adequate (interesting closure; main point reinforced)

3. So-so (uninteresting closure; main point reinforced)

4. Ineffective (no sense of closure; main point not reinforced)

Ask your group members to suggest how you could make your concluding paragraph more interesting and forceful. Use their suggestions and your own ideas to revise your conclusion, making sure that you reinforce your thesis and broaden your focus.

Connect Ideas

In addition to improving your introduction and conclusion when you revise your essay, be sure to show how your main idea and your supporting points are connected. You can do this by strengthening your thesis statement, by including topic sentences for each paragraph, and by using keywords and transitions.

Use Keywords   One way to connect your ideas is to repeat *keywords* — words that relate to the topic being discussed. By repeating a keyword, you keep your reader focused on the topic. In the following paragraph from "Hook, Line, and Television," notice how the repetition of a keyword (highlighted) contributes to the flow of ideas and reminds readers that the topic is ice fishing:

> First, find a spot on the lake where the ice is thick enough to support your car without its dropping through. If you're unsure, watch someone else drive out first. Next, auger a fishing hole in the ice. An ice auger is like a posthole digger with a large screwlike cutting blade rotated by hand or motor. In the fun department, the powered ice auger sits just behind the chain saw and way ahead of the power leaf blower.

In addition to repetition of the same keyword, you can use pronouns and synonyms as keywords. A *pronoun*, such as *it* or *them*, takes the place of the original word; a *synonym* is another word or phrase that refers to the same thing as the original keyword. In the following paragraph, notice how Nora Okja Keller's use of synonyms (highlighted) for the keyword *kim chee* helps connect her ideas:

> We went crazy for the smell of kim chee—a perfume that lured us to the kitchen table. When my mother hefted the jar of kim chee out of the refrigerator and opened the lid to extract the almost fluorescent strips of cabbage, she didn't have to call out to us, although she always did. "Girls, come join me," she would sing; even if we weren't hungry we couldn't resist. We all lingered over snacks that lasted two or three hours.

Add Transitions   Another way to connect your ideas is to use *transitions*. Transitions show your readers how one idea relates to the next, making your writing easy to follow.

Most commonly, transitions are words or phrases that connect sentences within a paragraph. Here is a list of the relationships expressed by some of the most common transitions:

to add information	additionally, and, also, as well, furthermore, in addition, too
to show differences	but, in contrast, on the other hand, whereas
to show similarities	as, in comparison, in the same way, similarly
to show time	after, at that time, before, by then, during, meanwhile, now, since, sometimes, soon, then, until then, when, while
to show cause and effect	as a result, because, consequently, hence, thereby, therefore, thus
to contradict or contrast	although, but, however, in contrast, nevertheless, or
to add emphasis	actually, furthermore, indeed, in fact, in truth, moreover, most important
to give an example	for example, for instance, specifically, such as
to show sequence	finally, first, last, next

When you use a transition, be sure it expresses the correct relationship between ideas. Notice how effectively Nora Okja Keller uses transitions (highlighted) to connect ideas about her daughter's reaction to her first taste of kim chee:

> When my daughter was fifteen months old, she took her first bite of kim chee. I had taken a small bite into my own mouth, sucking the hot juice from its leaves, giving it "mothertaste" as my own mother had done for me. Still, my daughter's eyes watered. "Hot, hot," she said to her grandmother and me. But the taste must have been in some way familiar; instead of spitting up and crying for water, she pushed my hand to the open jar for another bite.

In longer essays, writers sometimes use *transitional paragraphs* to make ideas flow smoothly. A transitional paragraph connects the main idea in one section of an essay to the main idea of a section that follows it. This type of paragraph is usually from one to three sentences in length and, unlike most paragraphs, does not need a topic sentence.

Nora Okja Keller, for instance, uses a transitional paragraph in "My Mother's Food":

So I erased my stink by eliminating kim chee. Though I liked the sharp taste of garlic and pepper biting my tongue, I stopped eating my mother's food.

In this transitional paragraph, the author connects her feelings about being Korean with how those feelings affected her relationship with her mother.

 Improve the flow of ideas

Use **bold** to highlight the keywords in each paragraph. Check that the keywords pertain directly to the topic of the paragraph. (The find-and-replace tool can help you locate these keywords.) Add, delete, or revise keywords as needed. Then use *italic* to highlight the transitions in each paragraph. Add transitions where the flow of thought seems disconnected or where there are no transitions in a long section. (Remember to remove the highlighting of keywords and transitions before printing your essay.)

▪ HOW TO Use Keywords and Transitions

Keywords and transitions provide a road map that can help readers connect your ideas.

- To help readers follow your main idea, repeat keywords, and use pronouns and synonyms.
- To move your readers to a new idea, use transitional words and phrases.
- To move your readers from one major part of your essay to another, write a brief transitional paragraph.

GROUP ACTIVITY 7 Add Keywords and Transitions

In the following paragraphs from *And the Beat Goes On: A Survey of Pop Music in America* by Charles Boeckman, keywords and transitions have been deleted. Work with your classmates to make the paragraphs more coherent by adding keywords and transitions.

In the 1950s, a revolution began in America. There was nothing quiet about it. It had happened before most people woke up to what was going on. It has been one of the most curious things in our history. The young people banded together, splintered off into a compartment totally their own. They formed their own culture, economy and morals. A generation of young people was totally immersed in its own music. It symbolized, reflected, dictated the very nature of its revolution.

The stage was set. Out of the wings stepped a young Memphis truck driver with a ducktail hair style and a sullen, brooding expression — Elvis Presley with his rock 'n' roll guitar. In 1954, a black group, the Chords, had played the rock 'n' roll style. In 1955, Bill Haley and a white group, the Comets, recorded the hit "Rock around the Clock." They lacked Elvis's charisma. They lacked his sex appeal. Elvis did more than sing. He went through a whole series of gyrations filled with sexual implications. It was just the thing for the mood of the hour. His voice trembled and cried out. His guitar thundered. His torso did bumps and grinds and shimmies. A whole generation of young people blew its cool.

> **GROUP ACTIVITY 8** Add Keywords and Transitions to Your Essay

Working in a group of three or four students, distribute copies of each group member's draft, and evaluate how well ideas are connected. On each draft, circle the keywords, synonyms, and pronouns, and underline the transitions. Your peers should do the same for your draft. Discuss with your classmates how each of you can improve the use of transitions. Then revise your draft, using your group's suggestions to add keywords and transitions.

A Student's Revised Draft

Throughout this chapter, you have been following Sandra Cordero as she gathered ideas and drafted an essay about El Grito de Dolores, a Mexican tradition she thought others would be interested in learning more about. Before you read Sandra's revised draft, review her discovery draft on page 135. Notice how Sandra revised by adding examples and process explanation to help her readers imagine themselves at the celebration. She inserted transitions to make her ideas flow more smoothly, and she added information about the cultural tradition that her readers may be unfamiliar with. (You may notice some errors in her revised draft; Sandra will correct these errors when she edits her essay.)

El Grito de Dolores

"¡Viva México! Viva México! Viva México!" hundreds of people cry out at the same time. Gathered in the town plaza at midnight on September 16, 1 they are celebrating one of Mexico's most important holidays, El Grito de Dolores. The holiday honors the men and women who fought for Mexico's independence. On this day, Mexicans feel united as they celebrate their history.

The keyword *holidays* is introduced.

What is El Grito de Dolores? This expression means "the cry from Dolores," and it refers to an important event that happened early in the morning on September 16, 1810. At this time, Mexico was ruled by the Spanish king. Because a priest named Miguel Hidalgo called together his parishioners at his church in Dolores, Guanajuato, Mexico. In a speech that was later called "El Grito de Dolores," Hidalgo urged his people to fight for freedom. This was the beginning of the Mexican revolution against Spain. Since then, the holiday is celebrated everywhere in Mexico. Even the smallest towns have their own celebrations.

2 Background information is added.

The transition *at this time* is added.

The transition *since then* is added.

The celebration begins in the main plaza exactly at midnight the governor of each city goes on top of the municipal building. "¡Viva Don Miguel Hidalgo!" he yells to honor the person who began the movement for independence. ("Viva" means "long live.") The people shout, "¡Viva México! Viva México! Viva México!" Fireworks light up the night sky. Everyone celebrates Mexico's independence.

3 The keyword *celebration* is repeated.

The keyword *celebrates* is repeated.

The next part of the celebration is a parade held on the morning of September 16. On the street called "16 de Septiembre." Every town in Mexico has a street with this name. The parade includes children, business leaders, government leaders, members of clubs, police officers, and firefighters. Green, red, and white streamers float through the air. People waving little Mexican flags to show their pride in their country.

4 The keyword *celebration* is repeated.

Examples are added.

Mexico is sometimes divided because of politics. The 16th of September is a day of unity. El Grito de Dolores brings the Mexican people together in a celebration of their ancestors who fought for freedom.

5

The keyword *celebration* is repeated.

GROUP ACTIVITY 9 Analyze Sandra's Revised Draft

Use the following questions to discuss with your classmates how Sandra improved her draft.

1. Is the purpose of Sandra's revised draft clear? What is her purpose?
2. What is Sandra's thesis statement? Could it be improved?
3. Does Sandra tell her readers enough to understand the cultural tradition? Explain.
4. How effective is Sandra's introduction? Conclusion?
5. Are the paragraphs in Sandra's revised draft better developed than those in her discovery draft? Do the ideas flow together better? Explain, and give examples.
6. How could Sandra's revised draft benefit from further revision?

135

GROUP ACTIVITY 10 Peer Review

Form a group with two or three other students, and exchange copies of your drafts. Read your draft aloud while your classmates follow along. Take notes on your classmates' responses to the following questions about your draft.

1. What did you like best about my essay?

2. How interesting is my introduction? Did you want to continue reading the essay? Why or why not?

3. What is my thesis statement? Do I need to make my essay's thesis clearer?

4. Where in the essay could I add examples and process explanation to help deliver my message?

5. How can I use keywords and transitions to make my ideas flow better?

6. Where can I combine sentences to improve the writing?

7. Where in the draft did my writing confuse you? How can I clarify my thoughts?

8. How effective is my conclusion? Do I end in a way that lets you know it's the end?

WRITING ACTIVITY 12 Revise Your Draft

Finish revising your discovery draft by using the work you completed for the activities in this chapter as well as your classmates' suggestions for revision. Make your introduction and conclusion as strong as they can be. In addition, develop your ideas with examples and process explanation, and use keywords and transitions to connect ideas. If you have time, look for irrelevant or unnecessary material that can be omitted, and experiment with moving sections of your draft to achieve the best presentation.

Step 4 Edit Your Sentences

So far in revising your paper, you have focused on improving your introduction and conclusion and on helping your ideas flow by using keywords and transitions. Now you're ready to make your sentences more readable and to edit your finished essay for correctness. Remember, errors distract your readers from what you have to say. In this section, you will learn how to combine sentences with conjunctive adverbs and how to identify and correct sentence fragments.

Combining Sentences Using Conjunctive Adverbs

For more on sentence combining, see Chapter 17.

By combining short, closely related sentences, you can clarify the relationship between ideas and make them easier to understand. Sentence combining also eliminates unnecessary words and keeps readers' interest by varying the types of sentences in an essay.

If your draft has short, complete sentences that are closely related, consider combining some of them with *conjunctive adverbs*—words and phrases that help readers understand how two ideas are related to each other. The following conjunctive adverbs are often used to combine sentences. Remember, a complete sentence has a subject and a verb.

Conjunctive Adverbs

also	meanwhile	specifically
besides	moreover	subsequently
consequently	nevertheless	then
finally	next	therefore
furthermore	otherwise	thus
however	similarly	

To combine sentences with a conjunctive adverb, place a semicolon before the adverb and a comma after it. Notice how the sentences in the following examples make more sense when they are combined this way.

DISCONNECTED My neighbor brings me flan whenever she makes a batch for her children. My pants are getting tight.

COMBINED My neighbor brings me flan whenever she makes a batch for her children; consequently, my pants are getting tight.

DISCONNECTED Hurricane Katrina devastated New Orleans. The first Mardi Gras after the disaster was a success.

COMBINED Hurricane Katrina devastated New Orleans; nevertheless, the first Mardi Gras after the disaster was a success.

The conjunctive adverb can also appear in the middle of the second sentence, as in this revised example from Sandra Cordero's draft:

DISCONNECTED Mexico is sometimes divided because of politics. The 16th of September is a day of unity.

COMBINED Mexico is sometimes divided because of politics; the 16th of September, however, is a day of unity.

As you can see from this example, commas are placed both before and after the conjunctive adverb when it is in the middle of the sentence.

> ## ■ **HOW TO** Combine Sentences Using Conjunctive Adverbs
>
> - Check that each of the two sentences you plan to combine has a subject and a verb and expresses a complete thought.
> - Select a conjunctive adverb that shows how the sentences are related.
> - Combine the two sentences with a semicolon, the conjunctive adverb, and a comma.
> - If a conjunctive adverb appears in the middle of the second sentence, put commas before and after it.

EDITING ACTIVITY 1 Combine Sentences Using Conjunctive Adverbs

Combine the following pairs of sentences with conjunctive adverbs. Be sure you punctuate the combined sentences correctly.

EXAMPLE In the United States, we play "soccer." The rest of the world calls the sport "football."

"soccer"; however, the

1. Sports competitions are some of the most important cultural traditions throughout the world. International sports competitions increase national pride.

2. In many countries, soccer is the most popular sport. The World Cup tournament draws huge crowds of fans.

3. Many fans watch the games with friends at neighborhood bars. Celebrations often spill into the streets.

4. Some fans drink too much. Others take the competition very seriously.

5. Violent behavior and riots have caused problems at past tournaments. Most countries vie for the honor of hosting the World Cup.

WRITING ACTIVITY 13 Combine Your Sentences

Examine your revised draft for short, closely related sentences. Where it makes sense to do so, combine them with conjunctive adverbs.

For additional practice with using conjunctive adverbs to combine sentences, go to **bedfordstmartins.com /choices** and click on **Exercise Central**.

Correcting Sentence Fragments

A *sentence fragment* is an incomplete sentence: it looks like a sentence, but something is missing.

For more on sentence fragments, see pp. 453–57.

A *complete sentence* contains a subject and a verb and expresses a complete thought. The subject tells who or what is doing the action. The verb explains the action or links the subject to the rest of the sentence.

The following are complete sentences. In each, the subject is italicized, and the verb is underlined.

Sentences

My *sister* <u>attended</u> graduation.

Jerry <u>enjoys</u> holidays.

I <u>left</u> class early.

He <u>is</u> my closest friend.

Unlike a sentence, a *sentence fragment* does not express a complete thought. A sentence fragment may be a *phrase*—a group of words that lacks a subject or a verb.

Phrases

Attended graduation. (missing subject)

Cinco de Mayo. Jerry's favorite holiday. (missing verb)

Left class early. (missing subject)

My closest friend. (missing subject and verb)

To correct a sentence fragment that is a phrase, add the missing subject, verb, or both.

Sentences

My *drill sergeant* attended graduation.

Cinco de Mayo *is* Jerry's favorite holiday.

Abrian left class early.

Liza is my closest friend.

A sentence fragment may also be a *dependent clause*—a group of words that contains a subject and a verb but doesn't express a complete thought.

Dependent Clauses

When my drill sergeant attended graduation.

Because it is Jerry's favorite holiday.

After Abrian left class early.

Since Liza is my closest friend.

There are three ways to correct a sentence fragment that is a dependent clause:

- Combine it with another sentence.
- Add information to make it a complete thought.
- Delete the conjunction or pronoun that starts it.

Sentences

I was proud when my drill sergeant attended graduation.

We went out for Cinco de Mayo because it is Jerry's favorite holiday.

Abrian left class early.

Liza is my closest friend.

▪ HOW TO Correct Sentence Fragments

To identify a sentence fragment, ask yourself the following questions about each sentence in your essay:

- Does the sentence have a subject?
- Does the sentence have a verb?
- Does the sentence express a complete thought?

If you answer No to any of these questions, you have a sentence fragment. To correct the sentence fragment

- Add the missing subject or verb or both.

  OR
- Combine the fragment with the sentence before or after it.

  OR
- Add information to make it a complete thought.

  OR
- Delete any words (such as conjunctions or pronouns) that make the clause dependent.

EDITING ACTIVITY 2 Correct Sentence Fragments

Correct each of the following sentence fragments by adding a missing subject or verb, by connecting a fragment to the sentence before or after it, or by adding information to form a complete thought.

1. My favorite custom is hiding Easter eggs. Because it's fun for everyone.

2. Since I left home. My mother calls me every other day.

3. Approaching my home.

4. Never a dull moment.

5. Forgot to celebrate my birthday!

For additional practice with eliminating sentence fragments, go to **bedfordstmartins.com /choices** and click on **Exercise Central**.

> **WRITING ACTIVITY 14** Edit Your Sentences

Read your essay word for word, looking for errors in sentence structure, grammar, spelling, and punctuation. Focus on finding and correcting sentence fragments. Also ask a friend or classmate to help you spot errors you might have overlooked. Then correct the errors you find, using a dictionary and the Handbook in Part Four of this book to help you.

A Student's Edited Essay

You probably noticed that Sandra's revised draft contained errors in sentence structure and punctuation. Sandra corrected these errors in her edited essay. Her corrections are noted in the margin.

Sandra Cordero
Professor Rowley
English 0311
6 Nov. 2011

El Grito de Dolores

"¡Viva México! Viva México! Viva México!" hundreds of people cry out at   1
the same time. Gathered in the town plaza at midnight on September 16,
they are celebrating one of Mexico's most important holidays, El Grito de
Dolores. The holiday honors the men and women who fought for Mexico's
independence. On this day, Mexicans feel united as they celebrate their
history.

What is El Grito de Dolores? This expression means "the cry from Dolores,"   2
and it refers to an important event that happened early in the morning on
September 16, 1810. At this time, Mexico was ruled by the Spanish king.
A priest named Miguel Hidalgo called together his parishioners at his church   *A sentence fragment is corrected.*
in Dolores, Guanajuato, Mexico. In a speech that was later called "El Grito de
Dolores," Hidalgo urged his people to fight for freedom. This was the
beginning of the Mexican revolution against Spain. Since then, the holiday is
celebrated everywhere in Mexico. Even the smallest towns have their own
celebrations.

The celebration begins in the main plaza. Exactly at midnight, the   3   *A run-on sentence is corrected.*
governor of each city goes on top of the municipal building. "¡Viva Don
Miguel Hidalgo!" he yells to honor the person who began the movement for
independence. ("Viva" means "long live.") The people shout, "¡Viva México!
Viva México! Viva México!" Fireworks light up the night sky as everyone   *Sentences are combined.*
celebrates Mexico's independence.

The next part of the celebration is a parade held on the morning of   4   *A sentence fragment is corrected.*
September 16 on the street called "16 de Septiembre." Every town in Mexico

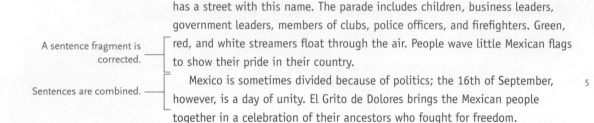

A sentence fragment is corrected.

Sentences are combined.

has a street with this name. The parade includes children, business leaders, government leaders, members of clubs, police officers, and firefighters. Green, red, and white streamers float through the air. People wave little Mexican flags to show their pride in their country.

Mexico is sometimes divided because of politics; the 16th of September, however, is a day of unity. El Grito de Dolores brings the Mexican people together in a celebration of their ancestors who fought for freedom.

5

(Step 5 Share Your Essay

In addition to sharing your final essay with your instructor and classmates, you can show it to other readers who might be interested in learning about a cultural symbol, tradition, or hero. You can easily get friends and family members to read it by attaching the document to your Facebook page. Another way to broaden your audience—and even to get people around the world interested in your subject—is to create a blog about your essay topic. A blog is different from a Web site because it is usually organized by date and category, with the most recent entry listed first. Blogs also allow for comments and feedback by readers. While you can "self host" a blog by creating your own domain name and paying for a Web host (ipage.com is the most common service), you can also create a blog for free on a site such as blogger.com or wordpress.com. These free sites also connect people to communities of other bloggers who are interested in similar subjects. The more people who read your essay, the more likely it is that it will help someone become more knowledgeable, considerate, or accepting of someone else's culture—a change in attitude that you will have made happen.

CHAPTER CHECKLIST

❑ I read essays about culture to explore and learn about this chapter's theme.

❑ I gathered ideas on a cultural symbol, tradition, or hero by clustering, asking questions, and freewriting.

❑ I developed the ideas in my paragraphs with examples and process explanation.

❑ I strengthened my introduction by hooking readers, narrowing my focus, and providing a thesis statement.

❑ I wrote a strong conclusion that reinforces my thesis and broadens the topic.

❑ I made my ideas easier to understand by connecting them with keywords and transitions.

❑ I combined closely related sentences by using conjunctive adverbs.

❑ I eliminated sentence fragments.

❑ I shared my finished essay with my instructor and classmates.

REFLECTING ON YOUR WRITING

To help you continue to improve as a writer, answer the following questions:

1. Did you enjoy writing about an aspect of your culture? Why or why not?

2. Which topic did you choose—a cultural symbol, tradition, or hero? Why?

3. What types of changes did you make to your essay when you revised?

4. If you had more time, what further revisions would you make to improve your essay? Why?

Using your answers to these questions, complete a Writing Process Report for this chapter (you can download a report form at **bedfordstmartins.com /choices**). Once you complete this report, freewrite about what you learned in this chapter.

"For me, nothing would be more satisfying than helping a child get well."
— KATHY CHU, "HELPING CHILDREN HEAL"

Analyzing
Occupations, Workplace Communication, and Job-Related Problems

When you analyze a topic, you define it, research it, and investigate how the parts come together to make up a whole. The goal of analysis is to study your topic or subject, revealing new information that will give you a deeper understanding of that subject. You can then share what you have learned with your readers, so they will be better informed about your subject. In this chapter, you will use this type of informative writing to investigate the workplace.

One of the first questions most of us ask when we meet someone new is, "What do you do?" This question shows the importance that we place on work. Most of us want our occupations to be satisfying and rewarding. After all, at some point in our lives, we are likely to spend at least forty hours a week in the workplace. Finding the right occupation is not an easy task, however. Most of us will hold many different jobs and change career fields a few times during our lives. Look at the résumés of just a few of America's presidents, for instance: Harry S Truman owned a clothing store, Jimmy Carter farmed peanuts, George W. Bush drilled for oil, and Barack Obama worked to improve living conditions in poor Chicago neighborhoods. You might already have had several

In this chapter, you will write about an occupation that interests you, a style of workplace communication, or a job-related problem. As you follow the steps of the writing process, you will

- Explore the chapter topic by reading essays about a work issue.
- Gather ideas by freewriting, brainstorming, and consulting with others.
- Develop your ideas using **classification** and **definition**.
- Practice using research material in your writing.
- Combine sentences with subordinating conjunctions.
- Learn how to correct pronoun reference and agreement.
- Submit your essay to a school, volunteer, or work-related newsletter.

jobs yourself, and if you're like most college students, you're probably preparing for a better future.

When you consider a particular occupation, you'll need to determine how well the job matches your interests and abilities. To succeed, you'll also need to understand the culture of a profession—how people think, dress, behave, and communicate. Finally, it helps to learn how people in an occupation go about analyzing the problems that they encounter in the workplace.

In this chapter, you'll have the chance to write about a job that interests you, to examine the communication styles in a given occupation, or to look for ways to analyze a problem you may have encountered in the workplace. You will also follow a student, Kathy Chu, as she writes about her chosen profession and what it takes to be a pediatrician. Because your investigations will uncover information that will be helpful to your peers, you will share what you learn with other students who have similar career interests. ■

GROUP ACTIVITY 1 Think about Workplaces

Examine the photograph on the chapter-opening page. What is this pediatrician doing? Would this type of work and workplace appeal to you? Why or why not? With your classmates, brainstorm a list of occupations that might interest you.

Getting Started   Reading Essays That Analyze a Work Issue

A good starting point for learning more about any occupation is to read about it. You can find information about a particular field in reference books and on Web sites, for example, as well as in personal essays and memoirs that describe people's experiences in the workplace.

Successful businesspeople and professionals often publish books and magazine articles filled with advice for overcoming problems and achieving their career goals. To get a feel for this kind of writing, read the following short essays that describe an occupation, examine communication in the workplace, or analyze problems on the job. As you read, pay attention to how the writers use classification and definition to explain their ideas. Notice, too, how the writers support their ideas with information from outside sources and expand on their topic through analyzing the ideas they present. (For additional essays about work and the workplace, see p. 564.)

An Occupation

HEATHER ROBINSON

I Am Not a Babysitter

Being a schoolteacher can be a very rewarding occupation, but teachers often struggle to earn respect. Before committing yourself to any occupation, find out what other people, both in and out of the profession, say about it. In the following essay, "I Am Not a Babysitter," Heather Robinson, a seventh grade science teacher, describes what people who are not in the profession sometimes think, compared to what it's really like to be a teacher. This article is from Newsweek .com, a Web site that publishes a variety of news stories, including personal essays from its readers.

As a teacher, I face many stereotypes about my job. But I wouldn't trade my career for any other. It is said that teaching is the profession that creates all other professions. That's a beautiful compliment for a job that often does not receive the respect one would predict given all of the platitudes bestowed upon teachers. "God bless you!" "What a noble profession" and "I couldn't do it, but thank goodness there are people like you out there" are a few that I've received.

Like many of my colleagues, I didn't attend college intending to become a teacher. I worked in a related profession in youth services, helping high-school dropouts find social and vocational outlets other than the streets and dead-end jobs. Though the work was often rewarding, I realized I could be more influential working with young people before they became a statistic. Thus began my career in education.

Some family and friends seemed to think the change was only temporary. Several asked, "How long do you think you'll teach?" Some inquired whether I had administrative aspirations. When one year became two, then three, etc., some friends actually questioned my sanity. Surely I wouldn't remain a lowly classroom teacher, they would insinuate, as if teaching is a stop-gap job. Unfortunately, too many people view teaching as a fallback, insurance, something stable to get them from their last corporate layoff to the next higher-paying job.

If those types of comments aren't bewildering enough, I still hear chiding responses about my "cream-puff" schedule. This always reminds me of a remark a salty veteran teacher once made to me: "If a teacher tells you she is done with her work any time before 7 p.m., she is lying or she isn't doing her job." What is sad about that statement is that it is not only true, it's sometimes an understatement. Eight or nine o'clock can be more like it, after a day that began at five or six a.m.

Summers off? Think again. Teachers who truly aspire to make their mark and contribute only their very best to our nation's future enroll in summer training courses and continue their education in a constant pursuit to perfect their craft. We are a profession of lifelong learners. In a continually changing world, it's not only advised but imperative that we never cease to improve and devour each new piece of research that reveals to us some small piece of the education puzzle.

1 The opening thesis statement immediately lets readers know what the essay is about.

A general definition of teaching is provided.

2 Background information explains why Robinson became a teacher.

3 Robinson begins to classify stereotypes about teaching. The first one: teaching is a stop-gap job. For each stereotype, she provides her own view of teaching.

4 The second stereotype: teaching is a "cream-puff" job. Quoting a veteran teacher gives credibility to her statement about teaching loads.

5 The third stereotype: teachers have summers off.

The fourth stereotype: teaching is a boring job.

"Don't you get bored doing the same thing each day?" is another question I   6
get a lot. It's a teacher's windfall if any two given class periods are identical and flow according to the lesson plan, let alone an entire day or more. What many people don't understand is that we teachers are working with wiggling, chatting children with varied needs. They are not robots who perform exactly as we direct without exception. Teachers are not on autopilot — we make thousands of decisions each day while working hard to produce a quality product that provides each student with what she needs and deserves. Teaching isn't simply perching at a lectern and pontificating to hungry minds; it's being an educator, a mentor, a parent, a nurse, a social worker, a friend, a diplomat and an expert on the curriculum. In short, we are professionals.

In these two sentences, Robinson provides a more comprehensive definition of teaching.

After all of the long hours, grueling days, mountains of paperwork, emotional   7
exhaustion and misperceptions about the profession that I dearly love and would trade for no other, we continue to pour ourselves into the work because it's too important not to. How can we not give all of ourselves, our intellect and our talents to this work? After all, it is our current students whom we will be voting for in a future presidential election, who will care for us when we're ill and who will educate our grandchildren.

Robinson explains why, in spite of all of the stereotypes, she remains a teacher.

The conclusion includes a call for action, asking readers to "respect" teachers.

Notice I've said nothing about increasing teachers' pay, improving benefits or   8
strong-arming uninvolved parents. Though those are all valid topics, they are not any more important than the need to increase an emergency medical technician's near minimum-wage compensation. What can easily be increased in education is the value placed upon the service that teachers provide to society. So the next time it's tempting to quiz a teacher about why she's not doing something more lucrative or supposedly more challenging with her talents, rib her about what is perceived to be a workday designed for the golf course or — worst of all — liken her job to a teenage babysitter's, offer up something utterly free: respect. A little of it goes a long way.

READING ACTIVITY 1 Build Your Vocabulary

Determine the meanings of the following words from the context of the essay. Then check their meanings by looking up the words in a dictionary: platitudes (1), aspirations (3), insinuate (3), salty (4), imperative (5), pontificating (6), lucrative (8).

GROUP ACTIVITY 2 Discuss the Reading

Discuss the following questions about "I Am Not a Babysitter" with your classmates.

1. In your own words, list the skills that a teacher needs to be successful in the classroom.
2. This essay classifies the different stereotypes that people have about teachers. How does this organizational pattern help readers understand what others think about teaching? Do you agree with any of these stereotypes? Why or why not?

3. In paragraphs 6 and 7, Robinson defines what teachers actually do and why they do it. Does this definition of teaching change your mind about the profession? Why or why not?

4. Based on this essay, do you have the characteristics and skills to be a teacher? Explain your answer.

> **WRITING ACTIVITY 1 Share Your Ideas**

Write a paragraph or two about an occupation that interests you. First, define the occupation. Then, describe some of the stereotypes that people have about this profession. Share what you have written with your classmates.

Workplace Communication

PERRI KLASS
She's Your Basic L.O.L. in N.A.D.

Often a doctor's work is hard for people to understand because it involves technical skills and terms. Because she's both a pediatrician and a writer, Perri Klass has helped her readers better understand her profession. In "She's Your Basic L.O.L. in N.A.D.," Klass explains her introduction to the language of medicine. Klass focuses on what the language means and also on why doctors use it.

"Mrs. Tolstoy is your basic L.O.L. in N.A.D., admitted for a soft rule-out M.I.," the intern announces. I scribble that on my patient list. In other words Mrs. Tolstoy is a Little Old Lady in No Apparent Distress who is in the hospital to make sure she hasn't had a heart attack (rule out a myocardial infarction). And we think it's unlikely that she has had a heart attack (a *soft* rule-out).   1

If I learned nothing else during my first three months of working in the hospital as a medical student, I learned endless jargon and abbreviations. I started out in a state of primeval innocence, in which I didn't even know that "s̄ C.P., S.O.B., N/V" meant "without chest pain, shortness of breath, or nausea and vomiting." By the end I took the abbreviations so for granted that I would complain to my mother the English professor, "And can you believe I had to put down *three* NG tubes last night?"   2

"You'll have to tell me what an NG tube is if you want me to sympathize properly," my mother said. NG, nasogastric — isn't it obvious?   3

I picked up not only the specific expressions but also the patterns of speech and the grammatical conventions; for example, you never say that a patient's blood pressure fell or that his cardiac enzymes rose. Instead, the patient is always the subject of the verb: "He dropped his pressure." "He bumped his enzymes." This sort of construction probably reflects that profound irritation of the intern when the nurses come in the middle of the night to say that Mr. Dickinson has disturbingly low blood pressure. "Oh, he's gonna hurt me bad tonight," the intern may say, inevitably angry at Mr. Dickinson for dropping his pressure and creating a problem.   4

When chemotherapy fails to cure Mrs. Bacon's cancer, what we say is, "Mrs. 5
Bacon failed chemotherapy."

"Well, we've already had one hit today, and we're up next, but at least we've got 6
mostly stable players on our team." This means that our team (group of doctors and
medical students) has already gotten one new admission today, and it is our turn
again, so we'll get whoever is next admitted in emergency, but at least most of the
patients we already have are fairly stable — that is, unlikely to drop their pressures
or in any other way get suddenly sicker and hurt us bad. Baseball metaphor is perva-
sive: a no-hitter is a night without any new admissions. A player is always a patient —
a nitrate player is a patient on nitrates, a unit player is a patient in the intensive-care
unit and so on, until you reach the terminal player.

It is interesting to consider what it means to be winning, or doing well, in this 7
perennial baseball game. When the intern hangs up the phone and announces, "I got
a hit," that is not cause for congratulations. The team is not scoring points; rather, it
is getting hit, being bombarded with new patients. The object of the game from the
point of view of the doctors, considering the players for whom they are already responsible, is to get as few new hits as possible.

These special languages contribute to a sense of closeness and professional 8
spirit among people who are under a great deal of stress. As a medical student, it
was exciting for me to discover that I'd finally cracked the code, that I could understand what doctors said and wrote and could use the same formulations myself.
Some people seem to become enamored of the jargon for its own sake, perhaps
because they are so deeply thrilled with the idea of medicine, with the idea of themselves as doctors.

I knew a medical student who was referred to by the interns on the team as Mr. 9
Eponym because he was so infatuated with eponymous terminology, the more ob-
scure the better. He never said "capillary pulsation" if he could say "Quincke's
pulses." He would lovingly tell over the multinamed syndromes — Wolff-Parkinson-
White, Lown-Ganong-Levine, Henoch-Schonlein — until the temptation to suggest
Schleswig-Holstein or Stevenson-Kefauver or Baskin-Robbins became irresistible to
his less reverent colleagues.

And there is the jargon that you don't ever want to hear yourself using. You 10
know that your training is changing you, but there are certain changes you think
would be going a little too far.

The resident was describing a man with devastating terminal pancreatic cancer. 11
"Basically he's C.T.D.," the resident concluded. I reminded myself that I had resolved
not to be shy about asking when I didn't understand things. "C.T.D.?" I asked
timidly.

The resident smirked at me. "Circling the Drain." 12

The images are vivid and terrible. "What happened to Mrs. Melville?" 13

"Oh, she boxed last night." To box is to die, of course. 14

Then there are the more pompous locutions that can make the beginning medi- 15
cal student nervous about the effects of medical training. A friend of mine was told
by his resident, "A pregnant woman with sickle-cell represents a failure of genetic
counseling."

Mr. Eponym, who tried hard to talk like the doctors, once explained to me, "An 16 infant is basically a brainstem preparation." A brainstem preparation, as used in neurological research, is an animal whose higher brain functions have been destroyed so that only the most primitive reflexes remain, like the sucking reflex, the startle reflex, and the rooting reflex.

The more extreme forms aside, one most important function of medical jargon 17 is to help doctors maintain some distance from their patients. By reformulating a patient's pain and problems into a language that the patient doesn't even speak, I suppose we are in some sense taking those pains and problems under our jurisdiction and also reducing their emotional impact. This linguistic separation between doctors and patients allows conversations to go on at the bedside that are unintelligible to the patient. "Naturally, we're worried about adeno-C.A.," the intern can say to the medical student, and lung cancer need never be mentioned.

I learned a new language this past summer. At times it thrills me to hear myself 18 using it. It enables me to understand my colleagues, to communicate effectively in the hospital. Yet I am uncomfortably aware that I will never again notice the peculiarities and even atrocities of medical language as keenly as I did this summer. There may be specific expressions I manage to avoid, but even as I remark them, promising myself I will never use them, I find that this language is becoming my professional speech. It no longer sounds strange in my ears — or coming from my mouth. And I am afraid that as with any new language, to use it properly you must absorb not only the vocabulary but also the structure, the logic, the attitudes. At first you may notice these new alien assumptions every time you put together a sentence, but with time and increased fluency you stop being aware of them at all. And as you lose that awareness, for better or for worse, you move closer and closer to being a doctor instead of just talking like one.

READING ACTIVITY 2 Build Your Vocabulary

Determine the meanings of the following words from the context of Perri Klass's essay. Then check their meanings by looking up the words in a dictionary: jargon (2), primeval (2), inevitably (4), metaphor (6), perennial (7), enamored (8), eponymous (9), locutions (15), jurisdiction (17), atrocities (18).

GROUP ACTIVITY 3 Discuss the Reading

Discuss the following questions about "She's Your Basic L.O.L. in N.A.D." with your classmates.

1. According to Klass, what are some examples of the jargon that health professionals use?

2. Why do medical practitioners use jargon in the workplace? For example, why do the interns say "He dropped his [blood] pressure" instead of "His [blood] pressure dropped"?

3. Explain the significance of the last sentence of the essay: "And as you lose that awareness, for better or for worse, you move closer and closer to being a doctor instead of just talking like one."

4. Have you ever heard medical professionals use terminology you couldn't understand? If so, describe what this experience was like.

> **WRITING ACTIVITY 2 Share Your Ideas**

Write a paragraph or two on jargon that you use or have used on the job, at school, or in your community. How has using this jargon helped you adapt to the culture of your workplace or organization? Share a few of these words with your classmates.

A Job-Related Problem

DONALD TRUMP
You're Hired!

How do you get ahead in your job? In "You're Hired!" Donald Trump—real estate tycoon, author, and reality TV star—suggests ways to analyze and solve workplace problems and get ahead. Trump has made a fortune in business, but most people know him more for the blunt, confident style he's displayed on television—a style he recommends to others.

1   I think it's funny that the phrase so closely associated with me these days is my line from *The Apprentice — You're fired*. The truth is, although I've had to fire employees from time to time, I much prefer keeping loyal and hard-working people around. At The Trump Organization, which has some 20,000 members at this point, Helen Rakotz has worked for me since I first moved to Manhattan, and she still puts in long hours. She's in her 80s. There's also a wonderful woman in her 90s, Amy Luerssen, who worked for my father, Fred, and still reports to work every day. Unless your boss is a total sadist, he or she doesn't want to fire you or cause hardship to your family. If you think you're in danger of losing your job, take control of the situation and ask for a meeting. Tell your boss you want to make sure you're communicating and doing your job to everyone's satisfaction.

2   Of course, if your boss *is* a sadist — or just a lousy communicator — you've got a problem. In that case, fire your boss and get a better job. There's no sense trying to cope with a bad situation that will never improve.

3   I never try to dissuade people from quitting. If they don't want to be here, I don't want them here either. People see how it works at The Trump Organization, and if it doesn't suit them, they move on. An experienced receptionist once worked here for a grand total of six hours. She realized right away that the pace just wasn't right for her, and she told us so and left. I appreciated her quick thinking and her ability to make a decision. She'll have a successful career somewhere else.

4   **Fine-Tune Your Timing.** When it comes to your career, certain moves shouldn't be made without careful consideration of the old and very apt saying "Timing is everything."

Jason Greenblatt, a brilliant young lawyer who works for me, is terrific at every-   5
thing he does, but one time, I swear, he must have been wearing a blindfold—and
earplugs. I was having an especially tough, vicious, terrible day that seemed never-
ending to me and everyone around me. It was a grand-slam rotten day. Late in the
afternoon, I heard a polite knock on my door. I yelled out, *"What?"* Nonchalantly
Jason entered my office and proceeded to ask me for a raise.

I could not believe a lawyer as smart as Jason could make such a dumb move. I use   6
his real name because Jason knows how much I like and respect him, despite this incred-
ible faux pas. But I have to tell you, I was ready to kill him. Was he joking? It's amazing,
but he wasn't. Did he get a raise? Not that day. He almost got fired for his stupidity. I
told him that although he might be brilliant, his timing on certain things needed work—
and that maybe he ought to pay more attention to what was going on around him.

Jason is still with me, and he gets lots of raises because he's great at what he   7
does. But now he waits for sunny days and blue skies before approaching me. I told
you he was smart.

The best way to ask for a raise is to wait for the right time. It indicates that you   8
have a certain amount of discernment and appreciation for what your boss might be
going through. If you knew your company was scheduled to give a major client presentation at 3 p.m., would you approach your boss at 2:45 to ask for a raise? Money,
like comedy, is all about timing.

Toot Your Own Horn. I was originally going to call Trump Tower by another name—   9
Tiffany Tower, for the famous jewelry store next door. I asked a friend, "Do you think
it should be Trump Tower or Tiffany Tower?" He told me, "When you change your
name to Tiffany, call it Tiffany Tower."

We've all seen the power of a brand name, especially quality brand names. Coco   10
Chanel became world famous some 80 years ago by naming her perfume Chanel No.
5, and it's still going strong in a competitive market. Her fragrance, as well as her
name, has become timeless. She proved the right ingredients can create a legend.

I've worked hard for decades to accomplish the same thing in my business. My   11
buildings are among the finest in the world, and that's not just bragging. Last year,
an article by *Chicago Tribune* columnist Mary Umberger attributed the sales for
Trump International Hotel and Tower in Chicago to "the Trump factor." She reported:
"The sales velocity surprises even experienced real-estate players, who told me at
the sales inaugural that they doubted Trump would gain enough momentum, because Chicago's luxury market was—and is—in a lull." And in an article by Herbert
Muschamp, architecture critic for the *New York Times*, the Trump World Tower was
described as "a handsome hunk of a glass tower." I was honored.

If you're devoting your life to creating something, and you believe in what you   12
do, and what you do is excellent, then you'd better damn well tell people you think
so. Subtlety and modesty are appropriate for nuns and therapists, but if you're in
business, you'd better learn to speak up and announce your contributions to the
world. Nobody else will.

Go with Your Gut. To be a success at anything, you have to trust yourself. You may   13
have superb academic credentials, but without instincts you'll have a hard time

reaching—and staying at—the top. This is one of those gray areas that remain an enigma even to those who have finely honed business instincts. There are inexplicable signs that can guide you to or away from certain deals and certain people.

For example, within a few seconds of meeting Mark Burnett, the creator of *The* 14 *Apprentice,* I knew he was 100 percent solid, both as a person and a professional, which is a remarkable accomplishment in the entertainment industry. On the other hand, I've met people I have an aversion to, and while I try not to be judgmental, I have reason by now to trust my instincts.

Keep Critics in Perspective. In any job, you'll be criticized at some point. While no- 15 body wants criticism, there is a smart way to assess it. First, consider the source. Should this person's opinion matter to you? If it does, take a few minutes to consider if you can learn anything helpful from the criticism. Others can often see things that you've overlooked. Use their observations to your advantage if you can.

Second, remember that critics serve their purpose. *American Idol* judge Simon 16 Cowell can be critical of the performers on the program, but he's fair and he's honest, and I don't think the show would work without him.

Third, understand everyone has an opinion. In most cases, it's not worth the 17 paper it's written on. But if it is, and if it's in a paper people are buying and reading, then realize that if people didn't find you interesting enough, they wouldn't be taking the time to criticize you in the first place.

Practice Straight Talk. If you equivocate, it's an indication that you're unsure of 18 yourself and what you're doing. It's also what politicians do all the time, and I find it inappropriate, insulting and condescending.

I try not to do it. Fortunately, I don't have to try too hard at this one, because 19 I've been known to be on the blunt (and fast) side, which is good.

When I need to know something about my Atlantic City casinos and hotels, 20 I can call Mark Brown, my CEO, and get a fast, informed answer. If I call Laura Cordovano at Trump Park Avenue and ask about sales, she'll give it to me exactly as it is. Allen Weisselberg, my CEO, will tell me what I need in 20 words or less. My senior counsel and *Apprentice* advisor, George Ross, can do it in 10 words or less.

Once I asked an executive with my organization to give me a synopsis of a new 21 development we were considering. He'd been to the city in question, spent time there, done careful investigation. He described the pros and cons of the site in great detail. He must've talked for ten minutes straight. There seemed to be as many reasons to drop the project as there were reasons to jump in and get going.

I asked more questions, and we ended up exactly where we were before. This 22 guy had a good track record, so finally I asked him to tell me what he really thought— in ten words or less. "It stinks," he said. He had eight words left, but he didn't need them.

All Ideas Are Welcome. If you're going to be bold enough to present an idea, make 23 it as clear as possible and don't take it casually. Think of it as a presentation that could cost your company money if you were to lose the client. Your boss's time is important; you won't win points by wasting it.

Also, remember this: The boss has the big picture; you don't. If your idea doesn't   24
meet with hurrahs, it could be that a similar idea is already in development, or your
idea is not in step with plans that have already been made. This shouldn't discourage
you, because your initiative will always be noticed.

I like people who don't give up. But being merely a pest is detrimental to every-   25
one. Know when to ease up. Keep your eyes open for another idea and a more appropriate opportunity.

There was one former employee I liked a lot, but he reminded me of a jumping   26
bean. He couldn't keep still for more than three seconds. Riding in the car with him
became an ordeal, because being in an enclosed space seemed to warm him up even
more. I finally learned to avoid him, and that's too bad, because he was a great guy.
But enough is enough. Going on and on will cause people to tune you out — or wish
that you would move to another state. Last I heard, the jumping bean was living in
Montana. I only hope they have enough space there to contain him, and every time
I hear about UFO sightings in Montana, I have to laugh. I know just who it is.

One more thing: No one ignores a terrific idea. If your boss says no to an idea   27
of yours, it might not be the *right* terrific idea for the company you're with. Maybe
you're meant to go off on your own as an entrepreneur. Let that be an indication to
you. It could be the beginning of your career, rather than the end of it.

READING ACTIVITY 3 Build Your Vocabulary

Determine the meanings of the following words from the context of Donald Trump's
essay. Then check their meanings by looking up the words in a dictionary: sadist (1), dissuade (3), apt (4), nonchalantly (5), faux pas (6), discernment (8), velocity (11), inaugural
(11), enigma (13), aversion (14), equivocate (18), synopsis (21), detrimental (25).

GROUP ACTIVITY 4 Discuss the Reading

Discuss the following questions about "You're Hired!" with your classmates.

1. List at least four job-related problems that Trump identifies, and summarize his
   solutions in your own words.

2. Reread paragraphs 4 to 8. How does Trump use a story from his past to define
   what good timing is?

3. In paragraph 11, the author includes quotations from two newspaper articles. How
   do these quotations support his advice for succeeding in the corporate world?

4. What have you learned about doing well at work that you could share with
   readers?

WRITING ACTIVITY 3 Share Your Ideas

Write a paragraph or two on a job-related problem you have identified at your place of
employment or at the college you attend. What would you propose to solve this problem? Share your writing with your classmates.

Writing Your Essay   A Step-by-Step Guide

Now that you've read some essays analyzing an occupation, workplace communication, or a job-related problem, it's time to write your own essay. First, read the writing assignment that follows. Then, use the step-by-step advice that follows to discover ideas, develop them as you draft, and polish your writing into a finished essay that readers will find both interesting and informative:

Step 1   Explore Your Choices 168
Step 2   Write Your Discovery Draft 173
Step 3   Revise Your Draft 175
Step 4   Edit Your Sentences 186
Step 5   Share Your Essay 192

Writing Assignment

Whether you are a full- or part-time student, have worked in just one or many jobs, or have no work experience, you will probably be thinking about a job or working toward a specific career goal while in college. So it's a good idea to think about potential careers and investigate your options. For this assignment, you'll help yourself and other students plan for the future by writing about a career field that interests you or with which you have experience. You (or your instructor) may decide to approach this assignment in one of several ways:

■ Examine an occupation that interests you.

OR

■ Analyze the ways people communicate in a place where you work now or have worked in the past, or analyze the communication styles at an organization to which you belong.

OR

■ Analyze a job-related problem.

◖Step 1 Explore Your Choices

Are you thinking about what kind of occupation you would like to have? You may have a specific career in mind already, or maybe you haven't decided yet. Perhaps learning more about how people communicate at their jobs will help you think about possible careers. Analyzing a workplace problem might also give you valuable information about a particular type of work. This chapter's writing assignment will help you think about the workplace, possibilities for careers, and ways to achieve your goals. Before you choose an occupation, communication issue, or job-related problem to write about, you will think about who your readers are and what you want them to learn. Then you will experiment with three techniques for gathering ideas as you apply one to each of the assignment's topic choices. Gathering ideas before you start to write will give you a wealth of material from which to work.

Analyzing Your Audience and Purpose

Before you begin gathering ideas about your topic, think about who will read your essay and what they might expect.

You are writing an essay that investigates the workplace for people who are interested in the same kind of work that appeals to you. Your readers, then, might be students in your major, members of a club or volunteer group that you belong to, or coworkers at your current place of employment. Before you begin writing for this audience, give some thought to their experiences and hopes, and ask yourself what will interest them. What can you tell them that they don't already know? How will they benefit from reading your essay?

Consider, also, what you want to accomplish by writing about the workplace. This chapter assignment asks you to *inform* your readers about an occupation, a style of workplace communication, or a job-related problem. You can include some expressive writing, but you don't need to persuade your readers to take action on what you say. Your purpose is primarily informative. Knowing your purpose before you begin writing will make it easier for you to write an essay that both you and your readers will value.

WRITING ACTIVITY 4 Analyze Your Audience and Purpose

Your responses to the following questions will help you decide how to approach this chapter's writing assignment. Be sure to come back to these questions after you have chosen a topic.

1. This assignment calls for primarily informative writing, but you could also include some expressive writing. What personal experience related to this topic could you share?

2. Who will read your essay? Will you share it with students in your major, members of a club or volunteer group, coworkers, or someone else?

3. What types of jobs have these readers had in the past?

4. What types of jobs do your readers want to have?

5. How do your job interests resemble or differ from those of your readers?

6. How can you interest your readers in an essay that deals with the workplace?

For more on audience and purpose, see pp. 7–11.

Gathering Ideas

Several techniques can help you find good ideas to write about, as you learned in Chapter 1. For this chapter's assignment, you will practice using three of these methods—freewriting, brainstorming, and consulting with others—as you explore your thoughts about workplace topics.

For more on gathering ideas, see pp. 11–16.

Feel free, however, to gather additional ideas using any other methods that work for you. Your goal at this stage is to collect as many ideas and details as you can to help you determine what you want to write about.

Freewriting about an Occupation

Many of us decide to pursue a particular occupation without thinking it through. For instance, being an actor appears to be glamorous until you realize that most actors are unemployed in their chosen profession. Or you might daydream of flying until you learn that pilots are away from their families for days at a time. Some people, such as the author of "I Am Not a Babysitter" (p. 159), change professions to find one better suited to their personalities. When thinking about a particular career, you need to consider whether the job matches your interests, needs, and personality.

One useful way to investigate an occupation that appeals to you is to freewrite about it. To freewrite, you write for a set period of time without worrying about what you have to say or how you say it. You simply put all of your thoughts down as they come to you. If your mind wanders, let it. The point of freewriting is to discover ideas you didn't know you had. You could continue to write about the occupation you wrote about after reading "I Am Not a Babysitter," or you could freewrite about a different occupation that also interests you.

If you either don't know where to start or get stuck, the following questions can help stimulate your thoughts:

- When did you first become interested in pursuing this occupation?
- If you're already in this occupation, in what way do you want to change (such as to obtain a higher position or go into another specialty)?
- List three things that interest you about this occupation.
- What aspects of your personality do you think will make you successful in this occupation?
- What don't you like about this occupation?
- List at least two things you want to learn about this occupation.

One student, Kathy Chu, freewrote about her desire to become a pediatrician.

> I've wanted to become a pediatrician ever since I was a little girl. The doctor seemed so nice and knew so much. Then when my brother had to spend

a week in the hospital, I got to see other pediatricians helping the sick children. My family is so grateful to the pediatricians who helped my brother get better. I know that being a pediatrician is hard. First you have to go through years of school. I guess I could handle that. But I'm not sure I could handle dealing with sick children all the time. It takes patience and dedication.

WRITING ACTIVITY 5 Freewrite about an Occupation

Gather ideas about an occupation you're interested in pursuing by freewriting about it for ten minutes. Follow your ideas without pausing, and do not stop, go back, or try to correct your writing. Just write.

Brainstorming about Workplace Communication

Put aside your writing about an occupation for a while so that you can gather ideas about another aspect of work.

Coworkers in every workplace develop their own way of communicating with one another, often by using specialized language known only to their peers. For instance, police officers use special terminology when referring to crimes, telemarketers label incoming and outgoing calls according to numerical codes, and attorneys write contracts that are difficult for non-specialists to understand. One of the first things a person entering a profession needs to learn is its jargon.

Whether you work at a job or belong to a student or community organization, you probably speak more jargon than you realize. To gather ideas for an essay that explains this language to others, try brainstorming a list of terms used in your field. You might continue to add to the list of words you used when writing about workplace jargon after reading "She's Your Basic L.O.L. in N.A.D." (p. 161). Write your general topic at the top of a page, and then list all of the words and phrases that come into your head. Jot down a brief definition for each term. Don't worry about whether your examples are good ones or not; just write down everything you think of.

One student, Javier, brainstormed about the jargon used by the teachers in the elementary school where he was a teacher's aide:

> TAAS test—the standardized test that the students have to take every year
> ADD—attention deficit disorder
> Hyper—a child with ADD
> SW—the "student of the week" award, also known as the "sweetheart" award
> Sub—substitute teacher
> Meeting with the Pal—a meeting with the principal
> Sight words—common words, like "dog" or "the," that students should know
> Portfolio—a collection of student work

In-service training — educational sessions to update experienced teachers

Eager Beaver — a new teacher who thinks he or she knows everything

> **WRITING ACTIVITY 6** Brainstorm about Communication at Work

Pick a job you're familiar with. It can be a job you've had or a job held by a friend or family member. Brainstorm about the jargon that you've encountered by listing words and their definitions. Alternatively, you may list examples of another aspect of communication that interests you, such as levels of formality, uses of humor, spoken versus written communication, or body language.

Consulting Others about a Job-Related Problem

Put aside the writing you've done on communication for a while so that you can consider one last aspect of the workplace.

No matter how much you like your job, you're always going to encounter difficulties. Perhaps your boss is hard to talk to, or one of your coworkers likes to gossip too much. Your hours might be long, or you might object to a recent change in policy. To be successful, you need to be able to find solutions to problems such as these.

An excellent way to analyze problems is to ask other people what they think about your situation and what solutions they suggest. You might ask people at the workplace or college you described after reading Donald Trump's "You're Hired!" (p. 164). You might also consult with an expert or two (as Trump describes in his essay), ask those who have had similar experiences, or simply choose to share your problem out loud and get reactions from people who can offer you a fresh perspective.

Student writer Alfredo was interested in writing about a problem he had been having at his job in a restaurant. He decided to describe the issue out loud to his classmates and ask for their suggestions. Here is what he told them:

> "Whenever I'm on the night shift at the restaurant where I work, I see other workers steal food. We're allowed to eat one meal after a shift, but what these people are doing goes way beyond that. They carry out bags of food! The owner is never there when we close up so I don't think she knows what's happening. If I tell on the workers they might hate me, but if I keep quiet my conscience bugs me. What should I do?"

Alfredo's classmates had these suggestions:

> BRENDA: I think you should tell the owner. Who cares what the workers think? What they're doing is wrong.
>
> JOE: But what if the other workers deny it? What if the owner doesn't believe Alfredo?
>
> BRENDA: It's a chance Alfredo will have to take. It's the right thing to do.
>
> ALFREDO: I make good tips at this job. I really don't want to lose it.

JOE:	Maybe you could talk to the people who are stealing? Tell them they should knock it off.
RUDY:	Can you change shifts? That way you won't see it being done.
KIM:	But it will still be happening. Do you know why they're stealing food? Maybe they don't think they're paid enough. Or would it be thrown out if they didn't take it home?

Alfredo used his classmate's comments to gather more ideas about his topic. Kim's questions, for example, made him realize that his coworkers might not think they were doing anything wrong. He decided to investigate how other area restaurants handled the problem of employee theft before talking to his boss.

> ◀ **GROUP ACTIVITY 5 Consult with Others about Your Topic** ▶
>
> Identify a problem or an issue related to a job — it could be your job or someone else's. For instance, you might have a problem with a work schedule, the attitudes of coworkers, or difficult customers. Describe the problem to your classmates, and ask them for suggestions. Or you might choose to interview an expert on the subject and ask how he or she would address the problem. Take notes on the responses. As you write your informative essay, you may want to include some of the proposed solutions to your problem, but remember that your main goal is to inform your readers of the possibilities, not to try to persuade them to accept a particular solution.

◖ Step 2 Write Your Discovery Draft

You have now gathered ideas about an occupation, workplace communication, and a job-related problem. The next step is to write a discovery draft that explains something you have learned about working.

For more on drafting, see pp. 16–20.

It's okay if your ideas and your writing are rough at this stage. The discovery draft is just your first try at putting your thoughts in essay form. You'll have plenty of time later to develop your ideas, add supporting information, and fix any mistakes.

Choosing a Topic

You have collected rich materials for writing, but you need to decide how to proceed. Keeping in mind that you are writing to share something you know with others who may be interested in a particular occupational field, you need to pick a topic for your essay. Look over the ideas you have gathered, and try to identify a topic that will enable you to give your readers useful information.

Remember that you have three general choices to work with: examining a specific occupation, analyzing workplace communication, or analyzing a job-related problem. You may select one of the topics you have already explored, gather ideas on a new topic, or even combine related topics. For example, while freewriting about an occupation, you may have discovered that you have some concerns about it. Rather than decide the job is no good for you, you could consult with some people and write about ways to address those problems. Whatever you do, be sure to select a topic that matters to you, that you have considered carefully, and that your readers will want to learn about.

> ◀ **WRITING ACTIVITY 7** Choose Your Topic ▶

Review your freewriting, brainstorming, and consultation notes, and choose or create a topic that will be interesting for you and your readers. If you're not confident that you have something to say about your topic, you may go back and freewrite, brainstorm, or consult some more on the topic of your choice.

Sharing Your Ideas

When you sit down to write your discovery draft, first write a preliminary thesis statement that says what your topic is and what you think your main point will be. You can always revise your thesis statement if your writing takes you in an unexpected direction, but having a general plan in mind will help get you started.

Keep your audience and purpose in mind as you draft, but remember that your main goal at this stage is to find out what you have to say. Focus on writing, and don't worry about every supporting detail or how you express yourself. You'll have a chance later on to expand, revise, and edit your discovery draft.

> ⏻ **Discuss your drafts online**
>
> E-mail your discovery draft to your fellow students or coworkers for feedback. Or if you have access to a course management system such as Blackboard or Moodle, post your draft online for other classmates to read. Ask for specific help where you need it most. For example, you might ask your readers to focus on how effectively you have used transitions.

A Student's Discovery Draft

Here's a discovery draft written by Kathy Chu, the student whose freewriting about her desire to be a pediatrician you read earlier in this chapter. Notice that her preliminary thesis statement (highlighted) expresses her main idea and maps out a few of the reasons she is interested in pursuing a career in medicine. (Like most discovery drafts, this one includes errors; Kathy will fix them later.)

Preliminary thesis statement: I want to be a pediatrician so I can help children, make a good living, and have an interesting job.

Ever since I was a child, I wanted to be a pediatrician, which is a doctor who specializes in children. I hated going to the pediatrician when I was a child, but I was also fascinated by the woman in the white jacket who seemed to have all the answers. I want to be a pediatrician so I can help children, make a good living, and have an interesting job.

Ever since I can remember, I've wanted to take care of children. My little brother used to get earaches. I'd pretend I was the doctor and hold a cup to his chest so I could hear his heartbeat. In high school I volunteered at Providence Hospital in the children's wing. Seeing a sick child made me sad. I felt better when I'd play with them and cheer them up.

As a pediatrician, I can make a good living. Making a good living is important to me. My parents have had to cope with many financial difficulties. I want to be able to provide for my parents when they get old. I want to take care of my own family, too.

Pediatricians work long hours. This might be a problem for some people, but not for me. Right now I help take care of my family, carry a full class load at college, and work about 30 hours a week. I wouldn't know what to do with myself if I had free time!

I think pediatricians have exciting jobs. You never know what might be making a child sick. They might have a runny nose or something more serious. It's your job to make sure they get the right treatment so they can get well. The job might make me tired or stressed, but never bored.

For me, nothing beats helping a child get well.

WRITING ACTIVITY 8 Write Your Discovery Draft

Write at least three to five paragraphs that state why you are interested in an occupation, that analyze workplace communication, or that discuss a job-related problem. Prepare a preliminary thesis statement, and use your prewriting materials to get started, but feel free to write anything that occurs to you while you're drafting. If you're not sure what to write about, that's fine. You may write drafts on several topics to see which one will be most productive for you.

Step 3 Revise Your Draft

Now that you have completed your discovery draft, it's time to make it better. Start by looking for anything you can improve by using the skills you have learned in other chapters of this book. For example, you can

For more on thesis statements, see pp. 18–19.

probably clarify and support your main ideas by improving your thesis statement and topic sentences (Chapter 4), making your ideas flow more smoothly by adding transitions (Chapter 5), organizing your paragraphs (Chapter 2), and strengthening your introduction and conclusion (Chapter 5).

As you revise your essay about the workplace, you will learn how to develop your ideas using classification and definition, and you will practice adding support with information from books, articles, and the Web. Keep your audience and purpose in mind as you revise by reviewing the analysis you completed in Writing Activity 4 (p. 169). What information do your readers need to know to understand your topic? How can you keep them interested as they read your essay?

Developing Your Ideas

Because you are writing to teach your readers something about the workplace, it's important that you explain your points clearly. Two methods of development—classification and definition—are especially useful when you want to help people unfamiliar with a topic understand what you have to tell them.

Classification

For more on classification, see pp. 64–65.

Classification shows the relationship between different people, things, or ideas by organizing them into logical categories. A single *principle*, or *theme*, links those categories together as a group. For instance, college students can be classified according to the principle of demographics: age, place of birth, marital status, income. Or they can be classified by participation in groups: fraternities or sororities, athletic teams, clubs. Because classification breaks a large concept into parts, it makes a topic easier to understand.

Classification is used in all three of the essays that open this chapter. In "I Am Not a Babysitter," Heather Robinson classifies stereotypes about teachers. Perri Klass, in "She's Your Basic L.O.L. in N.A.D.," classifies medical jargon according to how it helps health care professionals communicate. In "You're Hired!" Donald Trump classifies different kinds of strategies for succeeding in the workplace—such as "fine-tune your timing" and "toot your own horn"—and gives each category a heading to help readers follow his points. By using classification, these authors order their ideas logically and clearly.

When you classify, be sure to explain your principle of classification and to discuss each category separately. Although you might occasionally write one paragraph to classify the parts of your topic, you will usually need a full paragraph to identify and explain each category. (You may need to write two or three paragraphs to explain the most important category.)

> ### ■ **HOW TO** Use Classification
>
> - Decide on what basis you'll classify the topic. For example, the topic of "workplace stress" can be classified into "causes of workplace stress."
> - Break the topic down into parts. "Causes of workplace stress" can be grouped into "stress from coworkers," "stress from supervisors," and "stress from customers."
> - Discuss one category at a time.
> - Give examples to support the classification.

Student writer Kathy Chu reviewed her discovery draft and noticed that she had several specific reasons for wanting to be a pediatrician: to help children, to earn a good living, and to be challenged on a daily basis. For her revised draft, she thought of some additional reasons for her interest in pediatrics and decided to use classification to explain each of those reasons in detail.

GROUP ACTIVITY 6 Use Classification to Develop Your Ideas

With several classmates, brainstorm ways you could use classification to make your essay easier to understand. For instance, if you wrote a discovery draft about dealing with a difficult supervisor, you might classify difficult supervisors into categories (those who yell, those who expect too much, those who give confusing instructions, and so on). If appropriate, use your classmates' suggestions to organize your topic into categories for your revision.

Definition

To *define* something is to explain what it means. *Definition* is a helpful strategy to use when developing your essay because it can help you clarify important points. When you define a term, first place it in a general category. Then explain how it fits within that category according to what sets it apart—its distinguishing features. For example, in the introduction of her discovery draft, Kathy Chu defines *pediatrician* by placing it in a general category—doctors. She then explains the characteristics of this type of doctor (they work with children), which highlights the occupation's distinguishing features.

For more on definition, see pp. 65–66.

Although a simple one-sentence definition is always useful, writers often use more than one sentence to define complex terms or concepts. In "I Am Not a Babysitter," for example, the author first defines teaching in very general terms as "the profession that creates all other professions" and then later uses several sentences to describe what teachers do.

> ### ▪ HOW TO Use Definition
>
> - Introduce the word, phrase, or concept to be defined.
> - Place the word, phrase, or concept in a general category, and explain what sets it apart from others in that category.
> - Provide details (such as description, narration, examples, process explanation, or comparison and contrast) to explain your term.
> - Organize the details so that a reader will easily understand your definition.

GROUP ACTIVITY 7 Use Definition to Develop Your Ideas

Exchange your discovery draft with a classmate. Underline any words, phrases, or concepts in your partner's draft that you don't understand or that could be made clearer with a sentence or paragraph of definition. Your classmate should do the same for your paper. Use your partner's suggestions to add definitions to your own draft as necessary.

Building Your Essay

In addition to developing your own ideas fully, you need to make sure that you have provided enough information to keep your audience interested and informed. Because you may be writing about a topic that is new to you or unfamiliar to your readers, consider doing a little research to gather additional information that will help you explain something about the workplace. Used carefully, a handful of facts and opinions from reliable sources can make your ideas more convincing.

Find Information to Strengthen Your Support

To learn more about any aspect of an occupation, workplace communication, or a job-related problem, start by consulting a general reference—such as an encyclopedia, a dictionary, or a handbook—for basic facts. For instance, if you wrote your discovery draft about an occupation that interests you, you can look it up in the *Occupational Outlook Handbook*, updated every other year by the U.S. Department of Labor and available online at www.bls.gov/oco. The *Handbook* contains detailed information—such as job descriptions, educational requirements, and average salaries—about a wide variety of occupations. Some other useful references are listed on pages 339–43 of this book; your school librarian will be happy to suggest additional resources if you ask.

Also helpful are newspaper, magazine, and Web articles written by people with related experience in the workplace. Consider Donald Trump's essay "You're Hired!" which you read earlier in this chapter. Even though Trump is highly respected by his readers, he includes information from two newspaper articles to support his claim that his "buildings are among the finest in the world." Like Trump, you can include the opinion of another writer to make one of your own points more convincing.

To find additional information for your draft, search a library database or the World Wide Web for information about your topic. Use *keywords*, or words that pertain to your topic, to find useful articles. Keep in mind that you won't be able to use every source you find. As you read, look for facts, ideas, or opinions that can help you back up one of your points or explain one of your ideas.

For more on library databases and keywords, see pp. 341–42.

 Search a database or the Internet

For tutorials on how to use a library database or the Internet to conduct research, go to **bedfordstmartins.com/rewriting** and click on **The Bedford Research Room**.

 WRITING ACTIVITY 9 Locate Additional Information for Your Essay

Reread your discovery draft, and look for any ideas that could be better explained or made more convincing. Look for information to support these ideas by checking a reference work and reading some articles on your topic. Photocopy or print out any useful material that you find; you will refer to it in the next stage of revising your draft.

Outline Your Plan

Once you find facts, ideas, and opinions that can help you explain your topic to your readers, pay special attention to where you will include this information in your essay.

Review your discovery draft and your research notes, and make a rough outline of your major points. Indicate where you could add information from a book, an article, or a Web site to make your points clearer. Your outline should include the ideas you've already drafted and any additional support from your research that you plan to provide in each paragraph. Follow the outline format that works best for you. If you're unsure of how to make an outline, just create a simple list.

Student writer Kathy Chu, for example, found some good information about pediatrics in the online version of the *Occupational Outlook Handbook* and in a *Time* magazine article about the future of the profession. Here is the rough outline she put together to plan her revised draft. (Note that *P* in this outline stands for *paragraph*. The research information Kathy plans to add is underlined.)

P1: Introduce topic. Define *pediatrician*. Thesis: Pediatricians help children, make a good living, work hard, and enjoy challenges.

P2: My desire to help sick children. Experiences I've had with my brother and at the hospital.

P3: Pediatricians get to make decisions about treatment.

P4: Pediatricians make a good living. Why this is important to me. <u>Information about salaries from the *Occupational Outlook Handbook*</u>.

P5: Pediatricians work long hours. This doesn't bother me. <u>Information about number of hours per week and education requirements from the *Occupational Outlook Handbook* and article from *Time*</u>.

P6: Pediatricians face many challenges. This will keep me from getting bored. <u>Quote from *Time* magazine from pediatrician about challenges</u>.

P7: Conclusion. Go back to thesis. It's the job for me.

Remember that your outline, like Kathy's, is *tentative*—in other words, it is subject to change. As you revise, you might think of new ideas or a better way to order your points. Don't hesitate to rework your plan as needed.

 Use the outline view

To help you organize your outline, use the Outline View function found on many word-processing programs. This function will give you the option of outlining your ideas for the whole essay or for individual paragraphs. The Help function of your program will lead you through the appropriate steps.

 WRITING ACTIVITY 10 Outline Your Revision Plan

Outline your ideas for your revised draft. Use the format in Kathy's outline or a format of your own. List the major ideas that you will keep from your discovery draft, and note where you'll add new ideas and information from your research.

Correctly Use Research Material

As you revise your draft, remember that you are writing to express your own ideas about the workplace and not to give a report on what other people have said. Although it can be tempting to include several long chunks of research in your essay, select only the most pertinent ideas to support your points. Do not let the research take over your essay. As a rule of thumb, limit information from outside sources (articles, books, Web sites) to no more than 10 to 20 percent of your essay.

Keep the following three principles in mind when you add information from research to your own writing.

For more information on quoting and paraphrasing information, see pp. 351–53.

Put Information in Your Own Words Summarize or paraphrase—don't quote—facts or statistics from an article about your topic. You can select the key ideas that will support your point without having to repeat the whole of your source.

A *summary* is a short version of a piece of text that is written in your own words. To summarize, you explain the most important idea from a source while omitting the details. Suppose, for example, that you were writing an essay about your desire to be a teacher. To address any stereotypes that your family and friends may have, you could summarize information from the essay "I Am Not a Babysitter," which you read earlier in this chapter:

> As the author of "I Am Not a Babysitter" explains, there are a number of stereotypes about teaching, including that it is an easy, boring job that people do only until they can find something better. In reality, though, teaching is a challenging but rewarding profession that makes a real difference in students' lives.

When you *paraphrase*, you also put information from a source into your own words, but you use about the same number of words as the original source uses, as Kathy does in this example:

ORIGINAL	Over one-third of full-time physicians and surgeons worked 60 hours or more a week in 2004. (*Occupational Outlook Handbook*, page 1)
PARAPHRASE	According to the *Occupational Outlook Handbook,* more than 30 percent of all doctors work at least 60 hours a week (1).

Quote Sparingly A well-placed quotation can help you express an idea in a distinct way, but you should use another writer's exact words only to emphasize or explain an important point. One or two quotations are sufficient for a three-page essay.

When you do include a direct quotation, weave it smoothly into your sentences. Use an introductory phrase, and put quotation marks around your source's words, as Kathy does in her revised draft:

> *According to one pediatrician*, "I never know what I'll encounter with every patient I see. One child might just have a cold or flu. But the next child could have a bruise that won't heal. This could be a symptom of cancer" (Turner 53).

Document Your Sources Whether you summarize, paraphrase, or quote material from a source, you must always inform your readers that the ideas or words are not your own. Indicate where you obtained information by citing the source in the text of your essay and in a list of works cited at the end:

For more on documenting sources, see pp. 355–61.

- In most cases, introduce a summary, paraphrase, or quotation by identifying the author or title of the book, article, or Web site in which you found the information.
- At the end of a summary, paraphrase, or quotation, provide the author's last name and the page number where you found the

information in parentheses. (Exclude the author's name if you gave it when you introduced the material.)

■ At the end of the essay, include a Works Cited list that gives publication information for each source you used.

 Use color for research material

Use the Color feature on your word-processing program to highlight quotations in your draft. Use another color to highlight paraphrased and summarized material. This technique will help you monitor how much research material you have in your draft. For instance, if more than 10 to 20 percent of the draft is in color, you know that the research is taking over your own ideas.

■ **HOW TO** Use Research Material in an Essay

- Limit the amount of research material to no more than 10 to 20 percent of your essay.
- Use brief quotations only to emphasize or explain an important point.
- Summarize or paraphrase—put into your own words—information such as facts or statistics.
- Introduce most source material with a phrase such as *According to* or *In the words of.*
- Indicate where you obtained any quoted, summarized, or paraphrased information in the text of the essay and at the end of the essay.

For the most up-to-date information on documenting sources in MLA, go to **bedfordstmartins.com /resdoc** and click on **Humanities**.

GROUP ACTIVITY 8 Quote, Paraphrase, and Document Information

Quoting, paraphrasing, and documenting information are essential. Otherwise, you can be accused of plagiarism. For more help, see p. 355.

The following is a paragraph from a student essay about working while attending college.

Working your way through college has many advantages. Unlike students who depend on large checks from their parents, working students learn to be self-reliant and independent. Because they pay their own bills every month, they realize the value of a college education in getting a well-paid job. They learn how to manage time well, an important skill in the working world. They also gain excellent work experience for their résumés after they graduate. While they might be tempted to grumble about lack of free time or the old car they drive, working students have many advantages over students who don't work.

Here's a quotation from a magazine article on the same topic:

> I believe the fact that my husband and I are happy and financially stable is a direct result of our learning how to manage time and money in college.
> — "Pay Your Own Way! (Then Thank Mom)," by Audrey Rock-Richardson, page 12 in *Newsweek* on Sept. 11, 2000.

Working in groups of two or three students, first rewrite the paragraph by inserting the quotation into it. Be sure to introduce the quotation and correctly document the source in parentheses.

Then rewrite the paragraph again. Rather than inserting the quotation into the paragraph, paraphrase the information by putting it into your own words. Don't forget to document the source in the paragraph.

 WRITING ACTIVITY 11 Add Researched Information to Your Draft

Using the outline you prepared for Writing Activity 10 as a guide, add two or three summaries, paraphrases, or quotations to your draft. Be careful that you use this researched information to support your own points: don't expect it to speak for you. Also, make sure you correctly cite your sources in the body of your essay and in a Works Cited list.

A Student's Revised Draft

After writing a discovery draft about her desire to become a pediatrician, student writer Kathy Chu realized she needed more details to describe why she wants to be a pediatrician, so she did a little research to get more information. Before you read her revised draft, reread her discovery draft (p. 175). Notice how she has used classification to organize her ideas and added information from the *Occupational Outlook Handbook* and a magazine article to support her points. (You will also notice some errors in the revised draft; these will be corrected when Kathy edits her essay later.)

Helping Children Heal

When I was a child, going to the doctor was both frightening and exciting. I hated getting shots and seeing the crying babies. At the same time, the friendly doctor in the white jacket who seemed to have all the answers fascinated me. As an adult, I still admire the doctor from my childhood. Now I know that she was a pediatrician, which is a doctor who specializes in the health needs of children. I entered college and started to think of my future occupation. I thought more and more about becoming this kind of doctor. As a pediatrician, I can help children get well, make a good living, work hard, and enjoy challenges.

Ever since I can remember, I've wanted to take care of children. My little brother used to get earaches. I'd pretend I was the doctor and hold a cup to

For more help in using research material in your essay, go to **bedfordstmartins .com/rewriting** *and click on* **The Bedford Research Room**.

1 This introduction is more interesting.

Her thesis is clearer.

2

An example is added.

A reason is added to her classification categories.

his chest so I could hear his heartbeat. In high school, I volunteered at Providence Hospital in the children's wing. Seeing a sick child made me sad. I always felt better after playing with them and cheering them up. Being even a small part of a team that helped children heal, it made me feel worthwhile.

While volunteering at Providence Hospital, I observed many pediatric   3
nurses give children shots, examine their progress, and cheer up their patients. Pediatric nurses work one-on-one with children. Pediatricians spend less time alone with the patients. However, being a pediatrician appeals to me more than being a nurse because pediatricians diagnose children and decide on a treatment plan. Nurses have to carry out the decisions of doctors. I prefer to be the one who makes the decisions in the first place.

Summarized information from a Web site is added.

A source is cited in the body of the essay.

Paraphrased information from a Web site and an article is included.

Sources are cited in the body of the essay.

A reason is added to her classification categories.

As a pediatrician, I can make a good living. Making a good living is   4
important to me. My parents have had to cope with many financial difficulties. I remember bill collectors calling us and my mother's car being repossessed. A pediatrician doesn't have trouble finding a job, and their median salary is $133,000 a year (U.S. Dept. of Labor 6). This job security will let me provide for my parents when they get old, as well as take care of my own family.

Pediatricians work long hours. According to the *Occupational Outlook*   5
Handbook, published by the U.S. Department of Labor, more than 30 percent of all doctors work at least 60 hours a week (1). In addition, a pediatrician, like all doctors, must complete four years of college, four years of medical school, and then three to eight years of further training in a hospital (Turner 54). It takes a high grade point average and being especially good in science. Fortunately, I like to work hard.

A quotation is used to support a point.

A source is cited in the body of the essay.

Finally, as a pediatrician, I would encounter challenges every day. According   6
to one pediatrician, "I never know what I'll encounter with every patient I see. One child might just have a cold or flu. But the next child could have a bruise that won't heal. This could be a symptom of cancer" (Turner 53). I look forward to helping children heal whether they have a runny nose or something more serious. The job might make me tired or stressed but never bored.

The conclusion is extended.

While a pediatrician's job can be difficult, I think it's the job for me.   7
Getting into medical school is tough, but I like to aim high. For me, nothing would be more satisfying than helping a child get well.

Works Cited

Turner, Angela. "Pediatricians: An Endangered Species?" *Time* 7 Apr. 1999:
    53–54. Print.

United States. Dept. of Labor. Bureau of Labor Statistics. "Physicians and
    Surgeons." *Occupational Outlook Handbook, 2006–07 Edition.* Bureau
    of Labor Statistics, 2006. Web. 29 Mar. 2011.

A Works Cited list is added.

GROUP ACTIVITY 9 Analyze Kathy's Revised Draft

Use the following questions to discuss with your classmates how Kathy revised her draft.

1. How well has Kathy hooked the reader, given background information, and stated her thesis in her introduction?

2. What is Kathy's thesis statement? How much better is it than the thesis in her discovery draft? How can it be improved even more?

3. How has Kathy used classification and definition to develop her points? Are these revisions effective? Explain.

4. What kind of research did Kathy conduct on her topic?

5. How well has Kathy used research in her essay? Is the research connected to the ideas before and after it? Are quotations introduced? Is the research documented in her essay and in her Works Cited list?

6. In your view, what point or points are best supported with facts, examples, and statistics? Is there any idea that needs more support?

7. How could Kathy's draft benefit from more revision?

GROUP ACTIVITY 10 Peer Review

Form a group with two or three other students, and exchange copies of your current drafts. Read your draft aloud while your classmates follow along. Take notes on your classmates' responses to the following questions about your draft.

1. What did you like best about my essay?

2. How interesting is my introduction? Did you want to continue reading the essay? Why or why not?

3. What is my thesis statement? Do I need to make the essay's thesis clearer?

4. How well have I supported my points? Do I need to add facts, examples, or statistics to extend what I say?

5. How can classification or definition improve my supporting points?

6. How well have I used summaries, paraphrases, and quotations from my research? Have I given the correct information about my sources in the text of my essay and in the Works Cited list?

7. Where in the essay did my writing confuse you? How can I clarify my thoughts?

8. How effective is my ending? Do I end in such a way that you know it's the end?

WRITING ACTIVITY 12 Revise Your Draft

Using the plan you outlined in Writing Activity 10 and the research you added in Writing Activity 11 as a starting point, take your classmates' peer review suggestions into consideration, and revise your essay. Use researched information only to support your most important points, and summarize, paraphrase, and quote properly. Finally, document your sources — both in the text of your essay and in a Works Cited list at the end.

Step 4 Edit Your Sentences

At this point, you have worked hard to investigate an occupation, analyze workplace communication, or analyze a workplace problem. Now that you have finished developing and supporting your ideas, you're ready to focus on your words and sentences. Remember that the fewer errors you make, the more your readers will pay attention to what you have to say. In this section, you'll concentrate on two editing tasks — combining sentences using subordinating conjunctions and correcting pronoun reference and agreement.

Combining Sentences Using Subordinating Conjunctions

For more on subordination, see pp. 439–43.

By combining short, closely related sentences in your draft, you can eliminate unnecessary words, clarify connections between your sentences, and improve sentence variety. For now, you'll focus on combining sentences using subordinating conjunctions.

Often, one sentence in a paragraph is *subordinate* to — less important than — another, closely related sentence. Combining sentences with a subordinating conjunction tells the reader that one idea is less important than another. Here are some of the most frequently used subordinating conjunctions:

Subordinating Conjunctions

after	if	unless	where
although	since	until	wherever
because	that	when	whether
before	though	whenever	while

The subordinating conjunction comes at the beginning of the less important sentence, which is called a *subordinate clause*.

Student writer Kathy Chu's revised draft has several short, closely related sentences that can be combined with subordinating conjunctions. In the following examples, the less important sentence, or subordinate clause, is italicized:

ORIGINAL	*My little brother used to get earaches.* I'd pretend I was the doctor and hold a cup to his chest so I could hear his heartbeat.
REVISED	*When my little brother used to get earaches,* I'd pretend I was the doctor and hold a cup to his chest so I could hear his heart beat.
ORIGINAL	Making a good living is important to me. *My parents have had to cope with many financial difficulties.*
REVISED	Making a good living is important to me *because my parents have had to cope with many financial difficulties.*

As these examples illustrate, the subordinate clause can appear at the beginning or end of the sentence. When the subordinate clause comes at the beginning of the sentence, a comma divides it from the rest of the sentence. When the subordinate clause comes at the end of the sentence, no comma is used.

■ HOW TO Combine Sentences Using Subordinating Conjunctions

- Combine sentences that are short and closely related in meaning.
- Decide which sentence is subordinate to, or less important than, the other.
- Turn the less important sentence into a subordinate clause by beginning it with an appropriate subordinating conjunction.
- When the subordinate clause begins the sentence, use a comma to divide it from the main clause.
- Don't use a comma when the subordinate clause is at the end of the sentence.

EDITING ACTIVITY 1 Use Subordinating Conjunctions

Combine the following pairs of sentences. First, decide which sentence is less important in conveying the message; this sentence will become the subordinate clause. Then, select an appropriate subordinating conjunction to begin the subordinate clause. Finally, combine the two sentences. You may need to eliminate unnecessary words or move some words around.

because there
EXAMPLE For many people, it's hard to decide on a career/~~There~~ are so many careers

to choose from.

1. I'm studying to become a photojournalist. I like both photography and journalism.

2. I've always wanted to be a photojournalist. I remember wanting to be a

   photojournalist when I was a child.

3. A photojournalist takes photographs of current events. These photographs are

   published in print and online magazines and newspapers.

4. Often people read a magazine just for the photographs. This is why

   photojournalists are important to magazine editors.

5. Photojournalists have exciting jobs. They get to travel and take pictures of

   important people.

For additional practice with combining sentences with subordinating conjunctions, go to **bedfordstmartins .com/choices** and click on **Exercise Central**.

> **WRITING ACTIVITY 13 Combine Your Sentences**

Examine your revised draft for short, closely related sentences. Where it makes sense to do so, combine them with subordinating conjunctions.

Correcting Pronoun Reference and Agreement

A *pronoun* usually refers to or takes the place of a specific noun in a sentence. If a pronoun does not clearly refer to a specific noun or agree in number with the noun it replaces, your readers will be confused.

Here are some of the most common English pronouns:

I, me, mine, we, us, our, ours
you, your, yours
he, him, his, she, her, hers
it, its
they, them, their, theirs
this, these, that, those
who, whom, whose, which, that, what
any, anyone, anybody, each, everybody, everyone, everything
someone, something

Pronoun Reference

For more on pronoun reference, see pp. 430–31.

When you use a pronoun to refer to a noun, make sure the reference is clear, not vague. Here are two ways to correct vague pronoun reference:

- Replace the pronoun with the noun it refers to.
- Rewrite the sentence so that the pronoun is no longer needed.

VAGUE	In the article "Dealing with a Difficult Boss," *it* said that good communication between boss and employee is essential. [What does *it* refer to?]
CLEAR	In the article "Dealing with a Difficult Boss," *the author* said that good communication between boss and employee is essential.
VAGUE	Ms. Ortiz told Rachel *she* was going to be late. [Does *she* refer to Ms. Ortiz or to Rachel?]
CLEAR	Ms. Ortiz said, "I'm going to be late."
VAGUE	In the art world, *they're* used to unusual behavior and clothing. [Whom does *they* refer to?]
CLEAR	People in the art world are used to unusual behavior and clothing.
VAGUE	Raymond loved traveling with his band and recording a CD last summer. *It* made him decide to make music a career. [Does *it* refer to traveling with the band, recording a CD, or both?]
CLEAR	Because Raymond loved traveling with his band and recording a CD over the summer, *he* decided to make music a career.

Pronoun Agreement

Every pronoun must agree in number with the noun it takes the place of. That is, use a singular pronoun to replace a singular noun and a plural pronoun to replace a plural noun. Indefinite pronouns—such as *any, anybody, anyone, each, everybody, everyone, everything, someone,* and *something*— are singular. Here are two ways to correct pronoun agreement:

For more on pronoun agreement, see pp. 431–33.

- Make the pronoun and noun agree in number.
- Rewrite the sentence to eliminate the problem.

INCORRECT	A successful job applicant will prepare for *their* job interview.
REVISED	A successful job applicant will prepare for *his or her* job interview.
REVISED	Successful job applicants will prepare for *their* job interviews.
INCORRECT	To get a good job, *everyone* should try to get the best education *they* can afford.
REVISED	To get a good job, *everyone* should try to get the best education *he or she* can afford.
REVISED	To get a good job, *young people* should try to get the best education *they* can afford.

As these examples illustrate, you may wish to use a plural noun (such as *young people*) to avoid saying *he or she* or *his or her* throughout an essay.

> ### ■ HOW TO Correct Pronoun Reference and Agreement
>
> - Identify the pronouns in each sentence of your draft.
> - Identify the noun that each pronoun replaces. Make sure the noun is easy to identify and is close to the pronoun.
> - Check to see that the noun and pronoun agree in number.
> - Remember that indefinite pronouns (*any, anybody, anyone, each, everybody, everyone, everything, someone,* and *something*) are singular. Use singular nouns with them.

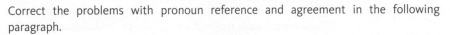

EDITING ACTIVITY 2 Correct Pronoun Reference and Agreement

Correct the problems with pronoun reference and agreement in the following paragraph.

Whenever I tell anyone my college major is food science, they get a puzzled look on their face. Most people haven't heard of it. I first read about food science in a magazine article about the invention of different varieties of corn for undeveloped countries. They said that scientists spend years in the laboratory and in greenhouses trying to get plants to grow in extreme climates or different types of soils. They take years to develop. Last semester in my Introduction to Food Science course, they had us experiment with making a type of yogurt that doesn't need refrigeration. It isn't available to consumers in poor countries. It didn't taste very good, but it was interesting to make. My ultimate goal is to contribute to the elimination of starvation throughout the world.

For additional practice with correcting pronoun reference and agreement, go to **bedfordstmartins.com /choices** and click on **Exercise Central**.

WRITING ACTIVITY 14 Edit Your Sentences

Read your essay word for word, looking for errors in spelling, punctuation, and grammar. Also ask a friend or classmate to help you spot errors you might have overlooked. Pay particular attention to vague pronoun reference and faulty pronoun agreement. Use a dictionary and the Handbook in Part Four of this book to help you correct the errors you find.

This essay shows how to give information about your sources in the body of the essay and in the Works Cited list. You can find another sample essay on pp. 361–64.

A Student's Edited Essay

You may have noticed that Kathy's revised draft contained some choppy sentences as well as errors in spelling, punctuation, and grammar. Kathy fixed these problems in her edited essay. Her corrections are noted in the margin.

Kathy Chu

Professor Mangelsdorf

English 0311

4 Apr. 2011

The correct MLA format is used.

Helping Children Heal

When I was a child, going to the doctor was both frightening and exciting.   1
I hated getting shots and seeing the crying babies. At the same time, the
friendly doctor in the white jacket who seemed to have all the answers
fascinated me. As an adult, I still admire the doctor from my childhood. Now
I know that she was a pediatrician, which is a doctor who specializes in the
health needs of children. When I entered college and started to think of my
future occupation, I thought more and more about becoming this kind of
doctor. As a pediatrician, I can help children get well, make a good living,
work hard, and enjoy challenges.

— Sentences are combined.

Ever since I can remember, I've wanted to take care of children. When my   2
little brother used to get earaches, I'd pretend I was the doctor and hold a
cup to his chest so I could hear his heartbeat. In high school, I volunteered
at Providence Hospital in the children's wing. Seeing sick children made me
sad, but I always felt better after playing with them and cheering them up.
Being even a small part of a team that helped children heal made me feel
worthwhile.

— Sentences are combined.

A vague pronoun reference is eliminated.

While volunteering at Providence Hospital, I observed many pediatric   3
nurses give children shots, examine their progress, and cheer up their
patients. Pediatric nurses work one-on-one with children, while pediatricians
spend less time alone with the patients. However, being a pediatrician appeals
to me more than being a nurse because pediatricians diagnose children and
decide on a treatment plan. Nurses have to carry out the decisions of doctors.
I prefer to be the one who makes the decisions in the first place.

— Sentences are combined.

As a pediatrician, I can make a good living. Making a good living is   4
important to me because my parents have had to cope with many financial
difficulties. I remember bill collectors calling us and my mother's car being
repossessed. Pediatricians don't have trouble finding jobs, and their median
salary is $133,000 a year (U.S. Dept. of Labor). This job security will let me
provide for my parents when they get old, as well as take care of my own
family.

— Sentences are combined.

A pronoun-agreement problem is fixed.

Pediatricians work long hours. According to the *Occupational Outlook*   5
Handbook, published by the U.S. Department of Labor, more than 30 percent
of all doctors work at least 60 hours a week (1). In addition, a pediatrician,
like all doctors, must complete four years of college, four years of medical

A vague pronoun reference is
eliminated.

school, and then three to eight years of further training in a hospital
(Turner 54). People who want to be accepted to medical school must have
a high grade point average and be especially good in science. Fortunately,
I like to work hard.

Finally, as a pediatrician, I would encounter challenges every day. 6
According to one pediatrician, "I never know what I'll encounter with every
patient I see. One child might just have a cold or flu. But the next child could
have a bruise that won't heal. This could be a symptom of cancer" (Turner
53). I look forward to helping children heal whether they have a runny nose or
something more serious. The job might make me tired or stressed but never
bored.

While a pediatrician's job can be difficult, I think it's the job for me. 7
Getting into medical school is tough, but I like to aim high. For me, nothing
would be more satisfying than helping a child get well.

Works Cited

Turner, Angela. "Pediatricians: An Endangered Species?" *Time* 7 Apr. 1999:
53–54. Print.

United States. Dept. of Labor. Bureau of Labor Statistics. "Physicians and
Surgeons." *Occupational Outlook Handbook, 2006–07 Edition*.
Bureau of Labor Statistics, 2006. Web. 29 Mar. 2011.

❰Step 5 Share Your Essay

You've worked hard to write an essay that will be useful to people who
share your interest in a particular occupation, so give them a chance to
read it. Many organizations distribute periodic newsletters that include articles of interest to their members. For example, your school might e-mail
news and career ideas to students every term, your volunteer group might
have a quarterly newsletter, or your employer might share monthly updates on staff activities. Whether these newsletters are printed, posted to
the Web, or e-mailed to a listserv, the people who distribute them are almost always looking for reader submissions. Find out who edits one of the
newsletters you receive, and send your essay to him or her. The other
members of your group will thank you!

CHAPTER CHECKLIST

❑ I read essays about work-related issues to learn about this chapter's theme.

❑ I gathered ideas on an occupation, workplace communication, and a job-related problem by freewriting, brainstorming, and consulting with others.

❑ I developed ideas using classification and definition.

❑ I located sources on my topic to help support my ideas.

❑ I wrote an outline before I revised.

❑ I correctly used summaries, paraphrases, and quotations in my draft.

❑ I documented source materials in the body and at the end of my essay in a Works Cited list.

❑ I combined short, closely related sentences using subordinating conjunctions.

❑ I corrected errors in pronoun reference and agreement.

❑ I submitted my essay to a newsletter.

REFLECTING ON YOUR WRITING

To help you reflect on the writing you did in this chapter, answer the following questions:

1. What did you learn from writing on your topic?

2. If you used research in your essay, what part of the research process was hardest? What was easiest?

3. Compare and contrast writing this essay with writing previous essays.

4. If you had more time, what further revisions would you make to improve your essay? Why would you make these revisions?

Using your answers to these questions, complete a Writing Process Report for this chapter (you can download a report form at **bedfordstmartins.com /choices**). Once you complete this report, freewrite about what you learned in this chapter.

"This is an effective and diverse display that is emotionally moving and often disturbing."
— PAUL LaPRADE, "THE DISAPPEARED"

Evaluating
Products, Performances, and Places

Evaluation is something you do every day, often without even thinking about it. In the morning, you may decide that a new brand of breakfast cereal tastes better than your old brand. During the school day, you may realize that this semester's chemistry instructor explains experiments more carefully than a previous instructor did. In the evening, you may channel-surf to find a television show that is worth watching.

When you *evaluate* something, you judge its value, worthiness, or merit. An evaluation is based on *standards*, or criteria: a breakfast cereal should taste good and be good for you, a chemistry instructor should know his subject and communicate it clearly, and a television show should entertain or inform you. When you evaluate, you apply standards like these to your subject. You taste the cereal and examine the nutritional label on the box. You listen to determine how well your chemistry instructor explains an experiment. You examine television shows for amusing plots or interesting settings. After applying the appropriate standards to your subject, you make a decision about its value, worthiness, or merit.

Everyday evaluations are usually simple, but you can apply standards to make decisions about less routine subjects—such as whether to buy a new computer game, to see

In this chapter, you will use evaluation to share your opinion of a product, a performance, or a place. As you follow the steps of the writing process, you will

- Explore the chapter topic by reading essays about a product, performance, or place.
- Gather ideas by brainstorming, asking questions, and freewriting.
- Develop your ideas using **comparison and contrast**.
- Practice expressing a judgment, giving criteria, providing evidence, and keeping a balanced perspective.
- Combine sentences with relative clauses.
- Learn how to correct comma splices.
- Consider posting your evaluation to a blog for consumers.

a movie that looks interesting, or to eat at a particular restaurant. When you have limited personal knowledge of a subject, you probably seek out other people's opinions and experiences to help form a judgment about it. You might ask friends or family members what they think, look for expert reviews in newspapers and magazines, or search the Web for comments.

Just as you seek out people's evaluations when you need to make a choice, other people are interested in knowing your opinions. In this chapter, you will learn how to write an essay that evaluates a product, performance, or place. You will begin by reading essays by professional writers who make evaluations. You will also follow a student, Paul LaPrade, as he writes about an art exhibit in his essay "The Disappeared." As you work through the readings and activities in this chapter, you will practice developing and supporting your opinions, which will help you write a convincing essay that shares your point of view with others and helps them make up their own mind. ■

GROUP ACTIVITY 1 Think about Subjects

The photo on page 194 shows an art exhibit called *The Disappeared* that focuses on the disappearances of hundreds of Latin American people who protested their oppressive governments. Student writer Paul LaPrade chose to write about this exhibit for an Introduction to Art course. With your classmates, discuss some products, performances, or places that you would like to evaluate. Compare your opinions with those of your classmates.

Getting Started   Reading Essays That Evaluate a Product, Performance, or Place

Evaluation essays, often called *reviews*, are popular with both readers and writers. Readers like them because they offer practical information; if you're planning a trip, for instance, you can read what other travelers have written about their experiences. Writers also like reviews because they provide an opportunity to influence what other people think and do. Because they're so popular, formal reviews are a regular feature of newspapers, magazines, radio and television broadcasts, blogs, and certain Web sites. Although reviewers might not agree with one another and readers might have their own opinions, disagreement is part of the fun.

Before you decide on a subject to evaluate, read the following professional reviews of a product (the iPad), a performance (Michael Jackson's rehearsal for his last concert), and a place (two new baseball stadiums). As you read them, try to identify some of the methods, such as comparison and contrast, that these writers use to explain their evaluations and to persuade their readers to agree with them. Notice, too, how the writers explain the criteria, or basis, for their evaluation, provide evidence to support their judgments, and try to show that they have a balanced perspective. Finally, pay attention to how you respond to the writers' arguments. Do they surprise you? Make you angry? Raise more questions? Jot down your reactions as they occur to you. (For addtional essays evaluating a product, performance, or place, see p. 000.)

Evaluation of a Product

NICHOLAS CARR
The PC Officially Died Today

Nicholas Carr writes on the effects of technology in our lives. In one of his best-known essays, "Is Google Making Us Stupid?" he argues that the Internet is making people less able to concentrate on ideas or contemplate spiritual matters. In addition to publishing articles, Carr is the author of three books. His latest, *The Shallows: What the Internet Is Doing to Our Brains*, expands on his idea that the Internet is changing (mostly for the worse) the way people think. You can read more about Carr on his blog, *Rough Type*, at roughtype.com. The following review of the iPad was originally published in *The New Republic* in January 2010. Steve Jobs, the founder of Apple, passed away on October 5, 2011, but his inspiring legacy lives on.

The PC era ended this morning at ten o'clock Pacific time, when Steve Jobs stepped onto a San Francisco stage to unveil the iPad, Apple's version of a tablet computer. Tablets have been kicking around for a decade, but consumers have always shunned them. And for good reason: They've been nerdy-looking smudge-magnets, limited by their cumbersome shape and their lack of a keyboard. Tablets were a solution to a problem no one had.

The rapturous reaction to Apple's tablet—the buildup to Jobs's announcement blurred the line between media feeding-frenzy and orgiastic pagan ritual—shows that our attitude to the tablet form has finally changed. Tablets suddenly look attractive. Why? Because the nature of personal computing has changed.

Until recently, we mainly used our computers to run software programs (Microsoft Word, Quicken) installed on our hard drives. Now, we use them mainly to connect to the vast databases of the Internet—to "the cloud," as the geeks say. And as the Internet has absorbed the traditional products of media—songs, TV shows, movies, games, the printed word—we've begun to look to our computers to act as multifunctional media players. The computer business and the media business are now the same business.

The transformation in the nature of computing has turned the old-style PC into a dinosaur. A bulky screen attached to a bulky keyboard no longer fits with

[Marginal annotations:]

1 This opening statement grabs the reader's attention.

2 Carr's judgment about the iPad is expressed here: it is a device that is suitable for the way people use computers today.

3 With these examples of traditional media, such as songs and TV shows, Carr is providing evidence to support his judgment.

By comparing the iPad to a PC, Carr strengthens his point that the iPad is the right answer to

4 how people communicate electronically.

the kinds of things we want to do with our computers. The obsolescence of the PC has spurred demand for a new kind of device — portable, flexible, always connected — that takes computing into the cloud era.

Suddenly, in other words, the tablet is a solution to a problem everyone has. 5 Or at least it's one possible solution. The computing market is now filled with all sorts of networked devices, each seeking to fill a lucrative niche. There are dozens of netbooks, the diminutive cousins to traditional laptops, from manufacturers like Acer and Asus. There are e-readers like Amazon's Kindle and Barnes & Noble's Nook. There are smartphones like Apple's iPhone and Google's Nexus One. There are gaming consoles like Nintendo's Wii and Microsoft's Xbox. In some ways, personal computing has returned to the ferment of its earliest days, when the market was fragmented among lots of contending companies, operating systems, and technical standards.

With the iPad, Apple is hoping to bridge all the niches. It wants to deliver the 6 killer device for the cloud era, a machine that will define computing's new age in the way that the Windows PC defined the old age. The iPad is, as Jobs said today, "something in the middle," a multipurpose gadget aimed at the sweet spot between the tiny smartphone and the traditional laptop. If it succeeds, we'll all be using iPads to play iTunes, read iBooks, watch iShows, and engage in iChats. It will be an iWorld.

But will it succeed? The iPad is by no means a sure bet. It still, after all, is a 7 tablet — fairly big and fairly heavy. Unlike an iPod or an iPhone, you can't stick an iPad in your pocket or pocketbook. It also looks to be a cumbersome device. The iPad would be ideal for a three-handed person — two hands to hold it and another to manipulate its touchscreen — but most humans, alas, have only a pair of hands. And with a price that starts at $500 and rises to more than $800, the iPad is considerably more expensive than the Kindles and netbooks it will compete with.

But whether it finds mainstream success or not, there's no going back; we've 8 entered a new era of computing, in which media and software have merged in the Internet cloud. It's hardly a surprise that Apple — more than Microsoft, IBM, or even Google — is defining the terms of this new era. Thanks to Steve Jobs, a bohemian geek with the instincts of an impresario, Apple has always been as much about show biz as about data processing. It sees its products as performances and its customers as both audience members and would-be artists.

Apple endured its darkest days during the early 1990s, when the PC had lost 9 its original magic and turned into a drab, utilitarian tool. Buyers flocked to Dell's cheap, beige boxes. Computing back then was all about the programs. Now, computing is all about the programming — the words and sounds and pictures and conversations that pour out of the Internet's cloud and onto our screens. Computing, in other words, has moved back closer to the ideal that Steve Jobs had when he founded Apple. Today, Jobs's ambitions are grander than ever. His overriding goal is to establish his company as the major conduit, and toll collector, between the media cloud and the networked computer.

Jobs doesn't just want to produce glamorous gizmos. He wants to be the impresario of all media. 10

> **READING ACTIVITY 1** **Build Your Vocabulary**

Determine the meanings of the following words from the context of "The PC Officially Died Today." Then check their meanings by looking up the words in a dictionary: cumbersome (1), rapturous (2), multifunctional (3), obsolescence (4), lucrative (5), ferment (5), impresario (8), utilitarian (9), conduit (9).

> **GROUP ACTIVITY 2** **Discuss the Reading**

Discuss the following questions about "The PC Officially Died Today" with your classmates.

1. Why does Carr think that the iPad is superior to the personal computer (PC)?
2. Why does Carr compare the iPad with the PC? Do you agree with his description of the PC?
3. What does Carr mean in paragraph 3 when he writes that "the computer business and the media business are now the same business"?
4. What do you think is Carr's strongest point in support of his evaluation of the iPad? What do you think is his weakest point? Explain your answers.
5. Based on this review, would you suggest that a friend buy an iPad, or would you recommend another electronic device? Why?

> **WRITING ACTIVITY 1** **Share Your Ideas**

In a paragraph or two, evaluate an electronic device that you use, such as a smartphone, a computer, or a video game. Express your opinion about the quality of the device, and explain why you have that opinion. Share what you have written with your classmates.

Evaluation of a Performance

RICHARD CORLISS
Michael Jackson's This Is It Review: He's Still a Thriller

Richard Corliss has been a writer for *Time* magazine since 1980, focusing on show business, sports, and, most notably, movies. As a movie reviewer, he has written cover stories for *Time* and contributed to *Time*'s annual list of the best movies of the year. He has a master's degree in film studies from Columbia University and currently lives in New York City.

    Death and resurrection. That's the scenario not just for gods but for pop stars   1
who earn fans' ardor with an electrifying presence and their sympathy with very

public private lives of addiction and misbehavior. The stars' talent makes them unique; their transgressions make them human. Michael Jackson, who died in June at age 50, outlived Edith Piaf and Judy Garland by three years, and Elvis by eight. (Forget Madonna — that woman is too smart to self-immolate.) Jackson's bizarre resculpting of his features, his litigious shenanigans with his youngest admirers, his obsession with being an eternal preadolescent, a petrified Peter Pan: all these eccentricities gave him an otherworldly cast. It took death to restore his standing as a one-of-a-kind entertainer — to bring him back to life.

Jackson is hot again. His old albums — now sacred relics, for which the faithful 2 did not pay so much as tithe — sold better after his death this summer than they had in this millennium. A poll of visitors to the Fandango website showed that the No. 1 movie costume for this weekend's Halloween revelers would be Michael Jackson. The singer, whose worldwide success was built on CDs and concerts, not movies, became his own fictional character. And like the runners-up — Wolverine from the *X-Men* films and the *Twilight* series' Edward — Jackson is a hero from the dark side.

But full redemption, not to mention true resurrection, requires a personal 3 appearance. And on the 125th day he rose from the dead, at least on screen, with *Michael Jackson's This Is It*, a docu-musical record of the star's rehearsals for his comeback London concert series that was to begin in July. Sony, the music and movie conglomerate that has had a decades-long stake in Jackson's economic fortunes, shrouded the project in mystery until its premiere, which was held simultaneously on Tuesday night and Wednesday in 16 cities around the globe. (Sony took over all 13 auditoriums of the Regal E-Walk Theater on New York City's 42nd Street to show the movie to 3,200 invitees.) Many of the venues had a satellite feed from the Nokia Theater in Los Angeles, where director Kenny Ortega, who had also been in charge of the planned concert, greeted surviving Jackson brothers Jermaine, Marlon, Tito and Jackie.

The only pre-premiere insights to the film came from two people who had 4 been close to Jackson. His father Joe told the British tabloid *News of the World*, "This movie features body doubles, no doubt about it." (Given Joe's wrangles with his family and with AEG, the concert's promoters, he may not be an unimpeachable source.) Michael's stalwart buddy Elizabeth Taylor, who attended an early screening last week, effusively tweeted that *This Is It* was "the single most brilliant piece of filmmaking I have ever seen." And she was in *The Sandpiper*.

So what is *This Is It*? A concert film without the concert. A backstage musical 5 that takes place almost entirely onstage. A no-warts hagiography that still gets the audience closer to the real Michael Jackson — MJ the performer, that is — than anything in the man's avidly documented history. Wisely and decently ignoring the circumstances of his death and the circus that followed it, Ortega focuses on the re-creation of about a dozen Jackson standards for the concert. ("Beat It," "Billie Jean," "Wanna Be Startin' Somethin'," "Black and White" and "I'll Be There" are all here.) At times several takes of a song are edited into one performance; you know because Jackson is sporting different rehearsal clothes. The footage was shot so the star could study his work and that of his crew, thus it has the artlessness of visual stenography. The art is in what we're privileged to watch: a perfectionist who quietly pushes himself to prove he's still got it.

The movie is worlds removed from another making-of concert doc, Madonna's calculatedly scandalous *Truth or Dare*, and closer to old let's-put-on-a-show musicals like the Busby Berkeley *42nd Street*, the Judy Garland–Mickey Rooney *Babes in Arms* and the Broadway standard *A Chorus Line*. It has all the elements: the big star (Jackson), the guiding impresario (Ortega) and, supporting them, a whole retinue of gifted, ambitious singers and dancers. The movie opens with the prospective dancers' declarations of the inspirational impact that Jackson has had on them. (O.K., they really need this job, but the effusions sound genuine.) Later, the men have to rehearse one of Jackson's more notorious dance figures. Apparently, grabbing your crotch while gliding across the stage is more difficult than it looks.   6

There are only two differences between *This* and the old musicals. Instead of the star breaking a leg, he dies after we see the fruit of his labors. And in *This Is It* the emphasis is not on love affairs — though Jackson proclaims a tender "I love you" to everyone in sight — but on the energizing, exhausting business of making a spectacle spectacular.   7

Ortega and Jackson had some Berkeley-size production numbers in mind. A version of "Smooth Criminal" interpolates Jackson into antique movie clips with Rita Hayworth, Humphrey Bogart and Edward G. Robinson. "They Don't Care About Us" sends 1,100 CGI soldiers marching down a kind of Champs-Elysées whose Arc de Triomphe is bent into an M for Michael. "Thriller" was to boast 3-D effects. And "Earth Song," the rain-forest-message number, has a dewy child (a girl, if you're wondering) facing down a bulldozer, which was then to motor toward the front of the stage, ready to devour the star. "Save Michael," he seemed to be saying, and save the planet.   8

But the coolest moments show Jackson unadorned and unplugged. He sings "Human Nature" nearly a cappella, blending vocal virtuosity and a choirboy's clarity; there's nothing false about his falsetto. His Terpsichore leads viewers through how-the-hell-does-he-do-that? astonishment into a mute appreciation of Jackson's ability to channel Fred Astaire's nonchalant elegance and fit it to the percussive drive of R&B. He gives dancing class *and* sex.   9

Jackson also plays well with others. There's a splendid duet with Judith Hill on "I Just Can't Stop Loving You" that's both a call-and-response act of communion and a little contest over who can show more soul. He urges his lead guitarist, the petite, blond Orianthi Panagaris, to release all the wildness her fingers can express. He's determined to get the best from everyone, and to think the best of them. Near the end, just before a powerful rendition of "Man in the Mirror," he thanks members of his family: "Jackie, Jermaine, Marlon, Tito, Randy…" Then, remembering his mother, he adds, "I should also say Katherine. I love you." He's got a lot of love he needs to express.   10

No question that Jackson, deeply in debt to Sony and other creditors, needed the money that the concerts would generate. But his heroic effort and attention to detail suggest that this was no take-the-money-and-run greatest-hits scam. He   11 saw *This Is It* as a career retrospective that would re-establish the value of his music and prove he still had the strength and the moves of 20, 30, 40 years ago. At times he tries to husband his resources: stinting on the vocalizing of one song, he apologizes, "I'm just trying to save my voice." Then the beat or the melody gets to him, and he helplessly transforms into the full-throttle kid.

For a modern entertainer who dies before his time, immortality is measured   12 in residuals — the money from commemorative projects like this. Michael Jackson will have no resurrection — in the end, that was that — but the movie does earn him a redemptive legacy. It proves that, at the end, he was still a thriller. Fans and doubters alike can look at the gentle, driven singer-dancer at the center of this up-close document and say admiringly, This was him.

READING ACTIVITY 2 Build Your Vocabulary

Determine the meanings of the following words from the context of Richard Corliss's movie review. Then check their meanings by looking up the words in a dictionary: transgressions (1), litigious (1), relics (2), redemption (3), hagiography (5), stenography (5), interpolates (8), a cappella (9), Terpsichore (9), retrospective (11).

GROUP ACTIVITY 3 Discuss the Reading

Discuss the following questions about "*Michael Jackson's This Is It* Review: He's Still a Thriller" with your classmates.

1. What is Corliss's opinion about *Michael Jackson's This Is It*? Identify the sentence or sentences where this opinion is best expressed.
2. Why does Corliss have this opinion about the movie? On what does he base his judgment?
3. Why does Corliss compare this movie to musicals made by other artists (such as Madonna)? How does this comparison help support his opinion?
4. In your view, where in the review does Corliss best support his point? Explain your answer.
5. Does this review make you want to see *Michael Jackson's This Is It*? Why or why not?

WRITING ACTIVITY 2 Share Your Ideas

Write a paragraph or two about one of your favorite movies, explaining why it is one of your favorites. On what do you base your opinion? Exchange your writing with your classmates, and compare the different movies that you each wrote about.

Evaluation of a Place

NICOLAI OUROUSSOFF

Two New Baseball Palaces, One Stoic, One Scrappy

As the architecture critic for the *New York Times,* Nicolai Ouroussoff writes about buildings all over the world. He originally wanted to be an architect himself, but when he realized how long it took for a building to actually be built, he decided to write about architecture instead. Ouroussoff has been nominated for the Pulitzer Prize—journalism's highest honor—three times. He has a bachelor's degree in Russian from Georgetown University and a master's degree from the Graduate School of Architecture at Columbia University. The following piece was published in the *New York Times* in 2009.

1   American stadium design has been stuck in a nostalgic funk, with sports franchises recycling the same old images year after year. Still, if you have to go with a retro look, New York City could have done worse than the new Yankee Stadium and Citi Field. Both were designed by Populous (formerly known as HOK Sport Venue Event) and are major upgrades over the stadiums they replaced, which had been looking more and more dilapidated over the years. Both should be fine places to spend a few hours watching a game.

2   What's more, each stadium subtly reflects the character of the franchises that built them. Yankee Stadium is the kind of stoic, self-conscious monument to history that befits the most successful franchise in American sports. The new home of the Mets, meanwhile, is scrappier and more lighthearted. It plays with history fast and loose, as if it were just another form of entertainment.

3   Yankee management started talking about replacing the old stadium more than a decade ago, and this seemed to be the tougher challenge: the stadium sparkled with the memories of 26 World Series championships. Architecturally, however, the stadium was charmless. Renovation in the 1970s may have made it more comfortable (fans loathed the painful wooden seats of the original version), but it also destroyed many architectural features. The original copper frieze that lined the stadium's upper deck was ripped out. (A partial concrete replica was added later.) The monuments that had once stood in the deepest recesses of center field were moved to an insipid space behind the left-center field fence and named Monument Park. The little personality the stadium had came from its site: a tight urban lot framed by elevated subway tracks on one side and a city park on the other.

4   The new stadium, which stands across the street from the old one, spruces up that image while reviving some of the lost history. The towering arched windows that dominated the original exterior, an echo of the Roman Colosseum, have been recast in a mix of limestone, granite and cast stone, and they are as imposing as ever. A small urban plaza, raised just above the level of the sidewalk, faces the bars

and souvenir shops along River Avenue and the entry to the elevated train, strengthening the structure's relationship to its urban setting.

The city has also promised to build a park and several ball fields just to the 5 south of the stadium in an effort to put a more community-friendly face on the project. A broad pedestrian walkway will eventually link the stadium to the fields and a Metro-North station farther to the south.

The biggest improvements, however, are the interiors, which have been orga- 6 nized with an eye to the fans. The concourses are broad open spaces, with concession stands set along the perimeter so that they don't obstruct views down to the field. More seats are concentrated below the mezzanine level, closer to the action. Even the luxury suites, which suddenly look like a holdover from the era of corporate excess, are discreetly set back so that they don't detract from the shared intimacy of watching the game.

There's history here, too, or at least a facsimile of it. The Yankees have brought 7 back the old manually operated scoreboards in left and right field, a feature that was last used in the 1960s. A replica of the old frieze sits along the top of the upper deck. Best of all, the slot that separated the scoreboard from the right-field stands in the old stadium has been re-created, so you can still catch glimpses of the subway rumbling by — a reminder that the stadium has been carved out of the heart of a living, thriving city.

All in all, the new Yankee Stadium may be an austere, even intimidating 8 place, but there's nothing tacky about it. It's straightforward, paint-by-numbers architecture.

Getting to Citi Field is a more drawn-out aesthetic experience. Descending 9 from the elevated 7 train in Queens, you have to cross a wide landscaped plaza before arriving at the main entry gate. A sea of parking stretches out in both directions. A pile of rubble (once the old Shea Stadium) currently lies just beyond the parking to the left. The building fits comfortably in this setting. Yankee Stadium's facade is dominated by vertical lines, which emphasize its monumentality. Citi Field's facade, which is loosely modeled on Ebbets Field, the former home of the Brooklyn Dodgers, is more low-key. Its brick cladding gives it a warmth that Yankee Stadium doesn't have. A pre-cast concrete band cuts across the arched exterior, breaking down the structure's scale and emphasizing its horizontality.

History also feels less heavy here. Like the Yankees, the Mets built broad 10 concourses that open up to the field so that you feel close to the game even while you're standing in line for a beer. But the design is far more eclectic. A porch that cantilevers out over right field is modeled on the old Tiger Stadium. Big steel trusses conjure the structure that supports the nearby elevated train. A soot-colored pedestrian bridge that spans the bullpen behind center field is a miniature version of the Hell Gate Bridge. Even the color of the seats — dark green — was copied from somewhere else: the Polo Grounds, where the New York Giants baseball team played and the Mets played their first two seasons. The casual mood is reinforced by a number of spaces that have little to do with watching a baseball game: an auditorium, a Wiffle ball field — even an event room for weddings or parties.

What saves the design from becoming completely hokey, however, is its 11
openness to the real world outside. Most of Queens, from the faded remnants of
the 1964 World's Fair to the Whitestone Expressway and the muddy waters of
Flushing Bay, is visible from the main concourse level. Farther up, you can see the
Manhattan skyline several miles away. The visitors' bullpen has a view of dilapidated garages and auto body shops across 126th Street to the northeast. The reality of this working-class landscape tempers the artificiality of the interior.

Even so, most serious architects today strive to create buildings that reflect the 12
values of their own era, not a nostalgic vision of the past, no matter how open they
may be toward their surroundings. And in that regard both stadiums will be a disappointment to students of architecture. For us, the buildings are just another reminder of the enormous gap that remains between high design and popular taste.

READING ACTIVITY 3 Build Your Vocabulary

Determine the meanings of the following words from the context of Nicolai
Ouroussoff's review. Then check their meanings by looking up the words in a dictionary:
dilapidated (1), franchises (2), stoic (2), scrappier (2), frieze (3), concourses (6), facsimile
(7), austere (8), aesthetic (9), eclectic (10).

GROUP ACTIVITY 4 Discuss the Reading

Discuss the following questions about "Two New Baseball Palaces, One Stoic, One
Scrappy" with your classmates.

1. What is Ouroussoff's overall view of these two stadiums? Where in the essay is
   this view best expressed?

2. What features or characteristics lead to an effective design for a stadium,
   according to the author?

3. Compare the basic features of Yankee Stadium and Citi Field. How are they
   different? How do these differences reflect the histories of the Yankees and the
   Mets baseball teams?

4. In what ways, according to the author, do both stadiums reflect the "living,
   thriving" city of New York?

5. Does "Two New Baseball Palaces, One Stoic, One Scrappy" make you want to visit
   these stadiums? Explain your answer.

WRITING ACTIVITY 3 Share Your Ideas

Write a paragraph or two about a sporting venue or another place you're familiar with,
such as a soccer field, an ice skating arena, a park, or a shopping mall. What are the good
and bad features of this place? How attractive is it? How suitable is the place for the
people who go there and use it? How could it be improved? Exchange your writing with
your classmates, and compare your ideas.

Writing Your Essay   A Step-by-Step Guide

Now that you've read some essays evaluating a product, performance, or place, it's time to write your own essay. First, read the following writing assignment. Then, use the step-by-step advice that follows to discover ideas, develop them as you draft, and polish your writing into a finished essay that readers will find both interesting and persuasive:

Writing Assignment

You make judgments and share your opinions all the time. For example, you may have complained to a friend that your expensive new athletic shoes don't provide enough arch support, argued with a co-worker about the results of *Top Chef*, or tried to persuade your family that Disney World would be a good vacation spot. Your task in this chapter is to share your opinion with a wider audience by writing an essay that evaluates something you feel strongly about. You (or your instructor) may decide to approach this assignment in one of several ways:

■ Evaluate a product you are familiar with.

OR

■ Evaluate a performance you have seen.

OR

■ Evaluate a place you have been to.

Step 1   Explore Your Choices

You can write an evaluation essay about almost anything that you have an opinion about, from topics as narrow as the latest smartphone or whole-grain snack to those as broad as the full run of a television series or the bus system in your city. So how should you begin? The first two things to consider are who might read your essay and why you're writing it for them. Even more so than other kinds of writing, reviews are written to inform and persuade people who are curious about a particular subject. As you gather ideas for possible topics, choose something that you have personal experience with, that you have a strong opinion about, and that others are interested in.

Analyzing Your Audience and Purpose

Your audience will include people who have sought opinions about the product, performance, or place you'll be writing about because they are directly affected by it. Your readers might include consumers deciding whether they should purchase a product or employees of the company that makes the product. They might include people who are considering a play, movie, or television show as well as those who have already seen it. Or they might include people interested in visiting a shopping mall, museum, or tourist attraction and possibly some of the managers or tour guides who are responsible for that site. Whatever your topic, your readers probably know something about it, but they are seeking other people's opinions to help themselves form a judgment or make improvements.

For more on audience and purpose, see pp. 7–11.

Knowing who your audience is will help you identify your purpose. What do you want your readers to do as a result of reading your essay? Do you want to encourage or discourage them from purchasing, watching, or visiting something? If your readers are in some way responsible for your subject, do you want to persuade them to change something about it?

 Use online surveys

To find out more about your audience, use an online survey tool. Create survey questions about readers' values, interests, and backgrounds, and send the survey to your potential readers. Use the survey responses to make your essay appealing to your audience.

 WRITING ACTIVITY 4 Analyze Your Audience and Purpose

Your responses to the following questions will help you select possible topics for your evaluation. Be sure to come back to these questions after you have chosen a topic to write about.

1. Does this assignment call for primarily expressive, informative, or persuasive writing?

2. Are you writing for an audience of consumers or for the people who make or manage something?

3. Have you recently purchased any consumer products that your audience might be interested in reading about?

4. What movies, television shows, music groups, or books might your readers be curious about?

5. What places — restaurants, shopping malls, museums, amusement parks — have you visited recently? Why would readers be interested in them?

6. How interested will your readers be in an essay that evaluates a product, performance, or place? How can you make sure you keep your readers' interest as they read your essay?

Gathering Ideas

For more on gathering ideas, see pp. 11–16.

Before you settle on a product, performance, or place to evaluate, explore your choices by gathering ideas for at least one subject in each of these three categories. Even if you already have a specific subject in mind for your essay, you may be surprised by where your explorations lead you.

To gather ideas for your evaluation, you may use any of the techniques you learned in Chapter 1 and applied in previous assignments. The student writers in this chapter will use brainstorming, asking questions, and freewriting.

Brainstorming about a Product

As a consumer, you evaluate products before purchasing them. If the product is inexpensive, such as a can of soup, your preliminary evaluation might be as simple as reading the label. If the product is a major purchase, such as an electronic device or a car, you might consult friends, check the reviews on a Web site like edmunds.com or epinions.com, read a magazine such as *Consumer Reports*, and comparison shop. Even after you purchase the product, you probably continue to evaluate it to confirm that you made a good choice.

To identify a product worth evaluating in your essay, try brainstorming a list of items you use every day or have recently purchased. Include the electronic device you wrote about after reading "The PC Officially Died Today." Don't worry yet about whether any of these items would make a good essay topic. Just write down as many products as you can think of.

Student writer Ellie, for example, brainstormed the following list of products by looking around her apartment:

Ramen noodles	foam pillow
Mary Kay hand-smoothing system	iPhone
coffeemaker	running shoes
school newspaper	fake butter spray
scanner/printer/fax machine	Red Bull
new laptop	digital photo frame
dead laptop	tennis racquet
George Foreman grill	

Once you have a list of products in hand, check off the items you have strong feelings about. Think of your audience as people who are interested in purchasing the product. Your evaluation will affect their decision to purchase (or not to purchase) the item. Select one product, and brainstorm a list of what you like and don't like about it. If you want to continue writing about an electronic device, refer to the paragraphs you completed after "The PC Officially Died Today." Student writer Ellie, for example, reviewed her list and realized that she had been telling friends how much she loved her new coffeemaker, which she received as a gift. Here is her brainstorming on the Cuisinart Automatic Grind and Brew:

I love this thing!

wanted it for ages

expensive: $69

couldn't bring myself to spend the money on it

has the coffee grinder built right in

and a timer

fresh ground coffee tastes so much better

grinder makes a lot of noise

scares the cat every time

wakes me up better than my alarm clock

automatic shut-off

can't figure out how to measure the beans for less than a full pot

a lot of parts

have to dismantle the pieces and wash them by hand every day

sometimes the parts jam from the wet coffee grounds

if you don't close the basket right, coffee pours all over the counter

more maintenance than my old coffeemaker

it's worth it

a luxury, but I don't think I could do without it now

WRITING ACTIVITY 5 Brainstorm about a Product

Brainstorm a list of products that you use every day or have recently obtained. Select one item from your list, and brainstorm again, this time writing down what you like and don't like about the product. You may brainstorm about as many products as you like, but focus on one at a time.

Asking Questions about a Performance

Put aside your writing about a product for now so that you can gather ideas for another type of evaluation—a performance.

As you probably know, newspapers, magazines, and Web sites carry reviews of all sorts of performances, including movies, concerts, art shows, dance performances, television programs, and sporting events. Readers often rely on these reviews to help them decide whether a performance is worth seeing or not. Before investing your hard-earned money in a movie ticket, for example, you may decide to read a few reviews at rottentomatoes.com or the Internet Movie Database (imdb.com). If the reviews are positive, you're more likely to see the film.

Because many professional critics are trained as reporters, they often use the journalist's questions as a starting point to gather ideas for their reviews:

- *Who* is (or was) involved in this performance? Include relevant producers, directors, and talent (such as actors, singers, dancers, and announcers).
- *What* is the show about?
- *Where* is (or was) the performance held or broadcast?
- *When* is (or was) the show performed or broadcast?
- *How* effective is (or was) the show?
- *Why* is (or was) this performance worth seeing or not worth seeing?

By using these questions as prompts, critics can be sure that their essays cover the basics that readers expect to find in a review. The questions also help writers gather details to explain what they liked or didn't like about a performance.

Here's how one student, Rob, used the journalist's questions to gather ideas about the cable television program *Mythbusters*. Here's a sample:

<u>Who</u> is involved?	Peter Rees, producer (Australian documentary filmmaker)
	Adam Savage, cohost (artist and model builder)
	Jamie Hyneman, cohost (Hollywood special-effects expert with a degree in Russian literature)
	Buster, subject of experiments (crash test dummy)
	Kari Byron, experimenter (sculptor, painter, actor)
	Grant Imahara, experimenter (electronics expert)
	Tory Belleci, experimenter (model builder)
	Scottie Chapman, experimenter (welder)
<u>What</u> is it about?	Cast members conduct science experiments to see if urban legends are true.
<u>Where</u> is it?	Discovery Channel
<u>When</u> is it?	Wednesdays at 9:00 p.m.
<u>How</u> effective is it?	I like that they use real science to bust the myths. The tests are really involved and over the top.

Lots of surprises: sometimes the urban legends are actually true! The experiments are creative and always very thorough, but sometimes they get carried away with themselves and forget the point. They'll redo an experiment if viewers write in and question their methods.

<u>Why</u> is it worth seeing?   Generally very informative, always entertaining. They manage to make science cool.

> **WRITING ACTIVITY 6** Ask Questions about a Performance

Select a performance that you might want to evaluate. The performance may be live (such as a concert, comedy show, sporting event, dance performance, or play) or recorded (such as a movie or television show). You may choose a past performance that you remember well or select a current performance and attend it in person. You could select the movie that you wrote about after reading "*Michael Jackson's This Is It* Review: He's Still a Thriller" if this topic still interests you. Answer each of the reporter's questions — *who, what, where, when, how, why* — about the performance to gather ideas for an evaluation essay.

Freewriting about a Place

Put aside your ideas about a performance for now so that you can gather ideas for one more type of evaluation.

A new shopping mall opens near your town, and you spend an afternoon visiting the stores, examining the layout, and sampling products from the food court. Afterward, you decide that you like the mall but wish it had a parking garage: you have just evaluated a place.

Other places you might evaluate include a museum, park, college or office building, classroom, theater, store, library, restaurant, or city. Almost any place you've been to and that other people might want to visit can be a good candidate for an evaluation essay.

Although a quick judgment of a place can be useful, a formal evaluation needs plenty of details to be convincing and useful for readers. To gather information to support a full essay that evaluates a place, consider freewriting (the practice of writing nonstop about a topic without trying to decide if your ideas are any good). Tell yourself that you will write for a certain amount of time or a certain number of pages, and keep writing. Don't pause to think, don't make corrections, and don't try to organize your thoughts. If you get stuck, write something like "I don't have anything to say" or "stuck! stuck! stuck!" until a new thought comes to you. Just keep writing, and see what you have to say.

Student writer Paul LaPrade decided to write about an art exhibit he had visited for his Introduction to Art class. Here is part of his freewriting:

Right at the entrance is a huge collection of portraits. The faces are blurred — I wonder what this means. "The Disappeared." I guess it means people who disappeared in Latin America because they were murdered by their governments. This series includes some interesting interrogation scenes. Huddled detainees. Surprising this happened so recently, and in Latin America. I didn't know what had happened. Hard to understand what some of these photos mean. There's no explanation. These family pictures seem so real. They make you see how awful it was. Why isn't there a fuller explanation of what these governments did somewhere?

WRITING ACTIVITY 7 Freewrite about a Place

Choose a place that is important to you and that others might want to know about, such as a new restaurant close to campus or an entertainment park that recently opened. You can also continue to write about the sports venue or other place you wrote about after reading "Two New Baseball Palaces, One Stoic, One Scrappy." Freewrite about this place for at least ten minutes. Follow your ideas without pausing, and do not stop, go back, or try to correct your writing. Just write.

Step 2 Write Your Discovery Draft

For more on drafting, see pp. 16–20.

At this point, you have explored at least three possible topics for your evaluation essay. It's time to choose a topic and prepare a rough draft.

Don't be concerned if you're not sure how you're going to evaluate a product, performance, or place. The purpose of writing a discovery draft is to discover what you have to say. For now, you'll focus on organizing what you already know and try to put it into words. As you draft, keep in mind that anything you write at this stage can (and should) be revised later.

Choosing a Topic

Now that you have gathered ideas for three different subjects you might evaluate, it's time to decide how you want to proceed.

When you choose a topic for an evaluation essay, it's crucial to remember your audience and your purpose. Gather your notes from brainstorming, asking questions, and freewriting, and look again at your responses to the writing activities earlier in this chapter. Review as well the writing you completed after reading the three professional essays that start this chapter. Of the topics you have considered for your essay, which one do you feel most strongly about? Even more important, which one would be most interesting and informative for your readers? After all, you don't want to put a lot of effort into evaluating something that nobody else cares about.

Because you will write a persuasive essay in which you make an evaluation, be sure to select a subject you feel confident about judging. As you contemplate your choices, remember that you may combine closely related topics and may gather additional ideas on any topic that interests you. For example, in reviewing your paragraphs about the movie you wrote about after the Michael Jackson review, you might realize that you had a strong positive reaction to the new stadium-style seating at the local multiplex. If you decide to evaluate the theater rather than the movie, you could use brainstorming, asking questions, or freewriting (or any other methods that work for you) to explore your thoughts.

WRITING ACTIVITY 8 Choose Your Topic

Review your responses to Writing Activities 5 to 7, and decide which of the topics you explored (a product, performance, or place) would be most useful to your readers. Be careful to select a topic you can judge. If you're not confident that you can turn any of your working ideas into a well-supported evaluation, use your favorite techniques to gather ideas on additional topic possibilities until you find one that will interest both you and your readers.

Sharing Your Ideas

Before you begin writing your discovery draft, narrow your topic and write a preliminary thesis statement that identifies your subject and expresses your judgment of it. You can always change your thesis later, but starting with a judgment in mind will help you focus and stay on track.

For more on narrowing your topic, see pp. 16–18.

As you write your draft, keep in mind that most readers expect an evaluation essay to address the following questions:

- What experiences have you had with the product, performance, or place you are writing about?
- What is your overall opinion of this product, performance, or place?
- Why do you have this opinion?
- What is good about your subject?
- What is bad about your subject?
- Compare your subject with other similar subjects: How is it better? How is it worse?

⏻ Use online rating systems

To get others' thoughts on your subject, refer to social media sites where people can post ratings such as "likes" or "+1." Many commercial sites (such as Amazon.com, Rotten Tomatoes, or Trip Advisor) allow customers and viewers to rate products, performances, and places.

Answering each of these questions in order is one way to create your draft, but don't hesitate to follow your train of thought as you write—even if it means revising your thesis statement later on. Keep your audience and purpose in mind, and remember that your main goal at the drafting stage is to get your ideas down on paper. You'll have time later to revise and edit your discovery draft.

A Student's Discovery Draft

Here's the discovery draft written by student writer Paul LaPrade, whose freewriting you read earlier. In this draft, Paul evaluates an art exhibit at his university. After reading the draft, discuss with your classmates what Paul might do to revise it. (Note that the example includes the types of errors that typically appear in a first draft.)

The Disappeared

The Rubin Art Gallery's current exhibit *The Disappeared* depicts the tragedy that occurred in Latin America in the last decades of the twentieth century, when military dictators in countries such as Argentina, Chile, and Guatemala kidnapped and killed thousands of people who resisted their dictatorships. The different types of art are prints, photos, video installations, and three-dimensional installations. The methods of expression here range from realistic documentation to symbolism, there are several works that fit into each of these categories. This display offers various artists' interpretations of these tragic events.

The first collection, "In Memoriam," by Antonio Frasconi, consists of forty-eight prints that personalize the tragic situation. These prints show victims of violence, their faces surrounded by dark colors as if they are vanishing in front of our eyes. "The Disappeared," also by Frasconi, consists of woodblock prints. The woodblock prints show people with bags over their heads, huddled as if they were in concentration camps.

Marcelo Brodsky's "Good Memory" is a large display of forty-three photographs and two videos. It includes a grade school portrait that shows his class with personal notes written beside the children. A video installation shows a school reunion in which ninety-eight missing class members are remembered in roll call.

The most moving and effective part of this exhibit is a series of photographs by Marcelo Brodsky. These photographs deal with his personal and family history. Pictures of Marcelo with his younger brother Fernando show happy family scenes. The two boys having fun on a boat or playing with bows and arrows and falling down and playing dead. Then photos of Fernando are shown in which he looks skinny and worn down. A caption says that Fernando was killed in a concentration camp.

On the whole, this exhibit very effectively represents the killings that have occured in South America over decades. Artists express this reality in various styles and mediums, including prints, sculpture, and photography. Its hard to forget what happened to these people.

> **WRITING ACTIVITY 9** Write Your Discovery Draft

Using your preliminary thesis statement and the questions on page 213 as a guide, write a discovery draft that evaluates a product, performance, or place. For now, focus on getting your ideas in writing; you'll have a chance to clarify and support your ideas when you revise. If you're not sure that the topic you've selected is a good one, remember that you may write separate drafts on two or three other topics to see which one gives you the best results.

Step 3 Revise Your Draft

Most writers find that the discovery draft of an evaluation needs additional information to make it interesting and informative.

Because reviews attempt to persuade readers, you'll also need to make sure that your ideas are clearly stated and well supported—from your audience's point of view.

How will you develop your ideas so that you communicate effectively with your readers? Start by applying the skills you acquired in earlier chapters: organize your paragraphs (Chapter 2), strengthen your focus (Chapter 4), outline your ideas (Chapter 6), and write an effective introduction and conclusion (Chapter 5). As you build your essay, you will learn how to use comparison and contrast to help your readers understand your points. You will then focus on expressing your judgment clearly while explaining your criteria, providing convincing evidence, and keeping a balanced perspective.

For more on revising, see pp. 20–22.

Developing Your Ideas with Comparison and Contrast

One good way to support an evaluation is to compare and contrast your subject with other subjects. Your audience may not know very much about the product, performance, or place that you are reviewing, but they probably have some knowledge of similar products, performances, or places. By relating what your readers know to what they don't know, you can support your judgment while helping your readers better understand your subject.

For more on comparison and contrast, see pp. 66–67.

When you compare two things, you point out similarities; when you contrast two things, you focus on differences. Comparison and contrast can be combined, as in this example from "*Michael Jackson's This Is It* Review: He's Still a Thriller":

> The movie is worlds removed from another making-of concert doc, Madonna's calculatedly scandalous *Truth or Dare*, and closer to old let's-put-on-a-show musicals like the Busby Berkeley *42nd Street*, the Judy Garland–Mickey Rooney *Babes in Arms* and the Broadway standard *A Chorus Line*.

You can also focus more on just similarities or just differences. Notice how Nicolai Ouroussoff contrasts the new Yankee Stadium with the new Citi Field:

> What's more, each stadium subtly reflects the character of the franchises that built them. Yankee Stadium is the kind of stoic, self-conscious monument to history that befits the most successful franchise in American sports. The new home of the Mets, meanwhile, is scrappier and more lighthearted. It plays with history fast and loose, as if it were just another form of entertainment.

When making comparisons, be sure that you focus on similar subjects and that you explain the basis of your comparison. In the previous example, Nicolai Ouroussoff compares the way that both stadiums reflect the teams that built them. If you were evaluating the new campus recreation center, you would not compare it to the college library (unless you are comparing the architecture of the buildings). Instead, you might contrast the new center with the old center to highlight the improvements that have been made. Once you have established the points of your comparison, provide several detailed examples to support each of those points, as Ouroussoff does later in his piece.

■ HOW TO Use Comparison and Contrast

- Use comparison to explain similarities, and use contrast to explain differences.
- Decide on what basis you will compare and contrast. For instance, you can compare and contrast energy drinks on the basis of ingredients, flavor, and effectiveness.
- Support the comparison and contrast with examples.

WRITING ACTIVITY 10 Draft Comparisons for Your Essay

For your topic, list several similar subjects. (If you're evaluating a product, list similar products; if your topic is a performance, list similar performances; if your essay is about a place, list similar places.) Choose one of these subjects, and write one or two paragraphs that compare or contrast it with the subject of your essay. Remember that the point of using comparison and contrast is to support your judgment and to help your readers understand your subject better.

Building Your Essay

When you revise an evaluation essay, you need to make sure that you have stated your opinion clearly and have provided enough information to persuade your readers that your opinion is reasonable. To do this, you'll first revise your thesis statement to ensure that it expresses a judgment. Next, make sure that readers understand the reasons for your opinion, and double-check that you have included enough evidence to support your points. Finally, reexamine your evaluation from your readers' perspective to ensure that your audience will accept your judgment as fair and carefully considered—even if they don't agree with it.

Express Your Judgment

As you may recall, the thesis statement does three things—announces the topic of your essay; shows, explains, or argues a particular point about the topic; and gives readers a sense of what the essay will be about. For an evaluation essay, the thesis statement argues a particular point. Specifically, it expresses your judgment of the product, performance, or place you are reviewing. Let's look in more detail at how to write an effective thesis statement for an evaluation.

For more on thesis statements, see pp. 18–19.

State an Opinion   A judgment is an opinion about the value or merit of something. It's not a fact. Notice the difference between fact and judgment in these statements:

> FACT   The Ford Mustang was among the most popular cars of the 1960s.
>
> JUDGMENT The Ford Mustang was one of the best cars made in the 1960s.

The first statement is factual because it can be verified by statistics about the best-selling cars in the 1960s. The second statement expresses an opinion about the worthiness of the car. Some but not all people will agree with this statement.

Focus on the Subject   A judgment focuses on the subject being evaluated, not on the writer.

> FOCUS ON THE WRITER   I really like the new thirty-minute circuit program at the local health club.
>
> FOCUS ON THE SUBJECT The new thirty-minute circuit program at the local health club is surprisingly effective.

In the first example, the first-person *I* emphasizes the writer. In the second example, the reference to the writer has been removed, shifting readers' focus to the product being evaluated—the new thirty-minute circuit program.

Be Moderate, Not Extreme   A good thesis statement for an evaluation essay gives a sensible opinion about the subject. A sensible opinion is moderate rather than extreme:

> EXTREME   Central College's library is the best library in the state.
>
> MODERATE   Central College's library has the most useful collection of business journals in Essex County.

The extreme statement cannot be proven without visiting every library in the state, whereas the moderate version is much easier to support.

Be Clear and Specific   A good thesis statement for an evaluation essay expresses a judgment that is immediately understandable. If your readers can't understand your thesis statement, they won't understand the rest of your evaluation either. To make your thesis statement clear, use standard written English, and tell readers why you have reached your judgment:

> UNCLEAR   The new Student Union is gross.
>
> CLEAR   The design of the new Student Union is disappointing because of its plain exterior and cold, gray cinderblock interior.

The nonstandard (in this context) *gross* has been replaced with *disappointing*, which is a more precise word. Details that explain the judgment have also been added to help readers understand the writer's opinion about the topic.

▪ HOW TO Write a Thesis Statement for an Evaluation Essay

- State an opinion about the value or merit of something.
- Focus on the subject, not yourself.
- Use a moderate rather than an extreme tone.
- Be clear and specific.

  Exchange thesis statements online

How do you know if your thesis statement expresses an opinion, focuses on the subject, and is moderate, clear, and specific? You can exchange thesis statements face-to-face with several classmates, or you can do this online through e-mail, texts, course management software, or Facebook. Ask your classmates to read and make suggestions for revision based on the criteria for a good thesis statement.

GROUP ACTIVITY 5 Express Judgments

Review the characteristics of a good thesis statement for an evaluation essay. Then, working with your peer response group, determine the problem in each of the following thesis statements. Revise the thesis statements to eliminate the problems.

1. The worst jeans ever made are manufactured by Salisbury, Inc.
2. Julia Roberts is an OK actor.
3. The Super Bowl is seen by millions of people around the world.
4. The National Air and Space Museum is my favorite museum.
5. The Bradley running shoe is one of the newest shoes on the market.

WRITING ACTIVITY 11 Express Your Judgment

Revise the thesis statement for your essay so that it meets the requirements for an evaluation essay. It needs to state an opinion about the value or merit of your subject, focus on the subject, be moderate and not extreme, and be clear and specific.

Give Criteria

To support your thesis statement in an evaluation essay, you must inform your readers of the *criteria*, or standards, on which you based your judgment. For example, in *"Michael Jackson's This Is It* Review: He's Still a Thriller," Richard Corliss uses singing ability as one criterion. According to Corliss, the movie showcases the high quality of Jackson's voice. Remember, you should include enough criteria to inform your readers, your criteria should suit the topic, and if your criteria are not obvious, you should explain them.

Include Enough Criteria An effective evaluation is based on having enough criteria. In most cases, a good evaluation essay will discuss three to five criteria. Judging a subject on the basis of only one or two criteria will usually not be enough to persuade your readers to accept your judgment. Imagine, for instance, if Richard Corliss had evaluated the movie only on the basis of Jackson's singing ability. As readers, we would have been left with unanswered questions about other aspects of the movie, such as how well Jackson dances and how he works with other performers.

Use Suitable Criteria The criteria on which your judgment is based should be suitable for your subject. Nicholas Carr, in "The PC Officially Died Today," does not claim that the iPad is good technology because he likes the colorful covers he can buy for it. Rather, the criteria that Carr uses— ease of use, attractiveness, and suitability for the new computer era—are appropriate because most potential buyers are interested in these features.

Suppose, however, that Carr was writing his review for an audience of elementary school teachers. In this case, the quality of educational apps designed for the iPad would be a suitable criterion. In other words, the criteria that are "suitable" depend on the characteristics or interests of your intended readers.

▪HOW TO Select Criteria

- Fill in the blanks: "I think that _____ is good/bad because _____."
- Identify between three to five reasons for your opinion.
- Review your reasons to make sure they're suitable for the topic and your audience.

Explain Your Criteria   If your readers might not understand your criteria, you'll need to explain them. For example, in an evaluation of a smartphone, you would probably need to explain the importance of a replaceable battery, an expandable storage capacity, and a unified in-box. Similarly, in evaluating a fashion show, you would need to explain why music is essential to the show's success.

Not all criteria require explanation. In evaluating *Michael Jackson's This Is It*, Richard Corliss does not explain why the quality of the music and dancing is an important criterion. Only when you think readers may have questions about a particular criterion should you explain it.

▪HOW TO Explain Criteria

- Will your readers automatically see why your criteria are suitable to your subject? If not, you need to explain the criteria.
- For readers familiar with your subject, include a brief explanation of the criteria (such as, "Jeans need to be comfortable because they're worn frequently").
- For readers unfamiliar with your subject, include a detailed explanation of the criteria (such as, "All the seats in a sports arena should give spectators good visibility. They shouldn't have to sit behind a post that partially obstructs their view").

GROUP ACTIVITY 6 Determine Criteria

Following is a list of subjects and audiences. Working with your classmates, determine the criteria to use for an evaluation essay for each subject and audience. Make sure that you provide enough criteria to evaluate the subject and that the criteria are appropriate for the audience.

EXAMPLE Subject: sports car

Audience: readers of *Consumer Reports*

Criteria: _____ handling, horsepower, style, price _____

1. Subject: grocery store chain

   Audience: readers of *Ladies' Home Journal*

   Criteria: _____

2. Subject: apartment

   Audience: readers of the classified ads in your local newspaper

   Criteria: _____

3. Subject: amusement park

   Audience: readers of *Parents* magazine

   Criteria: _____

4. Subject: the new Student Union at your college

   Audience: readers of the alumni magazine

   Criteria: _____

5. Subject: a television situation comedy

   Audience: potential advertisers

   Criteria: _____

WRITING ACTIVITY 12 Revise the Criteria in Your Essay

Examine the criteria in your discovery draft. Keeping your audience in mind, determine if you have enough criteria and whether your criteria are suitable. Then identify any criteria that need to be explained for your readers. Make any necessary changes, and add any necessary explanations.

Provide Evidence

An evaluation essay consists largely of evidence that supports a judgment. By presenting *evidence*—including examples, facts, and expert testimony—writers explain how a subject measures up to their criteria.

Examples Using *examples* to support your judgment makes your essay more interesting to a reader as well as more convincing. In "The PC Officially Died Today," Nicholas Carr gives examples of types of networked

> ⏻ **Write on two screens**
>
> If you need to gather more evidence to support your judgment, consider creating a new blank document where you can brainstorm ideas. This new screen will give you a fresh space to brainstorm ideas without worrying about how they will fit into your essay draft. After you have your ideas down, you can review them and decide which pieces of evidence will be effective in supporting your judgment.

devices to support his point that the iPad fills an important gap in the computer marketplace:

> There are dozens of netbooks, the diminutive cousins to traditional laptops, from manufacturers like Acer and Asus. There are e-readers like Amazon's Kindle and Barnes & Noble's Nook. There are smartphones like Apple's iPhone and Google's Nexus One. There are gaming consoles like Nintendo's Wii and Microsoft's Xbox. In some ways, personal computing has returned to the ferment of its earliest days, when the market was fragmented among lots of contending companies, operating systems, and technical standards.

Facts   *Facts* are a highly persuasive kind of evidence, primarily because they can be verified by readers. And because facts demonstrate your knowledge of the topic, including them makes readers more likely to trust your judgment. In *"Michael Jackson's This Is It* Review: He's Still a Thriller," Richard Corliss shows that he is an expert on the topic by demonstrating his knowledge of how the movie was released to the public:

> Sony, the music and movie conglomerate that has had a decades-long stake in Jackson's economic fortunes, shrouded the project in mystery until its premiere, which was held simultaneously on Tuesday night and Wednesday in 16 cities around the globe. (Sony took over all 13 auditoriums of the Regal E-Walk Theater on New York City's 42nd Street to show the movie to 3,200 invitees.) Many of the venues had a satellite feed from the Nokia Theater in Los Angeles, where director Kenny Ortega, who had also been in charge of the planned concert, greeted surviving Jackson brothers Jermaine, Marlon, Tito and Jackie.

Expert Testimony   *Expert testimony*—the opinion of people knowledgeable about a subject—can be used as evidence to confirm the significance of a topic or to support a writer's own judgment. In "The PC Officially Died Today," Nicholas Carr uses expert testimony when he describes Steve Jobs, the creator of Apple computers, unveiling the iPad to an audience of reporters and consumers. Because Jobs was such a significant figure in the development of digital technology, his presence lends importance to the topic of the iPad. Richard Corliss, in his review of *Michael Jackson's This Is It*, uses expert testimony when he refers to the opinions of people who have already seen the movie. Nicolai Ouroussoff, in his evaluation of Yankee Stadium and Citi Field, uses expert testimony for a different purpose: to contrast the way that architects and the general public view public buildings:

> Even so, most serious architects today strive to create buildings that reflect the values of their own era, not a nostalgic vision of the past, no matter how open they may be toward their surroundings. And in that regard both stadiums will be a disappointment to students of architecture. For us, the buildings are just another reminder of the enormous gap that remains between high design and popular taste.

As you revise your evaluation essay, consider looking for expert testimony that can help back up your judgment of a subject. In evaluating a product, you might refer to *Consumer Reports'* rating of the product. In evaluating a performance or a place, you could check a magazine or newspaper to see whether your subject has been evaluated by others. Awards can be considered a form of expert testimony because they're given by experts in a particular field. If a movie wins an Academy Award for best director, for example, it means that a team of successful movie directors thought highly of the film's director.

Be sure that your evidence is closely connected to your criteria. To help visualize this connection, create a chart with two columns. In the left column, list the criteria that you will use to make your judgment. In the right column, list the evidence that supports each criterion. Before revising your essay, review your chart to make sure you have enough evidence to support your judgment.

■ HOW TO Generate Evidence

- List examples that support your criteria.
- Identify facts that support your criteria by observing the subject carefully.
- Refer to expert testimony. Look in a library database and on the Internet for articles on the subject you're evaluating.

WRITING ACTIVITY 13 Provide Evidence for Your Judgment

Examine the evidence you used in your discovery draft. Is your judgment supported by sufficient examples, facts, and expert testimony? Where can you include additional evidence to support your criteria and make your points more convincing? Add evidence where needed.

Keep a Balanced Perspective

Readers know that few subjects are all good or all bad. Acknowledging both the negative and the positive aspects of your subject shows readers that your judgment is fair, reasonable, and believable.

You may recall from the evaluation of the iPad that Nicholas Carr describes these drawbacks to the iPad:

> The iPad is by no means a sure bet. It still, after all, is a tablet—fairly big and fairly heavy. Unlike an iPod or an iPhone, you can't stick an iPad in your pocket or pocketbook. It also looks to be a cumbersome device. The iPad would be ideal for a three-handed person—two hands to hold it and another to manipulate its touchscreen—but most humans, alas, have only a pair of hands. And with a price that starts at $500 and rises to more than $800, the iPad is considerably more expensive than the Kindles and netbooks it will compete with.

By sharing this information with readers, Carr maintains a balanced perspective and thereby strengthens the believability of his positive evaluation of the iPad.

You don't have to give equal space in an evaluation essay to the strengths and weaknesses of your subject. If your judgment about the subject is positive, briefly describe the negative aspects, as Carr does in his piece. If your judgment about the subject is negative, briefly describe the positive aspects.

Student writer Paul LaPrade, for example, decided to add a paragraph about what he didn't like about *The Disappeared* exhibit to balance his praise:

> While this exhibit is shocking and moving, it is also confusing because there is so little information given about the political situation in Latin America. This political situation led to these mass murders. Most people haven't kept track of all of the dictators that were in charge of Latin American countries in the 1970s and 1980s. This lack of information distracted me from the exhibits and kept me from totally appreciating them.

WRITING ACTIVITY 14   Chart Aspects of Your Subject

Gather ideas about the positive and negative aspects of your subject in a two-column chart. Label the columns "Positive Aspects" and "Negative Aspects." Then list the positive and negative features of your subject. Number the items in each column in the order that you plan to use them in your essay. As you revise your draft, use this chart to maintain a balanced perspective in your evaluation essay.

A Student's Revised Draft

After charting his criteria and evidence, student writer Paul LaPrade decided that he needed to give more details to help his readers understand why *The Disappeared* was such a moving exhibit. Before you read Paul's revised draft, reread his discovery draft (pp. 214–15). Notice, in particular, how Paul has expressed his judgment more explicitly, explained his criteria, and added evidence and comparison to improve his evaluation. (You will also notice some errors in the revised draft; these will be corrected when Paul edits his essay.)

The Disappeared

Most people, when they think of art, picture beautiful paintings of landscapes or portraits of important people. However, art can also be a way for people to record tragic events. Such is the case for the current exhibit at the Rubin Art Gallery, *The Disappeared*. This exhibit depicts the tragedy that occurred in Latin America in the last decades of the twentieth century, when military dictators in countries such as Argentina, Chile, and Guatemala kidnapped and killed thousands of people who resisted their dictatorships. The different types of art are prints, photos, video installations, and three-dimensional installations. The methods of expression here range from realistic documentation to symbolism, there are several works that fit into each of these categories. On the whole, this is an effective and diverse display that is emotionally moving and often disturbing.

An exhibit such as *The Disappeared* should contain skillfully made art, educate people about the political situation, and make people feel compassion for what happened. *The Disappeared* does all of these things. The first collection, "In Memoriam," by Antonio Frasconi, consists of forty-eight prints that personalize the tragic situation. These prints show victims of violence, their faces surrounded by dark colors as if they are vanishing in front of our eyes. "The Disappeared," also by Frasconi, consists of woodblock prints. The woodblock prints show people with bags over their heads, huddled as if they were in concentration camps. In one case, a skull seems to glow eerily through it's bag. The images that I found particularly powerful among Frasconi's prints are the dark nighttime shots of buildings. Drab cells are shown in red and grays, with the sky a twilight blue. These prints are similar to impressionist artwork with their use of colors and inexact drawings of real-life subjects, however, most impressionist works I have seen deal with more cheerful events or landscapes, not with tragic events, as in this exhibit.

1   The introduction contrasts this exhibit with other kinds of art.

The thesis statement gives a judgment about the quality of the exhibit.

2   Criteria have been added.

Facts and examples are added.

More comparison has been added.

Topic sentence has been added.

Photography plays an important role in this exhibit. Marcelo Brodsky's "Good Memory" is a large display of forty-three photographs and two videos. It includes a grade school portrait that shows his class with personal notes written beside the children. Some are among the disappeared, others reunite in photographic portraits in which they, as adults, blend into the class photo. Perhaps as images of the lost potential of those who were killed. A video installation shows a school reunion in which ninety-eight missing class members are remembered in roll call.

3

More facts have been added.

The most moving and effective part of this exhibit is a series of photographs by Marcelo Brodsky. The photographs deal with his personal and family history. Pictures of Marcelo with his younger brother Fernando show happy family scenes, such as the two boys having fun on a boat or playing with bows and arrows and falling down and playing dead. Then photos of Fernando are shown in which he looks skinny and worn down. A caption says that Fernando was killed in a concentration camp. This ties their young innocence to the horrors of mass murder. This is much more effective than just reading about tragic historical events in a textbook.

4

The significance of the exhibit is better explained.

While this exhibit is shocking and moving, it is also confusing because there is so little information given about the political situation in Latin America. This political situation led to these mass murders. Most people haven't kept track of all of the dictators that were in charge of Latin American countries in the 1970s and 1980s. This lack of information distracted me from the exhibits and kept me from totally appreciating them.

5

The limitations of the exhibit are explained.

On the whole, this exhibit very effectively represents the killings that have occured in South America over decades. Artists express this reality in various styles and mediums, including prints, sculpture, and photography. This exhibit makes viewers understand the effects that oppressive governments can have on individuals and their families. Its hard to forget what happened to these people.

6

The last sentence emphasizes the emotional impact the exhibit had on the writer.

GROUP ACTIVITY 7 Analyze Paul's Revised Draft

Use the following questions to discuss with your classmates how Paul has improved his discovery draft.

1. How has Paul improved his introduction?
2. Why is his thesis more effective now?
3. What criteria does Paul use to evaluate *The Disappeared*? Does he use enough suitable criteria? Are they obvious, or do they need explanation?

4. How well does Paul support his judgment with examples, facts, and expert testimony?

5. Does the comparison of the style of the "In Memoriam" prints with impressionism further support Paul's judgment? Why or why not?

6. How well does Paul maintain a balanced perspective? Explain.

7. How could Paul's revised draft benefit from further revision?

GROUP ACTIVITY 8 Peer Review

Form a group with two or three other students, and exchange copies of your revised drafts. Read your draft aloud while your classmates follow along. Then take notes on your classmates' responses to the following questions about your draft.

1. What did you like best about this essay?

2. How interesting is my introduction? Do you want to continue reading the essay? Why or why not?

3. What is my thesis statement? Is it effective? Does it express a judgment about the value or merit of my subject? Is it focused on the subject? Is it moderate rather than extreme? Is it clear and specific?

4. What are my criteria? Are there enough of them, and are they suitable? Are they obvious, or do I need to explain them?

5. How well do I support my judgment with examples, facts, and expert testimony?

6. Do I maintain a balanced perspective? Why or why not?

7. Do I make effective comparisons? Explain.

8. How effective is my ending? Do I conclude in such a way that you know it's the end?

WRITING ACTIVITY 15 Revise Your Draft

Building on the work you completed for Writing Activities 8 to 14, refer to your classmates' peer review suggestions as you finish revising your discovery draft. Focus on improving your thesis statement, criteria, and evidence. Add comparisons where they might be helpful, and ensure that your essay maintains a balanced perspective. You may also decide to omit unnecessary material or to rearrange parts of your essay more effectively.

⏻ Comment on your draft

Use the Comment function of your word-processing program to insert your own ideas for revising your draft. This function highlights the suggestions for revision (or comments) in your text, similar to your instructor's or classmates' handwritten comments.

(Step 4 Edit Your Sentences

At this point, you have worked hard to write a convincing evaluation of a product, performance, or place. But before you can share your essay with your audience, you must edit it for readability and correctness. Remember, an important part of the writing process is to revise your words and sentences to be clearer, more interesting, and free of distracting errors.

As always, consult a dictionary and the Handbook in Part Four of this book to check that your words are the right ones and that your sentences are structured correctly. As you edit your evaluation, you will practice combining sentences with relative clauses. You will also learn how to correct comma splices.

Combining Sentences Using Relative Clauses

Although short sentences can be powerful, using too many of them in a row can force you to repeat yourself. To eliminate unnecessary repetition and help your readers know which of your ideas are most important, consider using *relative clauses* to combine sentences.

You can turn a short sentence into a relative clause by beginning it with a relative pronoun (*who, whose, which,* or *that*). A relative clause contains a subject and a verb but cannot stand alone as a sentence.

Here's how student writer Paul LaPrade combined two pairs of sentences in his revised draft by using relative clauses:

> **ORIGINAL** "The Disappeared," also by Frasconi, consists of woodblock prints. The woodblock prints show people with bags over their heads, huddled as if they were in concentration camps.
>
> **REVISED** "The Disappeared," also by Frasconi, consists of woodblock prints that show people with bags over their heads, huddled as if they were in concentration camps.
>
> **ORIGINAL** The most moving and effective part of this exhibit is a series of photographs by Marcelo Brodsky. The photographs deal with his personal and family history.
>
> **REVISED** The most moving and effective part of this exhibit is a series of photographs by Marcelo Brodsky that deals with his personal and family history.

For more on combining sentences, see Chapter 17.

By combining these sentences, Paul eliminated unnecessary words and communicated his thoughts more clearly.

Notice that a relative clause can appear either in the middle or at the end of a combined sentence and that the revised sentence may or may not include commas. How do you know when to use commas?

■ Use commas when the relative clause gives information that's *not* essential to understanding the sentence, as in the following example:

The book, *which is on the table,* is by one of my favorite authors.

Commas are used in this example because the relative clause—*which is on the table*—is simply adding information. The sentence makes sense without it: *The book is by one of my favorite authors.*

- Don't use commas when a relative clause identifies who or what it is referring to, as in the following example:

The book *that is on the table* belongs to Wilbur.

No commas are used before or after the relative clause because it's a necessary part of the sentence: it tells which book—the one on the table—is the one that belongs to Wilbur.

- Avoid using commas with relative clauses that begin with the word *that:*

The bicycle *that has been sitting in the garage* is too small for my children to ride.

▪ HOW TO Combine Sentences Using Relative Clauses

- Turn the less important sentence into a relative clause by starting it with a relative pronoun: *who, whose, which,* or *that.*
- Check that the relative clause contains a subject and verb and cannot stand on its own.
- Add the relative clause to the middle or end of a complete sentence.
- Use a comma or commas when the relative clause adds information not necessary to the meaning of the sentence.
- Don't use commas when a relative clause identifies the word that it's referring to.
- Don't use commas when the relative clause begins with the word *that.*

▌ EDITING ACTIVITY 1 Combining Sentences Using Relative Clauses ▐

Combine the following pairs of sentences using relative clauses. You may need to eliminate unnecessary words or move words around. Use a comma or commas when the relative clause is unnecessary for the sentence to be understood.

EXAMPLE *North by Northwest* is one of my favorite movies. ~~It was directed by~~ , which Alfred Hitchcock directed in 1959,

~~Alfred Hitchcock. It was made in 1959.~~

1. Cary Grant plays an advertising executive. His name is Roger Thornhill.

2. Cary Grant is framed for killing a UN diplomat. He is mistaken for a man named George Kaplan.

3. James Mason plays a foreign spy. The spy's name is Phillip Vandamm. James Mason was a British actor.

4. Eva Marie Saint plays a beautiful blonde woman. The woman's name is Eve Kendall. Eve Kendall is actually Phillip Vandamm's lover.

5. *North by Northwest* is typical of many Hitchcock movies. It has mistaken identities, a cool blonde woman, and a man. The man is chased by people he doesn't know.

For additional practice with using relative clauses to combine sentences, go to **bedfordstmartins.com /choices** and click on **Exercise Central**.

> **WRITING ACTIVITY 16** Combine Your Sentences

Search your revised draft for short, closely related sentences that cause unnecessary repetition. Where it makes sense to do so, combine them with relative clauses.

Correcting Comma Splices

For more on comma splices, see pp. 461–64.

A *comma splice* is a common error that occurs when two complete sentences are combined *only* with a comma. (Remember that a complete sentence contains both a subject and a verb and expresses a complete thought.)

COMMA SPLICE The plot was full of twists, the ending of the movie was predictable.

There are three ways to correct a comma splice.

- Replace the comma with a period to make two sentences:

  The plot was full of twists. The ending of the movie was predictable.

- Add a coordinating conjunction after the comma:

  The plot was full of twists, *but* the ending of the movie was predictable.

- Replace the comma with a semicolon:

  The plot was full of twists; the ending of the movie was predictable.

When using a semicolon, many writers include a conjunctive adverb, such as *in addition, although, nevertheless, however, moreover, in fact,* or *for example.* The conjunctive adverb will tell your readers how the two parts of the sentence connect together. The conjunctive adverb comes after the semicolon and is followed by a comma:

The plot was full of twists; nevertheless, the ending of the movie was predictable.

Here is an example of a comma splice from Paul LaPrade's draft, followed by three different ways he could correct it:

COMMA SPLICE	The methods of expression here range from realistic documentation to symbolism, there are several works that fit into each of these categories.
CORRECT	The methods of expression here range from realistic documentation to symbolism. There are several works that fit into each of these categories.
CORRECT	The methods of expression here range from realistic documentation to symbolism, and there are several works that fit into each of these categories.
CORRECT	The methods of expression here range from realistic documentation to symbolism; there are several works that fit into each of these categories.

■ HOW TO Correct Comma Splices

- Break the comma splice up into two sentences.
  OR
- Use a comma and a coordinating conjunction (*for, and, nor, but, or, yet, so*).
  OR
- Use a semicolon instead of a comma. If you wish, you may follow the semicolon with a conjunctive adverb and a comma.

EDITING ACTIVITY 2 Correct Comma Splices

Correct each of the following comma splices.

EXAMPLE My next-door neighbor is a great singer/she's always entertaining my kids.
                                                  . She's

1. The chocolates are crunchy on the outside, they are soft on the inside.

2. Mexico City was polluted, it was also expensive.

3. Some people think hybrid cars are sluggish, they're actually pretty quick.

4. When I was in Rome, I saw the pope say Mass, it was inspiring.

5. Some people find the movie *Grandma's Boy* offensive, I think it's funny.

For additional practice with correcting comma splices, go to **bedfordstmartins .com/choices** and click on **Exercise Central**.

WRITING ACTIVITY 17 Edit Your Essay

Using the Handbook in Part Four of this book as a guide, edit your revised essay for errors in grammar, spelling, and punctuation. In particular, look for comma splices and correct them using any of the three techniques listed on page 230. Your classmates can help you locate and correct errors you might have overlooked. Add the errors you find and their corrections to your editing log.

A Student's Edited Essay

You might have noticed that Paul's revised draft contained some wordy sentences and a few errors in grammar, spelling, and punctuation. Paul fixed these problems in his edited essay. His corrections are noted in the margin.

Paul LaPrade

Professor Hall

English 0311

The correct MLA format is used.   21 Mar. 2011

The Disappeared

Most people, when they think of art, picture beautiful paintings of landscapes or portraits of important people. However, art can also be a way for people to record tragic events. Such is the case for the current exhibit at the Rubin Art Gallery, *The Disappeared*. This exhibit depicts the tragedy that occurred in Latin America in the last decades of the twentieth century, when military dictators in countries such as Argentina, Chile, and Guatemala kidnapped and killed thousands of people who resisted their dictatorships. The different types of art are prints, photos, video installations, and three-dimensional installations. The methods of expression here range from realistic documentation to symbolism; there are several works that fit into each of these categories. On the whole, this is an effective and diverse display that is emotionally moving and often disturbing.   1

Comma splice is corrected.

An exhibit such as *The Disappeared* should contain skillfully made art, educate people about the political situation, and make people feel compassion for what happened. *The Disappeared* does all of these things. The first collection, "In Memoriam," by Antonio Frasconi, consists of forty-eight prints that personalize the tragic situation. These prints show victims of violence, their faces surrounded by dark colors as if they are vanishing in front of our eyes. "The Disappeared," also by Frasconi, consists of woodblock prints that show people with bags over their heads, huddled as if they were in concentration camps. In one case, a skull seems to glow eerily through its bag. The images that I found particularly powerful among Frasconi's prints are the dark nighttime shots of buildings. Drab cells are shown in red and grays, with the sky a twilight blue. These prints are similar to impressionist artwork with their use of colors and inexact drawings of real-life subjects; however, most impressionist works I have seen deal with more cheerful events or landscapes, not with tragic events, as in this exhibit.   2

Sentences are combined with a relative clause.

Apostrophe mistake is corrected.

Comma splice is corrected.

Photography plays an important role in this exhibit. Marcelo Brodsky's "Good Memory" is a large display of forty-three photographs and two videos.   3

It includes a grade school portrait that shows his class with personal notes written beside the children. Some are among the disappeared, others reunite in photographic portraits in which they, as adults, blend into the class photo, perhaps as images of the lost potential of those who were killed. A video installation shows a school reunion in which ninety-eight missing class members are remembered in roll call.

The most moving and effective part of this exhibit is a series of photographs by Marcelo Brodsky that deals with his personal and family history. Pictures of Marcelo with his younger brother Fernando show happy family scenes, such as the two boys having fun on a boat or playing with bows and arrows and falling down and playing dead. Then photos of Fernando are shown in which he looks skinny and worn down. A caption says that Fernando was killed in a concentration camp, tying their young innocence to the horrors of mass murder. This is much more effective than just reading about tragic historical events in a textbook.

4 — Sentences are combined with a relative clause.

— Sentences are combined.

While this exhibit is shocking and moving, it is also confusing because there is so little information given about the political situation in Latin America that led to these mass murders. Most people haven't kept track of all of the dictators that were in charge of Latin American countries in the 1970s and 1980s. This lack of information distracted me from the exhibits and kept me from totally appreciating them.

5 — Sentences are combined with a relative clause.

On the whole, this exhibit very effectively represents the killings that have occurred in South America over decades. Artists express this reality in various styles and mediums, including prints, sculpture, and photography. This exhibit makes viewers understand the effects that oppressive governments can have on individuals and their families. It's hard to forget what happened to these people.

6 — Spelling error is corrected.

— Apostrophe error is corrected.

 Post your review on the Web

Many Web sites make it easy to publish your review online. For links to sites where you can post your evaluation essay, go to **bedfordstmartins.com/choices** and click on **Annotated Web Links**.

Step 5 Share Your Essay

You're ready to share your evaluation with your audience—your instructor, your classmates, and others interested in your topic. For instance, if you evaluated a product, people who are deciding whether to purchase that product will want to know your opinion of it. If you evaluated a movie, other moviegoers will be curious to read your review, whether they've already seen the film or are trying to decide what to see over the weekend. If you evaluated a place, you could share your essay with someone who is interested in going to that place.

An excellent way to share your evaluation with people interested in your subject is to post your review online. As you probably know, many Web sites provide a forum for consumer reviews of products, performances, and places. Sites such as Epinions (www.epinions.com), Rating Bar (www.ratingbar.com), and Trip Advisor (www.tripadvisor.com) consist entirely of user comments. Others, such as the Internet Movie Database (www.imdb.com) and Amazon.com, encourage visitors to add their own reviews to the site's professional content. The magazine *Consumer Reports* offers blogs about a variety of products (www.blogs.consumerreports.org). Major newspapers, such as the *New York Times* (www.nytimes.com) and the *Chicago Tribune* (www.chicagotribune.com), also provide blogs on products, performances, and places. Choose an appropriate Web site or blog, and add your essay to it. Be sure to check back for comments from other site visitors about how useful your review was for them.

 Writing for online sites

If you decide to post your evaluation to an online site, you might need to change the way you have written your evaluation essay. For example, if you decide to post to Amazon.com, you'll need to shorten the evaluation, include a title, and give a ranking of one to five stars.

CHAPTER CHECKLIST

- ❏ I read essays to learn more about evaluating a product, performance, and place.
- ❏ I gathered ideas for evaluating a product, performance, and place.
- ❏ I compared my subject with other similar subjects to support a judgment.
- ❏ I revised my thesis statement to express an opinion or a judgment about the value or merit of the subject, to focus on the subject and not the writer, to be moderate and not extreme, and to be clear and specific.
- ❏ I gave the criteria on which the judgment is based, used enough suitable criteria, and explained those criteria that weren't obvious.
- ❏ I provided evidence—examples, facts, and expert testimony—to support each criterion.

❏ I gave both the positive and negative aspects of my subject to maintain a balanced perspective.

❏ I combined short, closely related sentences with relative clauses.

❏ I edited to eliminate comma splices and other errors in grammar, punctuation, and spelling.

REFLECTING ON YOUR WRITING

To help you reflect on the writing you did in this chapter, answer the following questions:

1. Compare your experience writing an evaluation with writing an expressive or informative essay. What did you find easiest and most difficult about these assignments?

2. What did you learn from writing this essay?

3. How will your audience benefit from reading your essay?

4. If you had more time, what more would you do to improve your essay before sharing it with readers?

Using your answers to these questions, complete a Writing Process Report for this chapter (you can download a report form at **bedfordstmartins.com /choices**). Once you complete this report, freewrite about what you learned in this chapter.

"Universities are supposed to be a place where ideas are debated."
—REGINALD JONES, "NEWSPAPER AD SPARKS CONTROVERSY"

Arguing a Position

Censorship, Stereotypes, and Media in Our Lives

People have always tried to change other people's minds. The topic might be serious—land disputes that could lead to war—or minor—couples debating about where to go to dinner. Countless songs have been written about arguments between lovers, from George and Ira Gershwin's "Let's Call the Whole Thing Off" to Eminem's "Love the Way You Lie." In addition to songs, arguments can be expressed in speeches, essays, works of art, even refrigerator magnets—however people choose to express themselves and take a position. These arguments can also appear in a variety of media, including newspapers, books, magazines, radio, television, and the Internet.

Recently media options have expanded to include texting, e-mail, social Web sites, online shopping, blogs, tweets, video conferencing, chat groups, and podcasts. This interactive technology—often called *new media*— allows us to alter what we watch, listen, or read to suit our own tastes or to communicate with others. Instead of being vulnerable to the trickery of commercials, for instance, we can skip through them. We can create our own song playlists, shows, and videos and send them to people we've never met.

In this chapter, you will write an essay that argues your position on censorship, stereotypes, and media in our lives. As you follow the steps of the writing process, you will

- Explore the chapter topic by reading essays that argue a position about the media.
- Gather ideas by freewriting, brainstorming, and consulting with others.
- Develop your ideas using **cause-and-effect** analysis.
- Practice making an argument claim, generating pro and con points to support your ideas, and ordering your points effectively.
- Learn to avoid logical fallacies.
- Combine sentences using introductory phrases.
- Practice correcting problems with subject-verb agreement.
- Consider submitting your finished essay to a campus or local newspaper.

But do we really control the media, or do the media control us? Critics and consumers argue about many aspects of the media, such as the benefits and dangers of censorship, the ways that people are portrayed, and the media's effect on people's lives. Which is more important: freedom of speech or national security? How are viewers and performers affected when the media portray people in particular ways? Are our society's ever-changing forms of communication helpful or harmful to the people who use them?

In this chapter, you'll read and analyze argument essays on these issues. You will also follow a student, Reginald Jones, as he writes an argument about censorship on a college campus. Then you will join the debate by writing an argument on a media-related topic. Once you have completed your argument, you can share it with friends and classmates, or you can expand your audience by sending it to a campus or local newspaper. By writing this essay, you have the opportunity to affect the way people think about a topic you care about. ■

GROUP ACTIVITY 1 Think about the Media

The photograph on the chapter-opening page shows students protesting racism on a college campus. At various times, college students have protested wars, tuition increases, controversial speakers, and even bad food in the dining halls. What issue would make you want to protest on your college campus? How effective are these protests, in your view?

Getting Started   Reading Essays That Argue a Position about a Media Issue

Debates about the media have become intense, as the following three readings show. The authors of these essays each take a position on a controversial issue associated with censorship, stereotypes, or media in our lives. As you read, notice how they use cause-and-effect analysis to develop their points. Also note how these authors try to persuade their audience. What arguments do they make to support their points? How do they try to win over readers who disagree with them? How do they order their ideas? How logical are their arguments? Consider, too, how you react to their arguments. To what degree do these authors change your mind on these topics? You can use what you learn from reading these arguments to get started writing your own argument. (For additional essays on censorship, stereotypes, and the media in our lives, see p. 581.)

A Censorship Issue

ANNA QUINDLEN
Write and Wrong

Anna Quindlen—a Pulitzer Prize–winning essayist and novelist—currently writes a regular column for *Newsweek* magazine on important current events, and was one of the first woman columnists for the *New York Times*. In "Write and Wrong," originally published in *Newsweek* in 2008, Quindlen tackles the issue of censorship in schools.

Each year in the state of Indiana, librarians, teachers and students compile a list of 20 nominated books for the Eliot Rosewater Award, named after a character in the work of Kurt Vonnegut, a native of the state. This year one finalist was *The Freedom Writers Diary*, which makes even more bizarre what happened to Connie Heermann, tossed from her classroom for trying to use that same book as a teaching tool. In the months since Heermann was placed on an 18-month suspension without pay by the school board in Perry Township, her case has been ballyhooed as errant censorship. But it's really a cautionary tale about what's too often the ruling principle in American public education: the timidity and inefficiency of powerful bureaucracies far removed from the daily lives of either teachers or kids.

A bit about *The Freedom Writers Diary*: the book grew out of the work of Erin Gruwell, who was once a newbie teacher in a class of at-risk students in California. "At risk" is edu-code: it most often means the students in question are poor, minority, have chaotic home lives, are likely to drop out. Gruwell decided that the road to success for her students was to get them to write their lives. They kept diaries about everything from self-doubt to incest to gang membership. Some of the students used profanity and racial slurs, but a reader notices that as their writing improves, that disappears. As Gruwell says, "As they wrote more, they made better choices." They also had better lives. The students in Gruwell's classes started out believing they might not survive high school—literally. By the end of the book, they're heading to college.

Which brings us back to Heermann, whose students at Perry Meridian High School were not much different from the ones in the diary and who she hoped would see their struggles—and their potential—within its pages. After attending a training session last summer with Gruwell, she came home psyched. She persuaded a local businessman to pay for 150 copies of *The Freedom Writers Diary*, but her principal asked her to hold off using it until the central office could take a look. That's unusual—most teachers use materials other than approved textbooks in their classes, and Heermann had done so before—but she started the year with John Grisham's *The Street Lawyer* instead. A lawyer visited the classroom, and students wrote letters to the author. "My kids were loving it," Heermann says. "They were even reading ahead." The engagement that had led Gruwell's students to success in school was in full flower, and Heermann decided it was time for empowerment, and the diary.

1	Quindlen uses cause-and-effect analysis to describe what happened when a teacher tried to use an award-winning book in her class.
	Quindlen's introduction shows she is against censorship. But her claim is broader: she criticizes the educational system itself.
2	This paragraph gives background information necessary for understanding Quindlen's argument.
3	More important background information is given.
	This is Quindlen's first pro point (or point in support of her claim): *The Freedom Writers Diary* will help empower Heermann's students.

Again, cause-and-effect analysis shows the result of Heermann's assigning the book to her students.

Here are the bare facts of what happened next: Heermann sent out permission slips to parents, virtually all of whom signed them. She informed the central office that she would be distributing the books on Nov. 15, and did. Almost immediately she was told to collect the books, and to keep a list of the names of those who did not comply. Most of the kids refused to hand over their copies. And before you could say "free exchange of ideas," Heermann was told that if she didn't resign, she would be fired. 4

This brief paragraph, consisting of a single question, indirectly supports Quindlen's claim by showing Heermann's experience and dedication as a teacher.

Did I mention that she'd been teaching for 27 years, and that she paid for all those copies of the Grisham book herself? 5

This is Quindlen's first con point (or argument against her claim): the book should not be taught because it contains a racial slur. Quindlen refutes this by noting that such a slur offers a "teachable moment."

It's hard to unearth exactly why someone was so hell bent on keeping *The Freedom Writers Diary* out of this classroom. Maybe it was the use of a particular racial slur, the one that keeps getting people riled about *Huckleberry Finn* and that provides the perfect teachable moment for discussing racial divisions in America—at least if you're not paralyzed by cowardice. You have to wonder whether the school-board members even read the book. Maybe they never made it to the entry by the student who said, "Who would have thought of the 'at risk' kids making it this far? But we did, even though the educational system desperately tried to hold us down." It's a they said/she said situation, difficult to parse because so much took place behind closed doors. The board lawyer said Heermann was told not to use the book and she did so anyhow. She says after months of silence from higher-ups, she assumed they just didn't care. 6

Quindlen's second pro point: members of the educational system knew nothing about the book.

If the school board of Perry Township wanted to counter *The Freedom Writers Diary*, it certainly did. The book teaches that open discussion about challenging subjects is always best, that engagement always trumps silence. The members of that board were outraged by alleged insubordination when they should have been outraged by the glacial pace of decision-making by their top administrators. Insubordination is what built this country, and a glacial pace in education means you lose kids. 7

Another con point—that Heermann should have obeyed the school board—is refuted by noting that open discussion is the best policy.

Have I mentioned that it's hard to get really good people to become teachers? 8

Another one-question paragraph captures the reader's attention and makes another point: censorship of teachers will result in fewer good teachers.

Connie Heermann will be teaching three courses in the fall at a local community college. She'll be making less than $5,000, but she's grateful for the opportunity. She was forbidden to contact her students after her job was yanked out from under her, was forced to go overnight from a powerful presence in their lives to a complete cipher. What made it worse was that she knows they are kids who assume they'll get the shaft. That's what "at risk" means, too. She hears that some stopped going to class. It looks as though her students are not going to wind up the way Erin Gruwell's did. That makes her so sad, but she doesn't regret what she did. "You know what?" she says. "My students have the book. They kept the book!" And then her voice breaks. 9

This conclusion emphasizes the effects of censorship on both Heermann and her students.

This final sentence emphasizes Heermann's dedication to her students.

> ### READING ACTIVITY 1 Build Your Vocabulary

Determine the meanings of the following words from the context of Anna Quindlen's essay. Then check their meanings by looking up the words in a dictionary: ballyhooed (1), errant (1), bureaucracies (1), psyched (3), slur (6), insubordination (7), cipher (9).

Discuss the following questions about "Write and Wrong" with your classmates.

1. Why does the author think that Connie Heermann was unfairly dismissed as a teacher at Perry Meridian High School?

2. In your view, what is the best point that Quindlen makes to support her claim? Why is this the best point?

3. What facts does Quindlen give about Connie Heermann that make you sympathetic to her plight?

4. If you were a student in Heermann's class, what might be your reaction to Heermann's dismissal, based on Quindlen's account of what happened?

Write a paragraph or two in which you give your perspective on the following topic: When, if ever, should materials for high school students be censored? Give several reasons to support your point. Compare your ideas with those of your classmates.

A Stereotyping Issue

SAMUEL L. JACKSON
In Character

Actor Samuel L. Jackson is a graduate of Morehouse College and has appeared in more than ninety films, including *Do the Right Thing* (1989), *Jungle Fever* (1991), *Pulp Fiction* (1994), *Star Wars* (Episodes I–III; 1999, 2002, 2005), *Snakes on a Plane* (2006), and *Iron Man 2* (2010). He often works with directors Spike Lee and Quentin Tarantino. In the following essay, Jackson considers the issue of racism in Hollywood and argues that although roles for minority actors have improved over the last few decades, there's more work to be done.

I think it's significant for the growth of the [movie] business that a black actor   1
like me is being cast in race-neutral parts when 20 years ago I wouldn't have been.
It's significant for young actors who have aspirations to be things other than crimi-
nals and drug dealers and victims and whatever rap artist they have to be to get into
a film. The things I've done and Morgan's done and Denzel's done, that Fish has
done, that Wesley's* done, everybody's done, have allowed us to achieve a level of
success as other kinds of people. We've been successful in roles as doctors, lawyers,
teachers, policemen, detectives, spies, monsters — anything that we have been able
to portray on-screen in a very realistic way that made audiences say, I believe that,

---

*Jackson is referring to African American actors Morgan Freeman, Denzel Washington, Laurence Fishburne, and Wesley Snipes.

and that brought them into the theaters to see us do it. This has allowed young black actors the opportunity to become different kinds of characters in the cinematic milieu we're a part of.

Before, I used to pick up scripts and I was criminal number two and I looked to see what page I died on. We've now demonstrated a level of expertise, in terms of the care we give to our characters and in terms of our professionalism — showing up to work on time, knowing our lines, and bringing something to the job beyond the lines and basic characterizations. Through our accomplishments and the expertise we have shown, studios know there is a talent pool out there that wants to be like us, and hopefully, these young actors will take care to do the things we did.

As the fabric of our society changes in certain ways, the fabric of the cinematic world changes in the same ways. For a very long time, the people that were in power were white men. They tended to hire other white men, and when they saw a story, the people in those stories were white men or specific kinds of white women. As we get younger producers and younger people in the studios, we have a generation, or several generations, of people who have lived in a society where they have black friends. They have Asian friends. They have Hispanic friends who do a wide variety of jobs, who went into a wide variety of vocations. When the studio heads look at a script now, they can see their friend Juan or they can see their friend Kwong or they can see their friend Rashan. So all of a sudden you see a different look in the movies, as they reflect the way this younger generation of producers and studio executives live their lives. And consequently, through the worldwide network of cinema, you meet other top-quality actors from other cultures. The world of cinema brings us all together. And we've started to cast films in a whole other way that reflects the way we live and the pattern of our society. Outside of *Spider-Man*, all the big action heroes now seem to be ethnic. The new Arnold Schwarzenegger is The Rock, and the new Bruce Willis is about to be Vin Diesel. So we're doing something right. But it's difficult to do a film that's of a serious nature and that does not have guns, sex, and explosions in it if it's ethnic.

There are many ways to answer the question whether Hollywood is racist. The direct and honest answer, I guess, is yes, only because Hollywood is anti anything that's not green. If something doesn't make money, they don't want to be bothered with it. Therefore, it's still difficult to get a movie about Hispanics made; it's difficult to get a movie about blacks made that doesn't have to do with hip-hop, drugs, and sex. You can get a black comedy made. Eddie Murphy's funny, Will Smith is funny, Martin Lawrence is funny. We have huge black comics. But getting a film like *Eve's Bayou* made is practically impossible. For five years, nobody knew what that movie was. Like, what is it? It's a family drama. Yeah, but how do we market that? Nobody wanted to be bothered with it. Or *Caveman's Valentine*. What is it? It's a mystery, a murder mystery. But it's a black murder mystery. No, there's white people in it; it just happens that a black person is the lead. So Hollywood is racist in its ideas about what can make money and what won't make money. They'll make Asian movies about people who jump across buildings and use swords and swing in trees, like *Crouching Tiger*, but we can't sell an Asian family drama. What do we do with that? Or if we're going to have Asian people in the film, they've got to be like the tong, or they're selling drugs and they got some guns and it's young gang members. It's got to be that. And

Hollywood is sexist in its ideals about which women are appealing and which women aren't. It's a young woman's game. Women have got to be either real old or real young to be successful. If they're in the middle, it's like, what do we do with her? Put her in kids' movies, you know, with some kids.

Hollywood can be perceived as racist and sexist, because that's what audiences   5
have said to them they will pay their money to come see. It's difficult to break that cycle, because it's a moneymaking business and it costs money to make films. Hollywood tends to copy things that make lots of money. The first thing they want to know is how many car chases are there and what's blowing up. They're over the how-many-people-die thing, because of 9/11. Now it's like, how many people can we kill and get away with it? We can't blow up anything right now unless it's in the right context. We can blow something up over there, and the bad guy can be a guy with a turban. So there's all kinds of things that go into what people say about Hollywood being racist. There have been times I had to go in a room and convince people I'm the right person for their script and the fact that I'm black will not impact on the script in a negative way. I've had to explain that my being black won't change the dynamics of the interaction; it won't change the dynamics of the story in terms of my character's interaction with the other characters. I'll just happen to be a black guy who's in that story doing those things.

We [African Americans] need to produce our own films. We need to own our   6
own theaters in addition to producing our own films. The more theaters we own, the sooner we can have our own distribution chain. It's a matter of us having that kind of network [as major Hollywood studios do], so when we do make small films that we want to distribute to a specific group of people or to a wider audience, we're able to do it.

I want to be able to produce films for friends of mine who haven't had the op-   7
portunity to be seen in the way I've been seen. They're good at what they do, and they deserve an opportunity to be seen by a greater public.

READING ACTIVITY 2 Build Your Vocabulary

Determine the meanings of the following words from the context of Samuel L. Jackson's essay. Then check their meanings by looking up the words in a dictionary: cinematic (1), milieu (1), vocations (3), tong (4), dynamics (5).

GROUP ACTIVITY 3 Discuss the Reading

Discuss the following questions about "In Character" with your classmates.

1. According to Jackson, is Hollywood racist?

2. Name at least three reasons that Jackson gives to support his opinion.

3. In Jackson's view, how does the desire to make money affect the way movies portray minority characters?

4. Why is the situation in Hollywood about the representation of minorities improving, according to Jackson?

> **WRITING ACTIVITY 2 Share Your Ideas**
>
> Write a paragraph or two in which you agree or disagree with Jackson's claim about racism in Hollywood. In your view, are minorities and women fairly or unfairly represented? Give examples to support your points. Compare your viewpoint with those of several of your classmates.

An Issue about Media in Our Lives

TARA PARKER-POPE
An Ugly Toll of Technology: Impatience and Forgetfulness

Tara Parker-Pope writes a consumer health column and blog for the *New York Times*, where "An Ugly Toll of Technology: Impatience and Forgetfulness" was published in 2010. Previously she wrote for the *Wall Street Journal*, where she won several awards for her writing on women's health. Parker-Pope's book, *For Better: The Science of a Good Marriage*, gives advice based on scientific research for how to make a successful marriage.

1   Are your Facebook friends more interesting than those you have in real life? Has high-speed Internet made you impatient with slow-speed children? Do you sometimes think about reaching for the fast-forward button, only to realize that life does not come with a remote control? If you answered yes to any of those questions, exposure to technology may be slowly reshaping your personality. Some experts believe excessive use of the Internet, cell phones and other technologies can cause us to become more impatient, impulsive, forgetful and even more narcissistic.

2   "More and more, life is resembling the chat room," says Dr. Elias Aboujaoude, director of the Impulse Control Disorders Clinic at Stanford. "We're paying a price in terms of our cognitive life because of this virtual lifestyle." We do spend a lot of time with our devices, and some studies have suggested that excessive dependence on cell phones and the Internet is akin to an addiction. Web sites like NetAddiction.com offer self-assessment tests to determine if technology has become a drug. Among the questions used to identify those at risk: Do you neglect housework to spend more time online? Are you frequently checking your e-mail? Do you often lose sleep because you log in late at night? If you answered "often" or "always," technology may be taking a toll on you.

3   In a study to be published in the journal *Cyberpsychology, Behavior and Social Networking*, researchers from the University of Melbourne in Australia subjected 173 college students to tests measuring risk for problematic Internet and gambling behaviors. About 5 percent of the students showed signs of gambling problems, but 10 percent of the students posted scores high enough to put them in the at-risk category for Internet "addiction." Technology use was clearly interfering with the students' daily lives, but it may be going too far to call it an addiction, says Nicki Dowling, a clinical psychologist who led the study. Ms. Dowling prefers to call it "Internet dependence."

Typically, the concern about our dependence on technology is that it detracts   4
from our time with family and friends in the real world. But psychologists have become intrigued by a more subtle and insidious effect of our online interactions. It
may be that the immediacy of the Internet, the efficiency of the iPhone and the anonymity of the chat room change the core of who we are, issues that Dr. Aboujaoude
explores in a book, *Virtually You: The Internet and the Fracturing of the Self*, to be released next year.

Dr. Aboujaoude also asks whether the vast storage available in e-mail and on   5
the Internet is preventing many of us from letting go, causing us to retain many old
and unnecessary memories at the expense of making new ones. Everything is saved
these days, he notes, from the meaningless e-mail sent after a work lunch to the
angry online exchange with a spouse. "If you can't forget because all this stuff is
staring at you, what does that do to your ability to lay down new memories and remember things that you should be remembering?" Dr. Aboujaoude said. "When you
have 500 pictures from your vacation in your Flickr account, as opposed to five pictures that are really meaningful, does that change your ability to recall the moments
that you really want to recall?"

There is also no easy way to conquer a dependence on technology. Nicholas   6
Carr, author of the new book *The Shallows: What the Internet Is Doing to Our Brains*,
says that social and family responsibilities, work and other pressures influence our
use of technology. "The deeper a technology is woven into the patterns of everyday
life, the less choice we have about whether and how we use that technology," Mr.
Carr wrote in a recent blog post on the topic. Some experts suggest simply trying to
curtail the amount of time you spend online. Set limits for how often you check
e-mail or force yourself to leave your cell phone at home occasionally. The problem is
similar to an eating disorder, says Dr. Kimberly Young, a professor at St. Bonaventure
University in New York who has led research on the addictive nature of online technology. Technology, like food, is an essential part of daily life, and those suffering
from disordered online behavior cannot give it up entirely and instead have to learn
moderation and controlled use. She suggests therapy to determine the underlying
issues that set off a person's need to use the Internet "as a way of escape."

The International Center for Media and the Public Agenda at the University of   7
Maryland asked 200 students to refrain from using electronic media for a day. The
reports from students after the study suggest that giving up technology cold turkey
not only makes life logistically difficult, but also changes our ability to connect with
others. "Texting and I.M.'ing my friends gives me a constant feeling of comfort," wrote
one student. "When I did not have those two luxuries, I felt quite alone and secluded
from my life. Although I go to a school with thousands of students, the fact that I was
not able to communicate with anyone via technology was almost unbearable."

READING ACTIVITY 3 Build Your Vocabulary

Determine the meanings of the following words from the context of "An Ugly Toll of
Technology: Impatience and Forgetfulness." Then check their meanings by looking up
the words in a dictionary: narcissistic (1), cognitive (2), insidious (4), anonymity (4),
curtail (6), logistically (7).

> **GROUP ACTIVITY 4 Discuss the Reading**

Discuss the following questions about "An Ugly Toll of Technology: Impatience and Forgetfulness."

1. How does Parker-Pope attempt to attract readers' attention at the beginning of her piece?

2. What is Parker-Pope's thesis, or claim, about technology, and where does it appear in the essay?

3. In supporting her claim, Parker-Pope relies on information from recent scientific studies. In your view, what is her most persuasive point, and why is it persuasive?

4. Evaluate Parker-Pope's conclusion. How effective is it? Does it give you a sense of closure, or does it leave you hanging? Explain your answer.

> **WRITING ACTIVITY 3 Share Your Ideas**

Write a paragraph or two in which you express your views about the effect that cell phones, the Internet, and other technologies have had on your life. Are your experiences similar to Parker-Pope's analysis, or are they different? Explain your ideas, and compare them with the ideas of your classmates.

Writing Your Essay   A Step-by-Step Guide

Now that you've read some essays arguing a position on censorship, stereotypes, or media in our lives, it's time to write your own essay. First, read the following writing assignment. Then, use the step-by-step advice that follows to discover ideas, develop them as you draft, and polish your writing into a finished essay that readers will find both interesting and persuasive:

Step 1   Explore Your Choices 247
Step 2   Write Your Discovery Draft 252
Step 3   Revise Your Draft 254
Step 4   Edit Your Sentences 267
Step 5   Share Your Essay 272

Writing Assignment

Types of media are all around you. Even this textbook is a medium of communication. While you read this book, you might have a television on or music playing. Periodically, you take a break by texting a friend or checking your Facebook account.

These technologies can have a strong influence on us. In this chapter, you'll write a persuasive essay that takes a position on a controversial aspect of the media that interests you. You (or your instructor) may approach this assignment in one of several ways:

- Argue for or against some type of censorship.

  OR

- Argue a point about how a group of people is represented or stereotyped in the media.

  OR

- Argue about how a particular communication medium has changed our lives for good or bad.

Step 1 Explore Your Choices

Because the media encompass everything from "old" one-way media (newspapers, magazines, television, and radio) to "new" interactive media (such as blogs, wikis, social media sites, and texting), you have many possible topics to choose from for your essay. Remember that most writers do their best work when they really care about the topic. At the same time, the topic that you select needs to keep your readers engaged and willing to listen to what you have to say. Before you think about possible topics, take some time to think about who your readers are and what they care about. Consider also what you want them to believe or do after they read your essay.

For more on audience and purpose, see pp. 7–11.

Analyzing Your Audience and Purpose

Keep your readers in mind from the very beginning. For this assignment, you might want to submit your finished essay to your campus or local newspaper. The readers of your campus newspaper will be mostly students, while the readers of your local newspaper will be of various ages and have many kinds of occupations. The type of newspaper you select will affect the way you write your essay.

Also, consider your purpose for writing this essay. You may need to inform your readers about something they know little about, and you may want to express your feelings about the topic, but the primary purpose of an essay that argues a position is persuasive. Are you trying to persuade your readers to change their minds about some aspect of the media or to do something about it? What do you want them to think? To do? Knowing your purpose will help you stay focused and make it more likely that your essay will succeed.

> **WRITING ACTIVITY 4**   **Analyze Your Audience and Purpose**
>
> Your responses to the following questions will help you decide how to approach this chapter's writing assignment. Be sure to come back to these questions after you have chosen a topic.
>
> 1. Consider the readers of your campus newspaper. How old do they tend to be? What topics relating to censorship, stereotyping, or the media's effect on our lives might they be most interested in?
>
> 2. Consider the readers of your local newspaper. How old do they tend to be? What topics relating to censorship, stereotyping, or the media's effect on our lives might they be most interested in?
>
> 3. What types of media do the readers of your campus newspaper typically use? Are these types of media the same or different from the kinds that the readers of your local newspaper might use?
>
> 4. What, if anything, do you know about your readers' political views? Would most readers have conservative, moderate, or liberal views? Give examples.
>
> 5. How interested would your readers be in an essay on the media? Explain your answer.

Gathering Ideas

To make sure you choose a topic that works for you, take the time to gather ideas on each of the three possible topics for this essay—censorship, stereotypes, and the media's effect on our lives. Even if you already have an idea for a topic, it's good to experiment with other ideas so that you don't miss an even better one. The activities and examples in this chapter will focus on using freewriting, brainstorming, and consulting with others, but you may use any additional techniques for gathering ideas that work for you.

For more on gathering ideas, see pp. 11–16.

Freewriting about Censorship

Even though the U.S. Constitution guarantees freedom of expression, restrictions on the media have always existed. For example, the Federal Communications Commission (FCC) has always regulated the content of radio, film, and television. It applied a morality code to movies in the 1930s and recently fined television stations for indecency. School boards often remove controversial books (including *Huckleberry Finn* and *The Catcher in the Rye*) from library shelves and reading lists, and churches sometimes discourage their members from reading or watching certain books or movies. Most Internet providers offer to block sites (often of a sexual or violent nature) that might upset their customers, and parents can prevent their children from viewing materials they find objectionable or inappropriate.

What is your opinion about these kinds of restrictions? You may have strong feelings about censorship, or you may not be sure what you think. Freewriting can be a productive way to explore your thoughts and get a better sense of where you stand on the issue. As you know, to freewrite, you simply write for five or ten minutes without trying to make sense of your thoughts. By letting your mind wander on the page, you can discover ideas you didn't know you had.

If you've had a personal experience with some kind of censorship, try writing about that for a few minutes and see where it leads you. You can also refer to the writing you completed after reading Anna Quindlen's "Write and Wrong." If you're stuck for ideas, you might explore your reactions to any of the following questions:

- Should the government attempt to regulate material on the Internet? Why or why not?
- How effective is the rating system used for movies and the warning labels on television shows and CDs? What changes, if any, would you suggest?
- Should commercials aimed at young children be restricted? Explain your position.
- Should magazines that glorify certain body types (such as extreme thinness) be restricted so that young people can develop healthy self-images? If so, who or what should restrict them?

⏻ **Follow these tips for freewriting**

At this early point in the writing process, you should write down your ideas, not worry about the size of the margins or how many spaces you need after a sentence. When you freewrite, to avoid being distracted by the appearance of your document, consider using a word-processing program with no formatting tools, such as Notepad, TextEdit, or Pages. You can also log on to http://750words.com, a site created for people who want to freewrite every day.

One student, Reginald, was interested in a controversy that erupted over an unpopular ad that ran in his college newspaper. Here is his freewriting on the issue:

> A school newspaper ad states that blacks should not receive reparations (a method of making up for past injustices) for slavery. There were ten reasons given for why blacks aren't entitled to damages for the effects of slavery. As you can imagine, a lot of people were really worked up about this ad and wanted the paper to apologize. But the editor of the paper said that he wouldn't, stating freedom of speech as his reason. Well, I don't agree with the ad, either, but I agree with the editor that the paper doesn't have to apologize.

> **WRITING ACTIVITY 5** Freewrite about Censorship

Select a recent controversy about media censorship that interests you, and freewrite about it for at least ten minutes. If nothing comes to mind, you may use one or more of the questions on page 249 to stimulate your thinking.

Brainstorming about Stereotypes

Mass entertainment—music, gossip magazines, radio programs, movies, television shows, video games, and the like—has always represented people in ways that at least some audience members have considered unfair or unrealistic. In the early days of television, for example, the typical American family was a white mother, father, and children who lived in a large house in a safe suburb. Today, television families are depicted in a variety of ways. For another example, consider shows and movies that feature young working professionals. Typically, the characters are portrayed as if they had no money problems and enough spare time to regularly sit around and talk. In fact, many young professionals have limited incomes, are raising children, and have little spare time. What effect do inaccurate portrayals, such as this one, have on viewers? How are other groups of people portrayed by different kinds of media? As a starting point, think about the following questions:

- Do you believe that song lyrics that are hostile to women or gay people affect the way these people are treated in the real world?
- Do you agree with Samuel L. Jackson that today's movies portray minorities more realistically than earlier movies did?
- How do video games typically represent people? Can gamers develop a distorted view of the world as a result of how characters are depicted?
- What do you think of the ways that contestants are represented on reality television shows?

To explore ideas about media representations, pick one type of media, and consider how it portrays different types of people. Then brainstorm a list of thoughts and questions that occur to you. If you pick film, you might want to further develop the ideas from your writing in response to Samuel L. Jackson's "In Character." For example, one student, Hillary, was concerned about the ways that women are depicted in fashion magazines. She brainstormed the following list of ideas:

Skinny, skinny
Girls with different ethnicities
Still very skinny
Plastic surgery
Models look unhappy

Some look like druggies

Girls try to be like the models

Clothes are beautiful

Very expensive

I know it's fantasy, but girls still try to copy

Can't do anything about it

I'm always on a diet

I'm affected by it even though I know better

WRITING ACTIVITY 6   Brainstorm about Stereotypes

Pick a form of media you enjoy (such as a particular TV show, movie, or Web site), and think about how people are represented on it. Brainstorm your thoughts about this issue.

Consulting with Others about the Media in Our Lives

As new media emerge and become popular, they have changed how we live from childhood to adulthood. Children text and upload photos and videos onto their phones or other electronic devices. In online classes, college students chat online and tweet with their instructors and classmates without ever having any face-to-face interactions. Online dating profiles allow people to search databases for possible partners with specific character traits—and to reject undesirable dates without ever speaking to them. Social networking sites allow people to screen out groups of people who disagree with them, which limits their exposure to diverse ideas.

To what extent are such media interactions beneficial? To what extent are they damaging? You may already have explored this point when you wrote in response to "An Ugly Toll of Technology: Impatience and Forgetfulness." However, you don't need to rely on just your own experiences to decide. To understand how such changes have affected other people, it makes sense to ask them some questions.

To consult with others, first decide what you want to know more about. For instance, if you're interested in knowing how much time college students spend texting one another, you might want to survey your classmates, perhaps on your class Web site. If you're curious about the effect that advertising in schools has on children, you could interview an elementary school teacher. Prepare a few questions before you talk to this person, and keep careful notes of the discussion.

Student writer Marshall was concerned that using television to keep small children occupied might stunt their intellectual growth. To gather ideas on this topic, Marshall consulted with a friend, Miguel, who was studying for a master's degree in child development. In an e-mail message, Marshall asked Miguel what experts thought about children who watch a lot of television. Here is Miguel's response:

Most child development experts think that many children are being exposed to too much media. Some researchers have shown that more and more children have TV sets and video games in their bedrooms, and 53 percent of children ages 8 to 18 report that their parents don't restrict their TV watching. Children whose parents don't limit TV viewing report that they read less than children whose parents restrict their viewing. They're also more likely to be overweight, and they have fewer friends. In general, in households with parents who monitor children's TV viewing, the children are better off.

⏻ **Connect with others online to discuss your topic**

Consider using e-mail to consult with or interview others. You can also talk online about your topic using texts, blog comments, online discussion forums, or chat sessions. One advantage to online communication is that you have a written record of the interaction that you can refer to later.

WRITING ACTIVITY 7   Consult with Others about Media

After choosing a topic that interests you, consult with at least two people who are knowledgeable about the issue. Ask your consultants to give their opinions and describe their experiences with the topic.

❨Step 2 Write Your Discovery Draft

For more on drafting, see pp. 16–20.

At this point, you've gathered ideas for three possible topics for your persuasive essay: censorship, stereotypes, or media in our lives. You'll now choose one of these topics and write a discovery draft.

Choosing a Topic

You have explored three different topics, but which one should you pick for your discovery draft? When deciding on a topic to write about, keep these three points in mind:

- Choose a topic that you're interested in and that you know something about. Your knowledge can come from your personal experiences, the experiences of others, your reflections and observations, and your reading on the topic.

- Choose a topic that is controversial and about which you have a strong opinion. Keep in mind that your primary purpose is to persuade your readers.

- Choose a topic that you think would interest your audience, which might include readers of your campus or local newspaper.

Consider the writing you completed for Writing Activities 1–7, as well as the paragraphs you composed after the three professional readings at the beginning of this chapter. If one of these topics meets all three of these criteria, you're in a good position to start drafting. But if you're not completely happy with any of your ideas, consider gathering some more ideas, trying a new topic, or combining related topics for your essay.

Your topic should be narrow enough to be well developed in a short essay. For instance, if you want to write about how the media have affected our lives, you couldn't cover all the ways that all media have affected us. Instead, select just one change and just one medium.

For more on thesis statements and narrowing your topic, see pp. 16–19.

> **WRITING ACTIVITY 8   Choose Your Topic**

Review the writing you have completed for this chapter so far, as well as the three criteria for a good topic listed on pages 256–57. Then choose or create a topic for your essay, and narrow it as necessary. If you wish, you may gather additional ideas before you start drafting.

Sharing Your Ideas

Before writing your discovery draft, write a preliminary thesis statement that identifies the issue you are writing about and expresses your position on it.

As you write, follow your train of thought, even if it means you'll need to revise your thesis statement later on. Keep your audience and purpose in mind, but remember that your main goal at the drafting stage is to get your ideas down on paper. You'll have time later on to revise and edit your draft.

A Student's Discovery Draft

Here's a discovery draft written by a student, Reginald Jones, on the issue of censorship in his college newspaper. After reading the draft, discuss with your classmates what Reginald might do to revise it. (Note that the example includes the types of errors that typically appear in a first draft.)

> An advertisement ran in last weeks school newspaper that shocked a
> number of students and faculty. The title was "Ten Reasons Why Reparations
> for Blacks Is a Bad Idea for Blacks—and Racist." The ad stated a number of
> reasons why blacks should not receive any damages for the effects of slavery.
> Some of the reasons given were that not all blacks have suffered because of
> slavery and that welfare and affirmative action has served as reparations. Boy,
> did this ad rile everyone! Some people wanted to burn all of the newspapers,
> some wanted an apology from the editor, and some said the paper should
> never have run the ad in the first place. I don't like the ad and don't agree

with what it says, but I do believe in freedom of speech. For this reason, I defend the right of the school newspaper to run this ad.

The constitution of the United States provides for freedom of expression. If we value our Constitution, then we must protect it even if it means protecting "hate speech."

Universities are supposed to be a place where ideas are debated. If we eliminate every piece of writing that someone finds offensive, we will no longer have a free exchange of ideas. There are many examples of books that people would like to ban. If colleges had to remove from the library shelves every book that was offensive to someone, the free exchange of ideas would become nonexistent.

Burning the newspapers would be a crime just as burning books is. There are better ways to protest. Students could run an ad themselves or write to the author of the ad.

Rather than burning newspapers or demanding an apology, they should discuss the ideas expressed in the ad and not just refuse to run it. We must attack these ideas with better ideas of our own.

WRITING ACTIVITY 9   Write Your Discovery Draft

Using your preliminary thesis statement and the ideas you've gathered on your topic, write a discovery draft. Keep in mind that your purpose is to express and support your opinion. If you're unsure about your topic, consider writing two or three discovery drafts on different topics to see which topic will work best for you.

Step 3 Revise Your Draft

When you revise your draft, use the skills you acquired in the preceding chapters: organize your paragraphs (Chapter 2), strengthen your focus (Chapter 4), outline your plan (Chapter 6), and write an effective introduction and conclusion (Chapter 5). Also, consider conducting primary or secondary research to gather more information about your topic (Chapter 6).

In this chapter, you'll focus on writing a persuasive argument. You'll learn how to develop your ideas with cause-and-effect analysis, make a claim, develop support for that claim, respond to opposing arguments, and organize your points.

For more on revising, see pp. 20–22.

Developing Your Ideas with Cause-and-Effect Analysis

When you use cause-and-effect analysis, you explain the reason that something happened (the cause) or the result of something that happened (the effect). (For more on cause and effect, see pp. 67–68.) You use cause-and-effect analysis often in your daily life. You might notice that when your tires aren't correctly inflated (cause), your car gets worse gas mileage (effect). After starting to drink high-calorie smoothies every day for breakfast (cause), you discover you've gained a few pounds (effect). With cause-and-effect analysis, you show your readers a logical connection between two or more events.

The writers of the three essays at the beginning of this chapter all use cause-and-effect analysis to develop their arguments. In "Write and Wrong," Anna Quindlen explains the effects that censorship had on the lives of Connie Heermann and her students. Samuel L. Jackson, in "In Character," develops his views about the causes of racism in Hollywood movies. In "An Ugly Toll of Technology: Impatience and Forgetfulness," Tara Parker-Pope uses scientific research to argue how certain types of media can have a negative effect on the way people think.

When you use cause-and-effect analysis to develop your argument, remember that there is a difference between cause and coincidence. To prove that there is a true relationship between events, give evidence—in the form of examples, statistics, or facts—to show how they are related. Draw on your personal experiences and knowledge, and on the experiences and knowledge of people you know. You might also want to include expert testimony to support your points. Consider, for example, how Tara Parker-Pope uses expert testimony to support her point in this paragraph from her essay:

> The problem is similar to an eating disorder, says Dr. Kimberly Young, a professor at St. Bonaventure University in New York who has led research on the addictive nature of online technology. Technology, like food, is an essential part of daily life, and those suffering from disordered online behavior cannot give it up entirely and instead have to learn moderation and controlled use. She suggests therapy to determine the underlying issues that set off a person's need to use the Internet "as a way of escape."

This expert testimony, which compares excessive Internet use with an eating disorder, helps support Parker-Pope's claim that technology is having a negative effect on people's ability to think and function.

■ HOW TO Use Cause-and-Effect Analysis

- Use cause and effect to show why something happened or what the result was when something happened.
- Show a logical connection between the cause and the effect.
- Use examples, statistics, facts, and expert testimony to support your analysis.

WRITING ACTIVITY 10 Draft Cause-and-Effect Sentences

Write several sentences that contain cause-and-effect analysis for your essay. Refer to these sentences when you revise your draft.

Building Your Essay

To be persuasive, your essay must be well developed. In other words, it must contain supporting details that convince your readers that your position is valid. First, though, you need to make an effective claim.

Make a Claim

A *claim* is a statement asserting that something is true. In persuasive writing, a claim is a type of thesis statement. As you may recall from Chapter 1, the *thesis statement* announces the topic of your essay; shows, explains, or argues a particular point about the topic; and gives readers a sense of what you will discuss in your essay. For an argumentative essay, you announce your topic and the point you will argue. Let's look at each of the qualities of an effective claim in more detail.

Express an Opinion   An effective claim expresses an opinion, not a fact. An *opinion* is an idea that some but not all people share. In contrast, a *fact* is something that can be verified as true by an objective observer.

> FACT   There is a great deal of spam on the Internet.
>
> OPINION   Because spam wastes people's time and money, it should be better regulated by the government.

The first statement can be verified by turning on a computer. There's no need to prove that it's true. The second statement, however, is a claim because some people will disagree with it. Notice that the claim includes the word *should*. Similar words used in claims include *needs to, ought*, and *must*.

Relate to Your Readers   An effective claim also seeks to persuade readers by pointing out how the topic relates to their lives. A claim that conveys only your personal interests, tastes, or experiences is not likely to persuade or interest readers. Rather, connect the claim to some aspect of your readers' lives.

> PERSONAL   Drivers should be able to use cell phones when they drive because I've never been in danger when this has happened.
>
> PERSUASIVE   Drivers should be able to use cell phones when they drive because researchers have shown that this practice is no more dangerous than any other distraction, such as changing the channel on the radio.

The first statement focuses on the writer. But the second statement relates the topic—drivers' use of cell phones—to a concept relevant to readers' lives.

Narrow the Focus   An effective claim focuses the topic so that it can be fully developed and supported. If your claim isn't sufficiently focused, you won't be able to discuss it in detail in your essay.

> **UNFOCUSED** There's too much violence on television.
>
> **FOCUSED** The graphic violence on the television show *Dexter* glamorizes a grisly use of force.

To support the claim made in the first example, you would have to cover all types of violence on all types of television shows—a large topic that would be better suited for a book than an essay. The second claim requires only that you focus on one type of violence (graphic violence) on one television show (*Dexter*). Because it's narrowly focused, this claim could be fully supported in an essay.

In addition, a focused claim does not leave readers with unanswered questions.

> **UNFOCUSED** Pornography should be banned.
>
> **FOCUSED** To prevent the sexual abuse of children, Congress should pass a law banning child pornography on the Internet.

In the first example, readers might ask: What type of pornography? Why should it be banned? How should it be banned? In the second, readers are told the type of pornography, why it should be banned, and how it could be banned (through federal legislation).

▪ HOW TO Make a Claim

- Express an opinion.
- Be persuasive by relating the claim to readers' lives.
- Keep the claim narrowly focused.

WRITING ACTIVITY 11 Revise Your Claim

Revise the claim for your essay so that it expresses an opinion, relates to your readers' lives, and is sufficiently focused.

Provide Pro Points

Once you have an effective claim, you need to concentrate on developing support for that claim—your reasons or pro points (*pro* means "in favor of"). *Pro points* tell readers why you believe your claim is true or valid. Keep in mind that pro points should always be supported with details (such as examples, facts, and statistics) and that the best supporting material is up-to-date, relevant, and easily understood by readers. A brief argumentative essay will usually need between three and five pro points. You can generate and develop pro points from your experiences, observations, and research.

Pro and con points are usually stated in topic sentences. For more on topic sentences, see pp. 36–39.

■ HOW TO Support Pro Points

- **Use recent material.** Because you're probably writing about a current issue, be sure to use supporting material that is up-to-date. By using recent material, you show your readers you're knowledgeable about your topic.

- **Use relevant material.** If your information isn't directly related to your topic, your readers will dismiss or ignore it. For example, if your topic is the portrayal of disabled people in recent movies, don't use examples from 1990s' television shows as support.

- **Use understandable material.** You probably know more about your topic than your readers do. You may need to explain the plot of a book, the meaning of a term, or the lyrics of a song to readers who are not familiar with the subject.

Experience   When trying to persuade others, we often look first to our own experiences with the topic. This is what Samuel L. Jackson does when he describes the types of acting roles he was offered early in his career. Suppose, for example, you're writing about obscene lyrics in rock music and you believe the lyrics are harmless because listeners tend to focus on the music, not the words. Thus, you have one pro point:

> Because most listeners focus on the music and not the words, obscene lyrics in rock music don't harm listeners.

How would you support this pro point? You could detail your own experiences with music. For instance, you could point out that you don't know the lyrics to your favorite song. However, keep in mind that what might be true for you may not be true for others.

Observation   Personal experiences alone are not enough to support an argument convincingly. Your observations of how the issue has affected others can also lead to pro points. In "Write and Wrong," Anna Quindlen's argument is based on her observations of what happened when Connie Heermann tried to teach the book *The Freedom Writers Diary*. Imagine, for instance, that you're arguing against censoring literature in high schools. Books weren't censored in your high school, but your cousin attended a school that banned several classics, including John Steinbeck's *Of Mice and Men* and George Orwell's *1984*. Because your cousin was unable to study these books in school, she was poorly prepared for her college entrance exams. From observing your cousin's experiences, you generate this pro point:

> Censoring important works of literature can limit students' opportunities in higher education.

You can support this point by describing your cousin's experience with censorship. However, what happened to your cousin might not happen to everyone, and unless your cousin is still in high school, her example might not be up-to-date. Thus, to strengthen your case, you could interview other students about their experiences with censorship or conduct research to collect facts and statistics that support your position.

Research   As we have seen, you will usually want to conduct some research on your topic to strengthen points gathered from your own experiences and observations. To convince readers of the harmful effects of too much access to media, Tara Parker-Pope presented recent scientific research that supported her points. Perhaps you're arguing that cable television companies should fund public-access television because it provides a necessary forum for groups that are misrepresented or ignored by the mainstream media. You could interview producers, question viewers, or look for information about the kinds of programming that are available only on public-access TV. From your research, you might generate the following pro point:

> Because commercial television news programs present few positive portrayals of immigrant neighborhoods, cable TV providers should use some of their profits to give community groups access to production equipment and free air time.

To support this pro point, you could provide information about the cable company's budget or describe a public-access show that focuses on a community rarely seen in network news.

GROUP ACTIVITY 5 Evaluate Supporting Material

Working in a group, examine the following claims. Determine whether the supporting material given for them is up-to-date, relevant, and easily understandable.

CLAIM The current rating system for movies needs to be improved.

1. More and more television shows are showing scenes of graphic violence.
2. Owners of movie theaters are reluctant to enforce the current rating system.
3. In 2001, half of all profitable movies contained sexually oriented material.
4. The profit margin for R-rated movies is almost 21 percent of all movies when aggregated.
5. When I sold movie tickets, I almost never checked people's IDs.
6. Movie producers avoid the R rating by making two versions of the same movie: a mild version for movie theaters and an explicit version for DVD or electronic sales and rental.

> **WRITING ACTIVITY 12** List and Support Your Pro Points

Review the pro points in your discovery draft. Are they sufficient? Are they effectively developed? Draw on your experiences, observations, and research to add additional pro points if you need them, and make sure that each point is supported by recent, relevant, and understandable information.

Respond to Con Points

An argument essay is most persuasive when you anticipate readers' objections and argue against them. Therefore, in addition to presenting pro points, you need to argue against the *con points* (*con* means "against"). To do this, put yourself in the place of the readers who might not agree with your pro points. Con points tell readers why someone might object to your claim, how these objections might be stated, and how you would respond to them.

List Con Points   First, you need to identify the most important con points against your claim. To do this, imagine that you disagree with your claim, and then think of reasons you might disagree with it. Suppose this is your claim:

> Companies that send unwanted spam e-mails and pop-up advertisements should be heavily taxed and regulated so that they'll go out of business.

Now imagine that you disagree with this claim—that you think the government should leave these companies alone. Here are two reasons:

> Although these companies are annoying, they still have a right to exist.
>
> If the government starts regulating these companies, it can start regulating other companies as well, which isn't right in a free-market economy.

These are your con points—the points that someone might make against the claim you are making. List just the most important con points. Depending on your topic, you might end up with two or three con points.

Refute Con Points   Examine your list of con points, and consider how you would respond to readers' objections. You want to *refute*, or argue against, the con points so that you can persuade readers to accept your claim. First, acknowledge what, if anything, is true about the con point; then, explain what you think is not true about it.

Let's continue the example about spam and pop-up advertisements on the Internet. Here's your first con point:

> Although these companies are annoying, they still have a right to exist.

Here's what you can say to *refute*, or argue against, this point:

> At times, annoyances can't be avoided. This is not one of those times. Because the spam and pop-ups are so numerous, individuals and companies have to spend a lot of money and time to get rid of them, which hurts productivity and the economy.

Here's your second con point:

> If the government starts regulating these companies, it can start regulating other companies as well, which isn't right in a free-market economy.

Here's one way to refute this con point:

> Even a free-market economy needs some regulation to protect consumers. By taxing and regulating spam and pop-ups, we can protect consumers, just as we already protect consumers by outlawing false advertisements and regulating drugs.

As these examples show, when you refute your con points, you're actually arguing in support of your pro points.

> **GROUP ACTIVITY 6** List and Refute Your Con Points
>
> Read your claim aloud to the students in your group. Ask them to disagree with your claim and to explain their reasons. List their responses, and use them as the con points for your claim. Refute each con point in writing (you will use them when you revise your draft).

> ⏻ **Debate online**
>
> Using an instant messaging tool such as Yahoo! Messenger, Google Talk, or Facebook Chat, hold an online debate with several classmates. Post your claim and one pro point, and then ask your classmates to respond to your claim by adding a pro point, adding a con point, or refuting a con point. Do the same for your classmates' topics. Use the best ideas generated in this debate when revising your essay.

Organize Pro and Con Points

Now that you've developed the ideas in your draft, you're ready to begin organizing those ideas. If you order your pro and con points in a logical way, your readers will become more convinced of your claim as they read your essay.

Order Pro Points   Some of your pro points will be more persuasive than others. Save your most convincing pro point for last so that you leave readers thinking about it. You might begin a paper with the least convincing pro point and build up to the most convincing one. Or you might begin with the second most convincing point, place the less convincing points in the middle, and end with the most convincing one.

Arrange Con Points   Where should you put the con points? You have several options. You may put con points at different spots in an essay, particularly when certain con points are closely connected to certain pro points. This pattern can help make the pro and con points flow smoothly in an essay. You may also begin an essay with the con points. After refuting them, give your pro points. Finally, you may save your con points until the end of the essay, but only do so when you can refute those points well. You don't want readers to finish your essay agreeing with the opposition.

■ HOW TO Organize Pro and Con Points

Pro points

- Save your most convincing pro point for last.

  OR

- Begin your essay with the least convincing pro point, and build up to the most convincing point.

  OR

- Begin with a fairly strong point, put the weaker points in the middle, and end with the strongest point.

Con points

- Connect each con point to its related pro point.

  OR

- Begin with con points, and then refute them and give pro points.

  OR

- Save con points for near the end of the essay, and refute them all at one time.

GROUP ACTIVITY 7 Order Pro and Con Points

Review Reginald's discovery draft on pages 253–54. Working in a group, list his pro points, and then create several con points. Put these pro and con points in the order you think is the most effective. Finally, compare your group's ordering of the pro and con points with the order that Reginald uses in his revised draft (pp. 264–66). Notice how Reginald improved his pro and con points in the revised draft.

> **WRITING ACTIVITY 13** Order Your Pro and Con Points

Think about the pro and con points for your essay about the media. List your pro points in the order in which they should appear in your revised draft. Then decide where you can include your con points, and insert them in your list.

Avoid Faulty Logic

Even if your argument is well supported and organized, it won't be persuasive unless it logically makes sense. Your readers will find your ideas worthwhile if you base your points on logical reasoning rather than faulty logic. Let's look at three common forms of faulty logic.

Hasty Generalization   A *hasty generalization* is a conclusion drawn from too little evidence. Suppose, for example, that you discovered a factual error in your local newspaper. Based on that single experience, you conclude your local newspaper is always inaccurate. Your conclusion, based on insufficient evidence (this single occasion), would be a hasty generalization. Just because you discovered one inaccuracy doesn't mean that all of the articles are inaccurate. One instance can't prove a point.

Here's another example: you argue that advertising in public schools has no harmful effects because it didn't harm you as a child. Your conclusion is based on insufficient evidence (only one example). More convincing evidence would include studies conducted to determine the effects of advertising on schoolchildren or surveys of children and teachers.

Either-Or Reasoning   *Either-or reasoning* proposes only two possible alternatives even though more than two options actually exist. For instance, you would use faulty either-or reasoning if you said, "Either I lose ten pounds, or I won't get a date." The reasoning is faulty because more than these two alternatives exist. You might get a date without losing any weight. Or you might lose ten pounds and still not get a date. Or you could lose five pounds and get several dates.

Likewise, a writer who argues "Either we regulate cigarette advertisements, or more and more people will die from lung cancer" is using faulty logic because other alternatives also exist, such as efforts to decrease smoking through public-service announcements and educational programs. Because of these efforts, fewer people might get lung cancer, whether or not cigarette advertising is regulated.

Faulty Cause-and-Effect Reasoning   *Faulty cause-and-effect reasoning* attributes an event to an unrelated cause. Superstitions are based on faulty cause-and-effect reasoning, such as when we blame a bad day on the black cat that crossed our path, the salt we spilled, or the mirror we broke. Logically, these events couldn't have caused the bad day because they were unrelated to what we experienced. Thus, we cannot assume that one event was caused by another event simply because one took place before the other.

Political candidates often use faulty cause-and-effect reasoning: "Since my opponent has been in the Senate, your taxes have increased." However, just because taxes went up after the senator was elected doesn't mean the senator raised the taxes. Perhaps they were increased by the previous Congress. Similarly, an essay writer who argues "Ever since certain types of music have become popular, teenage suicide rates have risen" fails to acknowledge other possible causes for the rise in teenage suicides. Unless the writer provides evidence to support this point, the argument is based on faulty cause-and-effect reasoning.

> **WRITING ACTIVITY 14** Eliminate Faulty Logic in Your Draft

Exchange your draft with a partner. Ask your partner to point out any hasty generalizations, either-or reasoning, or faulty cause-and-effect reasoning in your draft. (You should do the same for your partner.) Correct any errors in logic that your partner identifies.

A Student's Revised Draft

Student writer Reginald Jones was relatively happy with his discovery draft about censorship in his campus newspaper, but his classmates weren't as persuaded by his argument as he thought they'd be. With their help, he added support for his pro points and identified con points that he needed to address. Before you read Reginald's revised draft, reread his discovery draft (pp. 253–54). Notice how his argument is stronger in the revision. (You will also notice some errors in the revised draft; these will be corrected when Reginald edits his essay later on.)

Newspaper Ad Sparks Controversy

An advertisement, "Ten Reasons Why Reparations for Blacks Is a Bad Idea   1
for Blacks — and Racist" ran in last weeks school newspaper. A reparation is a
repayment for damage done in the past. This ad stated a number of reasons
why blacks should not receive repayments from the United States government

The introduction is more interesting.

because of the damages done by slavery. Some of the reasons given were that
not all blacks have suffered because of slavery and that welfare and
affirmative action has served as reparations. This ad, which some call a "hate"
ad, upset a number of students and faculty. Some people wanted to burn all of
the newspapers, some wanted a formal apology from the editor, and some said

the paper should never have run the ad in the first place. As a supporter of
freedom of speech, I defend the right of the school newspaper to run this ad
whether I agree with it or not.

The editor of the school newspaper doesn't have to apologize for this ad.
Because the Constitution of the United States provides for freedom of
expression. The First Amendment to the Constitution states, "Congress shall
make no law respecting an establishment of religion, or prohibiting the free
exercise thereof; or abridging the freedom of speech, or of the press; or the
right of the people peaceably to assemble, and to petition the Government for
a redress of grievances." Linda Chavez, a writer for Creators Syndicate, says that
"the reparations debate has the potential of replacing affirmative action as the
most volatile race issue in America, with Americans deeply divided on the
topic" (6A). If we value our Constitution, then we must protect it even if that
means using our campus newspapers as the showcase for both sides of an issue.

Universities are supposed to be a place where ideas are debated. However,
when David Horowitz, the founder of the Center for the Study of Popular
Culture, requested ad space in 71 campus newspapers, only 21 would run the
ad (Chavez 6A). This is unfortunate, if we eliminate every piece of writing
that someone finds offensive, we will no longer have a free exchange of ideas.
There are many examples of books that people would like to ban. Some people
have called for the banning of the Harry Potter series of books because of
their focus on wizardry and witchcraft. Some computer labs attempt to block
students from visiting pornographic Web sites. If colleges remove every book
and Web site that someone finds offensive, the free exchange of ideas would
become very limited.

To those students who propose burning the newspapers, I remind them
that this would be a crime. We don't want to encourage people to commit
crimes just to ban material that make them uncomfortable. There are better
ways to protest. Students could run an ad themselves explaining their views
on the topic of reparations for blacks, or they could write to the author of the
ad to protest his views. The topic has been debated as part of Black History
Month activities. This has happened on our campus. We have set up debates
and had students present both sides of the reparation argument.

Rather than burning newspapers or demanding an apology, they should
discuss the ideas expressed in the ad and not just refuse to run it. We must
attack these ideas with ideas that are even stronger. Joan Bertin of the
National Coalition against Censorship says, "While student protests are an
appropriate way to explore controversy, when students take it upon themselves
to suppress ideas that they find objectionable they fail to meet the challenge

Margin annotations:

The claim is more specific.

2

A strong pro point comes first.

A pro point is supported with expert testimony.

3

A second pro point is supported by facts and observations.

Cause and effect are used.

A hasty generalization is eliminated.

4   A con point is refuted.

A third pro point is supported by observation.

5

A fourth pro point is supported by expert testimony.

A con point is refuted.

of a free society—to counter offensive ideas with more persuasive arguments of their own" (par. 4). We recently had a campus debate. We concluded that reparations are not likely to occur and that the discussion of them only divides Americans.

The conclusion restates the claim.

As students and teachers, we must protect freedom of expression even if it   6 means permitting some advertisements that we don't like to appear in our school newspapers. Instead of attempting to ban these advertisements, we must come up with constructive ways to encourage debate on the content of the ads themselves.

Works Cited

Bertin, Joan. "Free Speech Groups Express Concern over Student Reaction to Controversial Ad." *NCAC on the Issues*. National Coalition against Censorship, 1 Mar. 2002. Web. 3 Mar. 2002.

Chavez, Linda. "Reparations Issue Could Be Divisive." *El Paso Times* 3 Mar. 2002: 6A. Print.

GROUP ACTIVITY 8 Analyze Reginald's Revised Draft

Use the following questions to discuss with your classmates how Reginald has improved his draft.

1. Is Reginald's claim more effective now? Why or why not?
2. How has Reginald improved his pro points?
3. How well has he refuted his con points?
4. In your view, how well does he organize his pro and con points?
5. How well did he avoid faulty logic?
6. How could Reginald's draft benefit from further revision?

GROUP ACTIVITY 9 Peer Review

Form a group with two or three other students, and exchange copies of your drafts. Read your draft aloud while your classmates follow along. Take notes on your classmates' responses to the following questions about your draft.

1. What do you like best about my essay?
2. How interesting is my introduction? Do you want to continue reading the essay? Why or why not?
3. How effective is my claim? Suggest an improvement.
4. How well do I support my pro points? Is my supporting material recent, relevant, and easily understood?

5. How well do I refute the con points?

6. Are my pro and con points effectively organized? Can you suggest a better way to order them?

7. Did I avoid faulty logic?

8. Where in the draft does my writing confuse you? How can I clarify my thoughts?

9. How clear is the purpose of my essay?

> **WRITING ACTIVITY 15 Revise Your Draft**

Taking your classmates' suggestions for revision into consideration, revise your essay. Focus on using cause-and-effect analysis, making your claim more specific, supporting your pro points, refuting your con points, organizing these points, and avoiding faulty logic.

Step 4 Edit Your Sentences

At this point, you have worked hard to improve your essay's claim, development, and organization. Now you need to edit it to polish the language and eliminate distracting errors. In this section, you'll focus on combining sentences with introductory phrases and on correcting subject-verb agreement errors.

Combining Sentences Using Introductory Phrases

As you know from previous chapters, sentence combining is a good way to connect closely related, short sentences. Sentence combining can make your writing clearer and more interesting.

One way to combine short, closely related sentences is to turn the sentence with the least important information into an introductory phrase for the other. A *phrase* is a group of words that lacks a subject, a verb, or both. It cannot stand alone as a sentence. When you combine sentences with an introductory phrase, begin with the phrase, and follow the phrase with a comma.

In Reginald's discovery draft, for example, he wrote two sentences to describe his opinion of the ad:

> I don't like the ad and don't agree with what it says, but I do believe in freedom of speech. For this reason, I defend the right of the school newspaper to run this ad.

In his revised draft, he combined these two sentences by using an introductory phrase and eliminating unnecessary words to create a stronger thesis statement:

As a supporter of freedom of speech, I defend the right of the school newspaper to run this ad whether I agree with it or not.

> **■HOW TO Combine Sentences Using Introductory Phrases**
>
> - Combine two short, closely related sentences by turning the sentence with the least important information into a phrase (a group of words that lacks a subject, verb, or both).
> - Place the phrase at the beginning of the remaining sentence.
> - Use a comma after the introductory phrase.

EDITING ACTIVITY 1 Use Introductory Phrases

Use an introductory phrase to combine the following pairs or groups of sentences. You may need to eliminate unnecessary words, change words, or move words around.

EXAMPLE *Founded in 2001,* Wikipedia is an online, interactive encyclopedia. ~~It was founded in 2001.~~

1. Its founder was Jimmy Wales. He wanted to create an encyclopedia that everyone on the planet could access for free.

2. Anyone can create an entry or edit an entry that already exists. Wikipedia uses software called wiki.

3. Hundreds of thousands of people contribute to Wikipedia. These contributors come from a variety of backgrounds.

4. Some people prefer to correct or change information that is already posted to the site. They don't actually add information.

5. Some researchers have studied the entries in Wikipedia. They have found that it contains more errors than do traditional encyclopedias, such as *Britannica*. Some of these errors are major.

For additional practice with combining sentences, go to **bedfordstmartins.com /choices** and click on **Exercise Central**.

EDITING ACTIVITY 2 Combine Your Sentences

Examine your revised draft for short, closely related sentences. Where it makes sense to do so, combine them with introductory phrases. You may also use any of the other sentence-combining techniques you have learned (coordinating conjunctions, conjunctive adverbs, subordinating conjunctions, or relative clauses) if you wish.

Correcting Subject-Verb Agreement Problems

You may recall that a complete sentence contains a subject and a verb. The subject tells who or what is doing the action, and the verb tells the action or links the subject to the rest of the sentence. The subject and the verb must *agree* in number. In other words, a *singular subject* must have a *singular verb*, and a *plural subject* must have a *plural verb*.

To make sure that your subjects and verbs agree in number, you need to identify the subject of your sentence and know whether it is singular or plural. Problems in subject-verb agreement often happen when the subject and verb of the sentence are not obvious.

INCORRECT	*Harry don't* care for my podcasts.
CORRECT	*Harry doesn't* care for my podcasts.
INCORRECT	Talk-show *hosts* on the radio *is* meaner than they were a decade ago.
CORRECT	Talk-show *hosts* on the radio *are* meaner than they were a decade ago.

The following pronouns are all singular. When using any of them as the subject of a sentence, use a singular verb.

anybody	everyone	nothing
anyone	everything	somebody
anything	nobody	someone
everybody	no one	something

INCORRECT	*Anybody write* better than I do.
CORRECT	*Anybody writes* better than I do.
INCORRECT	*Someone need* to take care of this.
CORRECT	*Someone needs* to take care of this.

> **EDITING ACTIVITY 3 Correct Subject-Verb Agreement**

Circle the correct form of the verb in the following sentences.

EXAMPLE Everybody (needs, need) to be considerate of others in public places.

1. The movies I wanted to download (was, were) unavailable.

2. Nobody (feel, feels) the way I do about WiFi hotspots.

3. Of all the bands I listen to, my favorite one (is, are) Red House Painters.

4. Everyone I talk to (agrees, agree) with me on this.

5. The Chicago Bears (doesn't, don't) excite me.

For additional practice correcting subject-verb agreement problems, go to **bedfordstmartins.com /choices** and click on **Exercise Central**.

> **WRITING ACTIVITY 16** **Edit Your Essay**

Using the Handbook in Part Four of this book as a guide, edit your revised draft for errors in grammar, spelling, and punctuation. Your classmates can help you locate and correct errors you might have overlooked.

A Student's Edited Essay

You may have noticed that Reginald's revised draft contained errors in grammar, spelling, and punctuation. Reginald corrected these errors in his edited essay. His corrections are noted in the margin.

The correct MLA format is used.

Reginald Jones
Professor Heller
English 1301
2 Mar. 2012

Newspaper Ad Sparks Controversy

An advertisement, "Ten Reasons Why Reparations for Blacks Is a Bad   1
Idea for Blacks — and Racist" ran in last week's school newspaper. A

An apostrophe is corrected.

reparation is a repayment for damage done in the past. This ad stated a
number of reasons why blacks should not receive repayments from the United
States government because of the damages done by slavery. Some of the
reasons given were that not all blacks have suffered because of slavery and
that welfare and affirmative action have served as reparations. This ad, which
some call a "hate" ad, upset a number of students and faculty. Some people

A subject-verb agreement problem is corrected.

wanted to burn all of the newspapers, some wanted a formal apology from the
editor, and some said the paper should never have run the ad in the first
place. As a supporter of freedom of speech, I defend the right of the school
newspaper to run this ad whether I agree with it or not.

Because the Constitution of the United States provides for freedom of   2

A sentence fragment is corrected.

expression, the editor of the school newspaper doesn't have to apologize
for this ad. The First Amendment to the Constitution states, "Congress shall
make no law respecting an establishment of religion, or prohibiting the free
exercise thereof; or abridging the freedom of speech, or of the press; or the
right of the people peaceably to assemble, and to petition the Government for
a redress of grievances." Linda Chavez, a writer for Creators Syndicate, says
that "the reparations debate has the potential of replacing affirmative action
as the most volatile race issue in America, with Americans deeply divided on
the topic" (6A). If we value our Constitution, then we must protect it even if
that means using our campus newspapers as the showcase for both sides of
an issue.

Universities are supposed to be a place where ideas are debated. However, when David Horowitz, the founder of the Center for the Study of Popular Culture, requested ad space in 71 campus newspapers, only 21 would run the ad (Chavez 6A). This is unfortunate. If we eliminate every piece of writing that someone finds offensive, we will no longer have a free exchange of ideas. There are many examples of books that people would like to ban. Most recently, some people have called for the banning of the Harry Potter series of books because of their focus on wizardry and witchcraft. Some computer labs attempt to block students from visiting pornographic Web sites. If colleges remove every book and Web site that someone finds offensive, the free exchange of ideas would become very limited.

3

— A comma splice is corrected.

To those students who propose burning the newspapers, I remind them that this would be a crime. We don't want to encourage people to commit crimes just to ban material that <u>makes</u> them uncomfortable. There are better ways to protest. Students could run an ad themselves explaining their views on the topic of reparations for blacks, or they could write to the author of the ad to protest his views. On our campus, the topic has been debated as part of Black History Month activities. We have set up debates and had students present both sides of the reparation argument.

4

— A subject-verb agreement problem is corrected.

— Sentences have been combined.

Rather than burning newspapers or demanding an apology, students should discuss the ideas expressed in the ad and not just refuse to run it. We must attack these ideas with ideas that are even stronger. Joan Bertin of the National Coalition against Censorship says, "While student protests are an appropriate way to explore controversy, when students take it upon themselves to suppress ideas that they find objectionable they fail to meet the challenge of a free society — to counter offensive ideas with more persuasive arguments of their own" (par. 4). At our most recent campus debate, we concluded that reparations are not likely to occur and that the discussion of them only divides Americans.

5   A vague pronoun reference is corrected.

— A sentence is combined.

As students and teachers, we must protect freedom of expression even if it means permitting some advertisements that we don't like to appear in our school newspapers. Instead of attempting to ban these advertisements, we must come up with constructive ways to encourage debate on the content of the ads themselves.

6

Works Cited

Bertin, Joan. "Free Speech Groups Express Concern over Student Reaction to Controversial Ad." *NCAC on the Issues*. National Coalition against Censorship, 1 Mar. 2002. Web. 3 Mar. 2002.

Chavez, Linda. "Reparations Issue Could Be Divisive." *El Paso Times* 3 Mar. 2002: 6A. Print.

(Step 5 Share Your Essay

Now that you have gathered ideas on your topic and drafted, revised, and edited your essay, you're ready to share your essay. Interested readers might include friends and family members, but to reach a broader audience, consider submitting your essay to your campus or local newspaper. If your essay is about something that most college students are interested in, such as censoring campus speakers or privacy issues with social media sites, your campus newspaper might be most appropriate. If your topic is about something with a broader appeal, such as controversial Web sites or the effects of too much technology on the brain, your local newspaper might be best. By submitting your essay for publication, you can reach a wide audience and influence more people.

To submit your essay to a newspaper, first find out the newspaper's policy about submissions from the public. Most newspapers explain this policy somewhere on their editorial or opinion pages, where opinion pieces from the public are usually published. Typically an e-mail address is provided so that you can submit your essay electronically.

As an alternative to trying to get your entire essay published in a newspaper, you can shorten it to a paragraph or two and submit it as a letter to the editor. Most newspapers publish several letters from the public every day, so the chances of getting published are typically good. If you choose this method of sharing, limit your essay to your claim and several of your pro points. You can usually find directions for submitting a letter to the editor on the same pages that these letters are published.

By reaching out to a wider audience, such as the readers of a campus or local newspaper, you will be able to influence more people—which is what writing is all about.

⏻ Respond to a post

Many local newspapers and television stations have Facebook and Twitter sites on which people can post responses and ideas. If one of your local news organizations has a story on your topic, consider sending an online response. These sites allow only brief comments, so you'll be limited to stating a main idea. However, this is another way to share your viewpoint with a broad audience.

CHAPTER CHECKLIST

❑ I read essays that argued about censorship, stereotypes, and the media in our lives to explore and learn about this chapter's theme.

❑ I used cause-and-effect analysis, as well as other methods of development, to support my ideas.

❑ I wrote an effective claim that expresses an opinion, relates to my readers' lives, and is focused.

❑ I used pro points—which came from experiences, observations, and research—to support my claim.

❑ I supported pro points with material that is recent, relevant, and easily understood.

❑ I argued against con points, or objections, to a claim.

❑ I arranged pro and con points so that readers become more convinced of my claim as they read through my essay.

❑ I avoided faulty logic when arguing my points.

❑ I combined short, closely related sentences using introductory phrases or other techniques to improve my flow of ideas.

❑ I edited my draft to correct errors, including problems with subject-verb agreement.

❑ I submitted my essay to my campus or local newspaper—or to another print or online publication.

REFLECTING ON YOUR WRITING

To help you reflect on the writing you did in this chapter, answer the following questions:

1. How did you decide on your topic for this essay?

2. Which pro point do you think is your strongest?

3. How persuasive do you think your essay would be to someone who strongly disagrees with your claim?

4. How did you feel submitting your essay to your campus or local newspaper?

5. If you had more time, what more would you do to improve your essay before sharing it with readers?

Using your answers to these questions, complete a Writing Process Report for this chapter (you can download a report form at **bedfordstmartins.com /choices**). Once you complete this report, freewrite about what you learned in this chapter.

"If you make the choice to go vegan, you can take a big step toward improving the environment."

— ANDREA BENITEZ, "WHY GO VEGAN?"

Proposing a Solution
Health, Education, and the Environment

At the center of any argument is an *issue*—a question or topic on which people disagree. Because some issues—such as those involving health, education, or the environment—affect many people, we often read or hear about them in the media. What should be done about the increasing rate of childhood obesity? What steps should be taken to deal with climate change? Will school vouchers improve the educational system or undermine public schools? When budgets are being cut, how can students get the financial aid they need? How much money should be spent to protect endangered species? Should we drill for oil in Alaska's Arctic National Wildlife Refuge? Politicians, columnists, and talk-show hosts argue with one another and their audiences every day about problems and how to solve them.

People often argue about important issues because they want to make a difference. Writing is an especially effective way to accomplish this goal. You can help solve a problem by writing an essay that states your position on an issue, provides evidence that a problem exists, and proposes a solution. This chapter will show you how to write an argument that can convince your readers to take action on something that is important to you.

In this chapter, you will identify a health, education, or environmental problem that is important to you, and propose a solution for it. As you follow the steps of the writing process, you will

- Explore the chapter topic by reading essays that propose a solution.
- Gather ideas by relating aloud, consulting with others, and researching your topic.
- Practice adding outside sources to your essay.
- Develop your ideas using **argument**.
- Use appeals and a reasonable tone to help persuade your readers.
- Combine sentences using appositives.
- Practice correcting shifts in person.
- Send your essay to someone with the authority to act on your proposal.

You will begin by reading essays by professional writers that propose solutions to problems of importance to them. You will also follow a student, Andrea Benitez, as she writes about veganism and its impact on the environment. You will then write about an issue of importance to you and send your essay to someone in authority who can act on your proposal. ■

GROUP ACTIVITY 1 Think about Problems and Solutions

The woman in the photograph on the chapter-opening page looks passionate about fruits and vegetables. Do you think that eating more of them could be a solution to environmental pollution?

Getting Started   Reading Essays That Propose a Solution to a Problem

Writing an argument that identifies an issue and proposes a solution requires all of your writing skills. You must identify a problem, use evidence to illustrate the problem, investigate what has worked and not worked to solve the problem, propose a solution, and then convince your readers that your proposal will work.

As you read the following three argument essays, jot down the evidence that the authors present to convince you that the problems exist. Do these authors convince you that these problems are real and that their solutions are workable? Can you think of other possible solutions to these problems?

Notice how the authors use their own ideas but also use outside sources to provide additional information and strengthen their arguments. An outside source is an expert on a particular topic. You may have the opportunity to personally interview an outside source, but you usually learn by reading what the source has to say in a book, magazine, newspaper, print or online journal, or Web site. (For additional essays proposing a solution to a health, education, or environmental problem, see p. 589.)

A Health Problem

DARSHAK SANGHAVI

Quicker Liquor: Should We Lower the Legal Drinking Age?

Darshak Sanghavi is the chief of pediatric cardiology at UMass Medical School. He also writes health-related columns for the *New York Times Magazine* and *Slate* magazine and has written a book entitled *A Map of the Child: A Pediatrician's Tour of the Body*. In "Quicker Liquor: Should We Lower the Legal Drinking Age?" published in *Slate* in 2008, Sanghavi argues that lowering the drinking age from 21 to 18 will not reduce teen binge drinking on college campuses. Instead, he proposes more realistic solutions to the problem of teenage drinking. For an alternative perspective on this issue, read Elizabeth M. Whelan's essay "Perils of Prohibition" on page 589. Both essays were written before July 2009 when the National Minimum Drinking Age Act was renewed by Congress.

Last week, a coalition of presidents from more than 100 colleges and universities called on authorities to consider lowering the legal drinking age. The so-called Amethyst Initiative, founded by a fed-up former president of Middlebury College, asserts that "twenty-one is not working" because the current drinking age has led to a "culture of dangerous, clandestine binge-drinking" on college campuses. "How many times," they rhetorically ask, "must we relearn the lessons of prohibition?" (*Amethyst Initiative*).

These academic heavyweights — who include the presidents of institutions like Duke, Spelman, Tufts, and Johns Hopkins — believe that lowering the legal drinking age can promote more responsible alcohol use. The familiar argument is that singling out alcohol to make it off-limits is odd, since 18-year-olds may legally join the military, vote, buy cigarettes, and watch porn. Meanwhile over the past decades, binge-drinking has soared among young people. The 1984 federal law that helps determine the legal drinking age is up for renewal next year, and the college presidents believe this law "stifles meaningful debate" and discourages "new ideas" to stop binge-drinking, like allowing kids over 18 to buy alcohol after a course on its "history, culture, law, chemistry, biology, neuroscience as well as exposure to accident victims and individuals in recovery" (*Amethyst Initiative*).

It's nice to think that simply lowering the drinking age would make college students behave better (as well as cheer loudly). But the Amethyst Initiative — named for the gemstone believed by ancient Greeks to stave off drunkenness — has naively exaggerated the benefits of a lower legal drinking age. They ignore some of the implications of their recommendations, fail to acknowledge their own complicity in the campus drinking problem, and ultimately gloss over better solutions to bingeing. Kind of like addicts might.

1   Sanghavi explains the problem: students secretly binge drink because they can't drink legally. A large number of college presidents want to lower the drinking age to 18.

2   In this paragraph, Sanghavi describes the university presidents' position on the problem of binge drinking. He quotes from their Web site, Amethyst Initiative.

3   Sanghavi provides his response to the presidents' position.

For the next several paragraphs, Sanghavi provides evidence that binge drinking is a serious problem. Notice the number of outside sources he uses to support his position.

In truth, the higher drinking age saves lives and has little relation to college bingeing. Some history: After her daughter was killed by an intoxicated driver, Candy Lightner founded Mothers Against Drunk Driving and successfully lobbied for the 1984 National Minimum Drinking Age Act, which gave full federal highway funds only to states that set the minimum age to purchase or consume alcohol at 21 years. Most states immediately complied, setting the stage for a national experiment. **4**

Sanghavi introduces a number of facts and statistics to underscore his position.

According to the federal study Monitoring the Future, underage drinking dropped instantly. From 1977 to 2007, the percentage of 12th graders drinking at least monthly fell from 70 percent to 45 percent—almost immediately after the law was enacted, and lastingly. Fatal car crashes involving drunk young adults dipped 32 percent, resulting in 1,000 fewer lives lost per year. Impressively, this decrease occurred despite minimal efforts at enforcement; the mere presence of the law was protective ("Facts"). The relationship is likely causal. In 1999, by comparison, New Zealand lowered the drinking age from 20 to 18, and while alcohol-related crashes involving 15- to 19-year-olds subsequently fell, they declined far less than in the overall population (Kypri et al. 129). Today, all major public health authorities, including the American Medical Association, Centers for Disease Control, National Highway Traffic Safety Board, and surgeon general, support the higher drinking age. **5**

Here Sanghavi introduces another study that discredits a popular myth about teen drinking in other countries.

We also know that kids in more permissive parts of the world don't drink more responsibly. A magisterial 760-page review from the Institute of Medicine in 2004 noted dryly, "As the committee demonstrates in this report, countries with lower drinking ages are not better off than the United States in terms of the harmful consequences of youths' drinking" (Committee). Those romantic visions of Irish lasses demurely drinking a glass of ale or sophisticated French teens sipping wine just don't reflect reality. **6**

Sanghavi uses even more research to show how serious the problem is.

Still, the college presidents signing the Amethyst statement aren't hallucinating about the American version of the problem: There *are* more binge drinkers on campuses today. Among college students, the percentage of "frequent-heavy" drinkers remained stable from 1977 to 1989, at about 30 percent (Wechsler and Issac 2930). However, bingeing began increasing steadily throughout the late 1990s, long after the legal age was increased (Naimi et al. 71). **7**

So if we can't blame the drinking age, what's going on? It's key to understand that there are huge disparities in bingeing, depending on where you live and go to school. State bingeing rates vary three- to four-fold, with middle-American states like Michigan, Illinois, and Minnesota far outpacing coastal areas like Washington state, North Carolina, New York, and New Jersey (Naimi et al. 72). David Rosenbloom, a professor of public health at Boston University who studies alcohol use, told me bingeing rates at colleges even in the same city can differ dramatically. **8**

Again, Sanghavi uses outside sources to support his position.

The reasons aren't very complicated: The strongest determinants of college bingeing are weak state and campus alcohol control policies (the regulatory environment) and the presence of lots of bingeing older adults (a locale's overall drinking culture) (Nelson et al. 444). Impressively, states that severely restrict the **9** promotion of alcohol and its purchase in large quantities — for example, by requiring registration of keg sales, restricting happy hours and beer-pitcher sales, and regulating advertising like billboards — have half the college bingeing rate of states that don't.

In addition to lobbying for these kinds of local laws, college presidents could 10 also promote alcohol education (obviously) and racial and ethnic on-campus diversity (less obviously). As one might expect, alcohol education does help; for example, a brief educational program at the University of Washington reduced long-term binge-drinking in high-risk students (Baer et al. 1310). Additionally, young whites drink far more than young African-Americans and Latinos, men drink more than women, and younger students drink more than older students. When mixed, all the groups moderate their alcohol consumption; thus, colleges with greater student diversity have less bingeing across the board (Wechsler and Kuo 1929).

There's a faster and more effective way to reduce underage drinking — and 11 bingeing — as well: Forget the drinking age debate and sharply increase excise taxes on beer, the preferred choice of underage drinkers. (In real dollars, taxes on liquor, and especially beer, have dropped substantially over the past 30 years.) Just as higher cigarette taxes trump all other methods of curbing smoking among young people, higher alcohol taxes stop kids from drinking too much.

David Rosenbloom notes that the five states with the highest beer taxes have 12 half the binge drinking of other states. In 2004, the Institute of Medicine concluded, with characteristic understatement, that the "overall weight of the evidence" that higher taxes reduce alcohol abuse and related harm to young adults is "substantial." Just as gasoline taxes today don't fully reflect the societal costs of carbon emissions, alcohol taxes are too low, argue economists P. J. Cook and M. J. Moore, since they cover less than half of alcohol's external costs, including damage done by drunk young drivers (120).

Of course, in the end a lot of teens will binge-drink, no matter what the law 13 says. But that's not an argument against making the legal age 21 years old to buy and consume it. (After all, a third of high-schoolers have smoked marijuana, and few people want to legalize it for them.) Rather, the current law is best viewed as a palliative medical treatment for an incurable condition. Chemotherapy can't cure terminal cancer, but it can make patients hurt a little less and perhaps survive a little longer. Similarly, the current drinking age undeniably reduces teen binge-drinking and death a little bit, without any bad side-effects. When there's no complete cure, though, desperate people are vulnerable to the dubious marketing hype of snake-oil peddlers — which is all the Amethyst Initiative is offering up now.

Works Cited

Amethyst Initiative. Amethyst Initiative, 2008. Web. 15 July 2008.

Baer, John S., et al. "Brief Intervention for Heavy-Drinking College Students: 4-Year Follow-Up and Natural History." *American Journal of Public Health* 91.8 (2001): 1310–16. Print.

Sanghavi begins to introduce his proposed solutions to the problem of binge drinking.

For the next three paragraphs, Sanghavi continues to give possible solutions to the problem of binge drinking.

Notice the number of outside experts Sanghavi uses to strengthen his argument.

Sanghavi concludes by comparing the university presidents to snake-oil peddlers, a strong indictment of their position.

Committee on Developing a Strategy to Reduce and Prevent Underage Drinking. *Reducing Underage Drinking: A Collective Responsibility. The National Academies Press.* The National Academies, 2004. Web. 1 Feb. 2011.

Cook, Philip J., and Michael J. Moore. "The Economics of Alcohol Abuse and Alcohol-Control Policies." *Health Affairs* 21.2 (2002): 120–33. Print.

"Facts about Youth and Alcohol." *American Medical Association.* American Medical Association, n.d. Web. 7 Feb. 2011.

Kypri, Kypros, et al. "Minimum Purchasing Age for Alcohol and Traffic Crash Injuries among 15- to 19-Year-Olds in New Zealand." *American Journal of Public Health* 96.1 (2006): 126–31. Print.

Naimi, Timothy S., et al. "Binge Drinking among US Adults." *Journal of the American Medical Association* 289.1 (2003): 70–75. Print.

Nelson, Toben F., et al. "The State Sets the Rate: The Relationship among State-Specific College Binge Drinking, State Binge Drinking Rates, and Selected State Alcohol Control Policies." *American Journal of Public Health* 95.3 (2005): 441–46. Print.

Wechsler, Henry, and Nancy Issac. "'Binge' Drinkers at Massachusetts Colleges: Prevalence, Drinking Style, Time Trends, and Associated Problems." *Journal of the American Medical Association* 267.21 (1992): 2929–31. Print.

Wechsler, Henry, and Meichun Kuo. "Watering Down the Drinks: The Moderating Effect of College Demographics on Alchohol Use of High-Risk Groups." *American Journal of Public Health* 93.11 (2003): 1929–33. Print.

READING ACTIVITY 1 Build Your Vocabulary

Determine the meanings of the following words from the context of Darshak Sanghavi's essay. Then check their meanings by looking up the words in a dictionary: coalition (1), clandestine (1), rhetorically (1), stave off (3), complicity (3), disparities (8), moderate (10), palliative (13), vulnerable (13), dubious (13).

GROUP ACTIVITY 2 Discuss the Reading

Discuss the following questions about "Quicker Liquor: Should We Lower the Legal Drinking Age?" with your classmates.

1. According to Sanghavi, why wouldn't lowering the legal drinking age from 21 to 18 address the problem of teenage binge drinking?

2. Sanghavi says the Amethyst Initiative "has naively exaggerated the benefits of a lower legal drinking age. . . . Kind of like addicts might." What is the tone of these words: Angry? Humorous? Condescending? Why does he use this tone?

3. What does Sanghavi propose as a better solution to the problem of teenage binge drinking? Is his proposal workable?

4. Can you identify another health issue facing Americans? What is your solution?

> **WRITING ACTIVITY 1 Share Your Ideas**
>
> Write a paragraph or two about a health problem that interests you. First, describe the problem, provide evidence that the problem exists, and then propose a solution. Where might you find outside sources to support your position? Share what you have written with your classmates.

An Education Problem

AMANDA SCHAFFER

How to Buck Up the Science Ladies: An Easy Way to Boost Women's Scores in Physics

Amanda Schaffer, a graduate of Harvard University, writes science columns for *Slate* magazine and the *New York Times.* Her writing has also appeared in the *Washington Post,* the *Wall Street Journal,* and *Technology Review.* Her degree in science history has provided her with the background knowledge to write articles such as "How to Buck Up the Science Ladies," in which she argues that simple writing exercises can boost female science students' grades.

1   Last week, researchers at the University of Colorado published a psych experiment that seems almost too good to be true. They showed that two 15-minute writing exercises, administered to an intro physics class early in the semester, could substantially boost the scores of female students (Miyake et al. 1236). Even more curious: the exercises had nothing to do with physics. Instead, students were asked to write about things that mattered to them, like creativity or relationships with family and friends. How could a few paragraphs on personal values translate into enduring better mastery of pulleys and frictionless planes?

2   When it comes to math and science classes, women can be subtly hampered by negative stereotypes about their gender. This is the idea of stereotype threat, advanced by psychologists Joshua Aronson and Claude Steele, and now solidly established, as I've written in *Slate* before. Stereotype threat can roar into action when members of any stereotyped group are primed to think about belonging to it—in other words, when women focus on being female or African Americans on being black (Schaffer). It causes performance problems, but stereotype threat can also be countered, often in simple ways. As the Colorado writing exercises show, getting women to focus on things they care about can buck them up. The lesson is that small doses of affirmation can do a lot of good.

Here's what we know about how stereotype threat works: In the 1990s, researchers found that women taking a math exam who were told that the test had "shown gender differences in the past" scored lower than other women with equivalent math backgrounds. Similarly, women asked to watch commercials in which ditzy ladies gushed about brownie mix afterward expressed less interest in quantitative pursuits (Davies et al. 1623). Stereotype threat is a universal offender: It can sabotage white men on the basketball court or men more broadly on a test of social sensitivity. Whenever people are made to worry that they might confirm a negative assumption—for instance, that girls can't do math or that white men can't jump—they may be less likely to do their best. Frustratingly, the stereotypes they want so badly to avoid may instead become self-fulfilling. For women on a math-and-science track, the threat is likely to worsen the further along they get, both because they will have fewer female classmates and role models and because they may have stronger "math-equals-males implicit associations," as psychologist Cordelia Fine points out in her terrific new book, *Delusions of Gender* (35).

At the same time, in 2007, psychologists handily proved that stereotype threat isn't intractable with a study of top-tier calculus students at the University of Texas (Good, Aronson, and Harder 25). At the beginning of one exam, half the students read a statement that said, in part: "Analysis of thousands of students' test results has shown that males and females perform equally well on this test." The women who read this statement scored significantly higher on average than other women in the class. They also scored higher on average than the *men*.

Now, the Colorado researchers have shown that writing exercises can also make a difference for female science students. In a double-blind study published last week in *Science*, the researchers worked with 399 undergrads in a calculus-based physics class. They randomly assigned some of them to write about two or three items from a list that included "learning and gaining knowledge," "belonging to a social group," "athletic ability," "relationships with family and friends," and "sense of humor." They were then told to reflect on why these things mattered to them. (The other students received the same list of values, but were asked to choose the ones least important to them and write about why they might be important to other people.) Students completed these exercises early in the semester, at moments when they might be expected to feel uncertain about the class: the first week of school and then the week before the first midterm (Miyake et al. 1234–37).

The benefits were dramatic. Most of the women who received C's in the class were in the group that had written on values they cared about least. Most of the women who received B's had written on what they cared about most. (There was no effect for women who were getting A's, or for men in general.) Women who affirmed their own values also scored higher on a standardized exam of key physics concepts, taken at the end of the term. Strikingly, women who'd said they believed the stereotype that men are better at physics were the ones who benefited from the exercises the most.

How did all of this work? Psychologists Akira Miyake and Tiffany Ito and physicist Noah Finkelstein, who were among the study authors, said they didn't know for sure. But they speculated that the women who wrote about things they cared about early in the course felt slightly more comfortable or relaxed in class. Maybe this helped them to absorb more material or motivated them to work harder. And maybe that in turn meant they did slightly better on the first exam, which in turn boosted their confidence and motivated them even more. It's easy to imagine such a virtuous cycle.

The current study followed physics students for one semester. But it's pos-   8
sible the effects of this sort of writing exercise could be longer-lasting. In a 2006 paper in *Science*, Stanford psychologist Geoffrey Cohen showed that similar writing tasks boosted the grades of African American middle-school students. Two years later, after several follow-up exercises, the benefits were still apparent (1307–10).

Of course, stereotype threat isn't the only reason that women remain under-   9
represented in math and science. Previously, some of the co-authors of the new study found that differences in background explained 60 percent of the disparity between their male and female students' physics scores, with the men more likely to have taken physics in high school. After giving the affirming writing exercises, the researchers did another analysis that controlled for differences in prior math scores, which correlated with who'd done more or less past math and physics coursework. This time, they found no statistically significant gender disparities in the scores for the standardized physics test or other physics exams. The implication is that if women had the same background in science as men, on some measures, writing exercises like this one might close the rest of the gender gap—or at least come close. In a world where women may worry that they're not as good at science, it looks as if we have an easy-to-use tool for helping them zap their self-defeating demons.

Works Cited

Cohen, Geoffrey L., et al. "Reducing the Racial Achievement Gap: A Social-Psychological Intervention." *Science* 313.5791 (2006): 1307–10. Print.

Davies, Paul G., et al. "Consuming Images: How Television Commercials That Elicit Stereotype Threat Can Restrain Women Academically and Professionally." *Personality and Social Psychology Bulletin* 28.12 (2002): 1615–28. Print.

Fine, Cordelia. *Delusions of Gender: How Our Minds, Society, and Neurosexism Create Difference*. New York: W. W. Norton, 2010. Print.

Good, Catherine, Joshua Aronson, and Jayne Ann Harder. "Problems in the Pipeline: Stereotype Threat and Women's Achievement in High-Level Math Courses." *Journal of Applied Developmental Psychology* 29.1 (2008): 17–28. Print.

Miyake, Akira, et al. "Reducing the Gender Achievement Gap in College Science: A Classroom Study of Values Affirmation." *Science* 330.6008 (2010): 1234–37. Print.

Schaffer, Amanda. "The Sex Difference Evangelists: The Next Best-Seller." *Slate*. The Slate Group, LLC. 7 July 2008. Web. 11 Jan. 2011.

READING ACTIVITY 2 Build Your Vocabulary

Determine the meanings of the following words from the context of Amanda Schaffer's essay. Then check their meanings by looking up the words in a dictionary: subtly (2), hampered (2), affirmation (2), equivalent (3), quantitative (3), sabotage (3), implicit (3), intractable (4), double-blind (5), speculated (7), disparity (9), implication (9).

GROUP ACTIVITY 3 Discuss the Reading

Discuss the following questions about "How to Buck Up the Science Ladies" with your classmates.

1. What educational problem does Schaffer identify in her essay?
2. What is Schaffer's proposed solution? What supporting details does she use to convince you that her solution will work? What outside sources did she use to find these details?
3. What objections might you raise to Schaffer's proposal?
4. Identify three educational problems, and propose a solution to one of them.

WRITING ACTIVITY 2 Share Your Ideas

Write a paragraph or two on an education problem. Has this problem affected you personally? Why or why not? Share your proposed solution to this problem with your classmates. What research can you do to support your position that this solution is workable?

An Environmental Problem

DAVID SIROTA
Putting the "I" in the Environment

In this editorial, David Sirota argues that we can't wait for legislation to fix our environmental problems; instead, it is up to each of us to take action. David Sirota is a senior editor at *In These Times* and a columnist and author of *Back to Our Future: How the 1980s Explain the World We Live In Now—Our Culture, Our Politics, Our Everything*, released in March 2011.

For those who are not (yet) heartless cynics or emotionless Ayn Rand acolytes,   1
the now-famous photographs of sludge-soaked pelicans on the Gulf Coast are painful to behold. It's those hollow pupils peeking out of the brown death, screaming in silence. They are an avian version of the eyes of T. J. Eckleburg that F. Scott Fitzgerald once wrote about—and they implicate us all.

As President Obama correctly stated: "Easily accessible oil has already been 2
sucked up out of the ground"—and drilling companies must now use ever-riskier
techniques to find the oil we demand (Obama). While British Petroleum and federal regulators are certainly at fault for their reckless behavior, every American
who uses oil—which is to say, every American—is incriminated in this ecological
holocaust.

If we accept that culpability—a big "if" in this accountability-shirking society— 3
we can start considering how to reduce our oil addiction so as to prevent such holo-
causts in the future. And when pondering that challenge, we must avoid focusing
exclusively on legislation. As Colin Beavan argues in his tome *No Impact Man*, green
statutes are important, but not enough. Those oil-poisoned birds, choking to death
on our energy gluttony, implore us to also take individual action.

This does not necessarily mean radical lifestyle changes—good news for those 4
who remain locked into various forms of oil use. Millions, for instance, must drive or
fly to workplaces where no alternative transportation exists. And most of us don't
have the cash to trade in our cars for Priuses, and don't have the option of
telecommuting.

However, almost everyone regardless of income or employment can take steps 5
that are so absurdly simple and cost-effective that there's simply no excuse not to.

Here are two: We can stop using disposable plastic bags and stop buying 6
plastic-bottled water. Though no big sacrifice, doing this is a huge way to reduce oil
use. The Sierra Club estimates that Americans "use 100 billion plastic shopping bags
each year, which are made from an estimated 12 million barrels of oil" ("Plastic
Bags"). Likewise, the Pacific Institute reports that the equivalent of 17 million barrels
of oil are used to produce plastic water bottles—incredibly wasteful considering
that clean tap water is ubiquitously available in America ("Bottled Water").

Here's another: In a country that puts one-fifth of its fossil fuel use into agricul- 7
ture, we can make a difference by slightly reducing our consumption of animal flesh,
the culinary gas-guzzler.

Today, the average American eats 200 pounds of meat annually, "an increase 8
of 50 pounds per person from 50 years ago," according to the *New York Times*
(Bittman). Setting aside morality questions about executing 10 billion living beings
a year simply to satiate an epicurean fancy, the sheer energy costs of this dietary
choice are monstrous.

Quoting Cornell University researchers, *Time* magazine reports that producing 9
animal protein requires eight times as much fossil fuel as producing a comparable
amount of plant protein (Corliss). Carbon-emissions-wise (which roughly reflects
energy use), geophysicists Gidon Eshel and Pamela Martin find that cutting meat
consumption by just 20 percent—say, going meatless two days a week—is equal to
switching from a standard sedan to a hybrid (Rosenthal).

Using knapsacks at supermarkets, drinking free tap water and replacing meat 10
with comparatively inexpensive vegetable protein—these are easy steps. Sure, they
will not singularly end our oil dependence, but they will decrease it. As importantly,
they will begin building a national culture that takes personal responsibility for combating the ecological crisis we've all created.

Are we willing to make minimal behavioral reforms? Are we willing to assume   11
such responsibility? Those, of course, are the crucial questions — the ones nobody
wants to ask, but the ones those crude-drenched birds beg us to answer.

Works Cited

Beavan, Colin. *No Impact Man*. New York: Farrar, Straus, and Giroux, 2009. Print.

Bittman, Mark. "Rethinking the Meat-Guzzler." *New York Times*. New York Times,
27 Jan. 2008. Web. 7 Apr. 2011.

"Bottled Water and Energy: A Fact Sheet." *Pacific Institute*. Pacific Institute, 2008.
Web. 7 Apr. 2011.

Corliss, Richard. "Should We All Be Vegetarians?" *Time*. Time, Inc., 7 July 2002. Web.
7 Apr. 2011.

Obama, Barack. "Remarks by the President on the Gulf Oil Spill." U.S. Government.
The White House, Washington, D.C. 27 May 2010. Speech.

"Plastic Bags." *Sierra Club*. Massachusetts Chapter Sierra Club, n.d. Web. 7 Apr. 2011.

Rosenthal, Elisabeth. "Is Your Lunch Causing Global Warming?" *New York Times
Upfront*. New York Times, 18 Jan. 2010. Web. 7 Apr. 2011.

READING ACTIVITY 3 Build Your Vocabulary

Determine the meanings of the following words from the context of David Sirota's essay. Then check their meanings by looking up the words in a dictionary: acolytes (1), avian (1), holocaust (2), culpability (3), pondering (3), tome (3), statutes (3), gluttony (3), ubiquitously (6), culinary (7), satiate (8), epicurean (8).

GROUP ACTIVITY 4 Discuss the Reading

Discuss the following questions about "Putting the 'I' in the Environment" with your classmates.

1. What environmental problem does Sirota identify?

2. What evidence does he provide that the problem exists? Where did he get this evidence?

3. What solution does Sirota propose? What, if anything, is unrealistic about his proposed solution?

4. How does Sirota's choice of words make his argument more powerful?

5. What environmental issues are important to you? List your proposed solutions to the issues you identify.

WRITING ACTIVITY 3 Share Your Ideas

Write a paragraph or two on an environmental problem you have identified. What research might you do to find evidence that this is a problem? What solution would you propose? Share your writing with your classmates.

Writing Your Essay   A Step-by-Step Guide

Now that you've read some essays proposing a solution to a health, education, or environmental problem, it's time to write your own essay. First, read the following writing assignment. Then, use the step-by-step advice that follows to discover ideas, develop them as you draft, and polish your writing into a finished essay that readers will find both interesting and persuasive:

Writing Assignment

Think about the issues of health, education, and the environment. Is there a problem you often complain about or feel strongly about? Now is your chance to do something about it. By writing about a problem and suggesting a possible solution, you are both getting involved in important issues and honing your argument skills. In this chapter, you will select a problem, give your position on it, provide evidence that the problem exists, and propose a workable solution. You (or your instructor) may decide to do this assignment in one of several ways:

- Write about a health problem of particular importance to you.

  OR

- Write about an education problem that affects you or a person or group you care about.

  OR

- Write about an environmental problem that you both know and care about.

☾Step 1   Explore Your Choices

The radical civil rights activist Eldridge Cleaver once said, "You're either part of the solution, or you're part of the problem." You can, in fact, be part of the solution by writing a persuasive essay about an issue that is important to you.

To do this, start by identifying a problem and gathering evidence that supports a workable solution. If you want your essay to make a difference, you must be careful to choose a position that you can argue with some authority, both by drawing on your own knowledge and doing some re-search to learn more about it. But if you think you don't know enough about any problems to write an effective essay, don't worry. You will evalu-ate your audience, your purpose, and at least three potential topics before you settle on a problem and a solution to write about.

Analyzing Your Audience and Purpose

If you take the time to write about an important problem, you want someone to read your essay and do something about it. For example, if you choose a health problem, such as the need for a student health center on your campus, your audience might include a dean or the school's presi-dent. Similarly, for an education problem, such as the federal government's proposed cuts in financial-aid benefits to students, your audience could include your congressional representative and possibly even the president of the United States. For an environmental problem, such as the need to stop a local factory from polluting the air, your audience might include the factory owner, local government officials, or the state governor.

Because you're trying to convince at least one of your readers to act on your suggestions, your purpose is primarily persuasive. You'll want to ap-pear well informed, respectful, and fairly formal. You'll also need to con-sider how they might disagree with you and what information you should gather to help convince them to change their minds.

For more on audience and purpose, see pp. 7–11.

 WRITING ACTIVITY 4   Analyze Your Audience and Purpose

Your responses to the following questions will help you decide how to approach this chapter's assignment. Be sure to come back to these questions after you have chosen a topic.

1. Why does this assignment call for primarily persuasive writing?

2. What is the average age of your audience?

3. What is your audience's average educational level? Ethnic background? Economic level? Political orientation: conservative, moderate, or liberal?

4. How might your responses to the previous three questions affect how you write your essay?

Gathering Ideas

Before you decide which issue you want to write about, explore your choices by gathering ideas for at least one subject in three categories: health, education, and the environment. Even if you think you already know which problem you would like to write about, it's always a good idea to explore a few topics to be sure you have chosen the best one. To gather possible topics, you may use any of the techniques you learned in Chapter 1.

The student writers in this chapter gather ideas by relating aloud, consulting with others, and researching.

For more on gathering ideas, see pp. 11–16.

Relating Aloud about a Health Problem

Relating aloud means discussing your subject with others who might be able to give you additional insights into the problem or provide alternative solutions for you to consider. As you talk with others about your subject, you'll discover new ideas and gather additional evidence. Based on their responses, you'll also be able to determine if others are interested in this problem and if they think your solution is workable.

Here's how one student, Bruce, related his ideas about a health problem to his peer response group:

> My biggest concern is how the health-care system seems to ignore unwed mothers. Did you know that if a teenage girl becomes pregnant, she can't receive health care for her baby unless she moves out of her parents' home? Because of this law, teenage girls from poor families are forced to leave home and try to make it on their own. They not only have a rough time making it alone, but they also lose the emotional support of their family at a time they need it most. I would like to see this law changed.

Bruce's topic idea prompted several reactions from his classmates. One student, for example, said she had never heard of this law and couldn't believe it was true. Another student argued that free health care is available from private charities and asked why taxpayers should have to pay for it. A third student wondered if the law was intended to discourage teenage girls from becoming pregnant. In response to his group members' questions about his topic, Bruce admitted that he didn't know the answers and needed to do some additional research on his issue:

> I don't think we want to encourage unwed mothers to have babies, but if they do, I think they should be able to remain with their families and still receive health benefits. I'll need to find more about why the health-care system is set up this way and how it could be changed without costing taxpayers more money. I'm sure the idea is to save money, but I'm not sure how this works. I think I'll call my congressional representative and see if she has any information. Then I'll rethink my position.

⏻ **Create a video**

Ask someone to videotape you relating aloud about a health problem (or other issue). Upload the video to an online chat room, and ask your group members to respond. Use their questions and comments to add details to your essay.

GROUP ACTIVITY 5 Relate Aloud about a Health Problem

Relate your ideas about a health problem aloud to the members of your peer response group. You could talk about the health problem you wrote about in response to Darshak Sanghavi's "Quicker Liquor" piece, or you could choose another topic. One member should take notes on (or tape-record) group members' responses to your description of the problem and your proposed solution. Respond to questions about your topic as best you can. Then use the group's suggestions to gather additional ideas about your topic.

Consulting with Others about an Education Problem

Think about some of the problems affecting students on your campus or in your community. What could be done to improve education or campus life? Perhaps you would like to see more courses offered in photography or more school spirit among students. Maybe you want the state to fund a new medical research lab at your college or the federal government to increase financial aid benefits.

Even if you have a problem in mind, you may not yet be sure what kinds of solutions are possible. To unearth ideas you may not even know you have, try consulting with others. As you know from Chapter 1, *consulting with others* involves talking with people who can provide you with valuable insights into your topic. Consulting with others is a way of researching your topic, and then using the information you gather to help you develop your essay. In the area of education, for example, there may be fellow students who are experiencing the problem or experts who have researched the problem and its possible solutions. If you find yourself staring at a blank page without any idea of how to begin, consult with others to stimulate your thinking. For example, if you are writing on the need for more federal financial aid, you might interview the director of financial aid on your campus to find out more about the problem and to explore possible solutions. Before you conduct an interview, though, be sure that you have answered the following questions for yourself:

1. What is the problem I am interested in?
2. What do I already know about it?
3. What more do I need to know about the problem?
4. What do I think should be done?
5. Who has the power to act on my proposed solution?

Li Chiang, a student writer concerned about the computer lab on his campus, answered these questions before interviewing the vice president of academic affairs. Here's what Li wrote:

> I am concerned about the computer lab on campus. It does not serve the needs of students. Even though we pay a $150 user fee each semester, we don't get good service. I spend most of my spare time at the lab. I don't own

a computer and must use the lab to complete assignments. I really hate the computer lab it's so frustrating. The hardware is outdated. The software selection is inadequate. It's so dark in there. And it's always crowded. Long lines of people waiting for their turn. And there are definitely not enough computers! The students who work there are not very helpful. They ignore you and spend all their time on their own homework. Nice job if you can get it! I wonder if other students are as annoyed as I am.

Li decided to ask the vice president of academic affairs the following questions:

1. Why hasn't the college administration made any attempt to improve the computer lab?
2. How expensive would new computer equipment be?
3. Shouldn't part of the computer fee students pay each semester be used to update the computer lab on a regular basis?
4. What does the fee now pay for?
5. Why hasn't the university done anything about the old equipment?
6. Do you agree that it's a problem?
7. Do you agree that it's important to solve the problem?
8. What is the solution?

WRITING ACTIVITY 5   Consult about an Education Problem

Choose an education problem that concerns and interests you. It might be a problem specific to your school, an issue that affects college students all over the country, or perhaps a problem that involves grade school children or high school students. Or you could choose the problem you wrote about in response to Amanda Schaffer's "How to Buck Up the Science Ladies." Set aside ten or fifteen minutes to write your ideas on your topic. You may use the preceding questions as a starting point. Then generate a list of questions you might use to interview someone about the problem and its possible solutions.

For more on conducting an interview, see pp. 337–39.

Researching an Environmental Problem

Put aside your writing about an education issue for now so that you can gather ideas about an environmental problem. Radio, newspapers, magazines, the Web, and television all carry pieces on environmental issues, such as recycling programs, low-emission vehicles, and the destruction of the rain forests. You have probably noticed more local problems as well. Perhaps your neighbors insist on burning their leaves every fall. Maybe a local factory's wastewater leaks into the river, or nearby cities are taking water needed to irrigate farms in your county.

Sometimes writers think they know the solution to an environmental problem but can't provide evidence that the problem exists or that a solution is workable. Researching the issue can provide a lot of valuable information for an essay.

You can find magazine and newspaper articles on any environmental problem in the reference section of your library or on the Web. Before you begin to read, check your sources for reliability and relevance.

 Evaluate Web site sources

For a list of questions to help you evaluate Web site sources, go to Read Write Think at http://www.readwritethink.org/files/resources/lesson_images/lesson328/evalform.pdf.

Reliable Sources   A reliable source should present accurate information. Library reference materials are screened for accuracy, so they are usually reliable. Most students today, however, look for outside sources on the Web. Anyone can post information to the Web, so be sure that what you read was posted by an author you trust in a well-known source, such as a national magazine, a newspaper, an educational institution, or a government agency. You can follow the links provided on the site to learn more about the author and the organization sponsoring the information.

The authors of the readings at the beginning of this chapter used reliable sources, such as the *New York Times*, the *Washington Post*, *Slate* magazine, and *Science*. They also used reputable Web sites sponsored by the American Medical Association, the National Academies, and the U.S. government.

Relevant Sources   A relevant source should provide current information on your specific topic. To find relevant sources, use a keyword search to be sure the articles you find will be useful to you. Then look to see when the information was posted. It is usually best to avoid articles that are more than five years old, and you should resist the temptation to include material just because it was easy to find or interesting to read. To be relevant, it must relate to your specific topic for this essay.

For more information on how to conduct a keyword search, see p. 342.

For more information about finding and evaluating sources, see pp. 339–44.

If you look at the Works Cited of the readings at the beginning of this chapter, you'll see that the authors used recent newspaper and journal articles, mostly from the year in which they published their own article.

Use the following questions to evaluate the sources you find:

1. Do most of the articles support or oppose your solution to the problem?
2. Are these articles from reliable sources?

3. Is the information relevant to your specific topic?

4. Is the information current?

5. What supporting details do the authors use to convince readers of their views?

6. Can you add additional details to these arguments?

7. Do the authors propose any worthwhile solutions?

   Andrea Benitez, the student interested in writing about veganism, hoped to persuade fellow students to share her view that going vegan could help protect the environment. To learn more about the issue, Andrea researched her topic by first visiting her campus library to discuss her topic with a reference librarian. The librarian gave her suggestions for reliable print and Web sources she might use. Her statement of her topic and her answers to the preceding questions follow:

> **Preliminary thesis statement:** By avoiding the consumption of animal products such as meat, fish, dairy, or eggs and not wearing animal products such as fur or leather, you can take a big step toward improving the environment.
>
> 1. There are plenty of Web sites that explain how to go vegan. Most of the online articles I've read support the idea that veganism not only helps improve your health, but it also improves the environment.
>
> 2. I have to be careful because some of these Web sites really promote veganism, so they might not be completely objective. I'll go to their home pages to read more about the organization, and I'll pay attention to the tone of the Web site to be sure that they are providing reliable information.
>
> 3. It's pretty easy to find information on how veganism helps the environment; what will be difficult is to decide which information to include in my essay.
>
> 4. I'm going to limit myself to articles posted within the last five years, except that I will use *The Vegan Sourcebook* published in 1998 because it has some excellent basic definitions of veganism. I feel certain that I'm getting the latest information on veganism.
>
> 5. Most authors use statistics to support the view that veganism is helping the environment. Readers always respond well to facts and statistics, so I'll be sure to include some of these in my essay.
>
> 6. I can cite several specific examples of how veganism helps the environment.
>
> 7. One solution to the problem of how to protect the environment is to go vegan.

For more on conducting research, see Chapter 12.

> **WRITING ACTIVITY 6** Research an Environmental Problem

Identify an environmental problem that you might want to write about. If you like, you can expand on what you wrote about an environmental problem in response to David Sirota's "Putting the 'I' in the Environment." Or you can choose another topic. Locate at least three online newspaper or magazine articles on your topic, and read them carefully for ideas and supporting evidence. Use the questions on pages 292–93 to evaluate the articles.

Step 2 Write Your Discovery Draft

For more on drafting, see pp. 16–20.

You have explored at least three possible topics for your argument essay. It's time now to choose one health, education, or environmental issue and prepare a discovery draft that explains a problem and proposes your solution. The purpose of this draft is to discover what you have to say, so focus on organizing what you already know by trying to put it on paper. Remember that you will have the opportunity to revise later.

Choosing a Topic

As you get ready to write your discovery draft, choose a topic that concerns you, that you know something about, and that your readers can take action on if you convince them to accept your position. Start by reviewing your materials from the gathering-ideas step. Which topic—health, education, or the environment—generated the most ideas for you? If you find that you feel strongly about one of the topics, it's probably a good pick for your discovery draft. On the other hand, if you're not excited about any of the topics you've explored so far, go back and use your favorite idea-gathering technique to try out some other possibilities.

Once you have a topic that interests you, make sure it is narrow enough to handle in a short essay. You would not be able to address world hunger, the cost of a college education, or climate change thoroughly in one essay, but you could focus on one specific aspect of any of those problems. To write about the cost of college, for example, you could narrow the topic to a proposed tuition hike at your school and explain why and how the administration might avoid the increase.

> **WRITING ACTIVITY 7** Choose Your Topic

Review your responses to Writing Activities 1 through 6, and decide which of the three issues you explored (health, education, or the environment) is most important to you and would be most interesting to your readers. Be careful to select a problem for which you can propose a solution and for which you'll be able to do some research. If necessary, narrow your topic to something that can be fully addressed in the assigned length of your essay.

Sharing Your Ideas

Before you begin drafting, write a preliminary thesis statement that identifies a problem and proposes a solution. A working thesis statement will help keep you focused as you draft, but remember that you might change your mind about your topic as you write about it. You can always revise your thesis statement later on.

For more on thesis statements, see pp. 18–19.

Feel free to use material you've already gathered as part of your discovery draft. If you related your issue aloud to your classmates, for example, you might want to refer to your notes as you write. If you consulted with others, be sure to include some of what you learned. Using a few direct quotes from the people you interviewed will make your essay more interesting to read. Similarly, if you conducted other research on your topic during the gathering-ideas step, you might want to include these outside sources in your draft.

As you draft, remember to incorporate your outside sources into your essay by quoting directly, paraphrasing, or summarizing what you heard or read. Notice how the authors of the readings at the beginning of the chapter integrate their outside materials. In his article, David Sirota quotes President Obama by putting the president's exact words in quotation marks.

> As President Obama correctly stated: "Easily accessible oil has already been sucked up out of the ground"—and drilling companies must now use ever-riskier techniques to find the oil we demand (Obama).

Amanda Schaffer paraphrases from an article she wrote earlier. Notice how a paraphrase doesn't include quotations marks because the author is not quoting exactly what another person said but rephrasing the idea in different words.

> Stereotype threat can roar into action when members of any stereotyped group are primed to think about belonging to it—in other words, when women focus on being female or African Americans on being black (Schaffer).

Darshak Sanghavi summarizes how MADD was founded:

> Some history: After her daughter was killed by an intoxicated driver, Candy Lightner founded Mothers Against Drunk Driving and successfully lobbied for the 1984 National Minimum Drinking Age Act, which gave full federal highway funds only to states that set the minimum age to purchase or consume alcohol at 21 years.

Quoting, paraphrasing, and documenting information is essential. Otherwise, you could be accused of plagiarism. For more help, see pp. 345–46.

As these authors do, be sure to give credit to your sources both in your essay and in a Works Cited page at the end. If you use someone else's ideas without giving them credit, you have *plagiarized.*

By citing your sources, you let your reader know which ideas you learned from your research and which are original. You'll notice that the authors of the readings at the beginning of the chapter cite a lot of sources to

To learn how to cite your
sources in an essay and in
a Works Cited page, see
pp. 355–60.

strengthen their arguments. They know that these outside sources make their writing more interesting and convincing.

Although you may be incorporating sources at this stage, you may also choose to focus more on using sources to support your argument when you revise your draft. While writing your discovery draft, your main goal is to get your ideas down on paper, while also keeping your audience and purpose in mind.

A Student's Discovery Draft

Here's a discovery draft written by Andrea Benitez, the student whose writing about veganism you read earlier. You will notice that Andrea used some outside sources in her discovery draft. She will add more when she revises her essay. (Note, too, that Andrea's writing includes the types of errors that typically appear in a first draft.)

Why Go Vegan?

Most of us are not born vegan, so why should you go vegan? People often become vegans because they are concerned about the way society treats animals. Others don't want to eat meat or dairy products for health reasons. But the biggest reason to go vegan is to help our environment. According to Dr. Pamela Wood, professor in our university's Department of Public Health Science, "If you make the choice to go vegan, you can take a big step toward improving the environment. You do this by not consuming animal products such as meat, fish, dairy, or eggs, and not wearing animal products such as fur or leather." What really makes me angry, though, is that many people think veganism is a big joke. What gives with this attitude?

Not only does eating meat use many resources, but it also uses them very inefficiently. Livestock animals do not produce as many calories as they consume, making them a very inefficient way to get food. To produce an equivalent amount of vegetables and meat, the meat takes ten times as much land as the vegetables (Bittman). Its not just livestock on land — fishermen must throw away on average a third of what they catch.

Many assume it is very difficult to take on a vegan lifestyle because everything contains some kind of animal product. But then some crazy people think that any diet that doesn't include hamburgers is difficult! It can be difficult when you are just starting the transition to veganism because of the lack of available health information, like any new diet it is important to do research and make wise decisions about what you are consuming and how it will affect your body and health.

> **WRITING ACTIVITY 8   Write Your Discovery Draft**

Using your notes from the gathering-ideas step, write a preliminary thesis statement and a discovery draft to identify a problem and propose a solution on a health, education, or environmental issue of your choosing. If you included outside sources in your notes, you may want to practice putting these sources into your discovery draft. Most important is to focus on putting your ideas into words, and try not to worry about the details. If you wish, you may write drafts on two or three topics to see which one you prefer to continue working on.

Step 3 Revise Your Draft

Because convincing others to act on your proposed solution to a problem can be a challenge, you must ensure that your essay provides evidence of the problem and offers a workable solution. Refer to the audience analysis you completed in Writing Activity 4. What does your audience need to know to understand the problem? How can you propose your solution so that your readers will act on it? As you review your discovery draft, use the skills you acquired in earlier chapters of this book. In the pages that follow, you will learn how to further strengthen your draft by using argumentation, incorporating additional outside sources into your essay, appealing to your readers, and improving your tone.

For more on revising, see pp. 20–22.

Developing Your Ideas with Argument

Now that you have recorded some of your ideas in a discovery draft, you have probably noticed that you need to further develop what you have to say. For example, you may need to present evidence that illustrates the seriousness of the problem, and you may need to investigate any solutions that have already been tried. You may also need to explain how your solution will resolve the problem.

To do all of this, use the techniques of argument, or a *logical appeal*. First, revise your thesis statement to be sure that it states a problem and your position on it. Next, check that you have provided evidence that the problem exists and that you have proposed a workable solution. Be sure that you have included outside sources to help strengthen your argument. If necessary, return to the gathering-ideas stage of the writing process to do additional research on your topic. Let's see how these techniques of argumentation are put into action.

State the Problem

As you may recall from Chapter 1, the thesis statement announces your topic; shows, explains, or argues a particular point about the topic; and gives readers a sense of what the essay will be about. An effective thesis statement for a problem-and-solution essay also

- describes a specific problem or issue.
- conveys your position on the issue.

Here are some examples of vague and specific thesis statements:

VAGUE   Something should be done about students' health.
SPECIFIC Our college should develop a wellness program to encourage students to take care of their health.

VAGUE   Students need financial aid.
SPECIFIC Congress should reject proposed cuts to the Stafford Loan program because thousands of college students rely on it to finance their education.

VAGUE   Cement factories pollute the water.
SPECIFIC The local cement factory should be shut down because it is polluting Jacob's Creek.

GROUP ACTIVITY 6 Analyze Thesis Statements

Working in small groups, rewrite each of the following thesis statements to define the specific problem or issue at hand and to state a clear position on the issue.

1. Students shouldn't have to pay for vaccinations.
2. The cost of health care for illegal immigrants is an important issue.
3. The spotted owls in our area need protection.
4. Cigarette taxes should be raised.
5. Standardized testing is a bad idea.

WRITING ACTIVITY 9 Revise Your Thesis Statement

Evaluate the preliminary thesis statement you wrote for your essay about a health, education, or environmental issue. Does it identify a specific problem and clearly state your position? Revise your thesis statement accordingly.

Provide Evidence

When writing a persuasive essay, simply stating the problem isn't enough. You need to convince readers that the problem is serious enough to require a solution. Evidence—such as examples, facts, and expert testimony—can help you do this. You may also include a brief history of the problem, its causes, and the consequences of leaving it unsolved. If necessary, you can always do additional research to get more evidence to support your position.

Let's look at an overview of David Sirota's essay, "Putting the 'I' in the Environment," to see how he uses evidence to develop his argument that we are all responsible for fixing environmental problems, noting the statistical evidence he provides to convince his reader that environmental problems exist:

Problem

- British Petroleum and federal regulators are certainly at fault for the Gulf oil spill.
- But every American who uses oil is also part of the problem.

Why We Haven't Addressed the Problem

- Too often we expect legislation to fix the environment.
- Or we claim that there is nothing we can do to overcome dependence on oil.

Reliable and Relevant Evidence

- Too many plastic bags. The Sierra Club estimates that Americans "use 100 billion plastic shopping bags each year, which are made from an estimated 12 million barrels of oil."
- Too many plastic water bottles. The Pacific Institute reports that the equivalent of 17 million barrels of oil are used to produce plastic water bottles.
- Too much consumption of meat. *Time* magazine reports that producing animal protein requires eight times as much fossil fuel as producing a comparable amount of plant protein.

Solution

Each of us should take personal responsibility for combating the ecological crisis we've created by

- not using plastic bags.
- not buying plastic-bottled water.
- reducing consumption of animal flesh.

GROUP ACTIVITY 7 Examine Your Evidence

Share discovery drafts with two or three other students in your class, and examine the types of evidence each draft uses to support its problem statement. Does each draft provide enough supporting details to convince readers that the problem is serious and in need of a solution? Are the outside sources of information reliable and relevant? Ask your group members to suggest how you can revise to make your evidence more persuasive, and do the same for them.

Post supporting details to Facebook

Collect supporting details by asking your classmates for their suggestions. Create a Facebook group, and share your thesis statement and a list of your supporting details for your group members to review.

Propose a Solution

After you state the problem and provide evidence of it, you're ready to propose a solution. A good *solution* recommends specific and workable actions for correcting the problem or addressing the issue. If you are proposing a solution that you discovered while conducting research, be sure to give credit to the person who first proposed it.

Let's look again at the solutions proposed in this chapter's readings. Notice that in each case, the writer identifies a specific and workable resolution to the problem:

SANGHAVI'S PROBLEM	Lowering the drinking age from 21 to 18 will not reduce teen binge drinking on college campuses.
SANGHAVI'S SOLUTION	There are more realistic solutions, such as more regulation, higher alcohol taxes, education, and more student diversity to address the problem of teenage drinking.
SCHAFFER'S PROBLEM	Due to negative stereotyping, female science students don't do as well as their male counterparts.
SCHAFFER'S SOLUTION	Simple writing exercises can boost female science students' grades.
SIROTA'S PROBLEM	We all need to take responsibility for environmental problems.
SIROTA'S SOLUTION	Take simple steps: use cloth sacks at supermarkets, drink free tap water, and replace meat with vegetable protein.

■ HOW TO Propose a Solution

- Identify a problem.
- Provide evidence of the problem.
- Provide a specific solution.
- Make sure the solution is workable.

GROUP ACTIVITY 8 Revise Your Solution

Working with your peer response group, use the following questions to discuss the solution you proposed in your discovery draft about a health, education, or environmental problem.

1. Is the proposed solution to the problem specific? Why or why not?
2. Is the proposed solution workable? Why or why not?
3. How would you implement your solution? Are there outside sources that support your idea for how to implement a solution? Use your classmates' feedback to revise your solution accordingly.

Building Your Essay

When you revise an argument essay, it's important to consider whether you have done all you can to persuade your readers. Earlier in this chapter, you learned how to make a logical appeal. You need to make sure that your logical appeal makes sense. In addition, your argument will be more convincing if you appeal to your readers' emotions and trust. Finally, using a reasonable tone will further strengthen your position.

Persuade Your Readers

In identifying a problem or an issue and proposing a solution, you want your readers to understand the problem, accept your proposed solution, and perhaps take action on the issue. In addition to making a logical argument, two other types of appeals—emotional and ethical—can help you be persuasive.

Emotional Appeals   Sometimes even the tightest logic is not enough to spur readers to action. In this case, an *emotional appeal* may be more effective; it aims to make readers feel strongly about a problem or an issue—compassionate, proud, sad, angry, or intolerant, for example. But be careful when using an appeal to emotion. Readers dismiss appeals that are overly emotional because they assume that the writer is too close to the problem to propose an objective solution. Remember, too, that emotional appeals should be made in addition to a logical argument. You must always include logical evidence to support your thesis statement.

David Sirota, for example, uses several emotional appeals in "Putting the 'I' in the Environment." Even the title of his essay suggests Sirota's strong feelings about his topic. Sirota uses descriptions of the birds injured in the Gulf Coast oil spill as an emotional appeal, referring to "photographs of sludge-soaked pelicans on the Gulf Coast [that] are painful to behold. It's those hollow pupils peeking out of the brown death, screaming in silence." With this description, he hopes to foster a renewed conscience that will spur action.

Ethical Appeals   With an *ethical appeal*, you aim to gain your readers' trust by demonstrating your genuine concern about the problem or issue, your commitment to the truth, and your respect for others' differing opinions. You acknowledge that reasonable people might disagree with your proposal. Finally, you support your position with verifiable evidence (such as examples of facts, statistics, and expert testimony you discovered while researching your topic), and you ask readers to make a fair judgment based on that evidence.

Earlier in the chapter, you saw how several writers use ethical appeals in this way. Each demonstrates a genuine concern for the problem identified: Sanghavi for teenage drinking, Schaffer for low-scoring female science students, and Sirota for the environment. These writers also provide verifiable evidence to demonstrate their commitment to the truth and show respect for their readers' opinions. In return, they ask us, as open-minded readers, to evaluate their arguments fairly.

■HOW TO Use Logical, Emotional, and Ethical Appeals

- Use logical appeals to provide believable evidence for your position.
- Use emotional appeals to help readers feel strongly about your problem.
- Use ethical appeals to demonstrate your respect for your readers and your genuine concern about the problem.

WRITING ACTIVITY 10   Strengthen Your Appeals

Evaluate your draft to determine where an appeal to emotion or an appeal to ethics would make your logical argument more persuasive. Where in your essay might you appeal to your readers' compassion, pride, anger, or some other emotion to spur them to action? Do you demonstrate genuine concern about the issue, your commitment to the truth, and your respect for others' opinions? Add or revise your appeals as appropriate, and eliminate any details that are exaggerated or not factual.

Use a Reasonable Tone

Writers create *tone* through their choice of words and the structure of their sentences. You'll always want to strive for a reasonable tone, especially if you're proposing a solution. Readers rarely respond well to anger, sarcasm, accusation, hostility, or negativity. Calm, rational, and respectful language is always more effective.

Earlier you saw several examples of an angry and snide tone in Andrea Benitez's discovery draft, "Why Go Vegan?":

ANGRY TONE   What really makes me angry, though, is that many people think veganism is a big joke. What gives with this attitude?

SNIDE TONE   But then some crazy people think that any diet that doesn't include hamburgers is difficult!

Venting your anger in writing has the same effect as raising your voice, stomping your feet, or slamming the door in an argument. Remember, your goal is to persuade your readers to acknowledge the problem and to accept your solution. A harsh, negative tone won't accomplish this because it makes the writer look immature and puts readers on the defensive. To be persuasive, you must show respect for your readers' opinions by maintaining a reasonable tone.

Help others improve tone

Upload your essay to Google Docs. Ask each of your peer group members to read your essay for angry or snide statements and to boldface or underline any statements they think could be revised to improve the tone. Use their suggestions to improve your essay.

WRITING ACTIVITY 11   Improve Your Tone

Reread your draft, looking for remarks that come across as angry or that show a lack of respect for others' opinions. Revise as needed to create a reasonable tone.

A Student's Revised Draft

After considering the appeals she used and the tone of her essay, student Andrea Benitez decided that she could strengthen her appeals and moderate her tone. Before you read Andrea's revised draft, reread her discovery draft (p. 296). Notice how she researched her topic, added more outside evidence, and improved the tone in the revision. (You will still notice some errors in the revised draft; these will be corrected when Andrea edits her essay later on.)

Why Go Vegan?

It's no surprise that we are abusing our environment. We use too many natural resources that we can't replace, we polute our air and water, and we do very little to stop the effects of climate change. While there are lots of things you can do to treat the environment better, few people look at the food choices they make every day as a solution. The fact that animal products harm the environment is not heard all that often. According to Dr. Pamela Wood, professor in our university's Department of Public Health Science, "If you make the choice to go vegan, you can take a big step toward improving the environment. You do this by not consuming animal products such as meat, fish, dairy, or eggs, and not wearing animal products such as fur or leather."

Most of us are not born vegan, so why should you go vegan? People often become vegans because they are concerned about the way society treats animals. Others don't want to eat meat or dairy products for health reasons.

1   Andrea adjusts the tone of her introduction so that her reader will focus on the problem rather than on her feelings about it.

Andrea gives credit to the professor she interviewed about her topic.

2

Andrea clarifies the focus of her essay: veganism can help the environment.

But the biggest reason to go vegan is to help our environment. Modern animal agriculture uses vast amounts of natural resources, is an inefficient way to transfer those resources into calories, and is a major source of both polutants and greenhouse gases. By going vegan, you can personally reduce your own negative impact on the environment.

Andrea adds evidence, using facts and statistics she found in outside sources. These strengthen her appeals.

One major problem with our environment is that we are using too many resources without the ability to replace them quickly. This includes clean water, food, and land, and also sources of energy like oil and natural gas. According to a recent article in the *New York Times*, a full 30% of the land on earth not covered by ice is currently being used in some way in livestock production (Bittman). Livestock is also the largest source of water usage: all other uses of water in the United States combined are equivalent to the amount of water used in animal agriculture. Cattle ranching has caused a vast disappearance of rain forests in Central America. The United States imports millions of pounds of beef from Costa Rica, causing a loss of 83% of its forests (Stepaniak 250). Going vegan means not supporting this overuse of resources. If you do not consume or use animal products, you do not contribute to the demand for land, water, oil, and the earth's dwindling rain forests. 3

In this paragraph, Andrea uses emotional appeal to convince her readers that veganism can help protect the rain forests.

Andrea continues to add evidence to support her position.

Not only does eating meat use many resources, but it also uses them very inefficiently. Livestock animals do not produce as many calories as they consume, making them a very inefficient way to get food. To produce an equivalent amount of vegetables and meat, the meat takes ten times as much land as the vegetables (Bittman). Its not just livestock on land — fishermen must throw away on average a third of what they catch, as it dies or becomes contaminated in the process. A plant-based diet allows a direct line between the land and energy and your plate. Instead of having to feed an animal to produce a food that you then eat, as a vegan you simply eat what is grown, which is a far more efficient use of resources. 4

Andrea summarizes information she found on reliable Web sites.

Finally, animal agriculture is responsible for vast amounts of polution. According to the Web site vegansociety.com, one person going vegan could reduce carbon dioxide emissions by one and a half tons per year. In addition, runoff from concentrated feedlots polutes waterways. Cows are among the world's greatest producers of methane, which is the second most significant greenhouse gas in the world (Take Part). If you — and others — choose to become vegan, fewer of these animals would need to be raised, so both polution and greenhouse gas emissions could be reduced. 5

Andrea develops her conclusion by explaining how you can go vegan. She uses a moderate tone to strengthen both her logical argument and her ethical appeal.

Many assume it is very difficult to take on a vegan lifestyle because, after all, everything contains some kind of animal product. It can be difficult when 6 you are just starting the transition to veganism because of the lack of available health information, like any new diet it is important to do research and make wise decisions about what you are consuming and how it will affect your body and health. There are many resources available for a person who decides to become vegan, including cookbooks and several organizations, both local and national or international. Why go vegan? Each of us must follow our own conscience and live life as we see fit, but if you want to help protect the environment, you will continue to learn more about being vegan and join me in spreading the word about this valuable lifestyle.

Works Cited

Andrea adds a Works Cited list to her essay.

Bittman, Mark. "Rethinking the Meat Guzzler." *New York Times*. New York Times, 27 Jan. 2008. Web. 25 Feb. 2011.

Stepaniak, Joanne. *The Vegan Sourcebook*. Los Angeles, CA: Lowell House, 1998. Print.

Take Part. *ClimateCrisis*. Participant Media, 2011. Web. 25 Feb. 2011.

The Vegan Society. The Vegan Society. 2011. Web. 25 Feb. 2011.

Wood, Pamela. Personal Interview. 15 Mar. 2011.

GROUP ACTIVITY 9 Analyze Andrea's Revised Draft

Use the following questions to discuss with your classmates how Andrea improved her draft.

1. What is Andrea's thesis statement? Is it effective?
2. What kinds of evidence does Andrea provide to show that a problem exists?
3. Does her solution seem workable?
4. How does Andrea appeal to her readers logically, emotionally, and ethically?
5. How has Andrea adjusted her tone to make it more reasonable than it was in her discovery draft?
6. How could Andrea's revised draft benefit from further revision?

GROUP ACTIVITY 10 Peer Review

Read your draft aloud to the members of your peer response group. Take notes on your classmates' responses to the following questions about your draft.

1. What do you like best about this essay?
2. How effective is my thesis statement? Do I clearly state the problem?
3. Do I provide adequate evidence of the problem? Do I need to add more outside sources to strengthen my argument?

4. Do I propose a workable solution to the problem?

5. How could I improve my logical, emotional, and ethical appeals?

6. Where in my essay do I need to adjust my tone?

7. How clear is the purpose of my essay?

> ◖ **WRITING ACTIVITY 12**   **Revise Your Draft** ◗
>
> Using the work you have completed for Writing Activities 9 to 11 and Group Activities 7 and 8, and taking your classmates' suggestions for revision into consideration, finish revising your discovery draft. Focus on improving your thesis, evidence, and solution. Also evaluate your use of emotional and ethical appeals, and adjust your tone as needed. Finally, make sure you have supported your argument with outside sources that are reliable and relevant.

◖ Step 4   Edit Your Sentences

At this point, you have worked hard to communicate your position on a health, education, or environmental issue. Now that you're satisfied with the content of your revised draft, you're ready to edit it for correctness.

For more on editing, see pp. 22–24.

Editing is important because it removes errors that distract readers from focusing on the writer's ideas. Errors create the impression that a careless writer is untrustworthy. A clean, error-free essay, in contrast, suggests that a writer is careful and probably genuinely concerned about the topic. Therefore, edit your essay carefully before sharing it with your readers.

Combining Sentences Using Appositives

As you have learned, combining sentences can turn short, weak sentences into longer, stronger ones. Thus far, you have used several techniques for combining sentences. Another way to combine sentences is by using appositives. An *appositive* is a word or group of words that is set off by commas and that defines or renames a person or thing in the sentence.

For more on combining sentences, see Chapter 17.

> ▪ **HOW TO** Combine Sentences Using Appositives
>
> - Eliminate the subject and verb in one sentence.
> - Add the remaining phrase that describes the noun to the other sentence.
> - Set off the phrase with commas.

Here's how Andrea used appositives to combine sentences when she edited her draft:

ORIGINAL   One major problem with our environment is that we are using too many resources without the ability to replace them quickly. This includes clean water, food, and land, and also sources of energy like oil and natural gas.

REVISED   One major problem with our environment is that we are using too many resources, including water, food, land, oil, and natural gas, without the ability to replace them quickly.

▌ EDITING ACTIVITY 1 Combine Sentences Using Appositives ▐

Combine the following pairs of sentences by using appositives.

EXAMPLE   Jane ~~is my sister. She~~ $\overset{\text{, my sister,}}{\wedge}$ has type 2 diabetes.

1. The new campus plan is an improvement. It is called Student Access.

2. My biology book isn't difficult to understand. The title is *Life Science for Dummies*.

3. This holiday is important for the environment. It's called Arbor Day.

4. Jerry asked that the campus cafeteria serve more fresh vegetables. He is short and heavyset.

5. Don't even ask my girlfriend to go with you to the student council session. Luisa isn't interested in the college's problems.

*For additional practice with combining sentences, go to **bedfordstmartins.com/choices** and click on **Exercise Central**.*

▌ WRITING ACTIVITY 13 Combine Your Sentences ▐

Reread your discovery draft, looking for short, closely related sentences. Where it makes sense to do so, combine them using appositives.

Correcting Shifts in Person

Authors write in one of three persons: first *(I, we)*, second *(you)*, or third *(he, she, they)*. Here is a complete list of singular and plural pronouns in first, second, and third person:

SINGULAR

First Person	Second Person	Third Person
I	you	he, she, it, one
me	you	him, her, it
my, mine	your, yours	his, her, hers, its, one's

PLURAL

First Person	Second Person	Third Person
we	you	they
us	you	them
our, ours	your, yours	their, theirs

As a general rule, avoid shifting from one pronoun to another, because it confuses the readers:

> **CONFUSING** *I* never wanted to complain about the food served at the campus cafeteria. *You* know that it can be unhealthy. *I* finally wrote to the school newspaper to express *our* views. *We* believed something needed to be done about this situation, and so *I* took action.
>
> **REVISED** *I* never wanted to complain about the food served at the campus cafeteria even though *I* know that it can be unhealthy. *I* finally wrote to the school newspaper to express *my* views. *I* believed something needed to be done about this situation, and so *I* took action.

EDITING ACTIVITY 2 Correct Shifts in Person

Revise the following paragraph to correct unnecessary shifts in person.

> My favorite pastime is writing letters to the editor. I always have something to say about what's going on in our city. And there is plenty for you to write about: poor water quality, smog, and trash everywhere. They are always saying how much we need to improve the environment. You should never take a beautiful city for granted. I know I will continue to let people know how we feel about changing things around here.

For additional practice with correcting unnecessary shifts in person, go to **bedfordstmartins.com /choices** and click on **Exercise Central**.

WRITING ACTIVITY 14 Edit Your Essay

Edit your revised draft, looking for errors in grammar, spelling, and punctuation. Focus on finding and correcting any unnecessary shifts in person. If you know you often make a particular type of error, read the essay one time while you look only for that error. Ask a friend, family member, or classmate to help you spot errors you may have overlooked. Then use a dictionary and the Handbook in Part Four of this book to help you correct the errors you find.

A Student's Edited Essay

You probably noticed that Andrea's revised draft contained some errors in grammar, spelling, and punctuation. Andrea corrected these errors in her edited essay. Her corrections are noted in the margin.

Andrea Benitez

Professor Posey

English 1311

7 Apr. 2011

Why Go Vegan?

It's no surprise that we are abusing our environment. We use too many natural resources that we can't replace, we <u>pollute</u> our air and water, and we do very little to stop the effects of climate change. While there are lots of things you can do to treat the environment better, few people look at the food choices they make every day as a solution. The fact that animal products harm the environment is not heard all that often. If you make the choice to go vegan, you can take a big step toward improving the environment. According to Dr. Pamela Wood, professor in our university's Department of Public Health Science, "You do this by not consuming animal products such as meat, fish, dairy, or eggs, and not wearing animal products such as fur or leather."

Most of us are not born vegan, so why should you go vegan? People often become vegans because they are concerned about the way society treats animals. Others don't want to eat meat or dairy products for health reasons. But the biggest reason to go vegan is to help our environment. Modern animal agriculture uses vast amounts of natural resources, is an inefficient way to transfer those resources into calories, and is a major source of both <u>pollutants</u> and greenhouse gases. By going vegan, you can personally reduce your own negative impact on the environment.

One major problem with our environment is that we are using too many resources, including water, food, land, oil, and natural gas, without the ability to replace them quickly. According to a recent article in the *New York Times*, a full 30% of the land on earth not covered by ice is currently being used in some way in livestock production (Bittman). Livestock is also the largest source of water usage: all other uses of water in the United States combined are equivalent to the amount of water used in animal agriculture. Cattle ranching has caused a vast disappearance of rain forests in Central America. The United States imports millions of pounds of beef from Costa Rica, causing a loss of 83% of its forests (Stepaniak 250). Going vegan means not supporting this overuse of resources. If you do not consume or use animal products, you do not contribute to the demand for land, water, oil, and the earth's dwindling rain forests.

Not only does eating meat use many resources, but it also uses them very inefficiently. Livestock animals do not produce as many calories as they

Punctuation is added to
create a contraction.

consume, making them a very inefficient way to get food. To produce an equivalent amount of vegetables and meat, the meat takes ten times as much land as the vegetables. It's not just livestock on land—fishermen must throw away on average a third of what they catch, as it dies or becomes contaminated in the process. A plant-based diet allows a direct line between the land and energy and your plate. Instead of having to feed an animal to produce a food that you then eat, as a vegan you simply eat what is grown, which is a far more efficient use of resources.

Misspelled words
are corrected.

Finally, animal agriculture is responsible for vast amounts of pollution. According to the Web site vegansociety.com, one person going vegan could reduce carbon dioxide emissions by one and a half tons per year. In addition, runoff from concentrated feedlots pollutes waterways. Cows are among the world's greatest producers of methane, which is the second most significant greenhouse gas in the world (Take Part). If you—and others—choose to become vegan, fewer of these animals would need to be raised, so both pollution and greenhouse gas emissions could be reduced. 5

Run-on sentence
is corrected.

Many assume it is very difficult to take on a vegan lifestyle because, after all, everything contains some kind of animal product. It can be difficult when you are just starting the transition to veganism because of the lack of available health information; like any new diet, it is important to do research and make wise decisions about what you are consuming and how it will affect your body and health. There are many resources available for a person who decides to become vegan, including cookbooks and several organizations, both local and national or international. Why go vegan? Each of us must follow our own conscience and live life as we see fit, but if you want to help protect the environment, you will continue to learn more about being vegan and join me in spreading the word about this valuable lifestyle. 6

Works Cited

Bittman, Mark. "Rethinking the Meat Guzzler." *New York Times*. New York Times, 27 Jan. 2008. Web. 25 Feb. 2011.

Stepaniak, Joanne. *The Vegan Sourcebook*. Los Angeles, CA: Lowell House, 1998. Print.

Take Part. *ClimateCrisis*, Participant Media, 2011. Web. 25 Feb. 2011.

The Vegan Society. The Vegan Society, 2011. Web. 25 Feb. 2011.

Wood, Pamela. Personal Interview. 15 Mar. 2011.

Step 5 Share Your Essay

You're ready to share your solution to a health, education, or environmental problem with your audience. In addition to submitting your essay to your instructor and sharing it with your classmates, mail a copy of it to someone with the authority to act on your proposal.

According to an ancient Chinese proverb, "A journey of a thousand miles begins with a single step." Perhaps your essay will be the first step in bringing about a needed change in the areas of health, education, or the environment.

You may be surprised by the power of your writing. If you receive a reply, share it with your instructor and classmates. Student writer Andrea Benitez sent her essay to her campus newspaper. As a result, she was asked to start a vegan group on campus.

 Submit your essay online

Look for an online form or e-mail address where you might submit your essay to the person in authority who might act on your recommendations. Check for any special requirements for submitting the information online.

CHAPTER CHECKLIST

- ❏ I read essays about problems and proposed solutions to explore and learn about this chapter's theme.
- ❏ I analyzed my audience and purpose.
- ❏ I gathered ideas by relating aloud, consulting with others, and researching to find outside sources.
- ❏ I stated a specific problem and position in a thesis statement.
- ❏ I researched to find evidence to persuade my readers that the problem exists and merits their attention.
- ❏ I proposed a workable solution to the problem.
- ❏ I used logical argument and emotional and ethical appeals to persuade my readers to accept my position on the issue.
- ❏ I used a reasonable tone.
- ❏ I combined short sentences by using appositives.
- ❏ I corrected shifts in person.
- ❏ I edited to eliminate errors in grammar, punctuation, and spelling.

REFLECTING ON YOUR WRITING

To help you reflect on the writing you did in this chapter, answer the following questions:

1. Why did you choose the issue you did?

2. How did you determine the audience for your essay?

3. Which supporting details in your essay do you think provide the strongest evidence for your position? Why?

4. Which type of appeal—logical, emotional, or ethical—do you think you use most effectively in your essay? Why?

5. If you had more time, what would you do to improve your essay before sharing it with readers?

Using your answers to these questions, complete a Writing Process Report for this chapter (you can download a report form at **bedfordstmartins.com /choices**). Once you complete this report, freewrite about what you learned in this chapter.

PART THREE

Writing for Different Situations

Whether writing for personal enjoyment, for class, or for the workplace, you can use specialized writing strategies to help you do an even better job. In Part Three, you'll practice some of these writing strategies. You'll learn to keep journals as a way to gather ideas and practice your writing. You'll learn to write summaries to present information concisely. You'll learn how to conduct research to find outside sources to support what you have to say with interesting and informative details. You'll discover tips for doing your best on timed essay exams and standardized writing tests. And you'll learn how to write résumés and cover letters that will help you land that important job.

10

Keeping Journals

Imagine that you want to become a great musician or professional athlete. How would you go about it? First, knowing that achieving this goal takes hard work and a lot of time, you would have to be motivated to achieve your goal. Second, you would seek out a teacher or coach to work with you. Finally, you would do what great musicians and athletes do—practice: musicians rehearse, and athletes work out. The same is true if you want to be a writer. But you might think, "I don't want to become a great writer—another Shakespeare. I just want to write well enough to get better grades on my term papers or a promotion at work." But whether you're aiming for the major leagues, the minors, or a spot on your neighborhood sandlot team, the path is still the same—you'll need to make a commitment to study and practice.

> **In this chapter, you will begin your own journal. As you work on your journal, you will**
>
> - Discover why writers keep journals.
> - Learn how to keep a journal.
> - Practice keeping three types of journals.

You have demonstrated your motivation to improve your writing by enrolling in a writing course. In class, you'll have the opportunity to learn what you need to do to become a better writer. But to become a truly effective writer, you'll also need to practice what you have learned. Just as the musician practices scales and the athlete lifts weights, writers practice by writing. Often, writers do this in a *journal*, a notebook in which they express their thoughts and ideas.

You may ask, "Aren't some people just born musicians, athletes, or writers? Why should I bother to learn and practice if I wasn't born with this talent?" Some people may have more natural skill, but that doesn't mean the rest of us can't become better if we set our minds to it. Even people with natural talent must be willing to learn and practice to realize their potential. Musicians don't reach the concert hall, athletes don't reach the big time, and writers don't have their work published unless they are committed and willing to study and practice. ▪

Writing Assignment

Begin to keep a journal. You can write in a notebook or on your laptop, or you can even start a blog (see tip on p. 317). If you choose a notebook, be sure to use one that has at least one hundred pages so you can write in it daily.

You may choose to keep one or more of three types of journals: a personal journal, a dialogue journal, or a learning log. If a journal is required for one of your classes, your instructor may ask you to keep a particular type of journal. Once you decide which type of journal you will keep, set aside some time each day to write in it.

☽ Why Writers Keep Journals

Let's think more about practice. Would a musician wait until the night before a concert to practice the music? Would a basketball player wait until the day before the big game to practice slam dunks? Of course not. The same is true with writing. If you want to write well, you must start practicing now. Your tool—the equivalent to the musician's instrument or the athlete's equipment—is a journal. This could be a notebook, an electronic file, or an online space for jotting down your ideas, opinions, feelings, and memories. The more time you spend writing in your journal, the more practice you'll get as a writer.

LUCY McCORMICK CALKINS
From *The Art of Teaching Writing*

Lucy McCormick Calkins is a professor of education and children's literature, and the founding director of the Teachers College Reading and Writing Project at Columbia University. She is the author of several books on teaching and education, including *The Art of Teaching Reading* (2000); *One to One: The Art of Conferring with Young Writers* (2005); and her trademark *Units of Study* series, a set of curriculum guides for elementary school reading and writing teachers. In the following excerpt from *The Art of Teaching Writing* (1994), Calkins describes how she uses her notebook journal as a place to try out ideas.

I write to hold what I find in my life in my hands and to declare it a treasure. I'm   1
not very good at doing this. When I sit down at my desk, I'm like my students. "Nothing happens in my life," I say. I feel empty-handed. I want to get up and rush around, looking for something Big and Significant to put on the page.

And yet, as a writer I have come to know that significance cannot be found, it   2
must be grown. Looking back in my notebook I find a brief entry about how my son Miles uses one of my cotton T-shirts as his "pretend blanket," replacing the original blanket, which has disintegrated. My inclination is to dismiss the entry as trivial, or something only a mother could care about, but then I remember the writer Vicki Vinton saying, "It is an illusion that writers live more significant lives than non-writers; the truth is, writers are just more in the habit of finding the significance that is there in their lives."

Vicki's words hang over my desk, as do the words of the poet Theodore   3
Roethke, who said, "If our lives don't feel significant, sometimes it's not our lives, but our response to our lives, which needs to be richer." It's not only these quotations that nudge me to believe I can find significance in my son's "pretend blanket." I'm also instructed by memories of times when I've begun with something small, and seen significance emerge on my page. From my experiences as a writer and from the experiences of other authors, I have developed a small repertoire of strategies to draw on when I want to take a seed idea and grow it into a speech, a story, a book. This, for me, is what the writing process is all about.

Use your journal as a place to plant seeds of ideas, experiment with different ways of writing, and write without the pressure of being evaluated. Journal writing can help you find topics for writing. It can also help you clarify and organize your ideas. But most important, writing in a journal helps you become an active thinker, rather than being a passive reader or listener. This, in turn, will help you write better papers in college and get that promotion at work.

⏻ **Use a blog**

A blog is an online journal where writers can post entries and readers can post comments. Sites such as blogger.com, livejournal.com, myspace.com, wordpress.com, and typepad.com allow users to set up free accounts and post entries online. Keep in mind that unless your blog site allows for private entries, anyone will be able to read and comment on your blog.

Personal Journals

A *personal journal* is a collection of your thoughts and feelings. You write simply to express yourself. You don't need to be concerned about grammar, spelling, or punctuation, and you don't have to write in complete sentences. Just as the musician practices scales and the sprinter runs laps to loosen up, you develop fluency and the ability to express yourself smoothly and easily by writing in a personal journal. In addition to written entries, you may include lists, pictures, drawings, newspaper or magazine clippings, links to online sites—anything that gives you ideas for writing.

Because you don't share a personal journal, you can write without worrying about others' reactions to your writing. You can relax and write in your own style, using language that is natural to you. Here are some sample entries from student writer Alyssa's personal journal:

April 4

Here I am on a cloudy day headed to my house. My mom is driving at thirty-five miles per hour. She has always been a cautious driver. Every other car seems to be passing us. Some of the drivers turn, maybe wondering why my mother is driving so slow. Now we're passing the old factory. Sometimes it looks nice, especially at night. But today it looks really ugly. All the smoke is more noticeable because it is cloudy, too. I get sick just thinking about how many chemicals we breathe every day.

As I look around, I notice that this town is desperately in need of some trees. All I can see are poles, billboards, and dirt.

April 5

I called to see if I can get my old job back again. It's not exciting, but the pay's good and the people are nice. Maybe there'll be more part-timers around my age now. I hope I hear soon because otherwise I've got to get to work on finding something else.

April 7

I wrote this poem while I was waiting for the bus . . .

Wheels go, people go
Turning, turning, turning
Places to see and things to do
Waiting, waiting, waiting
Impatiently I check my watch
I have no book to pass the time
Just my journal

April 8

Got my summer job. Wow! That takes a load off of my mind.

GROUP ACTIVITY 1 Start a Personal Journal

To help you brainstorm ideas for starting a personal journal, form a group with several classmates, and answer the following questions. After the group has discussed the questions, have each member freewrite about his or her answer to one of the questions. Use this freewriting as the first entry in your new personal journal.

1. What are two things I would rather be doing right now?
2. Am I well organized? How often must I search for something that I have misplaced?
3. If I could change anything about the way I have been raised, what would it be?
4. If I could take a one-month trip anywhere in the world (and if money were not a consideration), where would I go, and what would I do?
5. What do I most strive for in life: accomplishment, security, love, power, excitement, knowledge, or something else?
6. Is there something I have dreamed of doing for a long time? Why haven't I done it?
7. Do I have long-term goals? What is one such goal, and how do I plan to reach it?
8. What is the greatest accomplishment of my life?
9. What is my most treasured memory?
10. What do I see myself doing in ten years' time?

(⏻) Turn off your word-processing tools

If you're keeping an online journal, consider turning off your word processor's grammar and spell checkers so you won't be distracted by the squiggly lines that appear under words as you type. You can turn them back on if you want to revise and edit your writing.

Dialogue Journals

The *dialogue journal* is a written conversation—or dialogue—between you and another person. As in a personal journal, your primary concern in a dialogue journal is expressing your thoughts. Unlike a personal journal, however, what you write in a dialogue journal will be read by someone else. You don't need to be overly concerned with grammar, spelling, and punctuation, but your thoughts and ideas should be complete enough for your reader to understand them. You may exchange your dialogue journal with one or more friends or classmates. You also may focus on one topic or change topics each time you exchange journals.

One advantage of a dialogue journal is that it allows you to clarify your understanding of an idea or issue by explaining it to someone else. Another advantage is that it allows you to determine how clearly you communicate your thoughts to someone else. You may even ask your reader specific questions.

In the following sample entry from a student's dialogue journal, Kirk writes about a school issue that concerns him. Because he is writing to get his thoughts down on paper, Kirk makes some errors in grammar and punctuation.

> One incident that really upset me this past week was the fact that on tests people are always cheating. It makes me mad that people expect others to always do their work for them. This might have been okay in high school but this is college and that means everyone has to make it on their own. We don't go to college expecting to "just pass." Well maybe some people do and those who do feel that way have no business in college.
>
> However what do my friends say. "Oh what a small classroom. Great for cheating. Come sit by me and let me see your paper, okay." What kind of people are they. They are wasting their parents money because it is obvious they don't plan to study or have a career.

Here's how Kirk's student reader, Michelle, responded to his journal entry:

> Kirk, rather than thinking so much about other people's cheating, concentrate on your own goals. In the long run, the cheaters will be the ones who lose out for not doing their own work. Just don't let them cheat off of you. Concentrate on not cheating yourself. Be honest to your own work, your own future.

And here's what Kirk's writing instructor had to say after reading the same journal entry:

> Kirk, I can see that you have strong feelings about cheating. You may want to write a persuasive letter to the editor of the campus newspaper about the problem of cheating on campus. Why do you suppose students cheat? Why do you say that cheating might have been okay in high school? Is cheating acceptable at some times but not at other times? How would you solve this problem? What do you think should happen to students who are caught cheating?

GROUP ACTIVITY 2 Start a Dialogue Journal

Write in your journal on a topic of interest to you. Then ask a classmate to respond to what you have written. In return, read and respond to your classmate's journal entry. If you need help getting started with your writing, try answering a few of the following questions.

1. What do I value most in a relationship?
2. Do I judge others by higher or lower standards than I use to judge myself?
3. When did I last yell at someone? Why? Did I regret it later?
4. Do I find it hard to say no to family and friends? Why or why not?
5. Who is the most important person in my life? Why?
6. Are there people whose lives I envy enough to want to trade places with them? Who are they?
7. Have I ever disliked someone? If so, why and for how long?
8. What do I most regret not having told someone? Why haven't I told that person yet?
9. What is my best advice for getting along with others?
10. How important is family life to me? Do I think of family as including only those people related to me by birth, or do I include close friends and neighbors as well?

 Keep a dialogue journal online

Dialogue online by posting entries to Facebook Notes. To encourage others to respond, end your entry with some questions for your readers. Be sure to also respond to other students' entries.

Learning Logs

A *learning log* is a journal that focuses on your responses to course content. In it, you summarize, synthesize, or react to a class lecture, discussion, or assigned reading. You may restate the objectives of each class or try to pinpoint what confuses you about a particular topic. By keeping a learning log, you'll improve not only your understanding of the subject but also your attitude toward the course in general. Asking questions and voicing your concerns in your log will help you become an active learner and contribute to class discussions. You'll also find yourself making connections between new ideas and previous knowledge.

Get into the habit of marking a *T* (for *Topic*) in the margin next to learning-log entries that you think might make good essay topics. What makes a good topic? A good topic is one that you're interested in and that others might also want to learn about. Consider, too, how much you already know about the topic and whether you can find additional information about it.

Student writer Tam's learning-log entry is about her first-year college composition class. By writing about her own writing class, Tam gains insight into how to become a better writer.

I am glad to hear that I am not expected to write excellently from the beginning. I now understand that everyone can improve their writing. I like the idea that we will be sharing our work with our classmates. I always thought that in college we would not have an opportunity to share.

Today we learned about freewriting, which means to write off the top of your head as fast as you can. We did freewriting in my English class. I liked it because it lets ideas flow out freely without worrying about grammar or punctuation. I'm glad we will be freewriting this semester.

The essays we have to do seem hard. I already feel the pressure of my first paper. Maybe freewriting will help me.

Tam keeps her learning log in a traditional full-page format. Some students, however, prefer to integrate their logs with their class notes in a double-column format. To do this, simply divide each page down the middle, with one column labeled *Notes* and the other *Thoughts*. In the Notes column, record key concepts, important details, and examples from class lectures and outside reading. In the Thoughts column, reflect on what you're learning: What does it mean to you? How do you feel about it? How will you use this information in the future? You may also summarize, keep a list of new vocabulary words, and jot down notes on upcoming assignments.

Keeping a two-column learning log helps you integrate what you're studying in college into the fabric of your own thinking and past experiences. Personal examples help you understand the course material and the ways it relates to your life. Whichever type of learning log you choose to keep, responding to your class notes will help you recall information when you need it for a class discussion or an exam.

Here's an entry from the two-column learning log that student writer Kevin kept for his psychology class:

Notes	Thoughts
Memory —	I never realized there were three
Where information is held.	kinds of memory. I'm not surprised
3 types	that we forget so much sensory
sensory	info: there's so much of it.
short-term	Short-term memory is what I am
long-term	thinking now, drawing on what is
sensory — all info that enters the senses	happening around me. I think of
short-term — where all conscious	long-term memory kind of like a
thought takes place	book in the library. If I want to
long-term — representation of all that	retrieve it, I hope that it is
is known	there.

▪ HOW TO Keep a Learning Log

- During class or as you read, take notes on the left-hand side of the paper.
- On the right-hand side, summarize, define words, connect to your own experiences, or jot down ideas about upcoming assignments.
- After class, write two or three paragraphs about what you learned using a full-page format (either with pen or in a computer file).

GROUP ACTIVITY 3 Start a Learning Log

During class, take notes as you always do. Afterward, along with a classmate, reflect in your logs by asking yourselves the following questions.

1. How can I summarize what I learned in class today?
2. What parts did I not understand?
3. How might I clarify this information?
4. What new vocabulary words do I need to look up?
5. What key points are likely to appear on an exam?
6. Which ideas would make good paper topics?
7. Do I agree or disagree with what I learned today?
8. How can I apply what I learned to other classes?
9. How can I apply what I learned to my work?
10. How will I use this information in the future?

 Keep a learning log on your computer

Using the Format command in your word-processing program, you can easily create a two-column learning log. Consider using a different font for summaries. Boldface new vocabulary words and concepts you don't understand so that you can look them up later.

▪ HOW TO Select the Right Journal for Your Writing

- Keep a personal journal if you want to explore your own thoughts and feelings.
- Keep a dialogue journal if you want to exchange ideas with others.
- Keep a learning log if you want to increase what you learn in your college classes.

CHAPTER CHECKLIST

❑ Use a journal to jot down ideas, opinions, feelings, and insights.

❑ A journal can be kept in a notebook or on a computer.

❑ There are three types of journals:

    ❑ the personal journal.

    ❑ the dialogue journal.

    ❑ the learning log.

❑ The personal journal is for its writer's eyes only and contains personal thoughts and feelings.

❑ The dialogue journal is shared with someone who reads and responds to it.

❑ The learning log is kept for a particular course and contains class notes, reading notes, and its writer's own thoughts, sometimes in a two-column format.

REFLECTING ON YOUR WRITING

You have practiced writing three types of journals: a personal journal, a dialogue journal, and a learning log. To help you decide which one you want to continue to keep throughout the semester, answer the following questions.

1. Do any of my instructors require a journal? If so, which type of journal is required?

2. How will keeping a personal journal be worthwhile to me as a student?

3. If I keep a dialogue journal, who will I ask to read and respond to it?

4. For which course would I keep a learning log?

5. How will keeping a journal help me discover topics for future papers?

6. How will journal writing give me practice as a writer?

Using your answers to these questions, complete a Writing Process Report for this chapter (you can download a report form at **bedfordstmartins.com /choices**). Once you complete this report, begin your journal by writing on what you learned in this chapter about journals and what you still hope to learn. Continue to add entries daily.

11

Writing Summaries

A *summary* is a condensed version of a piece of writing. Many of us have summarized the plot of a favorite book for a friend, and some of us have written summaries on the job and in college classes.

Instructors may ask you to summarize books, articles, essays, plays, television shows, movies, or speeches. These summaries help you condense important source information, reflect on what you have learned, and demonstrate your knowledge to others. You may also choose to write summaries of a reading assignment, a lecture, or other classroom materials for yourself as a way to learn and recall information for class discussions, reports, or exams.

A summary includes the main ideas and important supporting points from the original, and it leaves out overly specific details and examples. A summary is written in your own words but does not include your judgment or opinion. To summarize well, you must be able to analyze and evaluate the source information and then condense it, using your own words. Doing this can help you develop your writing, reading, listening, and thinking skills. Summaries test your understanding of the original information as well as your ability to effectively communicate what you have learned. ■

> In this chapter, you will write a summary of a favorite reading in this textbook. As you work on your summary, you will
>
> - Learn about the parts of a summary.
> - Practice using your own words to write a summary.

Writing Assignment

Your instructor is revising the syllabus for this course for next year and is asking students to give feedback about the essays in this book. Your instructor wants to know which readings interest students, which essays they understand fully, and which ones they do not understand. To help determine which essays students like best and how clearly students understand them, your instructor would like you and your classmates to select a favorite essay from any of the chapters in Part Two of this textbook and summarize it. Write a summary of your favorite essay, and share it with your instructor. (You may also select an essay from the Additional Readings at the back of the book.)

(Writing a Summary

As with other skills, writing a good summary takes practice. If you are writing an e-mail to a friend or family member in which you describe the movie you saw last night, you would draft quickly and hit the Send button. Other times—especially if you are summarizing a document for an employer or a textbook reading assignment for an instructor—you may need to use the writing process to gather ideas, write and revise several drafts, and edit your final summary to eliminate errors. A number of strategies will help you consistently write better summaries.

Reread the Original Text

Whether you are assigned a summary or decide to write one for yourself, go back and reread the original material. A summary allows you to condense a long piece of writing into one or a few paragraphs. This can be useful when your reader doesn't have time to read the original. When you summarize, you filter out unnecessary details and focus on main points only.

1. Preview the reading.
   - Think about the title and what it means to you.
   - Note the author's name.
2. Read the text.
   - Read carefully, underlining the most important points.
   - Circle and look up the meanings of words you don't know.
3. Write to comprehend and remember.
   - List the most important points.
   - Note the page numbers of the original text.

Check out movie review plot summaries

Most movie reviews contain a summary of the plot. Go to a Web site that posts reviews of movies, such as the Internet Movie Database, or IMDB. Select a movie that you have seen, and read the plot summary. How well does the summary communicate the essence of the plot?

Write the Summary

A summary helps you and your reader figure out what you do and don't know. You can write a good summary only if you fully understand the original text. A sure way for you and your reader to test whether you know a certain piece of material is to see whether you can summarize it accurately. Your summary will include the following parts:

Main Idea

In the first sentence, identify the title, the author's name, and the main idea of the original source in your own words. This is the sentence that tells your reader the source of the original text and its main topic. Remember, even when you use your own words, you must let the reader know that you borrowed the information from another source.

> In the essay "Prison Studies," Malcom X describes how he learned to love reading while serving time in prison.

Important Supporting Points

Learning to summarize helps you streamline the process of reading and recording information. Because you can't quote everything you read, you select and include only the most important points. Summaries also provide you with a version that you can reread later as you prepare for a class discussion, a report, or an exam.

Decide which pieces of information you need to include to get the main idea across quickly. Write these down in your own words. Try to stay true to the meaning the original author intended. Use direct quotes sparingly — no more than one or two.

For more on using direct quotations, see pp. 505–08.

> Malcolm X was impressed with one of his fellow inmate's knowledge, but he lacked the reading skills to effectively state his own opinions. To develop his vocabulary, he began copying the pages of a dictionary and then memorizing the meanings of the words. Once he learned some words, he began to read more and more books, often reading into the night after lights out. He states: "I knew right there in prison that reading had changed forever the course of my life."

Conclusion

Write a conclusion that restates the main idea or that restates the author's opinion or recommendations. The conclusion helps bring the summary to a close and helps your reader understand what you consider to be important.

> After Malcolm X was released from prison, he continued to read everything he could get his hands on and used what he learned to help his community. These prison studies helped him become an educated man (pp. 88–90).

GROUP ACTIVITY 1 Identify the Parts of a Summary

With several classmates, reread the essay "Quicker Liquor: Should We Lower the Legal Drinking Age?" on page 277, and then read the following summary. In the spaces provided, identify each element of the summary: write *M* for the main point of the summary, number each of the supporting points, and write *C* for the concluding sentence. Discuss how this summary condenses the original essay.

Summary Paragraph for Darshak Sanghavi's

"Quicker Liquor: Should We Lower the Legal Drinking Age?"

_____ In the essay "Quicker Liquor: Should We Lower the Legal Drinking Age?" author Darshak Sanghavi argues that the drinking age should not be lowered, in contrast to the views expressed by many college presidents. _____ He begins by describing the college presidents' arguments for lowering the drinking age to 18 because they think it will help prevent binge drinking. _____ He then points out why he thinks these college presidents are wrong. _____ According to Sanghavi, the 1984 law that resulted in the drinking age being raised from 18 to 21 has saved lives. _____ Sanghavi argues that binge drinking on college campuses results from local laws, lack of alcohol education, and a student body that is not diverse. _____ He believes that the best way to reduce binge drinking is to increase taxes on beer because states with a high beer tax have lower rates of binge drinking. _____ While he admits that binge drinking is a problem, he believes that there are better solutions than lowering the drinking age (pp. 277–80).

GROUP ACTIVITY 2 Write a Summary

Imagine that your class will be tested on the information in Tara Parker-Pope's essay "An Ugly Toll of Technology: Impatience and Forgetfulness" on pages 244–45. Write a summary that will help you remember this information. Share your summary with several classmates. Discuss ways to improve your summaries.

> ## ■ HOW TO Write a Summary
>
> - Reread the material to be summarized, underlining the important points.
> - Write a sentence that states the title, the author's name, and the main point of the original text.
> - In your own words, write the important supporting points.
> - Leave out overly specific details and examples.
> - Write a conclusion that restates the main point and includes the page numbers of the original text.

CHAPTER CHECKLIST

❑ A summary is a condensed version of a piece of writing.

❑ A summary has three sections:

    ❑ main idea.

    ❑ supporting points.

    ❑ conclusion.

❑ Use your own words to summarize someone else's writing.

❑ Give credit to the author of the original text.

REFLECTING ON YOUR WRITING

To help you continue to improve your summary writing, answer the following questions about the assignment.

1. Other than for this class, when have you been asked to write summaries?

2. Have you found writing summaries a useful way to study? Why or why not?

3. What elements of writing a summary do you need practice with? Why?

Using your answers to these questions, complete a Writing Process Report for this chapter (you can download a report form at **bedfordstmartins.com /choices**). Once you complete this report, freewrite about what you learned in this chapter about summary writing and what you still hope to learn.

Conducting Research

12

Imagine that you have received the following writing assignments in your college courses:

- Describe the life cycle of the diamondback rattlesnake.
- Analyze César Chávez's leadership of migrant farmworkers.
- Explain the origin of the Internet in the late 1970s.

How do you find information on these topics? Of course, you start looking online or head to the library. But then what? If you had looked for this information in a library thirty years ago, you would have consulted the card catalog to find the name of a book on your topic and to see where it was located. You also might have examined a reference book that listed magazine articles on your subject.

Today, however, most information is available electronically. Because of computer technology, libraries can now access information from around the world in seconds. How do you sort through this information to decide what is most useful and valid? How do you use this material in an essay? This chapter will give you strategies for conducting research and using information in your own essays. ■

In this chapter, you will write a brief researched essay. As you work on your essay, you will

- Prepare to research a topic.
- Make observations, survey others, and conduct interviews.
- Locate sources of information.
- Evaluate sources of information.
- Learn what plagiarism is and how to avoid it.
- Learn note-taking strategies.
- Quote, paraphrase, and summarize information.
- Document sources correctly.

Writing Assignment

The International Students Office on your campus is holding a public meeting to help students from other countries adjust to their new surroundings. Your psychology instructor has volunteered your class to participate in this forum. To prepare for the forum, your instructor has asked each student to write an essay with ideas for helping international students adjust to a new country and university. You and your classmates will present these essays at the forum at the end of the term.

◖ Preparing to Conduct Research

To conduct research, you first need to know what information you're seeking. Otherwise, you might spend a great deal of time finding information that doesn't pertain to your topic.

Narrow Your Topic

Before beginning your research, you need to narrow your topic so that your ideas can be well developed. If you choose a topic that is too broad, you will have difficulty communicating your ideas, supporting your points, and creating a clearly written, well-structured essay. For the International Students Office forum, you could explain aspects of U.S. culture that are important for international students to understand. You could also suggest how international students might increase their enjoyment of their new culture. Another choice would be to focus on the stress that people suffer when they encounter a new culture or setting—in other words, culture shock. Narrowing your topic to just one of these ideas will allow you to focus on an aspect of your topic, make the research process easier, and go into more detail in your essay. It will also help you know exactly what information you need to find to support your points.

For more on choosing and narrowing your topic, see pp. 16–18.

Write Research Questions

After you narrow your topic, think of questions that you want to answer. These *research questions* will guide you in conducting your research. For instance, if you are writing about culture shock, you might ask these questions:

- What is the definition of *culture shock*?
- Who gets culture shock?
- What are the emotional and physical effects of culture shock?
- How can culture shock be prevented?

As you research your topic, refer to your research questions to help you stay focused on the information you need.

> ### ■ HOW TO Plan a Research Project
>
> - Choose a topic that interests you.
> - Review your purpose and audience.
> - Narrow your topic.
> - State the following questions: Who? What? When? Where? Why? How?
> - Select a few of these questions to explore.
> - Establish a timeline for conducting research to answer these questions and for completing the project. Allow plenty of time to work on each part of the project.

◖ Primary Research

Research that you do on your own, rather than read about, is called *primary research*. Thus, when you conduct an experiment in science, you're doing primary research. When you ask friends to suggest a good movie, you're essentially taking a survey, another form of primary research.

Three common types of primary research involve making observations, surveying others, and conducting interviews. These types of primary research are used for different purposes:

- When you want to explain how something works or how something is done, consider making observations.
- When you want to explain your topic's importance in people's lives, consider surveying others.
- When you require specialized information or information known only to experts, consider conducting interviews.

Making Observations

To *observe* something is to watch it closely. Observations enable you to explain your points clearly to your readers. For example, if you're explaining cell mitosis, you can observe cell division under a microscope. In your essay, you can describe what you saw to make the process come alive for your readers. Similarly, in an essay about the Internet, you might describe your observations of some online conversations and include a quotation that illustrates a key point.

> ■**HOW TO** Make Observations
>
> - Obtain permission (if necessary) to observe an event relevant to your topic.
> - Remain visible, but do not participate in the event.
> - Decide what to focus on when you observe.
> - Take detailed notes as you observe the event.
> - Ask questions about what you observe but may not understand. You may need to ask more questions later.

⏻ **Record your observations in a blog**

While you observe your event, use a blog to record your observations. Later you can use these entries as sources of information for your essay, even copying and pasting from the transcript into your essay draft.

Surveying Others

A *survey* contains information collected from many people about a certain topic. Newspapers often conduct surveys to find out how citizens plan to vote in an upcoming election. Manufacturers hire market-research companies to survey users of their products and thereby learn how to improve them. In writing, a survey can help you gather people's opinions or knowledge about an issue and use these data in your essay. For example, if your topic for the International Students Office forum is culture shock, you could survey people to determine how many of them know the definition of the term. Your research findings might support the point that many people experience culture shock but few know what it is or how it can be overcome.

> ■**HOW TO** Conduct Surveys
>
> - Decide how you will conduct the survey—with an *oral survey* or a *written survey*. In an oral survey, respondents reply immediately but do not have much time to think about the questions. A written survey generates detailed responses, but many people may not have the time to fill out a questionnaire.
> - Decide where you will conduct the survey. You want to find a place where many people come and go, such as the entrance of the college library or student union.
> - Create five to ten survey questions. Make them brief and easy to understand. Also use various types of questions—that is, questions

that can be answered with yes or no mixed with questions that require short answers. Test questions on classmates for suggestions for improvement.

- Decide whom you will survey. For instance, do you want to survey both men and women from various age groups? Or do you want to narrow your survey to a specific group? Avoid surveying only people you know.

- Decide how many people you will survey. The more people you include in a survey, the more reliable your results will be. But you need to consider your time limitations as well.

- If you conduct an oral survey, write out your questions ahead of time, and either take careful notes or record the conversation (with the permission of the person you are recording).

 Conduct an online survey

A survey can be sent to people to fill in electronically via e-mail or via Web services such as SurveyMonkey or Google Forms. One of the benefits of an online survey is that the site will total the results for you. Consider sharing the results of the survey with those who participated in it.

Conducting Interviews

In addition to making observations and surveying others, you can conduct *interviews* to learn more about a research topic. By interviewing a knowledgeable person, you can collect information and gain an expert's perspective. If you're writing an essay on water quality in your region, for example, you could interview an environmental engineer who has studied this subject. For the topic of culture shock, you could interview international students, who can describe firsthand what it's like to experience culture shock.

Here's one more tip: if you're reluctant to contact a stranger for an interview, remember that most people enjoy talking about what they know and sharing their knowledge with interested students.

Interviewing others is a great way to gather information. For a review of how to consult with others, see p.15.

 Conduct an online interview

To conduct an interview with a person in a different location, consider conducting a face-to-face interview using Skype or Google+ Hangouts, or a text interview using e-mail or chat. Be sure to keep a copy of the video or a transcript of the conversation to view or read later.

■ HOW TO Conduct Interviews

- Choose a knowledgeable person to interview. To determine whether someone is an expert on your topic, check his or her credentials (such as academic degrees, professional activities, and published works). In some situations, a person's personal experience with your topic is more relevant than formal credentials.
- Contact the person in advance to set up an appointment.
- Prepare your interview questions.
- If you conduct the interview in person, dress appropriately and arrive on time.
- Keep the conversation focused on your questions. Be considerate of your interviewee's limited time.
- Listen carefully, and take good notes. Put quotation marks around the person's actual words. You may digitally record the conversation only if you obtain the interviewee's permission beforehand.
- Ask the interviewee to clarify anything you do not understand.
- Send a thank-you note to the person soon after the interview.

GROUP ACTIVITY 1 Conduct Primary Research

Discuss your writing topic with other students in your class. Determine the type of primary research that will best suit your topic. Then use the appropriate set of questions to discuss how members of your class can go about making observations, surveying others, or conducting interviews.

Questions about Making Observations

1. What information do you need to obtain from your observations?
2. Where will you make the observations?
3. Do you need permission to observe? If so, from whom?
4. What questions do you have about the event you want to observe?

Questions about Surveying Others

1. What information do you want the survey to provide?
2. Do you want your respondents to answer orally or in writing? Why?
3. Who will your respondents be, and how many people will you survey?
4. Where will you conduct the survey?
5. What questions will you ask in the survey?

Questions about Conducting Interviews

1. What information do you hope to obtain from the interview?

2. Who could give you this information?

3. What questions will you ask?

(Secondary Research

Secondary research involves reading what others have written about your topic. To conduct secondary research, you need to know how to locate relevant sources of information; how to evaluate sources; how to avoid plagiarism; how to take notes; how to quote, paraphrase, and summarize sources of information; and how to document the sources you cite in your research paper.

Locating Sources of Information

Use a Search Engine

When you are asked to do research, your first impulse might be to look up your subject on Wikipedia or conduct a Google search. While most professors will not consider this to be scholarly research, these sources may provide a helpful starting point. Keep in mind that "wiki" Web sites such as Wikipedia can be edited by anyone and so may contain inaccurate information. However, Wikipedia articles offer additional reference lists and links to external Web sites that may be helpful. Similarly, Google can be helpful when used properly. A Google search will yield a variety of commercial Web sites that may not provide the most reliable information. However, you can use a search filter to focus your results or an Advanced Search to limit your search to .edu, .gov, and .org sites. Google Scholar limits your search to scholarly articles, and Google Books allows you to read the full text of many books for free.

Visit Your Campus Library

Sources of information in libraries can be found in many formats, including books, newspapers, periodicals (popular magazines), journals, media (CDs, DVDs), as well as electronic (Web or Internet) resources and files. Periodicals are written by journalists for a general audience, while journals contain articles by experts for a more specialized audience. Both can be found in print, microform (fiche, microfilm), media, and electronic formats. Electronic formats are very popular, and many materials that once appeared only in print now also appear in electronic form. To do secondary research, you need to know how to access both print and electronic resources.

Consult a Reference Librarian

To help you find scholarly sources, you can talk to a reference librarian, either in person or online, or you can search the library's online catalog. This catalog will indicate which resources are available. The online catalog allows you to search by title, author, subject, keyword, call number, or ISSN/ISBN, and in some cases allows you to link directly to the abstract or full article.

Consult an Encyclopedia

If you have little experience doing research, or you don't know much about your topic or subject, you might want to start with a general resource such as an encyclopedia. Encyclopedias give broad descriptions, definitions, and background information about all kinds of topics. The library has print as well as electronic encyclopedias, such as the *Encyclopaedia Britannica*. There are also discipline-specific or specialized encyclopedias in many subject areas. Specialized encyclopedias are a better source of in-depth information because they cover specific fields. Some specialized encyclopedias are the *Encyclopedia of Computer Science and Technology*, *Encyclopedia of Psychology*, *Encyclopedia of the Biological Sciences*, and *Harvard Guide to American History*. To locate specialized encyclopedias, start by checking the library catalog or consult with a reference librarian. Print encyclopedias are usually for use in the library only and may not be checked out.

Consult an Index

After consulting an encyclopedia, you can find further information by checking an index, which lists magazine, journal, or newspaper articles by title, subject, or author. The library subscribes to many resources that will provide this sort of information, most of which are available online. Some of them provide not only citations and abstracts but full articles as well.

Find a Print Source

If you've located the title of a useful article but it is not available in full text, you will need to look for it in your college's library catalog (you should use a journal title search, not an article title search). Then, using a call number—the number the library assigns to each book, journal, or other item in its collection—you will need to physically locate the resource. Every item in the library will have a unique call number, arranged in alphabetical and numerical order. Books your library houses can also be searched for by topic, author, or subject, and they will also have call numbers and can be found on the shelves.

If the library doesn't have access to the periodical or book you need, you may request it through interlibrary loan. It can take anywhere from two to three days to two weeks to receive an item, so start your request in advance of when you need it.

Find an Electronic Source

In addition to the print versions, many books, encyclopedias, magazines, journals, and newspapers are available online. Both indexes and databases may contain full articles or only the titles and abstracts of articles from thousands of magazines, journals, and newspapers. Some databases, such as *Periodical Abstracts* and *Readers' Guide Abstracts*, list magazine and journal articles, whereas others, such as *InfoTrac Newspapers*, include only newspaper articles. A reference librarian is usually available to help you choose the databases that are most useful for your topic. Compared with print sources, electronic indexes and databases are generally more current because they are updated more frequently. You may also access your library's computer databases from your home or another campus computer.

Consult a Database

Your librarian will frequently direct you to an academic journal archive, like *JSTOR*, or an online research database, like *EBSCOhost*. These sites offer bibliographical information, abstracts, and full text links to thousands of scholarly articles. When consulting a database, use *keywords*, or words that pertain to your topic, to locate articles. The wrong keywords can give you either too many or too few items from the database. For her report on culture shock that you will read later in this chapter, one student, Leslie Lozano, visited *EBSCOhost* through her library's Web site and clicked on the link marked "Choose Databases." Some databases allow you to browse journals specific to your major or discipline. Leslie decided to choose *Academic Search Premier* because she wanted a database that would offer results across various disciplines and fields of study. Using the keywords "culture shock," she received a list of 2,645 articles—far too many for her to review. To narrow her search, she clicked on the "Advanced Search" option and used the keywords "culture shock AND international students." These keywords produced no relevant items for her to examine. On the advice of a librarian, she used "culture shock AND education." This produced 155 items for her to examine—a more manageable number.

A database often gives you an abstract, or a brief summary, of each article it contains. This abstract will help you determine whether the article is likely to answer one of your research questions. Leslie Lozano skimmed through a few abstracts and then found one that seemed related to her topic, "Native Identity and Community on Campus." Based on the abstract, she decided she might be able to use it in her report on culture shock. She was in luck. A link to the full article was included in the database, saving her the time of retrieving it from the periodical section of the library. See Figure 12.1 on the next page for Leslie's search results. After reading the article, she e-mailed a copy to herself and printed it out, so she could take notes on it at a later time.

Figure 12.1 Leslie's Search Results

■ **HOW TO** Use Keywords to Search

- Narrow your search by connecting keywords with the word *AND*, as in "culture shock AND education."

- You can also narrow your search by using the word *NOT*, as in "culture shock NOT immigration."

- If your keywords don't result in enough items for you to examine, broaden your search by using the word *OR*, as in "culture shock OR cultural studies."

- If you still can't find the right keywords, ask a reference librarian. He or she can then check the subject headings in the database for you.

■ **HOW TO** Find Electronic Resources

- Identify a database, such as *LexisNexis*, on which to search for information. A list of databases is available at your campus library.

- Enter keywords on your topic to access information.

- Read the abstract or summary to determine whether an article sounds useful.

- If the article seems useful, print or take notes on the information.

- Record the publication information for your Works Cited page.

Use Other Sources of Information

Secondary research need not be limited to written sources found in the library or on the Web. Check television listings for relevant documentaries or news shows. *All Things Considered*, broadcast daily on National Public Radio and digitally archived in podcasts on NPR.org, is another excellent source of current news.

GROUP ACTIVITY 2 Conduct Library Research

Team up with a classmate to do some library research on your topic. First, explain to your partner the type of information you need to find. Then, visit the campus library and, working together, locate Web sites or specialized encyclopedias, magazine and newspaper articles, and books on each of your topics. Don't hesitate to ask a librarian for assistance if you can't find the sources you need. Finally, record the titles and authors of the various sources you find on your topic.

1. Web site article (Give the author or compiler of the work, title of the work, title of the Web site, version or edition used, publisher or sponsor of the site, date of publication, medium of publication, and date you accessed this material.)

2. Specialized encyclopedia (Give the author's name, the title of the article, the title of the reference work, the edition, the year of publication, and the medium of publication.)

3. Magazine article (Give the author's name, title of the article, title of the magazine, date of publication — day, month, and year for a weekly magazine, or month and year for a monthly magazine — page number[s] of the article, and medium of publication.)

4. Newspaper article (Give the author's name, title of the article, name of the newspaper, city of publication unless it is a national paper, date it was published — day, month, and year — page number[s] of the article, and medium of publication.)

5. Book (Give the author's name, title of the book, city of publication, publisher, date of publication, and medium of publication.)

For a list of online sources of information for a researched essay, go to **bedfordstmartins.com /choices** and click on **Annotated Web Links**.

Evaluating Sources of Information

The credibility of the sources you consult is an important concern. A report isn't necessarily objective simply because it appears in print or on television. Many magazines have a political bias. The *National Review*, for instance, has a conservative slant, whereas the *Nation* is considered liberal. Recent sources (that is, those published within the last five years) are more up-to-date than older ones. Journal articles are often peer reviewed before being published—meaning they are evaluated by experts in that field— which makes them an excellent source of information. If you gather information from television sources, be especially skeptical about what you watch. Many television news discussion programs have a political bias, and some news-entertainment shows may exaggerate facts to make their stories more interesting to their audience. Avoid using material from a talk show unless you are certain it's not hearsay or gossip.

Evaluating sources you find on the Web is especially important. For the most part, no independent person or agency screens material before it is put on the Web. Therefore, *you* need to screen the material. When accessing information on culture shock, for instance, you might find Web pages advertising a therapist's treatment for culture shock, a site dedicated to a rock band named Culture Shock, and a high school student's research paper on this topic.

▪ HOW TO Evaluate Web Resources

- Determine who put the information on the Web site. Does this person have credentials, such as college degrees or university affiliations? If no author is named or if the author's credentials aren't given, find another source of information.

- Is the Web site trying to sell you something? If so, it might not contain objective information.

- Be cautious when accessing Web sites with *com* in their addresses, as in **elvispresley.com.** *Com* is an abbreviation for "commercial"; most of these Web sites are connected to commercial companies that are trying to sell you something.

- Web sites with *edu* in their addresses, as in **lib.iastate.edu**, are usually maintained by a college or university; Web sites with *gov* in their addresses, as in **lcweb.loc.gov**, are sponsored by a governmental agency; and Web sites with *org*, such as **votesmart.org**, are sponsored by nonprofit organizations. Information provided on such sites is likely to be reliable, although you still need to determine the author of the site and its purpose.

▪ GROUP ACTIVITY 3 Evaluate Web Sites

With a few of your classmates, evaluate several Web sites that deal in some way with culture shock. (To access these Web sites, use a search engine and type in the keywords "culture shock.") Which sites would be appropriate for an essay on culture shock? How did you determine their appropriateness?

⏻ Use favorites and bookmarks

Use the Bookmark feature in your browser to help you quickly access Web sites you plan to examine more than once. A bookmark allows you to link directly to a site rather than having to type in the entire URL address. You can return to the site by choosing it from your list of favorites or bookmarks.

Avoiding Plagiarism

A very serious offense, *plagiarism* is using another writer's ideas or words without giving credit to that writer as the source. Handing in someone else's work with your name on it is an obvious act of plagiarism. But using another writer's words or ideas in your paper without indicating where they came from, even if you do so unintentionally, is also an act of plagiarism.

Therefore, you must be careful to avoid plagiarism. Always identify your sources when you borrow ideas, information, or quotations so that your readers can clearly distinguish between what has been borrowed and what is your own.

■ **HOW TO** Avoid Plagiarism

- When you reproduce a writer's exact words, use quotation marks to enclose the quote. Be sure to name your source.
- When you restate an author's words in your own words, omit the quotation marks but still name your source.
- List all of the sources named in your paper in the Works Cited list.

The following sections on taking notes and on quoting, paraphrasing, summarizing, and documenting sources will also help you avoid plagiarism.

◖ GROUP ACTIVITY 4 Talk about Plagiarism

Plagiarism can come in many forms. Discuss the following situations with your classmates.

1. Because of her busy work schedule, Anne puts off writing a research paper until the night before the deadline. As a result, she doesn't take the time to identify the sources of borrowed words and ideas in her paper. A week later, her instructor calls her into his office and tells her that she has plagiarized.

   - Why is this plagiarism?
   - How might Anne be penalized?

2. Karita is on the Web doing research for her paper, and she finds an essay there on her topic. She copies several paragraphs from the essay, word for word, without indicating where they came from. Later, Karita's instructor asks her why part of her paper sounds as if someone else wrote it.

   - Why is this plagiarism?
   - How might Karita be penalized?

3. Coworkers Sam and Eloise are asked by their supervisor to write a report on the company's recent sales figures. Eloise volunteers to draft the report, and Sam

agrees to revise, edit, and submit it to the supervisor. The report that Sam submits, however, has only his name on it.

- Why is this plagiarism?
- How might Sam be penalized?

4. Kwan and Joe are roommates. Kwan is enrolled in the same history course that Joe took last semester. Kwan comes across one of Joe's old notebooks, and in it is the history paper that Joe wrote for last semester's course. Kwan reformats the paper and submits it as his own.

- Why is this plagiarism?
- If it is discovered, how might Kwan be penalized? If it isn't, how might Kwan's experience influence his behavior in the future?
- What advice would you give Kwan if you could?

For more help with understanding what plagiarism is and how to avoid it, go to **bedfordstmartins.com /plagiarismtutorial**.

Taking Notes

Once you locate a book, an article, or another source on your topic, skim it to see if it answers any of your research questions. To *skim* a source, simply read the introduction, the headings and subheadings, and the conclusion. If the source answers any of your research questions, take notes. You can also photocopy the relevant pages and highlight the important ideas. However, highlighting shouldn't replace taking careful notes. Note taking forces you to select only what is useful from a source, to restate the information in your own words, and thereby to reflect on its meaning.

Consider using index cards for your notes. Because they're small, index cards help you focus on the information you need. Also, you can arrange the cards in various ways, which can be helpful in organizing your ideas during revision. Take notes for only one source per note card.

For each source you use, be sure to record the author's name, the title, and the publication information you will need for your Works Cited page at the end of your essay. This information varies depending on the type of source you consult. For magazine, journal, and newspaper articles, encyclopedia entries, books, and Web sites, you must record the following information for each source you use:

MAGAZINE OR NEWSPAPER ARTICLE
- Author (if given)
- Title of article
- Name of magazine or newspaper
- Date of publication
- Page numbers of the whole article or printout
- Medium of publication

If you accessed the article on a database from your library, also record the following:

- Name of the database (such as *ProQuest*)
- Medium of publication
- Date that you accessed the article

Journal Article

- Author
- Title of article
- Name of journal
- Number of volume and issue
- Date of publication (year)
- Page numbers of the whole article or printout
- Medium of publication

If you accessed the article on a database from your library, also record the following:

- Name of the database
- Medium of publication
- Date that you accessed the article

Encyclopedia Article or Entry

- Author (if given, it usually appears at the end of the entry)
- Title
- Name of the encyclopedia (and edition)
- Year of publication
- Medium of publication

Book

- Author
- Title
- City and name of publisher
- Year of publication
- Medium of publication

Web Site

- Author
- Title
- Name of any institution or organization associated with the site
- Date of publication
- Medium of publication
- Date of access

Following is an example of a note card Leslie Lozano wrote based on Mark Rolo's article "Native Identity and Community on Campus." This article helped Leslie answer her research question, What can students do to help them cope with culture shock?

Side one of note card

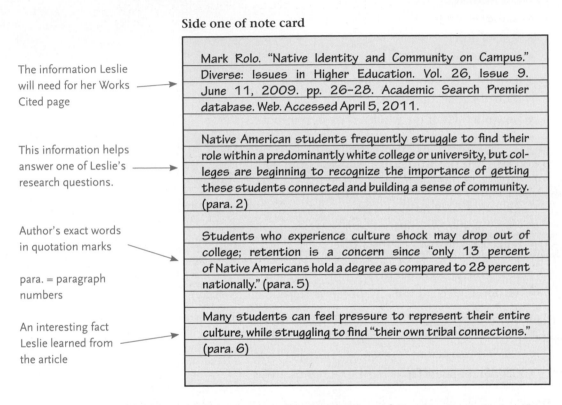

The information Leslie will need for her Works Cited page

Mark Rolo. "Native Identity and Community on Campus." Diverse: Issues in Higher Education. Vol. 26, Issue 9. June 11, 2009. pp. 26–28. Academic Search Premier database. Web. Accessed April 5, 2011.

This information helps answer one of Leslie's research questions.

Native American students frequently struggle to find their role within a predominantly white college or university, but colleges are beginning to recognize the importance of getting these students connected and building a sense of community. (para. 2)

Author's exact words in quotation marks

para. = paragraph numbers

Students who experience culture shock may drop out of college; retention is a concern since "only 13 percent of Native Americans hold a degree as compared to 28 percent nationally." (para. 5)

An interesting fact Leslie learned from the article

Many students can feel pressure to represent their entire culture, while struggling to find "their own tribal connections." (para. 6)

Figure 12.2 Leslie's Notes on "Native Identity and Community on Campus"

■ HOW TO Take Notes

- Refer frequently to your research questions to keep you focused on your topic.
- Don't just copy information from sources; add your own thoughts. You might note, for instance, where you could use the information in your essay.
- Use quotation marks to indicate where you record an author's exact words. Write the rest of your notes completely in your own words.
- When you change a source's words and sentence structure into your own words, you are *paraphrasing* the source. Most of your notes should be paraphrased.

> **GROUP ACTIVITY 5** Practice Taking Notes

Imagine that you're writing an essay on culture shock and that one of your research questions is, What can be done to help people cope with culture shock? To answer this question, take notes on an index card on the following essay. Compare your note card with several classmates' note cards. Did you answer the research question without giving unnecessary information? Did you put quotation marks around the authors' exact words? Did you record the necessary publication information for the source?

PHILIP ZIMBARDO AND ANN WEBER
Cross-Cultural Perspective: Culture Shock

Philip Zimbardo is professor emeritus of psychology at Stanford University and a former president of the American Psychological Association, the world's largest association of psychologists. Ann Weber is a professor of psychology at the University of North Carolina, Asheville. In the following excerpt from Zimbardo and Weber's college textbook *Psychology*, the authors discuss the causes and psychological effects of the experience known as culture shock.

Many people can point to a part of their culture that they consider *home*. Their 1
feelings of "home" include positive emotions, familiarity, knowledge about ways to satisfy everyday needs, and attachment to others who demonstrate acceptance and affection. Feelings that people have about home often are associated with the length of time they spend in one place. Because time spent in one place is connected to feelings of home, some people may not react positively to the concept of "home." For example, the children of migrant workers or the children of military families may never have lived in one place long enough to consider it home.

For those people who do have strong emotional ties to a home, moves from 2
their familiar surroundings can cause stress. Consider a time in your own life when you were away from home and felt discomfort because of your move. This may have occurred when you first went away to college. It could have occurred in years past when your family relocated due to a job transfer by one of your parents, or when you left home in the summer to attend summer camp or visit distant relatives. What were your feelings? Did you feel lonely, out-of-step with others, frustrated at your inability to satisfy everyday needs, or clumsy because you did not know how to behave in acceptable ways? With these thoughts in mind, consider the following situations.

1. An 18-year-old Navajo female from rural Arizona, who had won awards as a high-school basketball player, begins studies at one of the large state universities on an athletic scholarship.
2. An African-American businessman accepts a vice-presidential position in a large company where 95 percent of the upper-level executives are male Caucasians.
3. A student participates in a study-abroad program in Europe.
4. An American businesswoman travels to Japan to establish joint trade agreements for the marketing of computer hardware and software.

What do these experiences (including your own) have in common? All of these experiences involve moves away from familiar surroundings and the need to adjust to many new social situations. All of the individuals involved moved on their own, without others who had long shared their respective support groups. When faced with everyday demands such as finding food, housing, and local transportation, these people had only their own resources to help them cope. Often, such individuals feel overwhelmed in their new surroundings and experience high levels of stress (Barna, 1991). *Culture shock* is the term commonly used to describe the stress experienced by people who move to unfamiliar surroundings.

The term *culture shock* was originally coined to explain the intense experiences of people who found themselves on overseas assignments in roles such as diplomats, international students, technical assistance advisers, or businesspeople (Oberg, 1960).

Over the last thirty years, the term has expanded to include other types of experiences people have when they move across cultural boundaries *within any one country.* Occasionally, culture shock is used to explain reactions to the new and the unfamiliar. Examples include going away to college, getting married, or being forced to go on welfare after years of productive employment.

The complaints people have when experiencing culture shock are very similar, whether they are international students, overseas businesspeople, or members of an underrepresented ethnic group (Furnham & Bochner, 1986). Such individuals experience a sense of frustration and helplessness at their inability to meet their everyday needs. They feel lonely and find it hard to meet people and to develop good interpersonal relationships. Victims of culture shock often become suspicious of others and come to believe that others are "out to get them." People also report a predictable set of physical symptoms. They complain of stomachaches, inability to sleep, diarrhea, headaches, lack of sex drive, general feelings of tiredness, mild depression, and a lack of enthusiasm for life.

Many organizations now sponsor programs to help prepare people for life's transitions. Most commonly called *cross-cultural training programs* (Brislin, 1993), one of the goals of such curricula is to introduce people to the various experiences they are likely to encounter. During the programs, participants are commonly told that the experiences associated with "culture shock" are normal and are to be expected. Knowledge of what culture shock is, how frequently it is experienced, and effective coping strategies can aid in reducing people's stress.

Quoting Information

As a general rule, use quotations sparingly. But when an author uses an especially memorable phrase, you might want to quote it directly in your paper. You also might use quoted material to emphasize a point or sum up an idea. These should be brief quotations of one or two sentences.

Refer to pp. 505–08 for guidelines about punctuating quotations.

You should include an introductory phrase to tell your readers the source of each quotation. After the quoted information, put the page number of the source in parentheses. Here are some examples:

> According to psychologists Philip Zimbardo and Ann Weber, "Knowledge of what culture shock is, how frequently it is experienced, and effective coping strategies can aid in reducing people's stress" (425).

> Psychologists Philip Zimbardo and Ann Weber write, "Knowledge of what culture shock is, how frequently it is experienced, and effective coping strategies can aid in reducing people's stress" (425).

> "Knowledge of what culture shock is, how frequently it is experienced, and effective coping strategies can aid in reducing people's stress," write psychologists Philip Zimbardo and Ann Weber (425).

Also notice in the examples how the quotations are punctuated.

When you use a quotation, you can't just drop it into a paragraph. You need to explain its relevance to your topic or point. In the following paragraph from a student essay on culture shock, the writer quotes a phrase from the Zimbardo and Weber essay and then explains its relevance to his point:

> When you think of people who experience culture shock, you might picture immigrants moving to a new land or students studying in foreign countries. Not everyone who experiences culture shock, though, is in a foreign country. According to psychologists Philip Zimbardo and Ann Weber, "Over the last thirty years, the term has expanded to include other types of experiences people have when they move across cultural boundaries *within any one country*" (424). Therefore, people may experience culture shock when they leave home to go to college, lose their jobs, or move to a much bigger or smaller city.

Note, too, as this paragraph demonstrates, that the topic-illustration-explanation (TIE) pattern of organization is often used in paragraphs containing quotations.

For more information about using the TIE method of paragraph organization, refer to p. 41.

■ HOW TO Quote Information

- Use quoted information to repeat memorable phrases, to emphasize a point, or to sum up.
- Include a phrase that provides the source of the information.
- Add quotation marks at the beginning and end of the quoted material.
- Explain why the quotation is relevant to your topic.

> **GROUP ACTIVITY 6 Quote Sources**
>
> Working with several other students, write a paragraph about one of the main ideas in "Cross-Cultural Perspective: Culture Shock." Use a quotation from the essay to help you develop the paragraph. Then create an introductory phrase for the quotation, and consider using the topic-illustration-explanation pattern of paragraph organization. Compare your group's paragraph with those written by the other groups in the class.

Paraphrasing Information

To *paraphrase* is to restate a source in your own words. By paraphrasing information, you simplify complicated information and use your own writing style.

A paraphrase should be about the same length as the original passage and express the same ideas. Although when paraphrasing you might be tempted to simply substitute keywords with synonyms (words that have the same meaning), this can lead to plagiarism. Use your own writing style instead. This might mean changing the sentence structure or word order. Here's an example of an original passage, a poor paraphrase, and a good paraphrase. In the poor paraphrase, words from the original are in **bold-face type**:

ORIGINAL
: "Over the last thirty years, the term has expanded to include other types of experiences people have when they move across cultural boundaries *within any one country*" (Zimbardo and Weber 424).

POOR PARAPHRASE
: **Over the last thirty years,** the concept has broadened **to include other** kinds **of experiences people have when they** cross **cultural boundaries** *within any one country* (Zimbardo and Weber 424).

GOOD PARAPHRASE
: The meaning of this concept has broadened during the last three decades. Now it encompasses what happens to people crossing cultural borders *within a single country* (Zimbardo and Weber 424).

When paraphrasing, you don't need to use quotation marks because the words are your own. You must, however, indicate the source of the idea or information.

Here is the same student paragraph on culture shock you saw on page 351, except here the quotation is replaced with a good paraphrase (in bold-face type):

When you think of people who experience culture shock, you might picture immigrants moving to a new land or students studying in foreign countries. Not everyone who experiences culture shock, though, is in a foreign country.

The meaning of this concept has broadened during the last three decades. Now it encompasses what happens to people crossing cultural borders *within a single country* (Zimbardo and Weber 424). Therefore, people may experience culture shock when they leave home to go to college, lose their jobs, or move to a much bigger or smaller city.

Notice, too, that the TIE (topic-illustration-explanation) method of paragraph organization is used with the paraphrased information.

◾ HOW TO Paraphrase Information

- Read the material you want to paraphrase, then put it away. Write down the information or idea on a note card, using your own words and writing style.

- After the paraphrase, write the name of the author whose ideas you have borrowed (if you haven't already given the author's name) and the page number of the source.

- Reread the original passage to make sure you have accurately captured the author's information or ideas without plagiarizing.

GROUP ACTIVITY 7 Paraphrase Sources

Working with a group of students, paraphrase one or two paragraphs from "Cross-Cultural Perspective: Culture Shock." Compare your group's paraphrases with those of the other groups in your class.

Summarizing Information

A *summary* is a condensed version of a piece of text that contains that text's key ideas. A summary is always much shorter than the original because it omits most details. Summary writing is one of the most common types of writing used in college and the workplace. On the job, you might write a summary of sales over the past six months. In college courses, you might be asked to write summaries of lectures, lab experiments, or journal articles. In an essay, information summarized from primary or secondary research can provide good supporting examples, observations, definitions, facts, statistics, and expert testimony.

For more on summarizing, see Chapter 11.

Depending on your purpose for writing, a summary may be as short as a sentence or as long as a paragraph. Here's a one-sentence summary of "Cross-Cultural Perspective: Culture Shock."

In "Cross-Cultural Perspective: Culture Shock," Philip Zimbardo and Ann Weber explain what culture shock is, who experiences it, how it affects people emotionally and physically, and what people can do to cope with it.

Here's a longer summary of the same article:

> In "Cross-Cultural Perspective: Culture Shock," Philip Zimbardo and Ann Weber define *culture shock* as "the stress experienced by people who move to unfamiliar surroundings" (424). According to the authors, people may experience culture shock when they move to a new country or to a new place within their own country. A sudden life change, such as the loss of a job, can also create culture shock. This condition produces a variety of emotional problems, such as depression, loneliness, and unreasonable suspicions of other people. Culture shock can also cause physical problems, including stomach disorders and insomnia. Many programs now exist to help people about to undergo a life change that could result in culture shock.

When you summarize information in your essay, remember that your ideas come first. Summarized information should be used only to support your own points.

■ HOW TO Summarize Information

- Reread the source, and write down the main ideas. These ideas are usually expressed in the thesis statement, the topic sentences, and, at times, the conclusion. If the source has headings and subheadings, they may express main ideas as well.
- Focus on the main points only, and omit the details.
- At the beginning of your summary, give the title and author of the source.
- Write the summary in your own words. Use a quotation only to emphasize an important point that cannot be conveyed as powerfully in your own words.

GROUP ACTIVITY 8 Analyze Summaries

Read the following two summaries of "Cross-Cultural Perspective: Culture Shock." With your group, discuss how these summaries could be improved.

1. In "Cross-Cultural Perspective: Culture Shock," Philip Zimbardo and Ann Weber explain that culture shock is "the stress experienced by people who move to unfamiliar surroundings." People who might have culture shock are a Navajo student who moves to a large university, an African American businessman who takes a job in a company where 95 percent of the workers are Caucasians, a student who travels to Europe to study, and an American businesswoman who travels to Japan for her job.

2. According to Philip Zimbardo and Ann Weber in "Cross-Cultural Perspective: Culture Shock," many people feel attached to a place that they call "home." When they leave this comfortable place, they often experience stress, which is called *culture shock*. They have problems doing ordinary things, such as shopping or finding a place to live. When the term *culture shock* was coined, it referred to the stress felt by people who lived abroad.

For more help working with sources, go to **bedfordstmartins.com /bibliographer**.

Documenting Sources

Documentation of sources is an important aspect of the research paper. To *document* is to refer your reader to your primary and secondary research sources. Proper documentation allows readers to locate and verify your sources for their own future research. It also keeps you from inadvertently plagiarizing others' words or ideas. You document sources both in the essay itself (where you identify the author and page number for quotations, paraphrases, and summaries) and in a list of sources at the end of the paper (called a Works Cited page).

In-Text Documentation

You need to document whenever you quote, paraphrase, or summarize a secondary research source in the text of the paper itself. For each source you refer to, you will write a citation. Follow these guidelines for writing citations:

- Identify the author in an introductory phrase, and give the page number in parentheses.

  As psychologist Liu Chang has noted, "Students experiencing culture shock will benefit from participating in support groups" (107).

- If you don't give the author's name in an introductory phrase, include the author's last name along with the page number in parentheses.

  It is also true that "students experiencing culture shock will benefit from participating in support groups" (Chang 107).

- If the source has two or three authors, include all of the last names in the citation.

  According to Johnson and Hall, "Culture shock is an inevitable result of traveling to a new place" (189).

  Psychologists now understand that "culture shock is an inevitable result of traveling to a new place" (Johnson and Hall 189).

- If the source has four or more authors, either give the names of all the authors, or give the name of the first author followed by *et al.*, which is an abbreviation for "and others."

  As Gibson et al. have noted, "Culture shock can ultimately become a beneficial experience" (233).

  Experts point out that "culture shock can ultimately become a beneficial experience" (Gibson, Emerson, Chang, and Zimmerman 233).

- If no author is given for a source, give the title in an introductory phrase or a shortened version of the title in parentheses.

  According to "Tips for Success for New Students," a brochure produced by the International Students Office, culture shock will not "derail students' dreams of academic success" as long as they learn about this condition (3).

  Culture shock will not "derail students' dreams of academic success" as long as they learn about this condition ("Tips for Success" 3).

- If you're using a source in which no page numbers are given, such as a Web site, you may omit the page number, but be sure to include the author's last name. If there is no author, include the title of the work.

  Professor Caroline Edmunds has indicated that "even students who move away from home to attend a university only an hour away" can still experience culture shock.

  In fact, "even students who move away from home to attend a university only an hour away" can still experience culture shock (Edmunds).

- Remember that you need to include in-text documentation for paraphrased or summarized information, in addition to quoted information.

  In fact, students can experience culture shock even if they enroll in a university that's only sixty minutes from their homes (Edmunds).

- Use transitions or keywords to connect the documented material to the point being made. Some keywords and transitions used in the previous examples are "It is also true that," "psychologists now understand," and "in fact."
- Finally, study the format of the previous examples. Notice that only the number of the page is given (don't use *page* or *p.*). Also, put the period after the parentheses.

Works Cited Page

The *Works Cited page* is a list of sources that appears at the end of your paper. Every source you mention in your essay should be included in the Works Cited list.

Different fields of study use different formats and titles for the Works Cited list. The following discussion and sample entries are based on the format established by the Modern Language Association (MLA).

■ HOW TO Use MLA Format

- Put the Works Cited list on a separate page at the end of your paper.
- Arrange the source entries alphabetically by the authors' last names or by title if the author is not named.
- Double-space the entries.
- The first line of each entry should line up with the left-hand margin. The other lines of each entry should be indented one-half inch.
- Italicize the titles of books, journals, magazines, and newspapers.
- Put the titles of magazine and newspaper articles in quotation marks.

MLA format also requires that you present the information about your sources in a specific way. Books, magazines, journals, and newspapers require different formats. Encyclopedias are different still, and there is a particular way to list an interview. Also, the form varies slightly when a source has more than one author. Here are some sample MLA-style entries.

BOOK WITH ONE AUTHOR

Cooper, Catherine R. *Bridging Multiple Worlds: Cultures, Identities, and Pathways to College*. New York: Oxford UP, 2011. Print.

BOOK WITH MORE THAN ONE AUTHOR

Kottak, Conrad Phillip, and Kathryn A. Kozaitis. *On Being Different: Diversity and Multiculturalism in the North American Mainstream*. 3rd ed. New York: McGraw, 2007. Print.

CHAPTER OR ARTICLE FROM AN EDITED BOOK

Leung, S. Alvin. "Returning Home and Issues Related to Reverse Culture Shock." *A Handbook for Counseling International Students in the United States*. Ed. Hemla D. Singaravelu and Mark Pope. Alexandria: American Counseling Association, 2007. 137–51. Print.

Magazine Article (Print Source)

> Plagens, Peter. "These Days, It's the 'Old of the Shock.' " *Newsweek* 29 Dec.
> 1997: 89. Print.

Journal Article (Print Source)

After the author and title of the article, follow with the journal title, volume and issue numbers (if given), and the date.

> Schwarz, Adam. "Culture Shock." *Far Eastern Economic Review* 34 (1997):
> 63–68. Print.

In this example, "34" refers to the volume number.

> Chih-Ning Chang, Lynn. "My Culture Shock Experience." *ETC: A Review of*
> *General Semantics* 68.4 (2011): 403–05. Print.

In this example, "68.4" refers to volume 68, issue 4.

Newspaper Article (Print Source)

> Bartlett, Tom, and Karin Fischer. "Culture Shock." *New York Times* 6 Nov. 2011:
> ED24. Print.

If the article appears on more than one page, and the pages are not consecutive, add a plus sign after the number of the first page: *C4+*.

Encyclopedia Article (Print Source)

> O'Connell, John. "Culture Shock." *The Blackwell Encyclopedia of Management*.
> Ed. Cary L. Cooper. 2nd ed. Malden: Blackwell, 2005. Print.

Personal Interview

> Wucinich, Sophia. Personal interview. 10 Jan. 2006.

Telephone Interview

> Schroeder, Niels. Telephone interview. 14 Apr. 2006.

Article from an Online Database

To cite a source you obtained from a online database, give the same information you would give if you had used a print format. Additionally, give the name of the database, italicized; the medium (*Web*); and the date of access.

> Bulik, Beth Snyder. "Culture Shock." *Advertising Age* 8 Jan. 2001: 1–11.
> *Academic Search Premier*. Web. 8 Apr. 2002.

WORK FROM A WEB SITE

If you used information from a Web site, give the author's name (if included), the title of the document, and the title of the site (italicized); follow with the name of any institution or organization sponsoring the site (use *n.p.*, if none is given), the date of publication (use *n.d.*, if no date is given), the medium (*Web*), and the date you accessed the site.

> DeBenedictis, Jon. "Diversity and Multiculturalism on College Campuses."
> *TribunaCT.com*. Tribuna Connecticut, 19 Jan. 2011. Web. 12 Apr. 2011.

For more information on how to document sources, consult the *MLA Handbook for Writers of Research Papers*, Seventh Edition (2009), or the *MLA Style Manual and Guide to Scholarly Publishing*, Third Edition (2008). Both are available in the reference section of your library. These resources also give many more examples of documentation models, showing how to document e-mails, audio or video interviews, letters, reviews, blogs, paintings, films, and much more.

For help using MLA citation format and creating a Works Cited list, go to **bedfordstmartins.com /resdoc** and click on **Humanities**.

GROUP ACTIVITY 9 Create a Works Cited Page

With several classmates, write up a Works Cited page in the MLA format for the following five sources. All necessary information is given (as well as unnecessary information you need not use).

1. *What Do International Students Think and Feel? Adapting to U.S. College Life and Culture* by Jerry G. Gebhard. Page 23. 2010. University of Michigan Press, located in Ann Arbor, Michigan.

   _____

   _____

   _____

2. Interview by telephone with Helen Mar, who is Chinese, about her experiences as an international student. Boise, Idaho. June 30, 2011.

   _____

   _____

   _____

3. "Culture Shock" by Toni Mack, p. 188. Published in *Forbes* magazine in May 1997 on pp. 188–90.

   _____

   _____

   _____

4. Janice C. Simpson's article, called "Chronicler of Culture Shock," which appeared in *Time* on May 8, 2006, on p. 156. Obtained online from the *Academic Search Premier* database on Feb. 9, 2007.

_____

_____

_____

5. "Going to Teach in Prisons: Culture Shock" by Randall Wright. Published in a journal called *Journal of Correctional Education*, volume 56, issue 1, in March 2005 on pp. 19–38. Appeared online in the database *Academic Search Premier* on December 15, 2010.

_____

_____

_____

_____

Sample Researched Essay

The following essay was written by student writer Leslie Lozano for the International Students Forum on her campus. She used the writing process—exploring choices, drafting, revising, and editing—before presenting this essay to the audience at the forum. In order to have space to annotate her essay, we have reproduced it on these pages in a narrower and longer format than you will have on a standard eight-and-a-half-by-eleven-inch sheet of paper.

½"

1"

Leslie Lozano

Professor Lee

Psychology 101

1 May 2011

Culture Shock

 People who have the opportunity to live and study in a new country are usually eager to master a new language, taste different foods, and see new sights. But after a while they might begin to feel lonely and confused. They don't understand others, and others don't understand them. Nothing tastes right. They get lost easily. They have trouble doing even simple things, such as shopping or taking a bus. They realize that the way they speak, act, and perceive things is different from other people in their new environment. They are experiencing culture shock.

 People do not have to travel to another country to experience culture shock. At one point or another, everyone becomes uncomfortable in an unfamiliar environment or in the presence of people different from themselves. However, international students, in particular, are likely to experience culture shock because their culture and the host culture can be so different. Because culture shock can affect students' academic success, it is important for them to understand the four stages of culture shock: the honeymoon stage, the crisis stage, the recovery stage, and the adjustment stage. These stages were first described by anthropologist Kalvervo Oberg in 1960 (Thomas and Althen 213).

 The honeymoon stage takes place when people first arrive in their country. They feel excited about the new and different environment. After a few weeks, though, they become more aware of how different the new country is compared to their home country. They also begin to feel homesick. This is when the crisis stage begins. During this stage, students feel confused because they are confronting new behaviors and lifestyles (Thomas and Althen 221). Sometimes students disapprove of the values and beliefs of the new country. According to psychologists Philip R.

1"

1"

Note proper heading.

Note double-spacing throughout.

The introduction tries to attract the reader's attention. It also defines *culture shock*.

Thesis is given.

This citation shows where Leslie learned this information.

Source is paraphrased and cited.

Last name of authors and page number are given in parentheses.

Quote is introduced.

Lozano 2

Quotation is used to support the concept of negative evaluations.

Page number follows quotation.

Source is paraphrased, and cited.

Note that most of the essay consists of Leslie's ideas rather than information from the research.

Source is paraphrased.

No page number is given because the article was retrieved from an electronic database.

Quote is introduced.

These ideas are Leslie's, so no citations are needed.

Harris and Robert T. Moran, "Traditions provide people with a 'mindset' and have a powerful influence on their moral system for evaluating what is right or wrong, good or bad, desirable or not" (135). Because of their negative evaluations of the new culture, students can feel alienated from their surroundings. Other symptoms of the crisis stage include depression, boredom, trouble working or studying, and irritability (Schneider).

How can students help themselves during the crisis stage? They can begin by making friends with other international students at events organized by the International Students Office. They could even create an organization for international students experiencing culture shock. This is what Aaron Bird Bear did when he organized a group of Native American students at the University of Wisconsin–Madison, inviting them to recognize their unique traits within this cultural transition while also experiencing a sense of unity and community with students who shared and understood their heritage (Rolo). Sharing feelings with others in groups such as these can reduce loneliness. Also, students can always go to the campus counseling center for one-on-one help from a counselor.

Although getting together with students who share your background or cultural heritage is helpful, it doesn't mean that the new culture should be ignored. In fact, students will get over culture shock faster if they learn as much as they can about the new culture. Christina Bernal, a Mexican student advisor from the Office of International Programs, suggests that international students "should be like a sponge and absorb as much information as possible." Students suffering from culture shock should read local newspapers, watch television, and listen to the radio to learn about customs and habits that are foreign to them. They can also take advantage of opportunities to get to know people from the new culture. For instance, Bernal's university sponsors a host family program in which international students are paired up with families who get together with them regularly. This type of program allows the international students to educate members of the new

Lozano 3

culture about where they are from, which encourages mutual understanding and tolerance.

After a month or so, international students' anxieties begin to lower and they enter the recovery stage. During this stage, they still experience the symptoms of culture shock but not as intensely. The final stage of culture shock is the adjustment stage, when students begin to relax and enjoy being in the new culture, though they can still experience confusion and worries every once in a while (Thomas and Althen 221). By the time people reach the adjustment stage, they are usually more flexible and open-minded about cultural differences than they were before entering the new culture.

This information is summarized from the article by Thomas and Althen.

Although culture shock can feel overwhelming at times, students need to remember that the stress of culture shock can eventually lessen through proper cultural orientation and further integration (O'Connell). In the long run, the benefits of living in a different culture — such as being fluent in a second language, understanding a new value system, and getting around in a totally different environment — far outweigh the hardships.

This is an important idea, so Leslie paraphrases and cites O'Connell.

½"

1"   Lozano 4

Works Cited

Source from an interview

Bernal, Christina L. Personal interview. 25 Mar. 2011.

Source from a book with two authors

Harris, Philip R., and Robert T. Moran. *Managing Cultural Differences*. 4th ed. Houston: Gulf, 1996. Print.

Encyclopedia source: no page number is needed.

O'Connell, John. "Culture Shock." *The Blackwell Encyclopedia of Management*. Ed. Cary L. Cooper. 2nd ed. Malden: Blackwell, 2005. Print.

1"   1"

Source from an article that came from a database

Rolo, Mark. "Native Identity and Community on Campus." *Diverse: Issues in Higher Education* 26.9 (2009): 26–28. *Academic Search Premier*. Web. 5 Apr. 2011.

Web site source

Schneider, Katherine. "Cultural Difference: International Students Coping with Culture Shock." *Counseling Services*. University of Wisconsin–Eau Claire, 29 June 2010. Web. 20 Apr. 2011.

Thomas, Kay, and Gary Althen. "Counseling Foreign Students." *Counseling across Cultures*. Ed. Paul B. Pedersen, Juris G. Draguns, Walter J. Lonner, and Joseph E. Trimble. 3rd ed. Honolulu: U of Hawaii P, 1989. 205–41. Print.

Source from an edited book

Note double-spacing throughout.

CHAPTER CHECKLIST

❑ Narrow your topic before beginning research.

❑ Write research questions to help keep the research process focused.

❑ Conduct primary research by observing, surveying, and interviewing.

❑ Locate sources of information in the library and on the Internet.

❑ Avoid plagiarism by documenting sources.

❑ Use note taking as an effective research tool.

❑ Use quotation marks to indicate an author's exact words.

❑ Use your own words to paraphrase an author's ideas.

❑ Summarize an author's main ideas to condense lengthy passages.

❑ Document sources properly by identifying them in the essay and listing them on a Works Cited page at the end of the essay.

❑ Include a Works Cited entry with full publication information for every source cited in your essay. Format these entries correctly.

REFLECTING ON YOUR WRITING

To help you continue to improve as a writer, answer the following questions about the writing assignment for this chapter.

1. What was the easiest part of doing research?

2. What was the hardest part of doing research?

3. Compare writing a researched essay with writing an essay that doesn't contain research.

4. What information about your topic did you learn from conducting research?

5. If you could do the research for your essay over again, what would you do differently?

Using your answers to these questions, complete a Writing Process Report for this chapter (you can download a report form at **bedfordstmartins.com /choices**). Once you complete this report, freewrite about what you learned in this chapter about conducting research and writing a researched essay and what you still hope to learn.

13

Taking Timed Writing Tests

It's getting close to midterm, and you're feeling confident about your classes. Everything seems to be going well. As you read your syllabi, though, you begin to panic because in the next week you have three tests. Two of them include essay-exam questions, and the third is an in-class timed writing assignment about a reading you haven't even seen yet. You might have the same reaction as student writer Sherman, who wrote the following in his journal:

> Three tests in a week. Help! I've done all of the work (most of the reading), but I don't write well under pressure. How will I ever survive? I'm stressed out just thinking about all of these tests.

The most common type of timed writing you will do in college is the essay exam. But you may also be asked to do an in-class timed writing about a reading or to take a multiple-choice test on sentence structure, grammar, and punctuation.

The good news is that you can use everything you have already learned about writing to help you do well on these timed writing tests. For example, you can use the process of gathering ideas, drafting, revising, and editing when answering essay-exam questions or when writing in response to a reading. And you can use everything you have learned about grammar, spelling, and punctuation to help you do well on multiple-choice writing tests. ■

> **In this chapter, you will write a brief essay in which you describe your feelings about taking exams. As you work on your essay, you will**
>
> - Learn how to prepare for and take essay exams.
> - Learn how to prepare for and take in-class timed writings about readings.
> - Learn how to prepare for and take multiple-choice writing tests.

> ## Writing Assignment
>
> For this assignment, write an essay for your instructor and classmates in which you describe how you feel about taking exams. How do you reduce test anxiety, and what do you do during the test to ensure that you do your best? Share your responses with your classmates as a way to begin a discussion about how best to prepare for and take timed writing tests.

To review the writing process, see Chapter 1.

The Essay Exam

An essay exam includes questions to which you must respond in writing. Your responses must be written in sentences and paragraphs and should reflect your thoughts in an organized, clear way. The main difference between writing an essay outside of class and taking an in-class essay exam is that you must work through the first four stages of the writing process (gathering ideas, drafting, revising, and editing) in the time allowed for the exam.

Preparing for an Essay Exam

Learn about the Test

You will do your best on an essay exam if you know what to expect when you walk into class on exam day. If possible, find out what type of essay questions will be on the test, how long you will have to complete the test, and how it will be graded. You can find out about the test by reading your syllabus, asking your instructor, and talking with former students. If your instructor permits, obtain copies of old essay-test questions, or ask your instructor to provide sample test items.

> ### Look at exam questions online
>
> Ask your instructor if there is a class Web site or other online source of sample essay-test questions and student responses. If yes, access this source to learn as much as you can about the instructor's essay exams.

Anticipate the Questions

Whether or not you can look over copies of old essay-test questions, anticipate the questions for your upcoming exam. Remember, your instructor will probably ask only a few essay questions, so they will most likely be on the most important topics in the course. If your instructor provides a review session or gives you a study guide, either in print or on the course Web site, check these for possible essay questions. Most instructors take test items directly from these reviews or study guides. Reread your class notes, and mark the topics that your instructor spent the most time on in class. For example, if your history instructor discussed the Bill of Rights for an entire week, you could anticipate an essay question on this topic. If this same instructor defined the First Amendment to the Constitution and then gave you a list of First Amendment rights, you could expect an essay question on this topic.

Sherman, the student who wrote the journal entry on page 367, knew that one of his upcoming exams was in psychology. His instructor had spent a week lecturing on Abraham Maslow's hierarchy of needs. The textbook assignment also contained several pages on this topic. Because of the amount of class time devoted to this topic, Sherman predicted there would be an essay question on it. He was right. The instructor included this essay question on the test:

> Define Maslow's hierarchy of needs, classify these needs, and briefly describe each.

Develop a Study Routine

If you manage your study time wisely, you should have no difficulty studying for essay exams. You can manage your time wisely by setting aside two to three hours of study time a week for each hour that you are in class. During this time, review your lecture notes, read your textbooks, and complete any other assignments.

You might also consider forming a study group. Research suggests that studying in groups can increase your knowledge of course material because you and your classmates share the information you have learned. To form a study group, ask a few of your classmates to meet with you a week or two before a major exam. Share your class notes, and discuss the textbook readings.

As a group, discuss and write down what you expect the essay-exam questions to be. Then write your individual responses to these possible essay questions. Discuss the strengths and weaknesses of each response so that each group member leaves the study session with a better idea of how to respond to possible essay questions.

GROUP ACTIVITY 1 Prepare for an Essay Exam

With several classmates, take a moment to reflect and freewrite on how you have prepared for an essay exam in the past. As a group, discuss each member's study strengths and weaknesses. How could you improve? If you were to form a study group, how could you best help others? How could they best help you?

Taking the Essay Exam

Analyze the Questions

Most students have had the experience of writing an excellent answer that received no credit because it didn't answer the question asked. To prevent this from happening to you, use the following strategies to help you analyze the questions.

Quickly read over the exam. Notice the kinds of questions asked and the point value of each, and estimate the amount of time you will need to complete each response. With this information in mind, plan your answers, allowing the most time for questions with the most points.

As you read each essay question, be sure you understand what is expected of you. One way to be sure you understand the question is to mark it. Marking the question forces you to concentrate on what you need to do, reducing the chances that you will forget to answer part of the question or, even worse, write a response that doesn't answer the question at all. To mark the question, underline the keywords that indicate what the essay should be about, and then circle the words that explain how you should organize and develop your response. Here is how Sherman marked the psychology question on Maslow's hierarchy of needs:

(Define) Maslow's hierarchy of needs, (classify) these needs, and briefly

(describe) each.

You probably noticed that the words *define, classify*, and *describe* used in this essay question are all words you recognize as patterns of development. Just as you develop and organize essays using description, narration, examples, process explanation, classification, definition, comparison and contrast, cause and effect, and argument, you can develop and organize your essay-exam responses using these same patterns.

Following are some words you might see in essay-exam questions. Notice how each points to which pattern of development to use.

See Chapter 3 for additional information on the patterns of development.

Description	Describe the following . . .
	Explain . . .
	Illustrate . . .
	Give details of . . .
	Discuss . . .
Narration	Relate the events . . .
	Tell what happened . . .
	Tell what a character said . . .
	Describe the conversation between . . . .

Examples	Give examples of . . . Support with evidence of . . . Provide support for . . . Explain . . . Describe what the author says . . .
Process explanation	Provide the steps for . . . Outline the sequence of events in . . . Give the procedure . . . Analyze the following stages in . . .
Classification	List the types of . . . Analyze the parts of . . . List the kinds of . . .
Definition	Define . . . Give the meaning of . . . Identify . . .
Comparison and contrast	Compare and contrast . . . Discuss the similarities . . . Discuss the differences . . .
Cause and effect	Give the reasons for . . . Discuss the causes of . . . Describe the consequences of . . . Discuss the effects of . . . Explain why . . .
Argument	Argue for . . . Justify your opinion . . . Take a position . . .

Gather Ideas

Once you have analyzed the essay question, you might be tempted to begin writing your response right away. If you look at students around you, some of them may have already started writing. Resist the urge to begin writing before you gather ideas. Taking the time to gather ideas first will help you write an organized essay. Set aside five minutes to brainstorm a list of the points you want to make or to create a cluster of your main ideas and supporting details. Once you have a list or cluster, number the key points in the order you would like to write about them.

To review how to brainstorm and cluster, see pp. 12–14.

Here is an example of the list that Sherman brainstormed as he prepared to respond to the psychology question:

I <u>need</u> to do well on this test!

Abraham Maslow — 1970 I think

Described needs as part of a hierarchy

A hierarchy is something arranged in ranks or stages

Maslow's hierarchy

>> Hunger, thirst

>> Need to feel safe and secure

>> Need to feel loved

>> Need for recognition

>> Need to be all you can be!

But what are the stages? Help!

>> Physiological (sp?)

>> Safety

>> Belongingness

>> Esteem

>> Self-actualization

How would I define these needs?

Priorities to be met.

Write Your Response

Now that you have taken five minutes to brainstorm or cluster your ideas, you'll want to draft quickly but carefully. Organize your essay response just as you would an essay that you write outside of class. Begin with a brief introduction that includes a thesis statement that directly answers the exam question. Write your essay using complete sentences and paragraphs. Each paragraph should include a topic sentence or main idea, and each paragraph should include at least one or two specific details to support the topic sentence. Write a brief conclusion or concluding statement to sum up your essay.

More information on organizing an essay can be found on pp. 20–21.

Revise and Edit Your Response

When you have completed your essay exam, you may want to turn it in right away. However, you should allow five to ten minutes to reread the questions and your responses to be sure you have answered the questions completely. If you wish to add content, write it neatly in the margin or at the bottom of the page, and draw an arrow to the place where it belongs. For deletions or corrections, draw a line through the material to be deleted or corrected, and write the correction above the text. Where appropriate, you may wish to add transitions—such as *then, however, moreover,* or *in conclusion*—to help your instructor follow your train of thought.

As you reread your response, also proofread for errors in grammar, spelling, and punctuation. Remember, your responses are judged not only for content but also for how clearly they are written. Too many errors may make it difficult for your instructor to understand what you have written, resulting in a lower test grade. One more thing: be sure your name is on your exam before you turn it in.

Use word-processing tools

If you're writing an essay exam on a computer, make use of tools on your word-processing program, such as the spelling and grammar check and the thesaurus.

■ HOW TO Write an Essay Exam

- Read the exam. Divide your time according to the point value of each question.
- Mark up each question. Underline keywords that tell you what your essay should be about. Circle words (such as *classify*) that indicate how your essay should be developed.
- Take a few minutes to gather and organize ideas in a rough outline form.
- Write each essay. Include a brief introduction with a thesis statement that directly answers the exam question, body paragraphs with topic sentences and supporting details, and a short conclusion.
- After you finish writing, take a few minutes to read over the exam and make quick corrections.
- Keep track of the time.

Sample Essay Question and Student Response

Here's how Sherman responded to the psychology essay-exam question: "Define Maslow's hierarchy of needs, classify these needs, and briefly describe each." Notice that he made additions, deletions, and corrections neatly.

Abraham Maslow described five needs that each person has and ranked them in order of importance. This order is a hierarchy because a person must fulfill each need in order beginning with the most basic one. These needs are hunger and thirst, ~~love, safety,~~ safety, love, self-esteem, and the need to reach full potential.

The most basic need is hunger and thirst. What this means is that a person who is hungry or thirsty can't think of anything else. This was demonstrated during World War II when a researcher, Keys, fed 36 volunteers just enough food to maintain their weight and then cut their food in half. The effects showed that Maslow was correct. The men became obsessed with food and lost all interest in social activities.

The second need is for safety. A person who doesn't feel safe can't worry about the higher needs of love, ~~love,~~ self-esteem, and reaching full potential.

People must feel they can predict what will happen and that they have some control over it.

The third need is love. Humans form relationships with other people and like to hang on to those relationships. That is why when we meet people *at school or on vacation* we always promise to keep in touch. Most people like to be with other people. If they are deprived of this need, they often become depressed.

The ~~next~~ *fourth* need is self-esteem. A person needs to feel capable of achieving something in life and needs the respect of other people. Motivation is what causes a person to ~~fear~~ *work to earn* other people's respect. Intrinsic motivation is when a person does something just for the challenge of it. Extrinsic *motivation* is when a person does something to be rewarded or out of fear of punishment.

Maslow called the fifth need self-ac*u*talization. When Maslow studied people who had very successful lives, he discovered that they were open and loving and didn't worry about what other people think. They usually had a mission in life and had a few very good relationships instead of a lot of not-so-meaningful ones.

Maslow's hope was that developing this ~~heirarchy~~ *hierarchy* would help others think about how to motivate people to do their best.

GROUP ACTIVITY 2 Take an Essay Exam

Read and mark the following essay-exam questions. With several classmates, select one, and brainstorm or cluster to gather ideas for a response. Then draft, revise, and edit your response. Share your response with the other groups in your class. What suggestions do they have for improving your response?

1. Explain the stages of the writing process as described in *Choices: A Writing Guide with Readings*. Describe how you have used this process to improve your writing.

2. Compare and contrast an informative essay and a persuasive essay.

3. List the three types of journals. Give the advantages and disadvantages of each type.

4. Describe the process of preparing for and taking an essay exam.

In-Class Timed Writing about a Reading

Instructors occasionally ask students to read a short article or essay just before or during class and to respond to a question or questions about this reading during class. This type of timed writing assignment requires that you read and write well under pressure.

Preparing for In-Class Timed Writing about a Reading

Develop a Reading Routine

You will be most successful writing about a reading if you are already an active reader. Active readers think as they read. They ask questions, challenge the author, and look for the author's next point. They also know why they're reading (either for entertainment or for information) and stay focused on that purpose. Often, active readers write notes in the margins summarizing or commenting on what they have read.

Working with a study group can also help you become a more active reader. Ask study-group members to help you summarize readings, discuss difficult passages, and define unknown vocabulary words. Reviewing your reading assignments as a group will help each of you better understand the content.

Keep a Reading Journal

Keeping a reading journal is yet another way to become an active reader. Writing in a journal helps you explore your ideas more extensively than if you just think or talk about a text. By writing down your ideas, you can understand the reading more thoroughly. Reading journals also provide a place to reflect on what you have read. Writing in a reading journal helps you formulate questions and clarify ideas. Your journal is a place to collect and arrange your thoughts, draw conclusions, and evaluate what you have learned.

To begin keeping a reading journal, find a notebook that is comfortable to write in. One of the most effective types of reading journals is the two-column learning log. You write down the main points of the reading selection in one column and your thoughts about it in the other column. The advantage of the two-column learning log is that the two columns make it easier both to summarize and to think about the reading. If you decide to keep your reading journal on your computer, just use the word-processing feature that sets up columns.

For more information on learning logs, see pp. 321–23.

Keep a Vocabulary List

The larger your vocabulary, the greater your chances of understanding even the most difficult reading. As you read a text, circle unfamiliar words. Then look them up in a dictionary, or ask someone in your study group to tell you the meaning. Keep a list of these words, and review the list once a week. In addition to writing the definition of the word, use the word in a phrase or a sentence to help you remember it.

 Use an online dictionary

Make use of online dictionaries such as dictionary.com, which compiles information about a word from several dictionaries. You can also find the definition of a word by doing a search in your Web browser.

> **◀ GROUP ACTIVITY 3** Prepare for In-Class Writing ▶
>
> With several classmates, take a moment to reflect and freewrite on how you have read in the past. What are your strengths as a reader? What are your weaknesses? How could you improve your reading to ensure that you would do your best on an in-class timed writing in response to a reading?

Taking an In-Class Timed Writing Test about a Reading

Although active readers already have an advantage when assigned to write in class, all students can benefit from following these steps.

Read Carefully

Not all good readers read faster than others or fully understand what they read the first time through, but they have ways to improve their understanding. Important reading strategies include previewing, distinguishing between main and supporting ideas, annotating the text, and learning how to read confusing passages.

To fully understand a piece, you should preview it first. Quickly scan the entire article or essay for clues about the author's main ideas. Previewing helps you begin to think about the most important ideas even before you begin to read carefully. To preview,

1. Examine the title to determine what it suggests about the topic.
2. Look at the author's name. Do you know anything about this author?
3. If there's a headnote at the beginning of the reading, read it. What does it suggest about the topic?
4. Examine the headings and any illustrations. These are clues to what the author considers important.
5. Read the first paragraph.
6. Look at the first sentence of each remaining paragraph. This is where the author most often puts the topic sentence (the main point of the paragraph).
7. Read the conclusion. Authors often restate their main points in their conclusions.

Once you have previewed the reading selection, read it carefully to distinguish main ideas from supporting details. The main ideas are the writer's general points, and the supporting details are the specific points that explain or justify the main ideas. For example, one of the main ideas of this section is that you can use specific strategies to improve your under-

To review main ideas and supporting details, see Chapter 2.

standing of a reading; a supporting detail is that previewing is one of these strategies. Once you can distinguish between main ideas and supporting details, you can respond more effectively to a reading selection.

Another strategy is to annotate the text. Just as you read and mark essay-exam questions, you can read and mark the article or essay you are reading for a timed in-class writing. As you read, underline the main ideas. Once you have read the article or essay, look back at what you have underlined. Which is the author's thesis statement? Which are the main ideas and supporting details that help explain or justify the thesis statement? In the margin, you may also wish to write brief phrases that restate key ideas, note unfamiliar words to look up in the dictionary, and express your own thoughts about the reading.

One of the most difficult things to learn is how to read a confusing passage. You might be tempted to skip over it, or you might panic and stop reading altogether. Instead, use the following strategies to help you.

- Reread the confusing section again, sentence by sentence. Also, reread the paragraph just before and the one just after to provide you with a context.
- Underline words and phrases that seem significant.
- If permitted, use a dictionary to look up words that you don't know.
- If possible, ask your instructor for clarification of the confusing passage.

Write Your Response

Now that you have actively read the article or essay your instructor has assigned, you are ready to write a response to the question or questions that accompany the reading. Follow the same steps you use when answering essay-exam questions.

1. Analyze the question by marking it.
2. Gather ideas by brainstorming or clustering.
3. Write your response in an essay format.
4. Revise and edit it by making additions and deletions neatly.

Sample In-Class Writing Question and Student Response

Ofelia read the following essay titled "Beauty Is More Than Skin Deep: The Different Types of Attractiveness" as part of an in-class writing assignment.

RONALD E. RIGGIO

Beauty Is More Than Skin Deep: The Different Types of Attractiveness

Ronald E. Riggio, PhD, is a professor at Claremont McKenna College in Claremont, California. He has written many books and articles on the topic of leadership and social psychology, and he founded a column in the *Los Angeles Times* that deals with workplace problems and issues. Riggio is a regular blogger for the magazine *Psychology Today,* where this article first appeared in 2011.

There is more to being physically attractive than just good looks. Many believe   1
that people are born beautiful or handsome — that static qualities, such as a pretty face, nice hair, or a shapely body, are inherited. You either have it or you don't. Our research, however, suggests there is another type of attractiveness: what we call dynamic physical attractiveness.

What is dynamic attractiveness? Perhaps the Beatles song says it best . . .   2
"Something in the way she [or he] moves attracts me like no other lover . . ." In this research we focused on how the expression of a person's personality, physical grace, and body language impacted perceptions of who was attractive and who was not.

The idea that people have an expressive style goes back to the 1930s when early   3
social/personality psychologist, Gordon Allport, claimed that people have a consistency in how they express elements of themselves in how they walk, talk, and even in their handwriting. We also knew from our research, that people who were emotionally expressive — people who spontaneously express emotions (particularly positive emotions) were more attractive to others. So, we set out to examine how expressive style contributed to impressions that someone is physically attractive.

In order to look at different types of attractiveness we brought college students   4
into a lab where they were photographed and videotaped while meeting people or while giving a short speech. We then took the photos and videos, and by masking them, we showed only the faces, or only the bodies, and had different groups of judges rate attractiveness from only still photos of faces, bodies, and another group focused only on the attractiveness of how they were dressed. Other groups of judges rated different degrees of attractiveness, including how much they liked each individual, would want to be friends with them, and how attractive they were as a dating partner.

We were then able to statistically control for the different types of attractive-   5
ness. What we found was that in the videotaped interactions, dynamic expressive style (measured by the person's emotional expressiveness and social skills) predicted who was rated as physically attractive over and beyond the effects of static qualities of beauty (face, body, and dress attractiveness). We have found that dynamic expressive style is a major component of what makes a person charismatic.

So, what are the implications of this research?   6

First, personality, and the expression of personality, matters. As we all know, a   7
person can be beautiful on the outside, but not so nice on the inside, and vice versa. Moreover, our research suggests that dynamic expressive style might compensate

for lack of static physical attractiveness. In other words, there are plenty of people who are not classically beautiful or handsome, but are still very attractive to others.

Second, attractiveness can be "manipulated" to some extent. Dress, use of makeup, and keeping physically fit can affect perceptions of attractiveness. In one of our "charisma training" studies, we found that women who were trained to be better at expressing emotions and positive affect started to give greater concern to how they dressed and when they wore makeup, even though our training had not focused on that.   8

As they say, beauty is in the eye of the beholder, but attractiveness is complex, made up of both static and dynamic qualities, and both affect perceptions of attractiveness.   9

References

Allport, G.W. & Vernon, P.E. (1933). *Studies in expressive movement.* New York: Macmillan.

Riggio, R.E., Widaman, K.F., Tucker, J.S., & Salinas, C. (1991). Beauty is more than skin deep: Components of attractiveness. *Basic and Applied Social Psychology*, 12(4), 423–439.

Ofelia then responded to the following essay question: "What is the main point of Ronald Riggio's essay? Provide examples of the evidence the author uses to support his main point. What does this essay reveal about the way people decide who is beautiful?" Here is Ofelia's response:

> Ronald Riggio's main point is that beauty is more than just a person's face or body. Instead, beauty is more about people's personalities, physical movements, and body language. As a result, people can make themselves more attractive even if they can't change their face or their bodies.
>
> The main evidence for this point comes from a study that the author and his colleagues conducted in which they photographed and videotaped college students as they gave a short speech or met people. They then asked other people to rate the attractiveness of the college students, sometimes by just focusing on faces or bodies, and sometimes by looking at how they were dressed. Other people were asked to decide if they liked the college students or wanted to be friends with them or even date them. The results of the study showed that the people's social skills and the way they expressed themselves determined who was judged as physically attractive — more than the appearance of a person's face, body, or clothing.
>
> This study shows that beauty is based more on personality and personal style than on physical characteristics. It also shows that people can make themselves more attractive, even if they can't change their physical looks, by focusing on how they express themselves. This is an important point because our society is so obsessed with appearances.

■ HOW TO Take a Writing Test about a Reading

- Preview the reading for clues about the main ideas. Examine the title, headings, first paragraph, topic sentences, and conclusions.
- Read the text, distinguishing between main and supporting ideas.
- Annotate the text by taking notes in the margins about the main ideas. Look up unfamiliar words, and reread confusing passages.
- Before writing your response, analyze the question, gather ideas, and outline your answer.
- Use an essay format.
- After you write, take a few minutes to make corrections.
- Keep track of the time.

GROUP ACTIVITY 4 Respond to a Reading

Actively reread the essay "Beauty Is More Than Skin Deep: The Different Types of Attractiveness." Respond in writing to the following questions: To what extent do you agree with the results of the study that the author conducted? What, to you, are the different types of attractiveness? Share your response with members of your peer response or study group. What suggestions do they have for improving your response?

◖ Multiple-Choice Writing Tests

Some colleges require that students take multiple-choice writing tests to be placed in suitable classes or to advance to higher-level courses. Some writing instructors also administer multiple-choice writing tests as a way to determine each student's need for additional help with writing skills. For such tests, you may be asked to read a short passage and then determine the author's purpose and audience, to recognize main ideas and supporting details, and to recognize effective organization. A test on sentence structure may require that you identify sentence fragments, run-on sentences, incorrect subject-verb agreement, and incorrect word choice. You may also have to identify sentences that are poorly constructed because of too many words, misplaced words, or too few words. A test of grammar and punctuation skills requires that you identify standard sentence structure and standard punctuation.

Just as there are strategies for taking an essay exam and a timed in-class writing in response to a reading, there are strategies for doing your best on multiple-choice writing tests.

Preparing for a Multiple-Choice Writing Test

Learn about the Test

Review the skills that will be tested. For example, if you are not sure what the parts of speech are or what the phrases *standard sentence* and *standard punctuation* mean, you should review these. One way to review is to find out if there is a study guide for the test. Check with your college bookstore, tutoring center, or instructor. If a guide is available, review it before taking the test. Identify other resources, such as textbooks (including the Handbook in this book), workbooks, and worksheets that may be available to help you practice. Find out if you will be able to use any aids, such as a dictionary or thesaurus, during the test.

 Use an online study guide

If the test is standardized, there may be a computerized study guide available that tests and scores your present skills and tutors you on the skills you need to practice. Check online for the study guide you need.

Anticipate the Questions

Answer any sample test questions provided in study guides or provided by your instructor. Then score yourself on these sample questions. If you answer a question incorrectly, review the study materials to determine how you should have answered it. Using your overall score as a guide, assess your strengths and weaknesses, and plan a strategy for overcoming your weaknesses.

Develop a Study Routine

Consider the amount of time you have before the exam, the resources you have on hand, and the availability of instructors and tutors to help you. Then develop a study plan. To prepare for an essay exam, you focus on a few general topics, but to prepare for a multiple-choice writing exam, you must review everything that will be on the exam. Consequently, you may need to schedule several review sessions.

 GROUP ACTIVITY 5 Prepare for a Multiple-Choice Writing Test

With several classmates, take a moment to reflect on and freewrite about how you have prepared for multiple-choice writing tests in the past. What were your study strengths? What were your weaknesses? How could you improve?

Taking a Multiple-Choice Writing Test

Analyze the Questions

When taking a multiple-choice writing test, read the instructions carefully. Often there are both general instructions for taking the test and specific instructions for completing each part. Read each set carefully. If you don't understand any of these instructions, ask for clarification.

Read over the test items. Notice the kinds of questions asked and the point value of each. Estimate the amount of time you will need to complete each part of the test. With this in mind, plan your strategy, allowing the most time for the questions with the greatest point value.

Choose Your Responses

Once you begin the test, glance at your watch occasionally to ensure that you are working at a steady pace. Read each question carefully, and select the best answer to the question. To best manage your time, skip questions you can't answer right away. If there is a separate answer sheet, be sure that the number of the question on the test and the number on the answer sheet match.

When you have answered all the questions you know, return to the questions you skipped. If you are not penalized for guessing, choose the one that seems most reasonable. Reading and answering the other questions may have provided clues to the answers to the questions you skipped. If time still remains, double-check all your answers.

▪HOW TO Take a Multiple-Choice Writing Test

- Use study guides to learn about the types of questions that will be asked.
- Study for the test by reviewing what will be on it.
- When taking the test, read and follow the directions carefully.
- Save the most time for the questions with the highest point value.
- Skip questions you don't know, and return to them later.
- Keep track of the time.

GROUP ACTIVITY 6 Take a Multiple-Choice Writing Test

With several classmates, read the following three passages. Then read the questions that follow each passage, and as a group, choose the one best answer. (Note that the questions refer to the numbered sentences or word groups in the passages.)

[1]Archeologists are probably best known for discovering buried relics and ruins of ancient civilizations in faraway lands. [2]Many archeologists work right here in

the United States, however. [3]Scholars have learned much about human history from studying the remains of past societies, not only the origins of modern humans but also the origins of our own country. [4]Even though the original colonies and settlements that became the United States are young when compared to the centuries-old Mayan and Egyptian civilizations, there are still many questions left to be answered about what life in colonial America was like. [5]By investigating questions and researching evidence found at the sites of old European settlements, archeologists and historians alike hope to find enough evidence to answer their many questions.

[6]Among the questions to be answered is the nature of the relationship between the European settlers and the Native Americans. [7]Some people believe that the relationship between these two groups was usually hostile, while others believe it was often peaceful. [8]Building foundations, fragments of pottery, and bits of trash is the pieces of evidence archeologists are using to help learn more about how colonists and Native Americans got along. [9]Evidence discovered at the site of Jamestown Colony in Virginia suggests that the relations between the settlers and Native Americans were at times peaceful and at other times hostile.

[10]Although written records from colonial settlements have survived, these documents alone cannot tell the entire story.

1. Which of the following versions of sentence 5 eliminates the unnecessary repetition in the original?

   A. By investigating questions and researching evidence found at the sites of old European settlements, archeologists hope to find evidence to answer their many questions.

   B. Archeologists and historians, by investigating and researching evidence found at the sites of old European settlements, hope to find enough evidence to answer their many questions.

   C. By investigating and researching artifacts found at the sites of old European settlements, archeologists and historians alike hope to answer many questions about the settlements.

   D. Archeologists and historians alike hope to find evidence at the sites of old European settlements to answer their many questions.

2. Which of the following corrections should be made in the second paragraph?

   A. Sentence 6: Change "European" to "european."

   B. Sentence 7: Change "usually" to "usual."

   C. Sentence 8: Change "is" to "are."

   D. Sentence 9: Change "discovered" to "discovering."

3. Which of the following sentences is the best choice to use as a conclusion for the third paragraph?

   A. To find evidence, historians must always dig things up.

   B. Sometimes three-hundred-year-old garbage can be just as instructive as what has been written down.

    C. Nobody can trust the written word at all because the person writing it is always biased.

    D. Archeologists have a difficult and valuable job to perform.

Read the passage below, which has been taken from a student's essay, and answer the questions that follow.

[1]Aldo Leopold (1887–1948) was a well-known ecologist who believed that all life benefits when humans live in balance with nature and respect the environment. [2]His *Sand County Almanac*, a book of essays, is one of the most important books on ecology and conservation. [3]Observing the environment, the interconnected relationships among the animals, and the disruptions to the web of life caused by humans. [4]Leopold reached a number of important conclusions.

[5]After receiving a master's degree in forestry from Yale University, Leopold began his career by working for the Forest Service in the Southwest. [6]While there, he helped to establish the first protected wilderness area, the Gila National Forest in New Mexico. [7]He was also interested in landscape processes, such as fire and erosion, and the role of predators such as wolves in the wild. [8]Both interests helped shape his view of the natural world as an interconnected system, "a foundation of energy flowing through a circuit of soils, plants, and animals."

[9]<u>Several years later</u>, he bought and restored <u>an abandoned farm</u> where he worked on the land and studied nature. [10]He also <u>pioneered an effort</u> to re-create Wisconsin's <u>prairie-savanna ecosystem</u>.

[11]In 1948, as Leopold set out from his farm to help a neighbor put out a fire, he suffered a heart attack and died at sixty-one.

4. Which of the word groups from the first paragraph is not a complete sentence?

    A. Word group 1

    B. Word group 2

    C. Word group 3

    D. Word group 4

5. Which of the underlined words in the third paragraph should be replaced by more precise or appropriate words?

    A. "Several years later"

    B. "an abandoned farm"

    C. "pioneered an effort"

    D. "prairie-savanna ecosystem"

6. Which of the following sentences would best fit after sentence 11, as a conclusion for this passage?

    A. He had a wife and five children.

    B. Today his influence is greater than ever, though, and his book has sold over 1.5 million copies since its publication in 1949.

   C. The chicken coop on Leopold's farm, where he lived and worked, still exists.

   D. Leopold was born in Iowa in 1887.

Read the following passage, which is written in the style of a science textbook. Then answer the questions that follow.

[1]Alzheimer's disease, an illness that slowly deprives people of their memory, reasoning, judgment, and language skills, causes the gradual destruction of a person's brain cells. [2]For over ten years, scientists have known that this disease starts with the action of an enzyme. [3]This enzyme, beta-secretase, divides a protein that sticks out from brain cells in two. [4]Then gamma-secretase, another enzyme, further divides the resulting protein fragments. [5]This action creates the toxic A beta protein. [6]Theoretically, scientists could stop the production of A beta by blocking either enzyme, both enzymes have been difficult to block. [7]Recently, however, researchers have found the gene that causes cells to make beta-secretase. [8]Using a process of elimination, they started with a pool of one hundred genes and narrowed it down to one. [9]Having found this, scientists hope to be able to prevent Alzheimer's or slow its progress with medicine that can block beta-secretase. [10]Unfortunately, this next step may still be years away.

7. Which sentence is a comma splice?

   A. sentence 2

   B. sentence 4

   C. sentence 5

   D. sentence 6

8. Which of the following changes is needed in this paragraph?

   A. Change "causes" to "caused" in sentence 1.

   B. Change "then" to "also" in sentence 4.

   C. Change "Having found this" to "With this finding" in sentence 9.

   D. Change "slow" to "slowing" in sentence 9.

CHAPTER CHECKLIST

❑ Prepare for an essay exam by learning about the test, anticipating the questions, and developing a study routine.

❑ When taking an essay exam, analyze the questions, gather and outline ideas, use an essay format, and make corrections.

❑ Prepare for an in-class timed writing in response to a reading by developing a reading routine, keeping a reading journal, and keeping a vocabulary list.

❑ Write an in-class timed response to a reading by previewing the essay, identifying and taking notes on the main ideas, figuring out confusing passages, and using the writing process.

❑ Prepare for a multiple-choice writing test by learning about the test, anticipating the questions, and developing a study routine.

❑ Take a multiple-choice writing test by following the directions, reading the questions carefully, and selecting the best responses.

❑ For all tests, spend the most amount of time on items with the highest point value, and always keep track of the time.

REFLECTING ON YOUR WRITING

To help you reflect on your test-taking skills, answer the following questions.

1. Which type of timed writing test do you prefer to take? Why?

2. Does your college require such a test for placement?

3. Do any of your instructors give timed writing tests? If so, what do you know about the tests?

4. How will you study for each of these tests?

5. What strategies will you use during these tests?

Using your answers to these questions, complete a Writing Process Report for this chapter (you can download a report form at **bedfordstmartins.com /choices**). Once you complete this report, freewrite about what you learned in this chapter about taking timed writing tests and what you still hope to learn.

Writing Résumés and Cover Letters

What was your first job? You probably were hired because someone knew you personally — a neighbor who asked you to babysit, for instance. To get other types of jobs — such as delivering pizzas, waiting tables, or packing groceries — you might have filled out an application and had a brief interview. More professional jobs, however, require that you submit a résumé and cover letter. The word *résumé* derives from the Old French word for "to summarize." A *résumé* is a short account of your qualifications for a particular job. When you submit a résumé, you often include a cover letter that explains why you are the best person for the job. Typically, employers read submitted résumés and cover letters to select a few people to interview. Based on these interviews, they will select the best applicant for the job. ■

In this chapter, you will write a résumé and a cover letter. As you work on your résumé and cover letter, you will

- Learn about the sections of a résumé.
- Learn how to write a cover letter.
- Read a student's résumé and cover letter.

Writing Assignment

Write a résumé and cover letter for a job you have the skills for or are qualified to do. To find job listings, go to Web sites such as **monster .com**, or **careerbuilder.com**, look through classified ads in newspapers, or consult professional and trade publications. When you locate a job that interests you, learn more about the company or organization by going to its Web site. The more informed you are about a company, the more likely you are to get the job.

☾The Résumé

A résumé consists of several different sections intended to showcase your achievements. The most common type of résumé is called *chronological* because information is presented in time order, from most recent to least recent jobs and educational achievements. The required sections of a chronological résumé include your contact information, education, and work experience. Optional sections include objective, skills, honors and awards, and references. Keep in mind that a résumé is a persuasive document because you are trying to persuade your reader to grant you an interview. Unless you have significant work experience, it is best to keep your résumé to one page.

Required Information

You should include your contact information, education, and work experience in the résumé. The contact information should appear at the top of the page. The next section can be education or work experience, whichever one you feel will impress your reader the most.

Contact Information   Your contact information allows a potential employer to reach you.

- Give your name, address, phone number, and e-mail address.
- If you list more than one phone number, indicate whether it's a home, work, or cell number, and always include the area code: for example, (555) 123-4567 (cell).
- Be sure that your e-mail address sends a professional message. It should consist of some form of your name rather than a nickname. For example, it is more professional to list an e-mail address such as **j.rodriguez@gmail.com** than **hollyweirdo@gmail.com**.

⏻ **Create separate e-mail accounts**

You can create a free e-mail account through Google (**gmail.com**), Yahoo! (**mail .yahoo.com**), or Windows Live Hotmail (**hotmail.com**) and can access these accounts from any Internet-connected computer. Consider designating an e-mail address for professional correspondence to keep your personal and business messages separate.

Education   Include your college studies in this section. If you have just started college, you can also include your high school, especially if you had a good grade point average.

- Begin the list with the most recent achievement.
- List your college or university, your degree and major, and your expected graduation date.
- Indicate if you are on the dean's list or belong to an honor society.
- List particular courses you've taken that relate to the job you are applying for.
- Include any certificates or special training credentials you have earned.

Work Experience   Even if your work experience doesn't directly relate to the job you're applying for, your skills from one job can transfer to another job.

- List your most recent job first.
- List your job title, the company, the location, and the date for each of the jobs you've held.
- Following each job listing, briefly describe your responsibilities. Give facts, such as the number of employees you supervised, the amount of money you dealt with, the number of customers you served, and so on. Use sentence fragments that begin with action verbs: for example, "worked with technicians to fix breakdowns" or "designed Web pages."
- Include volunteer jobs if they consisted of a significant number of hours.

Optional Sections

Include the following sections in your résumé if you think they will help you get the job.

Objective   This section shows a potential employer what you can achieve in the job.

- "To create memorable advertisements that will sell Carsten cars"
- "To become a dynamic, highly rated DJ at KACL radio"
- "To break all sales records at Gale's Outdoor Wear"

■ HOW TO Write a Good Objective

- Begin with an infinitive form of a verb (*to sell, to make, to win*).
- Use strong verbs.
- Mention the name of the company or organization.
- Be concise.

Skills   This section highlights your special expertise.

- List computer skills ("Proficient with Word, Excel, and PowerPoint").
- Give languages you speak ("Fluent in spoken and written Spanish").
- Indicate other skills that relate to the job, such as typing speed, ability to lift heavy objects, or graphic design skills.

Honors and Awards   If you have won any academic awards, been voted employee of the month, or received other accolades, list them here.

References   Your references should be people such as supervisors and professors who can attest to your qualifications. Because they are biased, friends and family members are not considered good references. Due to space concerns, you may simply say "Available upon request" or omit this section altogether (the employer will contact you for a list of references). If you do list your references, give their names, titles, and contact information.

Format and Grammar

Your résumé represents you. Remember that any errors or sloppiness will send the message to the employer that you are careless and disorganized. Therefore, your résumé should be tidy, easy to read, and grammatically correct.

- Fill up the page.
- Use white space to make your résumé easy to read (but not so much white space that the résumé appears skimpy).
- Center your name in at least 14-point type. Use 12-point type for headings and 11-point type for the text.
- Edit carefully. Some employers will discard a résumé if it contains even one error.

 Use basic fonts for résumés

After your name, use no more than two font types or sizes, one for headings and one for the body. If you plan to print your résumé, use basic serif fonts such as Times New Roman. If you plan to submit your résumé online, use sans serif fonts such as Calibri. Don't use italics or fancy fonts such as **Comic Sans**, since these can be difficult to read.

Sample Résumé

One student, Rachel Serrano, applied for a job as a sales representative at a marketing company that sells restaurant supplies. As her résumé shows, she is a college student who is working her way through school.

Rachel Serrano

4115 Oakdale Avenue

El Paso, TX 79909

(555) 915-1544

rserrano@gmail.com

OBJECTIVE

To become an outstanding sales representative for Restaurant Marketing

EDUCATION

9/09–present   University of Texas at El Paso
- BA expected in May 2011
- Major: Business Marketing
- GPA: 3.0 (on a 4-point scale)

9/07–5/09   El Paso Community College
- AA, Business Administration, May 2009
- GPA: 3.1 (on a 4-point scale)

SKILLS

- Proficient in Microsoft Word, Excel, Access, and PowerPoint
- Fluent in spoken and written Spanish

WORK EXPERIENCE

10/06–present   Hostess/Cashier, Geppetto's Restaurant, El Paso, Texas
- Greet customers, answer phones, prepare carry-out orders
- Close and balance register at end of shift
- Train new personnel

6/04–9/04   Sales Associate, Western Cell Phones, El Paso, Texas
- Assisted customers in selecting cell phones and service providers
- Trained new personnel

HONORS AND AWARDS

- Employee of the month, Geppetto's Restaurant, March 2008
- Top seller, Western Cell Phones, July 2004

REFERENCES

Available upon request

Figure 14.1 Sample Résumé

> **GROUP ACTIVITY 1** Write a Résumé
>
> After carefully reading the job listing you've selected, draft a résumé for that job. Put the most impressive information early in the résumé. Ask classmates to make suggestions for revision. After revising the résumé, edit it carefully for format and grammar.

◖ Cover Letter

In your cover letter, make an argument about why you are the best person for the job. Rather than simply repeating information included in your résumé, add specific details that will make you stand out from other applicants.

A cover letter has an introduction, a body, and a conclusion.

- In your introduction, give the title of the job you're applying for, and explain where you found the listing. Then summarize your qualifications.

- In the body of the letter, explain why you can help the company meet its goals. Point to such experiences as managing people, dealing with difficult customers, and meeting deadlines. Demonstrate that you know important information about the company, such as its sales records or work in the community. You can usually find this information on the company's Web site.

- In your conclusion, restate your interest, give your contact information, and express appreciation for being considered.

As with any job-related document, be sure that the letter is correctly and clearly written. Use standard letter format, and limit the letter to one page. In addition, make sure your cover letter includes the specific information the job listing asks for, such as your salary requirements or your willingness to travel.

Sample Cover Letter

Rachel wrote the following cover letter for the Restaurant Marketing job. Notice the letter format she used, and follow this format when you write your own letter.

Rachel Serrano
4115 Oakdale Ave.
El Paso, TX 79909

September 15, 2010

Mr. Byron Millis
Restaurant Marketing
15313 Mesquite Ave.
Austin, TX 78734

Dear Mr. Millis:

Please consider this letter as an expression of my interest in the customer
sales and service position for Restaurant Marketing that was posted on
careerbuilder.com on September 13. As a marketing student, I am interested
in this opportunity to use my skills in the sales and marketing industry.
Through my experience working in the restaurant business as well as in
sales, I have learned the skills necessary to communicate to customers the
value of a product.

My experience in training personnel has taught me the value of teamwork,
and I pride myself on being a team leader. I am goal oriented, strive to be
the best, and enjoy motivating others to do the same. Because sales
representatives for Restaurant Marketing deal individually with the
customer, being able to communicate clearly is crucial. I am fluent in
Spanish, which will be of great advantage to Restaurant Marketing because
of its location in the Southwest. I am confident that I can contribute to your
company's current $180 million in sales.

I would appreciate the opportunity to meet with your company
representatives to discuss your company needs and what I can do to benefit
Restaurant Marketing. I can be reached by phone at (555) 915-1544 or by
e-mail at rserrano@gmail.com. Thank you for your consideration.

Sincerely,

Rachel Serrano

Rachel Serrano

Enclosure: Résumé

Figure 14.2 Sample Cover Letter

> **GROUP ACTIVITY 2** Write a Cover Letter
>
> Keeping in mind the job ad and your résumé, draft a cover letter. Make an argument — using information not included in the résumé — for why you're the best person for the job. Show the draft to your classmates for suggestions for revision. After revising the letter, edit it for format and grammar.

CHAPTER CHECKLIST

❑ Search for jobs for which you are qualified.

❑ A résumé includes your contact information, education, and work experience.

❑ Include other sections in your résumé when you think the extra information would help you land the job.

❑ Always draft, revise, and edit your résumé.

❑ A cover letter makes the argument for why you should be hired.

❑ In the cover letter, include information not given in your résumé, and organize it with an introduction, a body, and a conclusion.

❑ Always draft, revise, and edit your cover letters.

REFLECTING ON YOUR WRITING

To help you continue to improve as a writer, answer the following questions about the writing assignment for this chapter.

1. What was the easiest part about writing a résumé and cover letter? Explain.

2. What was the hardest part about writing a résumé and cover letter? Explain.

3. How are résumés and cover letters alike? How are they different?

4. How much did this assignment help prepare you for applying for a job?

Using your answers to these questions, complete a Writing Process Report for this chapter (you can download a report form at **bedfordstmartins.com /choices**). Once you complete this report, freewrite about what you learned in this chapter about writing résumés and cover letters and what you still hope to learn.

PART FOUR

Handbook with Exercises

When we write, we want to communicate our ideas clearly to demonstrate our knowledge of our topic and to ensure that our readers understand what we mean. In this Handbook, you'll find opportunities to practice and improve your writing. For example, you'll learn to improve your sentences and to combine short sentences into longer, more interesting ones. You'll learn how to vary your word choice and to eliminate errors. If you are a multilingual writer, you'll find an entire section devoted to helping you write more effectively.

Plan to use this Handbook in several ways. Use it as a reference guide when you have a question about sentence structure, grammar, spelling, or punctuation. Complete practice exercises to help you target specific errors that occur in your writing. Consult it during the editing stage. And, most important, use it as a resource to help you become the best writer you can be.

Handbook Contents

15

Writing Sentences

Every sentence needs to have a subject and a verb and to express a complete thought.

A. Subjects

The **subject** tells *who* or *what* is doing something or being something. Usually, the subject is a **noun**—a person, place, or thing. But a subject can also be a **pronoun**—a word that takes the place of a noun:

Anita laughs.

She is in a good mood.

Compound Subjects

Sometimes a sentence has more than one subject. A subject with more than one part is called a **compound subject**:

John and Emily planned the party.

The dog and the cat ran across the street.

■ **TIPS FOR MULTILINGUAL WRITERS**

Be careful not to leave out the subject in a sentence.

INCORRECT My brother likes his geology course. Is his favorite class.
CORRECT My brother likes his geology course. *It* is his favorite class.

INCORRECT Calls her best friend every day.
CORRECT *Kim* calls her best friend every day.

Remember not to include a pronoun that refers to the subject as part of the subject.

INCORRECT Greg he went fishing.
CORRECT Greg went fishing.

INCORRECT My neighbor she threw a rowdy party.
CORRECT My neighbor threw a rowdy party.

> **ACTIVITY 1 Add Subjects**

Complete each of the following sentences by adding a subject.

EXAMPLE The ___puppy___ chases his tail all day long.

1. My _____ served in the marines for twenty-five years.

2. The _____ complained about the slow service.

3. _____ and _____ lived together after college.

4. Every _____ deserves a quality education.

5. _____ attended the concert last weekend.

6. The dark _____ made the room feel small.

7. The _____ is very hot and spicy at that restaurant.

8. Lola's _____ is due tomorrow morning.

9. _____ and _____ want to visit the Grand Canyon.

10. The _____ is often crowded in the afternoon.

Subject Pretenders

Sometimes the subject of a sentence is hard to identify because the sentence contains other words that may look like the subject—called a **subject pretender**. The most common type of subject pretender is a prepositional phrase, which begins with a preposition.

Prepositions

A **preposition** is a word that expresses how other words are related in time, space, or another sense.

Common Prepositions

about	beside	into	to
above	between	like	toward
after	by	near	under
against	despite	next to	until
among	down	of	up
as	during	off	upon
at	except	on	with
before	for	out	within
behind	from	over	without
below	in	past	
beneath	inside	since	

■ **TIPS FOR MULTILINGUAL WRITERS**

Prepositions that show time—such as *for, during,* and *since*—may have differences in meaning.

For usually refers to an exact period of time that something lasts—one that has a beginning and an end:

> I worked as a cook *for* two years.

> We have been waiting *for* thirty minutes.

> I've been a nonsmoker *for* one month.

During usually refers to an indefinite period of time in which something happens:

> Several times *during* the week I thought of you.

> I want to go home *during* the holidays.

> It rained *during* the night, but I don't know exactly when.

Since usually refers to a period of time that has passed between an earlier time and the present:

> *Since* losing weight, I've been happy.

> Mae has been happy *since* she got married.

> Jason has been more confident *since* winning the race.

ACTIVITY 2 Identify Prepositions

Underline the prepositions in the following paragraph.

EXAMPLE   Nick and José drove to the library.

They had many questions for the reference librarian because they had a research project due in their history class the following week. Nick left the assignment directions in his car, but José had brought an extra copy with him in his backpack. The librarian found several history reference books on the shelves behind her desk. She helped Nick and José find newspaper and magazine articles by using the library databases and looking under the most useful subject headings. The boys sent copies of the best articles to their e-mail accounts. Then they copied entries from the reference books using the photocopier next to the library stairs. Driving home from the library, Nick suggested they stop for a snack before going back to their dorm.

ACTIVITY 3 Add Prepositions

Complete each of the following sentences by writing a preposition in the space provided.

EXAMPLE I never travel ___*without*___ my cell phone charger.

1. The swimmer dove _____ the pool.

2. The Harry Potter books were written _____ J. K. Rowling.

3. Kendra has several tattoos _____ her back.

4. Evan found a pen pal _____ the Internet.

5. _____ her last class, Berta checks her e-mail.

6. Zach never goes to sleep _____ midnight.

7. Hiding your house key _____ the doormat is a bad idea.

8. Jessica had Dr. Millhauser _____ her biology professor.

9. Jo suspected that everyone had been talking _____ her.

10. I walk _____ the playground every morning on my way to work.

Prepositional Phrases

A **prepositional phrase** consists of a preposition and its object. The object is a noun or pronoun, together with any words that describe or refer to the object. Here are some examples.

Preposition	+ Object	= Prepositional Phrase
into	the classroom	into the classroom
before	you	before you
on	a bright summer day	on a bright summer day

ACTIVITY 4 Write Prepositional Phrases

Complete each of the following sentences by adding a prepositional phrase.

EXAMPLE The babysitter took the children _____*for a walk*_____ .

1. Isaac bought his iPad _____ .

2. My economics study group meets _____ .

3. Movies _____ are very popular.

4. I ate the pasta that I found _____ .

5. When Sal called, I was _____ .

6. _____ , Lucy practiced her violin.

7. _____ , the plumber fixed the leak.

8. Zaini caught the train _____ .

9. The seagulls flew _____ .

10. Jesse and Sarah walked home _____ .

A prepositional phrase cannot be the subject of a sentence.

The children *in the bus* need to be brought inside.

In the sentence above, *in the bus* is a prepositional phrase. The subject of the sentence is *children*.

The dog *from across the street* chased my cat.

From across the street is a prepositional phrase. The subject of the sentence is *dog*.

Because you know that the subject of a sentence is never part of a prepositional phrase, you can find the subject easily. First, cross out all the prepositional phrases. Then decide which of the other words is doing something or being something.

The man in the photograph resembles like my grandfather.

The subject of the sentence is *man*.

The phone in Karen's office rang three times.

The subject of the sentence is *phone*.

> ### ■ HOW TO Find the Subject of a Sentence
>
> - Cross out all prepositional phrases.
> - Decide which of the remaining words is doing something or being something.

ACTIVITY 5 Find Prepositional Phrases and Sentence Subjects

In each of the following sentences, cross out the prepositional phrases and circle the subject.

EXAMPLE The box on the table was open.

1. The neighbors down the hall are very loud.

2. Darryl bought a netbook for five hundred dollars.

3. The pumpkins in that garden need to be picked.

4. After the midterm, the sociology class became more difficult.

5. Inside those drawers, you will find my old sweaters.

6. The guests at the wedding loved the food.

7. Without his friends, Nicky felt somewhat shy.

8. The information in that article is not very reliable.

9. The questions on the test covered the whole semester.

10. Two of Kristina's brothers joined the military.

⬛ **ACTIVITY 6 Identify Subject Pretenders**

In the following paragraph, cross out the prepositional phrases and circle the subject of each sentence.

EXAMPLE Ⓘentered the photographs ~~on that wall in the art show~~.

Everybody who participated in the student art show benefited from the experience. My friend Jill won a prize for one of her paintings. Consequently, three of her pieces are now on display in the student center. Although I did not win anything, I received lots of compliments on my photographs. A person who asked for my telephone number has purchased a photo from me. Around the campus green where the show took place were temporary walls made of plywood. Graffiti artists painted the walls with their best efforts. These walls were the most popular work of art at the show. They have been moved next to the art building and will remain on display.

For additional practice with using subjects, go to **bedfordstmartins.com /choices** and click on **Exercise Central**.

☾ B. Verbs

The **verb** in a sentence expresses action or links the subject to the rest of the sentence.

Action and Linking Verbs

Action Verbs

In the following sentences, the verb expresses action:

My grandmother *knits* quilts for family members.

The dog *ate* my homework.

That band always plays my favorite songs.

Linking Verbs

The most common linking verbs are forms of the verb *to be*: *am, are, is, was, were, be, been, being*. In the following sentences, the verb links the subject to the rest of the sentence:

I *am* short.

The children *were* grumpy.

Miriam *is* ready to perform.

Helping Verbs

Helping verbs include *am, are, is, was, were, be, have, has, had, do, does, did, may, might, must, can, could, shall, should, will, would*. A helping verb is used with another verb form, called the **main verb**, to form a phrase that acts as the verb of the sentence:

Moira *was helping* her brother prepare the meal.

Ramón *had studied* all morning.

You *must reply* this afternoon.

Compound Verbs

Sometimes a sentence has more than one verb. A verb with more than one part is called a **compound verb**:

Edgar Allan Poe *frightened* and *thrilled* readers.

The children *sat* and *waited* for their parents to get them.

I *can use* your help and *would be* grateful for it.

ACTIVITY 7 Find Subjects and Verbs in Sentences

In each of the following sentences, circle the subject and underline the verb.

EXAMPLE (I) enjoy performing in front of people.

1. My friends and I started a band a few years ago.

2. Currently, we are writing new songs.

3. We have enjoyed playing music together.

4. A neighbor helped us record our first demo on my computer.

5. She was happy to offer us advice.

6. We have played shows at a small club downtown.

7. The club owner has asked us to come more often.

8. Our bass player and our drummer are brothers.

9. They have written some of our best songs.

10. We have dreamed of stardom since we were kids.

ACTIVITY 8 Add Verbs

Complete each of the following sentences by adding a verb.

EXAMPLE A typical student ___*desires*___ many electronic devices, such as a cell phone, a laptop, and an e-reader.

1. An anonymous donor _____ a million dollars to the scholarship fund.

2. Lisa _____ student body president.

3. A flock of seagulls _____ overhead.

4. The children _____ free swimming lessons.

5. Armando _____ a rabbit hide behind the fence.

6. Our biology class _____ DNA last week.

7. Frederick _____ at a friend's house last night.

8. The soccer team _____ on the football field.

9. Police officers _____ the hillside for clues.

10. Many champion gymnasts _____ their training at a very young age.

Verb Pretenders

Verb pretenders (also called *verbals*) look like verbs but do not act as verbs in sentences. The most common verb pretenders are verb + *-ing* and *to* + verb combinations.

cooking	to cook
working	to work
studying	to study

Verb + *-ing*

When an *-ing* verb appears in a sentence without a helping verb, it does not act as the verb of the sentence. Instead, it modifies, or describes, other words in the sentence. These words are called **modifiers**.

I took a picture of the boy *swimming* in the fountain. [*Swimming* describes the boy.]

Working hard, we completed the job in a day. [*Working* describes the subject of the sentence, *we*.]

The *laughing* partygoers kept me awake at night. [*Laughing* describes the partygoers.]

ACTIVITY 9 Identify *-ing* Verbs

In the space provided, indicate whether the *-ing* verb in each of the following sentences acts as a modifier or as part of a verb.

EXAMPLE The panting dog needed to drink some water. _____modifier_____

1. Claudia is hiking the Appalachian Trail. _____

2. Joanne sent her father a singing telegram for his birthday. _____

3. That diving board is too high. _____

4. I was weeding the garden when I scraped my knee. _____

5. The cookie recipe requires a teaspoon of baking powder. _____

6. Stomping on the floor, William showed his displeasure. _____

7. Susan is moving to Las Vegas the day after tomorrow. _____

8. Nina went to the mall for a new pair of knitting needles. _____

9. Because of her back problems, Kata was sleeping on the floor. _____

10. Jumping up and down, the children showed their excitement. _____

ACTIVITY 10 Use Verbs and Verb Pretenders

For each of the following *-ing* verbs, write two sentences. In the first sentence, use the word as a verb. (You'll need a helping verb, too.) In the second sentence, use the word as a modifier to describe another word.

EXAMPLE drinking

Verb: _____I was drinking cranberry juice when you called._____

Modifier: _____Clean drinking water is harder and harder to find._____

1. viewing

Verb: _____

Modifier: _____

2. planting

Verb: _____

Modifier: _____

3. sleeping

Verb: _____

Modifier: _____

4. playing

Verb: _____

Modifier: _____

5. surfing

Verb: _____

Modifier: _____

To + Verb

The *to* + verb combination also looks like a verb but does not act as a verb in a sentence. Instead, it acts as either a noun or a modifier that describes something:

I can't wait to open my gifts. [Because *to* comes in front of *open, open* does not act as a verb. Instead, *to open* modifies *wait.*]

I always open my gifts before my birthday. [Here *open* acts as a verb.]

Stephanie had a plan to buy apples. [Because *to* comes in front of *buy, buy* does not act as a verb. Instead, *to buy* modifies *plan.*]

Stephanie buys apples from the farm. [Here *buys* acts as a verb.]

My goal is to study medicine. [Because *to* comes in front of *study, study* does not act as a verb. Instead, *to study* acts as a noun.]

Many Americans study medicine overseas. [Here *study* acts as a verb.]

▪ HOW TO Find the Verb in a Sentence

- Locate the word or words that express the action or link the subject to the rest of the sentence.
- Check that the word is not a verb pretender.
- When a verb + *-ing* combination appears in a sentence without a helping verb, it's a verb pretender.
- When a *to* + verb combination appears, it's a verb pretender.

ACTIVITY 11 Use *to* + Verb Combinations

Complete each of the following sentences with a *to* + verb combination.

EXAMPLE Mauricio used a hammer ___*to crack the coconut*___ .

1. Rebecca waited _____ .

2. _____ was the children's favorite thing to do.

3. Sunay promises _____ .

4. Half the apartments in this building do not seem _____ .

5. Before sitting down to breakfast, Erica's parents needed _____ .

6. _____ is Kyle's only chore this morning.

7. Bryan likes _____ .

8. After a day of skiing, Richard and Elizabeth want _____

_____ _____ .

9. Connie's old job was ___ _____ .

10. _____ may be Lon's greatest talent.

ACTIVITY 12 Find Subjects and Verbs

In each of the following sentences, circle the subject and underline the verb. Do not confuse verbs and verb pretenders.

EXAMPLE The smiling (woman) accepted the award.

1. Kim agreed to have the meeting at her house.

2. While taping the playoffs, Hugo watched a documentary.

3. Stepping carefully, Nizar tried to avoid the wet paint.

4. The hikers reached their campground by sunset.

5. Mosquitoes were annoying the hikers.

6. Adam washed his hands before kneading the bread dough.

7. The people on the street hoped to glimpse the famous actress.

8. Opening the newspaper, Maya began to read the classified ads.

9. After work, Tim and Linda lack the energy to cook dinner.

10. Slipping the diamond ring on Leticia's finger, Nahum asked her to marry him.

> **ACTIVITY 13 Identify Subjects and Verbs**

In the following paragraph, circle the subjects and underline the verbs.

EXAMPLE (Ivor) decided to major in music.

Ivor needed to interview a local drummer for a term project. Before contacting the musician, he read about her career. Feeling nervous, he wrote her an e-mail to request an appointment. To his surprise, the drummer invited him to watch a rehearsal. Her band was playing a new song. Ivor took many notes while listening to them. He wanted to describe his first impressions completely. After the rehearsal, the band kept asking him questions about his assignment. Answering the musicians politely, he wondered how to change the subject. Finally, the drummer told the band to let Ivor begin his interview.

Verb Tense

The **tense** of a verb shows the time that the action or condition takes place. The three basic tenses in English are *present, past,* and *future.*

The **present tense** shows an action or condition taking place at the time the writer is writing. The present tense can also show an action that happens more than once:

Anthony *has* a big kitchen.

He *cooks* every evening.

The **past tense** shows something that began and ended in the past. To form the past tense of most verbs, use the *-ed* form of the verb:

Last week, Anthony *cooked* for his friends and family.

The **future tense** shows something that will take place or will probably take place. To form the future tense, use *will, is going to,* or *are going to* and the present tense of the verb:

I *will learn* my lines by next week.

This extra credit assignment *is going to make* a difference in my grade.

As a general rule, stay with the tense you begin with at the start of a paragraph unless the time you are talking about changes. Avoid shifting from one tense to another for no reason, because these shifts may confuse your readers.

ACTIVITY 14 Correct Awkward Shifts in Verb Tense

Edit the following paragraph to correct unnecessary shifts in verb tense. The first sentence in the paragraph is correct.

EXAMPLE My stepson angered me, but I ~~try~~ ^tried^ to understand.

For a long time, my stepson, Jonathan, was unhappy to have me as part of his family. I try to get to know him better, but he will complain that I invade his privacy. As a newcomer, I understood that our relationship will require effort from both of us. It was not enough that I was friendly. Jonathan also has to want us to be friends. I am not happy with the two of us being strangers, but I can wait for him to feel more comfortable around me.

ACTIVITY 15 Correct Awkward Shifts in Verb Tense

Edit the following paragraph to correct unnecessary shifts in verb tense. The first sentence in the paragraph is correct.

EXAMPLE Anne Marie finds bottles on old farmland, where she ~~liked~~ ^likes^ to explore.

Anne Marie collects antique bottles. She will buy bottles if she liked them, but she prefers to find them in the ground. She will find bottles everywhere. However, she has the best luck at construction sites on old farmland. Often, bottles appeared on the surface after a good rain. She will use special tools for excavating bottles, including a set of brushes. She did not want to break the bottles as she removed them from the ground. After finding a new bottle, Anne Marie will add it to her display case.

Regular Verbs

Regular verbs are verbs whose past tense and past participle end in *-ed*. Past participles are forms of a verb that are used with *has, have,* or *had,* as in the following examples:

I *have studied* Portuguese for three years.
Niko *had drunk* all of the free champagne.

COMMON REGULAR VERBS

Verb	Past Tense	Past Participle
cook	cooked	cooked
measure	measured	measured
study	studied	studied
walk	walked	walked

Irregular Verbs

Irregular verbs are verbs whose past tense and past participle do not end in *-ed* but are formed in a variety of ways. As a result, they are often misused or misspelled. Review the forms of irregular verbs so you won't make errors.

COMMON IRREGULAR VERBS

Verb	Past Tense	Past Participle
be	was, were	been
begin	began	begun
catch	caught	caught
choose	chose	chosen
come	came	come
do	did	done
drink	drank	drunk
eat	ate	eaten
feel	felt	felt
fly	flew	flown
get	got	got, gotten
go	went	gone
leave	left	left
ride	rode	ridden
see	saw	seen

ACTIVITY 16 Identify Regular and Irregular Verbs

In each of the following sentences, underline the verb and identify it as a regular or an irregular verb.

EXAMPLE The letter carrier <u>knocked</u> on the door. _____regular_____

1. Kate placed the grapes in the bowl. _____

2. Nathan knew Robin and Simon already. _____

3. Somebody stole my purse! _____

4. Dwayne read comic books at night. _____

5. Chen baked a cake for his family. _____

6. The moths flew around the lamp. _____

7. Alice drank a bottle of water. _____

8. Zafir caught a cold on the airplane. _____

9. The mechanic looked under the hood. _____

10. The cell phone rang at midnight. _____

ACTIVITY 17 Use Regular and Irregular Verbs

In each of the following sentences, write the correct form of the verb in the space provided. If necessary, consult your dictionary for the correct form.

EXAMPLE Richard _____*lost*_____ his train ticket last night. *(lose)*

1. When she was young, Jayne _____ her money under her bed. *(hide)*

2. Isabel has _____ with a gospel choir for five years. *(sing)*

3. Last semester, Meg _____ about her grades. *(worry)*

4. Yesterday morning, the actors _____ very convincing in their costumes. *(look)*

5. Patrick and Hugh have _____ music at every school in town. *(teach)*

6. Experts say that the ocean liner *Titanic* _____ because it was too big. *(sink)*

7. My grandmother _____ that picture when she was ten years old. *(draw)*

8. Who has _____ my car without my permission? *(drive)*

9. The cousins _____ for hours at the family reunion last July. *(talk)*

10. Sigrid has _____ Naomi for her dance partner. *(choose)*

For additional practice with using verbs, go to **bedfordstmartins.com/choices** and click on **Exercise Central**.

C. Subject-Verb Agreement

A complete sentence contains a subject and a verb. The subject tells who or what is doing something or being something, and the verb either expresses the action or links the subject to the rest of the sentence. To maintain **subject-verb agreement**, a singular subject must have a singular verb form, and a plural subject must have a plural verb form.

Singular and Plural Forms

A singular subject consists of one thing:

the student

A singular verb form in the present tense usually ends in *-s:*

The student studies for the test.

A plural subject consists of more than one thing:

the students

A plural verb form in the present tense generally does not end in *-s:*

The students study for the test.

To check for subject-verb agreement, you must first identify the subject of the sentence. Remember that prepositions and other words sometimes occur between the subject and the verb. Once you identify the subject, you can add the correct verb form.

INCORRECT   Elaine go to the recycling center. [singular subject, plural verb form]

CORRECT   Elaine goes to the recycling center. [singular subject, singular verb form]

INCORRECT   The cars swerves to avoid hitting the dog. [plural subject, singular verb form]

CORRECT   The cars swerve to avoid hitting the dog. [plural subject, plural verb form]

ACTIVITY 18 Identify Subject-Verb Agreement

In each of the following sentences, underline the correct verb form.

EXAMPLE I (naps, nap) every afternoon.

1. This book (costs, cost) less online than at the store.

2. The swimmers (competes, compete) against one another every year.

3. The windows (sticks, stick) in humid weather.

4. The airlines (offers, offer) advice for children traveling alone.

5. Liam (works, work) as a computer help desk operator.

6. Strawberries (remains, remain) fresh for only a few days.

7. Dr. Perry (sees, see) new patients.

8. Phoebe (drives, drive) a vintage Ford truck.

9. Kathy and Lauren (attends, attend) an accelerated Spanish program.

10. Dancing (is, are) a form of art, a form of exercise, and a form of recreation.

ACTIVITY 19 Add Verbs That Agree

Add a singular or plural verb form to each of the following sentences as needed to maintain subject-verb agreement.

EXAMPLE My mother-in-law ___*bakes*___ the best vegan cookies.

1. At dusk, the city's skyline _____ especially beautiful.

2. I _____ your good grades.

3. This radio _____ only three AM stations.

4. Those magazines _____ the best information on fly-fishing.

5. Katie _____ French and Spanish fluently.

6. Empanadas _____ best when served fresh from the oven.

7. Professor Lopez _____ his students to write two research papers.

8. Bruce _____ at a gym several times a week.

9. Tracy and Lincoln _____ together at the soup kitchen.

10. Listening to soothing music _____ an effective way to relax.

To determine correct subject-verb agreement, be sure that you have correctly identified the subject. Watch out for subject pretenders such as prepositional phrases.

Read about subject pretenders on pp. 400–404.

> **INCORRECT** The cup of pencils *are* on the table. [The prepositional phrase *of pencils* is a subject pretender.]
>
> **CORRECT** The cup of pencils *is* on the table. [*Cup* is the subject of the sentence.]

ACTIVITY 20 Use Correct Verbs

In each of the following sentences, underline the correct verb form.

EXAMPLE The books on those shelves (belongs, <u>belong</u>) to my roommate.

1. To do one hundred sit-ups a day (is, are) my goal.

2. The pieces of gum (sticks, stick) to the roof of my mouth.

3. The keys lost in the backyard (needs, need) to be found.

4. The Halloween masks in the store (looks, look) scary.

5. The books that I like best (is, are) mysteries and thrillers.

6. One of the professors (has, have) a bad cold.

7. To beat my brother in checkers (is, are) my greatest wish in the world.

8. Lady Gaga's costumes (is, are) always in the news.

9. Movies of popular books often (becomes, become) very successful.

10. My pet ferrets, whose names are George and Laura, (eats, eat) more food than I do.

ACTIVITY 21 Maintain Subject-Verb Agreement

Add a singular or plural verb form to each of the following sentences as needed to maintain subject-verb agreement.

EXAMPLE The clothes in that box ____*belong*____ to Michael.

1. That cable channel always _____ reruns.

2. The vase of tulips _____ on the kitchen counter.

3. The applicants did not _____ a good first impression.

4. Those mushrooms around that tree _____ poisonous.

5. Our basement, filled with broken furniture and old toys, _____ to be cleaned out.

6. Professor Wu, joined by many of her students, _____ for animal rights.

7. The apples on that tree _____ ripe.

8. The nurses in the children's hospital _____ excellent care.

9. Poppy's collection of amusement park souvenirs _____ valuable.

10. A jar full of coins _____ in the back of my closet.

ACTIVITY 22 Insert Correct Verbs

In the following paragraph, underline the correct verb forms.

EXAMPLE Many people (is, are) interested in football, but few people (is, are) as obsessed as my husband.

Paul, who (has been, have been) my husband for three years, (is, are) in love with the sport. Being married to a football fanatic (has, have) its drawbacks. During the football season, each and every Sunday (is, are) dedicated to the sport. Paul and his friends (gather, gathers) at our house before noon to begin watching the games. Fortunately, his friend Rico, who is one of the best cooks I've ever met, (bring, brings) the snacks and drinks. All day, I (hear, hears) cheers and boos coming from the living room. Paul and his friends (take, takes) the game so seriously they get depressed when their teams lose. Personally, I'd rather have a hobby that is less stressful.

Indefinite Pronouns

Sometimes the subject of a sentence is an **indefinite pronoun**, a pronoun that refers to one or more unspecified beings, objects, or places. Here are some singular indefinite pronouns, which take singular verb forms:

See p. 399 for the definition of a pronoun.

anybody	everyone	somebody
anyone	everything	someone
anything	nobody	something
each	no one	
everybody	nothing	

INCORRECT   Each of us *need* to pay twenty dollars. [*Each* is singular and requires a singular verb form.]

CORRECT   Each of us *needs* to pay twenty dollars.

INCORRECT   Anyone *know* the answer. [singular pronoun, plural verb form]

CORRECT   Anyone *knows* the answer. [singular pronoun, singular verb form]

INCORRECT   Everybody *go* to the movies on Friday night. [singular pronoun, plural verb form]

CORRECT   Everybody *goes* to the movies on Friday night. [singular pronoun, singular verb form]

■ HOW TO Check for Subject-Verb Agreement

- Remember that singular subjects take singular verb forms and that plural subjects take plural verb forms.
- Be sure that you have correctly identified the subject.
- Watch out for subject pretenders, such as prepositional phrases.
- Most indefinite pronouns—such as *everyone, anyone, something,* and *no one*—are singular and take singular verb forms.

> **ACTIVITY 23 Identify Subject-Verb Agreement**

In each of the following sentences, underline the correct verb form.

EXAMPLE Something about that story (<u>makes</u>, make) me uneasy.

1. Nothing about that movie (is, are) worthwhile.

2. Everybody with a special permit (parks, park) in the same lot.

3. Somebody living on my street (plays, play) bongos in the middle of the night.

4. No one in that laboratory (has, have) a degree in science.

5. Something inside the car (makes, make) a strange clunking noise.

6. Everyone in Carmela's family (speaks, speak) English and Italian.

7. Everything remaining on the floor (does, do) not belong there.

8. Nobody with a new computer (uses, use) that outdated software.

9. Someone wearing strong perfume (leaves, leave) a trail of scent behind her.

10. Anything made of wood that is exposed to rain (requires, require) a waterproof finish.

> **ACTIVITY 24 Add Singular Verbs**

Add a singular verb form to each of the following sentences to maintain subject-verb agreement.

EXAMPLE No one in the room ____wants____ to stand up.

1. Everyone on the roller coaster _____ a little queasy.

2. Someone in this class _____ the answers to the test.

3. Anything in that store _____ a dollar or less.

4. Somebody _____ to clean the dishes in the sink.

5. Nobody _____ Suraj to pass his driving test.

6. Something in this room _____ like oranges.

7. Nothing _____ wrong with your plan.

8. Everything in the storage unit _____ to Lorraine and Howie.

9. No one in my class _____ group projects.

10. Everybody _____ to return next year.

ACTIVITY 25 Write Using Correct Subject-Verb Agreement

Complete each of the following sentences, making sure that the verb you add agrees with the subject that is provided.

EXAMPLE Everybody _____ *goes to the movies* _____ after work on Friday.

1. These young couples _____.

2. This Web site _____.

3. Everyone on this list _____.

4. We _____.

5. I _____.

6. None of the telemarketers _____.

7. The little boy who forgot his permission slip _____

   _____.

8. The director of the church choir _____.

9. The presidents of both classes _____.

10. Nobody _____.

ACTIVITY 26 Select Subjects and Verbs That Agree

In the following paragraph, underline the correct verb forms.

EXAMPLE Guo (feel, <u>feels</u>) proud of his Chinese heritage.

Guo (belongs, belong) to a troupe of lion dancers. Beginning in October, Guo meets once a week with the other lion dancers and (begins, begin) rehearsing for Chinese New Year. After being in the troupe for three years, Guo now (dances, dance) as the lion's head. He (shakes, shake) the mane and (pretends, pretend) to roar. Being the lion's head (is, are) a great honor as well as hard work. After Christmas, as Chinese New Year approaches, the troupe members, who all attend the same university, (rehearses, rehearse) every night. Everyone (looks, look) forward to the festivities. In addition to dancing in the Chinese New Year parade, the group of dancers (visits, visit) city schools to teach children about Chinese culture. The children sitting closest to the lion (screams, scream) when it approaches them.

The dancing creature, with his comical but threatening gestures, (delights, delight) and (frightens, frighten) young spectators.

> **ACTIVITY 27** Correct Subject-Verb Agreement

Revise the following paragraph as needed to correct errors in subject-verb agreement.

EXAMPLE Tanya's job of managing a plumbing supply business ~~satisfy~~ her.
_{satisfies}

Tanya manage her father's plumbing supply business. The first thing every morning, with the telephone already ringing, she turns on the computer and take the first orders of the day. The orders early in the morning is usually for emergency jobs and generates repeat business. Tanya's father, who has a good reputation among local plumbers, ask her to give these orders priority. No one, especially someone with clogged pipes, want to wait longer than necessary for repairs. Filling emergency orders are not Tanya's only job. She maintains the company budget and decide which bills to pay each day. Surrounded by boxes of hardware, Tanya admit that she had expected to work somewhere more glamorous after receiving her business degree. However, everybody who remembers the company before her improvements admire her work. Her decision to streamline office procedures have made the company more efficient and more profitable.

For additional practice with subject-verb agreement, go to **bedfordstmartins.com /choices** and click on **Exercise Central**.

16

Expanding Sentences

In addition to containing subjects and verbs, sentences can be expanded to include phrases, clauses, pronouns, adjectives, and adverbs. Using expanded sentences gives you the opportunity to express yourself effectively for a variety of audiences.

A. Phrases

See pp. 399–404 and 404–13 for more information about subjects and verbs.

If a group of words lacks a subject or a verb or both, it's called a **phrase**. A phrase is not a complete sentence. Notice the difference between phrases and sentences in these examples:

PHRASE	To get to class on time.
SENTENCE	To get to class on time, I need to leave my apartment at 8:30.
PHRASE	To come up with the right answer.
SENTENCE	Mel was unable to come up with the right answer.
PHRASE	Making her a good dinner.
SENTENCE	I want to please my girlfriend by making her a good dinner.
PHRASE	Such as a new backpack, a Barbie, a walkie-talkie, a stuffed lizard, and even a cell phone.
SENTENCE	My nine-year-old daughter wants a lot of things for her birthday, such as a new backpack, a Barbie, a walkie-talkie, a stuffed lizard, and even a cell phone.
PHRASE	On the shelf.
SENTENCE	I can't reach the box on the shelf.

ACTIVITY 1 Identify Phrases and Sentences

For each of the following items, write *S* next to the word groups that are sentences and *P* next to the word groups that are phrases.

EXAMPLE Within the last fifteen years. ___P___

1. To drive over the bridge at night. _____

2. Before sending the e-mail, she carefully reviewed it. _____

3. To find a new job, Frida updated her résumé. _____

4. On Friday my singing lesson. _____

5. The blog posting turned out to be a joke. _____

6. For example, a pencil, a notebook, and a flash drive. _____

7. Over there on the floor. _____

8. He used his keys to open the door. _____

9. To study for Spanish, English, algebra, biology, and economics. _____

10. The fire in the national forest was caused by a careless smoker. _____

ACTIVITY 2 Turn Phrases into Sentences

Expand each of the following phrases into a complete sentence.

EXAMPLE after the fire

After the fire, there was nothing left of the house.

1. talking with their parents

   _____

2. before the start of the semester

   _____

3. presented his oral report

   _____

4. due to the increase in gas prices

   _____

5. to maintain a good relationship

   _____

6. avoiding his old friends from high school

   _____

7. a flight of creaky stairs

   _____

8. the park in my family's neighborhood

   _____

9. an unusual but attractive hairstyle

_____

10. saving her wages from her after-school job

_____

ACTIVITY 3 Connect Phrases to Sentences

Revise the following paragraph to connect the phrases to the sentences that come before or after them.

EXAMPLE Families need to be flexible. ~~In~~ order to deal with hard times.
ⁱⁿ

Ever since my early teen years. My parents have had an untraditional marriage. My mother held a full-time job while my father stayed at home. Taking care of us kids. Until I was thirteen, both my parents worked full time. Then my dad lost his job. Mom earned enough to support the family as a buyer. For a large department store. She frequently had to travel. The whole family enjoyed her stories about the exciting places she visited. Including New York City, Paris, Hong Kong, and Milan. It was comforting having Dad there. Caring for us when we were sick and congratulating us when we did well at school. Because of this unconventional arrangement. We kids learned that people sometimes have to be flexible to succeed.

For additional practice with using phrases, go to **bedfordstmartins.com/choices** and click on **Exercise Central**.

B. Clauses

A **clause** can be a whole sentence or a part of a sentence. There are two kinds of clauses: independent and dependent.

Independent or Main Clauses

An **independent clause**, also called a *main clause*, is a group of words with a subject and a verb that can stand alone as a complete sentence. All sentences contain at least one independent clause, and some contain more than one:

Femi enjoyed her first piano lesson. [This sentence is an independent clause because it contains a subject and a verb and can stand alone as a sentence.]

She learned how to hold her hands, and she learned how to sit. [This sentence consists of two independent clauses.]

She decided to sign up for more lessons through the summer. [This sentence consists of one independent clause.]

■ HOW TO Identify an Independent Clause

- Check that the word group has a subject and a verb.
- Check that the word group can stand alone as a sentence.

ACTIVITY 4 Write Independent Clauses

Expand each of the following word groups into a sentence so that it contains an independent clause.

EXAMPLE After my divorce, *I felt determined not to make the same mistake again.*

1. The day my divorce became final _____.

2. Although my wife and I were not getting along, _____

   _____.

3. Because I had sworn to be with her forever, _____

   _____.

4. _____ even though we tried so

   hard to stay together.

5. Because we had no children, _____.

6. When we saw each other for the last time, _____

   _____.

7. _____ because the bad memories

   are fading.

8. A year after the divorce, _____.

9. Although I haven't found someone else to love, _____

   _____.

10. Because I don't want to make the same mistake again, _____

    _____.

Dependent or Subordinate Clauses

Although a **dependent clause** contains a subject and a verb, it cannot stand alone as a sentence. To be part of a complete sentence, it needs to be attached to or part of an independent clause. Dependent clauses are also called **subordinate clauses** because they often begin with one of these words, called **subordinating conjunctions**:

after	if	until
although	since	when
as	that	where
because	though	while
before	unless	

Because my car broke down, I had to reschedule my dentist appointment. [The subordinate clause at the beginning of the sentence contains a subject and a verb, but it cannot stand alone as a sentence.]

Before my uncle retired, he was a welder. [This sentence also starts with a subordinate clause.]

I didn't fly in a plane *until I was seventeen years old*. [This subordinate clause comes at the end of the sentence.]

As these examples show, you use a comma after a subordinate clause that begins a sentence. You generally do not use a comma before a subordinate clause that ends a sentence.

▪ HOW TO Identify a Subordinate Clause

- Check that the word group has a subject and a verb.
- Check that it begins with a subordinating conjunction (such as *because*, *until*, *before*, *after*, *although*, *when*, or *while*).
- Check that it cannot stand alone as a sentence.

ACTIVITY 5 Identify Subordinate Clauses

In each of the following sentences, underline the subordinate clause. One sentence contains two subordinate clauses.

EXAMPLE Though I had a bad cold, I still played in the championship game.

1. When the supervisor entered the office, Dean stopped playing his computer game.

2. On my street, the garbage is always collected before I wake up.

3. We toasted marshmallows and told ghost stories until the fire died.

4. If nobody has any questions, Ms. Skov will distribute the free samples.

5. Antonio wants to become a social worker because a social worker helped him through his long stay in the hospital.

6. While the turkey roasted in the oven, the family played touch football.

7. Unless you pay your parking fines, you will not be allowed to register for classes when the next semester begins.

8. Since Jazlynn began jogging, she has been having pain in her knees.

9. After he graduates, Achmed wants to tour Mexico.

10. I have hidden your birthday present where you will never find it.

> ◀ **ACTIVITY 6** Identify Subordinate Clauses ▶

In the following paragraph, underline the subordinate clauses.

EXAMPLE <u>Before he moved into his own apartment</u>, Brendan lived with his parents.

This year Brendan moved into his own apartment. After he moved in, he began to clean house regularly. In fact, he enjoys doing housework. If he cleans a little every day, his place always looks presentable. Solutions to his problems pop into his head while he is scrubbing something. When he was cleaning his bathtub, he thought of a better way to budget his paycheck. Although Brendan is not a perfectionist, he takes pride in his apartment because it represents a new stage in his adult life.

Relative Clauses

A subordinate clause may also begin with one of these words, called **relative pronouns**:

that	who
what	whoever
whatever	whom
which	whomever
whichever	whose

A subordinate clause that begins with a relative pronoun is often called a **relative clause**:

Whoever passes the obstacle course will be allowed to leave. [This relative clause is the subject of the sentence.]

Any soldier *who passes the obstacle course* will be allowed to leave. [This relative clause describes the subject and is essential to the meaning of the sentence.]

Private Mejia, *who passed the obstacle course*, was allowed to leave. [Here the relative clause also describes the subject but is not essential to the meaning of the sentence.]

As the last example shows, sometimes commas are used to set off relative clauses from the rest of the sentence. If the relative clause interrupts the flow of the sentence and could be removed without changing the basic meaning of the sentence, use a comma before it, and use another comma after it unless it is at the end of the sentence. Do not use a comma before or after a relative clause that is essential to the meaning of the sentence, as in the first two examples above.

HOW TO Identify a Relative Clause

- Check that the word group has a subject and a verb.
- Check that the word group begins with a relative pronoun (such as *that, who, what, which, whoever,* or *whichever*).
- Check that the word group cannot stand alone as a sentence.

ACTIVITY 7 Identify Relative Clauses

In each of the following sentences, underline the relative clause.

EXAMPLE I will support whomever you nominate for club president.

1. Alethea is the only student who talked to the professor on the first day of class.

2. Tom is one of those people who work at night and sleep all day.

3. I worry about students whose extracurricular activities interfere with their studies.

4. Whoever ate Asher's sandwich should fix him another one.

5. I recommend you buy the vehicle that has the least impact on the environment.

6. Jolene is the one student whose research paper received an A.

7. Whoever comes home last needs to let the cat out.

8. Frankie is the only boyfriend who ever gave me a bouquet of roses.

9. Miss Sweden was the contestant who played the accordion in the talent competition.

10. I feel sorry for the people whose jobs were eliminated last year.

ACTIVITY 8 Turn Relative Clauses into Sentences

Add information to each of the following relative clauses to make it a complete sentence.

EXAMPLE who can sing, dance, and act

The play requires performers who can sing, dance, and act.

1. that tasted the best

_____

2. who do not smoke

_____

3. whoever sits at the head of the table

_____

4. whom Elena admires

_____

5. who just left for vacation

_____

6. that leaves at 11:15 tonight

_____

7. who does not mind a little hard work

_____

8. that does not require batteries

_____

9. whose smile could light up a room

_____

10. that the dog ate

_____

ACTIVITY 9 Expand Sentences with Subordinate Clauses

Expand each of the following sentences by adding a subordinate clause.

EXAMPLE Andrew is studying geology.

Andrew is studying geology because he likes exploring caves.

1. Carmen wanted a new job.

   _____

2. The day-care center is having a bake sale.

   _____

3. Derek rode a bicycle to work.

   _____

4. The drugstore downtown is closed.

   _____

5. The coffee will not taste any better.

   _____

6. Demetria collects old magazines.

   _____

7. The roads have been undergoing repairs.

   _____

8. The Blumenfelds hired a gardener.

   _____

9. Monique wanted a laptop computer.

   _____

For additional practice with using clauses, go to **bedfordstmartins.com /choices** and click on **Exercise Central**.

10. You will not improve your physical condition.

    _____

◗ C. Pronouns

When you expand sentences, you'll be making grammatical choices about how you express your thoughts. One of these choices will concern the use of pronouns. A **pronoun** is a word that grammatically takes the place of a noun or another pronoun. Usually, it refers to a specific noun that appears earlier in the sentence or in a previous sentence. The following are common pronouns:

I, me, mine, we, our, ours

you, your, yours

he, him, his, she, her, hers

it, its

they, them, their, theirs

this, these, that, those

who, whom, whose, which, that, what

all, any, another, both, each, either, everyone

few, many, most, nobody, several, some, such

myself, yourself, himself, herself, itself

ourselves, themselves, yourselves

Pronoun Reference

For more information about pronoun reference, see pp. 188–89.

When you use a pronoun that refers to a noun, make sure that it's clear what the noun is. Don't use a pronoun that refers to a vague idea or that could refer to more than one noun.

VAGUE	In my history class, *they* claimed that the Vietnam War protesters were unpatriotic. [Who are *they*?]
CLEAR	In my history class, *a group of students* claimed that the Vietnam War protesters were unpatriotic.

UNCLEAR	John told Martin *he* needed to study. [Who needed to study?]
CLEAR	John told Martin, "I need to study."
CLEAR	John told Martin, "You need to study."
CLEAR	John needed to study, as he told Martin.
CLEAR	John thought Martin needed to study and told him so.

■ HOW TO Identify and Correct Vague Pronoun Reference

- Check that every pronoun clearly refers to a noun.
- If the reference isn't clear,
  - replace the pronoun with a noun, *or*
  - rewrite the sentence to delete the pronoun.

ACTIVITY 10 Correct Vague Pronoun Reference

In each of the following sentences, correct vague pronoun reference.

the characters
EXAMPLE On that television show, ~~they~~ are always saying the dumbest things.

1. At that office, they require both male and female employees to wear suits.

2. The musicians played a waltz and a traditional ballad. It was beautiful.

3. Fabiola confessed to Leah that she left her class notes at the restaurant.

4. At my health club, they recommend that we warm up before we do aerobics.

5. Seth told Andrew that he needed to drink less on the weekends.

6. There are too many scenes of violence and brutality. It should not have won the Academy Award.

7. In the documentary, it claimed that the mayor is corrupt.

8. While on vacation, I learned how to water ski and how to play croquet. It is not as easy as it looks.

9. In San Francisco, they have many landmarks of interest to tourists.

10. If Alicia tries to explain logarithms to Samia, she will become confused.

Learn more about pronoun agreement on pp. 189–90.

Pronoun Agreement

A pronoun should agree in number with the noun it refers to. To maintain pronoun agreement, use a singular pronoun to refer to a singular noun and a plural pronoun to refer to a plural noun. Remember that a singular noun also requires a singular verb form, and a plural noun requires a plural verb form.

INCORRECT PRONOUN AGREEMENT	My *friend* is bringing *their* own food to the picnic. [*Friend* is singular, but *their* is plural.]
CORRECT PRONOUN AGREEMENT	My *friend* is bringing *her* own food to the picnic.
CORRECT PRONOUN AGREEMENT	My *friends* are bringing *their* own food to the picnic.

Remember also to use a singular pronoun to refer to a singular indefinite pronoun. Singular indefinite pronouns include *anybody, anyone, anything, everybody, everyone, everything, nobody, somebody, someone,* and *something.*

INCORRECT PRONOUN AGREEMENT	My professor told *everyone* to take *their* laptop off the counter. [*Everyone* is singular, but *their* is plural.]
CORRECT PRONOUN AGREEMENT	My professor told the *students* to take *their* laptops off the counter.
CORRECT PRONOUN AGREEMENT	My professor told *everyone* to take *his or her* laptop off the counter.

ACTIVITY 11 Correct Errors in Pronoun Agreement

In each of the following sentences, correct the errors in pronoun agreement.

EXAMPLE A plumber will have to charge you more if they find cracks in the pipes.
(*Plumbers* written above *A plumber*, which is struck through)

1. A student will find more errors in an essay if they wait a few hours after writing it before proofreading it.

2. I need to talk to someone who has put snow chains on their tires.

3. Everybody brought their donation to the main office.

4. The player shouts "Bingo!" as soon as they have a winning card.

5. A psychiatrist must not betray their patients' confidentiality.

6. A movie star saves their biggest smile for the camera.

7. Nobody admitted that they had committed the vandalism.

8. Someone allows their dog to bark all day long.

9. Let me know when everyone has completed their questionnaires.

10. Every parent wants their children to be happy and successful.

■ HOW TO Correct Errors in Pronoun-Antecedent Agreement

- Check that singular pronouns (such as *I*, *he*, *she*, *his or her*, or *it*) refer either to singular nouns or to singular indefinite pronouns (such as *anyone, everyone, everybody, somebody,* and *someone*).
- Check that plural pronouns (such as *we, us, them,* and *their*) refer to plural nouns.
- Correct errors in pronoun agreement by making pronouns and nouns agree.

▶ ACTIVITY 12 Correct Pronoun Agreement

In the following paragraph, correct the errors in pronoun agreement.

EXAMPLE As long as we focus on the task at hand, each person in my study group can
              his or her
          get ~~their~~ needs met.

The last meeting of my statistics study group was disastrous. We met at the studio apartment of one of the group members, and they did not have enough chairs. Everyone who came was worried about their grade, but not everyone had completed their section of the homework problems. One person had loaned their calculator to a friend and had to share mine. Someone else only wanted us to do their work for them. A third person had to have every little thing explained to them.

Finally, one person got angry and left, saying they would save time by doing all the work themselves. This experience taught me something. The success of a study group requires every member to contribute as much as they can. Though each person must still understand the basic concepts for themselves, the group can help the individual refine what they already know.

For additional practice with using pronouns, go to **bedfordstmartins.com /choices** and click on **Exercise Central**.

☾ D. Adjectives

One of the best ways to expand sentences is to use adjectives, which can add interest to your writing. **Adjectives** modify nouns or pronouns by describing or adding information about them:

My *beautiful* mother never goes outside without makeup.

The *green* meadow is always restful on the eyes.

Adjectives may also show comparisons between things. When comparing two things, add *-er* to adjectives with one syllable or adjectives with two syllables ending in *-er*, *-le*, *-ow*, or *-ly*. Use the word *more* before all other adjectives with two, three, or more syllables.

This car is *smaller* than the one I owned before.

The seats are also *narrower*.

And, this car is *more unusual* than my other one.

When comparing three or more things, add *-est* to adjectives with one syllable or adjectives with two syllables ending in *-er*, *-le*, *-ow*, or *-ly*. Use the word *most* before all other adjectives with two, three, or more syllables.

This car is the *smallest* one I have ever owned.

This car has the *narrowest* seats of any car I have ever owned.

This car is the *most unusual* one on campus.

ACTIVITY 13 Identify Adjectives

In each of the following sentences, underline the adjectives. Some sentences have more than one adjective.

EXAMPLE Senator Johnson is a <u>powerful</u> person.

1. Professor Gupta teaches a worthwhile class.

2. The overdue book is a biography.

3. Andrea likes to eat dark chocolate with a glass of cold milk.

4. Jerome is the tallest person in his family.

5. The cold student pulled her wool hat over her ears while she waited for the next train.

6. Rene wears a waterproof jacket in rainy weather.

7. Among the three friends, Carlita is the best dancer.

8. Jamie owns a dented blue car.

9. I returned by the fastest route.

10. The defeated team ran off the muddy field.

ACTIVITY 14 Add Adjectives

Complete each of the following sentences by adding an adjective.

EXAMPLE The ____green____ coat fits you well.

1. The _____ cat sits in the window.

2. These cherries taste _____.

3. Alfredo took his _____ friend to the party.

4. Soraya has _____ brothers and sisters.

5. On _____ days, we wear _____ clothing.

6. I think that the _____ carpet looks pretty with the _____ wallpaper.

7. His family needs to move to a _____ house.

8. That hospital serves _____ meals to its patients.

9. That _____ child never seems to get what he deserves.

10. Arzella is one of the _____ workers but one of the best students.

For additional practice with using adjectives, go to **bedfordstmartins.com /choices** and click on **Exercise Central**.

E. Adverbs

Adverbs are another useful way to expand sentences. **Adverbs** modify verbs, adjectives, or other adverbs by describing or adding information about them. Adverbs usually answer the questions *how, when, where, why,* or *how often.* Many adverbs end in *-ly,* such as *slowly, noisily,* and *loudly*:

My favorite music is *never* played on the radio. [The adverb answers the question *How often is the music played?*]

The children played *nearby.* [The adverb answers the question *Where did the children play?*]

My wife *often* ate the dinner I made. [The adverb answers the question *When did the wife eat the dinner?*]

ACTIVITY 15 Identify Adverbs

In each of the following sentences, underline the adverbs.

EXAMPLE Doro <u>forcefully</u> threw the ball at the hitter.

1. The fans waited eagerly for concert tickets.

2. Is it true that crime never pays?

3. Traffic moved slowly on Van Ness Avenue.

4. The bored, complaining student soon dropped the class.

5. The pupils entered the school reluctantly.

6. My aunts and uncles secretly planned a surprise party for my grandfather.

7. The instructor of my Introduction to Ceramics class is very interesting.

8. My study group often remains in the library until it closes.

9. The candidate campaigned well in the urban neighborhoods.

10. Klaus speaks persuasively in front of large groups.

ACTIVITY 16 Add Adverbs

Complete each of the following sentences by adding an adverb.

EXAMPLE Guy practiced the saxophone ____*daily*____.

1. The customers _____ drank their iced tea.

2. You have _____ gotten to work on time.

3. Melina _____ eats at fast-food restaurants.

4. The punishment for plagiarism is _____ severe.

5. Darryl worked _____ on his English essay.

6. Winnie was talking _____ before she was interrupted.

7. My classmates _____ do their weekend homework on Sunday nights.

8. The football team _____ won the game.

9. Chong is _____ reliable.

10. Yolanda _____ sneaked up behind her boyfriend.

For additional practice with using adverbs, go to **bedfordstmartins.com /choices** and click on **Exercise Central**.

17

Combining Sentences

To express different kinds of ideas, you need to know how to write different kinds of sentences. One way to create different kinds of sentences is to combine them. In this chapter, you'll learn to combine sentences using sentence coordination and sentence subordination.

A. Coordination

When you have two or more short, closely related sentences in a row that are equally important, your ideas can seem choppy and unconnected. To avoid this problem, combine the sentences, making them *coordinate*, or equal. To join two equally important sentences, use a coordinating conjunction and a comma or a conjunctive adverb and a semicolon.

Coordinating Conjunctions and Commas

One way to combine equally important sentences is to use one of the **coordinating conjunctions**, which are *for, and, nor, but, or, yet,* and *so.* To remember these conjunctions, imagine the word *FANBOYS.* Each letter in this word is the first letter of one of the coordinating conjunctions.

COORDINATING CONJUNCTIONS

Conjunction	Definition
F—for	because
A—and	in addition, also
N—nor	not, neither
B—but	however, unless
O—or	as another possibility
Y—yet	however, unless
S—so	as a result

When you use a coordinating conjunction to combine short, closely related sentences, put a comma before the conjunction. Be sure to select a conjunction that logically connects the sentences.

CHOPPY SENTENCES	The traffic jam delayed us. We arrived on time for the party.
SENTENCES COMBINED WITH *BUT*	The traffic jam delayed us, *but* we arrived on time for the party.
CHOPPY SENTENCES	I braided my niece's hair. I ironed her dress.
SENTENCES COMBINED WITH *AND*	I braided my niece's hair, *and* I ironed her dress.
CHOPPY SENTENCES	Adam was hungry. He microwaved a slice of pizza.
SENTENCES COMBINED WITH *SO*	Adam was hungry, *so* he microwaved a slice of pizza.

■ HOW TO Combine Sentences Using Coordinating Conjunctions

- Use one of the *FANBOYS* conjunctions (*for, and, nor, but, or, yet,* and *so*).
- Put a comma before the conjunction.

(ACTIVITY 1 Combine Sentences Using Coordinating Conjunctions)

Combine each of the following pairs of sentences using a coordinating conjunction and a comma.

EXAMPLE Jorge has a law degree. <del>He</del> has never practiced law.
                                  , but he

1. Leigh was upset when she opened her cell phone bill. She owed more than four hundred dollars.

2. Rosa insisted on buying strawberry ice cream. I would have preferred chocolate chip.

3. I fell asleep in class. I missed next week's reading assignment.

4. Elizabeth carefully read the contract for the loan. She still couldn't understand it.

5. I went grocery shopping this morning. I did the laundry this afternoon.

6. Michael set his alarm clock for 7:30. He had an early class in the morning.

7. Hetty forgot to return the library book. She received a fine.

8. Malik worked really hard on his résumé. He got the job he wanted.

9. You can buy the racy red sports car. You can buy the practical brown sedan.

10. Adrianna spent hours looking over travel brochures. She ended up going to the same beach she had visited for the past three years.

Conjunctive Adverbs and Semicolons

Another way to join equally important sentences is to use a **conjunctive adverb** and a *semicolon*. The conjunctive adverb (often called a *transition*) shows how the two sentences fit together. A semicolon is used before the conjunctive adverb, and a comma is used after it.

Conjunctive Adverbs

Add an idea: *also, furthermore, in addition, moreover*

Show a different point: *however, instead, nevertheless, on the other hand, otherwise*

Show a similar point: *likewise, similarly*

Stress a key idea: *certainly, indeed, in fact, undoubtedly*

Show a consequence or result: *as a result, consequently, so, therefore, thus*

Point out a sequence: *first, second, next, finally*

CHOPPY SENTENCES	My daughter majored in psychology in college. She really wanted to be a writer.
SENTENCES COMBINED WITH *HOWEVER*	My daughter majored in psychology in college; *however*, she really wanted to be a writer.
CHOPPY SENTENCES	I am traveling to Argentina next summer. I want to learn Spanish.
SENTENCES COMBINED WITH *THEREFORE*	I am traveling to Argentina next summer; *therefore*, I want to learn Spanish.
CHOPPY SENTENCES	The neighborhood grocery store is small. It's very expensive.
SENTENCES COMBINED WITH *MOREOVER*	The neighborhood grocery store is small; *moreover*, it's very expensive.

■ HOW TO Combine Sentences Using Conjunctive Adverbs

- Select a conjunctive adverb that shows the logical connection between the sentences.
- Use a semicolon before the conjunctive adverb.
- Use a comma after the conjunctive adverb.

◀ ACTIVITY 2 Combine Sentences Using Conjunctive Adverbs ▶

Combine each of the following pairs of sentences using a semicolon and a conjunctive adverb. Be sure to include a comma after the conjunctive adverb.

; therefore,

EXAMPLE My hours at work have been increased,/ I have more money to save.
                                                              ^

1. Akio disliked the political ads during the last election. He decided to register as an Independent.

2. The children gathered roses, violets, and irises from their grandmother's garden. They ironed the flowers in waxed paper and labeled them with black ink.

3. Owners of small specialty stores find it hard to compete with large department stores. They need to advertise their products on television and the Internet.

4. Corinne was hired as a salesclerk. She got a better job the following week and quit.

5. Einstein had a reputation as an absentminded scientist. He could be very forgetful.

6. Landscape artists are more than just gardeners. They are both scientists and artists.

7. I stepped out into the foggy morning unable to see a thing. I heard something crunch beneath my feet.

8. This semester I'm working the graveyard shift at the food mart. I can barely stay awake in my 8:00 a.m. class.

9. Pacifists often demonstrate against warfare. They have been conscientious objectors during various wars.

10. Steve Jobs changed our lives with electronic devices such as the Apple computer and the iPhone. Some people call him this century's Thomas Edison.

For additional practice with using coordination, go to **bedfordstmartins.com /choices** and click on **Exercise Central**.

◖ B. Subordination

Use **sentence subordination** to combine two sentences that aren't equally important. Subordinating conjunctions and relative pronouns help you express the logical connection between the sentences.

Subordinating Conjunctions

One way to combine two sentences using subordination is to use an appropriate **subordinating conjunction**.

Subordinating Conjunctions

after	if	until	wherever
although	since	when	whether
because	though	whenever	while
before	unless	where	

The subordinating conjunction begins the part of the combined sentence that's less important to expressing the message.

CHOPPY SENTENCES	People are marrying later in life. The divorce rate hasn't decreased.
SENTENCES COMBINED WITH *ALTHOUGH*	*Although* people are marrying later in life, the divorce rate hasn't decreased.
CHOPPY SENTENCES	Greg made sure to save several thousand dollars. He did this before he quit his job.
SENTENCES COMBINED WITH *BEFORE*	Greg made sure to save several thousand dollars *before* he quit his job.
CHOPPY SENTENCES	You'll never understand the experience of being homeless. The only way to understand it is to live through it.
SENTENCES COMBINED WITH *UNLESS*	You'll never understand the experience of being homeless *unless* you live through it.

Sometimes you can just put the conjunction before the less important sentence of the original two, as in the first example. But often you'll also need to delete part of that sentence or change it in other ways, as in the second and third examples. Sometimes the conjunction you need will already be in the less important sentence, like *before* in the second example.

The word group that begins with a subordinating conjunction is called a **subordinate clause** or a *dependent clause*. Put a comma after a subordinate clause when it begins a sentence. In general, don't use a comma before a subordinate clause that ends a sentence.

COMMA	*After the children sat down*, the family began Thanksgiving dinner.
NO COMMA	The family began Thanksgiving dinner *after the children sat down*.

■HOW TO Combine Sentences Using Subordinating Conjunctions

- Decide which sentence is less important.
- Choose an appropriate subordinating conjunction to express the way the ideas in the two sentences are connected.
- Combine the sentences by putting the subordinating conjunction before the less important part of the new sentence and then deleting or changing any other words as necessary.
- Use a comma after the subordinate clause when it begins the combined sentence.
- In general, don't use a comma before the subordinate clause when it ends the sentence.

◖ **ACTIVITY 3 Combine Sentences Using Subordinating Conjunctions** ◗

Combine each of the following pairs of sentences using a subordinating conjunction. Add or delete words as necessary.

EXAMPLE I aced my art history exam,̸I studied for three hours last night.
                                    because

1. The number of arrests for drunk driving has increased. This has happened because there are stricter DUI laws.

2. The newspaper arrived late. I wasn't able to read about the big earthquake in Alaska.

3. I couldn't find the book at the library. Finally, I asked one of the librarians for help.

4. I saw my friends in the restaurant. They were gossiping about their coworkers.

5. I have a hard time recycling my garbage. The recycling center is too far from my house.

6. You have to create a secure password. Then, you can access your account again.

7. I kept the music low. My roommate left.

8. The politician finished her speech. Her followers cheered.

9. I would have stayed in class. The professor did not show up.

10. I didn't rent the apartment. The building didn't have a laundry room.

Relative Pronouns

Another way to combine choppy sentences is to use a **relative pronoun** to subordinate the information in the less important sentence.

Relative Pronouns

that	who
what	whoever
whatever	whom
which	whomever
whichever	whose

As with a subordinating conjunction, the relative pronoun goes before the part of the combined sentence that is less important to the meaning. The word group that begins with a relative pronoun is called a **relative clause**.

CHOPPY SENTENCES Athletes will stay in shape. They'll stay in shape if they work out regularly.

SENTENCES COMBINED WITH *WHO* Athletes *who* work out regularly will stay in shape.

CHOPPY SENTENCES	Ayana baked the cupcakes. They were moist and delicious.
SENTENCES COMBINED WITH *WHICH*	Ayana baked the cupcakes, *which* were moist and delicious.
CHOPPY SENTENCES	One of my favorite songs is "Big Yellow Taxi." I mean the version that the Counting Crows recorded.
SENTENCES COMBINED WITH *THAT*	One of my favorite songs is the version of "Big Yellow Taxi" *that* the Counting Crows recorded.

Don't use commas before or after a relative clause that is necessary to identify what it refers to, as in the following example:

The letter to the editor *that Anita wrote* was published in the local newspaper.

No commas are used before or after the relative clause because it's a necessary part of the sentence. It tells which letter to the editor—the one that Anita wrote—was published in the newspaper.

In contrast, use commas when the relative clause gives information that's not essential to the sentence:

The letter, *which is on the topic of school funding*, is somewhere in my backpack.

Commas are used in this example because the relative clause—*which is on the topic of school funding*—simply adds information about a letter that's already been mentioned. The meaning of the sentence is still clear without it: *The letter is still in my backpack*.

Don't use commas with relative clauses that begin with *that*:

The letter *that I wrote* was not published.

■ HOW TO Combine Sentences Using Relative Pronouns

- Decide which sentence is less important.
- Choose an appropriate relative pronoun to connect the information in the less important sentence to that in the other sentence.
- Use commas when the relative clause can be deleted and the sentence still includes all necessary information.
- Don't use commas when the relative clause is a necessary part of the sentence.

ACTIVITY 4 Combine Sentences Using Relative Pronouns

Combine each of the following pairs of sentences using a relative pronoun. Add or delete words as necessary.

EXAMPLE Jeans _, which are pants made out of denim,_ were often worn by cowboys because they were so sturdy. ~~Jeans are pants made out of denim.~~

1. Jeans have changed a great deal over the years. Jeans are still very popular.

2. Jeans were invented by Levi Strauss. They were first worn by miners in the 1850s.

3. The jeans never tore or fell apart. The jeans were worn by the miners.

4. In the 1950s, jeans became popular with teenagers. The teenagers thought that they were cool.

5. Jeans were a big part of the 1960s. Hippies started wearing them.

6. One popular style was bell-bottom jeans. This style was often decorated with flowers and peace signs.

7. I have a picture of my mother wearing jeans. The jeans have frayed hems and many holes.

8. Now just about everyone wears jeans. These jeans come in many styles.

9. Skinny jeans have very straight and tight legs. Skinny jeans are popular among teenage girls.

10. People wear jeans. These people live all over the world.

For additional practice with using subordination, go to **bedfordstmartins.com /choices** and click on **Exercise Central**.

C. Sentence-Combining Exercises

The following sentence-combining exercises will give you practice using sentence coordination and subordination.

Specific Methods of Combining Sentences

Use the methods identified in the directions for combining sentences in the following activities.

ACTIVITY 5 Combine Sentences Using Coordination

Combine each of the following pairs of sentences using either a comma and a coordinating conjunction or a semicolon, a conjunctive adverb, and a comma. Add or delete words as necessary.

EXAMPLE In 2007, *Keeping Up with the Kardashians* debuted on E!. ~~The~~ , and the show quickly became one of the highest-rated shows on television.

1. The reality show follows the lives of Bruce and Kris Jenner's combined family. Most of the episodes focus on the three oldest daughters, Kourtney, Kim, and Khloé Kardashian.

2. Bruce Jenner was famous for breaking the world record and winning a gold medal in the decathlon at the 1976 Olympics. His sons from a previous marriage, Brandon and Brody, have also appeared on their own reality shows.

3. The Kardashians' father, the late attorney Robert Kardashian, was famous for representing O. J. Simpson. His daughters gained recognition as American socialites.

4. Kim came into the national spotlight in 2007 after a sex-tape scandal and resulting *Playboy* appearance. The Kardashian fame grew into a profitable reality series.

5. The show depicts the daily routine of the Kardashians. Spin-off shows feature Kourtney, Kim, and Khloé's attempts to build their line of fashion boutiques.

6. The Kardashians' behavior at first seemed outrageous. They are a loving family.

7. The Kardashians squabble like typical siblings. Kris, the mother, holds the family together.

8. Kim's $10 million wedding to pro basketball player Kris Humphries in 2011 was seen by an estimated 10.5 million viewers. The marriage lasted only 72 days.

9. Some critics claimed that the wedding was arranged for publicity. The family denied this.

10. Despite the Kardashians' extravagant lifestyle and occasionally odd behavior, many people admire them. They clearly love one another very much.

ACTIVITY 6 Combine Sentences Using Coordination

Combine each of the following pairs of sentences using either a comma and a coordinating conjunction or a semicolon, a conjunctive adverb, and a comma. Add or delete words as necessary.

EXAMPLE   The station wagon used to be one of America's most popular vehicles. The ~~The~~
; however, the ^
SUV (sports utility vehicle) replaced the station wagon in popularity.

1. In the 1990s, SUVs became popular with many American consumers. They helped automobile companies make big profits.

2. At first, they were built for people to drive in extreme conditions and on dirt roads. Now, they are mostly used for city driving.

3. They are bought by parents who like the large size of the vehicles. They can fit their growing families into them with ease.

4. Some buyers imagine themselves driving off-road in a rugged, beautiful area of the country. They would never actually do that.

5. Increases in gas prices have influenced the size of SUVs. Many SUVs are now smaller and more energy efficient.

6. Americans prefer large cars. Europeans buy much smaller cars.

7. Gas in Europe Is much more expensive than in the United States. European consumers have good reason to use as little as possible.

8. At one time, Japanese-made SUVs were more popular with American consumers. The profits of American car companies declined.

9. In general, American-made vehicles have become more popular. Their resale rates are higher than they used to be.

10. Many Americans still love their SUVs. It will be interesting to see if this love affair continues when gas prices rise.

◀ ACTIVITY 7 Combine Sentences Using Subordination ▶

Combine each of the following pairs of sentences using a subordinating conjunction. Add or delete words as necessary.

EXAMPLE   Scientists often use placebos in experiments. They want to test the effective-
because they ^
ness of a new treatment.

1. A placebo is a fake treatment for an illness. Sometimes a placebo works as well as real medicine.

2. Scientists use placebos when they test the effectiveness of a new medicine. They do this to make sure the new medicine will really help patients get well.

3. In an experiment, one group of patients receives the medicine being tested. Another group of patients receives the placebo.

4. Both the medicine being tested and the placebo can be given in the form of a pill. The placebo pill might be made up entirely of sugar or some other harmless substance.

5. The patients who receive the new medicine are called the *experimental group*. The patients who receive the placebo are called the *control group*.

6. The patients don't know which group they're in. This process is called a "blind" experiment.

7. The new medicine must be very successful in treating the patients in the experimental group. The power of suggestion is so strong.

8. Sometimes the patients who receive placebos improve a great deal. The patients who receive the actual medicine improve less.

9. Scientists speculate that placebos work for some people. These people strongly believe that the placebo will make them get better.

10. The placebo effect can be very powerful. Scientists are beginning to study it seriously.

ACTIVITY 8 Combine Sentences Using Subordination

Combine each of the following pairs of sentences using a subordinating conjunction. Add or delete words as necessary.

EXAMPLE People who rush into marriage often end up divorced. ~~They~~ don't know their
partner well enough.
because they

1. The institution of marriage has changed greatly over the years. Most people still get married.

2. Most experts agree that people should take their time getting to know each other. They should do this before they get married.

3. The couple should know each other well. They have a better chance of not getting divorced.

4. Couples first come to understand the strengths and weaknesses of their potential partner. They do this when they are getting to know each other.

5. Couples find out if they have similar beliefs and interests. These similar beliefs and interests will help them have a happy marriage.

6. Couples should discuss each other's religious beliefs. They need to do this to prevent conflicts in the marriage.

7. Couples might have problems. This could happen if one partner is very conservative and the other is very liberal.

8. Couples also need to find out how responsible their potential partner is. They need to do this to make sure they can rely on their partner.

9. Couples need to learn to communicate well. Good communication will help them get through difficult times together.

10. Marriage is rewarding but often very difficult. It is important for couples to know each other well before the wedding day.

◀ ACTIVITY 9 Combine Sentences Using Subordination ▶

Combine each of the following pairs of sentences using a relative pronoun. Add or delete words when necessary.

EXAMPLE Rocky Mountain National Park Is located in one of the most beautiful areas ^, which in the country. It contains remote areas where you can find solitude.

1. Rocky Mountain National Park is in Colorado. It is one of America's favorite vacation spots.

2. This park is also one of America's most popular national parks. It is visited by 3 million people a year.

3. Several trails in the park are not well known. These trails are in remote locations.

4. The Tonahutu Creek trail follows the Continental Divide. The trail is 21 miles long.

5. The Never Summer Loop trail is well named. This trail has mountains that are almost 13,000 feet high.

6. Sometimes the snow never melts on this trail. The snow can be very deep.

7. Another trail people don't use very much is the Lost Lake trail. This trail is very steep.

8. The Lost Lake trail leads to Lost Lake. This lake is surrounded by breathtaking mountain scenery.

9. These three trails are great for backpacking. Not many people use these trails.

10. If you go backpacking, you can experience nature without crowds. Backpacking is strenuous and fun.

ACTIVITY 10 **Combine Sentences Using Subordination**

Combine each of the following pairs of sentences using a relative pronoun. Add or delete words when necessary.

EXAMPLE Teenagers $\overset{who}{\underset{\wedge}{are}}$ part of the abstinence movement. ~~These teenagers~~ don't have sex until they're married.

1. Abstinence has grown in popularity among young people. Abstinence refers to waiting until marriage to have sex.

2. This movement is being called a "sexual revolution." It is a sexual revolution very different from the sexual revolution of the 1960s.

3. The sexual revolution involved not waiting until marriage to have sex. The sexual revolution was the one that happened in the 1960s.

4. The current sexual revolution is a result of several factors. These factors include religion, family pressure, and health issues.

5. One reason for the interest in abstinence is that people are afraid of sexually transmitted diseases (STDs). STDs can cause illness and even death.

6. Other people remain abstinent until marriage because of religious beliefs. These beliefs discourage people from having sex outside of marriage.

7. Although abstinence is becoming more popular, most young people don't wait until marriage to have sex. These young people live in the United States.

8. Some people maintain that sex-education programs should promote only abstinence. These people are generally conservative.

9. Other people say that sex-education programs should mention abstinence as only one possibility. These people are generally liberal.

10. The abstinence movement is an interesting social trend. This social trend might continue to grow in popularity.

Various Methods of Combining Sentences

Up till now, you have practiced combining sentences using just one or two methods at a time. Now you will be given more choices about the best method to join particular sentences:

1. **a coordinating conjunction with a comma:**

   for, and, nor, but, or, yet, so

2. **a semicolon and a conjunctive adverb:**

   to add an idea: also, furthermore, in addition, moreover

   to show a different point: however, instead, nevertheless, on the other hand, otherwise

   to show a similar point: likewise, similarly

   to stress a key idea: certainly, indeed, in fact, undoubtedly

   to show a consequence or result: as a result, consequently, so, therefore, thus

   to point out a sequence: first, second, next, finally

3. **a subordinating conjunction:**

   after, although, because, before, even though, if, once, since, that, though, unless, until, when, whenever, where, whether, while, whomever

4. **a relative pronoun:**

   that, what, whatever, which, whichever, who, whoever, whom, whomever, whose

ACTIVITY 11 Combine Sentences Using Different Methods

Combine each of the following pairs of sentences using an appropriate method from the preceding list. Add or delete words as necessary.

EXAMPLE The recent economic downturn has changed the entire U.S. economy. The *, which* downturn has affected college students a great deal.

1. To cover their operating expenses, colleges and universities rely on money from the state and federal governments. State and federal government budgets have been cut because of the bad economy.

2. Most colleges and universities have had to raise tuition and fees. This increase in tuition and fees has made college much more expensive.

3. More and more students are applying for student loans. When they graduate, they owe more money than previous students owed.

4. The job market is also more challenging than it used to be. This is because of the high unemployment rate in many parts of the country.

5. College degrees are still very important for economic success. The degrees can be in any major.

6. People earn around $650,000 more over the course of their careers than do people with only a high school diploma. These are people who graduate from college.

7. People who go to college also tend to be healthier than those who don't go to college. They are healthier both physically and mentally.

8. College graduates also advance higher in the workplace than do those without college diplomas. They are more likely to become CEOs and other leaders.

9. Getting a college degree is more expensive than it has been in the past. This is because of the recent economic downturn.

10. In the long run, a college degree is worthwhile. A college degree now costs more.

ACTIVITY 12 Combine Sentences Using Different Methods

Combine each of the following sets of sentences using an appropriate method from the list on page 449. Add or delete words as necessary.

EXAMPLE Movies about spring break have been popular for years. ~~These movies often show college students partying on a beach.~~ *, which often show college students partying on a beach,*

1. To many people, spring break is a time when college students go wild. Spring break is a weeklong break in March or April.

2. Spring break is notorious for misbehavior. Some college students drink excessively at this time.

3. Not all college students party over spring break. Many college students don't have time to party.

4. Last spring break, I worked overtime to save up money. I needed the money to go to summer school.

5. This spring break, I'll probably catch up on my studies. I'm taking six courses. In three of these courses, I have to write research papers.

6. My friend Mike spent spring break taking care of his children. Mike is a single father. He has sole custody of the kids.

7. Some people think college students just goof off. Those people don't know what we go through.

8. Most college students have to work their way through college. They might have children to raise. They might have parents to support.

9. Nationwide, only a small percentage of college students are supported by their parents. Most college students pay their own way.

10. I wish spring break were a real break. It's really just a chance to do more work.

ACTIVITY 13 Combine Sentences Using Different Methods

Combine each of the following sets of sentences using an appropriate method from the list on page 455. Add or delete words as necessary.

EXAMPLE Blindness can lead to lifestyle restrictions. ~~These restrictions will occur~~ unless help is available.

1. Dan Shaw's life was changed. His doctor diagnosed him with retinitis pigmentosa. This is an incurable eye disease. This happened when Dan Shaw was seventeen.

2. Slowly he lost his sight. His life became very limited.

3. He wanted to be more involved with the world. He checked out his options.

4. He didn't want a seeing-eye dog. He had owned a dog. The dog died.

5. He heard about a program run by Janet and Don Burleson. They were training miniature horses as guides for the visually impaired.

6. Dan was interested in having a guide horse. Miniature horses have a life span of thirty to forty years. He would likely not have to endure the death of the horse.

7. His guide horse leads him everywhere. His guide horse is named Cuddles.

8. Cuddles responds to more than twenty-five voice commands. She is housebroken. She can see in the dark.

9. People are often curious. This happens when they see Dan being guided by Cuddles. They ask Dan questions about Cuddles.

10. Dan is happy to talk about Cuddles. He wants others to know about guide horses.

⬛ **ACTIVITY 14** **Combine Sentences Using Different Methods** ⬛

Combine each of the following sets of sentences using an appropriate method from the list on page 449. Add or delete words as necessary.

EXAMPLE *If people* ~~People~~ have a healthy lifestyle~~.~~ *, their* ~~Their~~ chances of getting diabetes will be reduced.

1. About 25.8 million children and adults in the United States are believed to have diabetes. Nearly 7 million of these people don't know they have diabetes.

2. Diabetes has no cure. It can be controlled.

3. Diabetes can cause heart disease, blindness, kidney failure, and amputations. It is a very serious disease.

4. Most diabetes is type 2. It is associated with obesity. It is also associated with poor lifestyle habits.

5. Children today are fatter. Children exercise less. They eat unhealthy food.

6. Obese children will develop serious health problems. This will happen if they don't lose weight.

7. Children are our future. We need to help children be healthier. We need to help them live long lives.

8. Many schools are teaching children about diabetes. They have many other subjects to teach.

9. Parents should be good role models. They are very busy. Parents should eat well and exercise regularly.

10. Diabetes is a major health problem. It will continue to get worse. We need to stop the spread of this disease.

For additional practice with combining sentences, go to **bedfordstmartins.com /choices** and click on **Exercise Central**.

18

Improving Sentences

To improve sentences, you'll need to eliminate sentence fragments, run-on sentences, and comma splices. Also, you should correct misplaced and dangling modifiers, try to use the active voice as much as possible, and use parallel sentence structure for groups of words that are part of a pair or series.

A. Sentence Fragments

A **sentence fragment** is an incomplete sentence that is presented as if it were a complete sentence. Some sentence fragments are **phrases:** they lack a subject or a verb or both.

The grocery store next to the bank.

Built a playhouse in the backyard.

At the bus station.

Other sentence fragments are **subordinate clauses:** they have a subject and a verb, but they begin with a subordinating conjunction or a relative pronoun.

Subordinating Conjunctions

after	since	where
although	that	wherever
because	though	whether
before	unless	while
even though	until	whomever
if	when	
once	whenever	

Here are three sentence fragments that begin with subordinating conjunctions:

For more about subordinate clauses, turn to pp. 425–26.

After the party is over.

Because it was raining outside.

When I come back from vacation.

Relative Pronouns

that	who
what	whoever
whatever	whom
which	whomever
whichever	whose

Here are three fragments that begin with relative pronouns:

That they ate at the bakery.

Who left the rambling message.

Which caused him to cry.

ACTIVITY 1 Identify Sentence Fragments

In the space provided, indicate whether each of the following word groups is a sentence fragment or a complete sentence.

EXAMPLE Since it will be rainy tomorrow. _____*fragment*_____

1. My son plays soccer and basketball. _____

2. In Mimi's old backpack. _____

3. Which was the first house constructed of recycled materials. _____

4. May I charge that to your credit card? _____

5. Because these french fries are too salty. _____

6. The shoe salesman earned a large commission. _____

7. Speaking as softly as she could. _____

8. A perfect score on the pop quiz. _____

9. This vacuum cleaner is effective on both deep carpets and bare floors.

_____

10. Vandalized mailboxes throughout the neighborhood. _____

How do you correct a sentence fragment? One way is to connect it to the sentence that comes before or after it.

> **FRAGMENT** *Although he had to get up early in the morning.* Kotoyo didn't get home until midnight.
>
> **SENTENCE** Although he had to get up early in the morning, Kotoyo didn't get home until midnight.

FRAGMENT Her favorite gift was the silk scarf. *That her grandmother had given her.*

SENTENCE Her favorite gift was the silk scarf that her grandmother had given her.

Another way to correct a sentence fragment is to turn it into a complete sentence. If the fragment is a phrase, add any missing subject or verb. If the fragment begins with a subordinating conjunction, delete the conjunction. If the fragment begins with a relative pronoun, change the pronoun to a noun.

FRAGMENT Running down the hall.
SENTENCE Matthew was running down the hall.

FRAGMENT *Because* the plane was late getting into Austin.
SENTENCE The plane was late getting into Austin.

FRAGMENT *Which* violated the drug laws in Michigan.
SENTENCE The prescription violated the drug laws in Michigan.

■ HOW TO Correct a Sentence Fragment

- Connect it to the sentence that comes before or after it.
- Rewrite it as a complete sentence.

ACTIVITY 2 Correct Sentence Fragments

Make each of the following fragments a complete sentence.

EXAMPLE ~~Polluting~~ our beautiful national parks.
Trash from campers is polluting

1. After taking a monthlong tour of Malaysia.

2. Because the batteries were low.

3. The load of sheets in the dryer.

4. The laptop next to the photocopier.

5. Who looked frightened enough to faint.

6. The car with the small scratch.

7. Although fried food is not very healthy.

8. While Victor was learning how to type.

9. If I knew these people better.

10. Surprised by the unexpected news.

ACTIVITY 3 Correct Sentence Fragments

Each of the following word groups contains one or more sentence fragments. Make each word group into a single complete sentence, either by connecting each fragment to a complete sentence or by rewriting each fragment as a complete sentence.

because
EXAMPLE Magda jogged every morning. ~~Because~~ she was preparing to run a marathon.

1. The concert that begins at 8:30 tonight.

2. Whomever Ryan picks as his wife. I'm prepared to like her.

3. That gave the children more freedom.

4. Alonzo cares for his sister's children on Wednesday and Thursday nights. Because he's free on those nights.

5. Let's try to go to the concert. If the tickets aren't too expensive and my car is working.

6. I'm jealous of Pilar. Who received an A on her report. Even though she didn't spend much time writing it.

7. I could clean my whole house. While the Web page loads.

8. His mother didn't like Jason's dyed blue hair. Said it was an embarrassment to the family.

9. I really liked my blind date. Until he lit up a cigarette.

10. Trying to keep my balance while standing on one foot, bending at the waist, and holding my arms in a graceful arc above my head.

ACTIVITY 4 Correct Sentence Fragments in a Paragraph

Edit the following paragraph to eliminate sentence fragments.

I am studying
EXAMPLE ~~Studying~~ to become an elementary school teacher.

• Because I want to teach my students to take care of themselves, I have a special interest in physical education. During my student teaching, I remembered my childhood experiences playing team sports like softball. Alone in left field. My classmates laughing at my mistakes. I should have been taught how to catch a fly ball. Without fear of being hit in the face. I never learned games like soccer and basketball. Which keep every player constantly involved in the game. I want P.E. to be better for my students. All children can learn to enjoy using their bodies. Though not everybody can become a professional athlete. I want my future students to enjoy a lifetime of fitness.

For additional practice with eliminating sentence fragments, go to **bedfordstmartins.com /choices** and click on **Exercise Central**.

B. Run-on Sentences

A **run-on sentence** occurs when two sentences (or sometimes more) are incorrectly presented as a single sentence, without any punctuation between them.

> **RUN-ON** The party was over it was time to go home.
> **CORRECT** The party was over. It was time to go home.

> **RUN-ON** I went to the store I forgot to get the flour.
> **CORRECT** I went to the store, but I forgot to get the flour.

ACTIVITY 5 Identify Run-on Sentences

In the space provided, indicate whether each of the following word groups is a run-on sentence or a correct sentence.

EXAMPLE Boyz II Men was a famous R&B band from the 1990s it was based in Philadelphia. _____run-on_____

1. David is friendlier than he appears he only frowns to hide his nervousness.

   _____

2. With her fingers poised over the piano keys, Carmel waited for the conductor's baton to drop. _____

3. That yogurt is too high in carbohydrates for my diabetic diet I need to have the low-fat cottage cheese. _____

4. Hard hats are required in this area the roof is being replaced. _____

5. No one volunteered to supervise the dance until the principal offered to buy the chaperones dinner. _____

6. My wife likes pizza my son likes hamburgers I prefer sushi. _____

7. Ray and Serena put a green decal on their black suitcase so that they could recognize it more easily at the airport. _____

8. Delia ran out the door in such a hurry that she left her coat draped over the sofa. _____

9. Kazuko welcomed the visitor into her office she asked her assistant to bring them both coffee. _____

10. Nigel was astonished when he received first prize he never thought that he would win an award. _____

One way to correct a run-on sentence is to turn it into two sentences, adding a period at the end of the first sentence and capitalizing the first word of the second sentence.

> **RUN-ON** The concert was supposed to begin at 8:00 it actually began at 9:30.
> **CORRECT** The concert was supposed to begin at 8:00. It actually began at 9:30.

> **RUN-ON** The digital camera is too expensive it costs more than three hundred dollars.
> **CORRECT** The digital camera is too expensive. It costs more than three hundred dollars.

See Chapter 17 to find out more about these methods of combining sentences.

A run-on sentence can also be corrected by putting a comma and a co-ordinating conjunction (*for, and, nor, but, or, yet,* or *so*) between the two sentences.

> **RUN-ON** The apartment is dirty the kitchen appliances are broken.
> **CORRECT** The apartment is dirty, and the kitchen appliances are broken.

> **RUN-ON** I registered for classes late I still got a good schedule.
> **CORRECT** I registered for classes late, but I still got a good schedule.

A third way to correct a run-on sentence is to put a semicolon between the two sentences. Often, you can also use a conjunctive adverb—such as *however, therefore, also, instead,* or *as a result*—after the semicolon. If you use a conjunctive adverb, put a comma after it.

> **RUN-ON** I've been working out I still haven't lost any weight.
> **CORRECT** I've been working out; however, I still haven't lost any weight.

> **RUN-ON** Computer technology is improving computers are getting cheaper.
> **CORRECT** Computer technology is improving; computers are getting cheaper.

> ### ■ HOW TO Correct a Run-on Sentence
>
> - Separate it into two sentences.
> - Add a comma and a coordinating conjunction.
> - Add a semicolon and, if appropriate, a conjunctive adverb and a comma.

ACTIVITY 6 Correct Run-on Sentences

Correct each of the following run-on sentences using a period and a capital letter; a comma and a coordinating conjunction; or a semicolon, a conjunctive adverb, and a comma.

EXAMPLE While Fred was watching the news, the electricity went out *, and* it was two hours before it came back on again.

1. Solange posed for the picture, the feather on her antique hat framing her face she found the waist and collar of the dress a little confining.

2. Before Benjamin applied for a job at Datacorp, he researched the company at the library he wanted to be well prepared for the interview.

3. Waiting for the tour bus, the family shivered on the windy corner they had expected warmer weather on their summer vacation.

4. Leland's motorcycle is his prized possession he had to sell it to pay his college tuition.

5. Because Olivia had never been surfing, she took lessons she felt ready to tackle the waves.

6. Paolo has thinning hair, glasses, and stooped shoulders everyone thinks he is a librarian he is a meteorologist at an Antarctic research station.

7. Toni gives her son a generous allowance and does not expect any help around the house from him Toni's brother expects his children to do chores if they want spending money.

8. Dark clouds gather overhead while trees toss in the wind rain does not fall.

9. Tai wanted to prove her trustworthiness to her parents she made it her responsibility to take her younger brother and sister to school.

10. Using a sharp jerk of his wrist, Simón flipped the pancake in the skillet his uncle taught him this trick when Simón was a child.

ACTIVITY 7 Correct Run-on Sentences

Correct each of the following run-on sentences using a period and a capital letter; a comma and a coordinating conjunction; or a semicolon, a conjunctive adverb, and a comma.

EXAMPLE Jake loved NASCAR races ; in fact, he had the autographs of several famous drivers.

1. Jasmine's parents made her return the prom dress they insisted she find one that was less revealing.

2. Aunt Edna poured tea into everyone's cup we sipped politely, although we would have preferred coffee.

3. I cannot sleep the shadows of the tree branches outside my window stretch across my bedroom wall like grasping fingers.

4. Damien put his ear to the door but heard nothing he wished doors still had keyholes that he could look through.

5. The rain began as soon as Kenneth washed his car it always rained after he washed his car.

6. Armend smiled at his bookshelf with pride it was his first one that was not made of boards and cinder blocks.

7. Not a single car at the dealership had been within Robert and Carolina's budget they drove their old car home in disappointment.

8. With the trees trimmed back, Malik enjoyed a better view from his living room the lights of the city twinkled below.

9. I turned in someone else's essay as my own the professor never found out.

10. Justin experimented with one hair color after another starting with burgundy, he then tried orange, blue, and purple none looked natural, but all looked funky.

ACTIVITY 8 Correct Run-on Sentences in a Paragraph

Edit the following paragraph to correct the run-on sentences.

EXAMPLE Watching the natural world is soothing ; in fact, it is as good for the soul as meditating.

The sun burns bright and hot however the world is shady and cool under the pine tree. Nestled within a deep hole in the thick needles underfoot, a turtle dozes. I look up a bird feeder is in my hand. The feeder weighs over four pounds I search for a strong, low branch. Two startled doves take flight their wings whistle as if to express their alarm. Three grackles hop from limb to limb, black and almost as big as crows. More grackles join the flock they scream their long, thick beaks gape menacingly. A tiny hummingbird darts between the large, black birds its bright patch of throat feathers flashes red in the flickering light. Several sparrows wait on a nearby telephone wire. Far from the trunk, I find a good branch and attach the feeder with sturdy twine. After I step back, a sparrow flies to the feeder another sparrow joins its companion. The grackles become quiet the doves return. I watch the birds gather on the branches around the feeder it is like a doorway to a world where I do not belong.

For additional practice with eliminating run-on sentences, go to **bedfordstmartins.com /choices** and click on **Exercise Central**.

(C. Comma Splices

A **comma splice** consists of two sentences incorrectly joined with only a comma.

COMMA SPLICE	Karima liked the aroma of coffee, she never liked the taste.
CORRECT	Karima liked the aroma of coffee, but she never liked the taste.
COMMA SPLICE	My daughter is based in Afghanistan, she'll be home for the holidays.
CORRECT	My daughter is based in Afghanistan. She'll be home for the holidays.
COMMA SPLICE	The domestic cat is a great pet, it's a ferocious hunter.
CORRECT	The domestic cat is a great pet; furthermore, it's a ferocious hunter.

One way to correct a comma splice is to make the comma splice into two separate sentences by changing the comma to a period and capitalizing the first word of the second sentence.

COMMA SPLICE	The Department of Homeland Security was created in 2002, it is responsible for the protection of the United States within its own borders.
CORRECT	The Department of Homeland Security was created in 2002. It is responsible for the protection of the United States within its own borders.

Turn to pp. 436–39 for more information about these ways of combining sentences.

Another way to correct a comma splice is to add a coordinating conjunction (*for, and, nor, but, or, yet,* or *so*) after the comma.

COMMA SPLICE	Our car trip across the country was exhausting, it was also exciting and educational.
CORRECT	Our car trip across the country was exhausting, but it was also exciting and educational.

A third way to correct a comma splice is to change the comma to a semicolon. You can also add a conjunctive adverb (such as *however*, *therefore*, *also*, *instead*, or *as a result*) after the semicolon. If you use a conjunctive adverb, put a comma after it.

COMMA SPLICE	Antibiotics have been widely used, they aren't as effective as they used to be.
CORRECT	Antibiotics have been widely used; as a result, they aren't as effective as they used to be.

■ HOW TO Correct a Comma Splice

- Separate it into two sentences.
- Add a coordinating conjunction after the comma.
- Change the comma to a semicolon and, if appropriate, add a conjunctive adverb with a comma after it.

ACTIVITY 9 Correct Comma Splices

Correct each of the following comma splices by making two separate sentences, adding a coordinating conjunction after the comma, or changing the comma to a semicolon and adding a conjunctive adverb and a comma.

EXAMPLE Graduating from college in four years is always good, but don't worry if you can't do it.

1. There were never two people more different than Arnulfo and Hadley, they have been best friends since the second grade.

2. The audience members jumped to their feet and would not stop applauding, I was very proud that I had started the Drama Club.

3. Frank set the tray of ice cream cones on the passenger seat to his right, the children would be delighted with his surprise.

4. Jessica gave the old dog a pat on the head, he thumped his tail in greeting without opening his eyes.

5. When we returned home, all the clocks were blinking, the power had gone off and come back on while we were away.

6. Adalena balanced her baby brother on her hip, almost three, he was becoming too big for her to carry.

7. Ceci inhaled the rich perfume of the cactus flower, the glowing white blossom would last less than a day.

8. Todd knew that there was a spare key hidden in the rock garden, he could not remember which rock concealed the key.

9. Ajamil bought several folk paintings while sailing around the Caribbean islands, his friends appreciated these colorful souvenirs.

10. Waiting for class to begin, Lei read her essay one last time, she found a few remaining errors.

ACTIVITY 10 Correct Comma Splices

Correct each of the following comma splices by making two separate sentences, adding a coordinating conjunction after the comma, or changing the comma to a semicolon and adding a conjunctive adverb and a comma.

EXAMPLE The number of young people who vote is declining*; however,* the number of elderly people who vote is increasing.

1. Akio immersed the spinach in a basin of water, he separated the leaves from the stems.

2. Our sixth-grade class collected starfish, sea urchins, and periwinkles on our field trip to the tide pools, we kept the animals alive in a saltwater aquarium.

3. When Noel was in high school, his aunt gave him five hundred dollars to invest in the stock market, six months later, he had doubled his money.

4. After Corinne became a salesclerk, she realized that she had not always been a very nice customer, she resolved to be more patient when she went shopping.

5. I got my first paycheck, the government deducted a lot in taxes.

6. The war in Iraq disrupted Neil and Joanna's wedding plans, they decided to marry at the courthouse and have a reception after Neil returned home.

7. I heard a sickening crunch, I realized I had stepped on another snail.

8. Tim appreciated the rich, nutty aroma of fresh coffee, he did not like its taste nearly as much.

9. The firefighters shook their heads in disgust, another pedestrian had tossed a lit cigarette onto a restaurant awning.

10. Reaching the top of the steep, narrow trail, Bronwen admired the view, the beauty of the green river valley made her forget her fear of heights.

ACTIVITY 11 Correct Comma Splices in a Paragraph

Eliminate the comma splices from the following paragraph.

EXAMPLE Single people always envy married people *, and* married people always envy single people.

    After Rachel became engaged, the first person she told was her sister, Bonnie. Rachel was hesitant to tell her parents because they wanted her to wait until after she graduated from college to get married, Bonnie would understand because she had married Kurt when she was Rachel's age. Rachel didn't want her parents to overhear her on the telephone, she went to her sister and brother-in-law's apartment to talk. Rachel did not mind helping her sister carry dirty clothes down to the laundry room, she did not mind giving Bonnie change for the machines, ever since she got married, Bonnie never seemed to have any money. Although the laundry room was hot and stuffy, Bonnie said it was a good place for them to talk. Kurt was studying for a midterm, the apartment was so small that Rachel and Bonnie's conversation would have disturbed him. Bonnie admired her sister's new diamond ring, she was even more interested in the ski trip that the engaged couple had planned. Bonnie and Kurt used to take weekend trips together when they each lived with their parents. Folding Kurt's worn jeans, Bonnie said that she envied Rachel, being engaged, according to Bonnie, is much more romantic than being married.

For additional practice with eliminating comma splices, go to **bedfordstmartins .com/choices** and click on **Exercise Central**.

D. Misplaced Modifiers

A **modifier** is a word or group of words that describes or adds information about another word. A modifier should appear as close as possible to the word it modifies:

Binh spent *almost* fifty dollars on her haircut. [The modifier appears next to the word it modifies, *fifty*.]

Spinach contains lutein, a vitamin *that strengthens the eyes*. [The modifier appears next to *vitamin*, which is the word it modifies.]

A modifier is *misplaced* when it appears in the wrong place in the sentence. Either it seems to modify a word other than the one the writer intended, or there's more than one word it could modify and the reader can't tell which one.

MISPLACED	The carpentry student nailed the plank to the floor *with red hair*. [Did the floor have red hair?]
CLEAR	The carpentry student *with red hair* nailed the plank to the floor.

MISPLACED	The restaurant *only* serves lunch on Sundays. [Is lunch the only meal served on Sundays, or are Sundays the only days that lunch is served?]
CLEAR	The restaurant serves *only* lunch on Sundays.
CLEAR	The restaurant serves lunch on Sundays *only*.

MISPLACED	Leo walked outside to smell the flowering rosemary plant *wearing his bathing suit*. [Is the plant wearing his bathing suit?]
CLEAR	*Wearing his bathing suit*, Leo walked outside to smell the flowering rosemary plant.

ACTIVITY 12 Identify Misplaced Modifiers

Underline the misplaced modifier in each of the following sentences.

EXAMPLE My supervisor said I needed to improve my attitude <u>in her office</u>.

1. The beer can almost hit my grandmother thrown out of the car window.
2. The new standards for graduation only required a low-level statistics class.
3. Boris found a pink and squirming nest of baby mice.
4. Aamir borrowed a shirt from his brother with long sleeves.
5. The waiter brought a steak to the man covered with mushrooms.

To correct a misplaced modifier, place the modifier closer to the word it describes.

MISPLACED	The Italian visitors drove a rental car *leaving on vacation*. [It appears the rental car is leaving on vacation.]
CLEAR	*Leaving on vacation*, the Italian visitors drove a rental car. [The modifier is placed closer to the word it describes, *visitors*.]

> ▪ **HOW TO** Correct Misplaced Modifiers
>
> • Place them as close as possible to the word they modify.

> ◖ **ACTIVITY 13** Correct Misplaced Modifiers ▷

Edit each of the following sentences to eliminate misplaced modifiers.

Wearing his expensive new suit,
EXAMPLE ‸Parker told the noisy employees to shape up ~~in his expensive new suit.~~

1. My boyfriend and I volunteered at the food bank with the best of intentions.

2. The volunteers put out the hillside fire from the next county.

3. The kids I was babysitting from next door played video games for hours.

4. Liam greeted the unexpected guests in his old pajamas.

5. My learning group always arranged to meet in the Student Union at my previous college.

6. Rosie almost spent two weeks in Las Vegas and went on to Reno for another week.

7. Dean took the rabbit to the veterinarian that had the sore paw.

8. Taka polished the antique cabinet standing on a stepladder.

9. Annick only told her coach what the doctor had said, but the coach told her parents.

10. The faucet dripped water all day that I need to replace.

For additional practice with eliminating misplaced modifiers, go to **bedfordstmartins .com/choices** and click on **Exercise Central**.

◖ E. Dangling Modifiers

A modifier is *dangling* when there's no word in the sentence that it can logically modify. Most dangling modifiers occur at the beginning of sentences.

DANGLING   *Smiling broadly*, the award fulfilled Renee's dreams. [It appears that the award is smiling.]

CLEAR   *Smiling broadly*, Renee accepted the award that fulfilled her dreams.

DANGLING   *In running for the taxi*, my foot tripped on the crack in the sidewalk. [Is the foot running for the taxi?]

CLEAR   *As I was running for the taxi*, my foot tripped on the crack in the sidewalk.

ACTIVITY 14 Identify Dangling Modifiers

Underline the dangling modifiers in each of the following sentences.

EXAMPLE <u>Deciding to join the team,</u> the coach enthusiastically shook Jennica's hand.

1. After finishing all of the basic classes, college became easier.
2. Staring into the distance, dark skies approach.
3. No one realized the problem with the proposal, pleased by the low cost.
4. To control your anger, a psychologist may be necessary.
5. Tired from the long flight, the crowds in the parking lot were depressing.

To correct a dangling modifier, rewrite the sentence so the reader knows what is being modified. You can add this information either to the modifier or to the rest of the sentence.

DANGLING	*Waiting in line,* the wind began to blow. [The reader can't tell who is waiting in line.]
CLEAR	*While I was waiting in line,* the wind began to blow.
CLEAR	Waiting in line, *I* felt the wind begin to blow.

HOW TO Correct Dangling Modifiers

- Add information about what or whom the modifier is describing.

ACTIVITY 15 Correct Dangling Modifiers

Edit each of the following sentences to eliminate dangling modifiers.

                    The wind, gusting   caused   to
EXAMPLE ~~Gusting~~ to forty-five miles an hour, the tree limb hit the tin roof loudly.

1. Shaking the principal's hand, Clarence's goal of earning a high school diploma became a reality.
2. Fed by hot winds and dry grass, the firefighters faced a difficult challenge.
3. Mom's jigsaw puzzle was complete, snapping the last piece into place.
4. Searching for a new way to treat diabetes, medical advances were made.
5. Seeing her nephew win a prize at the science fair, her heart was overwhelmed with pride.
6. Removing her foot from the accelerator, Diana's car rolled to a stop.
7. Having saved for years to buy a house, it was exciting that the Kangs' dream was coming true.

For additional practice with eliminating dangling modifiers, go to **bedfordstmartins.com /choices** and click on **Exercise Central**.

8. While window shopping at the mall, a sports watch caught my eye.

9. Deliriously happy, the newlyweds' limousine slowly drove to their hotel.

10. Water leaked into my boat while rowing as fast as possible.

F. Active and Passive Voice

In a sentence written in **active voice**, the subject performs the action; it does something. In a sentence written in **passive voice**, the subject receives the action; something is done to it. Readers prefer the active voice in most sentences because they normally expect the subject to be performing the action, so a sentence in which the subject doesn't perform the action takes longer to understand. The active voice is also less wordy than the passive voice.

> **PASSIVE VOICE** The tail of the kite *was caught by* the boy.
> **ACTIVE VOICE** The boy *caught* the kite by the tail.
>
> **PASSIVE VOICE** The newspaper *is read by* my mother each morning.
> **ACTIVE VOICE** My mother *reads* the newspaper each morning.

▸HOW TO Use Active Voice

- Decide who or what is performing the action in a sentence.
- Make the performer of the action the subject of the sentence.

ACTIVITY 16 Use the Active Voice

Edit each of the following sentences to eliminate passive voice.

       The tournament's sponsor gave
EXAMPLE Tiger Woods ~~was given~~ the green jacket by the tournament's sponsor.
         ^

1. The runners were encouraged by the spectators.

2. The memos had been signed by the manager.

3. A doctoral degree in physics was earned by Professor Patel.

4. An educational play about AIDS was performed by the juniors.

5. The baby was taken to the park by his older brother.

6. The party was planned by Milo, but all the work was done by his family.

7. The assignment was given at the beginning of class by the teaching assistant.

8. A swimming pool was installed by the previous owners of the house.

9. The movie was made by the Coen brothers, and the hero was played by George Clooney.

10. Our pets were fed by a neighbor.

ACTIVITY 17 Correct Passive Voice in a Paragraph

Edit the following paragraph so that all sentences are in the active voice.

EXAMPLE Because of the poor economy, my college money ~~was used~~ for rent and gas.
I used

    A university education must be paid for. School and work are balanced differently by my friends and me. Monica had both a full-time and a part-time job for two years following high school. Now a job isn't needed during college. She earns high grades because she doesn't have to divide her energies between work and school. A full-time night job was chosen by Bill, and only nine credits are taken by him. He does data entry for the business office of a department store. An administrative position in the same office will be taken by him after graduation. Bill earns enough money working at night to make payments on a new car. I don't need a car. However, money for college is needed. I chose to take out student loans to pay for my education. My friends and I live very different lives.

For additional practice with using active and passive voice, go to **bedfordstmartins.com /choices** and click on **Exercise Central**.

G. Parallelism

When two or more groups of words in a sentence are parts of a pair or series, these word groups should be **parallel**, or similar in their grammatical structure. The following sentences are written using parallel structure:

Today, we _drove to Philadelphia, visited the Liberty Bell,_ and _ate at our favorite restaurants._

The italic word groups in this sentence are parallel because they each follow the same grammatical structure: past-tense verb followed by words that modify the verb or complete its meaning.

My girlfriend is _smart in school, friendly to everyone,_ and _fun to be with._

The italic word groups in this sentence are parallel because they follow the same grammatical structure: adjective followed by words that modify the adjective.

Here are examples of sentences that do not have parallel structure, each followed by a revised sentence that has parallel structure. Notice that the revised sentences are easier to read and understand.

NOT PARALLEL I love going to the movies, reading, and to walk.

PARALLEL I love going to the movies, reading, and walking.

NOT PARALLEL He drove dangerously fast, missed the curve, and wrecks his car.

PARALLEL He drove dangerously fast, missed the curve, and wrecked his car.

NOT PARALLEL I don't like to fill out financial aid forms that are difficult, long, and have too many words.

PARALLEL I don't like to fill out financial aid forms that are difficult, long, and wordy.

■ HOW TO Write Using Parallel Structure

- Reread each sentence, looking for pairs or series of word groups in a sentence.
- Check that each of the groups of words in the pair or series has a similar grammatical structure.
- Rewrite any parts of the pair or series that are not parallel in structure.

◀ ACTIVITY 18 Use Parallelism ▶

Edit each of the following sentences for correct parallel structure.

EXAMPLE My favorite activities include horseback riding, hiking, and ~~to play~~ *playing* soccer.

1. My mother was a hairdresser, a taxi driver, and being a secretary.

2. In my University Studies class, I have learned how to study more effectively and preparing for an exam.

3. The bookstore has my favorite books: books about cooking, biographies, and novels.

4. I found the concert to be loud, expensive, and was not very entertaining.

5. Going to the dentist is worse than to go to the hospital.

6. The buffet included undercooked shrimp, limp lettuce, and the muffins were stale.

7. Haruko was filled with fear, anticipation, excited.

8. The squirrel peeked out, stole the nut, and then back to his home.

9. The Ferris wheel is my favorite carnival ride, but my sister prefers the haunted house and to ride the merry-go-round.

10. She likes to play basketball, but he prefers skiing.

ACTIVITY 19 Correct Faulty Parallelism in a Paragraph

Edit the paragraph so that all sentences are parallel.

EXAMPLE   We need a visionary leader in each of our groups, but ~~we're knowing~~ _we know_ this isn't likely.

    A visionary leader is someone who is not afraid to lead and of taking the group to a place it would not otherwise be. A visionary leader isn't necessarily the most dynamic person in the group but who is willing to listen to others. Such a leader works hard to improve conditions for every member of the group, seeks to put the needs of the group members first, and a desire to see the group succeed as a whole. The visionary leader is not always the group member with the most imaginative ideas but is the member who has the skills and energy to put these ideas into action. We could use more visionary leaders: they touch, inspire, and are changing the world we live in.

For additional practice with using parallelism, go to **bedfordstmartins.com/choices** and click on **Exercise Central**.

19

Improving Word Choice

Speaking and writing are key ways to communicate your thoughts and feelings to others, and different situations require different word choices. Just as you wouldn't go to a job interview in a wedding dress or to a football game in a bathing suit, you wouldn't write to your boss in the same way that you would write to a friend or daughter. You choose the best words for the person and the occasion. But how do you improve your word choice? Following are several strategies for expanding and improving the words you choose when you write.

A. Vocabulary

One way to expand your word choice and to better understand what you read is to develop a broad vocabulary. A **vocabulary** is a set of words you are familiar with and can use in your speech and writing. How can you tell if your vocabulary needs improvement? Do you have difficulty finding the words to express what you want to say or write in class? At a party, do you hesitate to join a conversation because you can't follow what others are saying? Do you find yourself skipping a lot of words in newspapers, magazines, or your college textbooks because you don't know what they mean? If you have answered yes to any of these questions, you'll want to work to improve your vocabulary.

HOW TO Improve Your Vocabulary

- **Read.** The more you read, the more words you'll learn.
- **Just ask.** If you are with friends or classmates, don't hesitate to ask the meaning of words you don't understand.
- **Play word games.** Try Scrabble, crossword puzzles, a Word of the Day calendar, or a Web site that sends you a word each day.

- **Keep vocabulary index cards**. Write each unfamiliar word on one side of an index card. On the other side, write the definition and use the word in a sentence. Keep these index cards with you for easy study and reference. If it's more convenient, you can record vocabulary words by using "sticky notes" or another note-taking application on your computer or smartphone.

ACTIVITY 1 Build Your Vocabulary

Using Chapters 15–18 of this Handbook, create vocabulary cards for unfamiliar grammar terms, such as *linking verbs*. Write the term on one side of the index card. On the other side, write the definition and a sentence that provides an example.

Meaning from Context

Reading is the most effective way to improve vocabulary. While reading, if you come across a word you don't know, see if you can determine the meaning of the word from the **context**—that is, from the other words in the sentence. For example, consider the following sentence:

Although Bree is often *morose*, she seems happy today.

What does *morose* mean? Because you know that the word *although* shows contrast and that Bree seems happy today, then *morose* must be the opposite of *happy*. Bree must often be sad.

ACTIVITY 2 Determine Meaning from Context

Read the following passage from an article about figure skating. Try to determine the meanings of the underlined words from the words around them. Write the meanings next to the words in the spaces provided.

There are many athletic and artistic <u>elements</u> in figure skating. <u>Initial</u> skills include the all-important basics—stroking forward, skating backward, and doing forward and backward crossovers. Jumps are so <u>predominant</u> in modern figure skating that we could say that this is the "jump era." In the six <u>preliminary</u> jumps, the skater <u>rotates</u> once in the air. Since their <u>inception</u> in the beginning of the twentieth century, these jumps have been doubled and now are commonly <u>trebled</u> by both men and women.

elements _____

initial _____

predominant _____

preliminary _____

rotates _____

inception _____

trebled _____

Learn Roots, Prefixes, and Suffixes

Another way to improve your vocabulary is to memorize the meanings of common word roots, prefixes, and suffixes. A **word root** is the main part of a word, a **prefix** is added to the beginning of a word or word root, and a **suffix** is added to the end of a word or word root. Following are the meanings of some common English word roots, prefixes, and suffixes.

ENGLISH WORD ROOTS

Root	Meaning	Examples
audi	to hear	audience, audio
bene	good, well	benefit, benevolence
geo	earth	geography, geometry
logo	word or thought	analogy, dialogue, logic
manu	hand	manufacture, manual
photo	light	photography, telephoto
tele	far away	telegraph, telepathy
vid, vis	to see	video, vision, visit

ENGLISH PREFIXES

Prefix	Meaning	Examples
ante-	before	antebellum, antedate
anti-	against	antibody, antisocial
bi-	two	bilateral, bipolar
de-	from	declaw, desensitize
hyper-	over, more	hypersensitive
mal-	bad	malpractice
post-	after	postscript, postwar
trans-	across	transition, transport
uni-	one	unicycle, uniform

ENGLISH SUFFIXES

Suffix	Meaning	Examples
-acy	state or quality	democracy, privacy
-dom	state of being	freedom, kingdom
-en	cause or become	blacken, cheapen

Suffix	Meaning	Examples
-ish	having the quality of	clownish
-less	lack of, without	childless, humorless
-ology	the study of	biology, psychology
-ment	condition of	impediment, payment
-sion, -tion	state of being	confusion, transition

ACTIVITY 3 Learn Roots, Prefixes, and Suffixes

Create a vocabulary card for each root, prefix, and suffix in the first column above. Write the root, prefix, or suffix on one side of the index card. Write the meaning and an example on the other side. Review these cards regularly until you have memorized them. Alternatively, you can use "sticky notes" or another note-taking application on your computer or smartphone.

B. Unnecessary Repetition

Repetition results from repeating the same idea in different words. Although repetition can help you emphasize and connect ideas as you write, too much repetition may cause you to lose your readers' attention. At times, you may not even realize that you're repeating words or using words that mean the same thing. Notice the unnecessary words in the following sentences:

REPETITION	There are several positive benefits to eating a healthy breakfast.
REVISED	There are several benefits to eating a healthy breakfast.
REPETITION	We tried to forget the sad events of that day and put them out of our minds.
REVISED	We tried to forget the sad events of that day.
REPETITION	When leaving the train, remember to take your personal belongings.
REVISED	When leaving the train, remember to take your belongings.

HOW TO Avoid Unnecessary Repetition

Check that each word in a sentence

- Adds interest.
- Is specific.
- Does not restate what you have already said.

ACTIVITY 4 Avoid Unnecessary Repetition

Revise each of the following sentences to avoid unnecessary repetition.

EXAMPLE I will never ~~ever~~ do anything like that again ~~in the future~~.

For additional practice with eliminating unnecessary repetition, go to **bedfordstmartins .com/choices** and click on **Exercise Central**.

1. My very favorite song I like the most is "I Can't Make You Love Me."
2. Jerry wanted to get caught up and be up-to-date on what was going on in class.
3. Don't confuse me with the facts and data!
4. We never knew or realized how important this event would be.
5. Let's just wait and pass the time until she returns.

C. Wordiness

Eliminating wordiness is similar to avoiding unnecessary repetition. **Wordiness** results from using too many words to say something or using "filler" phrases that don't contribute to the meaning of a sentence. Notice the wordiness in the following sentences:

> **WORDY** I would really very much like to go to that game.
> **REVISED** I would really like to go to that game.

> **WORDY** I get to make the choice of where I go.
> **REVISED** I get to choose where I go.

> **WORDY** I feel that we have a greater amount of freedom to choose these days.
> **REVISED** We have more freedom to choose today.

ACTIVITY 5 Eliminate Wordiness

Revise the following sentences to eliminate wordiness.

EXAMPLE ~~I believe that you~~ You are wrong.

1. I would like to say that I agree with you.
2. I am of the opinion that anyone who writes on this topic as a subject for an essay is not thinking straight.
3. A large number of students in the near future will agree with us.
4. At an earlier point in time, this wouldn't have happened, or it would have been postponed until a later time.
5. I believe that this is true for the reason that students feel differently today than they did at an earlier point in time.

20

Improving Spelling

As you edit your writing, you'll want to be sure to check your spelling. Misspelled words will cause your readers to focus on your lack of spelling skills rather than on the meaning of what you have written. You can often tell if a word is misspelled just by looking at it, or you can use a computer spell-check to catch errors. Because the spell-check can't catch every error, though, it's useful to improve your spelling.

A. Spelling Rules

One way to improve your spelling is to learn spelling rules that can help you master the spelling of commonly misspelled words.

Rule 1 Use *i* before *e* except after *c* or when sounded like *ay* as in *neighbor* and *weigh*.

believe, niece, piece, fierce

receive, ceiling, conceive, deceive

eight, freight, sleigh, weight

Exceptions: either, neither, leisure, height, seize, weird, science, counterfeit

ACTIVITY 1 Use *i* before *e* Except after *c*

In the space provided, correct each of the following misspelled words, or write "correct" if the word is spelled correctly.

EXAMPLE hieght _____*height*_____

1. conceited_____
2. recieve_____
3. neighbor_____
4. weigh _____
5. cieling _____

6. decieve _____
7. seize _____
8. beleive_____
9. niether _____
10. neice _____

ACTIVITY 2   Correct *i* before *e* Except after *c* Errors

Underline each of the misspelled words in the following sentences. Then write the correct spelling of these words in the space provided. If a sentence has no spelling errors, write "correct."

EXAMPLE Jerry has a <u>neice</u> and nephew. _____*niece*_____

1. Patrice asked Amando for a piece of paper. _____

2. It is important not to carry excess wieght when you are backpacking.

   _____

3. A good pair of shoes releived Kenia's backaches. _____

4. In his liesure time, Hal likes to go bow hunting. _____

5. Majel koncieved of a way to pass the exam without reading the textbook.

   _____

6. Terrelle was so concieted that people tried to avoid him.

   _____

7. On Christmas, Grandfather treated us to an old-fashioned sleigh ride.

   _____

8. My favorite beige jacket always looks dirty. _____

9. Tim decieved his teacher by forging his father's signature on his report card.

   _____

10. When we recieve your order, we will notify you by e-mail.

    _____

Rule 2   When adding an ending that begins with a vowel (such as *-ed* or *-ing*) to a word that ends with a consonant, double the consonant if it (1) is preceded by a single vowel and (2) ends a one-syllable word or stressed syllable.

   bet, betting
   stop, stopped
   commit, committed
   occur, occurrence

Exception: Even if the consonant ends a stressed syllable, do not double it if the syllable is no longer stressed when the ending is added: *refer, reference.*

ACTIVITY 3 Double the Final Consonant

In the space provided, add the correct ending to each of the following words.

EXAMPLE get + ing ____*getting*____

1. travel + ed _____
2. dig + ing _____
3. omit + ed _____
4. control + ing _____
5. prefer + ence _____
6. scan + er _____
7. nag + ing _____
8. persist + ence _____
9. defer + al _____
10. hop + ed _____

ACTIVITY 4 Correct Final Consonant Errors

Underline each of the misspelled words in the following sentences. Then write the correct spelling of these words in the space provided. If a sentence has no spelling errors, write "correct."

EXAMPLE The rabbit hoped to the side of the house. ____*hopped*____

1. Mary stoped kicking the bottom of Bill's chair when he fell asleep. _____
2. They never succeeded at ridding their house of ants. _____
3. Felicia admited that she was sad when her friend moved away. _____
4. After tiping over his glass, Lewis apologized and left the room. _____
5. Ron and Leni held hands and planed their future. _____
6. Efren made a referrence to his former girlfriend. _____
7. Delphine repeatted her name three times before the clerk said it correctly.

_____

8. The occurence of car theft in the parking lot has doubled in the last year.

_____

9. Pegeen believed that Neville was betting on a losing team. _____
10. Stuart laborred over his statistics homework for six hours. _____

Rule 3 Drop a final silent *e* from a word when adding an ending that begins with a vowel. Keep the final *e* if the ending begins with a consonant.

retire, retiring;   age, aging;   desire, desiring

hate, hateful;   state, statement;   lone, lonely

Exceptions: courageous, manageable, ninth, truly, argument, judgment

> **ACTIVITY 5 Drop the Final Silent *e***

In the space provided, add the specified ending to each of the following words.

EXAMPLE perspire + ing *perspiring*

1. bite + ing _____

2. encourage + ment _____

3. safe + ty _____

4. nine + th _____

5. care + ful _____

6. shine + ing _____

7. true + ly _____

8. fade + ing _____

9. use + able _____

10. state + ment _____

> **ACTIVITY 6 Correct Final Silent *e* Errors**

Underline each of the misspelled words in the following sentences. Then write the correct spelling of these words in the space provided. If a sentence has no spelling errors, write "correct."

EXAMPLE He thought he was ageing too quickly. _____*aging*_____

1. Mira's greatest achievment was hiking the entire Appalachian Trail.

   _____

2. This coat has a removable lining. _____

3. The lavish meal left us desireing nothing more. _____

4. Stan remained quiet to avoid an arguement with his friends in public.

   _____

5. The shoppers were hopeing to find bargains. _____

6. The audience made hatful remarks as the senator tried to speak. _____

7. Clarence used good judgement in choosing a roommate. _____

8. The surest way to be fired from a job is to not show up. _____

9. Denise found her courses in managment more interesting than those in marketing.

   _____

10. Sheldon spent the rest of the afternoon writeing his résumé. _____

Rule 4   When adding an ending other than *-ing* to a word that ends in *y*, you sometimes need to change the *y* to *i*. If the *y* is preceded by a consonant, change it to *i*:

easy, easiest;   duty, dutiful;   marry, married

If you're adding -s, also add an e after the i:

reply, replies;   dry, dries

If you're adding -ing or the y is preceded by a vowel, don't change it to i.

apply, applying;   dry, drying;   play, played;   monkey, monkeys

ACTIVITY 7 Change y to i

In the space provided, add the specified ending to each of the following words, and write the new word.

EXAMPLE carry + ed _____carried_____

1. pay + ing _____
2. turkey + s _____
3. say + ing _____
4. fry + ed _____
5. pretty + ily _____

6. plenty + ful _____
7. hurry ɪ s _____
8. fly + ing _____
9. happy + ness _____
10. play + ful _____

ACTIVITY 8 Correct y to i Errors

Underline each of the misspelled words in the following sentences. Then write the correct spelling of these words in the space provided. If a sentence has no spelling errors, write "correct."

EXAMPLE The couple's happyness left us inspired. ___happiness___

1. To find employment, he read the classified ads. _____

2. We were puzzled by the trickyness of the test question. _____

3. Lester has been studiing all day. _____

4. After several apologys, Wanda finally forgave her brother. _____

5. Rainer easly jumped over the puddle. _____

6. It was difficult to say which sister was most beautyful. _____

7. In warm weather, the clothes dryed very quickly on the line. _____

8. The sounds of the children playing in the street carryed into my sixth-floor apartment. _____

9. The two attornies made an agreement to avoid going to court. _____

10. After staying at campgrounds, I found the motel luxurious. _____

For additional practice with spelling, go to **bedfordstmartins.com /choices** and click on **Exercise Central**.

☾ B. Commonly Misspelled Words

The following are one hundred commonly misspelled words. Create spelling lists or cards to practice spelling them correctly.

absence	hoarse	privilege
accommodate	holiday	procedure
all right	hygiene	pursue
analyze	icicles	receipt
anoint	imagine	receive
anonymous	indispensable	recommend
benefit	innocent	repetition
boundary	irresistible	rhythm
business	irritable	ridiculous
category	jealousy	roommate
committee	league	schedule
conscience	leisure	seize
conscious	license	separate
corroborate	losing	sergeant
counterfeit	maneuver	sheriff
dealt	marriage	sophomore
definitely	meant	subtle
despair	minute	succeed
dilemma	misspelled	supersede
disappoint	necessary	surgeon
ecstasy	ninth	tongue
eighth	noticeable	tragedy
embarrass	occurrence	truly
exceed	often	tyranny
existence	optimistic	undoubtedly
fascinate	pamphlet	until
February	parallel	vacuum
forty	peculiar	vengeance
fulfill	perseverance	vicious
government	persistent	warrant
grammar	phenomenon	weird
guarantee	principal	wholly
guard	principle	yacht
height		

ACTIVITY 9 Correct Sentences for Spelling

Underline the misspelled words in each of the following sentences. Then write the correct spelling of these words in the space provided. (There may be more than one error in each sentence.)

EXAMPLE I always <u>recomended</u> <u>vacumming</u>, but I <u>definitly</u> see the <u>benafit</u> of it now.

recommended, vacuuming, definitely, benefit

1. When Rafa telephoned, Yoli was studing her chemistry, so he apologyzed for bothering her.

   _____

2. After beging for three weeks to be given a better work schedule, Steve stoped asking.

   _____

3. Gino had been liveing in his apartment for fifteen years when he recieved the eviction notice.

   _____

4. A counterfiet coin may wiegh less than a genuine one.

   _____

5. Shelley was carful when she tryed to remove the splinter from the child's finger.

   _____

6. You can easyly waste your liesure time on activities you don't really enjoy.

   _____

7. A student writeing a persuasive essay needs to construct a very strong arguement supporting his or her opinions.

   _____

8. Rasa prefered ordering from a Web site to shoping at the mall.

   _____

9. Unfortunately, Vincent omited his social security number when he applyed for a scholarship.

   _____

10. The dutys of the store manager never stoped at five o'clock.

   _____

C. Commonly Confused Words

Commonly confused words are words that sound similar but have different spellings and meanings.

accept: to agree to	I *accept* your offer.
except: excluding	Everyone *except* Joan was invited.
adapt: to adjust	Kenji had to *adapt* to his new town.
adopt: to take on	He realized that he would have to *adopt* a new attitude.
advice: a suggestion	Please take my *advice*.
advise: to suggest	I *advise* you to slow down.
affect: to influence	Her partying did not *affect* her grades.
effect: a result	The *effect*, though, was that she was under stress.
all ready: prepared	We are *all ready* for the holidays.
already: previously	We have *already* bought all of the food we need.
cite: to refer to	Jerome is always careful to *cite* his sources.
sight: vision	The eye surgery improved her *sight*.
site: a location	The article was about the *site* of the new museum.
complement: to well with; go something that goes well with something else	This tie does not *complement* your shirt.
compliment: to admire; an expression of admiration	I *compliment* you on your choice of pants.
conscience: moral principles	Josue's *conscience* wouldn't permit him to cheat.
conscious: aware	He was *conscious* of students cheating around him.
farther: a longer physical distance	My aunt lives *farther* away than my family can drive in one day.
further: additional; more	The committee agreed to *further* discussion of the issue.
loose: not tight or secure	Wasim's tooth was *loose*.
lose: to misplace	He didn't want to *lose* it if it fell out.
principal: head of a school; main or leading	The *principal* of my high school was one of the *principal* supporters of the new gym.
principle: a basic truth or belief	He believed in the *principle* of daily exercise.

to: toward	Aja ran *to* the lake.
too: excessively; also	Her brother, Ankur, was *too* slow to keep up and stopped along the way, *too*.
two: the number between one and three	The *two* of them arrived an hour apart.
weather: conditions such as sun, rain, and wind	The *weather* in Washington, D.C., was beautiful.
whether: a word indicating choice or possibility	I had to decide *whether* to leave or stay.

ACTIVITY 10 Correct a Paragraph for Spelling

Correct the misspelled words in the following paragraph by crossing them out and writing the correct spelling above each misspelled word.

EXAMPLE Ahmad wishes he knew more about this word-processing program because
affects
it ~~effects~~ the way he writes.

Ahmad feels the campus computer labs need improveing. Before geting his own computer, he relyed heavily on the labs. Although they were convient, they were to noisey and crowded. Computers were often unavailable because the maintance was so bad. Even when he found a free computer, he was often distractted by the rowdyness of the other students. After recieving a laptop from his father, Ahmad lookked foreward to his life being easyer. Unffortunatly, he still had problems when continueing projects he had begun at home. Once, he accidently reformated his hard drive, loosing all his data. He often had difficultys printing at the lab, discoverring pages of wierd symbols weather he wanted two or not. The technicians said that his laptop software isn't compattible with the software at the lab. Now he's more conscience of mistakes than ever before. Ahmad's father says that computers have all ready created new problems while solveing other ones.

21

Improving Punctuation

You use **punctuation** to make it easier for your readers to follow your meaning. Just as your car's taillights communicate that you are planning to stop, turn right, or turn left, punctuation communicates to your readers what to expect next. Readers depend on punctuation to guide them through your text. For example, what does the following sentence mean?

Don't let the snake eat Ryan.

Is the snake about to eat Ryan, or is Ryan supposed to prevent the snake from eating? Adding a comma to this sentence makes it clear.

Don't let the snake eat, Ryan.

The reader now understands that Ryan is supposed to prevent the snake from eating its food.

The following punctuation rules will help you make your meaning clear and communicate to your readers more effectively.

A. Commas

The **comma** (,) is used to separate parts of a sentence to make the meaning clear.

Rule 1   Use a comma after an introductory word, phrase, or clause.

Actually, snakes like to eat rodents.

After feeding the snake, you can leave for the NASCAR race.

As Ryan explained, snakes eat a variety of foods.

ACTIVITY 1 Use Commas with Introductory Words

Add a comma after the introductory word, phrase, or clause in each of the following sentences.

EXAMPLE Although I usually like the opera͜ I didn't like this one.

1. Smelling Janelle's perfume in the apartment Oscar knew that she was ready to go to the party.

2. First Corey fastened his seatbelt and put on his sunglasses.

3. Whether you agree or not I'm taking biology next semester.

4. In Wendy's opinion renting a large apartment is more convenient than owning a house.

5. While the children ate cake and played games their parents became better acquainted.

ACTIVITY 2 Write Using Commas with Introductory Words

In each of the following sentences, add an introductory word, phrase, or clause followed by a comma.

EXAMPLE *During the movie,*
Dan and Andrea would not stop talking.

1. I heard the drone of a small airplane overhead.

2. She put on more lipstick and mascara.

3. Your parents were watching you through the kitchen window.

4. We keep reams of paper and extra cartridges for the printer.

5. Philip admitted that he was wrong.

Rule 2   Use commas to separate three or more words, phrases, or clauses in a series. Do not use a comma before the first item in the series or after the last item.

Jane bought books, games, and DVDs at the bookstore.

Before leaving, she talked to her roommate, turned off her computer, and locked her desk.

Jane forgot to feed the dog, left her bed unmade, and didn't clean the bathroom.

ACTIVITY 3 Use Commas in a Series

Add commas as needed to each of the following sentences to separate words, phrases, or clauses used in a series.

EXAMPLE My favorite foods are salmon͜ fried rice͜ and chocolate cake.

1. All I had in the refrigerator was a pint of sour milk a block of moldy cheese and a jar of olives.

2. Eileen packed underwear jeans sweaters socks shoes and maps.

3. Vikram walked down the street past the supermarket and around the corner.

4. Jorge filled the sandbox Gunilla set up the swings Noah built the seesaws Calvin welded the slide and Mahela painted the benches.

5. Chewing gum pacing the floor and watching the clock were the only things to do in the waiting room.

ACTIVITY 4 Write Using Commas with a Series

For each of the following lists of items, write a complete sentence using the items in a series.

EXAMPLE hills, river beds, dusty trails

We hiked hills, river beds, and dusty trails.

1. pens, pencils, notebooks, folders, erasers

_____

2. a pad of paper, a pair of scissors, a bottle of glue

_____

_____

3. on the dashboard, under the front seat, in the trunk

_____

_____

4. decorating the house, preparing a festive meal, spending time with family

_____

_____

5. sang songs, told funny stories, did magic tricks, made balloon animals

_____

_____

Rule 3   Use a comma to separate two independent clauses joined by a coordinating conjunction.

I wanted to go to the concert, and I wanted to study for my exam.

I knew my exam was important, but Lady Gaga is my favorite singer.

I studied all afternoon, so I was able to go to the concert after all.

ACTIVITY 5 Use Commas with Coordinating Conjunctions

Add a comma to each of the following sentences to separate the two independent clauses joined by a coordinating conjunction.

EXAMPLE I wanted to leave early ‸ yet my husband wanted to leave at noon.

1. The wind howled and the snow fell more thickly.

2. Margarita stood on a stepladder but she could not reach the ceiling.

3. Julio drank a second bottle of water yet he was still thirsty.

4. Marcia couldn't sleep for the next day she was going to start a new job.

5. I wanted to call you on your birthday but you were out all night.

ACTIVITY 6 Join Sentences with Coordinating Conjunctions

Use a comma and a coordinating conjunction to join each of the following pairs of sentences into a single sentence.

EXAMPLE My mother loves to travel. ~~She's~~ _, but she's_ a little afraid of flying.

1. Yusef sat in the driver's seat. His brothers pushed the car.

2. Aurelia found the strength to run even faster. She saw the banners at the finish line.

3. I realized that I had answered the essay question on my history midterm badly. I had only enough time to write a brief concluding paragraph.

4. The doctor gave Samia a pair of crutches. She could walk without further injuring her foot.

5. You could come to the dance with me. You could watch reruns on television.

Rule 4   Use commas before and after an appositive (a noun that renames the noun right before it) or a descriptive word, phrase, or clause if the appositive, word, phrase, or clause interrupts the flow of the sentence or could be removed from the sentence without changing its meaning. If the appositive, word, phrase, or clause is at the end of the sentence, use a comma before it.

My high school reunion, sadly, was missing the person I most wanted to see.

Jessie, who was my high school sweetheart, doesn't live here anymore.

The reunion, held over the Thanksgiving weekend, wasn't nearly as much fun as the last one.

I would really like to see Jessie, my old flame.

 ACTIVITY 7 Use Commas with Descriptive Words and Phrases

Add commas to each of the following sentences to set off the appositive or the descriptive word, phrase, or clause.

EXAMPLE Johnny, my closest friend, never has to study.

1. Mateo the youngest child is the first in his family to attend a university.

2. The driver of the car in front of us ignoring the stop sign sped through the intersection.

3. Ricky's new saxophone which had cost him his life savings enabled him to join his favorite jazz band.

4. My date a massage therapist named Yolanda asked me in to meet her parents.

5. Janine's former roommate surprisingly was happy to see her.

 ACTIVITY 8 Add Descriptive Words and Phrases with Commas

Rewrite each of the following sentences by inserting the appositive or descriptive word, phrase, or clause provided. Include the required commas.

EXAMPLE Corky flew from his perch to my shoulder. (*my parakeet*)
Corky, my parakeet, flew from his perch to my shoulder.

1. Mr. Gardner ran unsuccessfully for state senator. (*my history teacher in middle school*)

_____

_____

2. Hector's grandchildren ran into the kitchen. (*smelling the cookies in the oven*)

_____

_____

3. The library book gathered dust at the back of my closet. (*which I had never read*)

_____

_____

4. Gavin's wife has just published a magazine article about their trip to Bhutan. (*an agricultural advisor*)

_____

_____

5. Sally could not afford a new truck. (*unfortunately*)

_____

_____

Rule 5   Use commas to set off transitional words and phrases from the rest of the sentence.

It wasn't until I visited the museum, however, that I realized how much I liked art.

For example, I discovered I really enjoyed Remington's sculptures.

My friend, on the other hand, preferred Monet's paintings.

ACTIVITY 9 Use Commas with Transitional Words and Phrases

Add commas as needed to each of the following sentences to set off the transitional words and phrases.

EXAMPLE Surely my car will be ready soon.

1. Subsequently the rest of the family came down with the flu.

2. Fritz likewise saved copies of his work in his e-mail files.

3. Furthermore the larger company has superior benefits.

4. The two-lane road alongside the freeway nevertheless is very scenic.

5. It wasn't until Belinda heard the applause however that she truly believed her speech was convincing.

ACTIVITY 10 Add Transitional Words and Phrases with Commas

Rewrite each of the following sentences by inserting the transitional word or phrase provided. Include the required commas.

EXAMPLE Sandy wants to try out for the marching band. (*nonetheless*)
      Sandy, nonetheless, wants to try out for the marching band.

1. Consuelo is allergic to feathers and animal fur. (*however*)

_____

_____

2. Farak prefers snorkeling to scuba diving. (*on the other hand*)

_____

_____

3. The people who arrived late waited in the lobby for the first intermission. (*meanwhile*)

_____

_____

4. Some members of the city council want to increase the budget for public parks. (*in addition*)

_____

_____

5. The tenants are pooling their money to buy the apartment building from the bank. (*as a result*)

_____

_____

Rule 6   Use a comma to separate the day of the month from the year. If the year is in the middle of a sentence, also use a comma after it.

I will start graduate school on September 4, 2012.

I was born on July 4, 1974, and immediately became the center of my grandmother's attention.

My goal is to have my master's degree by the time I turn forty on July 4, 2014.

ACTIVITY 11 Use Commas in Dates

Add commas as needed to each of the following sentences.

EXAMPLE My birthday is December 8 1987.

1. My father was born on September 18 1956.

2. The automobile accident occurred on October 30 2011.

3. February 29 2005 is a date that never existed.

4. I first filed an income tax return on April 15 2008.

5. November 8 1990 was the day my aunt and uncle were married.

ACTIVITY 12 Write Sentences Using Commas in Dates

Complete each of the following sentences, giving the month, day, and year. Use commas as necessary.

EXAMPLE I received my degree on <u>May 5, 2011</u>.

1. Today's date is _____.

2. _____ is my date of birth.

3. The first day I attended class this semester was _____.

4. _____ is the date of the last holiday I celebrated.

5. Next Saturday's date is _____.

Rule 7   Use commas in addresses and place names to separate the various parts, such as the street, city, county, state or province, and country. If the address or place name ends in the middle of a sentence, also use a comma after it.

I have lived at 400 Elm Street, Chicago, Illinois, all of my life.

My closest friend now lives at 402 Oak Avenue, Bexar County, Texas.

ACTIVITY 13 Use Commas in Addresses and Place Names

Add commas as needed to each of the following sentences.

EXAMPLE Another friend lives at 632 Pecan Street, Toronto, Canada.

1. His office is located at 4100 Manchester Drive Albany New York.

2. I have some relatives who live in Atlanta Georgia and some who live in Tampa Florida.

3. There is a large medical center in Dane County Wisconsin.

4. Tamara celebrated New Year's Eve in Paris France.

5. I mailed the warranty card to 762 Wallingford Boulevard Fremont Virginia.

ACTIVITY 14 Write Using Commas in Addresses and Place Names

Complete each of the following sentences, providing the information indicated. Use commas as necessary.

EXAMPLE My favorite relative lives at <u>13 Main Street, Phoenix, Arizona</u>.

(*street address • city • state*)

1. I know someone who lives at _____.

(*street address • city • state*)

2. I was born in _____ .

   (*county • state* or *city • country*)

3. A place I have visited is _____ .

   (*city • state*)

4. My dream vacation would be in _____ .

   (*city • state*)

5. My address is _____ .

   (*street address • city • state*)

Rule 8   Use commas to set off dialogue or a direct quotation from the rest of the sentence. Commas always go *before* quotation marks.

> "Go ahead and start your engines," the announcer said.

> According to my brother, "He didn't say it loud enough for all of the racers to hear."

> "I said it loud enough," the announcer replied, "for all of the other racers to hear."

ACTIVITY 15 Use Commas with Dialogue and Direct Quotations

Add commas as needed to each of the following sentences.

EXAMPLE My father always says ⌃ "Don't judge a book by its cover."

1. "I think Douglas likes you" Charlene whispered to Amber.

2. Jon Stewart said "Insomnia is my greatest inspiration."

3. "Don't kill that spider" Alberto told his son.

4. "You don't need to insure your car" Yasmin joked "if you never drive it."

5. Professor Ambrosini reminds us "Even if it's not on the test, you still need to know it."

ACTIVITY 16 Write Using Commas with Dialogue and Quotations

Complete each of the following sentences by providing a one-sentence piece of dialogue or quotation. Use commas as necessary.

EXAMPLE I heard a singer on the radio repeat , *"I'm a creep;*

   I'm a weirdo." _____

1. My friend always tells people _____

2. I like to say _____

3. My favorite movie character says _____

4. _____ according to someone in my family.

5. One memorable teacher often said _____

ACTIVITY 17 Use Commas Correctly in Sentences

Using all of the comma rules you have learned in this chapter, add commas as necessary to each of the following sentences.

EXAMPLE Since I had never been to that ski resort‸he explained that it was in Jackson

Hole‸Wyoming.

1. The oldest son Steven surprised his family by bringing home his new wife for they had not known that he had even been dating somebody special.

2. In high school Sofia amazingly decided to take a cooking class to learn how to read package labels how to select and store fresh vegetables and how to prepare quick meals from basic ingredients.

3. Because he knew that I was worried Alexei my oldest friend telephoned to announce "Jackie my new address is 1561 Kendall Avenue Minneapolis Minnesota."

4. Mastering new software therefore involves solving two important problems which are learning what the software can do and figuring out how to get the software to do it.

5. On July 20 1969 when Neil Armstrong stepped onto the surface of the moon he said "One small step for a man; one giant leap for mankind."

ACTIVITY 18 Use Commas Correctly in a Paragraph

Using all of the comma rules you have learned in this chapter, add commas as needed to the following paragraph.

EXAMPLE The day that John F. Kennedy died‸November 22‸1963‸remains important to

older Americans.

One of them remarked "On that day everything changed." Many people began working to end war racism sexism and poverty. Violence increased and two other leaders were shot and killed: Martin Luther King Jr. and Robert Kennedy the president's brother. Finally public figures lost their privacy. In a famous photograph

For additional practice with using commas, go to **bedfordstmartins.com /choices** and click on **Exercise Central**.

President Kennedy's son salutes the funeral procession. No situation should be more private than a boy saying good-bye to his father. However a child had to share this moment with millions of strangers.

(B. Semicolons

The **semicolon** (;) is used to join independent clauses and to make meaning clear.

Rule 1   Use a semicolon to join two related independent clauses that could each stand alone as a sentence. Semicolons work especially well if the two independent clauses are short and closely related.

I never liked science fiction; it just doesn't make sense to me.

Stephen King is my favorite writer; he knows how to grab his readers' attention.

I can't believe how many books King has written; *Carrie* is still my all-time favorite.

◀ ACTIVITY 19 Write Using Semicolons to Join Independent Clauses ▶

Add a semicolon and an independent clause to each of the following independent clauses.

EXAMPLE Candace is an accomplished figure skater ; *she studied ballet to add grace to her routines.*

1. For me, the morning is the most frustrating time of day _____

_____

2. My cousin is an excellent athlete _____

_____

3. They have a beautiful view from their window _____

_____

4. Every day, I put up with someone with an annoying habit _____

_____

5. Next semester, I will have an ideal schedule _____

_____

Rule 2   Use a semicolon to link two clauses that are joined by a transitional word.

> Some people think Stephen King is too gory; nevertheless, they read every one of his books.

> I wanted to send a copy of *Misery* to my cousin; however, my father wouldn't let me.

> I will buy every book King publishes; for example, I just bought *Mile 81*.

Rule 3   Use a semicolon to separate items in a series that already includes commas.

> My favorite places to visit are Des Moines, Iowa; Orlando, Florida; and Denver, Colorado.

ACTIVITY 20 Use Semicolons Correctly

Use a semicolon to correctly punctuate each of the following sentences.

EXAMPLE I always go to the movies on Friday night; that's the night new movies open.

1. It would be difficult to work full time while taking five classes however, Noe accepted the job.

2. In the heat of the afternoon, the flowers began to droop a single bee stirred the roses.

3. Next summer, Nadine will see Madrid, Spain Paris, France Rome, Italy and Athens, Greece.

4. Patrick did not have enough time to finish cooking dinner consequently, the stew is very watery.

5. We had to wait two hours to pose for the family photograph by that time, unfortunately, the children were no longer clean and neat.

For additional practice with using semicolons, go to **bedfordstmartins .com/choices** and click on **Exercise Central**.

C. Colons

The **colon** (:) is also useful for making meaning clear.

Use a colon to introduce a list or an explanation. However, use the colon only when the words before it are a complete sentence that could stand alone. Do not use a colon after expressions like *such as* or *for example*.

When you go to the movies, be sure to get the following snacks: popcorn, soda, and a candy bar.

There is only one way to please Brandon at the movies: buy the foods he loves.

His friends know this about Brandon: the food is more important to him than the film.

ACTIVITY 21 Use Colons Correctly

Add colons as needed in each of the following sentences to introduce a list, clause, or phrase that explains the independent clause. If the sentence is correct without a colon, write "correct" in the space provided.

EXAMPLE I went to the bookstore to buy supplies : a ruler, graph paper, and a calculator.

1. To make your own salsa, you need tomatoes, onions, chiles, cilantro, and salt.

   _____

2. I have to do many things to prepare for my guests clean the house, shop for groceries, buy concert tickets, and repair the brakes on my car. _____

3. Ian can play four different wind instruments flute, clarinet, oboe, and bassoon.

   _____

4. This afternoon, two-year-old Ryan was impossible he poured maple syrup on the floor, tore the pages out of a photo album, and flushed a doll down the toilet.

   _____

5. Vanessa's mother taught her many old popular dances, such as the twist, pony, swim, jerk, frug, and monkey. _____

ACTIVITY 22 Write Sentences Using Colons

To each of the following sentences, add a list, clause, or phrase of explanation. Introduce your list, clause, or phrase with a colon.

EXAMPLE Many courses fulfill your science requirement: *Crime and Chemistry, Urban Geography, and Celestial Myths.*

1. Ava has autographs from her favorite actors _____

2. There are many things we can do next Saturday _____

_____

3. That couple broke up for some very good reasons _____

_____

4. I have a lot of homework for tonight _____

_____

5. In spite of its reasonable prices, that Italian restaurant has its bad points

_____

For additional practice with using colons, go to **bedfordstmartins .com/choices** and click on **Exercise Central**.

◖ D. End Punctuation

The **period (.)**, the **question mark (?)**, and the **exclamation point (!)** are the three types of punctuation used to end sentences.

Rule 1   Use a period to end most sentences, including indirect questions and commands. An indirect question reports a question rather than asks one.

He never believed her lies.

He asked her where she had heard such things.

Never lie to me again.

Rule 2   Use a question mark to end a direct question.

Why didn't he realize that she was telling the truth?

How could she make herself any clearer?

Rule 3   Use an exclamation point to give emphasis or show emotion.

Don't ever doubt my word again!

I will always tell you the truth!

▸ ACTIVITY 23 Add End Punctuation to Sentences

Insert the correct end punctuation mark at the end of each of the following sentences.

EXAMPLE Would you like to go to the store_∧ ?

1. Now that he is an adult, Rogelio relies on his parents' good advice more than ever

2. When Vera stepped into the cabin that had been in her family for years, she noticed its old, familiar smell

3. Caleb and Genevieve were happy to see that Mr. Siegel had not changed much over the years

4. What did people do with their evenings before the invention of television

5. How dare you behave that way with my friends

ACTIVITY 24 **Revise for Correct End Punctuation**

Revise each of the following sentences as needed for end punctuation. If the end punctuation does not need to be changed, write "correct" in the space provided.

EXAMPLE Jessie likes me. ___correct___

1. Ah, this is the life! _____

2. Does anyone know where the nearest police station is? _____

3. I wondered what my boss had planned for me? _____

4. This coat appears to be in good condition! _____

5. Olga wanted to know whether a new director had already been chosen.

_____

ACTIVITY 25 **Add End Punctuation to a Paragraph**

In the following paragraph, insert the correct end punctuation in the spaces provided.

EXAMPLE Because of my cousin, Martin, our family just had the best reunion ever __!__

After leaving the army, Martin decided to go to college ____ Did he study something normal, like history or psychology ____ You don't know Cousin Martin ____ He majored in recreation ____ We all used to ask ourselves if this was a real major ____ It is very real, for our reunion was his senior project ____ He organized everything: transportation, accommodations, catering, and even our matching T-shirts ____ Among the games he invented for us, my favorite was the scavenger hunt ____ The family has become so big that many of us had never met before, so instead of finding objects in our scavenger hunt, Martin made us become acquainted with our more distant relatives ____ For example, I had to find a rocket scientist, and to my surprise, Gwen Zawada, my second cousin, works for NASA ____ Even the newest family members were involved; I met the very young man who had just learned to stand up unassisted ____ Who was that ____ The answer is on the family reunion Web page that Martin constructed as part of his project ____ What grade did he receive ____ The professor gave him an A, of course ____

For additional practice with using end punctuation, go to **bedfordstmartins .com/choices** and click on **Exercise Central**.

(E. Apostrophes

An **apostrophe** (') is used to show possession and to form contractions.

Rule 1   Use an apostrophe to show that something belongs to someone. If the thing belongs to one person, use *'s* after the noun that refers to the person, even if the noun already ends in *-s*.

> Jessica's nose ring is the topic of conversation in class.
>
> Her friend's ear stud, however, does not generate much interest.
>
> Classmates do not even know about Doris's belly-button ring.

Rule 2   If the thing belongs to more than one person and the noun that refers to these persons ends in *-s*, use only an apostrophe *after* the *-s*.

> All of the students' conversations are about Jessica.
>
> Her friends' body piercings never come up.

If the noun doesn't end in *-s*, use *'s* after it.

> The men's faces were painted with white streaks.
>
> The women's hair was braided with vines and flowers.

Rule 3   Do not use an apostrophe in the plural form of a name unless the word is also showing possession. In that case, use an apostrophe after the *-s* of the plural.

> We always enjoyed seeing the Kennedys.
>
> The Kennedys' house always seemed warm and welcoming.

Rule 4   Do not use an apostrophe in possessive forms of pronouns: *yours, his, hers, its, ours,* or *theirs.*

> The car was missing one of its rear hubcaps.
>
> Because our car was being repaired, our friends let us use theirs.

(ACTIVITY 26 Use Apostrophes to Show Possession

In each of the following sentences, add any missing apostrophes. If the sentence is not missing any apostrophes, write "correct" in the space provided.

EXAMPLE The Smiths home is located in town. _____

1. Donalds clothes were always neatly pressed. _____

2. The three professors worksheets needed to be photocopied. _____

3. The womans umbrella refused to open, but the rain came down steadily.

   _____

4. This couch is ours. _____

5. Seth Wilsons motorcycle fell over while he was in the restaurant. _____

6. Javiers favorite movie is *Inception*. _____

7. The Smiths always spend holidays together. _____

8. The Georges favorite holiday is Labor Day. _____

9. Jennys wedding will be on Labor Day weekend. _____

10. The Varelas and Fraires will be at the wedding. _____

ACTIVITY 27 Write with Apostrophes That Show Possession

Each of the following words has an apostrophe that shows possession. Use each word correctly in a sentence of your own.

EXAMPLE driver's

> **The driver's windshield was covered with dust and squished bugs.**

1. Doctor Rice's

   _____

2. children's

   _____

3. man's

   _____

4. baseball players'

   _____

5. Melissa's

   _____

6. Today's

   _____

7. girls'

   _____

8. Brandon's

_____

9. Joneses'

_____

10. club's

_____

Rule 5 Use an apostrophe to form a contraction. A contraction is formed by combining two words into one and omitting one or more letters, with an apostrophe taking the place of the omitted letter or letters. Some college instructors prefer that you not use contractions in college writing.

It's [it is] always fun to go hunting.

I don't [do not] care if others think that my father and I shouldn't [should not] hunt.

We've [we have] always enjoyed it and wouldn't [would not] stop for anything.

ACTIVITY 28 Use Apostrophes in Contractions

In each of the following sentences, correct any contractions that have missing apostrophes.

EXAMPLE I can̆t find my way home.

1. Perry doesnt think that its a good idea for his daughter to go swimming while shes getting over a cold.

2. When youre tired of shoveling snow, have some of the hot cocoa I just made.

3. Well arrive at Yellowstone National Park before sunset.

4. The Mitchells arent going to the restaurant tomorrow because they cant get a reservation for that night.

5. Because its breezy today, Ive decided to show you how to fly your new kite.

6. Dont even get me started on where theyre going.

7. Were never going to make it to the top of the hill.

8. Weve always wanted to try our hand at doubles racquetball, but we couldnt find anyone who wanted to play.

9. She isnt my favorite, but shes my brother's favorite singer.

10. Hell never come around to your way of thinking.

ACTIVITY 29 Identify Possible Contractions

In each of the following sentences, underline the words that can be made into common contractions. Then write the contractions in the space provided.

EXAMPLE It <u>does not</u> matter if <u>he is</u> ready to take the test. _doesn't, he's_

1. Although it is against the rules, we are going to allow you to photograph the science exhibit for your school newspaper. _____

2. Greg and Celine are not sure if the bridge is safe, because they cannot see very far ahead through the thick mist. _____

3. The Hendersons hope that they will stay with us. _____

4. After you are finished with the weight bench, please wipe it down with the towel.

   _____

5. Sidra and Darrell do not realize that it is easier to replace the toner in the copy machine before it warms up. _____

6. There is never enough bread in your house. _____

7. Who is going to the movies with me? _____

8. I would rather not have to take the dog's toy away. _____

9. You should not recommend that restaurant to someone if you would not eat there yourself. _____

10. It is hard to talk with Dylan because he does not seem to listen to what I say.

    _____

ACTIVITY 30 Use Apostrophes Correctly

Each of the following sentences contains apostrophe errors. Add apostrophes where necessary to correct those errors.

EXAMPLE I went with the Joneses to their summer cabin. The⌄yre really lucky to have such a place.

1. If I could earn my employers trust, Id be able to do more to improve her business.

2. If Isaac would accept that Jenny isnt interested in him, hed notice the other attractive women in his life.

3. After were finished with the days chores, we can go to the beach.

4. Because Colin still had Raquels car, she wasnt able to join us at the club.

5. Misty couldnt admit to the professor that she hadnt written the research paper herself.

ACTIVITY 31 Use Apostrophes Correctly in a Paragraph

The following paragraph contains several apostrophe errors. Add apostrophes where necessary to correct those errors.

EXAMPLE It isnt always pleasant for me and my son, Donnie, to visit my mother on
Sundays.

Donnie doesnt like dressing up, and Mom wont let him accompany her to church unless he wears slacks, a long-sleeved shirt, and a tie. Long before the ministers sermon, hes squirming in the pew and pulling at his collar. His grandmothers stern glances certainly dont help the situation. After church, she ignores her grandsons request to go out for hamburgers. My moms idea of a perfect Sunday lunch is a nice plate of liver and onions, which even I cant eat without a lot of ketchup. Mom believes that its childrens duty to obey their elders. As Donnies father, I believe that its an adults responsibility to make obedience fun and easy.

For additional practice with using apostrophes, go to **bedfordstmartins .com/choices** and click on **Exercise Central**.

F. Quotation Marks

Quotation marks (" ") are used to enclose the exact words of a speaker or writer and the titles of essays, articles, poems, songs, and other short works.

Rule 1   Use quotation marks to set off a speaker's or writer's exact words.

"I can't believe I said that!" Joshua exclaimed.

"I don't know what you were thinking," I replied, "when you said that."

According to my textbook author, "We often say things we don't mean when we're stressed."

As these examples show, a period or a comma always goes before closing quotation marks. A question mark or an exclamation point, on the other hand, sometimes goes before the quotation marks and sometimes after them. It goes before the quotation marks if the quotation itself is a question or an exclamation, as in the first example. It goes after the quotation marks if your sentence is a question or an exclamation but the quotation itself isn't, as in the following example:

When did people begin to say "Have a nice day"?

Do not use quotation marks around an **indirect quotation**—one that doesn't use the speaker's or writer's exact words. An indirect quotation is usually introduced with *that:*

Henry said that he had always wanted to study medicine.

ACTIVITY 32 Use Quotation Marks to Show Exact Words

In the following sentences, place quotation marks around each occurrence of a speaker's or writer's exact words.

EXAMPLE "That was my favorite blouse," she said to her roommate.

1. How was the play? my professor asked the class.

2. You should get more exercise, the doctor said.

3. I'll take popcorn and a soda, I said to the clerk.

4. My aunt always says, A bird in the hand is worth two in the bush.

5. Guess what? she said. I'm pregnant.

6. Kim cried, You should have told me that the dog would bite!

7. Harold shouted, Let's play ball!

8. Even though I didn't want to go, my brother said, Give it a try; you'll have a great time.

9. The officer stated the obvious: Don't drink and drive.

10. How did you respond when he said, Forget about it?

Rule 2 Use quotation marks to enclose the titles of articles, essays, book chapters, speeches, poems, short stories, and songs.

I especially enjoy the newspaper column "Our Views."

My last essay was entitled "Día de los Muertos."

Emily Dickinson wrote the poem "I Dwell in Possibility."

Sandra Cisneros wrote my favorite short story: "Woman Hollering Creek."

When we go caroling, we always sing "Deck the Halls."

Use italics or underlining, not quotation marks, for the titles of longer works, such as books, newspapers, and magazines.

ACTIVITY 33 Use Quotation Marks to Enclose Titles

In the following sentences, place quotation marks around the title of each short work. Some sentences do not require any quotation marks.

EXAMPLE Martin Luther King's "I Have a Dream" speech is often read aloud in history classes.

1. Her essay, Women in the Military, was a hit with the ROTC cadets.

2. Vivek's favorite column on the Web site is Latest in Health News.

3. I'm currently reading the novel *Best Friends* by Martha Moody.

4. I bought the *Wall Street Journal* to read the article Stocks You Can Bet On.

5. Edgar Allan Poe's poem The Raven is usually assigned in American literature courses.

6. Bruce read the chapter in his textbook titled Marketing Genius.

7. Shailendra never left home without reading her daily horoscope in *USA Today*.

8. Hugo wrote an essay titled Get the Most out of College While Jogging.

9. Adele's Someone Like You is an extremely popular song.

10. The short story Hills Like White Elephants is written almost entirely in dialogue.

ACTIVITY 34 Use Quotation Marks Correctly

In each of the following sentences, insert quotation marks as necessary.

EXAMPLE My favorite essay this term was "Giving It My All."

1. Dencil said, Ms. Levin will be sorry that she missed you.

2. Yes, Aunt Lydia agreed, the autumn leaves were prettier last year.

3. Why do you always wear purple clothing? asked Josh.

4. Angela recited Walt Whitman's poem A Noiseless Patient Spider at her eighth-grade graduation ceremony.

5. After we read the essay I Just Wanna Be Average by Mike Rose, our class had an interesting discussion.

> **ACTIVITY 35 Revise for Quotation Marks**

In the following paragraph, insert quotation marks as necessary.

EXAMPLE I recited John Gould Fletcher's poem "The Groundswell" for the challenge of

mastering the difficult pronunciation.

For additional practice with
using quotation marks,
go to **bedfordstmartins**
.com/choices and click
on **Exercise Central**.

In my speech class last fall, we began the semester by reciting short creative

works to practice using our voices well. Choose anything you like, Professor Keroes

told us, but make it sound like natural speech. I enjoyed the variety presented by my

classmates. Two students performed the husband and wife in the poem The Death

of the Hired Man by Robert Frost. Three classmates took turns telling Shirley

Jackson's short story The Lottery. Many students chose songs. Alan did a great job

reciting One of the Boys by Katy Perry. Professor Keroes seemed pleased. I wish I

had a copy of everything to read for fun, he said.

22

Improving Mechanics

Just as with punctuation, the correct use of the **mechanics** of writing—elements like capital letters, italics, abbreviations, and numbers—helps your readers understand your meaning. This chapter focuses on the correct use of these elements.

◖ A. Capital Letters

Rule 1 Capitalize **proper nouns**: nouns that refer to a specific person, place, event, or thing. Do not capitalize **common nouns**: nouns that refer to a general category of persons, places, events, or things.

Proper Noun	Common Noun
Ball State University	a university
Costa Rica	a country
Thursday	a day
Dad (used as a name)	my dad
President Obama	a president
Professor Lee	a professor
God	a god
the North	north of the city
Bill of Rights	amendments
Political Science 102	a political science class

Rule 2 Capitalize the names of organizations, institutions, and trademarks.

My father belongs to the Order of the Elks.

I always vote for the Independent Party candidate.

My next computer will be a MacBook Pro.

> **ACTIVITY 1 Correct Errors in Capitalization**

Correct the errors in capitalization in each of the following sentences.

                               The Four Agreements
EXAMPLE Have you read the book ~~the four agreements~~?

1. Gabriel has wanted to be a green beret since he was a little boy.

2. Pearl dreams of owning a lexus.

3. Rita's family goes to extremes when they decorate their house for halloween.

4. Among the police officers who helped me after my backpack was stolen, officer franklin was the most sympathetic.

5. Michael's Uncle is a transit worker in new york city.

6. At one time, president's day was two separate holidays, lincoln's birthday and washington's birthday.

7. There are better things for you to do than sit around watching soap operas and eating doritos.

8. Alfredo's Mother wants us to join her at the opera.

9. I rode the elevator to the top of the empire state building, but I took the stairs back down.

10. Is Deanna from kansas city, kansas, or kansas city, missouri?

> **ACTIVITY 2 Use Correct Capitalization in a Paragraph**

Correct the errors in capitalization in the following paragraph.

                Thursday   *Thanksgiving*
EXAMPLE On ~~thursday~~ night after our ~~thanksgiving~~ dinner, the family was sitting around.

    aunt edna, who teaches geography at middlefield junior high school, proposed a contest. The losers would have to clean up. We divided into teams to see who could name the most states of the united states. My team included my youngest cousins and uncle raymond, who always falls asleep after a meal, so we only had thirty-two states. The best team, which had both grandpa and aunt edna, named only forty-five, and all the teams together couldn't name every one. While little tracy insisted that mexico was a state, everyone forgot delaware. aunt edna said that we were all losers and distributed reese's pieces as a consolation prize. Then we all did the dishes together.

Rule 3   Capitalize all words in titles except articles (*a*, *an*, and *the*), coordinating conjunctions (*for, and, nor, but, or, yet,* and *so*), and prepositions (*of, on, in, at, with, for*) unless they are the first or last word in the title. Do not capitalize *the* before the names of newspapers.

For Whom the Bell Tolls
Law and Order
The Art of Possibility
the *Washington Post*

ACTIVITY 3 Capitalize Titles

Correct the errors in capitalization in each of the following sentences.

EXAMPLE Students from ~~westwood community college~~ Westwood Community College sold ~~Walnuts~~ walnuts and ~~Pecans~~ pecans before Thanksgiving.

1. Because we have pets, my children enjoyed the movie *Cats And Dogs*.

2. Henry was surprised to learn that *fight club* was a book before it was a film.

3. Because of the clever robotic toys she invented, Meredith was interviewed by a reporter from the *Christian science monitor*.

4. At my high school, a history teacher and an English teacher both discussed *a tale of two cities* during the same two weeks.

5. When I was a child, my favorite album was *Peter And The Wolf*.

6. My favorite teacher recommended that I read the *House of the seven Gables* by Nathaniel Hawthorne.

7. Naturally, the only holiday song that my grumpy sister likes is Elvis's "blue Christmas."

8. Harlan dreams of winning a lot of money by appearing on *fear factor*.

9. Chrissie always has the latest issue of *reader's digest* on her coffee table.

10. I had to reserve my niece's copy of *Harry Potter and the deathy hallows* before it arrived at the bookstore.

ACTIVITY 4 Capitalize Titles in a Paragraph

Correct the errors in capitalization in the following paragraph.

EXAMPLE During ~~study skills~~ 101, ~~professor~~ Weston used the materials we had with us

Study Skills   *Professor*

to demonstrate how readers use different techniques.

My instructor compared the *Campus sun* and the *New York times* to show that not even two newspapers should be read the same way. *Portrait Of The Artist As A Young Man* is a difficult book that should be read slowly because the sounds of the words help the meaning. The textbook *physics* also should be read slowly; its vocabulary is difficult, but the sounds of these words add little to their meaning. Both *Applications in electrical engineering* and *Western Architecture* have diagrams, but for different reasons. A student is not expected to construct a church from the floor plan in a textbook!

For additional practice with using capitalization, go to **bedfordstmartins.com/choices** and click on **Exercise Central**.

B. Italics

Italicize (or underline in handwritten copy) the titles of books, magazines, movies, television shows, newspapers, journals, computer software, and longer musical works, such as CDs. Do not italicize (or capitalize) *the* before the title of a newspaper.

I read *The Scarlet Letter* in my American literature class.

People magazine is always interesting to read while you're waiting for the doctor.

Captain America: The First Avenger is exciting to watch.

My sister and I love to watch *How I Met Your Mother*.

A copy of the *New York Times* is delivered to my door daily.

I have seen copies of the journal *College English* in my instructor's office.

Windows 7 works well on Jerry's computer.

Acapulco Sunrise by Santana is a departure from his past music.

ACTIVITY 5 Use Italics Correctly

Use underlining to indicate where italics are needed in each of the following sentences.

EXAMPLE <u>Bridesmaids</u> was a funny movie.

1. The first novel that I ever read was Treasure Island by Robert Louis Stevenson.

2. When Uriel and Shayna got married, they received a subscription to National Geographic magazine.

3. Every spring, the family gathers around the television to watch our favorite movie, The Wizard of Oz.

4. Brendan has every episode of the original Star Trek series on video.

5. Sarah reads the Wall Street Journal and the New York Times every day.

ACTIVITY 6 Use Italics Correctly in a Paragraph

In the following paragraph, underline to indicate where italics should be used.

EXAMPLE The reference librarians were happy to receive Professor David's complete Oxford English Dictionary.

When Professor David retired, he donated much of his large personal library to the university. For thirty years, he had subscribed to the Classical Journal. His copies filled a gap in the library's collection. He also donated extra copies of books that were important to his career, including the Iliad and the Odyssey, both translated by Richmond Lattimore. Friends of the professor say that his collection of vinyl jazz records is equally impressive. His copy of the album Kind of Blue, autographed by Miles Davis, is very valuable.

For additional practice with using italics, go to **bedfordstmartins .com/choices** and click on **Exercise Central**.

C. Abbreviations

An **abbreviation** is a shortened version of a word or phrase.

Rule 1   Use standard abbreviations for titles before or after proper names.

Dr. Charles Elerick
Ms. Nancy Chin
Peggy Sullivan, DDS
Josiah Washington Jr.

Rule 2   Use abbreviations for the names of organizations, corporations, and societies. The first time you use the name in a piece of writing, spell out the name and give the abbreviation in parentheses after it. If you mention the name again, you may use just the abbreviation.

National Broadcasting Company (NBC)
International Business Machines (IBM)
People for the Ethical Treatment of Animals (PETA)

Rule 3   Use abbreviations for specialized terms. If the term is unfamiliar to your readers, spell it out the first time you use it.

digital versatile disc (DVD)

random-access memory (RAM)

extrasensory perception (ESP)

ACTIVITY 7 **Use Common Abbreviations**

In each of the following sentences, underline the words that could be written as abbreviations. Write the abbreviation in the space provided.

EXAMPLE My favorite news station is <u>Cable News Network</u>. _CNN_

1. Doctor Koster is always very busy late in the afternoon. _____

2. The headquarters of the United Nations is in New York City. _____

3. The stores sold out of U2's latest compact disc before noon. _____

4. Many people observe the birthday of Martin Luther King Junior by going to church.

   _____

5. Don't forget to set the digital video recorder before we leave for the game.

   _____

For additional practice with using abbreviations, go to **bedfordstmartins.com/choices** and click on **Exercise Central**.

D. Numbers

When to spell out numbers and when to use numerals can be confusing. In general, spell out numbers from one through ninety-nine, numbers expressed in two words (two hundred, three thousand), or numbers that begin a sentence. Use numerals for all other numbers, including decimals, percentages, page numbers, years, and time of day.

Justin counted twenty-six people in his marketing class.

The football player weighed 280 pounds.

Three hundred people is a lot to invite to your wedding.

My GPA is now 3.25, but I hope to graduate with at least a 3.50.

Maya got 85 percent of the questions right on her psychology midterm.

His computer science professor asked the students to turn to page 48 in the text.

The yoga class was at 7:00 p.m.

ACTIVITY 8 Use Numbers Correctly

Using the preceding guidelines, underline the correct form in each of the following sentences.

EXAMPLE Page (thirteen/13) contains all of the information you need.

1. (One hundred/100) winners were selected at random.

2. Students who are in the top (10 percent/ten percent) of their graduating class in high school are guaranteed a place at state universities.

3. (3 out of 4/Three out of four) people who take the motivational training say that they notice significant benefits.

4. Becky intends to have (6/six) children.

5. Coatl bought a bottle of (50/fifty) aspirin for his desk drawer at work.

ACTIVITY 9 Decide How to Write Numbers

Complete each of the following sentences, inserting a spelled out number or a numeral as necessary.

EXAMPLE Bookings of international flights are down _____40_____ percent.

1. There are approximately _____ people in my smallest class.

2. When I was a child, _____ people lived with me.

3. I own _____ pairs of shoes.

4. Where I live, the sales tax is _____ percent.

5. I plan to graduate in _____ semesters.

For additional practice with using numbers, go to **bedfordstmartins .com/choices** and click on **Exercise Central**.

23

Guide for Multilingual Writers

If you are multilingual—in other words, if you speak more than one language—you have several advantages over people who can speak only one language. Because of the global marketplace, you are better prepared to work with people who come from different parts of the world. You also have a better understanding of other people's cultures and values. Recent scientific research has even shown that people who speak more than one language are less likely to get Alzheimer's disease when they get old. According to linguist David Crystal in his book *How Language Works*, most people worldwide are multilingual, and most people who speak English learned it as a second or foreign language. If English is not your first language, you are far from alone.

The English language developed from a mixture of languages spoken centuries ago by people who lived in Great Britain, Scandinavia, Germany, France, and Italy. As a result, some aspects of the English language, such as spelling, are difficult for native speakers and nonnative speakers alike. Other aspects of English are particularly challenging for nonnative English speakers from different language backgrounds. This chapter will provide you with step-by-step guidelines to help you with these challenges. After each section, activities will allow you to practice what you have learned. By focusing on these topics, you will be able to express yourself more clearly and confidently in English.

A. Articles

English has three articles: *the*, *a*, and *an*. *The* is the **definite article**; *a* and *an* are **indefinite articles**.

Any one of these articles appears before the noun it refers to. If the noun is preceded by one or more adjectives, the article comes before the adjectives.

- *The* is used with nouns that refer to one or more specific things.

  I love *the* beautiful Victorian house. [Here *the* is referring to a specific house.]

  I love beautiful Victorian houses. [No house in particular is being referred to.]

  The roses bloom in May. [Particular roses are indicated.]

  Roses bloom in May. [Roses in general bloom in May.]

- In many cases, *the* refers to a noun that has been mentioned before.

  In buying a *car*, Chon focused mainly on appearance.

  The car he purchased looked sleek and sporty.

- *A* and *an* are used with nouns that refer to things not specifically known to the reader, perhaps because they haven't been mentioned before.

  A bird swooped out of the sky. [The reader has no prior knowledge of the bird.]

  A factory can create both jobs and pollution. [No factory in particular is being mentioned.]

  A day in the sun would do me good. [This article refers to some day in the sun but not to a specific day.]

- *A* and *an* are used only with singular count nouns. Count nouns name things that can be counted, such as *book* or *cat*. They have plural as well as singular forms: *books, cats. The* is used with both singular and plural count nouns as well as with noncount nouns. Noncount nouns name things that can't be counted, such as *information, homework,* or *advice.*

- *A* comes before words that begin with consonant sounds (such as *b, c, d, f,* and *g*). Notice that even though the letter *u* is a vowel, *a* is used before some words beginning with *u,* in which the *u* is pronounced with a *y* sound before it.

  a book   a cat   a movie   a speech   a unicycle

  My husband said he will never wear *a* tie again.

  I plan to buy *a* uniform at the store.

- *An* comes before words that begin with vowel sounds (*a, e, i, o,* and *u*) to make them easier to pronounce. Notice that even though the letter *h* is a consonant, *an* is used before some words beginning with *h,* in which the *h* is silent (not pronounced).

  an effort   an honor   an illness   an opera   an umbrella

  An elephant is an interesting animal to watch.

  I wanted to give him *an* honest answer.

ACTIVITY 1 Add Missing Articles

In each of the following sentences, add the missing articles.

EXAMPLE ~~First~~ *The first* concert of the season is always held *the* first week in September.

1. I found wallet and key chain; wallet was leather, and key chain was brass.

2. On plane flight to Bangkok, Petcharat met old friend.

3. Only way to succeed as writer is to write and learn from your mistakes.

4. When she tripped over rock, Penny tore jeans she had bought day before.

5. When you finish with stationary bicycle, please let Howard use it.

6. Please come to our party on first Saturday of April.

7. Spices in bottles on shelf are too old to use.

8. Campground near beach is best place for us to spend night.

9. After hour, Yesenia decided to leave house and go to movie.

10. Sandor bought T-shirt and decal for his car at only bookstore on campus.

ACTIVITY 2 Add Missing Articles in a Paragraph

Revise the following paragraph to include the missing articles.

EXAMPLE Cynthia completed her homework for *the* last day of class.

Beryl is specialist in textiles. She can tell difference between handmade and machine-made lace and knows names of different kinds of lace. Mostly she works with antique rugs, because purchase of rug is big investment. When investor wants to buy rug, he or she consults Beryl. Beryl will tell buyer if rug was made from natural or synthetic fibers. She can also tell whether dyes used in rug were natural or synthetic. These factors will determine true value of rug. Beryl has prevented many people from making big mistake.

- Do *not* use an article before a noun that is used in a general sense to include all examples of that type of person, place, or thing.

  INCORRECT I'm trying to lose weight, but *the candy* is hard to resist.
  [No specific kind of candy is being referred to.]

  CORRECT I'm trying to lose weight, but *candy* is hard to resist.
  [Candy in general is being referred to.]

INCORRECT   *The horses* are my favorite animal. [No specific horses are mentioned.]

CORRECT   *Horses* are my favorite animal. [Horses in general are mentioned.]

- Do *not* use an article before the names of people, towns, streets, cities, states, countries, churches, mountains, parks, or lakes. *Do* use an article before the names of seas, rivers, and oceans.

INCORRECT   We traveled to *the Lake Erie.*

CORRECT   We traveled to *Lake Erie.*

- Do *not* use an article before the days of the week or the months of the year.

INCORRECT   My favorite day of the week is *the Saturday.*

CORRECT   My favorite day of the week is *Saturday.*

- Do *not* use an article before the names of sports, languages, or academic subjects.

INCORRECT   My sister is majoring in *the physics.*

CORRECT   My sister is majoring in *physics.*

ACTIVITY 3 Use Articles Correctly

Correct each of the following sentences by adding missing articles and crossing out incorrectly used articles.

EXAMPLE Our neighbor used to live in ~~the~~ Spain.

1. My classmates and I had picnic at the Reid Park.

2. Eating in an restaurant is not always a pleasant experience.

3. The going through security in airports can take a long time.

4. Everyone needs the water to survive.

5. The driving can be dangerous on slippery streets.

6. Most popular sport in the world is soccer.

7. My goal while in college is to learn the Chinese.

8. The paying attention to the instructions is always important.

9. Jobless rate is high even though the inflation is low.

10. Do you know the expression "The pigs fly"?

For additional practice with using articles, go to **bedfordstmartins .com/choices** and click on **Exercise Central**.

B. Count and Noncount Nouns

As mentioned earlier, **count nouns** can be singular or plural: *computer* or *computers*. **Noncount (or mass) nouns** can usually only be singular, even though their meaning may be plural. Here are some noncount nouns:

advice	mail	information	homework
equipment	education	knowledge	evidence
furniture	vocabulary	justice	poverty
anger	honesty	courage	employment

- Don't use indefinite articles (*a* and *an*) with noncount nouns.

  INCORRECT Molly's mother gave Molly *an advice* about her boyfriend.
  CORRECT Molly's mother gave Molly *advice* about her boyfriend.

- Noncount nouns can't be made plural, so don't add *s* or *es* at the end.

  INCORRECT I need to buy *furnitures* for my apartment.
  CORRECT I need to buy *furniture* for my apartment.

- To express a quantity for a noncount noun, use **quantifiers**, or words that indicate the amount of something. Quantifiers used with noncount nouns include *some, any, more, less, a little, all, a lot of,* and *a great deal of.*

  CORRECT Molly's mother gave Molly *some* advice about her boyfriend.
  CORRECT I need to buy *more* furniture for my apartment.
  CORRECT I need *a great deal of* information to finish my assignment.
  CORRECT I saw *a lot of* poverty when I traveled around the world.

ACTIVITY 4   Use Count and Noncount Nouns Correctly

Revise each of the following sentences in which there is an error in the use of count and noncount nouns. If a sentence is correct, write "correct" in the space provided.

EXAMPLE Cynthia completed her homeworks a few minutes before class started.

_____

1. All four of my grandparents experienced poverties when they were young.

   _____

2. Too much knowledges can be a dangerous thing. _____

3. My roommate showed more courage than I did by confronting the burglar in the kitchen. _____

4. I will buy furnitures after I move into my new apartment. _____

5. My mails arrived every day by 3:00. _____

6. I learned some vocabularies by keeping a list of words and their definitions.

   _____

7. My professor lets me use an equipment in the lab. _____

8. You will need more evidence to prove your hypothesis. _____

9. I gained so much informations just by reading the book about economics.

   _____

10. Martin Luther King Jr. fought for civil rights and a justice for African Americans.

    _____

For additional practice with using count and noncount nouns, go to **bedfordstmartins .com/choices** and click on **Exercise Central**.

◖ **C. Prepositions**

Prepositions always begin a **prepositional phrase**—that is, a phrase that includes a preposition and its object.

To learn more about prepositions, turn to pp. 400–404.

>   at her dinner   in her office   on his folder

In English, the most common prepositions are *in*, *on*, and *at*.

- *In* indicates an enclosed area; a geographical area such as a city, state, or country; or a period of time, such as a month, a year, a season, or part of a day.

in a box	in the car	in the fall
in Egypt	in the classroom	in 2002
in June	in the evening	in winter
in Chicago	in Texas	in the 1990s

>   He wanted to get the book that was in the math lab.
>
>   In Kathmandu, you can buy beautiful wool hats and scarves.
>
>   In 2013, I will graduate from college.
>
>   I hoped to take a short trip in June.

- *On* indicates the top of something, a street or road, a day of the week, or a specific date.

>   You'll find the envelope on the table.
>
>   I prefer to live on a mountain.
>
>   Harriet lives on Memorial Drive.
>
>   Let's go to a movie on Friday night.
>
>   I'll start my new job on September 18.

■ *At* indicates a specific address or location or a specific time.

I live at 100 Main Street.

You'll find the snowshoes at the sporting goods store.

I'll meet you at your favorite restaurant.

I'll see you at 7:30 p.m.

At midnight, the townspeople set off fireworks.

ACTIVITY 5 Use *in*, *on*, and *at* in Sentences

Fill in the blanks in each of the following sentences, using *in*, *on*, and *at* correctly.

EXAMPLE I arrived _____*at*_____ the party a few minutes early.

1. Calvin is always ready to leave the house _____ 7:15 a.m.

2. Professor Chen's office is _____ the Physical Sciences building.

3. Please don't leave your shopping bags _____ the floor.

4. There is a telephone _____ the kitchen.

5. We live _____ an apartment but are looking for a house to buy.

6. Elliot is paid _____ the first and fifteenth of the month.

7. Your lunch break is _____ 1:00.

8. The ice cream bars are _____ the freezer _____ the top shelf.

9. Geneva will leave for Taipei _____ June 5.

10. Like Easter, Passover is celebrated _____ the spring.

ACTIVITY 6 Use *in*, *on*, and *at* in a Paragraph

Fill in the blanks in the following paragraph, using *in*, *on*, and *at* correctly.

EXAMPLE I first met Mireille _____*at*_____ the university.

Last summer, I visited my friend Mireille, who lives _____ Québec City. She and I met _____ Toronto two years ago. I arrived _____ Jean Lesage International Airport _____ June 3 _____ 3:30 _____ the afternoon. That evening, she took me to dinner _____ a bistro _____ the Old City. The moonlight sparkled _____ the surface of the Saint Lawrence River. I stayed with Mireille for five days. While I was there, we made plans to see each other again _____ the fall. We plan to stay _____ a small hotel _____ Victoria.

Besides *in*, *on*, and *at*, the most common prepositions for showing time are *for*, *during*, and *since*.

- *For* usually refers to an exact period of time that something lasts, a period that has a beginning and an end.

  I went into the army for six years.

  It has been snowing for two hours.

  I've been jogging for a month.

- *During* usually refers to an indefinite period of time in which something happens.

  Several times during the hike, I stopped to catch my breath.

  I plan to climb Mount Everest sometime during the summer.

  It hailed during the night.

- *Since* usually refers to a period of time that has passed between an earlier time and the present.

  I've gained weight since the holidays.

  Since last spring, Nicola has been working at the zoo.

  Pete's been so happy since quitting smoking.

◄ ACTIVITY 7 Use *for*, *during*, and *since* in Sentences ▶

Fill in the blanks in each of the following sentences, using either *for*, *during*, or *since* correctly.

EXAMPLE I visited my mother _____*during*_____ spring break.

1. Madeline has been a vegetarian _____ thirteen years.

2. _____ he turned eighteen, Trent has been living on his own.

3. The telephone rang _____ dinner.

4. I haven't seen Benny _____ three weeks.

5. Advertisers make special commercials to show _____ the World Cup.

6. After taking the pills, you should not eat _____ two hours.

7. The air conditioner runs nonstop _____ the hottest weeks of summer.

8. Somebody in the audience started coughing _____ the performance.

9. Caronne has been feeling sick _____ last night.

10. Mr. Jensen will be out of town _____ five days.

ACTIVITY 8 Use *for*, *during*, and *since* in a Paragraph

Fill in the blanks in the following paragraph, using either *for*, *during*, or *since* correctly.

EXAMPLE Karate has been popular in the United States ___*for*___ many years.

Anthony has been practicing karate _____ seven years, _____ he was twelve years old. _____ the school year, he trains three days a week, and _____ vacations, he trains nearly every day. He intends to practice this martial art _____ the rest of his life.

Certain verbs are often followed by prepositions. The preposition is actually part of the verb, creating what is sometimes called a **phrasal verb**. Here are some common verb/preposition combinations:

apply for	eat out	look into	set off
believe in	feel up to	look up	smile at
concentrate on	get around	make up	succeed in
consist of	hand in	pass out	worry about
depend on	insist on	run into	
draw out	kick out	search for	

Junius *smiled at* the cute baby.

Mavis *applied for* a summer job at an insurance company.

At the mall, I *ran into* my best friend from high school.

Some adjectives are also followed by prepositions:

angry at	frightened of	responsible for
anxious about	good at	sad about
capable of	happy about	similar to
curious about	known for	sorry about
dedicated to	late for	tired of
disappointed with	opposed to	typical of
experienced in	proud of	

These adjective + preposition combinations are typically followed by a noun or a **gerund**—a verb that ends in *–ing* and acts as a noun:

Peter was *late for* the exam.

The children were *happy about* going to the park.

We were all *tired of* waiting for the bus to come.

I was *angry at* my new boss when she didn't give me a raise.

For additional practice with using prepositions, go to **bedfordstmartins .com/choices** and click on **Exercise Central**.

D. Omitted or Repeated Subjects

In English, every sentence has a subject and a verb. The **subject** tells who or what is doing the action; the **verb** expresses an action or a state of being.

For more help with subjects, turn to pp. 399–404.

Omitted Subjects

The subject of a sentence must be stated, even when the meaning of the sentence is clear without its being stated.

INCORRECT Want to get my degree in mechanical engineering.
CORRECT *I* want to get my degree in mechanical engineering.

INCORRECT My sister loves to read. Goes to the library twice a week.
CORRECT My sister loves to read. *She* goes to the library twice a week.

The subject of a dependent clause must also be stated. A **dependent clause** contains a subject and a verb but can't stand alone as a sentence because it begins with a subordinating conjunction (such as *because* or *although*) or a relative pronoun (such as *who, that,* or *which*).

A dependent clause is sometimes called a *subordinate clause*. To learn more about subordinate clauses, turn to pp. 425–26.

INCORRECT I already knew that wanted to major in math.
CORRECT I already knew that *I* wanted to major in math.

INCORRECT I threw the package away because was empty.
CORRECT I threw the package away because *it* was empty.

English sentences and dependent clauses often begin with the word *it* or *there* followed by a form of *be*, as in *it is, there is,* and *there were.* In such a sentence or clause, the *it* or *there* acts as a kind of subject and can't be omitted.

INCORRECT Is too late to hand in the paper.
CORRECT *It is* too late to hand in the paper.

INCORRECT Are three bottles on the shelf.
CORRECT *There are* three bottles on the shelf.

ACTIVITY 9 Add Missing Subjects to a Paragraph

Using the preceding guidelines, add a subject in each place where one is missing in the following paragraph.

EXAMPLE ~~Are~~ There are several different kinds of friends.

Every Friday evening, a group of us meet at a café. Enjoy the time we spend together. Formerly, we went to bars. Then my friend Cassie developed a problem with alcohol because was going to bars too often. We decided to stop drinking as a group. Is still fun sometimes to go to clubs to dance and to meet new people. Is a strange connection between dancing and alcohol.

Repeated Subjects

Be careful not to repeat a subject that has been stated earlier in the sentence.

INCORRECT	The lady in the store *she* was rude.
CORRECT	The lady in the store was rude. [The pronoun *she* repeats the subject *lady*.]

INCORRECT	Some people *they* like to go to parties.
CORRECT	Some people like to go to parties. [The pronoun *they* repeats the subject *people*.]

▌ **ACTIVITY 10** Identify Repeated Subjects

Draw a line through the repeated subjects in the following paragraph.

EXAMPLE The people in the class ~~they~~ decided to postpone the test.

The members of my fraternity we decided to give holiday presents to children in local hospitals. Cliff and Rodney, who suggested the project in the first place, they contacted businesses for contributions. Andre, whose family owns a discount store, he was able to purchase toys at wholesale prices. Several members with trucks and vans they delivered the gifts to hospitals. All of us who worked on this charitable project we enjoyed watching the children open their presents.

For additional practice with using subjects, go to **bedfordstmartins .com/choices** and click on **Exercise Central**.

◗ E. Word Order

In English, the basic word order of a sentence is *subject, verb, object*.

$\overset{S}{\text{Jordan}}$ $\overset{V}{\text{ironed}}$ the $\overset{O}{\text{dress}}$.

Jordan ironed the dress.

Adjectives and adverbs are placed close to the words they modify.

Jordan quickly ironed the blue dress.

Adjective Placement

In English, adjectives almost always come before the noun they modify.

An *important* thing to remember is to stop at stop signs.

George prepared to take the *difficult* test.

Ulie bought the *red* motorcycle.

See pp. 433–34 for more information about adjectives.

In addition, different kinds of adjectives appear in a particular order. Though exceptions exist, this order is usually followed:

Articles and pronouns: *a, an, the, my, your*

Words that evaluate: *ugly, handsome, honest, appealing, flavorful*

Words about size: *big, small, large*

Words about length or shape: *small, big, round, square, wide, narrow*

Words about age: *old, young, new*

Words about color: *red, blue, yellow*

Words about nationality: *Irish, Mexican, Canadian, Chinese*

Words about religion: *Muslim, Buddhist, Protestant, Jewish*

Words about the material of the noun: *wooden, glass, brick, adobe, stucco*

Nouns used as adjectives: *bathroom floor, track team*

Finally, the noun goes last: *book, car, movie, church, bench, computer.*

The handsome old house sat at the top of the hill.

My German Catholic grandmother died last year.

The square wooden jewelry box sat on the table.

■HOW TO Determine Whether to Use Commas between Adjectives

How do you decide whether you need a comma between two or more adjectives? If you can place *and* between the adjectives and the sentence still makes sense, then you need the comma.

Suppose you want to write this:

The tall fragile rosebush was blooming.

A comma is needed between *tall* and *fragile* because "the tall *and* fragile rosebush" makes sense.

The tall, fragile rosebush was blooming.

ACTIVITY 11 Revise Sentences to Use Adjectives Correctly

Revise each of the following sentences so that the adjectives are placed correctly and commas are used between them where necessary.

EXAMPLE Please hand me the brown ~~big~~ box.
                                          big

1. We bought the leather sofa most comfortable.

2. Curtis promised to throw out his plaid old pajamas.

3. The dark Belgian delicious chocolates were a gift.

4. A spotted big snake crawled under the house.

5. The car little red fit in the parking space.

6. After the movie, Marisol remembered her assignment boring and difficult.

7. I gave the cheerful friendly child a cookie.

8. His leather black beautiful jacket was ruined.

9. We admired the aluminum elegant animal sculptures.

10. My grandmother recited a Jewish short prayer over the candles.

ACTIVITY 12 Add Adjectives Correctly

In each of the following sentences, add the number of adjectives indicated in parentheses in the space provided. Use commas as necessary.

EXAMPLE A _____curved stone_____ path led to the house. (2)

1. I wanted a _____ car. (2)

2. Smoking is a _____ habit. (2)

3. The sight of the _____ tacos made my mouth water. (3)

4. Linda wanted to take one of the _____ puppies home. (2)

5. The _____ sweater fit Ivan perfectly. (2)

6. Whenever Kevin wanted to quit school, he remembered his _____ _____ parents back home. (2)

7. To be accepted into the program, I had to pass a _____ exam. (2)

8. Eunice refused to climb the _____ steps. (3)

9. Last year, I dated a _____ student. (2)

10. Our assignment was to read a chapter in our _____ textbook. (3)

Adverb Placement

Adverbs that modify verbs can appear at the beginning or end of a sentence, before or after the verb, or between a helping verb and the main verb. Most often, the adverb appears as close as possible to the verb.

For more information about adverbs, turn to pp. 434–35.

Hurriedly, we escaped out the back door.

The dog scratched *frantically* against the window.

Abner *eagerly* wrote the letter.

My brother has *often* stayed out after midnight.

Sarah has *never* been on an airplane.

Do not put an adverb between a verb and its direct object. A direct object receives the action of the verb.

INCORRECT Li put *quickly* the package on the table.
CORRECT   Li *quickly* put the package on the table.

INCORRECT The hairdresser cut *carefully* my hair.
CORRECT   The hairdresser *carefully* cut my hair.

ACTIVITY 13 Place Adverbs Correctly

Revise the following paragraph, adding at least one adverb to each sentence.

                        impatiently
EXAMPLE Many students wait in long lines during late registration.
                        ^

Some students complain to the people around them about the lack of classes. Other students, who had to bring their children, make sure the kids don't run around the building screaming. A few students laugh with their friends. Many students check their watches and smartphones and wonder how long they can wait. Everyone wishes the lines were shorter. One student realizes she has an appointment and rushes out of the building.

For additional practice with using correct word order, go to **bedfordstmartins .com/choices** and click on **Exercise Central**.

F. Verbs

A **verb** expresses an action (*smile, work, hit*) or a state of being (*be, seem, become*). Depending on your language background, verbs in English can be particularly challenging to master. This section will help you correctly use verb tenses, helping verbs, and verbs followed by gerunds or infinitives.

To learn more about verbs, turn to pp. 404–13.

Verb Tense

The **tense** of a verb indicates the time in which the action or condition that the verb expresses takes place or exists. All such actions or conditions are expressed as happening now, or in the **present;** at some point before the current time, or in the **past;** or at some point in time still to happen, or in the **future**.

Basic Tenses

The three basic tenses in English that are used most frequently are *simple present*, *simple past*, and *simple future*. These tenses are often referred to as simply *present*, *past*, and *future*.

Simple Present Tense   The **simple present tense** shows an action or a condition that is taking place at the time it is mentioned. The simple present can also show an action or a condition that occurs repeatedly or one that is scheduled to occur in the future. Except for *be* and *have*, the simple present uses the base form of the verb (*swim*, *work*), with an *-s* or *-es* added if the subject is a singular noun or *he*, *she*, or *it*.

Jamilla *seems* depressed recently.

Pierre *studies* at least five hours a day.

I *drive* my daughter to school every weekday morning.

The new store *opens* next week.

For a list of common irregular verbs and their past-tense forms, see p. 412.

Simple Past Tense   The **simple past tense** indicates an action or a condition that began and ended in the past. Except for irregular verbs like *go* or *teach*, the simple past consists of the base form of the verb with *-ed* added to the end.

Yesterday I *passed* my driver's test.

When he *was* a student, he *walked* wherever he *had* to go. [The action of walking happened more than once in the past, but it's not happening now.]

Simple Future Tense   The **simple future tense** shows an action or a condition that will take place or will probably take place. The future tense requires the use of *will* or *be going to* followed by the base form of the verb.

I *will spend* next summer in Kansas City.

These economic conditions *are going to continue* indefinitely.

Perfect Tenses

The perfect tenses show a completed action or condition. They are formed using the past participle of the verb and the appropriate form of *have*.

Present Perfect Tense   The **present perfect tense** shows an action or a condition that began in the past and that either is now finished or continues into the present. Unlike with the past tense, the specific time of the action or condition is not given. To form this tense, use *has* or *have* followed by the past participle. Except for irregular verbs, the past participle consists of the base form of the verb with *-ed* added to the end.

For a list of common irregular verbs and their past participles, see p. 412.

Alex *has cooked* the dinner.

The lawyers *have argued* their case.

When the present perfect expresses an action or condition that began in the past and continues into the present, it is usually used with an expression of time beginning with *since* or *for*.

Susan *has played* the trumpet since she was a child.

(Susan has played in the past and continues to play in the present.)

They *have been* in Seattle for three years.

(They went to Seattle in the past, and they are still there.)

Past Perfect Tense   The **past perfect tense** indicates an action or a condition occurring in the past before another time in the past. To form this tense, use *had* and the past participle of the verb.

I *had learned* the formulas by the day of the test.

They *had smelled* smoke before they saw the fire.

Future Perfect Tense   The **future perfect tense** indicates a future action or condition that will end by or before a specific future time. To form this tense, use *will have* and the past participle of the verb.

By next Tuesday, I *will have finished* all my classes for the semester.

Heather *will have left* the office before you get there.

Progressive Tenses

The progressive tenses show a continuing action or condition. They are formed using the present participle (the *-ing* form of the verb) and the appropriate form of *be*.

Present Progressive Tense   The **present progressive tense** indicates an action that is happening at the time it is mentioned or an action that is scheduled to happen in the future. To form this tense, use *am*, *is*, or *are* and the *-ing* form of the verb.

Eduardo *is helping* us move the furniture.

We *are leaving* for the beach tomorrow.

Past Progressive Tense   The **past progressive tense** shows an action or a condition that continued for some time in the past and is now over. To form this tense, use *was* or *were* and the *-ing* form of the verb.

Over the summer, I *was spending* my money mostly on food.

Last night, the sick man's words *were becoming* very faint.

Future Progressive Tense   The **future progressive tense** indicates a continuing action or condition in the future. To form this tense, use *will be* and the *-ing* form of the verb.

The judge *will be hearing* your case soon.

By next week, you *will be feeling* better.

Perfect Progressive Tenses

The perfect progressive tenses show an action in the process of occurring before a specific event or time.

Present Perfect Progressive Tense   In the **present perfect progressive tense**, the action continues from the past until the present. Usually the length of time from the past to the present is included. To form this tense, use *has been* or *have been* followed by the *-ing* form of the verb.

He *has been shopping* for three hours.

The students *have been studying* since midnight.

Past Perfect Progressive Tense   In the **past perfect progressive tense**, the action takes place during a specified length of time and ends at a specific time in the past. This tense is formed with *had been* and the *-ing* form of the verb.

My children *had been driving* for an hour when the bad weather started.

Rajendra *had been cooking* all afternoon when his wife called to say she would not be home until after dinner.

Future Perfect Progressive Tense   When the **future perfect progressive tense** is used, the length of the action already begun and the time in the future when the action will be completed are both indicated. To form this tense, use *will have been* and the *-ing* form of the verb.

By the end of the semester, they *will have been preparing* the report for three months.

By the time my children graduate high school, I *will have been serving* as a scout leader for ten years.

ACTIVITY 14 Identify Verb Tenses

Identify the verb tense in each of the following sentences.

EXAMPLE The cake *will be* ready tonight. _____future_____

1. Julian *has completed* all the prerequisites. _____

2. You *have wasted* the whole semester. _____

3. Before getting married, Bill and Jenny *had decided* to move to Colorado.

    _____

4. Last week, I *was recovering* from surgery. _____

5. The tomatoes *will be ripening* next week. _____

6. They *work* at City Hall. _____

7. *Will* Marcie *compete* in the next essay contest? _____

8. They *have taken* all morning to buy groceries. _____

9. Wayne *had been eating* for ten minutes before he noticed the bug in his salad.

    _____

10. Dolores *is talking* to her doctor. _____

ACTIVITY 15 Use Verb Tenses Correctly

For each of the following sentences, write the required verb tense of the verb in parentheses.

EXAMPLE You _____had been_____ (be) doing very well in that class until now. *(past perfect)*

1. I _____ (do) my best to make you happy. *(present progressive)*

2. Lillian _____ (whisper) her secret to Josie. *(past)*

3. The children _____ (play) for an hour. *(present perfect)*

4. Hans _____ (be) here tomorrow. *(future)*

5. We _____ (hire) a band for the party. *(future)*

6. Jonathan _____ (walk) for a half hour when it began to rain. *(past perfect progressive)*

7. I _____ (work) at the ski resort over the winter. *(past progressive)*

8. Before the day of the show, the advertisements _____ (say) the tickets would be thirty-five dollars apiece. *(past perfect)*

9. The politician _____ (decide) to run for reelection. *(present perfect)*

10. Fred _____ (take) the children to the circus. *(present pefect)*

Helping Verbs

See p. 405 for more information about helping verbs.

A **helping verb** is a verb that is used with another verb, called the **main verb**, to create a phrase that acts as a verb in a sentence. Sometimes, such a phrase includes two or even three helping verbs in addition to the main verb. Helping verbs are used for a number of different purposes, including to form the future, the perfect, and the progressive tenses and the passive voice; to ask questions and make negative statements; and to show that something is possible or required.

Micah has left the room. [*Has* is the helping verb; *left* is the main verb.]

You must wait for the train to leave the station. [*Must* is the helping verb; *wait* is the main verb.]

I have been sitting here for two hours. [*Have* and *been* are the helping verbs; *sitting* is the main verb.]

Modals

Some helping verbs, known as **modals**, are used only as helping verbs:

can	might	should
could	must	will
may	shall	would

When using a modal in a sentence, use the base form of the main verb after it unless the modal is followed by another helping verb.

Luisa *might travel* to Cambodia.

My sister *would sing* if she could read music.

Rupert *can carry* the suitcase.

Carlos *could have been* a better candidate.

Our chorus *may be performing* in New York next year.

Unlike other helping verbs, a modal does not change form to agree in number with the subject, and neither does the main verb that follows it.

INCORRECT He wills leave.
INCORRECT He will leaves.
CORRECT He will leave.

ACTIVITY 16 Identify Modals

Circle the modals in the following paragraph.

EXAMPLE Friends (should) help each other out.

Three of my best friends are leaving town next week. Frank is going to Los Ange-les, where he will begin his career as a movie editor. He should be able to find a job quickly. Janice is moving to Chicago to attend medical school. She might be able to afford her own apartment, should she be able to find one. Finally, Leroy is going to New York. Because he has very little money saved up, he must find a job right away.

Do, Does, Did

Like modals, the helping verbs *do, does,* and *did* are followed by the base form of the verb. These verbs are used

- To ask a question:

  Do you want to dance?

  Did my brother pick up his suit?

- To make a negative statement (when used with *not*):

  I did not request this car.

  Sammy does not eat broccoli.

- To emphasize a main verb:

  Once again, I do appreciate the gift.

  She does look beautiful.

Unlike modals, the helping verbs *do* and *does* change in number to agree with the subject of the sentence.

> INCORRECT He do not enjoy watching football.
> CORRECT   He does not enjoy watching football.

Have, Has, Had

The helping verbs *have, has,* and *had* are used to indicate the per-fect tenses. *Have* and *has* change form to agree in number with the subject.

> INCORRECT They has broken all the good plates.
> CORRECT   They have broken all the good plates.

Forms of *Be*

Forms of the verb *be*—*be, am, is, are, was, were, been*—are used as help-ing verbs for two purposes. Together with the present participle of the main verb, they are used to indicate the progressive tenses.

> I am taking calculus this year.

> The birds were singing in the tree near my window.

For more information about the passive voice, turn to pp. 468–69.

Together with the past participle of the main verb, forms of *be* are used to indicate the passive voice, in which the subject doesn't perform the action of the verb but receives the action. Here are some examples:

> Jonathan was hit by the flying glass.

> The book was written by Tom Wolfe.

> Parts of the city have been closed by the chief of police.

ACTIVITY 17 Use Helping Verbs

In each of the following sentences, fill in the blank with an appropriate helping verb followed by the correct form of the verb in parentheses.

EXAMPLE After our argument, my brother ___*did not speak*___ (speak) to me for two

years.

1. Nobody _____ (see) Caroline for the past few weeks.

2. Barney _____ (paint) the kitchen before his in-laws arrived.

3. Until November, the weather _____ (be) pleasant.

4. With this excellent progress, you _____ (convince) me that you are

   motivated.

5. For three years, I _____ (accept) these strict rules.

6. Until she took organic chemistry, Aunt Lucy _____ (want) to be a

   doctor.

7. To my surprise, Angel _____ (win) a spelling contest when he was in

   the fifth grade.

8. Johnny Depp _____ (act) in many unusual roles.

9. To be independent in many rural areas, you _____ (own) a car.

10. Shawna _____ (work) at McDonald's while she takes college classes.

ACTIVITY 18 Use Helping Verbs in a Paragraph

In the following paragraph, fill in each of the blanks with an appropriate helping verb followed by the correct form of the verb in parentheses.

EXAMPLE Elyse ___should thank___ (thank) her family for their support.

Later today, at the graduation ceremony, Elyse _____ (receive) her diploma from the university. She began her studies at the age of forty, after she _____ (work) for many years. Since then, she _____ (struggle) to earn her degree. Many obstacles _____ (interrupt) her education, mostly health and financial difficulties. However, nothing _____ (stop) her from reaching her goal. Indeed, she _____ (graduate) with honors. Throughout these difficult and rewarding years, her family _____ (remain) her first priority. She _____ (celebrate) tonight among her loved ones.

Verbs Followed by Gerunds or Infinitives

A **gerund** is a form of a verb that ends in *-ing* and is used as a noun.

I enjoy *walking*.
Cooking is his favorite hobby.

In contrast, an *infinitive* is the base form of a verb with the word *to* in front of it.

I decided *to stop* my car.
I went home *to wash* my clothes.

The following verbs can be followed by either a gerund or an infinitive without changing the meaning of the sentence:

begin	love
continue	stand
hate	start
like	try

I started *to like* him right away.
I started *liking* him right away.

With other verbs, the meaning changes depending on whether they're followed by a gerund or an infinitive.

She stopped *smoking* cigarettes. [She gave up the habit of smoking.]

She stopped *to smoke* a cigarette. [She paused so she could light up a cigarette.]

George remembered *to buy* the gift. [George had planned to buy the gift and did so.]

George remembered *buying* the gift. [George recalled the act of purchasing the gift.]

The following verbs may be followed by a gerund but not by an infinitive:

admit	escape	quit
appreciate	finish	recall
avoid	imagine	resist
deny	miss	risk
discuss	practice	suggest
enjoy	put off	tolerate

Jonah denied *witnessing* the car accident.

My father missed *opening* the presents.

The following verbs may be followed by an infinitive but not by a gerund:

agree	expect	mean	pretend	wish
ask	have	need	promise	
beg	hope	offer	wait	
decide	manage	plan	want	

She planned *to take* the 7 a.m. flight.

Fred asked *to leave* the room.

ACTIVITY 19 Use Verbs Plus Gerunds or Infinitives Correctly

Complete each of the following sentences with the gerund or infinitive form of the verb in parentheses, whichever is correct.

EXAMPLE Lucy enjoyed _____*seeing*_____ (see) her parents.

1. We decided _____ (take) the scenic road to the lake rather than the freeway.

2. Theodore can't stand _____ (wait) for an elevator, so he always takes the stairs.

3. April planned _____ (attend) the community college before transferring to a university.

4. Ward denied _____ (be) my secret admirer.

5. Nora practiced _____ (drive) in a parking lot before she went on the road.

6. Chester started _____ (collect) fossils when he was in high school.

7. The teens expected _____ (receive) a reward for returning the lost wallet.

8. Dorcas imagined _____ (win) the lottery.

9. Students resist _____ (use) the university library.

10. My little sister continues _____ (bother) me when my friends visit.

ACTIVITY 20 Use Verbs Plus Gerunds or Infinitives Correctly

Complete each of the following sentences with a gerund or an infinitive, as well as other words if necessary.

EXAMPLE Because of her age, my daughter avoided *taking the test* _____.

1. Tomorrow, Richie will finish _____.

2. Whenever possible, I avoid _____.

3. My children love _____.

4. You do not need to beg _____.

5. Sheila only pretended _____.

6. A busy student certainly appreciates _____.

7. I made a New Year's resolution to quit _____.

8. I never succeed when I try _____.

9. In one hour, Maurice will start _____.

10. My parents hope _____.

Two-Part Verbs

Many verbs in English consist of two words. Here are some of the most common ones:

ask out	give up	play around
break down	help out	put together
call up	keep up	shut up
clean up	leave out	wake up
drop in	make up	
get along	pick up	

For more on two-part verbs, see p. 524.

Be careful not to leave out the second word of such verbs.

INCORRECT Susan picked aspirin at the drugstore.
CORRECT Susan picked up aspirin at the drugstore.

INCORRECT When buying gifts, James left his cousin.
CORRECT When buying gifts, James left out his cousin.

ACTIVITY 21 Use Two-Part Verbs Correctly

For each of the following sentences, complete the two-part verb.

EXAMPLE Let me help you clean _____*up*_____ the kitchen.

1. Professor Zindell wants us to drop _____ for a visit whenever we wish.

2. Please pick _____ your dirty clothes before you go to sleep.

3. The cat and dog get _____ very well.

4. Whenever I make that fruit salad, I always leave _____ the bananas.

5. Children always want to help _____ in the kitchen when they are too young to be useful.

ACTIVITY 22 Add Two-Part Verbs

Use a two-part verb to complete each of the following sentences.

EXAMPLE Roland ____*called up*____ his girlfriend on his cell phone.

1. Mary Alice has _____ a professional wardrobe using a few basic garments.

2. I _____ my mess so well that nobody knew I had made one.

3. Yesterday, Jim _____ a story to amuse the neighbor's children.

4. The truck always _____ in hot weather.

5. If you do these assignments, you will be able to _____ your classmates.

Participles Used as Adjectives

The present and past participles of verbs that refer to feelings or senses are often used as adjectives. Such verbs include the following:

bore	disappoint	encourage	frighten
charm	disturb	excite	interest
confuse	embarrass	fascinate	tire

When the adjective refers to a person or an animal *having* the feeling, use the past participle form, the one that ends in *-ed*.

The *frightened* cat jumped on the shelf.

The student was *bored*.

The *confused* child began to cry.

When the adjective refers to a thing or person *causing* the feeling, use the present participle form, the one that ends in *-ing*.

The *frightening* movie scared the children.

The book was *boring*.

The *confusing* message was not conveyed.

INCORRECT I was *interesting in* the show.
CORRECT I was *interested in* the show.

INCORRECT The story was *excited*.
CORRECT The story was *exciting*.

ACTIVITY 23 Use Participles as Adjectives

Complete each of the following sentences with the correct participle of the verb in parentheses.

EXAMPLE I was _encouraged_ (encourage) by the positive reviews of my show.

1. I was _____ (fascinate) by the butterfly collection.

2. The butterfly collection was _____ (fascinate).

3. Jane, who was _____ (embarrass) by all the attention, wanted to be left alone.

4. The children's play was _____ (charm).

5. I have never seen such a _____ (disturb) collection of artwork in my life.

6. The spectators enjoyed the _____ (excite) fireworks display.

7. Frankly, I found the speech rather _____ (tire).

For additional practice with using verbs, go to **bedfordstmartins .com/choices** and click on **Exercise Central**.

8. The _____ (disappoint) viewers turned off the television.

9. I am _____ (charm) to meet you.

10. When will this _____ (embarrass) display of affection end?

(G. Active and Passive Voice

In English, **voice** refers to the way that the action in a sentence is expressed. In the **active voice**, the subject of the sentence is the person or thing performing the action, and the object is the person or thing receiving the action.

[subject doing the action] + [action verb] + [object receiving the action]

Joyce   lit   the candles.

[*subject doing the action*] [*action verb*] [*object receiving the action*]

Rajendra   cooked   the meal.

[*subject doing the action*] [*action verb*] [*object receiving the action*]

In the **passive voice**, the subject is the person or thing receiving the action; something is being done to it.

[subject receiving the action] + [be] + [past participle of the verb] + [thing or person doing the action]

The candles   were   lit   by Joyce.

[*subject receiving the action*] [*be*] [*past participle*] [*person doing the action*]

The meal   was   cooked   by Rajendra.

[*subject receiving the action*] [*be*] [*past participle*] [*person doing the action*]

Note that when you use the passive voice, you do not always include who or what is performing the action.

The car was driven by Samuel.

The car was driven.

In English, the active voice is more common than the passive voice. Readers normally expect the subject to be performing the action. Also, the active voice is more direct and not as wordy as the passive voice. At times, however, you need to use the passive voice.

Use the passive voice when you don't know who or what is performing the action.

I was shocked to discover that the truck had been stolen. [You don't know who stole the truck.]

All I know is that the floor was mopped. [You don't know who mopped the floor.]

Use the passive voice when you don't want to say who or what was performing the action.

A mistake was made. [You don't want to say who made the mistake.]

All I know is that the coat was lost. [You don't want to say who lost the coat.]

You can also use the passive voice when it does not matter who or what performed the action.

The candidate was elected. [You do not need to say that voters elected the candidate.]

The exam was taken. [You do not need to say that students took the exam.]

Keep in mind that the passive voice is commonly used in scientific or technical writing.

The calculation was performed.

The experiment was concluded.

ACTIVITY 24 Use the Active and Passive Voice

Each of the following sentences is written in the active or passive voice. If the sentence is in the active voice, change it to the passive voice. If it is in the passive voice, change it to the active voice.

EXAMPLE   My sister   the health club .
~~The health club was~~ visited daily ~~by my sister.~~

1. The cat scratched the sofa.

2. The watermelon was eaten by my nephew.

3. Calista played the clarinet at the concert.

4. Facebook was created by Mark Zuckerberg.

5. The police chased the protesters out of the street.

6. The college raised tuition by 3 percent.

For additional practice with using the active and passive voice, go to **bedfordstmartins** **.com/choices** and click on **Exercise Central**.

7. My grandmother's scrapbook was destroyed in the flood.

8. The apple trees were ruined by the bad weather.

9. The graduation ceremony was attended by over five hundred family members and friends.

10. Almost all politicians use social media extensively to communicate their message.

Additional Readings

In this Appendix you'll find essays by professional writers that supplement the readings in Chapters 4–9 of this book. Reading those essays and the additional pieces included here can help you learn strategies to more effectively deliver your message to your reader as you write your own essay.

For each Part Two chapter, there are three additional readings by professional writers on the themes in that chapter. Do you want to know more about how to use vivid description in your essay on a cultural symbol? Read "Rice" by Jhumpa Lahiri on p. 554. If you're writing an evaluation of a place, "A Palace of Rock" by Nicholas Jennings on p. 578 can show you how to develop your ideas. To learn how to propose a solution to a problem, refer to Elizabeth M. Whelan's "Perils of Prohibition" on p. 590.

In addition to helping you write, the readings in Chapters 4–9 and in this Appendix will help you become a better reader. After each reading you'll find a vocabulary exercise and comprehension questions to deepen your understanding of the piece. Finally, a writing activity on the topic of the reading will give you the opportunity to express your own perspective and ideas on important topics that concern your world.

Chapter 4 Remembering: *Significant People, Events, and Periods in Our Lives*

For more essays about a significant person, event, or period, see Chapter 4, pp. 82–90.

A Significant Person

THOMAS L. FRIEDMAN
My Favorite Teacher

Thomas L. Friedman has been a foreign affairs columnist for the *New York Times* since 1981. He holds a master's degree in modern Middle East studies from Oxford University in England, and he has won three Pulitzer Prizes for journalism. Friedman has written several best-selling books, including *From Beirut to Jerusalem* (1989), which won the National Book Award, and *Hot, Flat, and Crowded: Why We Need a Green Revolution—and How It Can Renew America* (2008). If we're lucky, we find someone in our lives who teaches us what is truly important. In "My Favorite Teacher," which first appeared in the *New York Times* on January 9, 2001, Friedman tells of such a person.

Last Sunday's *New York Times Magazine* published its annual review of people 1 who died last year who left a particular mark on the world. I am sure all readers have their own such list. I certainly do. Indeed, someone who made the most important difference in my life died last year—my high school journalism teacher, Hattie M. Steinberg.

I grew up in a small suburb of Minneapolis, and Hattie was the legendary jour- 2 nalism teacher at St. Louis Park High School, Room 313. I took her Intro to Journalism course in 10th grade, back in 1969, and have never needed, or taken, another course in journalism since. She was that good.

Hattie was a woman who believed that the secret for success in life was getting 3 the fundamentals right. And boy, she pounded the fundamentals of journalism into her students—not simply how to write a lead or accurately transcribe a quote, but, more important, how to comport yourself in a professional way and to always do quality work. To this day, when I forget to wear a tie on assignment, I think of Hattie scolding me. I once interviewed an ad exec for our high school paper who used a four-letter word. We debated whether to run it. Hattie ruled yes. That ad man almost lost his job when it appeared. She wanted to teach us about consequences.

Hattie was the toughest teacher I ever had. After you took her journalism 4 course in 10th grade, you tried out for the paper, *The Echo*, which she supervised. Competition was fierce. In 11th grade, I didn't quite come up to her writing standards, so she made me business manager, selling ads to the local pizza parlors. That year, though, she let me write one story. It was about an Israeli general who had been a hero in the Six-Day War, who was giving a lecture at the University of Minnesota. I covered his lecture and interviewed him briefly. His name was Ariel Sharon. First story I ever got published.

Those of us on the paper, and the yearbook that she also supervised, lived in 5 Hattie's classroom. We hung out there before and after school. Now, you have to understand, Hattie was a single woman, nearing 60 at the time, and this was the 1960's. She was the polar opposite of "cool," but we hung around her classroom like it was a malt shop and she was Wolfman Jack. None of us could have articulated it then, but it was because we enjoyed being harangued by her, disciplined by her and taught by her. She was a woman of clarity in an age of uncertainty.

We remained friends for 30 years, and she followed, bragged about and cri- 6 tiqued every twist in my career. After she died, her friends sent me a pile of my stories that she had saved over the years. Indeed, her students were her family—only closer. Judy Harrington, one of Hattie's former students, remarked about other friends who were on Hattie's newspapers and yearbooks: "We all graduated 41 years ago; and yet nearly each day in our lives something comes up—some mental image, some admonition that makes us think of Hattie."

Judy also told the story of one of Hattie's last birthday parties, when one man 7 said he had to leave early to take his daughter somewhere. "Sit down," said Hattie. "You're not leaving yet. She can just be a little late."

That was my teacher! I sit up straight just thinkin' about her.   **8**

Among the fundamentals Hattie introduced me to was the *New York Times*.   **9** Every morning it was delivered to Room 313. I had never seen it before then. Real journalists, she taught us, start their day by reading the *Times* and columnists like Anthony Lewis and James Reston.

I have been thinking about Hattie a lot this year, not just because she died on July   **10** 31, but because the lessons she imparted seem so relevant now. We've just gone through this huge dotcom-Internet-globalization bubble — during which a lot of smart people got carried away and forgot the fundamentals of how you build a profitable company, a lasting portfolio, a nation state or a thriving student. It turns out that the real secret of success in the information age is what it always was: fundamentals — reading, writing and arithmetic, church, synagogue and mosque, the rule of law and good governance.

The Internet can make you smarter, but it can't make you smart. It can extend   **11** your reach, but it will never tell you what to say at a P.T.A. meeting. These fundamentals cannot be downloaded. You can only upload them, the old-fashioned way, one by one, in places like Room 313 at St. Louis Park High. I only regret that I didn't write this column when the woman who taught me all that was still alive.

READING ACTIVITY 1 Build Your Vocabulary

Determine the meanings of the following words from the context of Thomas L. Friedman's essay. Then check their meanings by looking up the words in a dictionary: annual (1), lead (3), transcribe (3), comport (3), harangued (5), admonition (6), imparted (10), portfolio (10).

GROUP ACTIVITY 1 Discuss the Reading

Discuss the following questions about "My Favorite Teacher" with your classmates.

1. Select the one sentence in Friedman's essay that you think best captures the essence of Hattie M. Steinberg. Then explain why this sentence describes her well.

2. Explain the significance of this sentence in your own words: "She [Hattie] was a woman of clarity in an age of uncertainty" (5).

3. Why does the author believe that Hattie's lessons are still important in the information age?

4. Friedman writes at the end of his essay, "I only regret that I didn't write this column when the woman who taught me all that was still alive." If you could write a letter to someone who has influenced you, who would that person be?

WRITING ACTIVITY 1 Share Your Ideas

Write a paragraph or two about a significant teacher, describing what the teacher looked like and telling a story about him or her. As you write, think about why this teacher is important to you. Share what you have written with your classmates.

A Memorable Event

FRANCIS LAM
Killing Dinner

Francis Lam is a senior writer for an online magazine. On his Twitter page, Lam describes himself this way, "I write about food, cooking, and people for Salon .com." His writing has appeared in *Gourmet* magazine, *Wine and Spirits*, and the 2006–2009 editions of *Best Food Writing*. Lam enjoys examining the more unusual aspects of food, cooking, and eating. In the following essay, published on *Salon*, Lam describes his first experience with killing his own food.

After a tour of his garden, where tomatoes were bombing from the vines and melons lolled about like a bowling alley after close, my friend Shelby showed me his chickens. He opened the door to the coop, which he built in anticipation of this first batch of chicks. "Hey babes," he cooed to them. "Hey, buddies," he said. He pointed them out, introducing them by their variety. Then we strolled over to his wood-burning oven, which he also built — with dirt he dug from his yard — but we weren't done talking about the chickens. "One of them turned out to be a rooster," he said. "I can't have roosters; the neighbors get upset. I was thinking we'd kill it and cook it. Maybe Saturday," he said. 1

I think the feeling I felt at that moment could be called excitement. For years, since the day I found myself hurling invective toward people freaked out by fish served with their heads on, I've been saying that meat eaters should have to kill their dinner at least once. "Meat is animals. You can love eating it, but you're not allowed to forget that," I said, with no small amount of self-righteousness. Of course, I'd never done it myself, and I've eaten many times my body weight in meat since then. So I looked forward to absolving myself of hypocrisy and, I figured, who better to walk me through it than Shelby? He grew up on a farm. He has a tattoo of pigs and chickens circling his arm, and he has the thick, powerful hands of a man who seems comfortable with any kind of labor. He's the kind of friend who makes you stand up a little straighter because you don't want to feel like a wussy around him. 2

I also have to admit that, in a world where we romanticize farmers and food artisans, there was a certain fantasy to it. Shelby calls his little suburban Michigan home "The Homestead." It's a joke, but one morning, when I woke up on the living room floor to the sound of his roommate Daniel hand-milling flour from wheat to make bread in an oven heated by a fire he tended, the jokiness of it started to melt away. This was some country-type living, and I happily threw myself into the fantasy. Out in the country, the circle of life is bare before you. Out in the country, you're supposed to kill your own dinner. It's supposed to make you closer to your food, right? This is what they mean by knowing where your food comes from. 3

All week long, as I attended baking camp, I marveled at the yeasts and bacteria that we harness for bread, at the aliveness of bread. On the way in and out of the house, though, I'd take a peek over at the chickens, where it was hard not to notice aliveness. I watched their big, clawed feet feel and stalk the ground as gracefully as 4 their sudden, jerky heads were awkward. I watched them scratch in the garden and peck at the greens. They love the greens.

Saturday. We wake up, have toast from Daniel's bread and apricots he'd canned.   5
Shelby sets a big pot of water to boil outside and, over coffee, I can't help noticing a book on the shelf called "Basic Country Skills."

We let the chickens out of the coop. "Hey, babes," Shelby says, "Hey, buddies."   6
We follow them into the garden in bare feet. As Shelby calmly approaches the young rooster, angling toward him, the other chickens skirt out of the way. "They know, he knows," I'm thinking. The bird shifts away from Shelby and comes toward me. I feel the dirt under my toes, such an odd feeling for my city feet, and I feel myself tense up in fear of the chicken's claws. I hunch over, make a halfhearted lunge for him, and miss.

After a few absurd minutes, Shelby emerges from the garden, holding the bird   7
to his chest. "Hey, buddy, it's OK," he whispers to him, stroking his feathers. "It's OK, it's OK," he says, and I dumbly follow suit, stroking his soft back. "Hey, buddy, it's OK. It's OK." We lay him down.

Will I look into the bird's eye? I have a quick moment of thanks when he flops to   8
the side, his eye trained away from mine. I stare at his neck. I don't see the hatchet come down, but, as if in reverse, I see the blade moving away from the board. In its place, where it was, suddenly there are different colors — red, white, yellow. The hatchet came down again, and then the body jolts. I see blood on my arm, on my feet, and I hold on to the bird, knowing that it would buck and kick. I hold him, and Shelby drops the hatchet and comes over to put his hands on, too, and we stay with him, thinking this is the only thing we can do. The feet stretch, and I can see the chicken's neck straining, as if searching. Shelby goes back to stroking the feathers, in gentle gestures. "It's OK, it's OK, it's OK," he keeps saying to the dead bird. My feet and arm are suddenly covered in tiny flies taking in the blood. "Circle of life," I mutter. "It's OK, it's OK," Shelby keeps saying to himself.

We dip the chicken in the boiling water and pluck his feathers. Shelby guts him,   9
and I take him inside to wash him out afterward. In the business, they call this "processing," a blandly generic term you have to imagine is intentional. The process took hold, and, at some undefined point, I was dealing with this chicken as if it was like all other chickens. I was just a cook, and this chicken was just food. As I washed the bird, though, I put my hand inside the carcass. It was warm. I've never felt raw chicken so warm.

"How should we cook it?" Shelby came in to ask. "I'd say high heat, in the wood   10
oven, crisp the skin. It wouldn't take long." I washed the blood off my arm and my feet, and, coagulated, it came off slowly, leaving the confusingly good smell of fresh chicken on my hands. Shelby consulted "Basic Country Skills" to see how long we should let the meat rest. Forty-eight hours, it said, far longer than the time between now and dinner. I asked him why he needed to read it in the book. "I haven't done this since I was 9," he said. Then, "I could feel he was scared, when I held him," he said. He paused. "I almost cried out there. I couldn't have done it without you," he said.

We roasted the chicken along with a feast of garden vegetables, and we sat   11
down to dinner with friends. The smell was exquisite, the juices pooled in the plate

were stunningly good, and the meat was tough from our failure to let it rest properly. Is this what it means to know where your food comes from? To know why your chicken is chewy? I had trouble taking my second bite, putting the crook of its leg up to my lips, and yet, again, I recognized the superb flavor when I did, like there were two parts of my brain working in different rooms and not talking to one another.

I finished eating my piece of chicken leg and felt obligated to have a taste of   12 breast. For some reason, it felt less weird to tear off a bite of meat with my hands; I suppose not putting the bird to my face gives a bit of distance. Is this what it means to be closer to your food?

I have to admit that I am left only with questions. Will I think differently of   13 chicken in the supermarket after this? Or will this just be a memory, something to write about? Will it become easier if I do it again, and would that mean that I'd be in greater harmony with the "circle of life" or just that I'd become inured to killing animals? Did we honor or debase this bird any more or less than what Tyson does? I believe so — it had a good life, ran freely, was slaughtered by people who, for better or worse, feel badly about it. Cold comfort for the bird.

Yesterday, in a hurry at work and thinking about writing this story, I reflexively   14 got in line at a food cart for lunch. It came my turn, and without giving it a thought, I ordered. "Chicken and rice, extra sauce," I said.

READING ACTIVITY 2   Build Your Vocabulary

Determine the meanings of the following words from the context of Francis Lam's essay. Then check their meanings by looking up the words in a dictionary: invective (2), absolving (2), artisans (3), coagulated (10), inured (13), debase (13), reflexively (14).

GROUP ACTIVITY 2   Discuss the Reading

Discuss the following questions about "Killing Dinner" with your classmates.

1. In your own words, what is the main point of Lam's essay?
2. What effect did killing the chicken have on Lam? On his friend? How was the author changed by this event?
3. List five words that describe how Lam reacted to eating the chicken he had helped kill.
4. Focus on paragraph 8. Explain how these descriptive details help the author make his point.

WRITING ACTIVITY 2   Share Your Ideas

Write a paragraph or two about a time you did something that was not usual for you or that made you uncomfortable. Describe what happened, and let your classmates know whether you would do it again.

An Important Period

BRENT STAPLES
Black Men and Public Space

Have you ever noticed you were making someone else uncomfortable not because of anything you were doing but because of what you are—male or female, black or white, young or old, skinny or heavy, rich or poor? Perhaps you've even felt such discomfort about someone yourself. Some kinds of prejudice can be relatively harmless (an American who avoids french fries because France was against the war in Iraq). Other kinds can be deeply damaging. In "Black Men and Public Space," African American journalist Brent Staples uses examples from his own life to show how hurtful prejudice can be. This essay originally appeared in *Harper's* magazine.

1   My first victim was a woman—white, well dressed, probably in her early twenties. I came upon her late one evening on a deserted street in Hyde Park, a relatively affluent neighborhood in an otherwise mean, impoverished section of Chicago. As I swung onto the avenue behind her, there seemed to be a discreet, uninflammatory distance between us. Not so. She cast back a worried glance. To her, the youngish black man—a broad six feet two inches with a beard and billowing hair, both hands shoved into the pockets of a bulky military jacket—seemed menacingly close. After a few more quick glimpses, she picked up her pace and was soon running in earnest. Within seconds she disappeared into a cross street.

2   That was more than a decade ago. I was twenty-two years old, a graduate student newly arrived at the University of Chicago. It was in the echo of that terrified woman's footfalls that I first began to know the unwieldy inheritance I'd come into—the ability to alter public space in ugly ways. It was clear that she thought herself the quarry of a mugger, a rapist, or worse. Suffering a bout of insomnia, however, I was stalking sleep, not defenseless wayfarers. As a softy who is scarcely able to take a knife to a raw chicken—let alone hold one to a person's throat—I was surprised, embarrassed, and dismayed all at once. Her flight made me feel like an accomplice in tyranny. It also made it clear that I was indistinguishable from the muggers who occasionally seeped into the area from the surrounding ghetto. That first encounter, and those that followed, signified that a vast, unnerving gulf lay between nighttime pedestrians—particularly women—and me. And I soon gathered that being perceived as dangerous is a hazard in itself. I only needed to turn a corner into a dicey situation, or crowd some frightened, armed person in a foyer somewhere, or make an errant move after being pulled over by a policeman. Where fear and weapons meet—and they often do in urban America—there is always the possibility of death.

3   In that first year, my first away from my hometown, I was to become thoroughly familiar with the language of fear. At dark, shadowy intersections, I could cross in front of a car stopped at a traffic light and elicit the *thunk, thunk, thunk, thunk* of the driver—black, white, male, or female—hammering down the door locks. On less traveled streets after dark, I grew accustomed to but never comfortable with people

crossing to the other side of the street rather than pass me. Then there were the standard unpleasantries with policemen, doormen, bouncers, cabdrivers, and others whose business it is to screen out troublesome individuals *before* there is any nastiness.

I moved to New York nearly two years ago and I have remained an avid night walker. In central Manhattan, the near-constant crowd cover minimizes tense one-on-one street encounters. Elsewhere — in SoHo, for example, where sidewalks are narrow and tightly spaced buildings shut out the sky — things can get very taut indeed. 4

After dark, on the warrenlike streets of Brooklyn where I live, I often see women who fear the worst from me. They seem to have set their faces on neutral, and with their purse straps strung across their chests bandolier-style, they forge ahead as though bracing themselves against being tackled. I understand, of course, that the danger they perceive is not a hallucination. Women are particularly vulnerable to street violence, and young black males are drastically overrepresented among the perpetrators of that violence. Yet these truths are no solace against the kind of alienation that comes of being ever the suspect, a fearsome entity with whom pedestrians avoid making eye contact. 5

It is not altogether clear to me how I reached the ripe old age of twenty-two without being conscious of the lethality nighttime pedestrians attributed to me. Perhaps it was because in Chester, Pennsylvania, the small, angry industrial town where I came of age in the 1960s, I was scarcely noticeable against a backdrop of gang warfare, street knifings, and murders. I grew up one of the good boys, had perhaps a half-dozen fistfights. In retrospect, my shyness of combat has clear sources. 6

As a boy, I saw countless tough guys locked away; I have since buried several, too. They were babies, really — a teenage cousin, a brother of twenty-two, a childhood friend in his mid-twenties — all gone down in episodes of bravado played out in the streets. I came to doubt the virtues of intimidation early on. I chose, perhaps unconsciously, to remain a shadow — timid, but a survivor. 7

The fearsomeness mistakenly attributed to me in public places often has a perilous flavor. The most frightening of these confusions occurred in the late 1970s and early 1980s, when I worked as a journalist in Chicago. One day, rushing into the office of a magazine I was writing for with a deadline story in hand, I was mistaken for a burglar. The office manager called security and, with an ad hoc posse, pursued me through the labyrinthine halls, nearly to my editor's door. I had no way of proving who I was. I could only move briskly toward the company of someone who knew me. 8

Another time I was on assignment for a local paper and killing time before an interview. I entered a jewelry store on the city's affluent Near North Side. The proprietor excused herself and returned with an enormous red Doberman pinscher straining at the end of a leash. She stood, the dog extended toward me, silent to my questions, her eyes bulging nearly out of her head. I took a cursory look around, nodded, and bade her good night. 9

Relatively speaking, however, I never fared as badly as another black male journalist. He went to nearby Waukegan, Illinois, a couple of summers ago to work on a story about a murderer who was born there. Mistaking the reporter for the killer, 10 police officers hauled him from his car at gunpoint and but for his press credentials would probably have tried to book him. Such episodes are not uncommon. Black men trade tales like this all the time.

Over the years, I learned to smother the rage I felt at so often being taken for a 11 criminal. Not to do so would surely have led to madness. I now take precautions to make myself less threatening. I move about with care, particularly late in the evening. I give a wide berth to nervous people on subway platforms during the wee hours, particularly when I have exchanged business clothes for jeans. If I happen to be entering a building behind some people who appear skittish, I may walk by, letting them clear the lobby before I return, so as not to seem to be following them. I have been calm and extremely congenial on those rare occasions when I've been pulled over by the police.

And on late-evening constitutionals I employ what has proved to be an excel- 12 lent tension-reducing measure: I whistle melodies from Beethoven and Vivaldi and the more popular classical composers. Even steely New Yorkers hunching toward nighttime destinations seem to relax, and occasionally they even join in the tune. Virtually everybody seems to sense that a mugger wouldn't be warbling bright, sunny selections from Vivaldi's *Four Seasons*. It is my equivalent of the cowbell that hikers wear when they know they are in bear country.

█ READING ACTIVITY 3 Build Your Vocabulary

Determine the meanings of the following words from the context of Brent Staples's essay. Then check their meanings by looking up the words in a dictionary: uninflammatory (1), quarry (2), wayfarers (2), errant (2), elicit (3), warrenlike (5), bandolier (5), bravado (7), ad hoc (8), labyrinthine (8), give a wide berth (11), constitutionals (12).

█ GROUP ACTIVITY 3 Discuss the Reading

Discuss the following questions about "Black Men and Public Space" with your classmates.

1. What main point is Staples making about how black men in public spaces are perceived?
2. What examples does the author provide to support his main point?
3. Why do you think Staples ends his essay by describing the precautions he takes to avoid being mistaken for a criminal?
4. Have you ever felt that your presence was causing a stranger discomfort? Describe one or two of these moments and the feelings they evoked in you.

█ WRITING ACTIVITY 3 Share Your Ideas

Write a paragraph or two about an important period in your life when either you caused someone else to feel uncomfortable or someone made you feel uncomfortable. What experiences made this period uncomfortable? What helped you get through it? Does the same situation still bring about that same feeling? Why or why not? Compare your experiences with those of your classmates.

For more essays about a cultural symbol, tradition, or hero, see Chapter 5, pp. 117–126.

Chapter 5 Explaining: *Cultural Symbols, Traditions, and Heroes*

A Cultural Symbol

JHUMPA LAHIRI
Rice

Born in London and currently living in Brooklyn, Jhumpa Lahiri has published two collections of short stories—*Interpreter of Maladies* (1999) and *Unaccustomed Earth* (2008)—and one novel, *The Namesake* (2003). She has won many awards for her writing, including the Pulitzer Prize. Much of Lahiri's writing concerns the immigrant experience in the United States, in particular the attempt to maintain the "old" culture while gaining the "new" American culture. The following essay, "Rice," first appeared in the *New Yorker* in 2009.

My father, seventy-eight, is a methodical man. For thirty-nine years, he has had the same job, cataloguing books for a university library. He drinks two glasses of water first thing in the morning, walks for an hour every day, and devotes almost as much time, before bed, to flossing his teeth. "Winging it" is not a term that comes to mind in describing my father. When he's driving to new places, he does not enjoy getting lost. 1

In the kitchen, too, he walks a deliberate line, counting out the raisins that go into his oatmeal (fifteen) and never boiling even a drop more water than required for tea. It is my father who knows how many cups of rice are necessary to feed four, or forty, or a hundred and forty people. He has a reputation for *andaj*—the Bengali word for "estimate"—accurately gauging quantities that tend to baffle other cooks. An oracle of rice, if you will. 2

But there is another rice that my father is more famous for. This is not the white rice, boiled like pasta and then drained in a colander, that most Bengalis eat for dinner. This other rice is pulao, a baked, buttery, sophisticated indulgence, Persian in origin, served at festive occasions. I have often watched him make it. It involves sautéing grains of basmati in butter, along with cinnamon sticks, cloves, bay leaves, and cardamom pods. In go halved cashews and raisins (unlike the oatmeal raisins, these must be golden, not black). Ginger, pulverized into a paste, is incorporated, along with salt and sugar, nutmeg and mace, saffron threads if they're available, ground turmeric if not. A certain amount of water is added, and the rice simmers until most of the water evaporates. Then it is spread out in a baking tray. (My father prefers disposable aluminum ones, which he recycled long before recycling laws were passed.) More water is flicked on top with his fingers, in the ritual and cryptic manner of Catholic priests. Then the tray, covered with foil, goes into the oven, until the rice is cooked through and not a single grain sticks to another. 3

Despite having a superficial knowledge of the ingredients and the technique, 4

I have no idea how to make my father's pulao, nor would I ever dare attempt it. The recipe is his own, and has never been recorded. There has never been an unsuccessful batch, yet no batch is ever identical to any other. It is a dish that has become an extension of himself, that he has perfected, and to which he has earned the copyright. A dish that will die with him when he dies.

In 1968, when I was seven months old, my father made pulao for the first 5
time. We lived in London, in Finsbury Park, where my parents shared the kitchen, up a steep set of stairs in the attic of the house, with another Bengali couple. The occasion was my *annaprasan*, a rite of passage in which Bengali children are given solid food for the first time; it is known colloquially as a *bhath*, which happens to be the Bengali word for "cooked rice." In the oven of a stove no more than twenty inches wide, my father baked pulao for about thirty-five people. Since then, he has made pulao for the *annaprasans* of his friends' children, for birthday parties and anniversaries, for bridal and baby showers, for wedding receptions, and for my sister's Ph.D. party. For a few decades, after we moved to the United States, his pulao fed crowds of up to four hundred people, at events organized by Prabasi, a Bengali cultural institution in New England, and he found himself at institutional venues — schools and churches and community centers — working with industrial ovens and stoves. This has never unnerved him. He could probably rig up a system to make pulao out of a hot-dog cart, were someone to ask.

There are times when certain ingredients are missing, when he must use al- 6
monds instead of cashews, when the raisins in a friend's cupboard are the wrong color. He makes it anyway, with exacting standards but a sanguine hand.

When my son and daughter were infants, and we celebrated their *an-* 7
naprasans, we hired a caterer, but my father made the pulao, preparing it at home in Rhode Island and transporting it in the trunk of his car to Brooklyn. The occasion, both times, was held at the Society for Ethical Culture, in Park Slope. In 2002, for my son's first taste of rice, my father warmed the trays on the premises, in the giant oven in the basement. But by 2005, when it was my daughter's turn, the representative on duty would not permit my father to use the oven, telling him that he was not a licensed cook. My father transferred the pulao from his aluminum trays into glass baking dishes, and microwaved, batch by batch, rice that fed almost a hundred people. When I asked my father to describe that experience, he expressed no frustration. "It was fine," he said. "It was a big microwave."

◀ READING ACTIVITY 1 Build Your Vocabulary ▶

Determine the meanings of the following words from the context of Jhumpa Lahiri's essay. Then check their meanings by looking up the words in a dictionary: methodical (1), oracle (2), pulverized (3), cryptic (3), sanguine (6).

◀ GROUP ACTIVITY 1 Discuss the Reading ▶

Discuss the following questions about "Rice" with your classmates.

1. What are five words or phrases that describe Lahiri's father?

2. Why does Lahiri's father make pulao on so many different occasions?

3. What does pulao seem to symbolize to Lahiri's father? To Lahiri herself?

4. Examine the process explanation given in paragraph 3 about how Lahiri's father makes pulao. What details make this process clear to the reader?

> **WRITING ACTIVITY 1 Share Your Ideas**

Write a paragraph or two about a type of food that is important in your culture. Describe how the food is usually cooked and what kind of role it plays in your tradition.

A Cultural Tradition

LIZETTE ALVAREZ
Latinas Make Sweet 16-ish Their Own

Lizette Alvarez, a reporter for the *New York Times*, writes on topics ranging from war to politics to yoga. She received a master's degree in journalism from Northwestern University in 1987. In "Latinas Make Sweet 16-ish Their Own," published in 2009, Alvarez describes the impact that U.S. culture has had on the traditional Latin American coming-of-age tradition for girls.

Cathy Zuluaga rearranged her strapless pink froufrou gown, lightly touched her 1 updo and, to the recorded strains of a waltz, strode into the ballroom at Riccardo's catering hall in Astoria, Queens. As the applause from the crowd of Colombians, Puerto Ricans and Dominicans swelled, Cathy, 16, released her father's arm, twirled, curtsied and smiled. She glided past her court of honor, eight girls in long silver dresses and eight boys in Nehru tuxes, and positioned herself on the white swing festooned with tulle, ribbons and flowers. Then, in keeping with tradition, her father knelt and slid off Cathy's demure ballerina slippers, trading them for a pair of womanly high-heeled cha-cha sandals. Her mother gently placed a tiara on her head.

"She's putting the crown on her beautiful princess," announced the evening's 2 M.C. In a flash, Cathy, her boyfriend and the rest of the court, some with braces on their teeth, tentatively began the traditional waltz that is one mainstay of many Latin quinceañera parties: step-step-close, step-step-close. At that moment, Cathy crossed the threshold from girlhood to womanhood.

"It was a special moment," Cathy recalled a week later, referring to her party. 3 "It all looked dead cute." Plus, she added, "I got gifts, money and a Lexus."

Some say it is the boom in the Hispanic population, while others point to 4 today's party-mad, status-driven culture and the success of the MTV show "My Super Sweet 16." But there is no doubt that the Hispanic coming-of-age quinceañera is more popular, more lavish and, in subtle ways, more American than ever. Picture a souped-up debutante ball without the high-society trappings or a bat mitzvah with an extra dose of razzle-dazzle, and a portrait emerges of many modern-day quinceañeras, a term that derives from the word quince (pronounced KEEN-say), which means 15 in Spanish. "Quinceañeras have really taken off," said Will Cain, publisher of the new glossy, ad-filled magazine *Quince Girl*, a takeoff on bridal magazines. "Quinceañeras are something unique, something that ties Hispanics together."

Today a number of girls are shaking off a few time-honored quinceañera tradi-   5
tions, like the Catholic Mass that typically precedes the party, and adding new ones, like arriving as Belle from "Beauty and the Beast" or choreographing dance moves to hip-hop. Some teenagers, like Cathy, a 10th-grader at Sewanhaka High School on Long Island, are choosing to wait an extra year so they can ditch the old-fashioned "quinceañera" label for the hipper, more acculturated "Sweet 16" tag.

The quince-style coming-of-age parties have even managed to influence the   6
coming-of-age celebrations of other groups, including West Indians, African-Americans and Asians, who have grown infatuated with the party's choreographed nature and family tributes. This trend is particularly evident in multicultural New York, where the tradition of trading slippers for heels, lighting 16 candles and surrounding the birthday girl with a weddinglike "court" of friends is winning over non-Hispanic girls. "I am amazed at how many nationalities come in and want these Sweet 16's — Indians, Filipinas, Chinese," said Angela Baker-Brown, who runs Iatiana's Bridal in Queens, which sells quinceañera dresses and props, like the scepter the birthday girl carries. "It is a Hispanic tradition, but these other groups are going to these parties and wanting one as well."

The quinceañera party, long venerated for its wallet-busting tendencies, even   7
among families with modest incomes, is pricier and more flamboyant than ever, according to dress manufacturers and event planners. The trend has also spread to states like Georgia and North Carolina, where Hispanics now make up a larger percentage of the population.

Business owners have noticed the emerging market. In addition to *Quince*   8
Girl magazine, which is in Spanish and English, a number of bridal gown manufacturers like David's Bridal and the House of Wu now offer quinceañera lines. Event planners and choreographers are proliferating, carving out specialties in the quince party. And teenagers can frequent quinceañera expos, giant showcases for dresses, props and ideas, in Miami, Houston, Dallas and Los Angeles.

Girls celebrate their quinces at Disneyland, where Prince Charming will greet   9
them as they step out of Cinderella's coach. They go on cruises with friends and hold their parties aboard the ship, or book quince trips to Europe. If they choose to stay at home, many girls are sure to step out of a Humvee stretch limo, change their dresses midparty, present videos of their journey from infancy to womanhood and indulge in multilayered cakes.

Traditions vary depending on the culture. Cubans in Miami may not necessar-   10
ily do the slipper-to-shoe exchange, while Mexicans in Texas emphasize the Catholic Mass, during which the girls sometimes carry a doll (to be given up that night) and receive their tiara. Other traditions, though, are being tweaked, a nod to today's teenage consumerism and to teenage girls' sometimes exacting demands. The waltz, a holdover from European colonialism, is still popular at many parties,

but some girls are choosing to dance it alone, with their partner or father, rather than with their entire court of friends, a project that requires a lot of rehearsal and coordination. Persuading today's teenagers to waltz to "The Blue Danube," or something close to it, is not easy, so Latin music is creeping into the ritual.

The most dramatic departure has been in places like Miami, where the parties 11 have turned into extravaganzas. With price tags of $10,000 to $80,000, quince-añeras now rival weddings in cost and, in some respects, outpace them. "We have seen a lot more of the bigger productions," said Isabel Albuerne, who goes by the name Event Lady and whose company, Florida Weddings and Special Events, is based in Naples, Fla. "The Hispanic community treats it this way: I have one or two daughters. She may get married several times but a '15' happens only once. It's once in a lifetime. And there is no other half giving an opinion. It is the mom, the dad and the girl. You spend $40,000 on a wedding and in a year you are divorced."

Many families who can't really afford the party have them anyway. Tradition- 12 ally, quinceañera parties have cut across class lines. "They save for this for years," Ms. Albuerne said. Mexican-Americans often share the cost with the extended family, naming several godparents specifically to participate in the process. Cuban families open special savings accounts. "I know some Hispanics who have placed second mortgages on their home for this," she said. "It's important."

In Miami, home to moneyed Latin Americans and wealthy Cuban-Americans, 13 quinces are fancier than ever, with some parties now veering into Broadwayesque stagecraft. It is not uncommon for a young girl in belly-dancing attire to be carried aloft on a bejeweled "Arabian Nights" bed by four young men or to step out of a custom-built Cinderella castle. Birthday girls saunter across sandy floors as mermaids, à la "Under the Sea," or dance in Victorian regalia, or put on hip-hop routines. Masquerade parties are popular, and costume changes, as in stage productions, are au courant. Even when the party involves just the traditional waltz, a choreographer is a must. "Some wear short dresses underneath their big dresses and during the disco, they rip off the big dress," said Ana Ricolt, owner of Fantastic Fiestas in Miami, whose clientele is 80 percent Cuban-American. In September, Ms. Ricolt is putting together a Cinderella party and the girl "is coming in a Cinderella carriage mounted on the stage," she said. "It's a production. It can take us from 8 to 12 weeks to get everything done."

By Miami standards, Natasha Poupariña's celebration last October was no- 14 table. Hewing to the "Phantom of the Opera" theme, Natasha arrived on stage astride a white horse. Her escort was the Phantom. Natasha and her partner, a young man dressed like a prince, danced with their court, in masks and long ball gowns, to the "Phantom" theme song. All the details of the party, down to the cake's décor, revolved around the theme.

Some parents do still hold their parties in a church hall, cook their own food 15 and make their daughters' dresses. But that has quickly become a rare occurrence, particularly among girls who have grown up in America. At Tatiana's Bridal, the average cost of a dress is about $400. Choreographers charge at least $2,000 and photographers more than $3,000.

Milady Chaverra, Cathy's mother, who was born in New York and is half-   16
Puerto Rican, half-Colombian, said Cathy's party took more than a year of preparation, including finding dance halls for the waltz rehearsals. "It's a lot of planning
and a lot of money," said Mrs. Chaverra, who owns Flushing Express Car Service
with her husband, Adolfo. "It's a tradition. I didn't have one and Cathy really
wanted one. It's worth it. I get the memories."

▌ READING ACTIVITY 2 Build Your Vocabulary ▐

Determine the meanings of the following words from the context of Lizette Alvarez's
essay. Then check their meanings by looking up the words in a dictionary: froufrou (1),
demure (1), mainstay (2), infatuated (6), venerated (7), proliferating (8), saunter (13).

▌ GROUP ACTIVITY 2 Discuss the Reading ▐

Discuss the following questions about "Latinas Make Sweet 16-ish Their Own" with your
classmates.

1. What sentence or sentences best express the main idea of this essay?
2. Why do some girls wait until age 16 to celebrate their *quinceañeras*?
3. How have U.S.-style *quinceañeras* influenced coming-of-age traditions of other
   cultures?
4. Where is process explanation best used in this essay?

▌ WRITING ACTIVITY 2 Share Your Ideas ▐

Write a paragraph or two about a coming-of-age tradition that you are familiar with. In
U.S. culture, for example, getting a driver's license or being able to drink legally for the
first time can be considered coming-of-age traditions. Share what you have written with
your classmates.

A Cultural Hero

JOHN CULHANE
Oprah Winfrey: How Truth Changed Her Life

John Culhane is a journalist who writes about American culture and entertain-
ment. His articles have appeared in the *New York Times Magazine,* the *Los Angeles
Times,* the *Chicago Tribune, American Film, Reader's Digest,* and *Newsweek.* Many
Americans consider Oprah Winfrey a contemporary cultural hero because of the

way she triumphed over personal hardships and has encouraged others to do the same. In the following essay, Culhane describes one of Winfrey's most precious values: telling the truth.

In January 1984 a phenomenon hit the airwaves. Chicago's WLS-TV needed 1 someone to take over its floundering morning program, which ranked third in local competition for the 9 a.m. slot. So it brought in a little-known news anchor from Baltimore. Her name was Oprah Winfrey.

Earthy, articulate and spontaneous, Oprah seemed to have a knack for con- 2 necting emotionally with her guests, her studio audience and her viewers. In a single season, she brought the show to the number one spot in its time period. In 1985 the program was retitled *The Oprah Winfrey Show*, and in 1986 it was syndicated nationally. Oprah won an Emmy for the 1986–87 year, and her approximately 20 million loyal viewers have made her program television's most popular daytime show.

But hers is not the typical celebrity success story, by any means. Oprah actu- 3 ally calls her program "a kind of ministry." And there is something more, something intensely personal and powerful in the advice she often gives nervous guests before air time. "Just tell the truth," she says quietly, gazing directly into their eyes. "It'll save you every time."

It is a lesson Oprah learned against great odds. Significantly, this woman 4 noted for the unflinching honesty of her interviews learned the value of truth only after she tried — and failed — to lie her way to happiness.

As Oprah explains: She was born January 29, 1954, in Kosciusko, Mississippi, to 5 an unmarried 18-year-old farm girl. Vernon Winfrey, a soldier at Fort Rucker, didn't even know until much later that Vernita Lee had become pregnant with his child.

The infant was named after Orpah, the sister-in-law of Ruth in the Bible. (The 6 midwife misspelled the name "Oprah" on the birth certificate.) Shortly after, Vernita Lee left Oprah in the care of the child's grandmother and headed for Milwaukee, where unskilled black women could find jobs as maids.

On the farm where she was reared, little Oprah began her broadcasting ca- 7 reer declaiming to the pigs in the barnyard. At three, she was reciting in church. By the time her grandmother enrolled her in kindergarten, Oprah could already read and write well enough to send a note to her teacher: "Dear Miss New. I do not think I belong here." Agreeing, Miss New advanced her to the first grade, where envious classmates soon nicknamed her The Preacher.

"From the time I was eight years old," says Oprah, "I was a champion speaker. 8 I spoke for every women's group, banquet, church function — I did the circuit. Anybody needed anybody to speak anything, they'd call me." Oprah begins to recite, in the commanding voice she's had since childhood, from the famous old poem "Invictus" by William Ernest Henley:

Out of the night that covers me,
Black as the Pit from pole to pole,
I thank whatever gods may be,
For my unconquerable soul.

Oprah grins. "Very impressive, especially when you're eight."   9

Between ages six and nine, Oprah lived part-time with her mother in Milwau-   10
kee, part-time with her father in Nashville. But then she moved in full-time with
her mother. Perhaps her precociousness was one reason the relationship was
difficult. In Oprah's words, "My mama really wasn't prepared to take on this
child — me."

Oprah's childhood innocence came to a traumatic end when, at nine, she was   11
raped by a teen-age cousin. "Three people abused me from the time I was nine
until I was fourteen," she says. The horror of this sexual abuse would come out
years later on one of Oprah's famous talk shows, but at the time she kept it secret,
and it fed an enormous sense of shame and insecurity.

When Oprah was thirteen, she decided new, octagon-shaped glasses would   12
make her beautiful and popular. Her mother refused, telling Oprah they couldn't
afford such an extravagance. The next day, after her mother had gone to
work, Oprah smashed her old glasses on the floor. She pulled down the curtains,
knocked over a table and threw things around the room. Then she called the
police.

"I decided to be unconscious when they came in and to have amnesia."   13

At the hospital, the doctor brought her mother to her bed, but Oprah pre-   14
tended not to recognize her. "All we know is that someone broke into the apartment, hit her over the head and broke her glasses," explained the doctor.

"Broke her *glasses*?" asked Vernita Lee. "Do you mind if I'm alone with the   15
child for a few minutes?"

The mother glared at her daughter and counted to three. As Oprah tells it: 16
"She got to two, and I knew she was going to kill me. And so I said, 'It's coming
back to me now . . . you're my mother!' She dragged me from the bed and we went
home. Yes, I got the octagons."

But Oprah wasn't any happier. She ran away from home, only to be   17
brought back.

She tells these stories on herself with her usual candor and humor, but it   18
seems clear that the teen-age Oprah was using theatrical lies to win acceptance
and love, just as she had won admiration in the past through her dramatic speaking roles.

Finally, Vernita Lee had had enough. "And that's how I ended up with my   19
father."

Vernon Winfrey had married and grown into a responsible member of the   20
community, a barber and pillar of the Baptist church. He and his wife, Zelma, were
unsettled by the heavily made-up teen-ager with the tight skirt and belligerent
expression. "You will not live in this house unless you abide by my rules," he told
her. Those rules, and, more important, Vernon Winfrey's air of confidence and cer-
tainty, would change Oprah's life.

His first rule was that she had to be home by 11 p.m. Another was that she   21
read a book a week and submit a written report on it. When she came home with
Cs on her report card, he told her: "If you were a child who could only get Cs, then
that is all I would expect of you. But you are not. So in this house, Cs are not
acceptable."

Oprah found herself getting home by ten minutes before eleven. And she 22 became an honor student and president of the student council. But the most significant turn-around was her newfound honesty.

"I never told another lie. I wouldn't dream of making up a story to my dad. Let 23 me tell you, there is something about people who believe in discipline—they exude a kind of assurance and realism."

Five feet, seven inches tall, about 135 pounds, with the same dramatic eyes 24 and magnetic presence we see today, Oprah entered a Nashville beauty pageant in high school. She figured she would be asked what she planned to do with her life, and calculated the best answer would be: "I want to be a fourth-grade schoolteacher."

But on the morning of the interview, she happened to watch the *Today* show, 25 then featuring Barbara Walters. And when the judges asked her about her life's ambitions, she found herself stating firmly: "I believe in truth, and I want to perpetuate truth. So I want to be a journalist."

She won the contest and was offered a part-time news position at a local ra- 26 dio station. In an oratorical contest, sponsored by the Elks, she won a four-year scholarship that she used to attend Tennessee State University in Nashville.

Once she was in college, the management of the CBS affiliate in Nashville 27 offered her a job on television.

In 1976, the year she should have graduated, Oprah still had to make cur- 28 few—which her father had now extended to midnight. Later that year, she moved to Baltimore to join WJZ-TV; "her primary motive," according to her official biography, "was to escape her father's curfew." And in Baltimore, destiny—in the form of a Chicago TV station searching for a talk-show host—found her.

The topics on her nationally syndicated show have ranged from overcoming 29 weight problems (a longtime concern for Oprah, who recently shed more than 60 pounds) to racism. For her most famous show, in February 1987, she went to an all-white county in Georgia and asked an audience composed entirely of white residents some simple questions: "Why has Forsyth County not allowed black people to live here in 75 years? What is it you're afraid black people are going to do?" Though there were some dissenters, Oprah found many in her audience who believed in co-existence with blacks. The show made newspaper stories across America.

Through her show, Oprah won a substantial victory over herself. Her lawyer 30 had advised her against ever disclosing that she had been sexually abused as a child, arguing that many people still blame the victims of abuse. He didn't want his client to suffer from that stigma. Oprah agreed. Nevertheless, during a program in which victims of sexual abuse spoke of their experiences, Oprah suddenly decided to tell her story. She put her arms around another victim and wept with her. It was an honest, moving moment. . . .

Now there was just one more old fence to mend. Every time she visited, her 31 father warned her that she would not amount to anything without a college degree. Oprah had left Tennessee State without a diploma: she had finished all her course work, but not her senior project.

Through a friend, Oprah made discreet inquiries: Would Tennessee State Uni- 32 versity waive the senior-project requirement if Oprah did independent work or study? TSU would not.

Oprah had to re-enroll and then put together a project to fulfill her require- 33 ment in the media course. So she did it. TSU informed her that she would receive her diploma at the 1987 commencement ceremonies and invited her to address the graduating class.

Vernon Winfrey was in the audience that packed Howard C. Gentry complex 34 on TSU's North Nashville campus. "Even though I've done a few things in life, every time I've come home, my father has said, 'You need that degree,' " she told the crowd. "So this is a special day for my dad." With that, she announced she was establishing scholarships at the school in his name.

She was her father's daughter, too, in the advice she gave to fellow graduates: 35 "Don't complain about what you don't have. Use what you've got. To do less than your best is a sin. Every single one of us has the power for greatness, because greatness is determined by service — to yourself and to others."

She was Oprah the graduating senior, and she was also Oprah the famous 36 and wealthy entertainer. But she was still the Oprah they used to call The Preacher, who had herself learned the most valuable lesson of all: *Just tell the truth. It will save you every time.*

READING ACTIVITY 3 Build Your Vocabulary

Determine the meanings of the following words from the context of John Culhane's essay. Then check their meanings by looking up the words in a dictionary: floundering (1), earthy (2), articulate (2), unflinching (4), precociousness (10), octagon (12), candor (18), belligerent (20), abide by (20), dissenters (29).

GROUP ACTIVITY 3 Discuss the Reading

Discuss the following questions about "Oprah Winfrey: How Truth Changed Her Life" with your classmates.

1. What did you learn about Oprah Winfrey from this essay that you didn't already know?
2. Of the events that are described by Culhane, which one do you think had the most effect on Winfrey? Why?
3. According to the author, why is telling the truth so important to Winfrey?
4. Do you admire Winfrey? Why or why not?
5. How does Culhane keep his audience interested in his topic?

WRITING ACTIVITY 3 Share Your Ideas

Write a paragraph or two about telling the truth. To Oprah, telling the truth "will save you every time." Do you agree with this? Why or why not?

For more essays about work and the workplace, see Chapter 6, pp. 159–167.

Chapter 6 Analyzing: *Occupations, Workplace Communication, and Job-Related Problems*

An Occupation

DONNA McALEER
How a Soldier Takes on Community Health Care

What's the first thing that comes to mind when you think of military leadership? Many people think of an autocratic, top-down, do-as-you're-told environment, but there is more to military leadership. In the following essay, "How a Soldier Takes on Community Health Care," Donna McAleer describes how the skills she learned in the military helped her become an effective executive director of a civilian nonprofit organization. This essay was a posting to the blog *Frontline Leadership,* on the *Harvard Business Review* Web site.

When I was interviewing to be the executive director of a health-care non-profit, the People's Health Clinic (PHC), members of its board of directors questioned my experience. They wanted to know what someone coming from the U.S. Army, known for its hierarchy and "give-and-take orders" environment, could bring to a volunteer-based organization, particularly one with limited resources.   1

I told them that the skills I learned in the military would be directly transferable. Soldiers are taught to accomplish a mission by gathering information, understanding the resources available, analyzing the situation, and determining what the desired outcome is. From there, they set an order of battle, an operations plan, and a timetable with responsibilities delineated. They get buy-in from the chain of command, and when orders are given, they execute and react as things unfold. If I had to identify three skills essential to military success they would be team-building, communication, and delegation of responsibility. I knew I could use these skills to my advantage at the PHC.   2

In the military, building a team with complementary capabilities is critical to a mission, and to the safety of the men or women under your command. Once I was hired at the PHC, a group based in Park City, UT, that is committed to providing health care to the community's uninsured, I could see it needed three people: a medical director to establish protocols for care, a clinic manager to focus on the delivery of that care, including acquiring resources for staff, and an administrative manager to oversee day-to-day office activities. With less than six months of operating cash, we could not hire for those positions immediately. But, instead of   3 waiting, we filled the spots with volunteers and part-time employees. Eventually we had enough funding to hire three full-time executives, who have since expanded our services by more than 30%, adding two full-day clinics covering general medicine, pediatrics, prenatal and women's health, and a patient education program.

In the military, the measure of effective communication has long been whether each soldier understands his or her role and responsibilities in achieving the mission. Increasingly, however, particularly in Iraq and Afghanistan, it also means ensuring that affected communities understand what you are doing. At the PHC, employees and volunteers understood the mission — to provide quality health care for the uninsured — and their place in it. But outside stakeholders also had to be brought on board. We initiated an aggressive media and PR campaign expanding from a bi-annual snail-mail newsletter to a more comprehensive campaign that included not only direct mail but also print, radio, broadcast, a website and video. The message was received and in the first year contributions to the PHC increased 33%. We also reached out to businesses in the lodging, dining, construction and landscaping sectors, which typically employ part-time and seasonal (i.e. uninsured) workers to create a clinic sponsorship program.

Delegation is about understanding your resources and building skills in subordinates by giving them more responsibility. In the military it is imperative that one soldier be able to step up and assume the responsibilities of another in case he or she is re-assigned to another unit, or injured or killed in combat. In companies and non-profits, delegation is fundamental to building bench strength so anyone in the organization can assume the next higher level of responsibility at any time. This requires clear information, defined expectations, support and oversight. During my tenure at the PHC, I consistently worked with our medical director, clinic and administrative managers to develop financial, operational and administrative processes and metrics so that when I eventually left the clinic to pursue a new opportunity, all operations not only continued but grew from the foundation we collectively built.

When I arrived at the PHC in 2002, it was in financial distress. Now, it is a thriving, stable organization that logs more than 7,000 patient visits a year, reducing the demand that preventable, non-emergency care places on local hospitals. In reality, there are far more similarities than differences between military and non-profit leadership. Proper team-building, communication and delegation can help any organization perform better. It just takes leadership to point the way, and keep everyone moving in the right direction.

READING ACTIVITY 1 Build Your Vocabulary

Determine the meanings of the following words from the context of Donna McAleer's essay. Then check their meanings by looking up the words in a dictionary: non-profit (1), hierarchy (1), delineated (2), delegation (2), protocols (3), metrics (5).

GROUP ACTIVITY 1 Discuss the Reading

Discuss the following questions about "How a Soldier Takes on Community Health Care" with your classmates.

1. What three leadership skills does McAleer write about in this essay? How do they transfer from the military to civilian nonprofit leadership? Can you think of other leadership skills that might transfer?

2. It is generally believed that people who have served in the military make good civilian employees. Why do you suppose this is true?

3. Why does McAleer say that she had to "take on" community health care? How does one take on an entire profession?

4. How does McAleer use examples from Afghanistan and Iraq to support her points? In your view, are these effective or ineffective examples? Explain your answer.

WRITING ACTIVITY 1 Share Your Ideas

Write a paragraph or two describing your own leadership skills. Explain why these skills are important for a profession you might like to pursue.

Workplace Communication

RITA WARREN HESS
American Workplace Slang and Jargon

Slang and jargon help people in the workplace communicate quickly and effectively. Until people understand this language, however, they are at a disadvantage. "American Workplace Slang and Jargon" was originally published on the immigration resources Web site www.New2USA.com. In this essay, Rita Warren Hess helps people who are new to the United States understand some of the odd-sounding language used in the American business world.

Have you mastered the English language? Good! Can you also comfortably   1
speak business-ese, the sometimes-unusual words and phrases like those in the following fictional American workplace?

Mega Music is a **brick and mortar** business (a traditional company with an   2
actual building or store location, rather than an e-commerce business). Mega struggles to compete with online retailers, sometimes called **click and mortar** businesses. To remain financially sound, Mega Music used **headhunters**, paid recruiters who match hiring companies with employees or executives, to find a new

CEO. The headhunter found a young energetic **Yankee** (a person from the north-eastern region of the United States) named Bill Black.

Mega hired Bill because he possessed excellent **soft skills** (people skills). He interacted well with the public, was an excellent motivator and a good conversationalist. Soft skills are sometimes more important than **hard skills** (hands-on abilities) like programming or building cars.   3

The headhunter also located a **bean counter** to handle the company's funds (beans). People often refer to *accountants* as bean counters. The bean counter suggested Mega managers do some **number crunching** (performing complex calculations) to see if they could save the company money by lowering budget estimates or postponing planned projects. Mega's new accountant further recommended **across the board** budget cuts (reductions that applied to everyone equally). Slashing budgets by 10% across the board meant *every* department received a 10% budget cut.   4

When budget projections still did not align with income estimates, Mega Music **downsized** (went from one size to a smaller size by reducing the number of employees through terminations or retirements). Downsizing forced department managers to make difficult decisions. Janet had to reduce her engineering staff of four people by one. Each person was an excellent worker and played an important role in the group. Deciding which one to fire was hard for Janet.   5

All department managers were uncomfortable knowing certain employees would receive a **pink slip** (termination notice). A person being fired (also known as *getting the axe*) does not actually receive a pink slip terminating his/her employment. This term is one of many unusual phrases adopted by businesses.   6

One Mega employee reacted unfavorably to termination and charged the company with age discrimination. This was expected since the company had **deep pockets**, meaning they were a large and reasonably successful business. People contemplating **litigation** (legal charges) often target companies with deep pockets because they anticipate a large financial settlement.   7

Other employees welcomed the termination. They were tired of the **rat race**—methodically getting up, going to work, performing job duties, going home, sleeping, and repeating the process over again. They never felt refreshed, although they escaped the rat race on weekends by catching up on **R and R** (rest and relaxation).   8

What else did Mega Music do to prevent **going under** (going out of business)?   9

Bill, the new CEO, believed saving the company meant identifying previous   10
mistakes. He invited all managers to a **Monday morning quarterback** session. This phrase originated after weekend football games, when fans discussed what the **quarterback** (an important player on a football team) *should* have done or *could* have done differently to change the game's outcome. Bill felt that by evaluating past failures, they could avoid the same mistake(s) in the future.

Following Bill's Monday morning quarterback session, his staff presented a   11
list of ideas for improvement.

First, they found their method of valuing and managing warehouse products   12
was a disaster. They switched to **FIFO**, an inventory term meaning "first-in-first-out" and placing a value on items sold by using the cost of the oldest items

first. FIFO was chosen over another inventory valuation method called **LIFO** (last-in-first-out).

Bill and his team also decided to decrease their inventory by using a process 13 called **JIT** (just-in-time), in which they would stock little, if any, surplus goods or materials. Instead, buyers ordered items from suppliers to arrive just in time, or just before needed.

An internal investigation revealed that Mary, the warehouse manager, was 14 receiving **kickbacks** (illegal payments made between two parties to give one person an unfair advantage over competitors). Mary routinely sent bid packages to obtain quotes on CD cases. John Jones, an employee at a plastics company that manufactures CD cases, paid Mary $500 cash each time she arranged it so that his company got the contract to supply the cases.

Besides firing Mary, Mega Music **outsourced** purchasing, meaning they hired an 15 independent firm to provide the service rather than using employees on the company payroll. Financially, it benefited the company to outsource the function rather than having it done **in-house** (done by employees on the company payroll).

Bill's team also found that filling product orders was very **labor-intensive**, 16 meaning labor costs were disproportionately high. They devised a plan to ship inventory twice as fast with fewer employees by **working smarter** (getting the work done more efficiently). Working smarter is different from working harder. For example, if your job is to move bricks from Pile A to Pile B all day, you could work harder and move more bricks. But if you load them in a wheelbarrow, push them across the yard, then go back for another load, you are working smarter.

Finally, Mega Music changed their advertising strategy by studying the 17 **benchmark**, the best in their industry. Their largest competitor, Today's Tunes, had the ultimate advertising campaign for reaching young male audiences. Today's Tunes set the benchmark (the standard), so Mega used a similar format to devise a halftime Super Bowl Sunday commercial.

Mega encountered obstacles during the **eleventh (11th) hour**, the timeframe 18 just before a deadline but not necessarily the *hour* before. After spending six months preparing the new commercial, they made several changes during the last three weeks (their 11th hour) before the spot aired.

Mega's CEO wondered if the company's efforts would be in vain. If the Super 19 Bowl advertisement did not bring the anticipated returns, the company would **take a bath** (an unfavorable way of describing a person or group of people who did not fare well in some undertaking) and might face bankruptcy. Bill worried needlessly. Millions of viewers watched Mega Music's halftime commercial and the company telephones rang non-stop on Monday morning with new orders.

READING ACTIVITY 2 Build Your Vocabulary

Determine the meanings of the following words from the context of Rita Warren Hess's essay. Then check their meanings by looking up the words in a dictionary: business-ese (1), retailers (2), projections (5), align (5), termination (6), inventory (12), surplus (13), disproportionately (16).

GROUP ACTIVITY 2 Discuss the Reading

Discuss the following questions about "American Workplace Slang and Jargon" with your classmates.

1. What is Hess's purpose in this essay? Is this purpose stated directly? If it is stated directly, where does it appear? If it's not stated directly, why not?

2. Describe the audience that the author is writing for. How does her understanding of her readers affect the way the author explains slang and jargon? Do you disagree with any of her definitions? Select at least one and research its origin.

3. Why did the author decide to write a fictional story — rather than a standard essay — to explain specialized language in the business world?

4. Among the business terms defined in this article are *pink slip*, *deep pockets*, and *rat race*. How do you suppose these terms came to be?

WRITING ACTIVITY 2 Share Your Ideas

Research a phrase commonly used in a business — but not used in this essay — and write one or two paragraphs defining it and describing its origin. Explain why it's important for your classmates to understand the meaning of this phrase.

A Job-Related Problem

ELLEN GOODMAN
The Company Man

Ellen Goodman is a Pulitzer Prize–winning newspaper columnist. Her column in the *Boston Globe* was syndicated to more than 450 newspapers. With common sense and humor, Goodman writes about topics close to home. She focuses on families, women in the workplace, and the poor. In the essay that follows, Goodman provides a vivid definition of "the company man."

He worked himself to death, finally and precisely, at 3:00 a.m. Sunday morning.   1

The obituary didn't say that, of course. It said that he died of a coronary   2
thrombosis — I think that was it — but everyone among his friends and acquaintances knew it instantly. He was a perfect Type A, a workaholic, a classic, they said to each other and shook their heads — and thought for five or ten minutes about the way they lived.

This man who worked himself to death finally and precisely at 3:00 a.m. Sunday   3
morning — on his day off — was fifty-one years old and a vice-president. He was, however, one of six vice-presidents, and one of three who might conceivably — if

the president died or retired soon enough — have moved to the top spot. Phil knew that.

He worked six days a week, five of them until eight or nine at night, during a   4
time when his own company had begun the four-day week for everyone but the executives. He worked like the Important People. He had no outside "extracurricular interests," unless, of course, you think about a monthly golf game that way. To Phil, it was work. He always ate egg salad sandwiches at his desk. He was, of course, overweight, by twenty or twenty-five pounds. He thought it was okay, though, because he didn't smoke.

On Saturdays, Phil wore a sports jacket to the office instead of a suit, because   5
it was the weekend.

He had a lot of people working for him, maybe sixty, and most of them liked   6
him most of the time. Three of them will be seriously considered for his job. The obituary didn't mention that.

But it did list his "survivors" quite accurately. He is survived by his wife, Helen,   7
forty-eight years old, a good woman of no particular marketable skills, who worked in an office before marrying and mothering. She had, according to their daughter, given up trying to compete with his work years ago, when the children were small. A company friend said, "I know how much you will miss him." And she answered, "I already have."

"Missing him all these years," she must have given up part of herself which   8
had cared too much for the man. She would be "well taken care of."

His "dearly beloved" eldest of the "dearly beloved" children is a hard-working   9
executive in a manufacturing firm down South. In the day and a half before the funeral, he went around the neighborhood researching his father, asking the neighbors what he was like. They were embarrassed.

His second child is a girl, who is twenty-four and newly married. She lives   10
near her mother and they are close, but whenever she was alone with her father, in a car driving somewhere, they had nothing to say to each other.

The youngest is twenty, a boy, a high-school graduate who has spent the last   11
couple of years, like a lot of his friends, doing enough odd jobs to stay in grass and food. He was the one who tried to grab at his father, and tried to mean enough to him to keep the man at home. He was his father's favorite. Over the last two years, Phil stayed up nights worrying about the boy.

The boy once said, "My father and I only board here."   12

At the funeral, the sixty-year-old company president told the forty-eight-   13
year-old widow that the fifty-one-year-old deceased had meant much to the company and would be missed and would be hard to replace. The widow didn't look him in the eye. She was afraid he would read her bitterness and, after all, she would need him to straighten out the finances — the stock options and all that.

Phil was overweight and nervous and worked too hard. If he wasn't at the of-   14
fice, he was worried about it. Phil was a Type A, a heart-attack natural. You could have picked him out in a minute from a lineup.

So when he finally worked himself to death, at precisely 3:00 a.m. Sunday   15
morning, no one was really surprised.

By 5:00 p.m. the afternoon of the funeral, the company president had begun, discreetly of course, with care and taste, to make inquiries about his replacement. One of three men. He asked around: "Who's been working the hardest?"

READING ACTIVITY 3 Build Your Vocabulary

Determine the meanings of the following words from the context of Ellen Goodman's essay. Then check their meanings by looking up the words in a dictionary: obituary (2), extracurricular (4), board (12), deceased (13), discreetly (16).

GROUP ACTIVITY 3 Discuss the Reading

Discuss the following questions about "The Company Man" with your classmates.

1. What details about Phil make him the definition of "the company man"?

2. What point is Goodman trying to make by ending her piece with the line: "He [the president] asked around: 'Who's been working the hardest?' "

3. What about her style helps Goodman convince readers that Phil was a true "company man"?

4. In your view, does this essay accurately depict the modern workplace? Why or why not?

WRITING ACTIVITY 3 Share Your Ideas

Write a paragraph or two describing your workplace or college experience. Is the work you are doing causing you stress and affecting your health? Why or why not? Compare your experiences with those of your fellow students.

Chapter 7 Evaluating: *Products, Performances, and Places*

For more essays evaluating a product, performance, or place, see Chapter 7, pp. 197–205.

Evaluation of a Product

ANN HODGMAN
No Wonder They Call Me a Bitch

Ann Hodgman is a freelance writer whose articles have appeared in various print and online publications, including *Good Housekeeping*, *Spy*, *Smithsonian*, the *New Yorker*, and *Slate*. She is also the author of cookbooks, humor books, and more than forty children's books. In "No Wonder They Call Me a Bitch," Hodgman evaluates dog food with a humorous twist: she tastes it herself.

I've always wondered about dog food. Is a Gaines-burger really like a hamburger? Can you fry it? Does dog food "cheese" taste like real cheese? Does Gravy Train actually make gravy in the dog's bowl, or is that brown liquid just dissolved crumbs? And exactly what *are* by-products? 1

Having spent the better part of a week eating dog food, I'm sorry to say that I now know the answers to these questions. While my dachshund, Shortie, watched in agonies of yearning, I gagged my way through can after can of stinky, white-flecked mush and bag after bag of stinky, fat-drenched nuggets. And now I understand exactly why Shortie's breath is so bad. 2

Of course, Gaines-burgers are neither mush nor nuggets. They are, rather, a miracle of beauty and packaging — or at least that's what I thought when I was little. I used to beg my mother to get them for our dogs, but she always said they were too expensive. When I finally bought a box of cheese-flavored Gaines-burgers — after 20 years of longing — I felt deliciously wicked. 3

"Dogs love real beef," the back of the box proclaimed proudly. "That's why Gaines-burgers is the only beef burger for dogs with real beef and no meat by-products!" The copy was accurate: meat by-products did not appear in the list of ingredients. Poultry by-products did, though — right there next to preserved animal fat. 4

One Purina spokesman told me that poultry by-products consist of necks, intestines, undeveloped eggs and other "carcass remnants," but not feathers, heads or feet. When I told him I'd been eating dog food, he said, "Oh, you're kidding! Oh no!" (I came to share his alarm when, weeks later, a second Purina spokesman said that Gaines-burgers *do* contain poultry heads and feet — but *not* undeveloped eggs.) 5

Up close my Gaines-burger didn't much resemble chopped beef. Rather, it looked — and felt — like a single long, extruded piece of redness that had been chopped into segments and formed into a patty. You could make one at home if you had a Play-Doh Fun Factory. 6

I turned on the skillet. While I waited for it to heat up I pulled out a shred of cheese-colored material and palpated it. Again, like Play-Doh, it was quite malleable. I made a little cheese bird out of it; then I counted to three and ate the bird. 7

There was a horrifying rush of cheddar taste, followed immediately by the dull tang of soybean flour — the main ingredient in Gaines-burgers. Next I tried a piece of red extrusion. The main difference between the meat-flavored and cheese-flavored extrusions is one of texture. The "cheese" chews like fresh Play-Doh, whereas the "meat" chews like Play-Doh that's been sitting out on a rug for a couple of hours. 8

Frying only turned the Gaines-burger black. There was no melting, no sizzling, no warm meat smells. A cherished childhood illusion was gone. I flipped the patty into the sink, where it immediately began leaking rivulets of red dye. 9

As alarming as the Gaines-burgers were, their soy meal began to seem like an old friend when the time came to try some *canned* dog foods. I decided to try the Cycle foods first. When I opened them, I thought about how rarely I use can open- 10 ers these days, and I was suddenly visited by a long-forgotten sensation of can-opener distaste. *This* is the kind of unsavory place can openers spend their time when you're not watching! Every time you open a can of, say, Italian plum tomatoes, you infect them with invisible particles of by-product.

I had been expecting to see the usual homogeneous scrapple inside, but each 11 can of Cycle was packed with smooth, round, oily nuggets. As if someone at Gaines had been tipped off that a human would be tasting the stuff, the four Cycles really were different from one another. Cycle-1, for puppies, is wet and soyish. Cycle-2, for adults, glistens nastily with fat, but it's passably edible — a lot like some canned Swedish meatballs I once got in a care package at college. Cycle-3, the "lite" one, for fatties, had no specific flavor; it just tasted like dog food. But at least it didn't make me fat.

Cycle-4, for senior dogs, had the smallest nuggets. Maybe old dogs can't open 12 their mouths as wide. This kind was far sweeter than the other three Cycles — almost like baked beans. It was also the only one to contain "dried beef digest," a mysterious substance that the Purina spokesman defined as "enzymes" and my dictionary defined as "the products of digestion."

Next on the menu was a can of Kal-Kan Pedigree with Chunky Chicken. 13 Chunky chicken? There were chunks in the can, certainly — big, purplish-brown chunks. I forked one chunk out (by now I was becoming more callous) and found that while it had no discernible chicken flavor, it wasn't bad except for its texture — like meat loaf with ground-up chicken bones.

In the world of canned dog food, a smooth consistency is a sign of low 14 quality — lots of cereal. A lumpy, frightening, bloody, stringy horror is a sign of high quality — lots of meat. Nowhere in the world of wet dog foods was this demonstrated better than in the fanciest I tried — Kal Kan's Pedigree Select Dinners. These came not in a can but in a tiny foil packet with a picture of an imperious Yorkie. When I pulled open the container, juice spurted all over my hand, and the first chunk I speared was trailing a long gray vein. I shrieked and went instead for a plain chunk, which I was able to swallow only after taking a break to read some suddenly fascinating office equipment catalogs. Once again, though, it tasted no more alarming than, say, canned hash.

Still, how pleasant it was to turn to *dry* dog food! Gravy Train was the first I 15 tried, and I'm happy to report that it really does make a "thick, rich, real beef gravy" when you mix it with water. Thick and rich, anyway. Except for a lingering rancid-fat flavor, the gravy wasn't beefy, but since it tasted primarily like tap water, it wasn't nauseating either.

My poor dachshund just gets plain old Purina Dog Chow, but Purina also makes 16 a dry food called Butcher's Blend that comes in Beef, Bacon, and Chicken flavor. Here we see dog food's arcane semiotics at its best: a red triangle with a *T* stamped into it is supposed to suggest beef; a tan curl, chicken; and a brown *S*, a piece of bacon. Only dogs understand these messages. But Butcher's Blend does have an endearing slogan: "Great Meaty Tastes — without bothering the Butcher!" *You know, I wanted to buy some meat, but I just couldn't bring myself to bother the butcher. . . .*

Purina O.N.E. ("Optimum Nutritional Effectiveness") is targeted at people 17 who are unlikely ever to worry about bothering a tradesperson. "We chose chicken as a primary ingredient in Purina O.N.E. for several reasonings," the long, long essay on the back of the bag announces. Chief among these reasonings, I'd guess, is the fact that chicken appeals to people who are — you know — *like us*. Although our dogs do nothing but spend 18-hour days alone in the apartment, we still want them to be *premium* dogs. We want them to cut down on red meat, too. We also want dog food that comes in a bag with an attractive design, a subtle typeface and no kitschy pictures of slobbering golden retrievers.

Besides that, we want a list of the Nutritional Benefits of our dog food — and we get it on O.N.E. One thing I especially like about this list is its constant references to a dog's "hair coat," as in "Beef tallow is good for the dog's skin and hair coat." (On the other hand, beef tallow merely provides palatability, while the dried beef digest in Cycle provides palatability *enhancement*.)   18

I hate to say it, but O.N.E. was pretty palatable. Maybe that's because it has about 100 percent more fat than, say, Butcher's Blend. Or maybe I'd been duped by the packaging; that's been known to happen before.   19

As with people food, dog snacks taste much better than dog meals. They're better-looking too. Take Milk-Bone Flavor Snacks. The loving-hands-at-home prose describing each flavor is colorful; the writers practically choke on their own exuberance. Of bacon they say, "It's so good, your dog will think it's hot off the frying pan." Of liver: "The only taste your dog wants more than liver — is even more liver!" Of poultry: "All those farm fresh flavors deliciously mixed in one biscuit. Your dog will bark with delight!" And of vegetable: "Gardens of taste! Specially blended to give your dog that vegetable flavor he wants — but can rarely get!"   20

Well, I may be a sucker, but advertising *this* emphatic just doesn't convince me. I lined up all seven flavors of Milk-Bone Flavor Snacks on the floor. Unless my dog's palate is a lot more sensitive than mine — and considering that she steals dirty diapers out of the trash and eats them, I'm loath to think it is — she doesn't detect any more difference in the seven flavors than I did when I tried them.   21

I much preferred Bonz, the hard-baked, bone-shaped snack stuffed with simulated marrow. I liked the bone part, that is; it tasted almost exactly like the cornmeal it was made of. The mock-marrow inside was a bit more problematic: in addition to looking like the sludge that collects in the treads of my running shoes, it was bursting with tiny hairs.   22

I'm sure you have a few dog food questions of your own. To save us time, I've answered them in advance.   23

Q. *Are those little cans of Mighty Dog actually branded with the sizzling word* BEEF, the way they show in the commercials?   24

A. You should know by now that that kind of thing never happens.   25

Q. *Does chicken-flavored dog food taste like chicken-flavored cat food?*   26

A. To my surprise, chicken cat food was actually a little better — more chickeny. It tasted like inferior canned pâté.   27

Q. *Was there any dog food that you just couldn't bring yourself to try?*   28

A. Alas, it was a can of Mighty Dog called Prime Entree with Bone Marrow. The meat was dark, dark brown, and it was surrounded by gelatin that was almost black. I knew I would die if I tasted it, so I put it outside for the raccoons.   29

◖ READING ACTIVITY 1 Build Your Vocabulary ▶

Determine the meanings of the following words from the context of Ann Hodgman's essay. Then check their meanings by looking up the words in a dictionary: palpated (7), malleable (7), rivulets (9), unsavory (10), homogeneous (11), scrapple (11), callous (13), imperious (14), arcane (16), semiotics (16), tallow (18), palatability (18), loath (21).

◖ GROUP ACTIVITY 1 Discuss the Reading ▶

Discuss the following questions about "No Wonder They Call Me a Bitch" with your classmates.

1. What criteria does Hodgman use to evaluate different types of dog food?
2. How does the author show that she's knowledgeable about the topic?
3. List three of Hodgman's facts or examples that you think are effective in supporting her evaluation. Explain why you think they're effective.
4. Did this essay make you want to taste dog food or cat food yourself? Why or why not?

◖ WRITING ACTIVITY 1 Share Your Ideas ▶

Write a paragraph or two in which you evaluate a product that you like to use, such as a piece of clothing that you frequently wear or a type of food that you regularly consume. Why do you often use this product? To what extent do other people enjoy this product? Compare your response with those of your fellow students.

Evaluation of a Performance

DIANE HEIMAN AND PHYLLIS BOOKSPAN
Sesame Street: Brought to You by the Letters M-A-L-E

Diane Heiman is an attorney and public policy consultant, and Phyllis Bookspan is a law professor at Widener University School of Law in Wilmington, Delaware. Both Heiman and Bookspan are mothers, and when they wrote this article for the *Seattle Times* in 1994, their children were very young. In this evaluation of *Sesame Street,* Heiman and Bookspan explain how the popular children's television show could be more girl-friendly.

A recent report released by the American Association of University Women,   1
"How Schools Shortchange Women," finds that teachers, textbooks, and tests are, whether intentionally or unintentionally, giving preferential treatment to

elementary-school boys. As a result, girls who enter school with equal or better academic potential than their male counterparts lose confidence and do not perform as well.

An earlier study about law students, published in the *Journal of Legal Education*, found a similar disparity. "Gender Bias in the Classroom" found that male law students are called upon in class more frequently than females, speak for longer periods of time, and are given more positive feedback by law professors. 2

The article raised some disturbing questions about whether women and men receive truly equal education in American law schools. 3

Unfortunately, this insidious gender bias appears long before our children enter school and pervades even the television show *Sesame Street*. Yes, *Sesame Street* is sexist! But, just as in the story of the emperor and his new clothes, many of us do not notice the obvious. 4

The puppet stars of the show, Bert and Ernie, and all the other major *Sesame Street* animal characters—Big Bird, Cookie Monster, Grover, Oscar the Grouch, Kermit the Frog, and Mr. Snuffleupagus—are male. Among the secondary characters, including Elmo, Herry Monster, Count VonCount, Telemonster, Prairie Dawn, and Betty Lou, only a very few are girls. 5

The female Muppets always play children, while the males play adult parts in various scenes. In a recently aired skit "Squeal of Fortune," this disparity is evident when the host of the show introduces the two contestants. Of Count VonCount of Transylvania the host asks, "What do you do for a living?" to which the count responds authoritatively, "I count!" Of Prairie Dawn, he inquires, "And how do you spend your day?" Sure, it would be silly to ask a schoolgirl what she does for a living. But none of the female Muppets on *Sesame Street* are even old enough to earn a living. 6

Further, almost all the baby puppet characters on *Sesame Street* are girls. For example, Snuffie's sibling is Baby Alice; in books, Grover's baby cousin is a girl, and when Herry Monster's mother brings home the new baby—it's a girl. Since babies are totally dependent and fairly passive, the older (male) relatives take care of them and provide leadership. 7

Also, the female Muppets almost never interact with each other. In sharp contrast, consequential and caring friendships have been fully developed between male Muppets: Ernie and Bert; Big Bird and Snuffie; even Oscar the Grouch and his (male) worm, Squirmy. 8

Any parent of toddlers or preschoolers can testify that the "girls" on *Sesame Street* are not very popular. Children ask their parents for Bert and Ernie dolls, not Baby Alice. Is this just because the girls are not marketed via books, tapes, placemats and toy dolls the same way the boys are? Or is it that the *Sesame Street* writers simply have not developed the girls into the same types of lovable, adorable personalities that belong to the main characters? 9

Interestingly and peculiarly, the minor "girls" look more human than most of the well-loved animal roles. They are not physically cuddly, colorful or bizarre, as are the more important male characters. Prairie Dawn has ordinary blonde hair and brown eyes—nothing even remotely similar to Big Bird's soft yellow feathers or Cookie Monster's wild, bright blue, mane. 10

Yes, we believe that *Sesame Street* is one of the best shows on television for 11
small children. Our children — boys and girls — are regular viewers. In addition to its
educational value, lack of violence and emphasis on cooperation, the adult characters on the show are admirably balanced in terms of avoiding sexual stereotypes.

But even the best of the bunch has room for improvement. Just as elemen- 12
tary through professional school educators must learn to be more sensitive to
subtle and unintentional gender bias, so too should the folks at Children's Television Network. We can stop sexism from seeping into our children's first "formal" educational experience.

The message was brought to you by the letter F: fairness for females. 13

READING ACTIVITY 2 Build Your Vocabulary

Determine the meanings of the following words from the context of Diane Heiman and
Phyllis Bookspan's essay. Then check their meanings by looking up the words in a dictionary: disparity (2), insidious (4), authoritatively (6), inquires (6), consequential (8),
peculiarly (10).

GROUP ACTIVITY 2 Discuss the Reading

Discuss the following questions about "*Sesame Street:* Brought to You by the Letters
M-A-L-E" with your classmates.

1. What is the authors' opinion of *Sesame Street*? Do they express this opinion in a
   single sentence? If so, indicate what sentence this is.

2. What elements of a children's television program are important to Heiman and
   Bookspan? How well does *Sesame Street* meet their expectations of a good
   children's show?

3. Throughout the essay, the authors compare and contrast male and female
   characters on *Sesame Street*. Do they use point-by-point or subject-by-subject
   order (or both) to organize their ideas? How effective is this organization?

4. How do Heiman and Bookspan support their argument that *Sesame Street* is
   sexist? Is their evidence convincing? Why or why not?

WRITING ACTIVITY 2 Share Your Ideas

People may be stereotyped based on their ethnicity, body type, occupation, and so on.
For instance, a common stereotype is the "dumb jock." Write a paragraph or two in
which you evaluate a certain television show or movie according to how well it avoids
stereotyping people. Share your responses with your classmates.

Evaluation of a Place

NICHOLAS JENNINGS
A Palace of Rock

Nicholas Jennings lives and works in Toronto, Canada, where he writes about music and pop culture. His books include *Before the Gold Rush: Flashbacks to the Dawn of the Canadian Sound* (1998) and *Fifty Years of Music: The Story of EMI Music Canada* (2000). He is also a music critic for *Maclean's,* a Canadian magazine. In "A Palace of Rock," written soon after the Rock and Roll Hall of Fame and Museum opened in 1995 in Cleveland, Ohio, Jennings evaluates the museum's exhibits about rock and roll from its birth in the 1950s to the present.

1   As museum pieces, they are the most humble of artifacts: a few report cards, a black leather jacket, a pair of government-issue eye glasses. Yet for many, the three objects are priceless. Once the property of John Lennon, those treasures are now on display at the recently opened Rock and Roll Hall of Fame and Museum in Cleveland, Ohio, where they are already among its most popular exhibits. Looking at the articles, it is easy to see why: each of them brings the viewer closer to the real Lennon. His elementary school report card reveals that one of his teachers found rock's future genius "hopeless," while the well-worn, sloppy jacket somehow perfectly captures the musician's irreverent charm. And Lennon's wire-rimmed spectacles trigger a flood of emotions because they are so evocative of the artist, who was fatally shot by a crazed fan in December, 1980. "Rock music has a power that makes you want to be a part of it," says museum director Dennis Barrie. "Hopefully, we represent some of that."

2   Judging by the scores of fans who flooded into the facility during its Labor Day weekend opening—an estimated 8,000 on the first day—Barrie need not worry: despite a once-shaky history, the Rock and Roll Hall of Fame and Museum is now a resounding success. Visitors can feast on more than 3,500 items, ranging from posters, album jackets and handwritten lyric sheets to movies and interactive exhibits that play requested songs and videos. Among the most memorable displays: a replica of the old Sun Studios in Memphis, Tenn., where Elvis Presley made his first records; a piece of Otis Redding's private airplane, which crashed in 1967; and the 1945 Magnavox tape recorder that pioneering musicologist Alan Lomax used to record blues legends such as Lead Belly and Muddy Waters. And Hall of Fame inductees Neil Young and The Band are reminders that rock has also thrived in Canada.

3   Meanwhile, hundreds of photographs, instruments and costumes—including Michael Jackson's famed sequinned glove and Madonna's gold bustier—are also housed in the museum's impressive, seven-level structure, a $123-million geometric shrine designed by New York City–based architect I. M. Pei, whose other accomplishments include the additions to the National Gallery of Art in Washington and the Louvre in Paris. From the air, the lakefront building resembles a record player with turntable, tonearm and a stack of 45s. But from the ground level, the

elaborate structure is a cheeky mix of pyramid-like facades, rectangular towers and trapezoidal extensions that boldly jut out over Lake Erie.

The contents of the museum, like the all-star concert that launched it on   4
Sept. 2 — the roster of performers included Chuck Berry, James Brown, The Kinks, Creedence Clearwater Revival, Robbie Robertson and Bruce Springsteen — reflect rock in all of its ragged glory. For some, the very idea of chronicling the history of rock 'n' roll in a serious, curated institution is offensive. They argue that, like caging a wild beast, it runs counter to the laws of nature, as though rock music should always be allowed to roam free of commerce and academia. "Absolute nonsense," scoffs Rob Bowman, a professor of rock at Toronto's York University. "Rock has been institutionalized for at least the last 40 years, by record companies, radio stations and other media. Anyone who doesn't understand that is a hopeless romantic." Still, it is difficult to ignore some of the contradictions raised by the museum. Thirty years ago, The Who's Pete Townshend was smashing his guitar in a display of anarchic frenzy, yet the museum has one of his instruments respectfully encased in a glass cabinet. The irony is not lost on Ron House of the Columbus, Ohio–based band Thomas Jefferson Slave Apartments. The musician has written a punk protest song called "RnR Hall of Fame" that angrily tackles the subject. "I don't want to see Eric Clapton's stuffed baby / I don't want to see the shotgun of Kurt Cobain," sings House. "I don't want to see the liver of David Crosby / Blow it up before Johnny Rotten gets in."

Although Rotten's Sex Pistols have yet to be inducted by the Hall of Fame   5
Foundation (artists become eligible 25 years after their first recording), the British punk band is part of the museum's "Blank Generation" exhibit, which examines punk's birth in London and New York City between 1975 and 1980. Included is an 11-inch Sid Vicious doll, complete with chains, ripped T-shirt and swastika, that was used as a prop in the 1980 documentary *The Great Rock 'n' Roll Swindle*, made a year after his death from a heroin overdose.

In fact, the museum strives mightily to keep up to date with rock's more re-   6
cent developments, charting the rise of rap music and Seattle's grunge scene. According to chief curator James Henke, a former editor at *Rolling Stone*, the museum's collection will be in constant flux. That is partly due to the fact that most display items are on loan, partly due to the nature of its subject matter. Says Henke: "Like the music, it'll always be evolving."

However, the collection is shamelessly skewed to the past. Above the en-   7
trance to the main exhibition area is a neon sign quoting Chuck Berry: "Roll Over Beethoven." Berry and other such pioneers as Little Richard and Presley are well represented in a noisy, arcade-like space that includes small cinemas, record booths and computer screens. Amateur musicologists can trace the 500 songs that the museum has deemed to have shaped the history of rock 'n' roll. Among the oldest entries: Woody Guthrie's 1956 folk anthem "This Land Is Your Land" and Louis Jordan's jump-blues classic "Caldonia," written in 1945. But the most revealing exhibit is The Beat Goes On, which traces musical family trees. Touch-screen computers allow museum-goers to click on images of musicians and discover their influences through video clips and songs. In some cases, the technology bridges generations. Lucy Schlopy, an 82-year-old visitor from Bradford, Pa., found that

her favorite artist, Roy Orbison, had in turn influenced one of her great-niece's musical heroes, Bruce Springsteen. "I'm learning all kinds of things," said Schlopy.

Responses like that, says director Barrie, who previously worked at the Smith- 8
sonian Institution in Washington and Cincinnati's Contemporary Arts Center, prove that the museum is a success. "People are actually reading, taking in the content of the exhibits," he beamed. "They're not just looking at the glittery costumes, which is very gratifying." At the same time, the costumed mannequins throughout the museum are proving to be among the biggest draws. Especially popular are Presley's leather stage outfit from his 1968 comeback TV special, Lennon's lime-green Sgt. Pepper's uniform and the "butterfly dresses" of Motown's The Supremes. For the kids, rock's schlock meister Alice Cooper, standing next to a guillotine and a bloody, severed head, is an awesome, cartoonish highlight.

By contrast, the actual Hall of Fame, housed on the top floor, is a model of 9
decorum. To get there, visitors climb a long, spiral staircase to reach a darkened room honoring the inductees (123 so far). Images of such legends as Buddy Holly and Bob Marley dissolve on tiny video screens like ghosts, while their signatures, etched on backlit glass plaques, seem to float in the ether. After the musical cacophony and video chaos downstairs, the Hall of Fame is a welcome sanctuary.

For the Hall of Fame's creators, the museum was a pipe dream that almost 10
never materialized. Founders Jann Wenner, editor of *Rolling Stone*, and Ahmet Ertegun, president of Atlantic Records, steered the project through three directors and one site change before the groundbreaking two years ago. Cleveland was chosen over Memphis and New York after residents collected 600,000 signatures and local businesses raised $87 million. But the city had already earned a place in rock history: Alan Freed, its famous deejay, popularized the term rock 'n' roll in the 1950s.

At the museum's ribbon-cutting ceremony, Jimi Hendrix's version of "The 11
Star Spangled Banner" played over the loudspeakers. The guitarist's rendition, conceived as an anti-Vietnam statement at Woodstock in 1969, is full of feedback and guitar distortions designed to simulate war sounds. But suddenly, Hendrix's tortured notes were punctuated by the real-life sounds of two Marine Corps Harrier jets flying overhead. The irony was not lost on some in the crowd, including Wenner, who later addressed the issue of how rock has now joined the establishment. The hall, said Wenner, standing next to Lennon's widow Yoko Ono, was built to remind people of the "power of innocence, rebellion and youth," but also the value of "maturity and growth and perspective." Rock 'n' roll, once scruffy and rebellious, is all grown up. Although it will strike some as contradictory, a hall of fame and museum is simply a natural step in its evolution.

◀ READING ACTIVITY 3 Build Your Vocabulary ▶

Determine the meanings of the following words from the context of Nicholas Jennings's essay. Then check their meanings by looking up the words in a dictionary: artifacts (1), irreverent (1), replica (2), roster (4), contradictions (4), anarchic (4), inducted (5), skewed (7), sanctuary (9), scruffy (11).

GROUP ACTIVITY 3 Discuss the Reading

Discuss the following questions about "A Palace of Rock" with your classmates.

1. What is the author's evaluation of the Rock and Roll Hall of Fame and Museum? Where in the essay is this evaluation expressed?

2. What criteria does Jennings use to support his evaluation?

3. Explain in your own words what Jennings means when he writes in paragraph 4 that "it is difficult to ignore some of the contradictions raised by the museum." What are these contradictions? Give an example.

4. Rock and roll artists can be inducted into the museum twenty-five years after their first recording. In your opinion, what current rock and roll groups or performers will be inducted into the Hall of Fame when they become eligible?

WRITING ACTIVITY 3 Share Your Ideas

Write a paragraph or two in which you evaluate a museum, gallery, monument, or similar place. Decide on suitable criteria, such as the quality of the exhibits, the accessibility of the site, and the attractiveness of the structure or layout. Exchange your writing with several classmates, and discuss the evaluations that each of you wrote.

Chapter 8 Arguing a Position: *Censorship, Stereotypes, and Media in Our Lives*

For more essays on the media, see Chapter 8, pp. 239–45.

A Censorship Issue

PETER SINGER

Let's Hope the WikiLeaks Cables Move Us Closer to Open Diplomacy

Australian philosopher Peter Singer is best known for his writing on the animal liberation movement. He coined the phrase "speciesism," defined as when human beings see their own interests as justifying cruelty to other living beings. As a result of his beliefs, he is a vegetarian who argues against any act that causes harm to animals. As an ethicist, he frequently publishes arguments on a variety of current events. In "Let's Hope the WikiLeaks Cables Move Us Closer to Open Diplomacy," published in the British newspaper the *Guardian*, he writes about the secret international documents released in 2010 by Julian Assange, the controversial creator of the Web site WikiLeaks.

At Princeton University, Woodrow Wilson, who was president of the university before he became president of the United States, is never far away. His larger-than-life image looks out across the dining hall at Wilson College, where I am a fellow, and Prospect House, the dining facility for academic staff, was his family home when he led the university.

So when the furor erupted over WikiLeaks' recent release of a quarter-million diplomatic cables, I was reminded of Wilson's 1918 speech in which he put forward "Fourteen Points" for a just peace to end the first world war. The first of those 14 points reads: "Open covenants of peace must be arrived at, after which there will surely be no private international action or rulings of any kind, but diplomacy shall proceed always frankly and in the public view."

Is this an ideal that we should take seriously? Is WikiLeaks founder Julian Assange a true follower of Woodrow Wilson?

Wilson was unable to get the Treaty of Versailles to reflect his 14 points fully, although it did include several of them, including the establishment of an association of states that proved to be the forerunner of today's UN. But Wilson then failed to get the US Senate to ratify the treaty, which included the covenant of the League of Nations.

Writing in the *New York Times* earlier this month, Paul Schroeter, an emeritus professor of history, argued that open diplomacy is often "fatally flawed," and gave as an example the need for secret negotiations to reach agreement on the Treaty of Versailles. Since the treaty bears substantial responsibility for the resurrection of German nationalism that led to the rise of Hitler and the second world war, it has a fair claim to being the most disastrous peace treaty in human history.

Moreover, it is hard to imagine that if Wilson's proposals had formed the basis of the peace, and set the tone for all future negotiations, the history of Europe in the 20th century would have been worse than it actually was. That makes the Treaty of Versailles a poor example to use to demonstrate the desirability of secrecy in international negotiations.

Open government is, within limits, an ideal that we all share. US President Barack Obama endorsed it when he took office in January 2009. "Starting today," he told his cabinet secretaries and staff, "every agency and department should know that this administration stands on the side not of those who seek to withhold information but those who seek to make it known." He then noted that there would have to be exceptions to this policy to protect privacy and national security.

Even secretary of defense Robert Gates has admitted, however, that while the recent leaks are embarrassing and awkward for the US, their consequences for its foreign policy are modest.

Some of the leaked cables are just opinion, and not much more than gossip about national leaders. But, because of the leak, we know, for example, that when the British government set up its supposedly open inquiry into the causes of the Iraq war, it also promised the US government that it would "put measures in place to protect your interests." The British government appears to have been deceiving the public and its own parliament.

Similarly, the cables reveal that President Ali Abdullah Saleh of Yemen lied to 10 his people and parliament about the source of US airstrikes against al-Qaida in Yemen, telling them that Yemen's military was the source of the bombs.

We have also learned more about the level of corruption in some of the re- 11 gimes that the US supports, like those in Afghanistan and Pakistan, and in other countries with which the US has friendly relations, notably Russia. We now know that the Saudi royal family has been urging the US to undertake a military attack on Iran to prevent it from becoming capable of producing nuclear weapons. Here, perhaps, we learned something for which the US government deserves credit: it has resisted that suggestion.

Knowledge is generally considered a good thing; so, presumably, knowing 12 more about how the US thinks and operates around the world is also good. In a democracy, citizens pass judgment on their government, and if they are kept in the dark about what their government is doing, they cannot be in a position to make well-grounded decisions. Even in non-democratic countries, people have a legitimate interest in knowing about actions taken by the government.

Nevertheless, it isn't always the case that openness is better than secrecy. 13 Suppose that US diplomats had discovered that democrats living under a brutal military dictatorship were negotiating with junior officers to stage a coup to re-store democracy and the rule of law. I would hope that WikiLeaks would not pub-lish a cable in which diplomats informed their superiors of the plot.

Openness is in this respect like pacifism: just as we cannot embrace complete 14 disarmament while others stand ready to use their weapons, so Woodrow Wilson's world of open diplomacy is a noble ideal that cannot be fully realized in the world in which we live.

We could, however, try to get closer to that ideal. If governments did not 15 mislead their citizens so often, there would be less need for secrecy, and if leaders knew they could not rely on keeping the public in the dark about what they are doing, they would have a powerful incentive to behave better.

It is therefore regrettable that the most likely outcome of the recent revela- 16 tions will be greater restrictions to prevent further leaks. Let's hope that in the new WikiLeaks age, that goal remains out of reach.

READING ACTIVITY 1 Build Your Vocabulary

Determine the meanings of the following words from the context of Peter Singer's essay. Then check their meanings by looking up the words in a dictionary: cables (2), covenants (2), legitimate (12), coup (13), pacifism (14), disarmament (14).

GROUP ACTIVITY 1 Discuss the Reading

Discuss the following questions about "Let's Hope the WikiLeaks Cables Move Us Closer to Open Diplomacy" with your classmates.

1. What is Singer's argumentative claim, and where does he express this claim in his essay?

2. Why does Singer begin his piece by referring to President Woodrow Wilson's 1918 speech?

3. What are Singer's pro points that support his argumentative claim?

4. Does Singer ever admit that at times governments need to maintain secrecy? If so, why does he think this is so?

5. Consider the characteristics of an argumentative essay, and rank Singer's piece from 1 to 5 (5 being high) in quality based on those characteristics. Explain your ranking.

◀ WRITING ACTIVITY 1 Share Your Ideas ▶

Write a paragraph or two about the ethics of secret or private documents being released for anyone to access on the Internet. In addition to government documents, consider private information concerning celebrities, as well as information about ordinary individuals, such as their addresses, phone numbers, and credit ratings. Do you think information such as this should be regulated so that privacy can be maintained? Why or why not?

A Stereotyping Issue

ALLISON SAMUELS
The Case against Celebrity Gossip

Allison Samuels, an award-winning national correspondent for *Newsweek* magazine, writes about entertainment and sports. During her career, she has interviewed and written about such celebrities as Kobe Bryant, Denzel Washington, and Oprah Winfrey. Her book *Off the Record* (2007) is a collection of back stories on the subjects of these interviews. In "The Case against Celebrity Gossip," Samuels makes the argument that exposure to celebrity gossip can affect the way we view our favorite artists.

As I sat under the hair dryer this past week at my favorite salon perusing my 1 regular supply of weekly entertainment glossies, I remarked out loud how breathtaking I thought singer Alicia Keys looked in her one-shoulder Vera Wang–designed wedding gown. On one particular tabloid cover, Keys seemed to glow as she kissed her new husband, Swizz Beatz, in front of a fabulous island. Now, usually a comment about a popular celebrity elicits an immediate response in my chatty salon. Not this day. My complimentary words about Keys were met with an odd silence that lasted five minutes or more. (For those who aren't familiar with the African-American beauty-salon etiquette, that's an eternity.)

Finally, the young lady under the dryer next to mine calmly turned to me and 2 asked how I could admire a husband-stealing "floozy" like Keys. Before I could process that question, the woman on the other side chimed in by adding that Keys had one less fan now that she'd broken up someone else's home.

To say I was floored by the callous reactions of these seemingly sensible   3
women would be an understatement. Yes, I'd read all the blog accounts of how Keys allegedly began an affair with her then-married record producer, Beatz, while recording her most recent album. I'd even read interviews in which Beatz's "jilted" wife claimed Keys became pregnant months before she and her husband had officially divorced. (Keys has not commented publicly on any of this.) I skimmed most of the stories about Keys but only partially retained the scandalous and racy tidbits because, frankly, I just don't care much about the intimate details of Alicia Keys's life. I just really love her music.

When I explained my point of view to the women around me, they were   4
clearly appalled at my lack of outrage. They pointed out the contradiction of Keys's private life and her pro-female lyrics and classy onstage persona. As they listed the many ways in which Keys had disappointed them, they spoke as if they personally knew her—as if she were a friend they had drinks with every Friday night after work.

And therein lies the looming problem we as fans now face. Because of the   5
mass influx of social-media networks, celebrity blogs, and endless celebrity-based reality shows, Americans have been lulled into a dangerously false sense of intimacy with the people meant only to entertain us. It's allowed us to have detailed opinions on the actions and lives of people who used to be just fleeting and mysterious images on a video or in a film. Having "inside" knowledge about stars, their comings and goings, dating habits, and even shopping choices has somehow made us feel we share similarities with the faces that flawlessly grace magazine covers, light up the big screen, and sell millions of albums.

Accordingly, that so-called knowledge also appears to have given us the right   6
to judge celebs as harshly as we would our actual friends without ever considering the fact that blogs, magazines, and even the celebs themselves rarely tell anyone the full story. Just take the sad predicament of Fantasia Barrino, the former *American Idol* winner who recently attempted suicide after the details of her alleged relationship with a married man were revealed in a lawsuit. Barrino was reportedly so distraught by the news—and the vicious and mean comments posted by fans on celebrity blogs—that she took a mix of sleeping pills and aspirin to shut it all out. That's an interesting and sad turn for a celebrity who was created by a television show that allowed viewers to call in and vote on her success—now they're apparently voting on her morality as well.

But where does that leave us as fans when we decide we won't support the   7
career of some imperfect person whose talent or intellect has profoundly affected us? Is anyone out there really able to live up to society's standard of being a "good person" and the perfect role model? Is there even such a thing? Thinking about all this led me to reflect on the lives of my all-time favorite singers, Marvin Gaye and Sam Cooke—men whose music I simply couldn't fathom being without. Both were involved in a number of scandalous affairs while still married, and both died violent deaths. Cooke was shot and killed by a hotel manager under mysterious circumstances, while Gaye was gunned down by his own father during an

argument — not exactly the peaceful lives one would expect from men who wrote such iconic and thought-provoking songs as "A Change Is Gonna Come" and "What's Going On." During their lifetimes in the '50s, '60s, and '70s, only bits and pieces of their personal stories surfaced for public consumption. While fans of that generation surely heard the rumors, they never seemed to allow them to affect their love for the true genius of the artist in question. They simply separated the man or woman from their music. Maybe it's time we do the same.

READING ACTIVITY 2 Build Your Vocabulary

Determine the meanings of the following words from the context of Allison Samuels's essay. Then check their meanings by looking up the words in a dictionary: glossies (1), callous (3), retained (3), looming (5), fleeting (5), distraught (6), iconic (7).

GROUP ACTIVITY 2 Discuss the Reading

Discuss the following questions about "The Case against Celebrity Gossip" with your classmates.

1. What is Samuels's argumentative claim, and where in the essay does she express it?

2. In her essay, Samuels gives the example of what happened to Fantasia Barrino, the former *American Idol* winner. How well does this example help Samuels support her point?

3. In addition to discussing Fantasia Barrino, Samuels describes the lives of Sam Cooke and Marvin Gaye, musicians from the 1950s, 1960s, and 1970s. Are these examples too old to be persuasive to her audience? Explain your answer.

3. In her piece, Samuels writes that fans should separate artists' private lives from their work. Assume that you disagree with this point. What would you say to Samuels to get her to change her mind?

4. Samuels has published many articles based on interviews she has conducted with celebrities. Does this make her argument more or less convincing? Explain your answer.

WRITING ACTIVITY 2 Share Your Ideas

Write a paragraph or two about whether or not we should judge artists according to the way they lead their personal lives. To what extent are you influenced by artists' personal lives?

An Issue about Media in Our Lives

JANNA MALAMUD SMITH
Online but Not Antisocial

Ever since it became available to the general public in the 1990s, the Internet has been controversial. In "An Ugly Toll of Technology: Impatience and Forgetfulness" (p. 244), Tara Parker-Pope argues about some of the negative effects of computer technology on people's lives. In contrast, Janna Malamud Smith, a psychotherapist and writer, focuses on the positive aspects of spending time online. In "Online but Not Antisocial," originally published in the *New York Times*, she argues that being online instead of being with people can sometimes be a good thing. Smith is the daughter of the late novelist Bernard Malamud; her memoir of him, *My Father Is a Book*, was published in 2006.

1   The Internet is a member of our family. According to my monthly bill, each of us spent about 5.4 hours a week online, which makes us pretty much average American Net users. I can't speak for the rest of my family, but I relish my online time. A new study tells me that I should feel bad about that. Bourbon, red meat, whole milk and the Internet, too?

2   According to the study, by Norman Nie, a political scientist at Stanford University, the Web makes us even lonelier and more isolated than we already are. "The more hours people use the Internet, the less time they spend with real human beings," Professor Nie said. There is a danger, he claimed, of worsening social isolation and creating a deadened and atomized world without human emotion.

3   Could that be possible? Or are we perhaps confusing the bandage with the wound? For starters, it seems that Professor Nie is assuming that hours with real human beings are an unqualified good thing. Call me a curmudgeon, but I often find them to be something of a mixed bag.

4   Did I miss fighting the shopping mall crowds this Christmas to buy one of my sons a hat he had really wanted? Not at all. Spending 15 minutes online as opposed to two hours (minimum) searching for parking, then trudging from store to store to have indifferent teenage clerks shrug their shoulders and mutter, "No problem," is not a human contact I crave.

5   The days when a trip to the milliner's meant a nice exchange with a friendly proprietor you've known for years are long gone in my neighborhood. On the other hand, thanks to Net shopping I was able to buy my husband a beautiful bow tie made by hand by a woman in Maine.

6   Online in the last couple of weeks, I've kept in touch with busy friends, some of whom live halfway around the world, and tracked temperatures in Seville, Spain, which we are visiting next month. I've easily located and purchased out-of-print books from small secondhand dealers and looked up some useful exercises for a knee I had hurt.

7   Each of these little solitary outings made me shamefully happy. In fact, learning that it was 65 degrees in Seville when it was 10 above zero and icy in

Massachusetts was the single most mood-elevating discovery made in the first two weeks of February.

Driving to work this week, I listened to callers on a radio talk show discuss a   8
novel about transsexuals. Several callers who identified themselves as transsexuals talked about how much comfort and communion they felt from visiting certain Web sites just for them. You can't tell me that this is worse than spending endless hours interacting with the real people around them who may think they are nuts. While "atomizing" culture can be a problem, it can also allow more diverse stories to emerge and so reduce the silent suffering of the tellers.

When I came home tonight, my 14-year-old son was ecstatic because he had   9
finally gotten access to the chat room his school friends visit. Rather than sitting in front of the television to unwind after his homework was done, he happily chatted with his buddies. Yes, it would be better if all his friends lived on the same block so they could all hang out together in person. But connecting online may be the best alternative.

People already spend a lot of time alone, even when they are with their fami-   10
lies. I've heard many parents with multiple televisions in their homes talk about how everyone scatters after supper to watch a separate program.

According to the Stanford report, of the people in the study who are online   11
five or more hours a week (about 20 percent of those surveyed), 59 percent are spending less time watching television. Is that making life worse? Online, some of the conversations are two-way.

I grant that there are concerns. My husband, who teaches at a boarding   12
school, told me about an interesting faculty discussion about the pros and cons of wiring each dormitory room for Internet access. Would it help the students, or pull them away from their studies and their friends?

I recently told my 14-year-old that he couldn't put his computer in his bed-   13
room, and had to keep it in the family room. I didn't explain that I had made that decision because I wanted to keep an eye on what he was downloading, nag him when he has spent too much time online and pat his head occasionally, but I think he guessed. Yes, we all need to monitor this powerful tool.

When people gain more money and more choices, it seems they often choose   14
to move farther apart. Out of the one-room tenement, out of the bed shared with siblings, off the subway.

Why? Part of the answer is that privacy and solitude are very attractive and   15
often emotionally salubrious states. People enjoy being unobserved and left in peace — some of the time. And I think "some of the time" is the vital point that's being lost. Privacy and solitude, even anonymity, feel wonderful when they are chosen. When they're imposed, they tend to feel awful. Then they mutate into isolation, loneliness, depression and anomie, and Prozac sales skyrocket.

But the problem isn't the Internet. The suburbs and the long automobile   16
commutes to our workplaces have fragmented our lives and perhaps left us too far apart. And, yes, some people are too isolated and lonely. (Though I hold that in the past, many people were made equally miserable by too much forced contact.) So I suggest that we turn some attention to helping people find pleasurable ways

to get back together. And helping them make time to do it. Even Ralph Waldo Emerson recommended "Society and Solitude."

To prosper emotionally, people need to feel wanted, needed and valued. Our   17
failure to offer this prospect to many citizens long precedes the World Wide Web. And making sensational and premature proclamations about the Internet's harm simply distracts us from addressing those social conditions that drive us apart. Let's not go for the virtual damage when the real thing is before us.

READING ACTIVITY 3 Build Your Vocabulary

Determine the meanings of the following words from Janna Malamud Smith's essay. Then check their meanings by looking up the words in a dictionary: atomized (2), curmudgeon (3), milliner's (5), proprietor (5), transsexuals (8), ecstatic (9), salubrious (15), anonymity (15), imposed (15), anomie (15), virtual (17).

GROUP ACTIVITY 3 Discuss the Reading

Discuss the following questions about "Online but Not Antisocial" with your classmates.

1. What is Smith's thesis? State this in your own words.

2. What are Smith's pro points?

3. What are the arguments against the author's thesis (the con points)? How does she refute these?

4. Explain the last sentence of Smith's essay: "Let's not go for the virtual damage when the real thing is before us." What is "the real thing"?

WRITING ACTIVITY 3 Share Your Ideas

Write a paragraph or two about how you view the time you have spent online, whether you are on the Internet or texting. Do you think this time has been mostly beneficial or mostly harmful? Explain your answer.

For more essays on proposing a solution to a health, education, or environmental problem, see Chapter 9, pp. 277–86.

Chapter 9 Proposing a Solution: *Health, Education, and the Environment*

A Health Problem

ELIZABETH M. WHELAN
Perils of Prohibition

Solutions to health problems often require imaginative ideas. In "Perils of Prohibition," Elizabeth M. Whelan, president of the American Council on Science and Health, identifies a problem: the legal drinking age of twenty-one encourages irresponsible drinking. She then proposes a surprising solution: lower the drinking age to eighteen, and educate teens about alcohol abuse. (For an opposing viewpoint on this issue, read Darshak Sanghavi's "Quicker Liquor: Should We Lower the Drinking Age?" on p. 277.)

1   My colleagues at the Harvard School of Public Health, where I studied preventive medicine, deserve high praise for their recent study on teenage drinking. What they found in their survey of college students was that they drink "early and . . . often," frequently to the point of getting ill.

2   As a public-health scientist with a daughter, Christine, heading to college this fall, I have professional and personal concerns about teen binge drinking. It is imperative that we explore why so many young people abuse alcohol. From my own study of the effects of alcohol restrictions and my observations of Christine and her friends' predicament about drinking, I believe that today's laws are unrealistic. Prohibiting the sale of liquor to responsible young adults creates an atmosphere where binge drinking and alcohol abuse have become a problem. American teens, unlike their European peers, don't learn how to drink gradually, safely and in moderation.

3   Alcohol is widely accepted and enjoyed in our culture. Studies show that moderate drinking can be good for you. But we legally proscribe alcohol until the age of 21 (why not 30 or 45?). Christine and her classmates can drive cars, fly planes, marry, vote, pay taxes, take out loans and risk their lives as members of the U.S. armed forces. But laws in all 50 states say that no alcoholic beverages may be sold to anyone until that magic 21st birthday.

4   We didn't always have a national "21" rule. When I was in college, in the mid-'60s, the drinking age varied from state to state. This posed its own risks, with underage students crossing state lines to get a legal drink. In parts of the Western world, moderate drinking by teenagers and even children under their parents' supervision is a given. Though the per capita consumption of alcohol in France, Spain and Portugal is higher than in the United States, the rate of alcoholism and alcohol abuse is lower. A glass of wine at dinner is normal practice. Kids learn to

regard moderate drinking as an enjoyable family activity rather than as something they have to sneak away to do. Banning drinking by young people makes it a badge of adulthood — a tantalizing forbidden fruit.

Christine and her teenage friends like to go out with a group to a club, comedy show or sports bar to watch the game. But teens today have to go on the sly with fake IDs and the fear of getting caught. Otherwise, they're denied admittance to most places and left to hang out on the street. That's hardly a safer alternative. Christine and her classmates now find themselves in a legal no man's land. At 18, they're considered adults. Yet when they want to enjoy a drink like other adults, they are, as they put it, "disenfranchised."

Comparing my daughter's dilemma with my own as an "underage" college student, I see a difference — and one that I think has exacerbated the current dilemma. Today's teens are far more sophisticated than we were. They're treated less like children and have more responsibilities than we did. This makes the 21 restriction seem anachronistic. For the past few years, my husband and I have been preparing Christine for college life and the inevitable partying — read keg of beer — that goes with it. Last year, a young friend with no drinking experience was violently ill for days after he was introduced to "clear liquids in small glasses" during freshman orientation. We want our daughter to learn how to drink sensibly and avoid this pitfall. Starting at the age of 14, we invited her to join us for a glass of champagne with dinner. She'd tried it once before, thought it was "yucky" and declined. A year later, she enjoyed sampling wine at family meals. When, at 16, she asked for a Mudslide (a bottled chocolate-milk-and-rum concoction), we used the opportunity to discuss it with her. We explained the alcohol content, told her the alcohol level is lower when the drink is blended with ice and compared it with a glass of wine. Since the drink of choice on campus is beer, we contrasted its potency with wine and hard liquor and stressed the importance of not drinking on an empty stomach.

Our purpose was to encourage her to know the alcohol content of what she is served. We want her to experience the effects of liquor in her own home, not on the highway and not for the first time during a college orientation week with free-flowing suds. Although Christine doesn't drive yet, we regularly reinforce the concept of choosing a designated driver. Happily, that already seems a widely accepted practice among our daughter's friends who drink.

We recently visited the Ivy League school Christine will attend in the fall. While we were there, we read a story in the college paper about a student who was nearly electrocuted when, in a drunken state, he climbed on top of a moving train at a railroad station near the campus. The student survived, but three of his limbs were later amputated. This incident reminded me of a tragic death on another campus. An intoxicated student maneuvered himself into a chimney. He was found three days later when frat brothers tried to light a fire in the fireplace. By then he was dead.

These tragedies are just two examples of our failure to teach young people how to use alcohol prudently. If 18-year-olds don't have legal access to even a beer at a public place, they have no experience handling liquor on their own. They feel "liberated" when they arrive on campus. With no parents to stop them, they have a "let's make up for lost time" attitude. The result: binge drinking.

We should make access to alcohol legal at 18. At the same time, we should   10 come down much harder on alcohol abusers and drunk drivers of all ages. We should intensify our efforts at alcohol education for adolescents. We want them to understand that it is perfectly OK not to drink. But if they do, alcohol should be consumed in moderation.

After all, we choose to teach our children about safe sex, including the ben-   11 efits of teen abstinence. Why, then, can't we — schools and parents alike — teach them about safe drinking?

READING ACTIVITY 1 Build Your Vocabulary

Determine the meanings of the following words from the context of Elizabeth M. Whelan's essay. Then check their meanings by looking up the words in a dictionary: binge (2), imperative (2), predicament (2), proscribe (3), per capita (4), tantalizing (4), disenfranchised (5), dilemma (6), exacerbated (6), anachronistic (6), prudently (9).

GROUP ACTIVITY 1 Discuss the Reading

Discuss the following questions about "Perils of Prohibition" with your classmates.

1. Why does Whelan believe the current legal drinking age is a problem?
2. What supporting details does she use to convince her readers that the problem exists?
3. What is her proposed solution to the problem?
4. Does Whelan persuade you that the problem exists? Why or why not?
5. Do you think Whelan's solution is workable? Why or why not?

WRITING ACTIVITY 1 Share Your Ideas

Write a paragraph or two about a health problem for which people have strong opinions about how to solve. First, describe the problem, then provide evidence that there is more than one reasonable solution, and finally present your position on the most workable solution. Share what you have written with your classmates.

An Education Problem

MARY SHERRY

In Praise of the F Word

In the following essay, "In Praise of the F Word," first published in *Newsweek*, Mary Sherry identifies the problem of high school graduates who are poorly prepared for work or higher education. Sherry, who teaches in adult literacy programs, suggests that the threat of failure can be a valuable way to teach students that they must take responsibility for their own learning.

Tens of thousands of 18-year-olds will graduate this year and be handed meaningless diplomas. These diplomas won't look any different from those awarded their luckier classmates. Their validity will be questioned only when their employers discover that these graduates are semiliterate. 1

Eventually a fortunate few will find their way into educational-repair shops — adult-literacy programs, such as the one where I teach basic grammar and writing. There, high-school graduates and high-school dropouts pursuing graduate-equivalency certificates will learn the skills they should have learned in school. They will also discover they have been cheated by our educational system. 2

As I teach, I learn a lot about our schools. Early in each session I ask my students to write about an unpleasant experience they had in school. No writers' block here! "I wish someone would have made me stop doing drugs and made me study." "I liked to party and no one seemed to care." "I was a good kid and didn't cause any trouble, so they just passed me along even though I didn't read well and couldn't write." And so on. 3

I am your basic do-gooder, and prior to teaching this class I blamed the poor academic skills our kids have today on drugs, divorce, and other impediments to concentration necessary for doing well in school. But, as I rediscover each time I walk into the classroom, before a teacher can expect students to concentrate, he has to get their attention, no matter what distractions may be at hand. There are many ways to do this, and they have much to do with teaching style. However, if style alone won't do it, there is another way to show who holds the winning hand in the classroom. That is to reveal the trump card of failure. 4

I will never forget a teacher who played that card to get the attention of one of my children. Our youngest, a world-class charmer, did little to develop his intellectual talents but always got by. Until Mrs. Stifter. 5

Our son was a high-school senior when he had her for English. "He sits in the back of the room talking to his friends," she told me. "Why don't you move him to the front row?" I urged, believing the embarrassment would get him to settle down. Mrs. Stifter looked at me steely-eyed over her glasses. "I don't move seniors," she said. "I flunk them." I was flustered. Our son's academic life flashed before my eyes. No teacher had ever threatened him with that before. I regained my composure and managed to say that I thought she was right. By the time I got home I was feeling pretty good about this. It was a radical approach for these times, but, well, why 6 not? "She's going to flunk you," I told my son. I did not discuss it any further. Suddenly English became a priority in his life. He finished out the semester with an A.

I know one example doesn't make a case, but at night I see a parade of students who are angry and resentful for having been passed along until they could no longer even pretend to keep up. Of average intelligence or better, they eventually quit school, concluding they were too dumb to finish. "I should have been held back" is a comment I hear frequently. Even sadder are those students who are high-school graduates who say to me after a few weeks of class, "I don't know how I ever got a high-school diploma."

Passing students who have not mastered the work cheats them and the employers who expect graduates to have basic skills. We excuse this dishonest behavior by saying kids can't learn if they come from terrible environments. No one seems to stop to think that—no matter what environments they come from— most kids don't put school first on their list unless they perceive something is at stake. They'd rather be sailing.

Many students I see at night could give expert testimony on unemployment, chemical dependency, abusive relationships. In spite of these difficulties, they have decided to make education a priority. They are motivated by the desire for a better job or the need to hang on to the one they've got. They have a healthy fear of failure.

People of all ages can rise above their problems, but they need to have a reason to do so. Young people generally don't have the maturity to value education in the same way my adult students value it. But fear of failure, whether economic or academic, can motivate both.

Flunking as a regular policy has just as much merit today as it did two generations ago. We must review the threat of flunking and see it as it really is—a positive teaching tool. It is an expression of confidence by both teachers and parents that the students have the ability to learn the material presented to them. However, making it work again would take a dedicated, caring conspiracy between teachers and parents. It would mean facing the tough reality that passing kids who haven't learned the material—while it might save them grief for the short term—dooms them to long-term illiteracy. It would mean that teachers would have to follow through on their threats, and parents would have to stand behind them, knowing their children's best interests are indeed at stake. This means no more doing Scott's assignments for him because he might fail. No more passing Jodi because she's such a nice kid.

This is a policy that worked in the past and can work today. A wise teacher, with the support of his parents, gave our son the opportunity to succeed—or fail. It's time we return this choice to all students.

![Build Your Vocabulary icon] **READING ACTIVITY 2 Build Your Vocabulary**

Determine the meanings of the following words from the context of Mary Sherry's essay. Then check their meanings by looking up the words in a dictionary: validity (1), impediments (4), flustered (6).

> **GROUP ACTIVITY 2** Discuss the Reading

Discuss the following questions about "In Praise of the F Word" with your classmates.

1. What problem does Sherry identify?
2. What evidence of the problem does the author provide? She says that students "have been cheated by our educational system." Do you think that these words set a reasonable tone?
3. What is Sherry's proposed solution?
4. Is the solution specific and reasonable?

> **WRITING ACTIVITY 2** Share Your Ideas

Write a paragraph or two on high school students' lack of preparation for college. This lack of preparation could be educational, financial, or social. Has the lack of preparation affected you personally? Why or why not? Share your proposed solution to the problem with your classmates. What research can you do to support your position that your solution is workable?

An Environmental Problem

MARK HERTSGAARD
A Global Green Deal

Mark Hertsgaard has written "A Global Green Deal" to encourage governments to develop incentives for businesses and consumers to use environmentally friendly technologies. Hertsgaard is an independent journalist who has written numerous other articles and six books.

The bad news is that we have to change our ways — and fast. Here's the good news: it could be a hugely profitable enterprise. 1

So what do we do? Everyone knows the planet is in bad shape, but most people are resigned to passivity. Changing course, they reason, would require economic sacrifice and provoke stiff resistance from corporations and consumers alike, so why bother? It's easier to ignore the gathering storm clouds and hope the problem magically takes care of itself. 2

Such fatalism is not only dangerous but mistaken. For much of the 1990s I traveled the world to write a book about our environmental predicament. I returned home sobered by the extent of the damage we are causing and by the speed at which it is occurring. But there is nothing inevitable about our self-destructive behavior. Not only could we dramatically reduce our burden on the air, water and other natural systems, we could make money doing so. If we're smart, 3 we could make restoring the environment the biggest economic enterprise of our time, a huge source of jobs, profits and poverty alleviation.

What we need is a Global Green Deal: a program to renovate our civilization 4 environmentally from top to bottom in rich and poor countries alike. Making use of both market incentives and government leadership, a twenty-first-century Global Green Deal would do for environmental technologies what government and industry have recently done so well for computer and Internet technologies: launch their commercial takeoff.

Getting it done will take work, and before we begin we need to understand 5 three facts about the reality facing us. First, we have no time to lose. While we've made progress in certain areas — air pollution is down in the U.S. — big environmental problems like climate change, water scarcity and species extinction are getting worse, and faster than ever. Thus we have to change our ways profoundly — and very soon.

Second, poverty is central to the problem. Four billion of the planet's 6 billion 6 people face deprivation inconceivable to the wealthiest 1 billion. To paraphrase Thomas Jefferson, nothing is more certainly written in the book of fate than that the bottom two-thirds of humanity will strive to improve their lot. As they demand adequate heat and food, not to mention cars and CD players, humanity's environmental footprint will grow. Our challenge is to accommodate this mass ascent from poverty without wrecking the natural systems that make life possible.

Third, some good news: we have in hand most of the technologies needed to 7 chart a new course. We know how to use oil, wood, water and other resources much more efficiently than we do now. Increased efficiency — doing more with less — will enable us to use fewer resources and produce less pollution per capita, buying us the time to bring solar power, hydrogen fuel cells and other futuristic technologies on line.

Efficiency may not sound like a rallying cry for environmental revolution, but 8 it packs a financial punch. As Joseph J. Romm reports in his book *Cool Companies*, Xerox, Compaq and 3M are among many firms that have recognized they can cut their greenhouse-gas emissions in half — and enjoy 50 percent and higher returns on investment through improved efficiency, better lighting and insulation and smarter motors and building design. The rest of us (small businesses, homeowners, city governments, schools) can reap the same benefits.

Super-refrigerators use 87% less electricity than older, standard models while 9 costing the same (assuming mass production) and performing better, as Paul Hawken and Amory and L. Hunter Lovins explain in their book *Natural Capitalism*. In Amsterdam the headquarters of ING Bank, one of Holland's largest banks, uses one-fifth as much energy per square meter as a nearby bank, even though the buildings cost the same to construct. The ING center boasts efficient windows and insulation and a design that enables solar energy to provide much of the building's needs, even in cloudy Northern Europe.

Examples like these lead even such mainstream voices as AT&T and Japan's 10 energy planning agency, NEDO, to predict that environmental restoration could be a source of virtually limitless profit. The idea is to retrofit our farms, factories, shops, houses, offices and everything inside them. The economic activity generated would be enormous. Better yet, it would be labor intensive; investments in energy efficiency yield two to 10 times more jobs than investments in fossil fuel and nuclear power. In a world where 1 billion people lack gainful employment, creating jobs is essential to fighting the poverty that retards environmental progress.

But this transition will not happen by itself — too many entrenched interests 11 stand in the way. Automakers often talk green but make only token efforts to develop green cars because gas-guzzling sport-utility vehicles are hugely profitable. But every year the U.S. government buys 56,000 new vehicles for official use from Detroit. Under the Global Green Deal, Washington would tell Detroit that from now on the cars have to be hybrid-electric or hydrogen-fuel-cell cars. Detroit might scream and holler, but if Washington stood firm, carmakers soon would be climbing the learning curve and offering the competitively priced green cars that consumers say they want.

We know such government pump-priming works; it's why so many of us have 12 computers today. America's computer companies began learning to produce today's affordable systems during the 1960s while benefiting from subsidies and guaranteed markets under contracts with the Pentagon and the space program. And the cyberboom has fueled the biggest economic expansion in history.

The Global Green Deal must not be solely an American project, however. 13 China and India, with their gigantic populations and ambitious development plans, could by themselves doom everyone else to severe global warming. Already, China is the world's second largest producer of greenhouse gases (after the U.S.). But China would use 50% less coal if it simply installed today's energy-efficient technologies. Under the Global Green Deal, Europe, America and Japan would help China buy these technologies, not only because that would reduce global warming but also because it would create jobs and profits for workers and companies back home.

Governments would not have to spend more money, only shift existing sub- 14 sidies away from environmentally dead-end technologies like coal and nuclear power. If even half the $500 billion to $900 billion in environmentally destructive subsidies now offered by the world's governments were redirected, the Global Green Deal would be off to a roaring start. Governments need to establish "rules of the road" so that market prices reflect the real social costs of clearcut forests and other environmental abominations. Again, such a shift could be revenue neutral. Higher taxes on, say, coal burning would be offset by cuts in payroll and profits taxes, thus encouraging jobs and investment while discouraging pollution. A portion of the revenues should be set aside to assure a just transition for workers and companies now engaged in inherently anti-environmental activities like coal mining.

All this sounds easy enough on paper, but in the real world it is not so simple. 15 Beneficiaries of the current system — be they U.S. corporate-welfare recipients, redundant German coal miners, or cutthroat Asian logging interests — will resist. Which is why progress is unlikely absent a broader agenda of change, including real democracy: assuring the human rights of environmental activists, and neutralizing the power of Big Money through campaign-finance reform.

The Global Green Deal is no silver bullet. It can, however, buy us time to make 16 the more deep-seated changes — in our often excessive appetites, in our curious belief that humans are the center of the universe, in our sheer numbers — that will be necessary to repair our relationship with our environment.

None of this will happen without an aroused citizenry. But a Global Green 17 Deal is in the common interest, and it is a slogan easily grasped by the media and the public. Moreover, it should appeal across political, class and national boundaries, for it would stimulate both jobs and business throughout the world in the name of a universal value: leaving our children a livable planet. The history of environmentalism is largely the story of ordinary people pushing for change while governments, corporations and other established interests reluctantly follow behind. It's time to repeat that history on behalf of a Global Green Deal.

READING ACTIVITY 3 Build Your Vocabulary

Determine the meanings of the following words from the context of Mark Hertsgaard's essay. Then check their meanings by looking up the words in a dictionary: passivity (2), fatalism (3), profoundly (5), deprivation (6), retrofit (10), entrenched (11), abominations (14).

GROUP ACTIVITY 3 Discuss the Reading

Discuss the following questions about "A Global Green Deal" with your classmates.

1. What problem does Hertsgaard identify?

2. What evidence of the problem does the author provide? How does he use logical, emotional, and ethical appeals?

3. What is the proposed solution? Is the solution specific and reasonable?

4. What environmental problem would you like to see eliminated?

WRITING ACTIVITY 3 Share Your Ideas

Write a paragraph or two on a global environmental problem. Where can you find research that supports your position that this is a problem? What solution would you propose? Can you think of any experts who share your proposed solution? Share your writing with your classmates.

Acknowledgments

Lizette Alvarez. "Latinas Make Sweet 16-ish Their Own" from the *New York Times*, May 11, 2006. Copyright © 2006 the New York Times. All rights reserved. Used by permission and protected by the copyright laws of the United States. The printing, copying, redistribution, or retransmission of this content without express written permission is prohibited.

Joshua Bell. "My Maestro" from *Reader's Digest*, April 2004. Copyright © 2004 by the Reader's Digest Association, Inc. Reprinted with permission from Reader's Digest.

Lucy Calkins. Reprinted with permission from *The Art of Teaching Writing* by Lucy Calkins. Copyright © 1986, 1994 by Lucy McCormick Calkins. Published by Heinemann, Portsmouth, NH. All rights reserved.

Nicholas Carr. "The PC Officially Died Today" from the *New Republic*, January 27, 2010. Copyright © 2010 by Nicholas Carr. Reprinted by permission of the New Republic.

Richard Corliss. "*Michael Jackson's This Is It* Review: He's Still a Thriller" from *TIME* magazine, October 28, 2009. Copyright © 2009, Time Inc. Reprinted by permission. *TIME* is a registered trademark of Time Inc. All rights reserved.

John Culhane. "Oprah Winfrey: How Truth Changed Her Life" from the February 1989 *Reader's Digest*. Copyright © 1989 by the Reader's Digest Association, Inc. Reprinted with permission from Reader's Digest.

James Dillard. "A Doctor's Dilemma" from *Newsweek* June 12, 1995. Copyright © 1995 the Newsweek/Daily Beast Company LLC. All rights reserved. Used by permission and protected by the copyright laws of the United States. The printing, copying, redistribution, or retransmission of the material without express written permission is prohibited. www.newsweek.com.

Thomas L. Friedman. "My Favorite Teacher," originally published in the *New York Times,* January 9, 2001. Copyright © 2001 the New York Times. All rights reserved. Used by permission and protected by the copyright laws of the United States. The printing, copying, redistribution, or retransmission of this content without express written permission is prohibited.

Henry Louis Gates, Jr. "Samuel L. Jackson: In Character" from *America Behind the Color Line* by Henry Louis Gates, Jr. Copyright © 2004 by Henry Louis Gates Jr. Reprinted by permission of Grand Central Publishing. All rights reserved.

Ellen Goodman. "The Company Man" from *Value Judgments* by Ellen Goodman. Copyright © 1993 by Ellen Goodman. Reprinted by permission of International Creative Management, Inc.

Diane Heiman and Phyllis Bookspan. "*Sesame Street*: Brought to You By the Letters M-A-L-E" from the *Seattle Times*, July 28, 1992. Copyright © 1992. Reprinted by permission of authors.

Mark Hertsgaard. "A Global Green Deal" from *TIME*, April/May 2000. Copyright © 2000 by Mark Hertsgaard. Reprinted by permission of the author.

Rita Hess. "American Workplace Slang and Jargon." First published at www.coming2america.com. Reprinted by permission of the author.

Ann Hodgman. "No Wonder They Call Me a Bitch" from *Spy Magazine*. Copyright © 1989 Sussex Publishers. Reprinted by permission of the author.

Andrea L. Houk. Excerpt from "The Honor Principle" from *Newsweek*, January 12, 1998. Copyright © 1998 the Newsweek/Daily Beast Company LLC. All rights reserved. Used by permission and protected by the copyright laws of the United States. The printing, copying, redistribution, or retransmission of the material without express written permission is prohibited. www.newsweek.com.

Nicholas Jennings. "A Palace of Rock" from *Maclean's*, September 18, 1995. Copyright © 1995 Nicholas Jennings. Reprinted by permission of the author.

Art Credits

A QUICK REFERENCE TO EDITING SYMBOLS

adj	adjective error 433, 527
adv	adverb error 434, 529
awk	awkward wording
cap	capital letter needed 509
coord	correct coordination in sentence 108, 148, 436
cs	comma splice 230, 461
dm	dangling modifier 466
frag	sentence fragment 150, 453
jar	avoid jargon
lc	use lowercase letter 509
mm	misplaced modifier 464
no cap	no capital 509
pass	avoid passive voice 468, 542
prep	preposition error 400, 521
pr agr	pronoun agreement error 188, 429
ref	error in pronoun reference 188, 430
rep	repetitious 475
r-o	run-on sentence 110, 457
-s	s needed at the end of word
sp	spelling error 477, 482
sub	correct subordination in sentence 186, 228, 425
s-v agr	error in subject-verb agreement 269, 413
trans	transition needed 143, 148
v or vb	verb error 404, 529
vt	shift in verb tense 410
w	too wordy 476
ww	wrong word 484
¶	begin new paragraph 35
?	meaning unclear
√	good idea or expression
x	error marked or crossed out
^	insert
ℯ	delete